MANAGEMENT OF HUMAN RESOURCES

THE ESSENTIALS

GARY DESSLER
FLORIDA INTERNATIONAL UNIVERSITY

NITA CHHINZER
UNIVERSITY OF GUELPH

GARY GANNON
UNIVERSITY OF TORONTO

FIFTH CANADIAN EDITION

 Pearson

Toronto

VICE PRESIDENT, EDITORIAL: Anne Williams
ACQUISITIONS EDITOR: Karen Townsend
MARKETING MANAGER: Lisa Gillis
CONTENT MANAGER: John Polanszky
PROJECT MANAGER: Sarah Gallagher
CONTENT DEVELOPER: Jennifer Murray
MEDIA EDITOR: Rachel Stuckey
MEDIA DEVELOPER: Kelli Cadet

PRODUCTION SERVICES: iEnergizer Aptara®, Ltd.
PERMISSIONS PROJECT MANAGER: Joanne Tang
PHOTO PERMISSIONS RESEARCH: Integra
TEXT PERMISSIONS RESEARCH: Integra
INTERIOR DESIGNER: Anthony Leung
COVER DESIGNER: Anthony Leung
COVER IMAGE: © Rawpixel.com / Shutterstock
VICE-PRESIDENT, DIGITAL STUDIO: Gary Bennett

Pearson Canada Inc., 26 Prince Andrew Place, North York, Ontario M3C 2H4.

Dedication

To my mother

—G.D.

I would like to dedicate this book to those students who consistently demonstrate the ability to integrate, analyze and transfer knowledge, both within the classroom and outside of it.
Your excellence keeps me inspired.

—N .C.

To my wife Deborah whose patience and encouragement made this effort possible.

—G.G.

978-0-13-430506-6

1   18

Library and Archives Canada Cataloguing in Publication

Dessler, Gary, 1942–, author
   Management of human resources : the essentials / Gary Dessler, Florida International University, Nita Chhinzer, University of Guelph, Gary Gannon, University of Toronto.—Fifth Canadian edition.

ISBN 978-0-13-430506-6 (softcover)

   1. Personnel management—Textbooks.   2. Personnel management—Canada—Textbooks.
3. Textbooks.   I. Chhinzer, Nita, author   II. Gannon, Gary L. (Gary Lawrence), 1951–, author   III. Title.

HF5549.D495 2017   658.3   C2017-907343-5

Brief Contents

Preface   ix

Part 1   Human Resources Management in Perspective   1

Chapter 1   The Strategic Role of Human Resources Management   1

Chapter 2   The Changing Legal Emphasis: Compliance and Impact on Canadian Workplaces   20

Part 2   Meeting Human Resources Requirements   46

Chapter 3   Designing and Analyzing Jobs   46

Chapter 4   Human Resources Planning   69

Chapter 5   Talent Acquisition   89

Part 3   Developing Effective Human Resources   128

Chapter 6   Onboarding and Training   128

Chapter 7   Performance Management   152

Part 4   Total Rewards   177

Chapter 8   Strategic Pay Plans   177

Chapter 9   Employee Benefits and Services   210

Part 5   Building Effective Employee–Employer Relationships   236

Chapter 10   Occupational Health and Safety   236

Chapter 11   Managing Employee Separations: Foundations of Employee Engagement, Communication, and Turnover Management   264

Chapter 12   Labour Relations   282

Part 6   Global Issues in Human Resources Management   308

Chapter 13   Managing Human Resources in a Global Business   308

Notes   328

Glossary   348

Name and Organization Index   358

Subject Index   360

Table of Contents

Preface   ix

| PART ONE | Human Resources Management in Perspective   1 |

Chapter 1   **The Strategic Role of Human Resources Management   1**

The Strategic Role of Human Resources Management   2

The Evolution of HRM   3

    Strategic HR   The HR Role Continues to Evolve   7

Professionalism in HRM   9

Environmental Influences on HRM   11

Chapter 2   **The Changing Legal Emphasis: Compliance and Impact on Canadian Workplaces   20**

The Legal Framework for Employment Law in Canada   21

Legislation Protecting the General Population   25

    Workforce Diversity   Gender Identity in the BC Human Rights Code   27

Legislation Specific to the Workplace   37

| PART TWO | Meeting Human Resources Requirements   46 |

Chapter 3   **Designing and Analyzing Jobs   46**

Fundamentals of Job Analysis   47

Steps in Job Analysis   49

    Entrepreneurs and HR   A Practical Approach to Job Analysis and Job Descriptions   64

Chapter 4   **Human Resources Planning   69**

The Strategic Importance of Human Resources Planning   70

The Steps in Human Resources Planning   72

    Strategic HR   Pumping Up People Supply   77

Chapter 5   **Talent Acquisition   89**

Talent Acquisition   90

Recruitment   90

The Recruitment Process   92

Recruiting a More Diverse Workforce   101

    Workforce Diversity   The Disconnect in Recruiting People with Disabilities   104

Recruitment Metrics   104

The Strategic Importance of Employee Selection   105

PART THREE   Developing Effective Human Resources   128

Chapter 6   **Onboarding and Training   128**
Become a Learning Organization   129
Onboarding Employees   130
The Training Process   135
Career Planning and Development   144
Workforce Diversity Career Development for Older Workers   145
Managing Internal Employee Movement   148

Chapter 7   **Performance Management   152**
The Strategic Importance of Performance Management   153
The Performance Management Process   153
Global HRM Performance Appraisal Criteria in China   155
Strategic HR Jaguar Land Rover Formal Appraisal Discussion Training   164
Performance Appraisal Problems and Solutions   164
Who Should Do the Appraising?   169
Legal and Ethical Issues in Performance Management   172
The Future of Performance Management   173

PART FOUR   Total Rewards   177

Chapter 8   **Strategic Pay Plans   177**
The Strategic Importance of Total Employment Rewards   178
Money and Motivation   179
Basic Considerations in Determining Pay Rates   182
Pay Equity   183
Establishing Pay Rates   183
Pay for Knowledge   192
Developing Effective Incentive Plans   194
Types of Incentive Plans   195
Strategic HR Generational Preferences in Rewards, Recognition, and Incentives   196

Chapter 9   **Employee Benefits and Services   210**
The Strategic Role of Employee Benefits   211
Government-Mandated Benefits   212
Voluntary Employer-Sponsored Benefits   218
Global HRM Defined Benefit Pension Problems and Solutions around the World   226
Employee Services   228
Flexible Benefits Programs   232
Benefits Administration   233

PART FIVE   Building Effective Employee–Employer Relationships   236

Chapter 10   **Occupational Health and Safety   236**

Strategic Importance of Occupational Health and Safety   237
   Entrepreneurs and HR Small Business Safety Calculator   238
Basic Facts about Occupational Health and Safety Legislation   238
What Causes Accidents?   241
   Workforce Diversity Guiding Young Workers in Health and Safety   246
How to Prevent Accidents   246
Occupational Health and Safety Challenges in Canada   249
   Strategic HR Fidelity Investments Canada Focuses on Employee Health   250
Employee Wellness Programs   260

Chapter 11   **Managing Employee Separations: Foundations of Employee Engagement, Communication, and Turnover Management   264**

The Importance of Managing Employee Separations   265
Managing Turnover   265
   Strategic HR Employers Owed Reasonable Notice for Voluntary Turnover   268
Employee Engagement and Fairness in Employee Separations   274

Chapter 12   **Labour Relations   282**

Introduction to Labour Relations   283
   Workforce Diversity Collective Agreement Puts Aboriginals First   285
   Strategic HR UFCW's Social Media Campaign to Engage and Educate Young Canadian Workers   286
The Labour Relations Process   288
   Strategic HR NHL Lockout Timeline (2012–2013 Season)   299
The Impact of Unionization on HRM   305

PART SIX   Global Issues in Human Resources Management   308

Chapter 13   **Managing Human Resources in a Global Business   308**

The Globalization of Business and Strategic HR   309
How Intercountry Differences Affect HRM   309
Global Relocation   312
Considerations in Global HRM   315
Managing Global Workers within Canada   321

Notes   328
Glossary   348
Name and Organization Index   358
Subject Index   360

Preface

Management of Human Resources: The Essentials, Fifth Canadian Edition, recognizes that human resources are now among the most important organizational assets, and thus brings both human resources and non-human resources readers into a current and comprehensive discussion about human resources today. The term *human resources* refers to the employee–employer relationship in the workplace. The knowledge, skills, assets, and competencies employees bring to their work help the organization achieve its objectives; these resources provide a source of competitive advantage for organizations in a hyper-competitive, global environment.

The strategic importance of human resources management (HRM) activities is emphasized throughout the book, using recent examples from the Canadian employment landscape. This textbook highlights fundamental knowledge of HRM that is important for employees, supervisors, and managers in every field—not just those working in HR departments or aspiring to do so in the future.

The fifth Canadian edition provides extensive coverage of all HRM topics, such as job analysis, HR planning, recruitment, selection, onboarding and training, career management, compensation and benefits, performance management, occupational health and safety, labour relations, and international HRM.

New to the Fifth Canadian Edition

- **NEW!** Expert Opinion boxes in each chapter provide interviews with leading Canadian researchers in the field of HR as well as industry experts from various well-known companies about critical issues in HR in Canada. Each interview aligns with the topics discussed in the chapter.

- A revised discussion of formerly separate chapters on recruitment and selection into a new consolidated chapter entitled Talent Acquisition (Chapter 5).

- Improved and updated graphics and figures in the chapters dealing with designing and analyzing jobs (Chapter 3); balancing labour supply and demand considerations (Chapter 4); and developing pay wage curves and pay structures (Chapter 8).

- Updated Canadian data showing trends in corporate objectives for employee benefit programming (Chapter 9), union density, and collective bargaining demands (Chapter 12).

- Updated end-of-chapter *Experiential Exercises* to support classroom and independent learning activities.

Key Features

Comprehensive Introductory Chapter. Chapter 1 provides a comprehensive overview of the strategic importance of HR, highlighting the evolution of HR over the years, the advances in measuring HRM's contribution to the bottom line, and HRM's critical role in strategy implementation. It also highlights HR-related professional designations in Canada.

Legal Emphasis. Chapter 2 provides a clear understanding of the often overlapping areas of legislation that affect the employment relationship. This includes a discussion of key legal cases, potential outcomes, and remedies to violations, as well as a discussion about employer rights related to employment.

Significant Discussion of Managing Labour during Dynamic Times. Chapters 1, 4, and 11 focus on the impact and management of labour in dynamic times when organizations must compete for talent. Chapter 11 focuses on turnover (quits, layoffs, termination, etc.), including legal, psychological, and communication issues.

More Coverage on the Impact of Globalization on HR. Further discussion of the impact of globalization on HR was added throughout this edition, with a focus on both Canadian organizations' interactions on a global scale and the impact of immigrants on the Canadian labour force. Specific sections, such as performance management (in addition to performance appraisal), the impact of immigration on the labour force, and employability skills, are introduced.

Integrated Chapters. Rather than approaching topics as isolated silos, the book highlights areas of overlap in order to present HRM as an integrated set of topics.

HR by the Numbers. This feature focuses on the impact of HR practices and policies. The format of these sections is more magazine style and visually enticing for the students.

Highlighted Themes

- **Workforce Diversity.** The *Workforce Diversity* boxes describe some of the issues and challenges involved in managing the diverse workforces found in Canadian organizations. The broad range addressed includes generational/ age, ethnic, gender, racial, and religious diversities.

- **Strategic HR.** The *Strategic HR* boxes provide examples that illustrate the ways in which organizations are using effective HRM policies and practices to achieve their strategic goals.

- **Entrepreneurs and HR.** Suggestions, examples, and practical hints are provided to assist those in smaller businesses who have limited time and resources to implement effective HRM policies and procedures.

- **Global HRM.** In recognition of the increasing impact of globalization, topics highlighted in the *Global HRM* boxes include cultural issues in retirement plans, employment contracts in Europe, and the importance of personal relationships for business success in China.

Additional Features

Learning Outcomes. Specific learning goals are defined on each chapter-opening page.

Key Terms. Key terms appear in boldface within the text, are defined in the margins, and are listed at the end of each chapter.

Current Examples. Numerous real-world examples of HRM policies, procedures, and practices at a wide variety of organizations, ranging from small service providers to huge global corporations, can be found throughout the text.

Full-Colour Figures, Tables, and Photographs. Throughout each chapter, key concepts and applications are illustrated with strong, full-colour visual materials.

Web Links. Helpful Internet sites are provided throughout the text and are featured in the margins.

End-of-Chapter Summaries. At the end of each chapter, the summary reviews key points related to each of the learning outcomes.

End-of-Chapter Review and Discussion Questions. Each chapter contains a set of review and discussion questions.

Critical Thinking Questions. Each chapter contains end-of-chapter questions designed to provoke critical thinking and stimulate discussion.

Experiential Exercises. Each chapter includes a number of individual and group-based experiential exercises that provide learners with the opportunity to apply the text material and develop some hands-on skills.

Student Supplements

MyLab Management delivers proven results in helping individual students succeed. It provides engaging experiences that personalize, stimulate, and measure learning for each student. Students and instructors can make use of the following online resources:

- **NEW MediaShare:** Consisting of a curated collection of videos and customizable, auto-scored assignments, MediaShare helps students understand why they are learning key concepts and how they will apply those in their careers. Instructors can also assign favorite YouTube clips or original content and employ MediaShare's powerful repository of tools to maximize student accountability and interactive learning, and provide contextualized feedback for students and teams who upload presentations, media, or business plans.

- **Personal Inventory Assessment (PIA).** Students learn better when they can connect what they are learning to their personal experience. PIA is a collection of online exercises designed to promote self-reflection and engagement in students, enhancing their ability to connect with concepts taught in principles of management, organizational behaviour, and human resource management classes. Assessments can be assigned by instructors, who can then track students' completions. Student results include a written explanation along with a graphic display that shows how their results compare to those of the class as a whole. Instructors will also have access to this graphic representation of results to promote classroom discussion.

- **Study Plan:** As students work through the MyLab Study Plan, they can clearly see which topics they have mastered—and, more importantly, which they need to work on. Each question has been carefully written to match the concepts, language, and focus of the text, so students can get an accurate sense of how well they've understood the chapter content.

- **Pearson eText:** MyLab Management also includes an eText version of *Management of Human Resources: The Essentials*, including a complete Glossary and Index. This dynamic, online version of the text is integrated throughout MyLab Management to create an enriched, interactive learning experience for students. Users can create notes, highlight text in different colours, create bookmarks, zoom, and click hyperlinked words and phrases to view definitions and go directly to weblinks. The Pearson eText allows quick navigation to key parts of the eText using a table of contents and provides full-text search.

Instructors and students can also access quizzes, cases, simulations and other, study tools designed to engage learners and improve student understanding.

Instructor Supplements

These instructor supplements are available for download from a password-protected section of Pearson Canada's online catalogue (www.pearson.com/higher-education). Navigate to your book's catalogue page to view a list of those supplements that are available. Speak to your local Pearson sales representative for details and access.

Computerized Test Bank. Pearson's computerized test banks allow instructors to filter and select questions to create quizzes, tests, or homework. Instructors can revise questions or add their own, and may be able to choose print or online options. These questions are also available in Microsoft Word format.

Instructor's Manual. The Instructor's Manual includes Learning outcomes, chapter summaries, chapter/lecture outlines, discussion box summaries, ethical dilemmas, key terms from the text, and answers to the end of chapter questions.

PowerPoint Slides. This practical set of PowerPoint slides outlines key concepts discussed in the text, and includes selected tables and figures from the text.

Learning Solutions Managers. Pearson's Learning Solutions Managers work with faculty and campus course designers to ensure that Pearson technology products, assessment tools, and online course materials are tailored to meet your specific needs. This highly qualified team is dedicated to helping schools take full advantage of a wide range of educational resources, by assisting in the integration of a variety of instructional materials and media formats. Your local Pearson Canada sales representative can provide you with more details on this service program.

Acknowledgments

The manuscript was reviewed at various stages of its development by a number of peers across Canada, and we want to thank those who shared their insights and constructive criticism.

Ian Gellatly, University of Alberta

Noel Genoway, Langara College

Janet Latremouile, Humber College

Robin McQueen, Camosun College

Grace O'Farrell, University of Winnipeg

April Wallace, Queen's University

Qi Wang, George Brown College

Dileeni Weerasinghe, University of Guelph–Humber

At Pearson Canada, we are very grateful to Karen Townsend, Acquisitions Editor; Leigh-Anne Graham, Darcey Pepper/Lisa Gillis Marketing Managers; Jennifer Murray, Content Developer; Sarah Gallagher, Project Manager; and all the other people behind the scenes who have helped make this edition possible.

A special note of thanks is extended to research assistant Rachelle Phillips.

Gary Dessler
Florida International University

Nita N. Chhinzer
University of Guelph

Gary L. Gannon
University of Toronto

About the Canadian Authors

Dr. Nita N. Chhinzer

Dr. Nita N. Chhinzer is an Associate Professor in the Department of Management, University of Guelph. She was recognized as one of the top 25 HR professionals in Canada in 2016. Her research is concentrated on Strategic Human Resources Management, with a strong focus on downsizing practices, procedures, and ethics. Her program of research includes securing a stronger understanding of downsizing activity in the Canadian context, with an aim to affect public policy and legislation regarding layoffs. She has gained international recognition with conference participation in such places as Athens, Greece; Paris, France; Dubai, UAE; and many North American speaking engagements. From May 2012 to 2017, Dr. Chhinzer was the recipient of the prestigious Fellowship in Leadership, HRM and Work.

Dr. Gary L. Gannon

Dr. Gary L. Gannon (PhD, CHRL) has 18 years of experience in progressive HR management roles in the health care and higher education sectors. He is recognized as an expert in building and revitalizing HRM services in medium and large organizations in order to fulfill strategic business objectives. Dr. Gannon is a certified member of the Human Resources Professionals Association (HRPA) and serves on the Association's Academic Standards Committee. He has also advised several not-for-profit organizations on HRM-related matters as part of his involvement in the local community. In 2015, Dr. Gannon was awarded Durham College's Faculty Excellence Award. He presently teaches HR management and Labour Relations courses in the School of Continuing Studies at the University of Toronto.

THE STRATEGIC ROLE OF HUMAN RESOURCES MANAGEMENT

LEARNING OUTCOMES

AFTER STUDYING THIS CHAPTER, YOU SHOULD BE ABLE TO:

DEFINE human resources management (HRM), and **ANALYZE** the strategic significance of HRM.

DESCRIBE the evolution of HRM, and **EXPLAIN** how HRM has changed over recent years to include a higher-level advisory role.

EXPLAIN how HRM has taken on the characteristics of a profession.

DISCUSS the internal and external environmental factors affecting HRM policies and practices, and **EXPLAIN** their impact.

©Shutterstock

1

1.1 THE STRATEGIC ROLE OF HUMAN RESOURCES MANAGEMENT

human resources management (HRM) The management of people in organizations to drive successful organizational performance and achievement of the organization's strategic goals.

Human resources management (HRM) refers to the management of people in organizations. Human resources professionals are responsible for ensuring that the organization attracts, retains, and engages the diverse talent required to meet operational and performance commitments made to customers and shareholders. Their job is to ensure that the organization finds and hires the best individuals available, develops their talent, creates a productive work environment, and continually builds and monitors these human assets. They have the primary responsibility for managing the workforce that drives organizational performance and achieves the organization's strategic goals.[1]

The aim of this book is to help every manager develop the skills he or she needs to carry out the HRM–related aspects of his or her job, such as recruiting, selecting, training, appraising, and incentivizing employees, as well as providing them with a safe and fulfilling work environment.[2] In addition, establishing an awareness of the factors (strategic, legal, political, structural, etc.) that impact how individuals, teams, or units are recruited, selected, evaluated, developed, compensated, and removed from the employment relationship can be helpful for the reader in his or her role as an employee.

More specifically, HRM involves formulating and implementing HRM systems (such as recruitment, performance management, and compensation) that are aligned with the organization's strategy to ensure that the workforce has the competencies and behaviours required to achieve the organization's strategic objectives. In practice, the various HR topics are not isolated but interact with and affect other areas of HR. For example, hiring people who don't have the potential to learn the job will doom their performance, regardless of how much training they get. Similarly, each HRM function, from job analysis to recruiting, selecting, training, and rewarding employees, should aim to produce the employee behaviours and competencies that the company needs to achieve its strategic goals. Accordingly, it is crucial that the HR strategy be aligned with the company's strategic plan (see **Figure 1.1**).

human capital The knowledge, education, training, skills, and expertise of an organization's workforce.

Just as important as the financial capital that is required for an organization to operate, the knowledge, education, training, skills, and expertise of a firm's workers represent its increasingly valuable **human capital**. More and more organizations are awakening to the importance of human capital as the next competitive advantage.[3]

Research studies over the past two decades have confirmed that effective HR practices are related to better organizational performance.[4] Organizational benefits range from employee empowerment to extensive training that affects the productivity of employees.[5] The resource-based view of the firm suggests that practices in human resources contribute to the development of embedded knowledge of a firm's culture, history, processes, and context, which are non-imitable.[6] More specifically, three HR practices (profit sharing, results-oriented performance management, and employment security) are strongly related to important accounting measures of performance (return on assets and return on equity).[7] High-performance HR practices (comprehensive employee recruitment and selection procedures, incentive compensation and performance management systems, and extensive employee involvement and training) have a positive relationship with turnover, productivity, and corporate financial performance (gross rate of return on capital).[8]

FIGURE 1.1 Linking Company-Wide and HR Strategies

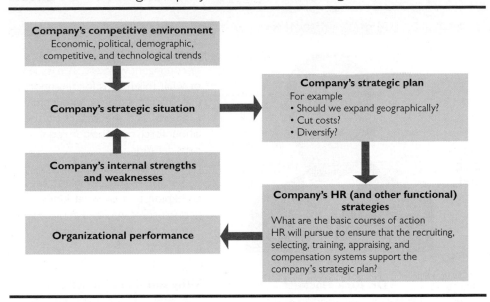

Source: © Gary Dessler, Ph.D., 2007.

1.2 THE EVOLUTION OF HRM

Is it accurate to say that HRM existed tens of thousands of years ago? Ancient armies and organized efforts always required attracting, selecting, training, and motivating workers. But personnel tasks like these were mostly just part of every manager's job, something that lasted in most countries until the late 1800s. At that time, labour problems began arising in many of the post–industrial revolution's new factories. Soon employers were setting up "welfare offices" and "welfare secretaries" to manage activities like factory washrooms, and "safety bureaus" to oversee plant safety. By 1900, employers set up the first "hiring offices," training programs, and factory schools. These early stages of HRM were known as personnel management.[9]

In these early firms, personnel managers took over hiring and firing from supervisors, ran the payroll departments, and administered benefits plans. As expertise in testing emerged, personnel departments played a greater role in employee selection and training.[10] New union laws in the 1930s added "Helping the employer deal with unions" to personnel management's tasks. New equity-oriented laws in the 1970s and 1980s made employers more reliant on personnel management to avoid discrimination claims.[11]

Around that time, globalization made gaining a competitive edge through engaged employees—and therefore personnel management—increasingly important. Today economic and demographic trends (recall the diminishing workforce participation rate and aging population, for instance) make finding, hiring, and motivating employees more challenging, while the existence of more high-tech and service jobs means employers must excel at managing employees' knowledge, skills, and expertise (human capital) through aptly renamed HRM departments.[12] Many HR experts (industry and academic) recognize the changing face of HR. Dr. Rick Hackett's perspectives on the profession and hot topics for the future are highlighted in the Expert Opinion box.

Academic Viewpoint
EXPERT OPINION

Focus: Executive/managerial assessment, leadership, HR recruitment, testing, selection, work attitudes, absenteeism, and performance assessment.

1. In your expert opinion, who is responsible for managing the added value associated with human resources (employees) in an organization?

My one-word answer: Everyone. Responsibility for managing employees in an organization might start at the executive level (executives develop the mission and vision that essentially drive the organizational strategy), but all stakeholders (employees, managers, specialists) facilitate the execution of that vision or mission. We rely on people to express the values required to meet the goals and objectives of the organization, which involves alignment of culture, incentives, process, and practices that often permeate through HR.

2. What are some of the hot topics being researched in the world of HRM now, which existing and future managers should know about?

I. Data Analytics: In recent years there has been a lot of discussion of big data, specifically about how we can harness the volume of

Dr. Rick Hackett

Identification:
Dr. Rick Hackett
Professor and Canadian Research Chair in Organizational Behaviour and Human Performance, and Fellow of Canadian Psychological Association

Affiliation:
DeGroote School of Business, McMaster University

---

data accessible through HR systems. Big data in HR changes in real time; it's dynamic, with constantly changing algorithms.

II. Technology for Performance Management: This is linked with data analytics, but addresses how we harness technology to make HR more effective. For example, HRIS requires packages tailored to the needs of specialized workers.

III. Contingent Workforce: Organizations have a smaller core

workforce with an increasing use of contingent workers. The issues of what this means for retention, information security, intellectual property, and the impact on the labour force composition requires consideration.

IV. Intrepreneurship: Innovation within the organization requires an exploration of what kinds of infrastructure we need in place to support new information and innovation.

3. Why should those who manage human resources in an organization use academic articles in peer-reviewed journals to inform their decisions?

Pressing demands of the day-to-day job requirements make it hard for practitioners to manage information overload. Instead, researchers should work with media teams at their research centres (e.g., universities, government agencies) or develop industry-oriented papers to communicate information in a meaningful way outside of the research community. Recent research grant applications have started asking about plans for research dissemination, but we can also build in incentive systems to recognize research communicated in practitioner forums.

Source: Reprinted by permission from Dr. Rick Hackett.

1.2.1 Critical Competencies for HR Professionals

A 2011 national survey of HR professionals identified five critical pieces of knowledge required by HR professionals today. Presented in order of priority, they are business acumen, an understanding of employment law and legislation, talent management, broad HR knowledge, and employee–labour relations knowledge.[13] The results align with an overall trend towards increased expectations of HR professionals, suggesting that there are six core competencies that those responsible for HR activities (within the HRM department and outside of it) must secure to help deliver value to the organization.

1.2.1.1 Credible Activist

A core HR competency is that of being both credible (respected, listened to, trusted) and active (a person who takes a position and challenges assumptions). Both of these qualities are required to help an organization optimize the value added from its human resources.

The activist role is shared with non-HR positions as well. For example, a recent study conducted by Monster.com found that 73 percent of CEOs spend more than 25 percent of their time on talent-related activities, with three in every five identifying employee satisfaction/engagement as a key goal for their job, and three of every four identifying retention of high-performing employees as one of their goals.[14]

1.2.1.2 Culture and Change Steward

The ability to appreciate, help shape, and articulate an organization's corporate culture includes understanding, guiding, and reacting to both internal and external stakeholder expectations. HR staff has a responsibility to shape and support a culture of change, as well as develop programs, strategies, or projects to embed desired change throughout the organization.

Intense global competition and the need for more responsiveness to environmental changes put a premium on **employee engagement**: the emotional and intellectual involvement of employees in their work, and the intensity, focus, and involvement they bring to their jobs and organizations. Engaged employees drive desired organizational outcomes—they go beyond what is required; understand and share the values and goals of the organization; perceive that there are opportunities for growth, development, and advancement; enjoy collegial relationships with managers and co-workers; trust their leaders; and regard the success of the organization as their success.[15] According to an analysis of a Hewitt Associates database (over 4 million employees from almost 1 500 companies), there is a strong positive relationship between employee engagement and organizational performance (sales growth and total shareholder return).[16] Similarly, a recent Global Workforce Study of 32 000 employees found that companies with engaged employees secured profit margins almost three times higher than companies with disengaged employees.[17]

employee engagement The emotional and intellectual involvement of employees in their work, and the intensity, focus, and involvement they bring to their jobs and organizations.

1.2.1.3 Talent Manager and Organizational Designer

Traditional linear career paths are changing, and the importance of an HR professional's ability to effectively manage human resources has become more critical as employees enter, exit, or move up, down, or across the organization. Accordingly, HR specialists must embed theory, research, and practice into the processes, policies, and structures of an organization.

HR professionals and line managers play a pivotal role in *lowering labour costs*, the single largest operating expense in many organizations, particularly in the service sector. Doing so might involve introducing strategies to reduce turnover, absenteeism, and the rate of incidence of occupational illnesses and injuries. It could also mean adopting more effective recruitment, selection, and training programs. At one international tire manufacturing firm, adopting a behaviour-based interview strategy as the basis for selection of entry-level engineers resulted in savings of $500 000 in three years. These savings were due to lower turnover, lower training costs, and improved capabilities of the engineering staff because of a better fit.[18]

1.2.1.4 Strategy Architect

HR professionals significantly contribute to strategy by integrating internal stakeholder and external stakeholder expectations. By identifying, forecasting, and facilitating organizational responses to an ever-changing internal workforce and often volatile external pressures, HR plays an active role in the establishment and execution of overall strategy.

strategy The company's plan for how it will balance its internal strengths and weaknesses with external opportunities and threats to maintain a competitive advantage.

Traditionally, **strategy**—the company's plan for how it will balance its internal strengths and weaknesses with external opportunities and threats to maintain a competitive advantage—was formulated without HR input. But today, HR professionals are increasingly involved in both formulating and implementing organizational strategy. A recent survey of over 1 100 corporate managers in Canada found that three-quarters of them strongly believe that the HR function contributes significantly to the overall success of their company and view having an HR professional on staff as a strategic advantage.[19]

1.2.1.5 Operational Executor

Leading HR researcher Brian Becker says, "It isn't the content of the strategy that differentiates the winners and losers, it is the ability to execute."[20] HR specialists are expected to be **change agents** who lead the organization and its employees through organizational change. Making the enterprise more responsive to product or service innovations and technological change is the objective of many management strategies. Flattening the pyramid, empowering employees, and organizing around teams are ways in which HRM can help an organization respond quickly to its customers' needs and competitors' challenges.

change agents Specialists who lead the organization and its employees through organizational change.

Drafting, adapting, and implementing policies, as well as dealing with employees' administrative needs, were traditional roles that HR fulfilled. In recent years, the efficiency in dealing with operational issues has significantly improved through the use of technology, shared services, or outsourcing. However, much of the expertise in operational aspects of employee-related policies remains largely within the HR professional's realm of responsibility.

© Cartoonresource/Fotolia

"I need someone in SuperHuman Resources."

1.2.1.6 Business Ally

Organizational goal setting and development of business objectives is highly dependent on external opportunities or threats. HR professionals, together with other organizational managers, play a role in what strategic planners call **environmental scanning**, which involves identifying and analyzing *external* opportunities and threats that may be crucial to the organization's success. These managers can also supply competitive intelligence that may be useful as the company formulates its strategic plans. Details regarding a successful incentive plan being used by a competitor, impending labour shortages, and information about pending legislative changes are examples.

environmental scanning Identifying and analyzing external opportunities and threats that may be crucial to the organization's success.

HR professionals can also add value to the strategy-formulation process by supplying information regarding the company's *internal* strengths and weaknesses, particularly as they relate to the organization's workforce. HR professionals not only understand the value and social context of the business, but they are also increasingly relied on to determine how an organization should be structured and how work can be integrated to ensure financial success.

As highlighted in the Strategic HR box, the evolution of HR is far from done. HR's transformation has been underway for several years, but progress has been somewhat inconsistent because of lack of senior management support and the fact that many non-HR managers still view HR as a cost centre. Many HR professionals need to acquire more broad-based business knowledge and skill sets to be considered and respected as equal business partners by other executives in the company.[21] In some organizations, HR remains locked in an operational mode, processing forms and requests, administering compensation and benefits, managing policies and programs, and overseeing hiring and training.[22]

Table 1.1 illustrates the differences in the focus of operational versus strategic HR activities.

STRATEGIC   HR

The HR Role Continues to Evolve

The current shift in human resources management as a department and as a profession will continue to undergo evolution well into the 2020s. There are five major forces driving this change:

1. **Changing Technology:** Technology has helped automate basic HR functions, including managing day-to-day transactions and employee self-service systems. Rather than maintain HR technology experts in-house, nearly half of companies outsource operational functions of HR (payroll, benefits administration, employee education, recruitment processes, and workforce analytics).

2. **New Rules:** Corporate accounting scandals that plagued the early 2000s resulted in a more focused alignment of organizational activities with new laws and compliance expectations. The financial crisis that started in 2008 included a series of additional regulations and expectations of organizational accountability. In this highly volatile environment with high accountability expectations, HR's role is increasingly strategic, including helping the organization recover from changes and comply with new regulations.

3. **Succession Planning:** Fifty percent of companies do not have a succession plan in place for their CEO. HR's role extends significantly beyond operational

tasks to think critically about the complexities, time, and contingencies that must be considered in succession planning. Thus, HR executives are critical to organizational success through development and management of a comprehensive succession planning process.

4. **Identifying Top Talent:** While some companies argue that all employees must be motivated, educated, rewarded, and evaluated, others argue that a better return on investment can be secured by focusing on a smaller portion of workers (for example, the top 3 percent of all employees). HR is continually asked to establish a commitment to talent development that is fair, realistic, aware of limitations, and sustainable.

5. **A New Breed of HR Leaders:** The rise of the CHRO (Chief HR Officer) or CTO (Chief Talent Officer) confirms the seriousness and intent of many boards of directors in elevating and recognizing the role and capabilities of HR in an organization's leadership. HR's participation at the highest level of organizational decision making marks the transformation of the role of HR from operational expert to strategic expert in a concrete way.

Source: Reprinted from *Human Resource Executive.* Copyright 2012. All rights reserved.

TABLE 1.1   Operational versus Strategic HR

Operational	Strategic
Skills	Concepts
Administrative tasks	Planning
Reactive	Proactive
Collecting metrics/measurements	Analyzing metrics/measurements
Working to achieve goals and objectives	Setting the goals and objectives
Following the laws, policies, and procedures	Interpreting, establishing, and revising the laws, policies, and procedures
Employee focus	Organizational focus
Explaining benefits to employees	Designing benefit plans that help the organization achieve its mission and goals
Setting up training sessions for employees	Assessing training needs for the entire organization
Recruiting and selecting employees	Workforce planning and building relationships with external resources
Administering the salary/wage plan	Creating a pay plan that maximizes employees' productivity, morale, and retention
Always doing things the same way	Recognizing that there may be better ways of doing things; recognizing how changes affect the entire organization—not just HR
Works within the organizational culture	Attempts to improve the organizational culture

Source: D.M. Cox and C.H. Cox, "At the Table: Transitioning to Strategic Business Partner," *Workspan* (November 2003), p. 22. Used with Permssion.

1.2.2 Measuring the Value of HR: Metrics

metrics   Statistics used to measure activities and results.

Today's HR professionals need to be able to measure the value and impact of their organization's human capital and HRM practices. The use of various **metrics,** or statistics to measure the activities and results of HR, is now quite common. Traditional operational measures focused on the amount of activity and the costs of the HR function (such as number of job candidates interviewed per month, cost per hire, and so on), but today's measures need to reflect the quality of people and the effectiveness of HRM initiatives that build workforce capability. These new measures provide critical information that can be linked to organizational outcomes such as productivity, product or service quality, sales, market share, and profits. For example, the percentage of first-choice job candidates accepting an offer to hire indicates the strength of the organization's employment brand in the marketplace and directly affects the quality of the workforce.[23]

balanced scorecard   A measurement system that translates an organization's strategy into a comprehensive set of performance measures.

Many organizations are using the **balanced scorecard** system that includes measures of the impact of HRM on organizational outcomes. The balanced scorecard approach translates an organization's strategy into a comprehensive set of performance measures. It includes financial measures that tell the results of actions already taken. It complements the financial measures with operational measures of organizational, business unit, or department success that will drive future performance. It balances long-term and short-term actions and measures of success relating to financial results, customers, internal business processes, and human capital management.[24]

1.3 PROFESSIONALISM IN HRM

Today, HR practitioners must be professionals in terms of both performance and qualifications.[25] Every profession has several characteristics: (1) a common body of knowledge; (2) benchmarked performance standards; (3) a representative professional association; (4) an external perception as a profession; (5) a code of ethics; (6) required training credentials for entry and career mobility; (7) an ongoing need for skill development; and (8) a need to ensure professional competence is maintained and put to socially responsible uses. **Certification** by a professional body indicates that certain professional standards have been met. Professionalism of the HR practitioner can be signalled through certification.

certification   Recognition for having met certain professional standards.

The HR professional designation in Canada is in the midst of a major change. Traditionally, those working in HR could be professionally certified, with the nationally recognized Certified Human Resources Professionals (CHRP) designation. In the past, the provincial associations governing the professional designation worked relatively cohesively, promoting and recognizing the common CHRP designation under the Canadian Council of Human Resources Associations (CCHRA). However, as a result of recent changes, Ontario has formed its own association and is governed independently from the other jurisdictions. In 2015, the Ontario-based Human Resources Professionals Association (HRPA) replaced CHRP with a three-tiered designation: (1) Certified Human Resources Professional (CHRP), (2) Certified Human Resources Leader (CHRL), and (3) Certified Human Resources Executive (CHRE).

Accordingly, in 2016, the CCHRA (covering all jurisdictions in Canada, except Ontario) renamed itself Chartered Professionals in Human Resources (CPHR). It replaced the CHRP designation across Canada with a new designation of Chartered Professional in Human Resources (CPHR, the same name and acronym as the governing body). This was due in part to the representation of CHRP as a junior or entry-level designation by the Ontario association (thereby depreciating the value of the CHRP), and in part as a reaction to market confusion regarding the designations in Canada. Those who secured the CHRP designations in the affiliated associations outside of Ontario in the past are now recognized with the CPHR designation instead. **Table 1.2** provides clarity on the designations and associations in HR in Canada as of 2017.

At the time that this chapter was last updated, the impact of the multiple designations on the labour market perceptions of the professional designation were unknown. Pragmatically, most HR professionals feel that a common national designation would be in the best interest of HR professionals but also understand the complex political and structural environment of professional associations. In 2017, advertised positions in HR appeared either to value CHRL and CPHR designations equally, or to suggest that a professional designation in HR was a desired attribute, rather than a requirement, without referring to which designation would be considered. The impact of this change should be unfolding in the labour market in the near future.

Other important associations for HR specialists include the Canadian Industrial Relations Association; WorldatWork for compensation and rewards issues; health and safety associations, such as the Industrial Accident Prevention Association, the Construction Safety Association, and Safe Communities Canada; and Institute for Performance and Learning (formerly the Canadian Society for Training and Development).

In addition to the international- and national-level broad HR designations, a series of more specialized or specific professional designations in Canada allows

TABLE 1.2   HR Associations by Province and Designation

Jurisdiction	HR Association	Designation	Link
British Columbia and Yukon	Human Resources Management Association (HRMA)	CPHR	www.hrma.ca
Alberta, Nunavet, and Northwest Territories	Human Resources Institute of Alberta (HRIA)	CPHR	www.hria.ca
Saskatchewan	Saskatchewan Association of Human Resource Professionals (SAHRP)	CPHR	www.sahrp.ca
Manitoba	Human Resource Management Association of Manitoba (HRMAM)	CPHR	www.hrmam.org
New Brunswick	Human Resources Association of New Brunswick (HRANB)	CPHR	www.hranb.org
Nova Scotia and Prince Edward Island	Human Resources Association of Nova Scotia (HRANS)	CPHR	www.hrans.org
Newfoundland and Labrador	Human Resources Professionals of Newfoundland and Labrador (HRPNL)	CPHR	www.hrpnl.ca
Quebec	Ordre des counseillers en ressources humaines et en relations industrielles agréés du Québec (ORHRI)	CPHR	portailrh.org
Ontario	Human Resources Professionals Association of Ontario (HRPAO)	CHRP, CHRL, CHRE	www.hrpa.ca

those who may be interested in specialized areas to gain recognition for a deeper level of subject matter expertise. These include the Group Benefits Associate (GBA), Registered Professional Recruiter (RPR), Canadian Payroll Manager (CPM), Certified Employee Benefits Specialist (CEBS), Canadian Management Professional (CMP), and Certified Training and Development Professional (CTDP) designations.

1.3.1 Ethics and Corporate Social Responsibility

ethics The principles of conduct governing an individual or a group; specifically, the standards you use to decide what your conduct should be.

Ethics means the standards someone uses to decide what his or her conduct should be. However, what is ethical or unethical is generally open to debate (except in a few very clear-cut cases such as willful misrepresentation). Most codes do not tell employees what they should do. Rather, codes provide a guide to help employees discover the best course of action by themselves.[26] Increasingly, HR departments are being given a greater role in providing ethics training and monitoring to ensure compliance with the code of ethics. Some organizations have such a commitment to ethics that they have a full-time ethics officer. However, others are less committed: A 2008 survey of HR professionals found that 78.2 percent indicated that they had been coerced into doing something morally or legally ambiguous at least once in their careers.[27]

An Ethical Dilemma

Can or should an employee reveal information that was disclosed in confidence about a troubled co-worker, and if so, under what circumstances?

The most prevalent ethical issues confronting Canadian organizations today pertain to security of information, employee and client privacy, environmental issues, governance, and conflicts of interest.[28] The major reasons for the failure of ethics programs to achieve the desired results are lack of effective leadership and inadequate training. Positive outcomes associated with properly implemented ethics programs include increased confidence among stakeholders, such as clients, partners, and employees; greater client/customer and employee loyalty; decreased vulnerability to crime; reduced losses due to internal theft; and increased public trust.[29]

In recent years, the concept of **social responsibility** has frequently been discussed as an important manifestation of ethics. A company that exercises social responsibility attempts to balance its commitments, not only to its investors but also to its employees and customers, other businesses, and the community or communities in which it operates. Mountain Equipment Co-op (MEC) is an example of a company that considers socially responsible approaches to all aspects of its business—selecting and designing products, manufacturing MEC-brand products, transporting products and people, greening operations, engaging employees, equipping members, supporting the community, driving economic performance, and governing the cooperative. It examines every aspect of a product's life cycle from a social responsibility perspective, from the resources that go into making and shipping it, to the satisfaction of the employees and the members who take the products home.[30]

social responsibility   The implied, enforced, or felt obligation of managers, acting in their official capacities, to serve or protect the interests of groups other than themselves.

1.4 ENVIRONMENTAL INFLUENCES ON HRM

There are numerous external and internal environmental influences that drive the strategic focus of HRM. To be effective, all managers, including those with responsibility for HR, must monitor the environment on an ongoing basis, assess the impact of any changes, and be proactive in responding to such challenges. Table 1.3 illustrates the major external and internal environmental influences on HRM.

1.4.1 External Environmental Influences

Six major external environmental influences on HRM will be discussed: economic conditions, labour market issues, technology, government, globalization, and environmental concerns.

TABLE 1.3   External and Internal Environmental Influences on HRM

External	Internal
Economic Conditions: affect supply and demand for products, impacting quantity and quality of employees required and ability to pay/give benefits	Organizational Culture: values, beliefs, and norms of organizational members
Labour Diversity: protected groups (visible/ethnic minorities, women, Aboriginal, disabled) and generational differences (traditionalists, baby boomers, Gen X-ers, Gen Y-ers)	Organizational Climate: the atmosphere's impact on employee motivation, job performance, and productivity
Technology: controlling data and privacy	Management Practices: organizational structure and employee empowerment
Government: abiding by provincial and national standards	
Globalization: managing the workforce in an intense, hypercompetitive global economy	
Environment: managing sustainability and corporate social responsibility	

1.4.1.1 Economic Conditions

Economic conditions affect supply and demand for products and services, which, in turn, have a dramatic impact on the number and types of employees required as well as on an employer's ability to pay wages and provide benefits. When the economy is healthy, companies often hire more workers as demand for products and services increases. Consequently, when unemployment rates fall, there is more competition for qualified employees, and training and retention strategies increase in importance. Conversely, during an economic downturn, some firms reduce pay and benefits to maintain workers' jobs. Other employers are forced to downsize by offering attractive early retirement and early-leave programs or by laying off or terminating employees. Unemployment rates rise, and employers are often overwhelmed with applicants when vacancies are advertised.

Productivity refers to the ratio of an organization's outputs (goods and services) to its inputs (people, capital, energy, and materials). Canada's relatively low productivity growth rate is of concern because of increasing global competition. To improve productivity, managers must find ways to produce more outputs with current input levels or use fewer resources to maintain current output levels. In most organizations today, productivity improvement is essential for long-term success.

Employment trends in Canada have been experiencing dramatic change. The **primary sector**, which includes agriculture, fishing and trapping, forestry, and mining, now represents only 4 percent of jobs. Employment in the **secondary sector** (manufacturing and construction) has decreased to 19 percent of jobs. The sector that has grown to represent 77 percent of jobs, dominating the Canadian economy, is the **tertiary or service sector**, which includes public administration, personal and business services, finance, trade, public utilities, and transportation/communications.

Since all jobs in the service sector involve the provision of services by employees to individual customers, effectively managing and motivating human resources is critical. Although there are some lesser-skilled jobs (in housekeeping and food services, for example), many service-sector jobs demand highly knowledgeable employees.

1.4.1.2 Labour Market Issues

Increasing Workforce Diversity Canada's workforce is among the most diverse in the world. *Diversity* refers to the attributes that humans are likely to use to tell themselves "that person is different from me." These attributes include demographic factors (such as race, gender, and age), as well as values and cultural norms.[31] In Canada, while there are four protected groups (visible and ethnic minorities, women, Aboriginals, and persons with disabilities), the concept of diversity is used broadly to describe differences in many aspects (e.g., gender identification, nationality, age, etc.) that are identified with the individual regardless of his or her place of employment.

Generational Issues Another aspect of diversity is generational differences. There are four generations in the workplace, and nearly half of all Canadians say they have experienced a clash with workers older or younger than themselves. However, about one-quarter of workers say they don't notice age differences and another one-quarter think this situation provides an excellent learning opportunity. **Table 1.4** outlines attitudes, key characteristics, and expectations of the four generations.

productivity   The ratio of an organization's outputs (goods and services) to its inputs (people, capital, energy, and materials).

primary sector   Jobs in agriculture, fishing and trapping, forestry, and mining.

secondary sector   Jobs in manufacturing and construction.

tertiary or service sector   Jobs in public administration, personal and business services, finance, trade, public utilities, and transportation/communications.

TABLE 1.4   The Four Generations

	Traditionalists 1922–1945	Baby Boomers 1946–1964	Gen X-ers 1965–1980	Gen Y-ers 1981–2000
Notes	Grew up in an era of hardship, including a war and the Great Depression.	The largest group in the workforce. Grew up in a time of major optimism and change amidst the moon landing and the women's movement.	This group grew up as divorce rates skyrocketed. First technology-literate generation.	Beginning to enter the workforce. Expect to change jobs frequently.
Attitudes, Values, and Expectations	• Loyalty • Respect for authority • Dedication • Sacrifice • Conformity • Honour • Privacy • Stability • Economic conservatism	• Optimism • Involvement • Team oriented • Personal growth and gratification • Youthfulness • Equality • Career focused	• Independence • Self-reliance • Pragmatism • Skepticism • Informality • Balance	• Confidence • Diversity • Civic duty • Optimism • Immediate access to information and services
Key Characteristics	• Compliant • Detail oriented • Hard-working • Fiscally frugal • Trustworthy • Risk averse • Long-term focused	• Driven to succeed • Team player • Relationship focused • Eager to add value • Politically savvy in the workplace • Competitive	• Tech-literate • Flexible and adaptable • Creative • Entrepreneurial • Multitasker • Results driven • Individualistic	• Tech-savvy • Collective action • Expressive and tolerant of differences • Eager to accept challenges • Innovative and creative

Source: Reprinted with permission from *HR Professional* magazine and the Human Resources Professionals Association (HRPA). www.hrpa.ca.

Education Approximately 54 percent of Canada's population has some postsecondary education (trades, college, or university).[32] Given the higher expectations of the better-educated labour force, managers are expected to ensure that the talents and capabilities of employees are fully utilized and that opportunities are provided for career growth.

On the other hand, a startlingly high proportion of the population (26 percent) has only marginal literacy skills, meaning that their ability to understand and use printed and written documents in daily activities to achieve goals and to develop knowledge and potential is limited. A frightening reality is that inadequate reading and writing skills have replaced lack of experience as the major reason for rejecting entry-level candidates.[33] **Figure 1.2** provides a recent breakdown of literacy levels in Canada. Functional illiteracy is exacting a toll not only on individual social and economic opportunities, but also on organizations' accident rates and productivity levels.

Non-Standard or Contingent Workers The labour market has undergone major structural changes with the growth of **contingent (or "non-standard") workers**, that is, workers who do not fit the traditional definition of permanent, full-time employment with the same employer on an indeterminate basis. These non-traditional workers are often used by companies to provide flexible, on-demand labour, without the same guarantees for continued employment, employee development, or benefits that regular full-time employees are given.

The forms of employment involving part-time, fixed-term, temporary, home, and standby workers, those who

contingent/non-standard workers Workers who do not have regular full-time employment status.

An Ethical Dilemma

The maintenance department supervisor has just come to you, the HR manager, voicing concern about the safety of two of her reporting employees whom she recently discovered to be functionally illiterate. What are your responsibilities to these employees, if any?

FIGURE 1.2   Literacy and Income Levels of Canadians (16–64 Years Old)

Level 1: 17% of adults: 29% in low income bracket, with median household income of $49 696

This level represents individuals with very low levels of literacy skills. They may be unable to follow written instructions at work or determine correct measurements required for task completion.

Level 2: 32% of adults: 17% in low-income bracket, with median household income of $63 520

This level includes individuals who can comprehend material that is is simple and straightforward. While they can read, they generally score poorly on tests involving reading. They can cope on a non-complex, daily level but face difficulty with more complex demands, such as learning new job skills.

Level 3: 37% of adults: 11% in low-income bracket, with median household income of $74 568

The majority of Canadians are at the level 3 literacy level. This skill level involves the ability to integrate multiple sources of information or solve complex problems.

Level 4 & 5: 13% of adults: 8% in low-income bracket, with median household income of $84 583

This is the highest literacy level. Individuals at this level have higher-order information processing skills.

Source: Adapted from Alison Campbell, *All Signs Point to Yes: Literacy's Impact on Workplace Health and Safety* (Ottawa: Conference Board of Canada, September 2008), p. 4. Based on data from A. Heisz, G. Notten, and J. Situ, "The Association between Skills and Low Income," *Insights on Canadian Society* (February 2016), http://www.statcan.gc.ca/pub/75-006-x/2016001/article/14322-eng.htm.

Increased Use of Contract Workers

HR by the Numbers

63% of companies have seen an increase in the use of contract workers in their organization in the last five years

51.2% identify that contract workers in their company receive no benefits at all

23.6% feel company does not have well-defined processes in place to manage contract workers

have more than one job, and the self-employed have become so significant numerically that they now affect about one-third of the workforce. More women fall into this category than men.[34] Non-standard work is often poorly paid, offers little or no job security, and is generally not covered by employment legislation. The HR by the Numbers box identifies some core metrics associated with the use of contingent workers in Canada.

1.4.1.3 Technology

Twitter, Facebook, videoconferencing, and other technology-aided setups can make it seem as if everyone were in the same room. Technology can make working in and managing a dispersed workforce easier and can enable people to work anywhere and everywhere. The workplace of today includes "hotels, cafes and conference venues, as well as public areas of lounges and airports."[35] However, it has also brought new concerns as the line between work and family time has become blurred.[36]

Questions concerning data control, accuracy, the right to privacy, and ethics are at the core of a growing controversy brought about by the new information technologies. In some firms, sophisticated computerized control systems are used to monitor employee speed, accuracy, and efficiency. More firms are also monitoring employee email, voice mail, telephone conversations, and computer usage, and some now monitor employee behaviour using video surveillance.[37]

1.4.1.4 Government

Various laws enacted by governments have had, and will continue to have, a dramatic impact on the employer–employee relationship in Canada. One of the factors that makes employment law in Canada so challenging is that there are 14 different jurisdictions involved. Each of the ten provinces and three territories has its own human rights, employment standards, labour relations, health and safety, and workers' compensation legislation. In addition, about 10 percent of the workforce (including employees of the federal government and Crown corporations, chartered banks, airlines, national railways, and the Canadian Armed Forces) is covered by federal employment legislation.

Although there is some commonality across jurisdictions, there is also considerable variation. Minimum wage, overtime pay requirements, vacation entitlement, and grounds protected under human rights legislation, for example, vary from one province/territory to another. Furthermore, some jurisdictions have pay equity and employment equity legislation while others do not. This means that in companies with employees in more than one jurisdiction, different rules apply to different employees. There are, however, certain laws that apply to all employers and employees across Canada, such as employment insurance and the Canada/Quebec Pension Plan.

1.4.1.5 Globalization

Globalization refers to the emergence of a single global market for most products and services. There are increasing numbers of multinational corporations—firms that conduct a large part of their business outside the country in which they are headquartered and that locate a significant percentage of their physical facilities and human resources in other countries. For example, Toyota has a large market share in the United States, Europe, and Africa, and is the market leader in Australia. Toyota has factories all over the world, manufacturing or assembling vehicles like the Corolla for local markets. Notably, Toyota has manufacturing or assembly plants in the United States, Japan, Australia, Canada, Indonesia, Poland, South Africa, Turkey, the United Kingdom, France, and Brazil, and has recently added plants in Pakistan, India, Argentina, the Czech Republic, Mexico, Malaysia, Thailand, China, and Venezuela.[38]

Globalization means that HR professionals need to become familiar with employment legislation in other countries and need to manage ethical dilemmas when labour standards are substantially lower than those in Canada. Companies doing business in sub-Saharan Africa, for example, have to deal with a high death rate among employees with AIDS. Some companies are paying for antiretroviral drugs to keep their employees alive.[39]

© Lubafilatova/Fotolia

Employees are increasingly concerned about social responsibility, including environmental responsibility, on the part of their employers.

1.4.1.6 Environmental Concerns

Environmental concerns have suddenly (some might say finally) emerged as an issue for people, particularly the younger generations.[40] Sustainability, climate change, global warming, pollution, carbon footprints, extinction of wildlife species, ecosystem fragility, and other related issues are increasingly important to people around the world. There is increasing evidence that interest in environmental issues is motivating the behaviour of employees, and that they are concerned about whether they work for environmentally responsible companies. Companies like Fairmont Hotels have made environmental stewardship a priority for almost 20 years. They have found that developing a reputation as an environmental leader and demonstrating corporate social responsibility have not only helped them to gain market share, but have also been a strong employee retention tool.[41]

1.4.2 Internal Environmental Influences

How a firm deals with the three internal environmental influences of organizational culture, organizational climate, and management practices has a major impact on its ability to meet its objectives.

1.4.2.1 Organizational Culture

organizational culture   The core values, beliefs, and assumptions that are widely shared by members of an organization.

Organizational culture consists of the core values, beliefs, and assumptions that are widely shared by members of an organization. Culture is often conveyed through an organization's mission statement, as well as through stories, myths, symbols, and ceremonies. It serves a variety of purposes:

- Communicating what the organization "believes in" and "stands for"
- Providing employees with a sense of direction and expected behaviour (norms)
- Shaping employees' attitudes about themselves, the organization, and their roles
- Creating a sense of identity, orderliness, and consistency
- Fostering employee loyalty and commitment

© Ministr-84/Shutterstock

Employees in fast-food establishments are taught how to provide courteous, efficient customer service.

All managers with HR responsibilities play an important role in creating and maintaining the type of organizational culture desired. For example, they may organize recognition ceremonies for high-performing employees and be involved in decisions regarding symbols, such as a logo or the design of new company premises. Having a positive culture has a positive impact on employer branding, recruitment, retention, and productivity.

1.4.2.2 Organizational Climate

organizational climate   The prevailing atmosphere that exists in an organization and its impact on employees.

Organizational climate refers to the prevailing atmosphere, or "internal weather," that exists in an organization and its impact on employees.[42] It can be friendly or unfriendly, open or secretive, rigid or flexible, innovative or stagnant. The major factors influencing the climate are management's leadership style, HR policies and practices, and the amount and style of organizational communication. The type of climate that exists is generally reflected in the level of employee motivation, job satisfaction, performance, and productivity.

HR professionals play a key role in helping managers throughout the firm establish and maintain a positive organizational climate.

1.4.2.3 Management Practices

Management practices have changed considerably over the past decade, with many HRM implications. For example, the traditional bureaucratic structure with many levels of management is being replaced by flatter organizational forms, using cross-functional teams and improved communication. Since managers have more people reporting to them in flat structures, they cannot supervise their employees as closely, and employee **empowerment** has greatly increased.

> **empowerment**   Providing workers with the skills and authority to make decisions that would traditionally be made by managers.

CHAPTER SUMMARY

1. Human resources management (HRM) refers to the management of people in organizations. Strategic HRM involves linking HRM with strategic goals and objectives to improve business performance. In more and more firms, HR professionals are becoming partners in strategy formulation and execution.

2. The two major stages in the evolution of HR management thinking were (1) personnel management, which focused on administrative tasks, and (2) HRM, in which it was recognized that organizational success is linked to operational and strategic management of labour.

3. Core roles that HR professionals must fulfill today include those of talent manager, culture/change steward, strategic architect, operational executor, business ally, and credible activist. These roles are shared with managers and executives in the organization, with HR professionals often assuming roles of advisers or subject-matter experts.

4. There are numerous professional designations that will boost a career trajectory in human resources from various provincial/territorial HR associations in Canada. However, additional designations exist that are important and may be influential in building expertise and careers in management or HRM.

5. Activities of employee management, empowerment, training, and guidance are often shared between managers in the organization (executive and line managers) and HR professionals. Therefore, managers, executives, and HR personnel are all influential in effective HRM.

6. A number of external factors have an impact on HRM, including economic factors, labour market issues, technology, government, globalization, and environmental concerns. Internal factors impacting HRM include organizational culture, organizational climate and management practices.

MyLab Management

Visit MyLab Management to access a personalized Study Plan, Personal Inventory Assessments (PIA), and a collection of videos and assignments within MediaShare.

KEY TERMS

balanced scorecard *(p. 8)*
certification *(p. 9)*
change agents *(p. 6)*
contingent/non-standard workers *(p. 13)*
employee engagement *(p. 5)*
empowerment *(p. 17)*
environmental scanning *(p. 6)*
ethics *(p. 10)*
human capital *(p. 2)*
human resources management (HRM) *(p. 2)*

metrics *(p. 8)*
organizational climate *(p. 16)*
organizational culture *(p. 16)*
primary sector *(p. 12)*
productivity *(p. 12)*
secondary sector *(p. 12)*
social responsibility *(p. 11)*
strategy *(p. 6)*
tertiary or service sector *(p. 12)*

REVIEW AND DISCUSSION QUESTIONS

1. Describe the transformation that HR has undergone over the years. Discuss how changes in internal and external factors have contributed to the evolution in HR.

2. Describe the role of HR in strategy formulation and strategy implementation.

3. Describe how the external environment influences HR.

4. Differentiate between organizational culture and organizational climate.

5. Describe the multiple jurisdictions related to employment legislation affecting HRM in Canada.

6. Discuss the six core competencies required of HR professionals. Identify how these competencies are also embedded in the roles of line managers, senior managers, and C-level executives in an organization.

7. Explain how HR has become professionalized, and describe the value of this professionalization.

CRITICAL THINKING QUESTIONS

1. Explain how demographics and workforce diversity have had an impact on the organization in which you are working or one in which you have worked. What policies or practices did managers or HR in the organization have in place to help assist with the management of a diverse internal labour force?

2. Explain how changing economic and competitive pressures have had an impact on the organization in which you are working or one in which you have worked. How has your business responded to these pressures?

3. A firm has requested your assistance in ensuring that its multigenerational workforce functions effectively as a team. What strategies or programs would you recommend? Why?

4. Choose a non-HR role you have had in your previous jobs. Identify how you used the core competencies of HR professionals in that role and how it affected your job performance.

EXPERIENTIAL EXERCISES

1. Working alone or with a small group of classmates, interview an HR manager and prepare a short essay regarding his or her role in strategy formulation and implementation.

2. Review job ads for five executive roles (such as CEO, vice-president, or president) on job posting websites or corporate websites. Identify common competencies required for those roles as per the ads. Contrast these required competencies (both implied and explicit) with the core HR professional competencies highlighted in this chapter. Discuss the most consistently required competency and how it is important in non-HR roles.

3. According to a 2016 study of the world's most attractive firms (released by Universum), the top 10 employers for career seekers with a business background were (in priority order): Google, Apple, Ernst & Young (EY), Goldman Sachs, PricewaterhouseCoopers (PwC), Deloitte, Microsoft, KPMG, L'Oréal Group, and J.P. Morgan. In groups, review the company websites of these organizations to determine the corporate strategy, objectives, and markets that these organizations target. As a team, discuss the similarities and differences among the strategies, objectives, and markets of these 10 employers. Explain how these factors might affect

Generation Y's perception of these companies as desirable employers.

4. Using the sample balanced scorecard template provided by your professor or found online, in pairs develop a balanced scorecard measure for a well-known company in the retail urban clothing sector. As you develop your measures, be sure to take into consideration current economic conditions.

Exchange your completed set of measures with that of another student team. Compare and contrast your measures. Is one set "better" than the other? Why or why not? Debrief as instructed.

2

THE CHANGING LEGAL EMPHASIS:
Compliance and Impact on Canadian Workplaces

LEARNING OUTCOMES

AFTER STUDYING THIS CHAPTER, YOU SHOULD BE ABLE TO:

EXPLAIN how employment-related issues are governed in Canada.

DISCUSS at least five prohibited grounds for discrimination under human rights legislation, and **DESCRIBE** the requirements for reasonable accommodation.

DESCRIBE behaviour that could constitute harassment, and **EXPLAIN** the employer's responsibilities regarding harassment.

DESCRIBE the role of minimums established in employment standards legislation and the enforcement process.

2.1 THE LEGAL FRAMEWORK FOR EMPLOYMENT LAW IN CANADA

A survey of 451 HR professionals in Canada indicates that the most critical pieces of knowledge required in HR are business acumen, followed by employment law/legislative awareness and talent management.[1] HR professionals are expected to provide guidance, training, programs, and policy developments that are legally defensible. In addition, the actions of supervisors and managers, as agents of the organization, must also comply with legislated rules and regulations. Given the risk of expensive lawsuits and their impact on employer branding or reputation, knowing and following employment law is important to both HR and non-HR persons in the workplace.

A number of distinct sets of responsibilities, including formal and informal expectations, exist between the employee and employer. There is a mutual expectation of each party to maintain the employment relationship by fulfilling their own responsibilities within the relationship, and these are difficult to manage or correct if one party (employer or employee) feels that the other has violated the expectations of the relationship. For example, employees might have an implied, informal expectation that as long as they work for the scheduled number of hours and have adequate performance, they won't be fired. Industry experts also recognize a shared responsibility towards ensuring employee and employer compliance with legislation, as highlighted in the Expert Opinion box.

The primary objective of most employment legislation in Canada is to prevent employers from exploiting paid workers, assuming that that the employer has more power than the employee.[2] **Figure 2.1** illustrates the balance between employer,

FIGURE 2.1 It Is the Government's Role to Balance Employer and Employee Needs

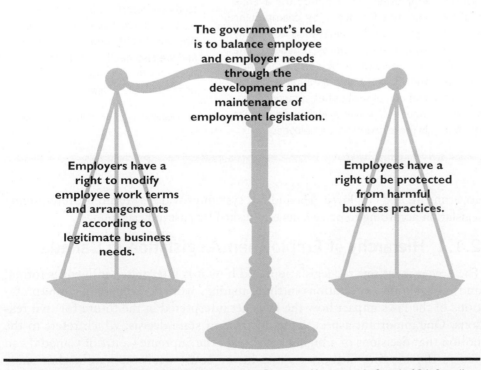

Source: Data from Gary Dessler and Nita Chhinzer, *Human Resources Mangement in Canada,* 13th Canadian ed. (Toronto, ON: Pearson, 2013), Chapter 2.

Industry Viewpoint
EXPERT OPINION

1. While the focus of employment law in Canada is to protect both employer and employees rights, most of what we read or hear is focused on protecting employees. What are some of the core legal obligations employees have to their employers?

Most employee obligations come through common law rather than legislation. There is an expected duty of loyalty. Employers contract employees to work, which requires being honest and productive (e.g., don't spend work hours texting). In addition, the employee is expected to not engage in a conflict of interest, which means the employee cannot steal company information, start a new business, or take that information to competitors.

2. In your opinion, who is responsible for compliance with employment laws within an organization?

Everybody. Some laws affect employees, such as health and safety (the employee has a responsibility to comply) or human rights laws (the employee cannot engage in discriminatory behaviour). Management has the responsibility to enforce and apply the law. Human resource teams share responsibility for

Lauren Bernardi

Identification:
Ms. Lauren Bernardi (LLB)
Principal at Bernardi Human Resource Law and author of *Powerful Employment Policies*, published by Canada Law Book

compliance, but they also serve an advisory role.

The leadership and the owners of the business have to take a top-down approach to compliance, and they genuinely need to care about their employees. They can be the avenue HR uses for buy-in by championing the value of adherence to legally sound best business practices. The leadership team should also recognize the business opportunity proactive and compliant business practices provide (e.g., progressive discipline results in more productive employees).

3. Based on your experience, what areas of concern are most overlooked by employers?

I. The impact of the negative work environment, which can be formed when management and employers disregard harassment claims or toxic workplaces. These affect the bottom line through decreased productivity, and increased turnover and absenteeism.

II. Rather than appreciating the strategic and business benefits of managing HR issues, employers often use the legal system to reactively investigate a complaint. Employers need to consider a more proactive approach to developing policies, procedures, and decision-making within the legal framework.

III. Psychosocial factors that affect the health of the organization and its employees as well as the bottom line are often neglected. Recently, an initiative by the Mental Health Commission of Canada was created aimed at bringing awareness to these factors. The initiative suggests that we have to consider physical health and safety laws, and we also need to consider psychosocial factors, such as respect, engagement, and leadership.

Source: Reprinted by permission from Lauren Bernardi.

government, and employee. The judicial system provides a forum for interpreting legislation according to precedents established by past judicial rulings.

2.1.1 Hierarchy of Employment Legislation in Canada

The government sets the legislation, and how it is interpreted influences formal and information expectations in the Canadian workplace. Previous interpretations of the laws impact how the laws get interpreted in the future for two reasons. One important aspect is the doctrine of **stare decisis**, which refers to the notion that decisions of a higher court (e.g., the Supreme Court of Canada) can act as the binding authority on a lower court decision within that same

stare decisis   Decisions of a higher court can act as the binding authority on a lower court decision within that same jurisdiction.

jurisdiction (e.g., provincial courts). The second important consideration is **precedent**, which refers to how the decision or interpretation of a court of one jurisdiction can act as a persuasive authority regarding how legislation is to be interpreted and applied in other jurisdictions.

precedent The decision or interpretation of a court of another jurisdiction can act as a persuasive authority regarding how legislation is to be interpreted and applied in other jurisdictions.

1. As highlighted in **Figure 2.2**, at the broadest level all persons residing in Canada are guaranteed protection under constitutional law, particularly the Charter of Rights and Freedoms. The regulations set forth in the Charter are not employment specific, but all employers must abide by them because they are fundamental, guaranteed rights to all persons residing in Canada.

2. Provincial human rights codes ensure that the rights of every Canadian are protected and that all persons are treated with equality and respect. Discrimination based on protected grounds highlighted in the legislation is prohibited in not only the employment relationship but also the delivery of goods and services. Therefore, while the Charter of Rights and Freedoms and human rights codes extend beyond just the employment relationship, they both have a significant impact on workplace practices.

3. In Canada, employers must abide by a series of employment-specific legislation, such as the Employment Standards Act, which vary slightly by jurisdiction. There is a great deal of commonality to the legislation, but there are also some differences. For example, vacations, statutory holidays, and minimum wage standards are provided by all jurisdictions, but specific entitlements may vary from one jurisdiction to the next. Therefore, a company with employees in more than one province/territory must monitor the legislation in each of those jurisdictions and remain current as legislation changes. Ensuring legality across multiple jurisdictions can be complex, since it is

FIGURE 2.2   Multiple Layers of Canadian Legislation Affecting Workplace
Practices

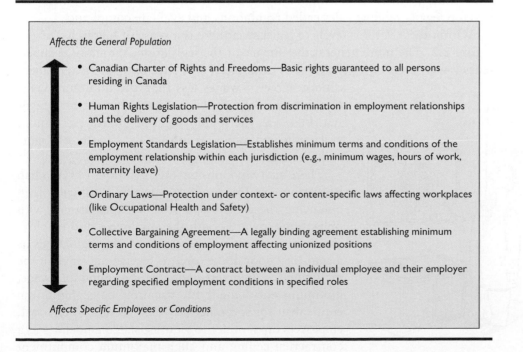

Affects the General Population

- Canadian Charter of Rights and Freedoms—Basic rights guaranteed to all persons residing in Canada

- Human Rights Legislation—Protection from discrimination in employment relationships and the delivery of goods and services

- Employment Standards Legislation—Establishes minimum terms and conditions of the employment relationship within each jurisdiction (e.g., minimum wages, hours of work, maternity leave)

- Ordinary Laws—Protection under context- or content-specific laws affecting workplaces (like Occupational Health and Safety)

- Collective Bargaining Agreement—A legally binding agreement establishing minimum terms and conditions of employment affecting unionized positions

- Employment Contract—A contract between an individual employee and their employer regarding specified employment conditions in specified roles

Affects Specific Employees or Conditions

Source: Based on Nita Chhinzer (2011).

possible for a policy, practice, or procedure to be legal in one jurisdiction yet illegal in others.

4. There are laws that specifically regulate some areas of HRM—occupational health and safety (occupational health and safety acts are reviewed in Chapter 10), union relations (labour relations acts are reviewed in Chapter 12), as well as pensions and compensation (pay equity acts, the Income Tax Act, and others are discussed briefly in Chapters 8 and 9).

5. Even more specific is the issue of contract law, which governs collective agreements and individual employment contracts. Such laws impose specific requirements and constraints on management and employee policies, procedures, and practices. For example, a collective bargaining agreement is a contract regarding the terms and conditions of employment that both employees and employers must abide by legally. In non-unionized situations, individual employment contracts are often signed prior to the commencement of the employment relationship and constitute individualized legal agreements that employees and employers must abide by.

Government of Canada
http://canada.gc.ca

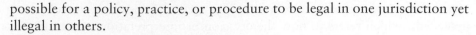

2.1.2 Tort Law

In addition to the legislation above, Canada has also inherited the English system of tort law. **Tort law** is primarily judge-based law, whereby the precedent and jurisprudences set by one judge through his or her assessment of a case establishes how similar cases will be interpreted. Tort laws are often separated into two categories: intentional torts (for example, assault, battery, trespass, intentional affliction of mental distress) and unintentional torts (for example, negligence based on events in which harm is caused by carelessness).

tort law Primarily judge-based law, whereby the precedent and jurisprudences set by one judge through his or her assessment of a case establishes how similar cases will be interpreted, as either intentional torts or unintentional torts.

To avoid flooding the courts with complaints and the prosecutions of relatively minor infractions, the government in each jurisdiction creates special regulatory bodies to enforce compliance with the law and aid in its interpretation. Such bodies, which include human rights commissions and ministries of labour, develop legally binding rules called **regulations** and evaluate complaints.

regulations Legally binding rules established by special regulatory bodies created to enforce compliance with the law and aid in its interpretation.

Within these various levels of legislation there is a sense of hierarchy, as per **Figure 2.2.** The more general the impact of the legislation, the more it supersedes lower levels of legislation. For example, a collective bargaining agreement cannot agree to wages less than the minimum wage established in the provincial Employment Standards Act. Likewise, the Employment Standards Act cannot violate the minimums set forth in the Charter of Rights and Freedoms.

There are two opposing interpretations of Canadian legislation, and HR professionals play a critical role in balancing these divergent sets of expectations, with obligations towards both the employees and employers. Employees often choose to view the regulations as a statutory floor and expect to receive higher than the minimum requirements (more than the minimum wage, minimum entitlement for vacation days, minimum entitlement for severance pay, and so on). In contrast, employers often prefer to view legislated guidelines as a contractual ceiling and align maximum commitment levels to the minimums established in the guidelines.

"See that dark spot? That's potential litigation."

© Cartoonresource/Fotolia

2.2 LEGISLATION PROTECTING THE GENERAL POPULATION

Human rights legislation makes it illegal to discriminate, even unintentionally, against various groups. Reactive (complaint driven) in nature, the focus of such legislation is on the types of acts that employers should I *not engage* in. Included in this category are the following:

1. *The Charter of Rights and Freedoms*, federal legislation that is the cornerstone of fundamental human rights in Canada
2. *Human rights legislation*, prohibits intentional and unintentional discrimination in employment situations and in the delivery of goods and services in every jurisdiction present in every jurisdiction

2.2.1 The Charter of Rights and Freedoms

The cornerstone of Canada's legislation pertaining to issues of human rights is the Constitution Act, which contains the **Charter of Rights and Freedoms**. The Charter applies to the actions of all levels of government (federal, provincial/territorial, and municipal) and agencies under their jurisdiction as they go about their work of creating laws. The Charter takes precedence over all other laws, which means that all legislation must meet Charter standards; thus, it is quite far-reaching in scope.

Charter of Rights and Freedoms Federal law enacted in 1982 that guarantees fundamental freedoms to all Canadians.

There are two notable exceptions to this generalization. First, the Charter allows laws to infringe on Charter rights if the law can be demonstrably justified as reasonable limits in a "free and democratic society." Since "demonstrably justified" and "reasonable" are open to interpretation, many issues challenged under the Charter eventually end up before the ultimate interpreter for the Charter, the Supreme Court of Canada. The second exception occurs when a legislative body invokes the "notwithstanding" provision, which allows the legislation to be exempted from challenge under the Charter.

Supreme Court of Canada
www.scc-csc.gc.ca

The Charter provides fundamental rights and freedoms to every Canadian, including but not limited to the following:

1. Freedom of conscience and religion
2. Freedom of thought, belief, opinion, and expression, including freedom of the press and other media of communication
3. Freedom of peaceful assembly
4. Freedom of association

equality rights   Section 15 of the Charter of Rights and Freedoms, which guarantees the right to equal protection and benefit of the law without discrimination.

In addition, the Charter provides Canadian multicultural heritage rights, First Nations' rights, minority language education rights, equality rights, the right to live and work anywhere in Canada, the right to due process in criminal proceedings, and the right to democracy.[3]

Section 15—**equality rights**—provides the basis for human rights legislation, as it guarantees the right to equal protection and benefit of the law without discrimination, in particular without discrimination based on race, national or ethnic origin, colour, religion, sex, age, or mental or physical disability.[4]

The freedom of religion is protected under the Charter of Rights and Freedoms and applies to all levels of government.

© Eray/Fotolia

2.2.2 Human Rights Legislation

human rights legislation
Jurisdiction-specific legislation that prohibits intentional and unintentional discrimination in employment situations and in the delivery of goods and services.

Every person residing in Canada is protected by **human rights legislation,** which prohibits intentional and unintentional discrimination in employment situations and in the delivery of goods and services. The human rights legislation supersedes the terms of any employment contract or collective agreement;[5] therefore, supervisors and managers must act in accordance with the human rights legislation of their jurisdiction. For these reasons, supervisors and managers must be thoroughly familiar with the human rights legislation of their jurisdiction and their legal obligations and responsibilities as specified therein.

To review each of the provincial and territorial human rights laws would be confusing because of the various, but often minor, differences among them. For example, some provinces use the term "creed," others "religion." Most provincial/territorial laws are similar to the federal statute in terms of scope, interpretation, and application. All jurisdictions prohibit discrimination on the grounds of disability, race, colour, religion/creed, sex, sexual orientation, marital status, and age. Some, but not all, jurisdictions further prohibit discrimination on the basis of family status, nationality or ethnic origin, political belief, association, and various other grounds. This creates a challenging situation for organizations operating in more than one jurisdiction since protected grounds for discrimination varies by jurisdiction. **Figure 2.3** indicates the types of complaints received by the Canadian Human Rights Commission (federal level) in 2016 by category. It is important to know that 29 percent of complaints associated with disability were related to mental health. This will be discussed in detail later in this section.

Canadian Human Rights Tribunal
www.chrt-tcdp.gc.ca

FIGURE 2.3   Types of Complaints Received by the Canadian Human Rights Commission in 2016, by number of complaints

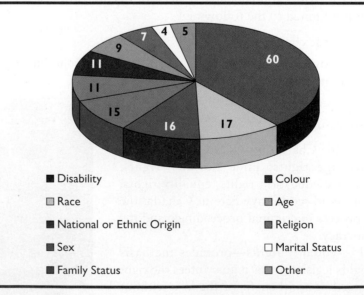

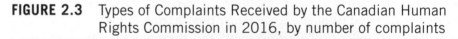

Source: Based on *People First: The Canadian Human Rights Commission's 2016 Annual Report to Parliament* (Ottawa, ON: CHRC, 2017), p. 57, figure 9, http://www.chrcreport.ca/assets/pdf/CHRC-Annual-2016-EN-web.pdf (accessed July 6, 2017).

2.2.2.1 Discrimination Defined in Human Rights Legislation

Central to human rights laws is the concept of **discrimination**. Recent research exploring the conceptual underpinnings of discrimination refers to employment discrimination as intergroup biases that occur because of social group memberships,[6] which often creates an identity of how we define and see ourselves versus others. The concept of self versus others develops prejudice or stereotype that can manifest into acts of discrimination. Most of the research on employment discrimination since 2000 has focused on the concept of social identity.

The law prohibits unfair discrimination—making choices on the basis of perceived but inaccurate differences to the detriment of specific individuals or groups. When someone is accused of discrimination, it generally means that he or she is perceived to be acting in an unfair or prejudiced manner within the context of prohibited grounds for discrimination, either intentionally or unintentionally. For example, if an employee were discriminated against based on his or her ethnicity/race or gender, then this would be a violation of the human rights laws since ethnicity, race, and gender are protected grounds. In comparison, if a person were discriminated against for wearing a purple top to work, this would fall outside the scope of human rights legislation, and therefore the human rights legislation would not be directly violated. Standards pertaining to unfair discrimination have changed over time, as highlighted in the Workforce Diversity box.

discrimination As used in the context of human rights in employment, a distinction, exclusion, or preference based on one of the prohibited grounds that has the effect of nullifying or impairing the right of a person to full and equal recognition and exercise of his or her human rights and freedoms.

WORKFORCE DIVERSITY

Gender Identity in the BC Human Rights Code

In July 2016, the BC government amended the BC Human Rights Code to include "gender identity or expression" as a ground protected from discrimination. While many managers and human resource professionals felt that this was already implied under the protected grounds of sex or sexual orientation, identification of gender along a spectrum (male, female, both, neither, etc.) and gender expression mean that employers have to ensure that they have at least one gender neutral restroom, look at unconscious biases that create barriers for people based on these grounds, and ensure that forms, benefits, uniforms, and so on are gender neutral.

Sources: N. Byres, "Revisiting the 2016 Changes to the *BC Human Rights Code*," Miller Thomson website, December 22, 2016, http://www.millerthomson.com/en/blog/canadian-labour-employment-law-blog/revisiting-2016-changes-bc-human-rights-code (accessed July 7, 2017); Government Communications and Public Engagement, "B.C. Human Rights Code to Include Explicit Protection for Gender Identity, Expression," news release, July 25, 2016, https://news.gov.bc.ca/releases/2016JAG0025-001352 (accessed July 6, 2017).

Intentional Discrimination Except in specific circumstances known as bona fide occupational requirement (that will be described later), intentional discrimination is prohibited. An employer cannot discriminate *directly* by deliberately refusing to hire, train, or promote an individual, for example, on any of the prohibited grounds. It is important to realize that deliberate discrimination is not necessarily overt. In fact, overt (blatant) discrimination is relatively rare today. But subtle, indirect discrimination can be difficult to prove. For example, if a 60-year-old applicant is not selected for a job and is told that there was a better-qualified candidate, it is often difficult for the rejected job seeker to determine whether someone else truly did more closely match the firm's specifications or the employer discriminated on the basis of age.

differential or unequal treatment   Treating an individual or group differently in any aspect of terms and conditions of employment based on any of the prohibited grounds.

An employer is also prohibited from intentional discrimination in the form of **differential or unequal treatment**. Legally, no individuals or groups may be treated differently in any aspects or terms and conditions of employment based on any of the prohibited grounds. For example, it is illegal for an employer to request that only female applicants for a factory job demonstrate their lifting skills or to insist that any candidates with a physical disability undergo a pre-employment medical, unless all applicants are being asked to do so.

It is also illegal for an employer to engage in intentional discrimination *indirectly* through another party. This means that an employer may not ask someone else to discriminate on his or her behalf. For example, an employer cannot request that an employment agency refer only male candidates for management training programs or instruct supervisors to exclude racial minorities from consideration for promotions.

discrimination because of association   Denial of rights because of friendship or other relationship with a protected group member.

Discrimination because of association is another possible type of intentional discrimination listed specifically as a prohibited ground in several Canadian jurisdictions. It involves the denial of rights because of friendship or other relationship with a protected group member. An example would be the refusal of a firm to promote a highly qualified male into senior management on the basis of the assumption that his wife, who has recently been diagnosed with multiple sclerosis, will require too much of his time and attention and that her needs may restrict his willingness to travel on company business.

unintentional/constructive/ systemic discrimination   Discrimination that is embedded in policies and practices that appear neutral on the surface and are implemented impartially, but have an adverse impact on specific groups of people for reasons that are not job related or required for the safe and efficient operation of the business.

Unintentional Discrimination   This type of discrimination, also known as **constructive or systemic discrimination**, is the most difficult to detect and combat. Typically, it is embedded in policies and practices that appear neutral on the surface and that are implemented impartially, but have an adverse impact on specific groups of people for reasons that are not job related or required for the safe and efficient operation of the business. Examples of **unintentional discrimination** include maximum height and weight requirements, limited accessibility to company premises, job evaluation systems that are not gender-neutral, and lack of a harassment policy or guidelines.

Existing research on discrimination is largely focused on gender, race/ethnicity, age, disability, and sexual orientation. Collectively, studies since 2000 indicate that employment discrimination still exists and that experiencing discrimination has a negative impact on mental health, job attitudes, job performance, and career progression.[7] Some research provides evidence that genuine differences between social groups (e.g. intelligence levels, physical ability) accounts for difference between groups on selection tests and job performance.[8] In contrast, other research suggests that no genuine group differences occur and that biases in testing procedures and stereotypes in performance appraisal processes are based on differential validity embedded in the HR or organizational processes.[9]

2.2.2.2 Permissible Discrimination via Bona Fide Occupational Requirements

bona fide occupational requirement (BFOR)   A justifiable reason for discrimination based on business necessity (that is, the discrimination is required for the safe and efficient operation of the organization) or a requirement that can be clearly defended as intrinsically required by the tasks an employee is expected to perform.

Employers are permitted to discriminate if employment preferences are based on a **bona fide occupational requirement (BFOR)**, defined as a justifiable reason for discrimination based on business necessity, such as the requirement for the safe and efficient operation of the organization. For example, a person who is blind cannot be employed as a truck driver or bus driver. In some cases, a BFOR exception to human rights protection is fairly obvious. For example, when casting in the theatre, there may be specific roles that justify using age, sex, or national origin as a recruitment and selection criterion. The terms bona fide occupational requirement (BFOR) and bona fide occupational qualification (BFOQ) are often used interchangeably to represent a reasonably necessary qualification or requirement that results in discrimination but is imposed in a sincere belief that it is fundamentally related to job performance.

The Meiorin case (Supreme Court of Canada, 1999) established three criteria that are now used to assess whether the discrimination qualifies as a bona fide occupational requirement:

1. Question of rationale: Was the policy or procedure that resulted in the discrimination based on a legitimate, work-related purpose?

2. Question of good faith: Did the decision makers or other agents of the organization honestly believe that the requirement was necessary to fulfill the requirements of the role?

3. Question of reasonable necessity: Was it impossible to accommodate those who have been discriminated against without imposing undue hardship on the employer?

The Royal Canadian Mounted Police has a requirement that guards be of the same sex as prisoners being guarded; this is considered a bona fide occupational requirement.

The issue of BFORs gets more complicated in situations in which the occupational requirement is less obvious; the onus of proof is then placed on the employer. There are a number of instances in which BFORs have been established. For example, adherence to the tenets of the Roman Catholic Church has been deemed a BFOR when selecting faculty to teach in a Roman Catholic school.[10]

2.2.2.3 Reasonable Accommodation

An important feature of human rights legislation is the requirement for **reasonable accommodation.** Employers are required to adjust employment policies and practices so that no individual is prevented from doing his or her job on the basis of prohibited grounds for discrimination. Accommodation may involve scheduling adjustments to accommodate religious beliefs or workstation redesign to enable an individual with a physical disability to perform a particular task.

Employers are expected to accommodate to the point of **undue hardship,** meaning that the financial cost of the accommodation (even with outside sources of funding) or health and safety risks to the individual concerned or other employees would make accommodation impossible.[11] Failure to make every reasonable effort to accommodate employees is a violation of human rights legislation in all Canadian jurisdictions. The term "reasonable" is relatively vague and open to interpretation, which can be found in the precedent that has been established in the legal system. The Supreme Court of Canada recently clarified the scope of the duty to accommodate by stating that it does not require an employer to completely alter the essence of the employment contract, whereby the employee has a duty to perform work in exchange for remuneration. For example, if the characteristics of an illness are such that the employee remains unable to work for the foreseeable future, even though the employer has tried to accommodate the employee, the employer will have satisfied the test of undue hardship.[12]

reasonable accommodation The adjustment of employment policies and practices that an employer may be expected to make so that no individual is denied benefits, disadvantaged in employment, or prevented from carrying out the essential components of a job because of grounds prohibited in human rights legislation.

undue hardship The point to which employers are expected to accommodate employees under human rights legislative requirements.

The Job Accommodation Network
http://askjan.org

2.2.2.4 Human Rights Case Examples

In claims of discrimination, it does not matter if the protected grounds were the primary or heaviest weighted factor in the decision being challenged or if it was one of many considerations made in the decision. If there were 20 criteria used to make a decision, and even one of those criteria violated protection against discrimination as per the applicable human rights legislation, then the entire decision made by the employer can be deemed illegal. Employees who feel that they have been discriminated against based on a protected ground in the applicable human rights legislation can contact the jurisdiction-specific human rights commissions or tribunal to formally register their concerns/complaints. **Figure 2.4** indicates some core metrics around the activity of the Canadian Human Rights Commission (federal level jurisdiction) in recent years.

disability A protected ground in human rights legislation, including a wide range of conditions, some which are visible and some which are not. A disability may be present from birth, be caused by an accident, or develop over time.

Disability In human rights legislation, **disability** includes a wide range of conditions, some which are visible and some which are not. A disability may be present from birth, caused by an accident, or develop over time.

Claims of discrimination based on disability make up almost half of all human rights claims. In general, a distinction can be drawn between a physical disability and a mental one. A disability may include (depending on the jurisdiction) physical, mental, and learning disabilities; mental disorders; hearing or vision disabilities; epilepsy; drug and alcohol dependencies; and environmental sensitivities; as well as other conditions. Temporary illnesses are generally not considered to be disabilities under human rights legislation (unless related to a workplace safety claim), but mental disorders, even temporary ones, are included in the definition of a disability. The intent of providing protection from discrimination based on past, present, or perceived disabilities is largely based on the principle of having an inclusive society with a barrier-free design and equal participation of persons with varying levels of ability.[13] Because employers set standards or requirements, they therefore "owe an obligation to be aware of

FIGURE 2.4 Canadian Human Rights Commission Key Metrics in 2016

1 488 discrimination complaints received, of which 1 394 complaints included allegations that were employment related:

- 268 complaints settled
- 164 dismissed
- 47 referred to a tribunal

For 234 cases, the commission indicated one of the following outcomes:

- the complainant should pursue alternative processes for resolution
- the complaint was out of the tribunal's jurisdiction
- the incident occurred too long ago
- the incident was considered too trivial or vexatious to pursue

Complaints came from many regions:

- 41% of complaints originated from Ontario
- 16% from BC
- 11% from Quebec
- 10% from Alberta

Sources: Based on *People First: The Canadian Human Rights Commission's 2016 Annual Report to Parliament* (Ottawa, ON: CHRC, 2017), pp. 46–47, http://www.chrcreport.ca/assets/pdf/CHRC-Annual-2016-EN-web.pdf (accessed July 6, 2017); *Canadian Human Rights Commission, 2015–16, Departmental Performance Report* (Ottawa, ON: Minister of Justice, 2016).

both the differences between individuals, and differences that characterize groups of individuals. They must build conceptions of equality into workplace [or other] standards."[14]

Case According to the Supreme Court of Canada, the focus of a disability is not simply the presence of it but the effect of the disability. In a case heard by the Supreme Court of Canada in 2000 against the City of Boisbriand and the Communauté urbaine de Montréal, the city had dismissed an employee, Palmerino Troilo, from his position as a police officer because he suffered from Crohn's disease. Crohn's disease is linked to problems with a person's immune system response, and people with it have (ongoing) inflammation of the gastrointestinal tract. There is no known cure for Crohn's at the moment.[15] Medical evidence presented in the case indicated that Troilo could perform the normal functions of his job, but the city argued that his illness was permanent and could be interpreted subjectively as an indication of future job-related challenges. The judge found that the illness did not actually result in any functional limitations and held that Troilo had been a victim of discriminatory exclusion. In this case, it was not the presence of a disability that was of concern to employment-related legislation, but the impact of that disability on creating job-related functional limitations.

In some jurisdictions, a dependency on alcohol is considered a disability.

© Igor Klimov/Fotolia

The Supreme Court of Canada has suggested three broad inquiries to determine if discrimination has taken place:

1. Differential treatment: Was there substantively differential treatment due to a distinction, exclusion, or preference, or because of a failure to take into account the complainant's already disadvantaged position within Canadian society?

2. An enumerated ground (a condition or clause that is explicitly protected by legislation): Was the differential treatment based on a ground enumerated in the legislation?

3. Discrimination in a substantive sense: Does the differential treatment discriminate by imposing a burden upon or withholding a benefit from a person? Does the differential treatment amount to discrimination because it makes distinctions that are offensive to human dignity?

Duty to Accommodate   Although each situation is unique, there are general principles for accommodating persons with disabilities.

1. Providing equal access to employment is largely based on the removal of physical, attitudinal, and systemic barriers. The accommodation should be provided in a manner that most respects the dignity of the person, including an awareness of privacy, confidentiality, autonomy, individuality, and self-esteem. Each person's needs are unique and must be considered independently. Persons with disabilities have the fundamental right to integration and full participation; therefore, barriers should be removed to the point of undue hardship. Workplace programs and policies should be designed by inclusion to combat "social handicapping," in which societal attitudes and actions create non-inclusive thinking against people who have no or few limitations. Even when all of these factors are considered, there might still be a need for accommodation.

Alberta Human Rights Commission
www.albertahumanrights.ab.ca
British Columbia Human Rights Tribunal
www.bchrt.bc.ca
Manitoba Human Rights Commission
www.gov.mb.ca/hrc
New Brunswick Human Rights Commission
www.gnb.ca/hrc-cdp/index-e.asp
Newfoundland and Labrador Human Rights Commission
www.justice.gov.nl.ca/hrc
Northwest Territories Human Rights Commission
www.nwthumanrights.ca
Nova Scotia Human Rights Commission
www.gov.ns.ca/humanrights
Nunavut Human Rights Tribunal
www.nhrt.ca
Ontario Human Rights Commission
www.ohrc.on.ca
Prince Edward Island Human Rights Commission
www.gov.pe.ca/humanrights
Québec Commission des droits de la personne et des droits de la jeunesse
www.cdpdj.qc.ca
Saskatchewan Human Rights Commission
www.shrc.gov.sk.ca
Yukon Human Rights Commission
www.yhrc.yk.ca

2. If discrimination does exist, the company must demonstrate individualized attempts to accommodate the disability to the point of undue hardship. The Meiorin test discussed earlier is used to establish if a company has reached the point of undue hardship. Employers have the legal duty to accommodate persons with disability, and the employees have a responsibility to seek accommodation, cooperate in the process, exchange relevant information, and explore accommodation solutions together.[16] Examples of the employer's duty to accommodate include requesting only information required to provide the accommodation, taking an active role in finding accommodation solutions, ensuring confidentiality is not breached, and providing a timely resolution to requests for accommodation. Employees also have a responsibility to inform the employer of disability-related needs that may impact work or require accommodation, provide supporting evidence in a timely manner, and explore options to accommodate solutions. Often, accommodations can be made easily and at minimal cost, for instance, by increasing flexibility in work hours or break times; providing reading material in digitized, Braille, or large-print formats; installing automatic doors and making washrooms accessible; job restructuring, retraining, or assignment to an alternative position within the company.

3. The duty to accommodate requires that the most appropriate accommodation be undertaken to the point of undue hardship. The principle underlying this condition is that accommodations are unique, numerous, part of a process, and a matter of degree. An accommodation can be considered appropriate if it results in equal opportunity to attain the same level of performance, benefits, and privileges that others experience, or if it is adopted for the purpose of achieving equal opportunity and meets the individual's disability-related needs. In cases in which alternative options preserve the same level of dignity and respect, employers are entitled to select the less expensive or less disruptive option.

Harassment Harassment includes unwelcome behaviour that demeans, humiliates, or embarrasses a person and that a reasonable person should have known would be unwelcome.[17]

The most historic battle for protection against harassment was initiated in 1982, at a time when it was largely interpreted that sexual harassment was not a form of sex discrimination (therefore not illegal), and it was perceived that employers were not responsible for the actions of their employees. Perspectives on sexual harassment and employers' responsibilities towards protecting employees from sexual harassment have shifted significantly over the last three decades, largely due to a Supreme Court ruling on a case initiated by two young waitresses.

Case In August 1982, a cook at Pharos Restaurant in Winnipeg, Manitoba, started groping the women and making sexual advances during each woman's shift at work. When the women approached the owner, he commented that they "needed to get laid." In mid-1989, the case was reviewed by the Supreme Court of Canada. In this historic case, the Supreme Court agreed that the women were sexually harassed at work, that sexual harassment is a form of sex discrimination (and is therefore illegal), and that employers are responsible for their employees' actions.[18]

One type of intentional harassment that is increasingly receiving attention is bullying, which involves repeated and deliberate incidents of negative behaviour

harassment Unwelcome behaviour that demeans, humiliates, or embarrasses a person and that a reasonable person should have known would be unwelcome.

that cumulatively undermine a person's self-image. This psychological form of harassment is much more prevalent and pervasive in workplaces than physical violence.[19] In 2004, a Quebec law prohibiting workplace psychological harassment came into effect with the intent of ending bullying in the workplace. In addition, the concepts of harassment and bullying are included in occupational health and safety legislation, as detailed in Chapter 10 of this book.

Employer Responsibility The Supreme Court has made it clear that protecting employees from harassment is part of an employer's responsibility to provide a safe and healthy working environment. If harassment is occurring and employers are aware or ought to have been aware, they can be charged as well as the alleged harasser.[20] Employer responsibility also includes addressing employee harassment by clients or customers once it has been reported.

   Case In a recent Ontario case, Bell Mobility was ordered to pay an employee more than $500 000 after a male supervisor assaulted a female employee in the office. The employee developed post-traumatic stress disorder. The company was found vicariously liable for the supervisor's aggressive behaviour and was found to have breached its duty of care to provide a safe and harassment-free working environment.[21]

The Supreme Court of Canada has determined that sexual harassment at work is a form of sex discrimination (and is therefore illegal), and that employers are responsible for their employees' actions.

© Gina Sanders/Fotolia

Sexual Harassment The type of harassment that has attracted the most attention in the workplace is **sexual harassment**. Sexual harassment is offensive or humiliating behaviour that is related to a person's sex, as well as behaviour of a sexual nature that creates an intimidating, unwelcome, hostile, or offensive work environment or that could reasonably be thought to put sexual conditions on a person's job or employment opportunities.

   Sexual harassment can be divided into two categories: sexual coercion and sexual annoyance.[22]

   Sexual coercion involves harassment of a sexual nature that results in some direct consequence to the worker's employment status or some gain in or loss of tangible job benefits. Typically, this involves a supervisor using control over employment, pay, performance appraisal results, or promotion to attempt to coerce an employee to grant sexual favours. If the worker agrees to the request, tangible job benefits follow; if the worker refuses, job benefits are denied or taken away.

   Sexual annoyance is sexually related conduct that is hostile, intimidating, or offensive to the employee but has no direct link to tangible job benefits or loss thereof. Rather, a "poisoned work environment" is created for the employee, the tolerance of which effectively becomes a term or condition of employment.

Harassment Policies To reduce liability, employers should establish sound harassment policies, communicate such policies to all employees, enforce the

sexual harassment Offensive or humiliating behaviour that is related to a person's sex, as well as behaviour of a sexual nature that creates an intimidating, unwelcome, hostile, or offensive work environment or that could reasonably be thought to put sexual conditions on a person's job or employment opportunities.

sexual coercion Harassment of a sexual nature that results in some direct consequence to the worker's employment status or some gain in or loss of tangible job benefits.

sexual annoyance Sexually related conduct that is hostile, intimidating, or offensive to the employee but has no direct link to tangible job benefits or loss thereof.

policies in a fair and consistent manner, and take an active role in maintaining a working environment that is free of harassment. Effective harassment policies[23] should include:

1. an anti-harassment policy statement, stating the organization's commitment to a safe and respectful work environment and specifying that harassment is against the law;

2. information for victims (for example, identifying and defining harassment);

3. employees' rights and responsibilities (for example, respecting others, speaking up, reporting harassment);

4. employers' and managers' responsibilities (for example, putting a stop to harassment, being aware, listening to employees);

5. anti-harassment policy procedures (what to do if you are being harassed, what to do if you are accused of harassment, what to do if you are a third-party employee, investigation guidelines, remedies for the victim and corrective action for harassers, guidelines for handling unsubstantiated complaints and complaints made in bad faith, confidentiality);

6. penalties for retaliation against a complainant;

7. guidelines for appeals;

8. other options such as union grievance procedures and human rights complaints; and

9. how the policy will be monitored and adjusted.

Race and Colour   Discrimination on the basis of race and colour is illegal in every Canadian jurisdiction. Colour refers to skin colour, and often impacts visible minorities. Race often refers to ethnic origin (country or region of birth) or ancestry (family descent).

Case   The British Columbia Human Rights Tribunal found that two construction companies had discriminated against 38 Latin American workers brought in to work on a public transit project; the Latin Americans were treated differently than workers brought in from European countries in that they were paid lower wages and provided with inferior accommodation. As a result, the Tribunal awarded each worker $100 000.[24]

Racism and Racial Harassment:
Your Rights and Responsibilities
www.ohrc.on.ca/en/racial-harassment-know-your-rights

Religion   Discrimination on the basis of religion can take many forms in Canada's multicultural society. It is a violation of human rights laws across Canada to deny time to pray or to prohibit clothing recognized as religiously required (for example, hijabs for Muslim women or turbans for Sikh men). An organization should never ask an employee about their religious affiliation, but employees have the right to disclose such affiliations and ask for reasonable accommodation regarding their religious commitments in the workplace.

Case   A well-recognized case on religion involved Canadian National Railway (CN). An employee, Mr. Bhinder, worked as a maintenance electrician in the Toronto coach yard. As a practicing Sikh, he wore a turban both on and off work premises. Four years after Bhinder first started working for CN, the company introduced a rule requiring all employees working in the coach yard to wear a hard hat, citing safety reasons. Bhinder informed management that he was unable to wear the hard hat, since his faith prohibited him from wearing anything on his head other than the turban and there was no way he could wear anything under or over it. He was fired and subsequently launched a discrimination case against CN. In 1995, the Supreme Court of Canada found that the rule discriminated against Bhinder on religious grounds, but that the requirement was bona fide for safety reasons. This established the precedent that safety considerations are a higher priority than protection from unintentional discrimination. Therefore, CN did not have a duty to accommodate Bhinder.

Sexual Orientation Discrimination on the basis of sexual orientation is prohibited in all jurisdictions in Canada. As a result of lawsuits by same-sex couples, the Supreme Court ruled that all laws must define "common-law partners" to include both same-sex and opposite-sex couples.[25]

Case In a recent federal case, a lesbian employee alleged that she was harassed by a co-worker. She made a complaint to her supervisors but felt the complaint was not investigated properly. She alleged that she was given a poor performance review because of her complaint and that her request for a transfer to another work site was denied. The Canadian Human Rights Commission ordered her employer to provide a letter of apology, financial compensation for pain and suffering, and a transfer to another work site. The Commission also ordered a meeting with the employer's harassment coordinator to talk about the complainant's experiences with the internal complaint process.[26]

Age Many employers believe that it is justifiable to specify minimum or maximum ages for certain jobs. In fact, evidence is rarely available to support the position that age is an accurate indicator of a person's ability to perform a particular type of work.[27]

Case During an economic downturn, an Ontario company was forced to lay off staff. Two foremen (aged 56 and 57) were terminated with generous retirement packages. The two foremen who remained were younger than the two released. The vice-president of the organization had prepared a note indicating that the two older workers who were terminated were told that the company "hoped to keep people with career potential." The Ontario Human Rights Tribunal found that the company had engaged in discrimination based on age.[28]

In the case of Bhinder vs. CN, the Supreme Court determined that wearing a hard hat was a BFOR and therefore CN did not have a duty to accommodate Bhinder, positioning safety as a higher priority than protection from unintentional discrimination.

Sexual Orientation: Your Rights and Responsibilities
www.ohrc.on.ca/en/sexual-orientation-and-human-rights

An Ethical Dilemma

Your company president tells you not to hire any gay or lesbian employees to work as part of his office staff because it would make him uncomfortable. What would you do?

The Canadian Council on Rehabilitation and Work
www.workink.com

2.2.2.5 Enforcement

Enforcement of human rights acts is the responsibility of the human rights commission in each jurisdiction. It should be noted that all costs are borne not by the complainant but by the commission, which makes the process accessible to all employees, regardless of financial means. The commission itself can initiate a complaint if it has reasonable grounds to assume that a party is engaging in a discriminatory practice.

Challenges of human rights legislation are heard by the human rights tribunal. The tribunal's primary role is to provide a speedy and accessible process to help parties affected by discrimination claims resolve the conflict through mediation. Once a claim is filed with the human rights commission or tribunal, the organization is notified and given a relatively short period of time (for example,

FIGURE 2.5   A Checklist for Employers when Selecting a Workplace Investigator

1. ◯ **Internal or external investigators:** Many employers select trained internal HR experts to conduct workplace investigations, while others rely on external investigators. Selection is dependent on the resources (*time and money*) of the firm, the complexities of the case (*potential conflicts of interest*), the expertise of the in-house staff, and the severity of the case.

2. ◯ **One investigator or two:** The nature of the case may warrant the involvement of more than one investigator (*e.g., one male and one female in the case of a sexual harassment claim*).

3. ◯ **Respecting the mandate:** Investigators should be able to maintain the role within the mandate of the task they have been assigned (*e.g., fact finder or adviser*) and not stray too far off track. Assigned investigators are perceived as agents of the organization; therefore, the organization can be held partially accountable for investigator actions.

4. ◯ **Impartiality or neutrality:** Investigators should have no conflict of interest vested in the conditions, persons, or context of the case they are handling.

5. ◯ **Reliable, thorough, and professional:** Although these qualities should go without saying, an investigator is expected to be a competent, effective, and professional communicator throughout the investigation, and must be capable of making credible assessments.

6. ◯ **Quality of the written report:** The details and word selection in the written report can become evidence in a case. Therefore, a high-quality report details "what happened" and assists counsel in their defence.

7. ◯ **Respects confidentiality:** The investigator should discuss the investigation only when required and respect the confidentiality of all parties affected by the investigation.

Source: N. Chhinzer, summary from Module 4 at the HR Law Certificate Program at Osgoode Hall Law School, 2011.

30 calendar days) to prepare its case. Regardless of whether a formal complaint or an informal accusation has been filed against a company, the employer has a duty to investigate claims of discrimination. Fulfilling the duty to investigate starts with the selection of an appropriate investigator. A checklist to be reviewed when selecting an investigator is provided in **Figure 2.5**.

An employer's obligations include the following:

1. Demonstrating an awareness of the issues of discrimination or harassment, including having an antidiscrimination/anti-harassment policy in place, a complaint mechanism, and training available for employees

2. Fulfilling post-complaint actions, including assessing the seriousness of the complaint, launching an investigation promptly, focusing on employee welfare, and taking actions based on the complaint

3. Resolving the complaint by demonstrating reasonable resolution and communication

If discrimination is found, two forms of remedies can be imposed. **Systemic remedies** (forward-looking remedies) require the respondent to take positive steps to ensure compliance with legislation, both with respect to the current complaint and with respect to any future practices. If a pattern of discrimination is detected, the employer will be ordered to cease such practices and may be required to attend a training session or hold regular human rights workshops. **Restitutional remedies** include monetary compensation for the complainant to put him or her back to the position he or she would be in if the discrimination

systemic remedies   Forward-looking solutions to discrimination that require respondents to take positive steps to ensure compliance with legislation, with respect to both the current complaint and any future practices.

restitutional remedies   Monetary compensation for the complainant to put him or her back to the position he or she would be in if the discrimination had not occurred (this includes compensation for injury to dignity and self-respect); a written letter of apology may be required.

had not occurred (this includes compensation for injury to dignity and self-respect). A written letter of apology may also be required.

The most common reason for restitutional remedies is compensation for lost wages; others include compensation for general damages, complainant expenses, and pain and humiliation. The violator is generally asked to restore the rights, opportunities, and privileges denied the victim, such as employment or promotion. The total compensation received by the complainant is generally between $0 and $20 000, with a general range of $10 000 to $20 000 for cases in which evidence has confirmed that discrimination occurred and a restitution was ordered.

2.3 LEGISLATION SPECIFIC TO THE WORKPLACE

2.3.1 Employment Equity Legislation

The Charter of Rights and Freedoms legalizes employment equity initiatives, which go beyond human rights laws in that they are proactive programs developed by employers to remedy past discrimination or prevent future discrimination. Human rights laws focus on prohibiting various kinds of discrimination; however, over time it became obvious that there were certain groups for whom this complaint-based, reactive approach was insufficient. Investigation revealed that four identifiable groups—women, Aboriginal people, persons with disabilities, and visible minorities—had been subjected to pervasive patterns of differential treatment by employers, as evidenced by lower pay on average, occupational segregation, higher rates of unemployment, underemployment, and concentration in low-status jobs with little potential for career growth. An example of **occupational segregation** is the fact that the majority of women worked in a very small number of jobs, such as nursing, teaching, sales, and secretarial/clerical work. Advancement of women and other designated group members into senior management positions has been hindered by the existence of a **glass ceiling**, an "invisible" barrier caused by attitudinal or organizational bias that limits the advancement opportunities of qualified individuals. As you can see in **Figure 2.6**, a survey from 2017 confirmed that the glass ceiling is still intact.

An **employment equity program** is designed to achieve a balanced representation of designated group members in the organization. It is a major management exercise because existing employees must become comfortable working with others from diverse backgrounds, cultures, religions, and so on, and this represents a major change in the work environment. A deliberately structured process is involved, which can be tailored to suit the unique needs of the firm. The employment equity process usually takes six months. The first step is the demonstration of senior management's commitment and support, which leads to data collection and analysis of the current workforce demographics. Following that, there is an employment systems review, which leads to plan development and eventual plan implementation. The last step is monitoring, evaluating, and revising the plan.

Although embracing employee equity or diversity offers opportunities to enhance organizational effectiveness, transforming an organizational culture presents a set of challenges that must be handled properly. Diversity initiatives

occupational segregation The existence of certain occupations that have traditionally been male dominated and others that have been female dominated.

glass ceiling An invisible barrier, caused by attitudinal or organizational bias, that limits the advancement opportunities of qualified designated group members.

employment equity program A detailed plan designed to identify and correct existing discrimination, redress past discrimination, and achieve a balanced representation of designated group members in the organization.

FIGURE 2.6   The Catalyst Pyramid—Canadian Women in Business

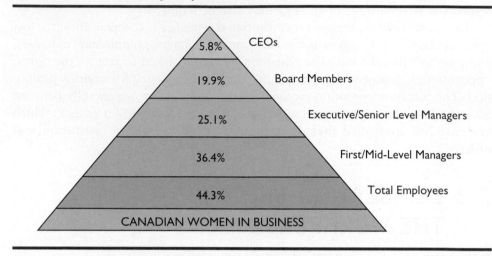

5.8%	CEOs
19.9%	Board Members
25.1%	Executive/Senior Level Managers
36.4%	First/Mid-Level Managers
44.3%	Total Employees

CANADIAN WOMEN IN BUSINESS

Source: Catalyst, *Pyramid: Women in S&P 500 Companies* (New York, NY: Catalyst, June 14, 2017), http://www.catalyst.org/knowledge/women-sp-500-companies (accessed July 7, 2017).

should be undertaken slowly, since they involve a complex change process. Resistance to change may have to be overcome, along with stereotyped beliefs or prejudices and employee resentment.

2.3.1.1 The Plight of the Four Designated Groups

Women Women accounted for 48 percent of the employed workforce in 2016.[29] Two-thirds of all employed women were working in teaching, nursing and related health occupations, clerical or other administrative positions, and sales and service occupations. There has been virtually no change in the proportion of women employed in these traditionally female-dominated occupations over the past decade. Women continue to be under-represented in engineering, natural sciences, and mathematics, a trend unlikely to change in the near future since women are still under-represented in university programs in these fields.[30]

Every jurisdiction in Canada has legislation incorporating the principle of *equal pay for equal work*. In most jurisdictions, this entitlement is found in the employment (labour) standards legislation; otherwise, it is in the human rights legislation. **Equal pay for equal work** specifies that an employer cannot pay male and female employees differently if they are performing the same or substantially similar work.

Pay differences based on a valid merit or seniority system or employee productivity are permitted; it is only sex-based discrimination that is prohibited. This principle makes it illegal, for example, for the Canadian government to employ nurses (mostly women) as "program administrators" and doctors (mainly men) as "health professionals" to do the same job adjudicating Canada Pension Plan disability claims and pay the men twice as much.[31] There is also the concept of equal pay for work of equal value, which is also discussed in Chapters 8 and 9, which indicates that men and women who do jobs that are valued equally based on skills, effort, responsibility, and working conditions cannot be paid differently, even if they do different jobs (e.g., administrative assistant and shipping clerk may be of same value, but represent different jobs). All of these evaluations are part of the compensation system, as discussed in detail in Chapter 8.

Canadian Association of Administrators of Labour Legislation
www.caall-acalo.org

Workplace Standards
www.workplace.ca/laws/employ_standard_comp.html

equal pay for equal work
Specifies that an employer cannot pay male and female employees differently if they are performing the same or substantially similar work.

Aboriginals There are more than 600 First Nations/Indian bands in Canada, and Aboriginal people account for 4.3 percent of Canada's total population.[32] In 2011, Bill C-3 (Gender Equity in Indian Registration Act) was amended to ensure that the grandchildren of Aboriginal women who lost their Aboriginal status when they married a non-Aboriginal man would be entitled to Indian status.[33] Most Aboriginal employees in the workforce are concentrated in low-skill, low-paid jobs such as trades helpers. According to the National Household Survey in 2011, the employment rate for Aboriginal people (aged 24–64) was 62.5 percent, while the employment rate among non-Aboriginals was 75.8 percent.[34]

People with Disabilities The definition of a person with a disability is well established in Canadian legislation and includes both physical and mental disabilities (e.g., vision, hearing, mobility, psychological/mental disorders, etc.). In 2011, Canadians (aged 25–64) with a disability had a significantly lower employment rate (49 percent) than those without disabilities (79 percent). Even among comparable university educated males in full-year, full-time jobs, average employment income was $69 200 for males with a disability, but $92 700 for males with no disability. The difference is less among comparable university educated women ($64 500 for women with a disability and $68 000 for women without a disability).[35]

Visible Minorities According to the federal Employment Equity Act, a visible minority is defined as "persons, other than Aboriginal peoples, who are non-Caucasian in race or non-white in colour." Often the terms "visible minority" and "immigrant" are used interchangeably, but these two terms are actually distinct. An immigrant is a person who was not born in Canada but resides in Canada for the purpose of settlement. In the 2011 Canadian census, over 6 million persons identified as immigrants in the Canadian population.[36] Almost 6.3 million persons self-identified as visible minorities,[37] with the largest representation among South Asians and Chinese, followed by persons who self-identified as black, Filipino, and Latin American. More than three out of every ten members of the visible minority population are not immigrants.

It is illegal in every jurisdiction in Canada to discriminate on the basis of disability.

Visible minorities have typically been unable to obtain employment that took full advantage of their knowledge, skills, and abilities (**KSAs**), and thus faced **underemployment.** As a result, visible minorities were included as a designated group. A recent study on diversity in the Greater Toronto Area (GTA) highlighted the continuing disadvantaged status of visible minorities. The study looked at 3 257 leaders in the GTA in all sectors and found that just 13 percent were from visible minorities (even though visible minorities make up half of the GTA population).[38]

KSAs Knowledge, skills, and abilities.

underemployment Employment in a job that does not fully utilize one's knowledge, skills, and abilities (KSAs).

employment (labour) standards legislation Laws present in every Canadian jurisdiction that establish minimum employee entitlements and set a limit on the maximum number of hours of work permitted per day or week.

2.3.2 Employment/Labour Standards Legislation

All employers and employees in Canada, including unionized employees, are covered by **employment (labour) standards legislation.** The intent of an employment or labour standards act (ESA/LSA) is to establish minimum terms and conditions for workplaces pertaining to such issues as wages; paid holidays and vacations; maternity, parental, or adoption leave (or some mix thereof); bereavement leave; compassionate care leave; termination notice; and overtime pay. They also set the maximum number of hours of work permitted per day or week and when overtime pay is required. The purpose of the ESA/LSA is to be prescriptive, meaning that employers and employees have clear minimum guidelines for basic terms and conditions of work. Any item not explicitly detailed in the ESA/LSA (e.g., clothing policies, rules about computer surveillance) would not be an issue covered under the ESA/LSA.

Employer and employee agreements or practices can *exceed* minimums established in the ESA. This can happen through collective bargaining agreements (in unionized positions), based on common law (precedent established by the judicial system), or through individual negotiations between employee and employer. However, the terms and conditions cannot be less than the minimums established in the ESA/LSA. For example, if the ESA minimum requirement establishes a minimum vacation rate equivalent to 4 percent of pay, then an employer or employee can agree to 5 percent of pay as vacation pay without violating the ESA/LSA; but even if both parties consent, an employment agreement cannot have a provision for only 3 percent of pay as vacation pay, since that is below the minimum established in the legislation. Essentially, neither party can choose to opt out of or waive their rights as established in the ESA/LSA.

If there is a conflict between the ESA/LSA and another contract, the principle of greater benefit is applied, meaning that the employee is entitled to the better of the two options. An example of this would be an employment policy or contract that is communicated to employees, stating that in the case of a layoff, employees will be provided with one month's notice for every year that they have worked for the employer. In this example, the applicable ESA/LSA minimum might indicate that the employee is only entitled to only one week's notice per year that an employee has worked; an employee who has worked for 10 years would be given the greater benefit (10 months of notice before a layoff), aligning with the employment contract, not the minimum under the ESA/LSA, to preserve the greater benefit to the employee.

While the ESA/LSA provides minimum terms and conditions of employment, it is not totally inclusive. Depending on the jurisdiction, students on work exchange programs, inmates on work projects, police officers, independent officers, and others may be explicitly excluded from protection under the ESA/LSA. In addition, regulations for specific occupations such as doctors, lawyers, managers, architects, and specific types of salespersons modify the applicability of certain sections of the ESA/LSA.

2.3.2.1 Enforcement of the ESA/LSA

Enforcement commissions for labour/employment standards across Canada
www.cic.gc.ca/english/work/labour-standards.asp
Privacy Commissioner of Canada
www.priv.gc.ca
Information and Privacy Commissioner of Ontario
www.ipc.on.ca

Governed by the applicable jurisdiction (federal, provincial, or territorial), enforcement of the ESA/LSA is complaint based, and violators can be fined. Enforcement is initiated through the filing of a formal written or electronic complaint against the violator to the appropriate authorities (often the provincial or territorial ministry of labour). A link to the various jurisdictions enforcement agencies is provided in the page margin. Complaints regarding violations can be filed with the appropriate ministry by individual employees, the union representing the employee, or corporations, given that the ESA/LSA has an interest in mitigating conflicts in the employment relationships between employees and employers.

Generally, employees are required to give up their rights to sue an employer in civil court once a claim is filed under the ESA/LSA governing bodies. This protects employers from dual proceedings on the same issue, and protects courts from being overwhelmed with duplicate cases. There are also strict limitation periods, establishing the maximum amount of time that can elapse between the violation and the filing of a complaint, with these limits differing based on the violation (unpaid wages, vacation pay, and so on). There is also a general maximum claim limit for unpaid wages. Under the ESA/LSA, employees have been awarded compensation for actual unpaid wages and direct earnings losses, time required to find a new job and expenses to seek a new job, benefit plan entitlements, severance pay, and loss of "reasonable expectation" of continued employment.

2.3.3 Respecting Employee Privacy

Today's employers are grappling with the problem of how to balance employee privacy rights with their own need to monitor the use of technology-related tools in the workplace. Employers must maintain the ability to effectively manage their employees and prevent exposure to risk for the company, which can be held legally liable for the actions of its employees.[39] The company would want to eliminate time wasted (surfing the web, playing computer games, and so on) and abuse of company resources (such as using the Internet and email at work for personal and possibly illegal uses, such as gambling or visiting pornographic sites).[40] Another concern is employee blogging, because although a posting that includes confidential company information or comments about management may be intended to be seen by only a few friends, it can easily make its way to a national media outlet without the author even knowing it.[41]

Employees are concerned with privacy—their control over information about themselves and their freedom from unjustifiable interference in their personal life. The Personal Information Protection and Electronic Documents Act (PIPEDA) governs the collection, use, and disclosure of personal information across Canada, including employers' collection and dissemination of personal information about employees. Any information beyond name, title, business address, and telephone number is regarded as personal and private, including health-related information provided to insurers. Employers must obtain consent from employees whenever personal information is collected, used, or disclosed.[42] A recent media leak regarding a questionnaire used to assess integrity of applicants to the Canadian Border Services Agency provides an example of questions that may be considered a violation of an individual's privacy, as provided in **Figure 2.7** below. The onus is on the company to prove that any information collected from applicants is legitimately linked to job requirements, and the debate about whether these questions are related to job requirements for border agents is currently quite active.

Some employers have resorted to electronic monitoring, which is becoming easier and less expensive as new software is developed, that can track websites visited by workers and the time spent on each.[43] In general, courts in Canada have permitted electronic surveillance as long as there is proper balancing of opposing interests. Employers are given substantial leeway in monitoring their employees' use of the Internet and email, and they are in an even stronger position if there is a written policy in place. The policy should be updated regularly to reflect changes in technology and should address the use of all company

FIGURE 2.7   Sample Questions from the CBSA Integrity Questionnaire

- Do you knowingly associate with anyone who uses illegal drugs?
- Have you ever been subjected to blackmail?
- Have you ever threatened the use of violence against your spouse, partner, parents, children, siblings, pets, etc.?
- Have you ever pointed a weapon such as a knife or firearm whether loaded or not, at yourself or another person?
- Have you ever viewed child pornography or bestiality?
- Have you ever associated with organized crime or a terrorist group?
- Have you ever hacked into a computer system?

Source: A. Silliker, "Border Guards Asked to Declare Drug Use, Unlawful Sexual Activity," *Canadian HR Reporter*, Nov 5, 2012, Vol. 25(19), p. 1.

© Arcady/Fotolia

Employees must be made aware of video surveillance.

An Ethical Dilemma

Is it ethical to use video surveillance of employees? Do you think employees need to be told of surveillance tools if they are used?

technological equipment away from the employer's premises, including laptops, cellphones, and so on.[44]

A recent example of how monitoring systems are being used to identify the misappropriation of work time and resources occurred with the City of Hamilton workers. GPS surveillance revealed that, rather than engaging in roadwork (pothole repairs), some employees were working as little as 30 minutes per day—running errands, visiting their homes, and frequenting coffee shops for the remainder of the day. The surveillance helped identify 29 employees whose abuse of company time and resources was so severe that the company decided to terminate their employment, while 2 other employees were given 30-day suspensions.[45]

2.3.3.1 Video Surveillance

Some employers install video surveillance equipment to prevent employee theft and vandalism and to monitor productivity. Employees must be made aware of the surveillance. Unions often file grievances against video surveillance, and arbitrators have been reluctant to support it because of privacy concerns. Courts typically assess whether the surveillance was reasonable and whether there were reasonable alternatives available. Generally, they have decided that video surveillance is not reasonable and that other means could be used.[46] Federal, British Columbia, and Alberta privacy commissioners have jointly issued video surveillance guidelines, available from the Office of the Privacy Commissioner of Canada.

CHAPTER SUMMARY

1. The legal framework in Canada attempts to balance employee and employer rights using multiple overlapping legislative pieces, including legislation aimed at protecting the general public (the Charter of Rights and Freedoms, human rights legislation), as well as more specific

legislation (employment equity legislation, employment standards acts, and privacy legislation).

2. The responsibility for employment-related law resides with the provinces and territories; however, employees of the federal civil service, Crown corporations and agencies, and businesses engaged in transportation, banking, and communications are federally regulated. Thus there are 14 jurisdictions for employment law in Canada—ten provinces, three territories, and the federal jurisdiction. Ninety percent of people employed in Canada fall under provincial/territorial employment legislation, and 10 percent are covered by federal employment legislation.

3. Harassment includes a wide range of behaviours that a reasonable person *ought to know* are unwelcome. Employers and managers have a responsibility to provide a safe and healthy working environment. If harassment occurs and it is felt that employers were aware or ought to have been aware of it, they can be charged along with the alleged harasser. To reduce liability, employers should establish harassment policies, communicate these to employees, enforce the policies, and play an active role in maintaining a work environment free of harassment.

4. All jurisdictions prohibit discrimination on the grounds of race, colour, sexual orientation, religion/creed, physical and mental disability, sex, age, and marital status. Employers are required to make reasonable accommodation for employees by adjusting employment policies and practices, so that no one is disadvantaged in employment on any of the prohibited grounds, to the point of undue hardship. Employers can only have employment-related conditions related to employment that discriminate if these conditions are bona fide occupational requirements.

5. Employment/labour standards legislation establishes minimum terms and conditions for workplaces in each jurisdiction, and violations of these terms are identified in a complaint-based process, whereby the ministry of labour will investigate violations once employees file a complaint.

6. Privacy legislation focuses on how to balance employee privacy rights with an employer's need to monitor the use of technology-related tools in the workplace. The Personal Information Protection and Electronic Documents Act (PIPEDA) governs the collection, use, and disclosure of personal information across Canada.

MyLab Management

Visit MyLab Management to access a personalized Study Plan, Personal Inventory Assessments (PIA), and a collection of videos and assignments within MediaShare.

KEY TERMS

bona fide occupational requirement (BFOR) *(p. 28)*
Charter of Rights and Freedoms *(p. 25)*
differential or unequal treatment *(p. 28)*
disability *(p. 30)*
discrimination *(p. 27)*
discrimination because of association *(p. 28)*
employment (labour) standards legislation *(p. 39)*
employment equity program *(p. 37)*
equal pay for equal work *(p. 38)*
equality rights *(p. 25)*
glass ceiling *(p. 37)*
harassment *(p. 32)*
human rights legislation *(p. 26)*
KSAs *(p. 39)*
occupational segregation *(p. 37)*

precedent *(p. 23)*
reasonable accommodation *(p. 29)*
regulations *(p. 24)*
restitutional remedies *(p. 36)*
sexual annoyance *(p. 33)*
sexual coercion *(p. 35)*
sexual harassment *(p. 33)*
stare decisis *(p. 22)*
systemic remedies *(p. 36)*
tort law *(p. 24)*
underemployment *(p. 39)*
undue hardship *(p. 29)*
unintentional/constructive/systemic discrimination *(p. 28)*

REVIEW AND DISCUSSION QUESTIONS

1. Explain how the legal system in Canada is different from the legal system in the United States.

2. Describe the impact of the Charter of Rights and Freedoms on HRM.

3. Differentiate among the following types of discrimination, and provide one example of each: direct, differential treatment, indirect, because of association, and systemic.

4. Provide five examples of prohibited grounds for discrimination in employment in Canadian jurisdictions.

5. Explain the purpose of employment standards legislation and the concept of "the greater good" when assessing minimums.

6. Define "sexual harassment," and describe five types of behaviour that could constitute such harassment.

7. Define the concepts of occupational segregation, underemployment, and the glass ceiling.

8. What is the test to define if a bona fide occupational requirement exists? What are the three elements of this test?

9. What is the role of privacy legislation in Canada? Describe the act that protects employees' privacy.

CRITICAL THINKING QUESTIONS

1. Go to your provincial or territorial employment (labour) standards website and determine the following:
   - minimum legal age to work in this jurisdiction
   - minimum hourly wages
   - maximum number of hours that can be worked in a week before overtime must be paid

2. How does this information apply to you and your friends and family? Did you notice anything else that caught your interest that you were previously unaware of?

3. Prepare a report outlining legally acceptable questions that may be asked at a selection interview with a young female engineer applying for the job of engineering project manager at an oil field in rural northern Alberta with an otherwise all-male group. (Refer to Appendix 5.1 on page 000 for help.)

4. Working with a small group of classmates, use Statistics Canada to find updated information regarding labour market outcomes for one of the four protected groups in Canada. Based on your research, what inequities exist for the group you selected? What are some direct and indirection organizational decisions or actions that can possibly explain these inequities? What legislation(s) provides protection for people in your selected designated group?

5. The organization you are working for is relatively new and growing, and has no HR department. They have asked you to prepare a briefing about what can and cannot be asked during an employment interview. Given that it is a small organization, management usually conducts interviews. You notice a number of managers huffing about how the law doesn't apply to them and about how their actions can't result in a lawsuit. In addition to preparing a briefing about the types of questions that can and cannot be asked in an interview, prepare a response to the perception that the law does not apply to the managers in this situation.

EXPERIENTIAL EXERCISES

1. You are an HR manager at a women-only fitness centre. The owner of your company has just informed you that he or she would like to only employ women trainers and staff, to accommodate the demands of clientele (some clients prefer this gym over a co-ed one for religious or personal comfort reasons). Do you think this is a BFOR? How would you handle men who apply for the position? How will you ensure a legally defensible position for the company?

2. An employee who has been off work for two months with a stress-related ailment has just contacted you indicating that she would like to return to work next week but won't be able to work full-time for another month or so. How would you handle this?

3. A supervisor has just approached you to indicate a concern she has with an employee. The supervisor indicates that the employee is often surfing the Internet while at work and fears that not only is this affecting productivity negatively, but it is also a violation of the company's rules for Internet surfing using a company computer. The supervisor would like you to ask the IT team to investigate how many hours a day are logged to non-work-related activities for that employee and also wants the team to create a list of websites that the employee visits. What is the role of privacy legislation from the employer and employee perspectives? What additional information would you need in order to make a decision about next steps? What recommendations can you make to the supervisor to help her deal with the situation in the short term?

CHAPTER

3 DESIGNING AND ANALYZING JOBS

LEARNING OUTCOMES

AFTER STUDYING THIS CHAPTER, YOU SHOULD BE ABLE TO:

EXPLAIN the steps in job analysis and the difference between a job and a position.

DESCRIBE the evolution of job design and how organizational structure influences job design.

EXPLAIN the three reasons why competency-based job analysis has become more common.

DESCRIBE and evaluate multiple methods of collecting job analysis information.

EXPLAIN the difference between a job description and a job specification.

3.1 FUNDAMENTALS OF JOB ANALYSIS

In everyday conversations, we may use the terms "job" and "position" interchangeably. For example, "I just was told that I will be getting a new position at work!" or "My job leaves a lot to be desired." From a human resources (HRM) standpoint, each term has a specific meaning.

A **job** consists of a group of related activities and duties. Ideally, the duties of a job should be clear and distinct from those of other jobs, and they should involve natural units of work that are similar and related. This approach helps minimize conflict among assigned work roles and enhance employee performance. A job may be held by a single employee or may have a number of incumbents. The collection of tasks and responsibilities performed by one person is known as a **position**. To clarify, in a department with 1 supervisor, 1 clerk, 40 assemblers, and 3 tow-motor operators, there are 4 jobs and 45 positions.

> **job**   A group of related activities and duties, held by a single employee or a number of incumbents.

> **position**   The collection of tasks and responsibilities performed by one person.

3.1.1 Uses of Job Analysis Information

Job analysis, sometimes referred to as the cornerstone of HRM, is the procedure organizations use to determine the tasks, duties, and responsibilities of each job, and the human attributes (in terms of knowledge, skills, and abilities) required to perform it. Once this information has been gathered, it is used for developing job descriptions (what the job entails) and job specifications (what the human requirements are). As illustrated in **Figure 3.1**, the information gathered, evaluated, and summarized through job analysis is the basis for a number of interrelated HRM activities.

> **job analysis**   The procedure for determining the tasks, duties, and responsibilities of each job, and the human attributes (in terms of knowledge, skills, and abilities) required to perform it.

3.1.1.1 Human Resources Planning

Knowing the actual requirements of an organization's various jobs is essential for planning future staffing needs. When this information is combined with knowledge about the skills and qualifications of current employees, it is possible

FIGURE 3.1   Uses of Job Analysis Information

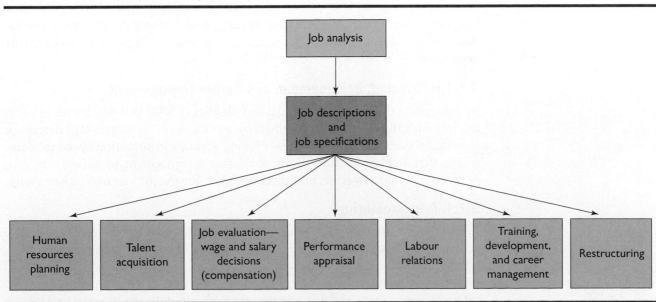

to plan the right number of jobs at the right time in support of corporate objectives.

3.1.1.2 Talent Acquisition

The job description and job specification information should be used to decide what sort of person to recruit and hire. Identifying bona fide occupational requirements and ensuring that all activities related to talent acquisition and selection (such as advertising, screening, and testing) are based on these requirements is necessary for legal compliance in all Canadian jurisdictions.

3.1.1.3 Compensation

Job analysis information is also essential for determining the relative value of, and appropriate compensation for, each job. Job evaluation should be based on the required skills, physical and mental demands, responsibilities, and working conditions—all assessed through job analysis. The relative value of jobs is one of the key factors used to determine appropriate compensation and justify pay differences if they are challenged under human rights or pay equity legislation. Information about the actual job duties is also necessary to determine whether a job qualifies for overtime pay and for maximum-hours purposes, as specified in employment standards legislation.

3.1.1.4 Performance Management

To be legally defensible, the criteria used to assess employee performance must be directly related to the duties and responsibilities identified through job analysis. For many jobs involving routine tasks, especially those of a quantifiable nature, performance standards are determined through job analysis. For more complex jobs, performance standards are often jointly established by employees and their supervisors. To be realistic and achievable, such standards should be based on actual job requirements as identified through job analysis.

3.1.1.5 Labour Relations

In unionized environments, the job descriptions developed from the job analysis information may be subject to union approval before being finalized. Such union-approved job descriptions then become the basis for classifying jobs and bargaining over wages, performance criteria, and working conditions. Once job descriptions are approved, significant changes to them may have to be negotiated.

3.1.1.6 Training, Development, and Career Management

By comparing the knowledge, skills, and abilities (KSAs) that employees bring to the job with those that are identified by job analysis, managers can determine gaps that require training programs. Having accurate information about jobs also means that employees can prepare for future advancement by identifying gaps between their current KSAs and those specified for the jobs to which they aspire.

3.1.1.7 Restructuring

Job analysis is useful for ensuring that all of the duties that need to be done have actually been assigned and for identifying areas of overlap within duties. Also, having an accurate description of each job may lead to the identification of unnecessary requirements, areas of conflict or dissatisfaction, or health and safety concerns that can be eliminated through job redesign or restructuring.

3.2 STEPS IN JOB ANALYSIS

There are six critical steps involved in analyzing jobs. Organizations collect details about jobs on a relatively continuous basis for many uses, such as the ones outlined above (planning, talent acquisition, performance management, compensation, and so on). Traditionally, organizations would first determine the intended use of job analysis information, since this determined the types of data that should be collected and the techniques used. However, this preliminary step has been largely abolished in practice, given the diverse uses of job analysis information and the continual need for such information.

The six steps involved in job analysis are as follows:

1. Relevant organizational information is reviewed.

2. Jobs are selected to be analyzed.

3. Using one or more job analysis techniques, data are collected on job activities.

4. The information collected in Step 3 is then verified and modified, if required.

5. Job descriptions and specifications are developed based on the verified information.

6. The information is then communicated and updated on an as-needed basis.

The structure of the rest of this chapter aligns with the six steps of job analysis.

3.2.1 Step 1: Review Relevant Organizational Information

An organization consists of one or more employees who perform various tasks to accomplish business goals and objectives. The relationships between people and tasks must be structured so that the organization achieves such ends in an efficient and effective manner through a motivated and engaged workforce. There are many ways to distribute work among employees, and careful consideration of how this is done can provide a strategic advantage over competitors.

Organizational structure refers to the formal relationships among jobs in an organization. An **organization chart** is often used to depict the structure. As illustrated in **Figure 3.2**, the chart indicates the types of departments established and the title of each manager's job. By means of connecting lines, it clarifies the chain of command and shows who is accountable to whom. An organization chart presents a "snapshot" of the firm at a particular point in time, but it does not necessarily provide details about actual communication patterns, degree of supervision, amount of power and authority, or specific duties and responsibilities. In the example provided in **Figure 3.2**, there may be the expectation that Auditor Plant A will have to report some information to Manager Plant A; however, the incumbent reports directly to the VP Finance. Often an organizational chart will exclude this information or identify secondary reporting responsibilities using a dotted line.

Designing an organization involves choosing a structure that is appropriate, given the company's strategic goals. **Figure 3.3** shows the three common types of organizational structures: bureaucratic, flat, and matrix. Bureaucratic organizations are typically represented as an organizational pyramid. This hierarchical organizational design sees a narrowing of positions and increased authority as one move higher in structure. Rapid organizational change and the need to curb

organizational structure   The formal relationships among jobs in an organization.

organization chart   A "snapshot" of the firm, depicting the organization's structure in chart form at a particular point in time.

Online Organization Charts
www.lucidchart.com

FIGURE 3.2   A Sample Organization Chart

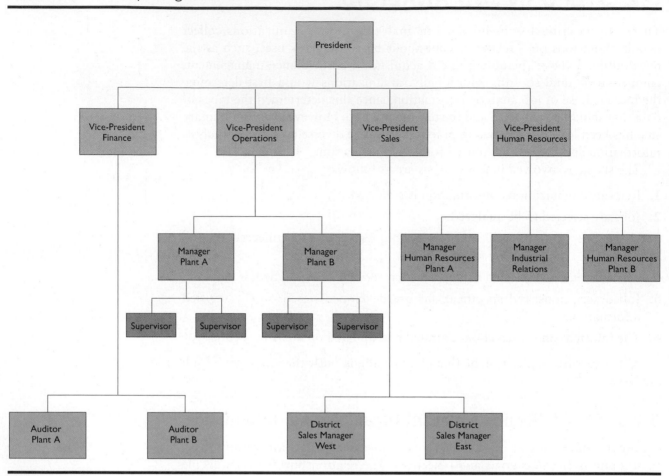

operating expenses may create the need for a flatter organization structure. In such settings, managers have increased spans of control (the number of employees reporting to them) and thus less time to manage each one. Therefore, employees' jobs involve more responsibility. A matrix organizational structure sees dual reporting relationships for certain employees. For example, a project engineer in an aerospace company would report to both the Director of Engineering Services at the corporate head office and the Divisional Manager, Western Canada in Edmonton.

Step 1 includes the review of relevant background information, such as organization charts, process charts, and existing job descriptions.[1] A **process chart** shows the flow of inputs to and outputs from the job under study. For example, for the process chart in **Figure 3.4**, the inventory control clerk is expected to receive inventory from suppliers, take requests for inventory from the two plant managers, provide requested inventory to these managers, and give information to the plant accountant on the status of in-stock inventories.

3.2.2 Step 2: Select Jobs to Be Analyzed

The next step involves the selection of representative positions and jobs to be analyzed. This selection is necessary when there are many incumbents in a single job and when a number of similar jobs are to be analyzed, because it may be too time-consuming to analyze every position and job.

Example of Online Organization Charts
www.forces.gc.ca

process chart   A diagram showing the flow of inputs to and outputs from the job under study.

FIGURE 3.3   Bureaucratic, Flat, and Matrix Organizational Structures

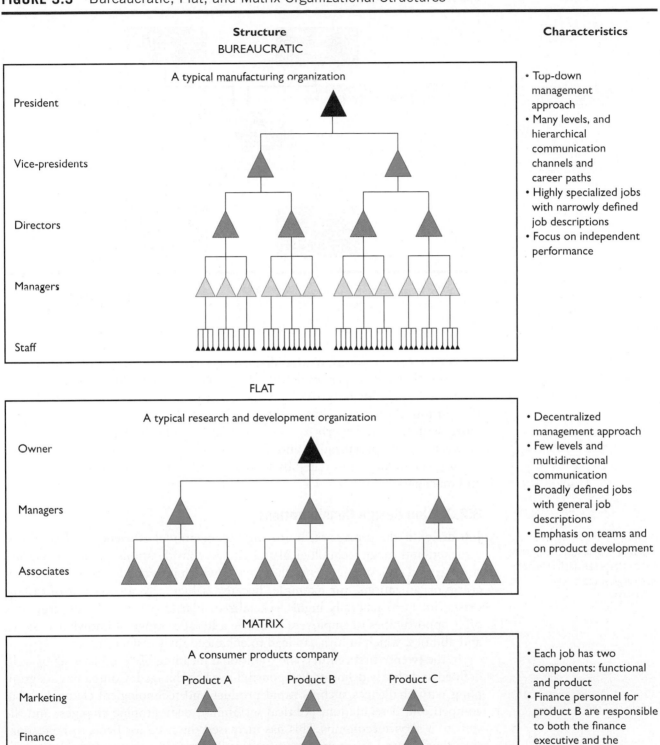

Structure

BUREAUCRATIC

A typical manufacturing organization

President

Vice-presidents

Directors

Managers

Staff

FLAT

A typical research and development organization

Owner

Managers

Associates

MATRIX

A consumer products company

Product A   Product B   Product C

Marketing

Finance

Sales

Production

Characteristics

- Top-down management approach
- Many levels, and hierarchical communication channels and career paths
- Highly specialized jobs with narrowly defined job descriptions
- Focus on independent performance

- Decentralized management approach
- Few levels and multidirectional communication
- Broadly defined jobs with general job descriptions
- Emphasis on teams and on product development

- Each job has two components: functional and product
- Finance personnel for product B are responsible to both the finance executive and the product B executive

FIGURE 3.4   Process Chart for Analyzing a Job's Workflow

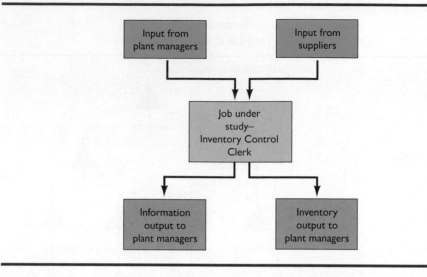

Source: Henderson, Richard I., *Compensation Management in a Knowledge-based World*, 10th ed. (c) 2006, p. 114. Reprinted and electronically reproduced by permission of Pearson Education, Inc., Upper Saddle River, NJ.

In most organizations, work is divided into manageable units and, ultimately, into jobs that can be performed by employees. The term "job" as it is known today is largely an outgrowth of the efficiency demands of the Industrial Revolution. As the substitution of machine power for people power became more widespread, experts wrote glowingly about the positive correlation between (1) job specialization and (2) productivity and efficiency.[2] The popularity of specialized, short-cycle jobs soared—at least among management experts and managers.

3.2.2.1 Job Design Considerations

job design The process of improving organizational efficiency and employee satisfaction through technological and human considerations.

Job design is the process of improving organizational efficiency and employee satisfaction through technological and human considerations. An organization's strategy and structure influence the ways in which jobs are designed. In bureaucratic organizations, for example, because a hierarchical division of labour exists, jobs are generally highly specialized. Flatter organizational structures offer opportunities to employees to utilize a broader range of knowledge, skills, and abilities, which in turn can lead to enhanced job satisfaction.

In the twenty-first century, the traditional meaning of "job" as a set of well-defined and clearly delineated responsibilities has changed. Companies are grappling with challenges such as rapid product and technological change, global competition, deregulation, political instability, demographic changes, and the shift to a service economy. This has increased the need for firms to be responsive, flexible, and much more competitive. In turn, the organizational methods that managers use to accomplish this have challenged the traditional definition of a "job." Requiring employees to limit themselves to narrow jobs runs counter to the need to have them readily available to switch from task to task as jobs and team assignments change.

All these changes have led to work becoming more cognitively complex, more team-based and collaborative, more dependent on social skills, more dependent on technological competence, more time pressured, more mobile, and less dependent on geography.[3] This situation has led some organizations to focus on personal competencies and skills in job analysis, hiring, and compensation management, rather than on specific duties and tasks.

Work Simplification **Work simplification** evolved from scientific management theory. It is based on the premise that work can be broken down into clearly defined, highly specialized, repetitive tasks to maximize efficiency. This approach to job design involves assigning most of the administrative aspects of work (such as planning and organizing) to supervisors and managers, while giving lower-level employees narrowly defined tasks to perform according to methods established and specified by management.

Work simplification can increase operating efficiency in a stable environment and may be very appropriate in settings employing individuals lacking education and training (as in some operations in the developing world); it is not effective, however, in a changing environment in which customers/clients demand custom-designed products and/or high-quality services, or one in which employees want challenging work. Moreover, among educated employees, simplified jobs often lead to lower satisfaction, to higher rates of absenteeism and turnover, and sometimes to a demand for premium pay to compensate for the repetitive nature of the work.

Industrial Engineering Another important contribution of scientific management was the study of work. **Industrial engineering**, which evolved with this movement, is concerned with analyzing work methods and establishing time standards to improve efficiency. Industrial engineers systematically identify, analyze, and time the elements of each job's work cycle and determine which, if any, elements can be modified, combined, rearranged, or eliminated to reduce the time needed to complete the cycle.

Too much emphasis on the concerns of industrial engineering—improving efficiency and simplifying work methods—may result in human considerations being neglected or downplayed. For example, an assembly line, with its simplified and repetitive tasks, embodies the principles of industrial engineering but may lead to repetitive strain injuries, high turnover, and low satisfaction because of the lack of psychological fulfillment. Thus, to be effective, job design must also satisfy human psychological and physiological needs.

Job Enlargement (Horizontal Loading) By the mid-1900s, reacting to what they viewed as the "dehumanizing" aspects of highly repetitive and specialized jobs, various management theorists proposed ways of broadening the activities engaged in by employees. **Job enlargement**, also known as **horizontal loading**, involves assigning the worker additional tasks at the same level of responsibility to increase the number of tasks they have to perform. Thus, if the work was assembling chairs, the worker who previously only bolted the seat to the legs might take on the additional tasks of assembling the legs and attaching the back as

work simplification An approach to job design that involves assigning most of the administrative aspects of work (such as planning and organizing) to supervisors and managers, while giving lower-level employees narrowly defined tasks to perform according to methods established and specified by management.

industrial engineering A field of study concerned with analyzing work methods; making work cycles more efficient by modifying, combining, rearranging, or eliminating tasks; and establishing time standards.

job enlargement (horizontal loading) A technique to relieve monotony and boredom that involves assigning workers additional tasks at the same level of responsibility to increase the number of tasks they have to perform.

Industrial engineering improves efficiency and simplifies work methods but neglects human considerations, such as repetitive strain and lack of psychological fulfillment.

© Nejron Photo/Fotolia

well. Job enlargement reduces monotony and fatigue by expanding the job cycle and drawing on a wider range of employee skills.

Job Rotation   Another technique to relieve monotony and employee boredom is **job rotation**. This involves systematically moving employees from one job to another. For example, an auto assembly line worker would rotate among several jobs associated with building the interior of an automobile, including installation of seats, interior trim, carpeting, and dashboard components. Such rotation schedules could be set within a single work day or designed to rotate after one or more days in a given period. Although the jobs themselves don't change, workers experience more task variety, motivation, and productivity. The company gains by having more versatile, multi-skilled employees who can cover for one another efficiently.

Job Enrichment   It has also been suggested that the best way to motivate workers is to build opportunities for challenge and achievement into jobs through **job enrichment,** also known as **vertical loading.**[4] This is defined as any effort that makes an employee's job more rewarding or satisfying by adding more meaningful tasks and duties. Job enrichment involves increasing autonomy and responsibility by allowing employees to assume a greater role in the decision-making process.

Enriching a job can be accomplished through activities such as

- increasing the level of difficulty and responsibility of the job;
- assigning workers more authority and control over outcomes;
- providing feedback about individual or unit job performance directly to employees;
- adding new tasks requiring training, thereby providing an opportunity for growth; and
- assigning individuals entire tasks or responsibility for performing a whole job rather than only parts of it, such as conducting an entire background check rather than just checking educational credentials.

Job enrichment is not always the best approach. It is more successful in some jobs and settings than in others; for example, not all employees want additional responsibilities and challenges. Some people prefer routine jobs and may resist job redesign efforts. In addition, job redesign efforts almost always fail when employees lack the physical or mental skills, abilities, or education needed to perform the additional tasks required post job enrichment.

Ergonomics   In addition to considering psychological needs, effective job design also requires taking physiological needs and health and safety issues into account. **Ergonomics** seeks to integrate and accommodate the physical needs of workers into the design of jobs (further discussed in Chapter 10). It aims to adapt the entire job system—the work, environment, machines, equipment, and processes—to match human characteristics. Doing so results in eliminating or minimizing product defects, damage to equipment, and worker injuries or illnesses caused by poor work design.

3.2.2.2 Competency-Based Job Analysis

Not coincidentally, many employers and job analysis experts say that traditional job analysis procedures are limited in how they impact HRM, as highlighted in the Expert Opinion box.[5] Their basic concern is this: In high-performance work environments in which employers need workers to seamlessly move from job to

job rotation   A technique to relieve monotony and employee boredom that involves systematically moving employees from one job to another.

job enrichment (vertical loading)   Any effort that makes an employee's job more rewarding or satisfying by adding more meaningful tasks and duties.

ergonomics   An interdisciplinary approach that seeks to integrate and accommodate the physical needs of workers into the design of jobs. It aims to adapt the entire job system—the work, environment, machines, equipment, and processes—to match human characteristics.

Industry Viewpoint
EXPERT OPINION

1. How do you think job descriptions are different in entrepreneurial firms or dynamic firms than in larger, more structured organizations?

Job descriptions that are task based, job specific, and static in nature can be constraining or narrowing in dynamic firms. Instead, we look at how the role helps the organization achieve its goals, and compose a few bullet points of core competencies required for each position where vacancy comes up. Rather than calling these job descriptions, we refer to these as the operating plans. Each of the 75 employees in the organization has an individualized operating plan that is embedded in the large organizational operating plan. There's a large focus on cultural alignment and the business focus on the individual's competencies. So rather than aligning an individual with a specific position, we focus on alignment of the person's competencies with the organization's operating plan.

2. What challenges do you face when trying to identify the core requirements for a job in an innovative firm?

First, there is a very competitive labour market for technical competencies, so the use of networking and the ability to move quickly on

Identification:
Scott Dolson
People Operations Specialist at
Miovision Technologies

opportunities as they're presented is critical to filling vacancies and growing the firm.

Second, with a high speed of change, it is critical that we maintain clarity on the main projects the individual will be involved in, and share that information with candidates to look for synergies and identify what knowledge is needed to be successful.

Third, we are also a very engineering-centric company, and we take a lot of direction from the engineers in everything from operations to project management. In order to help open up lines of communication and make sure that we're understanding the situation correctly, we include the engineering hiring manager in multiple traditional human resource processes, such as recruitment, selection, training, development, and career planning.

3. Within your company, how do you provide clarity as to employee's job responsibilities while maintaining flexibility to alter the job requirements as the market and organization changes?

Rather than creating and then shelving job descriptions until annual performance review times, we treat our operating plan and employee job descriptions as live documents. Accordingly, we update our version of the job description monthly. This process involves both employee and manager input and consensus.

Parallel to this is the culture of continuous feedback to identify opportunities for growth and help provide clarity on career trajectory options. Essentially, in dynamic organizations you need lots of communication platforms for the employee to learn about company projects, share information, learn about new initiatives, etc., as well as full transparency as to where employees fit in the organization. We provide this communication and transparency by giving access to all operating plans in the organization.

Source: Reprinted by permission from Dr. Scott Dolson

job and exercise self-control, job descriptions based on lists of job-specific duties may actually inhibit (or fail to encourage) the flexible behaviour companies need. Employers are therefore shifting toward newer approaches for describing jobs, such as competency-based analysis.

Competency-based job analysis basically means writing job descriptions based on competencies rather than job duties. It emphasizes what the employee must be capable of doing, rather than a list of the duties he or she must perform.

Competencies are demonstrable characteristics of a person that enable performance. Job competencies are always observable and measurable behaviours

competencies Demonstrable characteristics of a person that enable performance of a job.

competency-based job analysis Describing a job in terms of the measurable, observable behavioural competencies an employee must exhibit to do a job well.

that comprise part of a job. The job's required competencies can be identified by simply completing this sentence: "In order to perform this job competently, the employee should be able to . . ."

Competency-based job analysis involves describing the job in terms of the measurable, observable behavioural competencies (knowledge, skills, or behaviours) that an employee doing that job must exhibit to do the job well. This contrasts with the traditional way of describing a job in terms of job duties and responsibilities. Traditional job analysis focuses on "what" is accomplished—on duties and responsibilities. Competency-based analysis focuses more on "how" the worker meets the job's objectives or actually accomplishes the work. Traditional job analysis is thus job focused; competency-based analysis is worker focused—specifically, what must he or she be competent to do?

Three Reasons to Use Competency Analysis There are three reasons to describe jobs in terms of competencies rather than duties. Giving someone a job description with a list of specific duties may simply breed a "that's-not-my-job" attitude by pigeonholing workers too narrowly.

1. Traditional job descriptions (with their lists of specific duties) may actually backfire if a *high-performance work system* is the goal. The whole thrust of these systems is to encourage employees to work in a self-motivated way by organizing the work around teams, encouraging team members to rotate freely among jobs (each with its own skill set), pushing more responsibility for things like day-to-day supervision down to the workers, and organizing work around projects or processes in which jobs may blend or overlap. Employees here must be enthusiastic about learning and moving among jobs.

2. Describing the job in terms of the skills, knowledge, and competencies the worker needs is *more strategic*. For example, a company with a strategic emphasis on miniaturization and precision manufacturing should encourage some employees to develop their expertise in these two strategically crucial areas.

3. Measurable skills, knowledge, and competencies support the employer's *performance management process*. Training, appraisals, and rewards should be based on fostering and rewarding the skills and competencies required to achieve work goals. Describing the job in terms of skills and competencies facilitates understanding of those required competencies.

Examples of Competencies In practice, managers often write paragraph-length competencies for jobs and organize these into two or three clusters. For example, the job's required competencies might include *general or core competencies* (such as reading, writing, and mathematical reasoning), *leadership competencies* (such as leadership, strategic thinking, and teaching others), and *technical/task/functional competencies* (which focus on the specific technical competencies required for specific types of jobs or occupations).

Some technical competencies for the job of systems engineer might include the following:

- Design complex software applications, establish protocols, and create prototypes.
- Establish the necessary platform requirements to efficiently and completely coordinate data transfer.
- Prepare comprehensive and complete documentation, including specifications, flow diagrams, process patrols, and budgets.[6]

Similarly, for a corporate treasurer, technical competencies might include the following:

- Formulate trade recommendations by studying several computer models for currency trends and using various quantitative techniques to determine the financial impact of certain financial trades.

- Recommend specific trades and when to make them.

- Present recommendations and persuade others to follow the recommended course of action.[7] (Note: Exhibiting this competency presumes the treasurer has certain knowledge and skills that one could measure.)

3.2.2.3 Comparing Traditional versus Competency-Based Job Analysis

In practice, in almost any job description today some of the job's listed duties and responsibilities are competency based, while most are not. For example, consider the typical duties you might find in a marketing manager's job description. Which of the duties would complete this phrase: "In order to perform this job competently, the employee should be able to . . ."?

Some familiar duties and responsibilities would not easily fit these requirements. For example, "work with writers and artists and oversee copywriting, design, layout, and production of promotional materials" is not particularly measurable. How can the extent to which the employee "works with writers and artists" or "oversees copywriting, design, and layout" be measured? Put another way, in analyzing this job, how would one determine whether the person had been adequately trained to work with writers and artists? In fact, what sort of training would that duty and responsibility even imply? It's not clear at all.

On the other hand, some of the job's typical duties and responsibilities are more easily expressed as competencies. For example, the phrase "to perform this job competently, the employee should be able to . . ." could easily be completed with "conduct marketing surveys on current and new-product concepts; prepare marketing activity reports; and develop and execute marketing plans and programs."

3.2.2.4 Team-Based Job Designs

A logical outgrowth of job enrichment and the job characteristics model has been the increasing use of **team-based job designs**, which focus on giving a **team**, rather than an individual, a whole and meaningful piece of work to do. Team members are empowered to decide among themselves how to accomplish the work.[8] Often they are cross-trained and then rotated through different tasks. Team-based designs are best suited to flat and matrix organization structures. Increasingly, organizations are using "virtual teams"—people working together effectively and efficiently across boundaries of time and space and using software to make team meetings more productive.[9]

© Andy Levin/Photo Researchers, Inc./Science Source

At a Nissan factory in Tokyo, Japan, workers meet at a productivity session, surrounded by unfinished car frames hanging along the assembly line. Work teams like this are part of the trend toward a multi-skilled, cross-functional, self-directed team organization that allows workers greater autonomy in meeting goals. In plants like these, broadly described jobs that emphasize employees' required competencies are replacing narrowly defined jobs.

team-based job designs Job designs that focus on giving a team, rather than an individual, a whole and meaningful piece of work to do and empowering team members to decide among themselves how to accomplish the work.

team A small group of people with complementary skills who work toward common goals for which they hold joint responsibility and accountability.

3.2.3 Step 3: Collecting Job Analysis Information

Various qualitative and quantitative techniques are used to collect information about the duties, responsibilities, and requirements of the job; the most important ones will be discussed in this section. In practice, when the information is being used for multiple purposes, ranging from developing recruitment criteria to making compensation decisions, several techniques may be used in combination.

Collecting job analysis data usually involves a joint effort by a human resources (HR) specialist, the incumbent, and the incumbent's supervisor. The HR specialist (an HR manager, job analyst, or consultant) might observe and analyze the work being done and then develop a job description and specification. The supervisor and incumbent generally also get involved, perhaps by filling out questionnaires. The supervisor and incumbent typically review and verify the job analyst's conclusions regarding the job's duties, responsibilities, and requirements.

3.2.3.1 The Interview

The interview is probably the most widely used method for determining the duties and responsibilities of a job. Three types of interviews are used to collect job analysis data:

1. *Individual interviews* with each employee;
2. *Group interviews* with employees who have the same job; and
3. *Supervisory interviews* with one or more supervisors who are thoroughly knowledgeable about the job being analyzed.

The group interview is used when a large number of employees are performing similar or identical work, and it can be a quick and inexpensive way of learning about the job. In order to allow candid input by participating employees, job analysts will ask the supervisor not to participate in such discussions. However, in such cases, the supervisor would be asked to review the results of such interviews, verify the gathered data, and provide his or her perspectives before "signing off" on the job analysis interview results.

The most fruitful interviews follow a structured or checklist format. A job analysis questionnaire may be used to interview job incumbents or may be filled out by them. It includes a series of detailed questions regarding such matters as the general purpose of the job; responsibilities and duties; the education, experience, and skills required; the physical and mental demands; and working conditions.

Interview Guidelines When conducting a job analysis interview, supervisors and job analysts should keep five major considerations in mind:

1. The job analyst and supervisor should work together to identify the employees who know the job best, as well as those who might be expected to be the most objective in describing their duties and responsibilities.
2. Rapport should be established quickly with the interviewee by using the individual's name, speaking in easily understood language, briefly reviewing the purpose of the interview (job analysis, not performance appraisal), and explaining how the person came to be chosen.
3. A structured guide or checklist that lists questions and provides spaces for answers should be used. Using a form ensures that crucial questions are identified ahead of time, that complete and accurate information is gathered, and that

all interviewers (if there is more than one) glean the same types of data, thereby helping to ensure comparability of results. However, leeway should also be permitted by including some open-ended questions, such as "Describe other important aspects of your job that we have not covered so far in this interview."

4. When duties are not performed in a regular manner—for instance, when the **incumbent** doesn't perform the same tasks or jobs over and over again many times a day—the employee should be asked to list his or her duties *in order of importance and frequency of occurrence*. This will ensure that crucial activities that occur infrequently—such as a nurse's occasional emergency room duties—aren't overlooked.

5. The data should be reviewed and verified by both the interviewee and his or her immediate supervisor.

3.2.3.2 Questionnaire

Having employees or supervisors fill out questionnaires to describe job-related duties and responsibilities is another good method of obtaining job analysis information. Questionnaire formats are usually structured with specific questions, checklists, or numeric rating scales regarding frequencies of duties. To capture unique information about the job, a "comments" section is typically provided in relevant sections of the job analysis to allow the incumbent or supervisor to include additional information.

One of the most popular pre-developed, structured job analysis questionnaires is the **Position Analysis Questionnaire (PAQ)**.[10] The PAQ itself is filled in by a job analyst, who should already be acquainted with the particular job to be analyzed. The PAQ contains 194 items, each of which represents a basic element that may or may not play an important role in the job. The job analyst decides whether each item plays a role in the job and, if so, to what extent (using a five-point scale). If, for example, "written materials" received a rating of four, this would indicate that materials such as books, reports, and office notes play a considerable role in this job.

The advantage of the PAQ is that it provides a quantitative score or profile of the job in terms of how that job rates on six basic dimensions: (1) information input, (2) mental processes, (3) work output (physical activities and tools), (4) relationships with others, (5) job context (the physical and social environment), and (6) other job characteristics (such as pace and structure). Because it allows the assignment of a quantitative score to each job based on these six dimensions, the PAQ's real strength is in classifying jobs. Results can be used to compare jobs with one another; this information can then be used to determine appropriate pay levels.[11]

Functional Job Analysis (FJA) is also a regularly used pre-established questionnaire that rates a job on responsibilities for data, people, and things from simple to complex. For example, working with "things" literally means the physical interaction with tangibles such as desktop equipment (pencils, paper clips, telephone), groceries, luggage, or a bus. Physical involvement with tangibles such as a telephone may not seem very important in tasks primarily concerned with data (such as data analysis) or people (such as nursing), but its importance is quickly apparent for a worker with a disability. This technique also identifies performance standards and training requirements. Thus, FJA allows the analyst to answer the question: "To do this task and meet these standards, what training does the worker require?"[12]

incumbent Individual currently holding the position.

Position Analysis Questionnaire (PAQ) A questionnaire used to collect quantifiable data concerning the duties and responsibilities of various jobs.

PAQ Services Inc.
www.paq.com

Functional Job Analysis (FJA) A quantitative method for classifying jobs based on types and amounts of responsibility for data, people, and things. Performance standards and training requirements are also identified.

3.2.3.3 Observations

Observation involves watching employees perform their work and recording the frequency of behaviours or the nature of performance. This can be done using information that is prepared in advance (structured), or in real time with no advance information provided to the observer (unstructured), or a combination of the two.

Direct observation is especially useful when jobs consist mainly of observable physical activities. Jobs like those of a janitor, assembly-line worker, and accounting clerk are examples. Third-party observation focuses more on reality than perception. As a result, third-party observation is often viewed as having more credibility, since there is minimal incentive to distort the results.

A challenge in using this job analysis method is that observations by the job analyst can influence the employee's job behaviour. Additionally, observation is usually not appropriate when the job entails a lot of immeasurable mental activity (e.g., practicing law or design engineering). Nor is it useful if the employee engages in important activities that might occur only occasionally, such as compiling year-end reports. Often, direct observation and interviewing are used together.

3.2.3.4 Participant Diary/Log

Another technique involves asking employees to keep a **diary/log** or list of what they do during the day. Each employee records every activity in which he or she is involved (along with the time spent) in a log. This can produce a very complete picture of the job, especially when supplemented with subsequent interviews with the employee and his or her supervisor. The employee might, of course, try to exaggerate some activities and underplay others. The incumbent may also forget to record certain tasks or duties. However, the detailed, chronological nature of the log, plus proper training in how to complete this job analysis method, tends to minimize this problem.

3.2.3.5 The National Occupational Classification

The **National Occupational Classification** (NOC), the product of systematic, field-based research by Employment and Social Development Canada (ESDC), is an excellent source of standardized job information. It was updated and revised in 2016, and contains comprehensive descriptions of approximately 30 000 occupations and the requirements for each. To illustrate the types of information included, the NOC listing for specialists in human resources is shown in **Figure 3.5**.

Organizations can readily access information regarding the activities, requirements, competencies, and so on required by job title. However, it is highly recommended that companies who use external sources such as the NOC

1. adjust information based on their organizational strategy and structure;
2. update information as required; and
3. engage in the verification techniques in detail as per Step 4 (which we will discuss below).

The NOC and its counselling component, the *National Occupation Classification Career Handbook* (2nd ed.), both focus on occupations rather than

© Auremar/Fotolia

Work observation is helpful in identifying work activities performed but is not useful for jobs that change tasks or fluctuate significantly over short periods of time.

diary/log   Daily listings made by employees of every activity in which they engage, along with the time each activity takes.

National Occupational Classification (NOC)   A reference tool for writing job descriptions and job specifications. Compiled by the federal government, it contains comprehensive, standardized descriptions of about 30 000 occupations organized into 500 Unit Groups according to four skill levels and ten skill types.

FIGURE 3.5   NOC Job Description for Specialists in Human Resources

---

1121 Human resources professionals

Human resources professionals develop, implement and evaluate human resources and labour relations policies, programs and procedures and advise employers and employees on human resources matters. Human resources professionals are employed throughout the private and public sectors, or they may be self-employed.

Example Titles

- classification officer – human resources
- classification specialist
- compensation research analyst
- human resources consultant
- human resources research officer
- job analyst

Included Titles

- employment adviser – human resources

Main duties

Human resources professionals perform some or all of the following duties:

- Plan, develop, implement and evaluate human resources and labour relations strategies including policies, programs and procedures to address an organization's human resource requirements
- Advise employers and employees on the interpretation of human resources policies, compensation and benefit programs and collective agreements
- Research and prepare occupational classifications, job descriptions, salary scales and competency appraisal measures and systems
- Manage programs and maintain human resources information and related records systems

Employment requirements

- A university degree or college diploma in human resources management or a related field, such as business administration, industrial relations, commerce or psychology
  or
  Completion of a professional development program in human resources administration is required.
- Some employers may require human resources professionals to hold a Certified Human Resources Professional (CHRP) designation.

Additional information

- Progression to management positions is possible with experience.

Adapted from Employment and Social Development Canada, National Occupational Classification, 2016.
Source: Based on http://noc.esdc.gc.ca/English/NOC/ProfileKeyword.aspx?val=1&val1=1121&val11=Human &val12=0&val13=0&val14=&val15=0&val16=0&ver=16&val65=human+resources+professional (accessed June 27, 2017).

jobs. An **occupation** is defined as a collection of jobs that share some or all of a set of main duties. The list of examples of job titles within each of the 520 Unit Groups in the NOC provides a frame of reference for the boundaries of that occupational group. The jobs within each group are characterized by similar skills.

To provide a complete representation of work in the Canadian economy, the NOC classifies occupations into Major Groups based on two key dimensions— skill level and skill type. The Major Groups, which are identified by two-digit numbers, are then broken down further into Minor Groups, with a third digit added, and Unit Groups, at which level a fourth digit is added. Within these

occupation   A collection of jobs that share some or all of a set of main duties.

Occupational Information Network
www.job-analysis.net

three levels of classification, a Unit Group provides the actual profile of an occupation.[13] For example:

> Major Group 12—Administrative and financial supervisors and administrative occupations
>
> Minor Group 122—Administrative and regulatory occupations
>
> Unit Group 1223—Human resources and recruitment officers

3.2.3.6 Using Multiple Sources of Job Analysis Information

Job analysis information can be obtained from individual workers, groups, supervisors, observers, and, on occasion, subject matter experts. Interviews, observations, or questionnaires can be used. Some firms use a single approach. However, it is suggested that using only one source is not wise, because each approach has drawbacks. For example, some group members in a group interview may feel pressure to go along with the group's consensus; or an individual employee may be careless about how he or she completes a questionnaire. Thus, since collecting job analysis data from only one source may lead to inaccurate conclusions, job analysis data should be collected from several sources whenever possible.

An Ethical Dilemma

If a job analyst is working for a global company and is on the other side of the world from an employee who completed a web-based job analysis questionnaire, is it appropriate for another method of job analysis also be used to confirm the accuracy of the information? Why?

3.2.4 Step 4: Verifying Information

The job analysis information should be verified with any workers performing the job and with the immediate supervisor. This corroboration will help to confirm that the information is factually correct and complete, and it can also help gain employees' acceptance of the job analysis data.

The knowledge that information will be verified increases the reliability and validity of the results in two ways. First, areas of inconsistency or concern can be further probed to develop awareness as to why the inconsistency exists and what should be done about it. Second, knowing that they may later be held accountable for their contributions, participants in the data collection techniques will be more honest and consistent.

3.2.5 Step 5: Writing Job Descriptions and Job Specifications

3.2.5.1 Job Descriptions

job description   A list of the duties, responsibilities, reporting relationships, and working conditions of a job—one product of a job analysis.

A **job description** is a written statement of *what* the jobholder actually does, *how* he or she does it, and *under what conditions* the job is performed. The description is quite comprehensive and includes such essential elements as job identification, summary, and duties and responsibilities, as well as the human qualifications for the job.

No standard format is used in writing job descriptions, but most include the following types of information: job identification, job summary, duties and responsibilities, and working conditions. As mentioned previously, job specifications (human qualifications) may also be included.

Job Identification   The job identification section generally contains several categories of information that are of particular relevance to the employer. The *position title* specifies the title of the job, such as vice-president, marketing manager, recruiter, or inventory control clerk. The *department* and *location* are also indicated, along with the title of the immediate supervisor—in this case under the heading *reports to*. Administrative information such as job classification code, location, and pay band may also be contained in this section.

Job Summary The *job summary* should describe the general nature of the job, providing a concise overview of its major functions or activities. For example, for the job of talent acquisition specialist, the summary might state that he or she will "complete the full talent acquisition cycle for assigned positions including but not limited to candidate sourcing, screening, selection, and job offer creation," while the summary for a customer service representative may require the employee to "ensure an accurate and timely response to standard product sales calls and provide technical sales support, including product knowledge, quotations, and recommendations in line with customer needs and specifications."

Duties and Responsibilities This section presents a detailed list of the job's major duties and responsibilities. Each of the job's major duties should be listed separately and written in a manner that illustrates job behaviours or actions. For example, a key responsibility for a labour relations consultant might be that the consultant "provide evidence and arguments in favour of management's position at an

An Ethical Dilemma

In view of the fact that job descriptions are not required by law and some organizations have found them no longer relevant, would abolishing job descriptions raise any moral or legal concerns? Give an example to support your viewpoint.

FIGURE 3.6   Sample Job Description for a Front Desk Clerk at a Resort Hotel

---

Job Identification

Job title: Front Desk Clerk   **Reports to:** Guest Services Manager
Department: Guest Services   **Location:** Western Canada Division
Job code: C-07   **Job analyst:** Marcie Smith
Date analyzed: 03/04/17

Job Summary

The Front Desk Clerk makes room reservations, provides information and services to guests, and receives payments for hotel services. The clerk also tracks and produces certain reports as required by the Guest Services Manager.

Duties and Responsibilities

1. Registers arriving guests and assigns rooms. (30%)
2. Answers inquiries regarding hotel services, provides information to guests, and addresses complaints. (30%)
3. Presents statement of charges to departing guests and processes payments. (20%)
4. Maintains up-to-date inventory of vacancies, reservations, and assigned rooms using an automated booking system. (10%)
5. Compiles and checks daily records, guest accounts, receipts, and vouchers using an automated booking and related computerized systems. (10%)

Working Conditions

1. Prolonged periods of standing at guest services counter.
2. Peak periods for check-in and check-out of guests requires the ability to prioritize tasks and effectively deal with guests who may be upset or exhibit aggressive behaviours.
3. Evening and weekend shift work schedules posted every two months.

Approval

Supervisor's signature   *Moshed Khan*
HR manager's signature   *P. J. Brookings*
Date: *April 30, 2017.*

ENTREPRENEURS and HR

A Practical Approach to Job Analysis and Job Descriptions

Without their own job analysts or even their own HR managers, many small-business owners need a more streamlined approach to job analysis. A resource that includes all of the possible positions that they might encounter, with a detailed listing of the duties normally assigned to these positions, exists in the National Occupational Classification (NOC) mentioned above. The practical approach to job analysis for small-business owners presented next is built around this invaluable reference tool.

Step 1: Develop an Organization Chart

Drawing up the organization chart of the present structure comes first. Then, depending on how far in advance planning is being done, a chart can be produced that shows how the organization should look in the immediate future (say, in two months), as well as two or three other charts showing how the organization is likely to evolve over the next two or three years.

Step 2: Use a Job Analysis Questionnaire

Next, a job analysis questionnaire can be used to determine what each job entails. A shorter version of one of the more comprehensive job analysis questionnaires may be useful for collecting job analysis data.

Step 3: Obtain a Copy of the National Occupational Classification (NOC)

Next, standardized examples of the job descriptions needed should be obtained from the NOC website at http://noc.esdc.gc.ca/English/noc/welcome.aspx?ver=16.

Step 4: Choose Appropriate Job Titles and Job Descriptions and Copy Them for Reference

For each department, the NOC job titles and job descriptions that are believed to be appropriate should be chosen. The NOC definition will provide a firm foundation for the job description being created. It will provide a standardized list and a constant reminder of the specific duties that should be included.

Step 5: Complete the Job Description

An appropriate job description for the job under consideration can then be written. The job analysis information, together with the information from the NOC, can be used to create a complete listing of the tasks and duties of each of the jobs. The working conditions section can be completed once all of the tasks and duties have been specified.

arbitration hearing." Some job description formats include the average percentage of time devoted by the incumbent to each listed responsibility.

Most experts state unequivocally that "one item frequently found that should *never* be included in a job description is a "cop-out clause" like "other duties, as assigned." This phrase leaves open the nature of the job and the people needed to staff it, and it can be subject to abuse.[14]

Working Conditions and Physical Environment   The job description should also list the general working conditions involved in the job. This section generally includes information about noise level, temperature, lighting, degree of privacy, frequency of interruptions, hours of work, amount of travel, and hazards to which the incumbent may be exposed.

Writing Competency-Based Job Descriptions   Defining the job's competencies and writing them up involves a process that is similar in most respects to traditional job analysis. In other words, the manager will interview job incumbents and their supervisors, ask open-ended questions regarding job responsibilities and activities, and perhaps identify critical incidents that pinpoint success on the job. These job descriptions can be particularly useful in organizations that use competency-based pay, as discussed in Chapter 8.

3.2.5.2 Job Specifications

Writing the **job specification** involves examining the duties and responsibilities of the job and answering the question, "What human traits and experience are required to do this job?" Much of this information can be obtained from the job analysis questionnaire. The job specification clarifies what kind of person to recruit and which qualities that person should be tested for. It is sometimes included with the job description.

Having a clearly defined job description and an understanding of the essential job specifications provides a solid basis for designing rules and standards, providing accommodation, assessing the performance of applicants and employees, and making decisions on hiring, promotions, discipline, and termination. Organizations that have not defined the essential duties of a position, provided required accommodation, and individually assessed ability to perform the essential duties will have difficulty defending themselves if a human rights complaint is filed.[15]

Complying with human rights legislation means keeping a few pointers in mind:

- All listed qualifications are bona fide occupational requirements (BFORs), meaning each was developed in good faith or genuine, based on the current job duties and responsibilities.

- Unjustifiably high educational or lengthy experience requirements can lead to systemic discrimination.

- The qualifications of the current incumbent should not be confused with the minimum requirements, since he or she might be underqualified or overqualified.

- For entry-level jobs, identifying the actual physical and mental demands is critical. For example, if the job requires detailed manipulation on a circuit-board assembly line, finger dexterity is extremely important and is something for which candidates should be tested. A **physical demands analysis**—which identifies the senses used and the type, frequency, and amount of physical effort involved in the job—is often used to supplement the job specification. Having such detailed information is particularly beneficial when determining accommodation requirements. The mental and emotional demands of a job are typically missing from job analysis information. They should be specified so that the mental and emotional competencies of job applicants can be assessed and any need for accommodation can be identified.

Identifying the human requirements for a job can be accomplished through a judgmental approach (based on educated guesses of job incumbents, supervisors, and HR managers) or statistical analysis (based on the relationship between some human trait or skill and some criterion of job effectiveness). Basing job specifications on statistical analysis is more legally defensible. For example, the Personality-Related Position Requirements Form (PPRF) is a survey instrument designed to assist managers in identifying potential personality-related traits that may be important in a job. Identifying personality dimensions is difficult when using most job analysis techniques, because they tend to be much better suited to unearthing human aptitudes and skills, such as manual dexterity. The PPRF uses questionnaire items to assess the relevance of such basic personality dimensions as

job specification   A list of the "human capital requirements," that is, the requisite knowledge, skills, and abilities needed to perform the job—another product of a job analysis.

physical demands analysis   Identification of the human senses used and the type, frequency, and amount of physical effort involved in a job.

An Ethical Dilemma

Is it proper for an employer to use personality traits as part of the KSAs and the bona fide occupational requirements/essential duties of a job? Explain your reasoning.

agreeableness, conscientiousness, and emotional stability to the job under study. The relevance of these personality traits can then be assessed through statistical analysis.[16]

Completing the Job Specification Form   Once the required human characteristics have been determined, whether using statistical analysis or a judgmental approach, a job specification form should be completed.

3.2.6 Step 6: Communication and Preparations for Revisions

Organizations are often affected by internal and external factors, as described in Chapter 1, that influence organizational strategy, structure, or processes. Most organizations adopt strategies with a three- to five-year target, and many are forced to adjust according to environmental factors much sooner. Significant organizational changes such as restructuring, new product development, technological changes, and competition modify the way in which work is done, resulting in a need for revisions to existing job descriptions and specifications.

Job analysis must be structured enough to allow modifications as required while still providing current and future employees with an understanding of what they are expected to do. Once a system is developed to collect data, an organization may choose to (1) regularly update the data collected in a proactive manner, (2) develop systems to collect data on an ongoing basis, or (3) adjust job analysis activities in a reactive manner after a significant organizational change has been initiated.

Information provided from the job analysis must be communicated to all relevant stakeholders. For example, employees must be aware of the core job requirements if they are to achieve a desired performance. Line managers must be aware of information provided in the job analysis to help align expectations of various jobs, judge employee performance, and manage HR planning activities. Recruiters use this information to determine and assess the desired knowledge, skills, abilities, and other characteristics (KSAOs) of potential candidates and to develop job ads. Compensation specialists can use this information to develop or modify pay scales according to job-related activities. Overall, the job analysis process is a fundamental component of HRM and a cornerstone that is critical to other organizational activities related to labour and work processes.

CHAPTER SUMMARY

1. In any organization, work has to be divided into manageable units (e.g., a production department) and ultimately into jobs (e.g., machinist) that can be performed by employees. The process of organizing work into tasks that are required to perform a specific job is known as job design. The term "job" means a group of tasks and duties, and several employees may

   have the same job. The collection of tasks and responsibilities performed by one person is known as a "position."

2. Job analysis involves six steps: (1) collecting background information, (2) selecting the representative positions and jobs to be analyzed, (3) collecting data, (4) reviewing the information collected with the incumbents and their

supervisors, (5) developing job descriptions and job specifications, and (6) communicating and reviewing on an ongoing basis.

3. Techniques used to gather job analysis data include interviews, questionnaires (including the PAQ and FJA), direct observation, participant diaries/logs, and the National Occupational Classification (NOC), to list just a few.

4. Competency-based job analysis, focusing on how the job is done (the behaviours required) more than on task requirements, has become more common for three reasons. First, traditional job descriptions may not be appropriate in organizations requiring more flexibility in job design. Second, describing the job in terms of the skills, knowledge, and competencies the worker needs is more strategic. Third, competency-based job analysis supports the employer's performance management process.

5. A job description is a written statement of what the jobholder actually does, how he or she does it, and under what conditions the job is performed. The job specification involves examining the duties and responsibilities and answering this question: "What human capital requirements (that is, what knowledge, skills, and abilities) are needed to perform the job?"

MyLab Management

Visit MyLab Management to access a personalized Study Plan, Personal Inventory Assessments (PIA), and a collection of videos and assignments within MediaShare.

KEY TERMS

competencies *(p. 55)*
competency-based job analysis *(p. 56)*
diary/log *(p. 60)*
ergonomics *(p. 54)*
Functional Job Analysis (FJA) *(p. 59)*
incumbent *(p. 59)*
industrial engineering *(p. 53)*
job *(p. 47)*
job analysis *(p. 47)*
job description *(p. 62)*
job design *(p. 52)*
job enlargement (horizontal loading) *(p. 53)*
job enrichment (vertical loading) *(p. 54)*

job rotation *(p. 54)*
job specification *(p. 65)*
National Occupational Classification (NOC) *(p. 60)*
occupation *(p. 61)*
organization chart *(p. 49)*
organizational structure *(p. 49)*
physical demands analysis *(p. 65)*
position *(p. 47)*
Position Analysis Questionnaire (PAQ) *(p. 59)*
process chart *(p. 50)*
team *(p. 57)*
team-based job design *(p. 57)*
work simplification *(p. 53)*

REVIEW AND DISCUSSION QUESTIONS

1. Explain how job analysis provides important information that is required for at least three different HRM (human resources management) programming areas.

2. Differentiate among job enlargement, job rotation, and job enrichment, and provide an example of each job design option.

3. Describe a negative consequence to the employer or an employee if an organization pays little attention to ergonomic job design.

4. Several methods for collecting job analysis data are available: interviews, questionnaires, diaries, and observation. Explain one "pro" and one "con" for any two of these methods.

5. Although not legally required, having job descriptions is highly advisable. Provide two reasons to support the argument for a business ensuring such documents exist for all jobs in the company.

6. Present your rationale for describing jobs in terms of competencies rather than duties. How is this approach different from the traditional approach?

CRITICAL THINKING QUESTIONS

1. Why is it sometimes undesirable or inappropriate to use job enrichment when designing jobs? How would you determine how enriched an individual employee's job should be?

2. Assume that you are the job analyst at a bicycle manufacturing company in British Columbia and have been assigned responsibility for preparing job descriptions (including specifications) for all the supervisory and managerial positions. One of the production managers has just indicated that he will not complete the job analysis questionnaire you have developed.

   a. How would you handle this situation?

   b. What arguments would you use to attempt to persuade him to change his mind?

   c. If your persuasion efforts fail, how would you go about obtaining the job analysis information you need to develop the job description for his position?

3. Because the top job in a firm (such as president, executive director, or CEO) is by nature more strategic and broader in scope than any other job, is competency-based job analysis more appropriate? Why or why not?

4. Give examples of working conditions that should be included in the job descriptions for each of the following: emergency room nurse; animal control officer; telephone repair technician; road maintenance worker; air traffic controller; metal stamping press operator.

5. If a supervisor reviews the job analysis information provided by an employee and says that the job duties and responsibilities have been inflated, but the employee says that the supervisor does not really know what the job entails, explain the approach you would take to ensure that the final job analysis information is accurate.

EXPERIENTIAL EXERCISES

1. Using the examples of organizational structures in **Figure 3.3** in this chapter, prepare a sketch of the structure that matches a current or recent company where you have held a job. Once you have completed this task, form a group with several of your classmates. Taking turns, have each member show his or her organization chart to the group and, briefly, (i) describe the structure depicted; (ii) explain whether or not the structure seems to be appropriate; and (iii) identify at least one advantage and one disadvantage he or she experienced working within this structure.

2. Working individually or in groups and using the Employment and Skills Development (ESDC) website, find the National Occupational Classification (NOC) job descriptions for both an architect (NOC# 2151) and an architectural technologist (NOC# 2251). Compare the two descriptions, noting two similarities and two differences between these related but different jobs.

3. Working individually, use the Physical Demands Analysis sample form provided by the Industrial Accident Prevention Association (www.iapa.ca/main/documents/pdf/FreeDownloads_PDA.pdf). Complete it based on a current or former job (one you have held in the last two years). Once completed, share your working conditions information with someone else in the class.

HUMAN RESOURCES PLANNING

LEARNING OUTCOMES

AFTER STUDYING THIS CHAPTER, YOU SHOULD BE ABLE TO:

DEFINE human resources planning (HRP), and **DISCUSS** its strategic importance.

DISCUSS briefly the three strategies used to forecast internal human resources supply and three types of external conditions assessed when forecasting external human resources supply.

DESCRIBE four quantitative and two qualitative techniques used to forecast human resources demand.

EXPLAIN how organizations deal with labour surpluses and labour shortages.

4.1 THE STRATEGIC IMPORTANCE OF HUMAN RESOURCES PLANNING

human resources planning (HRP)   The process of forecasting future human resources requirements to ensure that the organization will have the required number of employees, at the right time, with the necessary skills, knowledge, and abilities to meet its strategic objectives.

Human resources planning (HRP) is the process of forecasting future human resources requirements to ensure that the organization will have the required number of employees, at the right time, with the necessary skills, knowledge, and abilities to meet its strategic objectives. Effective HRP helps an organization achieve its strategic goals and objectives by forecasting the supply of, and demand for, employees under changing conditions. Those responsible for HR planning, at a very fundamental level, oversee a series of related processes that predict the flow of necessary human capital in, through, and out of the organization.

HRP has recently become a key strategic priority not just for HR departments but for strategic business planners as well. The Government of Canada regularly tracks labour market conditions along with projections of job openings and job seekers. For the period of 2013–2022, a total of 5.8 million job openings (those due to economic growth plus those due to replacement needs) are forecasted. Demographic forces, particularly in the area of retirements, will see a greater demand than the supply of labour, particularly in occupations in health, management, trades, transport and equipment, and the primary sector. About one-third of these projected job openings will be in occupations requiring high school education or on-the-job training.[1] These national projections of labour force supply and demand are further detailed by provincial labour forecasts. For example, for the period 2016 to 2022, Manitoba is estimated to create 167 700 job openings with 67 percent of these openings resulting from worker retirements and deaths. This province estimates that 165 500 new workers will join the labour force during this same period. For all these occupational groups, except health occupations (where expansion demand is greater) replacement demand in Manitoba is more prominent than expansion demand over this forecast period.[2] Anticipated labour competition in the coming decades underscores the importance of effective HRP as an essential tool for successful strategy implementation.[3]

As illustrated in **Figure 4.1**, key steps in the HRP process include analyzing forecasted labour supply, forecasting labour demands, and then planning and implementing HR programs to balance supply and demand.

Lack of or inadequate human resources planning within an organization can result in significant costs when unstaffed positions affect productivity and quality customer service. It may also negatively affect an organization's financial performance due to severance pay owed to large numbers of employees who have received termination notices. It can also create situations in which one department is laying off employees while another is hiring individuals with similar skills, which can reduce morale or productivity and can often increase turnover. The greater concern is that ineffective HRP can lead to an organization's inability to accomplish short-term operational plans or long-range strategic objectives.

4.1.1 The Relationship between HRP and Strategic Planning

An HR plan (HRP) does not occur independently of the other departments within an organization (such as finance, marketing, and research and development). The HRP must align with the overall goals of the organization as well as

FIGURE 4.1   Human Resources Planning Model

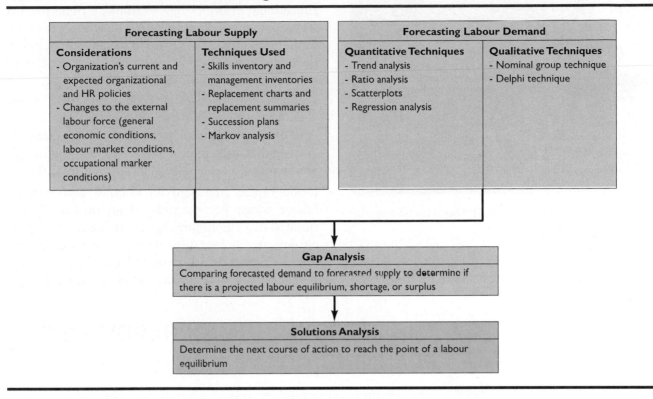

both the long-term and short-term strategic plans set by the organization. Fundamental to the business planning process is the impact and alignment of HRP (as discussed in detail in Chapter 1). An organization's strategic decision to expand, redirect, divest, or merge will have an associated effect on the HR expectations and plans of the organization.

4.1.2 The Importance of Environmental Scanning

Environmental scanning is a critical component of HRP and strategic planning processes; the most successful organizations are prepared for changes before they occur. **Environmental scanning** involves assessing factors that affect the external labour market as well as an organization's ability to find and secure talent from outside of the organization. The external environmental factors most frequently monitored include the following:

- Economic conditions (local, regional, national, international): For example, if the unemployment rate in a region is low, an organization would have to be more aggressive in recruiting job candidates, as availability of talent may be more scarce.

- Market and competitive trends: For example, compensation policies that lag behind competitors' policies may result in higher turnover or more difficulties in attracting talent.

- New or revised laws and the decisions of courts and quasi-judicial bodies: For example, a raise in the minimum wage rate can inflate the cost of labour in an organization, therefore creating budgetary pressure to reduce labour expenses.

environmental scanning Identifying and analyzing external opportunities and threats that may be crucial to the organization's success. In the context of human resources management, environmental scanning is an assessment of external factors influencing the organization's ability to find and secure talent from the external labour market, including economic, competitive, legislative, social, technological, and demographic trends.

A trend toward higher education can reduce the size of the available external workforce in the short term.

- Social concerns such as health care, child care, and educational priorities: For example, a trend toward securing higher education can reduce the size of the available external workforce in the short run, but in the longer run can result in retaining applicants with more specialized training.

- Technological changes affecting processes, products, and people: For example, a new technology developed can be implemented in the organization and significantly reduce labour demands through automation of a previously labour-intensive process.

- Demographic trends of an internal and external labour force: For example, if an organization is situated in a community largely inhabited by senior citizens, it may face difficulties securing a diverse or full-time workforce from the local area. In addition, HR planning can assist with meeting employment equity goals, as legislated (as per Chapter 2).

4.2 THE STEPS IN HUMAN RESOURCES PLANNING

HRP is critical to an organization's success as it aligns forecasted labour supply (provided by the human resources department) with the predicted labour demands of the organization (such as the number of employees needed and the skill sets required). An element of HR planning that is often taken for granted is the availability and accuracy of information regarding the current HR situation. Understanding the current internal labour force is the basis for a number of demand and supply estimates. Therefore, before embarking on an HR planning exercise, current HR levels (quantity and quality) must be assessed.

There are numerous sources of information available to identify existing talent or human resources in an organization. An organization chart can provide HR planners and managers with an understanding of the organizational structure, business units, and possible career paths. This macro-level information can be linked to more micro-level information, such as how many employees the company currently has at each level, what existing skill sets the employees have, and the demographic data and job-related information about the existing employee base.

An organization must forecast not only future HR demand (the number of employees and the skill sets needed in the future) but also future HR supply (internal and external availability of workers). These two forecasts can occur simultaneously or one after the other, depending on the resources available (time, money, people, and so on). Only after demand and supply have been forecast can an organization identify potential labour imbalance issues, after which plans to balance HR can be developed and implemented.

4.2.1 Step 1: Forecasting the Availability of Candidates (Supply)

Short-term and long-range HR demand forecasts only provide half of the staffing equation by answering the question, "How many employees will we need?"

The next major concern is how projected openings will be filled. There are two sources of supply:

1. *Internal*—present employees who can be trained, transferred, or promoted to meet anticipated needs
2. *External*—people in the labour market not currently working for the organization, including those who are employed elsewhere, recent graduates from secondary and postsecondary educational settings, and those who are unemployed, who can be expected to join the organization to meet anticipated needs

While internal forecasting identifies which members of the internal workforce will remain within the organization and where they will work, an awareness of the external labour force can help organizations identify challenges that the expected recruitment of candidates into the internal labour force may bring. Such challenges could include the number of graduates in specific educational or training programs, the literacy levels of the local or target population, and general economic trends. These external factors can impact how much compensation an organization must provide to secure top talent. As well, in times of low unemployment the internal workforce may be more inclined to seek employment elsewhere, perceiving favourable ease of movement. Therefore, trends in the external labour force have a direct impact on projections of the internal labour force.

4.2.1.1 Forecasting the Supply of Internal Candidates

Before estimating how many external candidates will need to be hired, management must determine how many candidates for projected openings will likely come from within the firm. This is the purpose of forecasting the supply of internal candidates. This can be accomplished using tools such as a skills/management inventory, replacement plan/summaries, succession plans, or Markov analysis. Each of these is discussed in detail below.

Skills Inventories and Management Inventories **Skills inventories** contain comprehensive information about the capabilities of current employees. Data gathered for each employee include name, age, date of employment, current position, present duties and responsibilities, educational background, previous work history, skills, abilities, and interests. Information about current performance and readiness for promotion is generally included as well. Data pertaining to managerial staff are compiled in **management inventories**. Records summarizing the background, qualifications, interests, and skills of management employees, as well as information about managerial responsibilities and management training, are used to identify internal candidates eligible for promotion or transfer opportunities.

To be useful, skills and management inventories must be updated regularly. Failure to do so can lead to present employees being overlooked for job openings. Updating every two years is generally adequate if employees are encouraged to report significant qualifications changes (such as new skills learned or courses completed) to the HR department as they occur.

Replacement Charts and Replacement Summaries **Replacement charts** are typically used to keep track of potential internal candidates for the firm's most critical positions. An organizational chart format is often used to depict reporting

skills inventories   Manual or computerized records summarizing employees' education, experience, interests, skills, and so on, which are used to identify internal candidates eligible for transfer or promotion.

management inventories   Records summarizing the qualifications, interests, and skills of management employees, along with the number and types of employees supervised, duties of such employees, total budget managed, previous managerial duties and responsibilities, and managerial training received.

replacement charts   Visual representations of who will replace whom in the event of a job opening. An organizational chart format is typically used to depict reporting relationships, relevant jobs, and job incumbents. Such charts indicate the current performance level of the employee and his or her promotion potential.

relationships, relevant jobs, and job incumbents. Such charts indicate the current performance level of the employee and his or her promotion potential. The latter is based on the employee's future career aspirations and a supervisory assessment of readiness for promotion. **Figure 4.2** provides an example of this internal supply-forecasting tool.

To provide a more objective estimate of potential, this information may be supplemented by results of psychological tests, interviews with HR specialists, and other selection techniques.

Although replacement charts provide an excellent quick reference tool, they contain very little information. For that reason, many firms prefer to use **replacement summaries**. Such summaries list likely replacements for each position and their relative strengths and weaknesses, as well as information about current position, performance, promotability, and experience. These additional data can be extremely helpful to decision makers.

Succession Plans Forecasting the availability of inside candidates is particularly important in succession planning. **Succession planning** refers to the plans a company makes to fill important management and other key positions. It extends beyond the replacement chart by focusing on developing people rather than simply identifying potential replacements. As a result, there is a stronger focus on skills development for a specific list of potential successors within an organization.

In the days when companies were hierarchical and employees tended to remain with a firm for years, executive succession was often straightforward. Staff climbed the organizational ladder one rung at a time, and it was common for someone to start on the shop floor and end up in the president's office. Although that kind of ascent is still possible, employee turnover and flatter structures mean that the lines of succession are no longer as direct. For example, potential successors for top positions might be routed through the top jobs at several key divisions, as well as overseas, and sent through a university graduate-level, advanced management program.

replacement summaries   Lists of likely replacements for each position and their relative strengths and weaknesses, as well as information about current position, performance, promotion potential, and experience.

succession planning   The process of ensuring a suitable supply of successors for current and future senior or key jobs so that the careers of individuals can be effectively planned and managed.

FIGURE 4.2   Personnel Replacement Chart Showing Development Needs of Potential Future Divisional Vice-Presidents

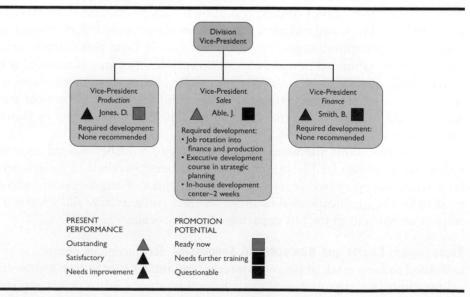

Succession planning is extremely important today, affecting both large and small organizations. This HR planning strategy is also key to developing the leaders of tomorrow, passing knowledge from one generation to the next.[4] However, there is concern that small business owners belonging to the baby-boom generation are not attending to this important HR planning function. A TD Waterhouse 2012 survey of small business owners found that only 24 percent had a succession plan worked out for their retirement.[5] In 2012, a CIBC World Markets report indicated that by the year 2022 at least \$3.7 trillion in business assets will change hands as 550,000 owners of small businesses exit their organizations. Given the magnitude of this figure, a faulty or poorly executed succession planning process could produce a ripple effect in the Canadian economy through reduced productivity, job losses, premature sales, and increased bankruptcy rates.[6]

Small business owners can take steps to create a succession plan that provides them with financial independence following retirement and creates a continuing opportunity for success and growth for the organization. One step in such planning involves the identification of successors from among company managers and business owners. In family-run businesses, succession planning should identify specific active and non-active roles for the family members, as well as note what support from family members should be given to the successor.[7]

It should be noted that replacement charts, replacement summaries, and succession plans are considered highly confidential in most organizations.

Markov Analysis Estimating internal supply involves much more than simply calculating the number of employees. Some firms use the **Markov analysis** technique to track the pattern of employee movements through various jobs and develop a transitional probability matrix for forecasting internal supply by specific categories, such as position and gender. As illustrated in **Figure 4.3**, such an analysis shows the actual number (and percentage) of employees who remain in each job from one year to the next, as well as the proportions promoted, demoted, transferred, and leaving the organization. These proportions (probabilities) are used to forecast human resources supply.

In the example provided, there were 35 employees in the foreperson occupation in 2017. Out of these, 82 percent (28 employees) are expected to remain in that position next year (based on past levels of activity). The organization can anticipate that 8 percent of the foreperson population (which would be 3 out of the 35 employees in 2017) would be promotable to the role of plant manager. In addition, the past trends show that 10 percent of employees at this level are lost to turnover (representing 4 employees who are expected to leave the organization before the start of next year). Further, out of the 110 team leaders (the level below), 11 percent (12 employees) would be eligible for promotion to a foreperson position. Therefore, next year's projected supply of forepersons would be the 28 from this year who are projected to stay in that role plus the 12 team leaders who are projected to be eligible for promotion over the year, for a total supply of 40 forepersons.

To complement such quantitative data, the skills and capabilities of current employees must be assessed and skills inventories prepared. From this information, replacement charts or summaries and succession plans can be developed.

An Ethical Dilemma

You are asked to identify one employee on your team as a worthy candidate to align with a new company program offering top performers intensive management skills training. The employee you identified for this role is unaware of the program. This morning, she confided in you that she has just applied for graduate school. Five months from now, she will find out if she has been accepted, and she would start the program one month after that. Would you change your identification of this nominated employee based on this new information? Why or why not?

Markov analysis   A method of forecasting internal labour supply that involves tracking the pattern of employee movements through various jobs and developing a transitional probability matrix.

FIGURE 4.3   Hypothetical Markov Analysis for a Manufacturing Operation

2017 \ 2018	Plant Manager	Foreperson	Team Leader	Production Worker	Exit
Plant Manager (n = 5)	80% / 4				20% / 1
Foreperson (n = 35)	8% / 3	82% / 28			10% / 4
Team Leader (n = 110)		11% / 12	70% / 77	7% / 8	12% / 13
Production Worker (n = 861)			6% / 52	72% / 620	22% / 189
Projected Supply	7	40	129	628	

Percentages represent transitions (previous year's actuals).
Actual numbers of employees are shown as whole numbers in each block (projections for 2018 based on current staffing).

4.2.1.2 Forecasting the Supply of External Candidates

Some jobs cannot be filled with internal candidates because no current employees are qualified (such as those holding entry-level jobs) or they are jobs that experience significant growth. In these situations, the firm looks for external candidates. Employer growth is primarily responsible for the number of entry-level openings. A key factor in determining the number of positions that must be filled externally is the effectiveness of the organization's training, development, and career-planning initiatives. If employees are not encouraged to expand their capabilities, they may not be ready to fill vacancies as they arise, and external sources must be tapped.

To project the supply of outside candidates, employers assess general economic conditions, labour market conditions, and occupational market conditions.

General Economic Conditions   The term "general economic conditions" refers to natural fluctuations in economic activity, which have an impact on all businesses. These include factors such as interest rates, wage rates, rate of inflation, and unemployment rates. In general terms, the lower the rate of unemployment, the smaller the labour supply and the more difficult it will be to recruit employees. This is sometimes referred to as a "tight" labour market. It is important to note that unemployment rates vary by occupation and geographic location, and can result in an organization's inability to fill certain positions.

Labour Market Conditions   "Labour market conditions" refers to the demographics of those in the population, such as education levels, age, gender, marital status, and so on. Demographic conditions remain stable and can be forecast with a relatively high degree of accuracy. Fortunately, a wealth of national labour market information is available from Statistics Canada and other government or private sources. Regional chambers of commerce and provincial/local development and planning agencies can be excellent sources of local labour market information. The baby boom generation, school leavers (graduates), and immigrants are three key demographic groups influencing current labour market conditions in Canada.

Statistics Canada
www.statcan.gc.ca

The aging of the Canadian workforce will lead to a rising number of people leaving the labour market. Of special interest is the baby boom generation (born between born between 1946 and 1965), which currently accounts for about 30 percent of the total population and over 45 percent of the labour force. This cohort has begun to enter the retirement years (a pressure that will continue well beyond the forecasting horizon of 2017).

In 2007, there were an estimated 432 000 new entrants into the labour market from Canadian educational institutions (with or without a degree). The number of these school leavers is expected to reach 457 000 in 2017.

In the 1980s, Canada welcomed an average of 123 000 new immigrants each year. This number rose to an annual average of 220 000 in the 1990s and 236 000 since 2000. It is estimated that approximately 96 000 of all new immigrants to Canada in 2007 entered the labour market. This number is expected to increase at an average annual rate of 1 percent to reach close to 105 000 in 2017.[8] An example of a company that has come to realize the benefits of new immigrants as a major source of talent is provided in the Strategic HR box.

STRATEGIC   HR

Pumping Up People Supply

According to Judith Thompson, senior manager of HR at Burnaby, BC–based Sorin Group, "Canada isn't well known for its biomedical engineers so even when we hire now, to ask for medical device experience, we wouldn't get it. So we hire an engineer or scientist and train on the rest of it." The company has come to realize the benefits, and necessity, of new immigrants as a major source of talent. "Our culture is very diverse. About 90 percent of our staff speak English as a second language, from production people to vice-presidents, so we don't look for Canadian-born, Canadian-educated, Canadian experience because in these economic times that would set us back," she says. "I would never have filled 60 positions last year with those criteria."

Training is extensive, as it takes three or four months before workers, wearing gowns and gloves in a super-clean environment, can make a product that is usable. Even then, it takes another six months to ramp up to regular production, says Thompson. Sorin supports its employees with in-house English-language training, through a partnership with immigration services, and provides subsidies to foreign-trained engineers who want to pursue an engineering degree in British Columbia.

"We're getting better feedback on problems on the floor because the employees are more comfortable speaking to the researchers and scientists and surgeons who come in on tours. The confidence level of the group has gone up and they are very devoted to the company and the product they make," says Thompson.

Source: Adapted with permission from S. Dobson, "Pumping Up People Supply at Sorin Group Canada to Build Heart Valves," *Canadian HR Reporter,* February 23, 2009.

Occupational Market Conditions In addition to looking at the overall labour market, organizations also generally want to forecast the availability of potential candidates in specific occupations for which they will be recruiting. Current projections show that an excess supply for some occupations will coexist with excess demand for others. The largest number of occupations with significant imbalances will be in management and the health sector, and shortage pressures should be especially acute for managers in health and education, physicians, and nurses. In some cases, supply would need to double or even triple to meet projected demand. Other occupations showing signs of excess demand include senior managers, human resources professionals, contractors, and supervisors of trades and occupations related to oil and gas drilling and services. However, an excess supply situation is projected over the medium term in occupations (mainly low-skilled) specific to the primary sector and to processing, manufacturing, and utilities.[9]

4.2.2 Forecasting Future Human Resources Needs (Demand)

A key component of HRP is forecasting the number and type of people needed to meet organizational objectives. Managers should consider several factors when forecasting such requirements. From a practical point of view, the demand for the organization's product or service is paramount. Thus, in a manufacturing firm, sales are projected first. Then the volume of production required to meet these sales requirements is determined. After this, the staff needed to maintain this volume of output is estimated. In addition to this basic requirement for staff, several other factors should be considered, including the following:

1. **Projected turnover** because of resignations or terminations
2. **Quality and nature of employees** in relation to what management sees as the changing needs of the organization
3. **Decisions to upgrade** the quality of products or services *or enter into new markets,* which might change the required employee skill mix
4. **Planned technological and administrative changes** aimed at increasing productivity and reducing employee head count, such as the installation of new equipment or introduction of a financial incentive plan
5. The **financial resources** available to each department: For example, a budget increase may enable managers to pay higher wages or hire more people; conversely, a budget crunch might result in wage freezes or layoffs.

In large organizations, forecasting demand is primarily quantitative in nature and is the responsibility of highly trained specialists. *Quantitative techniques* for determining human resources requirements include trend analysis, ratio analysis, scatter plot analysis, and regression analysis. These are often viewed as numerically or mathematically grounded, and therefore more objective in nature. *Qualitative approaches* to forecasting range from sophisticated analytical models to informal expert opinions about future needs, often involving subjective interpretations or estimates, such as the nominal group technique or the Delphi technique.

4.2.2.1 Quantitative Approaches

Trend Analysis **Trend analysis** involves studying the firm's employment levels over the last three to five years to predict future needs. The purpose is to identify employment trends that might continue into the future, assuming that the past is a strong predictor of the future. Trend analysis is valuable as an initial estimate only, since employment levels rarely depend solely on the passage of time. Other factors (such as changes in sales volume and productivity) will also affect future staffing needs; thus, trend analysis is an approach used in relatively static and non-changing environments.

trend analysis   The study of a firm's past employment levels over a period of years to predict future needs.

Ratio Analysis **Ratio analysis** involves making forecasts based on the ratio between some causal factor (such as sales volume) and the number of employees required (for example, the number of salespeople). Ratio analysis can also be used to help forecast other employee requirements. Like trend analysis, ratio analysis assumes that productivity remains about the same; it is, however, more useful than trend analysis if there are significant changes between past patterns and future expectations. For example, suppose a salesperson traditionally generates $500 000 annually in sales and that the firm's plans call for increasing sales by $3 million in the coming year. If the sales revenue–salespeople ratio remains the same, six new salespeople would be required (each of whom would produce an extra $500 000 in sales). With ratio analysis, additional consideration can be given to changes in productivity. Using the example above, if we expect that the launch of a new technology and additional training programs will increase productivity by 20 percent, we can determine that in the future sales per employee will be $600 000. Based on the projected $3 million increase in sales, we would now need five additional employees rather than the six predicted when things were static.

ratio analysis   A forecasting technique for determining future staff needs by using ratios between some causal factor (such as sales volume) and the number of employees needed.

The Scatter Plot **Scatter plots** can be used to determine whether two factors (e.g., a measure of business activity and staffing levels) are related. If they are, then when the measure of business activity is forecast, HR requirements can also be estimated.

scatter plot   A graphical method used to help identify the relationship between two variables.

An example to illustrate follows. Legislative changes to the Canadian health-care system require that two 500-bed hospitals be amalgamated. Both previously had responsibility for acute, chronic, and long-term care. The government's plan is for Hospital A to specialize in acute care while Hospital B assumes responsibility for chronic and long-term care. In general, providing acute care requires staffing with registered nurses (RNs), while chronic and long-term care facilities can be staffed primarily with registered practical nurses (RPNs).

By the end of the calendar year, 200 beds at Hospital A must be converted from chronic and long-term care beds to facilities for acute patients. At the same time, Hospital A's 200 chronic and long-term patients must be transferred to Hospital B. In a joint meeting, the directors of nursing and HR decide that a good starting point in the planning process would be to calculate the relationship between hospital size (in terms of number of acute beds) and the number of RNs required. After placing telephone calls to their counterparts at eight hospitals in larger centres across the country, they obtain the following information:

Size of Hospital (Number of Acute Beds)	Number of Registered Nurses
200	240
300	260
400	470
500	500
600	620
700	660
800	820
900	860

To determine how many RNs would be needed, they use the data obtained to draw the scatter plot shown in **Figure 4.4,** in which hospital size is shown on the horizontal axis and number of RNs is shown on the vertical axis. If the two factors are related, then the points will tend to fall along a straight line, as they do in this case. Carefully drawing a line that minimizes the distances between the line and each of the plotted points (the line of best fit) permits an estimate of the number of nurses required for hospitals of various sizes. Thus, since Hospital A will now have 500 acute-care beds, the estimated number of RNs needed is 500.

regression analysis   A statistical technique involving the use of a mathematical formula to project future demands based on an established relationship between an organization's employment level (dependent variable) and some measurable factor of output (independent variable).

Regression Analysis **Regression analysis** is a more sophisticated statistical technique to determine the line of best fit, often involving multiple variables (rather than just two, as per the example above). Using this statistical tool to determine the effect of one variable on another, the investigator is able to determine the magnitude and direction of the relationship between variables to develop future predictions. In the context of HRP, regression analysis involves the use of a mathematical formula to project future demands based on an established rela-

FIGURE 4.4   Determining the Relationship between Hospital Size and Number of Registered Nurses

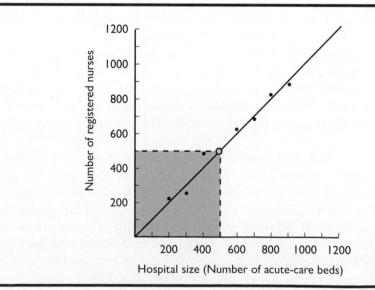

Note: After fitting the line, the number of employees needed, given the projected volume, can be extrapolated (projected).

tionship between an organization's employment level (dependent variable) and some measurable factors of output (independent variables), such as revenue, sales, or production level.

4.2.2.2 Qualitative Approaches

In contrast to quantitative approaches, which use statistical formulas, qualitative techniques rely solely on expert judgments. Two approaches used to forecast human resources demand (or supply) are the nominal group and Delphi techniques. Although managerial judgment is central to qualitative forecasting, it also plays a key role when quantitative techniques are used. It is rare that any historical trend, ratio, or relationship will continue unchanged into the future. Judgment is therefore needed to modify the forecast based on anticipated changes.

Nominal Group Technique The **nominal group technique** involves a group of experts (such as first-line supervisors and managers) meeting face to face. Although one of its uses is human resources demand forecasting, this technique is used to deal with issues and problems ranging from identifying training needs to determining safety program incentives. The steps involved are as follows:[10]

1. Each member of the group independently writes down his or her ideas on the problem or issue (in this case, estimates of demand).

2. Going around the table, each member then presents one idea per round. This process continues until all ideas have been presented and recorded, typically on a flipchart or chalkboard. No discussion is permitted during this step.

3. Clarification is then sought, as necessary, followed by group discussion and evaluation.

4. Finally, each member is asked to rank the ideas. This is done independently and in silence.

The advantages of this technique include involvement of key decision makers, a future focus, and the fact that the group discussion involved in the third step can facilitate the exchange of ideas and greater acceptance of results. Drawbacks include subjectivity and the potential for group pressure to lead to a less accurate assessment than could be obtained through other means.

Delphi Technique Although managers generally handle short-term forecasting, the **Delphi technique** is useful for long-range forecasting and other strategic planning issues. It typically involves outside experts as well as company employees, based on the premise that outsiders may be able to assess changes in economic, demographic, governmental, technological, and social conditions, and predict the potential impact of these external changes more objectively. The Delphi technique involves the following steps:[11]

1. The problem is identified (in this case, estimates of demand), and each group member is requested to submit a potential solution by completing a carefully designed questionnaire. Direct face-to-face contact is not permitted.

2. After each member independently and anonymously completes the initial questionnaire, the results are compiled at a centralized location.

nominal group technique   A decision-making technique that involves a group of experts meeting face to face. Steps include independent idea generation, clarification and open discussion, and private assessment.

In the nominal group technique, each member presents ideas independently, followed by group discussion and evaluation of ideas.

Delphi technique   A judgmental forecasting method used to arrive at a group decision, typically involving outside experts as well as organizational employees. Ideas are exchanged without face-to-face interaction, and feedback is provided and used to fine-tune independent judgments until a consensus is reached.

© Monkey Business/Fotolia

In the Delphi technique, after each member independently and anonymously provides their forecast, the results are compiled at a centralized location.

3. Each group member is then given a copy of the results.

4. If there are differences in opinion, each individual uses the feedback from other experts to fine-tune his or her independent assessment.

5. The third and fourth steps are repeated as often as necessary until a consensus is reached.

As with the nominal group technique, the advantages of the Delphi technique include involvement of key decision makers and a future focus; in addition, though, it permits the group to critically evaluate a wider range of views. Drawbacks include the fact that judgments may not efficiently use objective data, the time and costs involved, and the potential difficulty in integrating diverse opinions.

4.2.3 Gap Analysis: Summarizing Human Resources Requirements

The result of the forecasting process is an estimate of short-term and long-range HR requirements. Long-range plans are general statements of potential staffing needs and may not include specific numbers.

staffing table A pictorial representation of all jobs within the organization, along with the number of current incumbents and future employment requirements (monthly or yearly) for each.

Short-term plans—although still approximations—are more specific and are often depicted in a **staffing table**. A staffing table is a pictorial representation of all jobs within the organization, along with the number of current incumbents and future employment requirements (monthly or yearly) for each.

4.2.4 Planning and Implementing HR Programs to Balance Supply and Demand

Once the supply and demand of human resources have been estimated, program planning and implementation begin. To successfully fill positions internally, organizations must manage performance and careers. Performance is managed through effectively designing jobs and quality-of-working-life initiatives; establishing performance standards and goals; coaching, measuring, and evaluating; and implementing a suitable reward structure (compensation and benefits).

To manage careers effectively, policies and systems must be established for recruitment, selection, and placement (including transfer, promotion, retirement, and termination), as well as training and development. Policies and systems are also required for job analysis, individual employee assessment, replacement and succession planning, and career tracking, in addition to career planning and development.

Specific strategies must be formulated to balance supply and demand considerations. As illustrated in **Figure 4.5**, there are three possible scenarios.

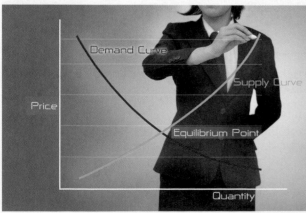

Once the future demand and supply of human resources have been established, managers and HR experts work together to determine actions required to reach the equilibrium point.

FIGURE 4.5   Balancing Labour Supply and Demand Considerations

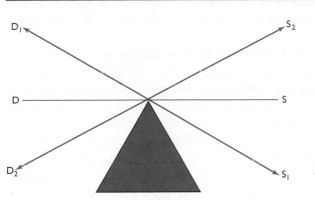

The choice of staffing "rebalancing" strategies depends on the estimate length of time of the imbalance of labour demand and supply.

D – S (Labour supply equilibrium) Vacancies filled internally through training, transfers, promotions, or external recruiting methods (see Chapter 5).

D₁ – S₁ (Labour shortage) Depending on estimated length of labour shortage, the company may schedule overtime, hire temp workers, subcontract work, promote or transfer staff internally, or seek new permanent FT or PT staff.

D₂ – S₂ (Labour surplus) Depending on estimated length of labour surplus, the company may utilize attrition and a hiring freeze, early retirement incentives, job sharing, reduced work hours, layoffs, buy-outs, unpaid leave of absences, or terminations.

4.2.4.1 Labour Equilibrium

Although it is extremely rare to have a labour equilibrium, when the expected supply matches the actual demand, organizations do not need to change their course of action. Existing plans to replace outgoing employees should be maintained by promoting or transferring internal members of the organization and recruiting external labourers.

4.2.4.2 Labour Surplus

A labour surplus exists when the internal supply of employees exceeds the organization's demand. Most employers respond initially by instituting a **hiring freeze**, which means that openings are filled by reassigning current employees, and no outsiders are hired. The surplus is slowly reduced through **attrition**, which is the normal separation of employees because of resignation, retirement, or death. When employees leave, the ensuing vacancies are not filled and the staffing level decreases gradually without any involuntary terminations. In addition to the time it takes, a major drawback of this approach is that the firm has no control over who stays and who leaves.

Some organizations attempt to accelerate attrition by offering incentives to employees to leave, such as **early retirement or buyout programs**. Staffing levels are reduced and internal job openings created by offering attractive buyout packages or the opportunity to retire on full pension with an attractive benefits package at a relatively early age (often 55 or 60). To be successful, buyouts must be handled carefully. Selection criteria should be established to ensure that key people who cannot be easily replaced do not leave the firm. A drawback of

hiring freeze   A common initial response to an employee surplus; openings are filled by reassigning current employees, and no outsiders are hired.

attrition   The normal separation of employees from an organization because of resignation, retirement, or death.

early retirement or buyout programs   Strategies used to accelerate attrition that involve offering attractive buyout packages or the opportunity to retire on full pension with an attractive benefits package.

job sharing   A strategy that involves dividing the duties of a single position between two or more employees.

buyouts and early retirement packages is that they often require a great deal of money up front. Care must also be taken to ensure that early retirement is voluntary, since forced early retirement is a contravention of human rights legislation.

Another strategy used to deal with an employee surplus involves reducing the total number of hours worked. **Job sharing** involves dividing the duties of a single position between two or more employees. Reducing full-time positions to part-time work is sometimes more effective, especially if there are peak demand periods. Creating a job-share position or offering part-time employment can be win–win strategies, since layoffs can be avoided. Although the employees involved work fewer hours and thus receive less pay, they are still employed, and they may enjoy having more free time at their disposal, while the organization benefits by retaining good employees. Planning this supply reduction option should involve consultation with the organization's legal advisor to be sure that the required notice period relating to this change is provided to the affected employees.

work sharing   Employees work three or four days a week and receive EI benefits on their non-workday(s).

reduced workweek   Employees work fewer hours and receive less pay.

Twenty-five years ago, the federal government introduced a **work-sharing** scheme, a layoff-avoidance strategy that involves employees working three or four days a week and receiving employment insurance (EI) benefits on their non-workday(s). Similar to work sharing, but without a formal arrangement with the government regarding EI benefits, is a **reduced workweek**. Employees simply work fewer hours and receive less pay. The organization retains a skilled workforce, lessens the financial and emotional impact of a full layoff, and reduces production costs. One potential drawback is that it is sometimes difficult to accurately predict in advance how many hours of work should be scheduled each week. A significant number of organizations use work arrangements other than the traditional Monday-to-Friday, nine-to-five schedule, as highlighted in the Expert Opinion box.

layoff   The temporary or permanent withdrawal of employment to workers for economic or business reasons.

Another strategy used to manage an employee surplus is a **layoff**: the temporary withdrawal of employment to workers for economic or business reasons. Layoffs may be short in duration (for example, when a plant closes for brief periods in order to adjust inventory levels or to retool for a new product line), but can last months or even years at a time if the organization is negatively affected by a major change in the business cycle. Employment standards legislation may stipulate that a temporary layoff of a specific duration may become a deemed termination from employment for affected workers. Layoffs are not easy for managers, who have to reduce the number of employees to the required level, or for workers, but are usually necessary to ultimately reduce the impact of the organization's economic downturn. Layoffs and terminations are discussed in depth in Chapter 11.

termination   Permanent separation from the organization for any reason.

Termination is a broad term that encompasses the permanent separation of the worker from the organization. Termination is often triggered by a management decision to sever the employment relationship for job performance reasons. Purging poorly performing employees is an ongoing activity in any organization, regardless of any projected labour surpluses; however, the rate of termination may increase if there is a projected surplus of labour.

leave of absence   Allows an employee who may be interested in taking time away from work for a variety of reasons (e.g., personal, educational, etc.) to have a set period of time away from their position without pay, but with a guarantee that their job will be available upon their return.

The option of a voluntary **leave of absence** can also be used if the labour surplus is temporary in nature. A leave of absence allows those who may be interested in time off for personal, educational, or other reasons to have a set period away from their position, with a guarantee that their job will be available

Industry Viewpoint
EXPERT OPINION

Identification:
Ms. Renee Paquin
Director, Corporate Human
Resources & Diversity Services,
Yukon Public Service Commission

1. What is the government of Yukon's approach to employees' use of flex time?

There are a number of flexible arrangements available for employees. We can average hours over two weeks or one month terms, use traditional flex time, and allow compressed workweeks, job sharing, and part-time positions; some seasonal or auxiliary positions are usually limited to spring and summer (e.g., firefighters, campground crews).

This works best when clients want flexibility, and when the nature of work is such that we can allow some flexibility. We recognize that candidates choose employers according to a number of issues, including the job, the work environment, and some non-work considerations such as the local community and climate. A number of our employees enjoy physical activity associated with the region, and flexible arrangements can allow people to engage in activities that support work–life balance and that they are passionate about. We believe that our employees should live healthy and fulfilling lives, for overall physical and mental well-being. In addition, there are a number of employees who require flex time in order to care for others such as dependents and aging parents.

2. What benefits has this employer experienced through flex time options?

We have noticed an increase in interest of individuals outside of Yukon for a job, so there is a recruitment benefit. We also see a retention benefit, given that these arrangements help keep us competitive with local external employers. Initially, some new hires believe they will be here for one to two years, but stayed because they love the nature of the work and the options for work–life balance.

3. What obstacles have you experienced when

implementing flexible work arrangements, and how can these be overcome?

I. At times, we can have up to 100 percent of our staff in a specific unit on a compressed workweek. We have to modify the days that employees can take off, in order to ensure that we're staffed to appropriate levels throughout the week. We learn to create clear decision rules around why or how to move requested days off, and also use a written agreement to approve flexible hours on an individual basis.

II. Internal mobility can be a challenge at times. An employee currently on flex time may apply for a job somewhere else in the organization that may not have flex time options. In this case, we are careful to communicate which positions allow flex time and which ones do not.

III. Locally, there is a demand for teleworking, but the technology infrastructure doesn't exist to support teleworking consistently. This creates an external limitation that prevents the use of teleworking regularly, although we still allow it on days with severe weather.

Source: Reprinted by permission from Renee Paquin, Director, Corporate Human Resources & Diversity Services Yukon Public Service Commission

---

upon their return. A leave of absence can be paid or unpaid, but often seniority and benefits remain intact. Terms of the leave and expected return must be clearly outlined, including potential conflicts of interest and mutual expectations from each party.

4.2.4.3 Labour Shortage

A labour shortage exists when the internal supply of human resources cannot meet the organization's needs. Internal solutions to correct this shortage are planned by the HR department, based on the estimated length of time for such shortages. Such options range from offering overtime for a period of a few days when the shortage is seen on an occasional basis to permanent hiring when additional employees are required to meet the labour needs due to a long-term increase in demand for goods or services. Employers may also subcontract work on a temporary or permanent basis. Another short-term solution is to hire temporary employees.

As vacancies are created within the firm, opportunities are generally provided for employee transfers and promotions, which necessitate performance management, training (and retraining), and career development. Of course, internal movement does not eliminate a shortage, which means that recruitment will be required. It is hoped that resultant vacancies will be for entry-level jobs, which can be filled more easily externally.

transfer Movement of an employee from one job to another that is relatively equal in pay, responsibility, or organizational level.

Internal Solutions to a Labour Shortage   A **transfer** involves a lateral movement from one job to another that is relatively equal in pay, responsibility, or organizational level. Transfers can lead to effective use of human resources, broaden an employee's skills and perspectives, and help make him or her a better candidate for future promotions. Transfers also offer additional technical and interpersonal challenges and increased variety of work, which may enhance job satisfaction and motivation.

promotion Movement of an employee from one job to another that is higher in pay, responsibility, or organizational level, usually based on merit, seniority, or a combination of both.

A **promotion** involves the movement of an employee from one job to another that is higher in pay, responsibility, or organizational level. Such a move may be based on merit, seniority, or a combination of both. Merit-based promotions are awarded in recognition of a person's outstanding performance in his or her present job or as an assessment of his or her potential.

A focus on employee retention initiatives can also mitigate potential labour shortages. The HRP process often highlights challenges the organization is having with turnover or retention at specific levels. This may warrant further investigation into why employees are leaving and which types of employees are leaving. Rather than a broad focus on retention, organizations can benefit from focusing on retaining key employees or employees with strong job performance. A discussion of career planning to assist with internal solutions in response to a labour shortage is provided in Chapters 6 (Onboarding and Training) and 7 (Performance Management).

"How could anyone think that this department is under staffed?"

External Solutions to a Labour Shortage   External solutions to managing a labour shortage involve recruiting the right quality and quantity of talent needed in an organization to meet the long-term goals and strategy of the company. Options for selection related to managing a labour shortage are provided in Chapter 5 (Talent Acquisition).

CHAPTER SUMMARY

1. Human resources planning (HRP) is the process of reviewing HR requirements to ensure that the organization has the required number of employees with the necessary skills to meet its strategic goals. Forecasting future labour demand and supply is a critical element of the strategic planning process. HRP and strategic planning become effective when a reciprocal and interdependent relationship exists between them.

2. Four quantitative techniques for forecasting future HR demand are trend analysis, ratio analysis, scatter plots, and regression analysis. Two qualitative techniques used to forecast demand are the nominal group technique and the Delphi technique.

3. Four strategies used to forecast internal HR supply are a skills/management inventory, replacement plan/summaries, succession plans, and Markov analysis. Forecasting external HR supply requires an assessment of general economic conditions, labour market conditions, and occupational labour conditions.

4. Strategies to manage a labour surplus include a hiring freeze; downsizing through attrition; early retirement or buyout programs; reduced hours through job sharing, part-time work, work sharing, or reduced workweeks; leaves of absence; and termination of employment.

5. Strategies to manage a human resources shortage include internal and external solutions, such as allowing overtime hours, hiring employees, employee transfers and promotions, and retention programs.

MyLab Management

Visit MyLab Management to access a personalized Study Plan, Personal Inventory Assessments (PIA), and a collection of videos and assignments within MediaShare.

KEY TERMS

attrition *(p. 83)*
Delphi technique *(p. 81)*
early retirement or buyout programs *(p. 83)*
environmental scanning *(p. 71)*
hiring freeze *(p. 83)*
human resources planning (HRP) *(p. 70)*
job sharing *(p. 84)*
layoff *(p. 84)*
leave of absence *(p. 84)*
management inventories *(p. 73)*
Markov analysis *(p. 75)*
nominal group technique *(p. 81)*
promotion *(p. 86)*

ratio analysis *(p. 79)*
reduced workweek *(p. 84)*
regression analysis *(p. 80)*
replacement charts *(p. 73)*
replacement summaries *(p. 74)*
scatter plot *(p. 79)*
skills inventories *(p. 73)*
staffing table *(p. 82)*
succession planning *(p. 74)*
termination *(p. 84)*
transfer *(p. 86)*
trend analysis *(p. 79)*
work sharing *(p. 84)*

REVIEW AND DISCUSSION QUESTIONS

1. Name and briefly describe two undesired consequences to an organization that lacks a proper human resources planning (HRP) process.

2. Environmental scanning involves assessing external factors that may affect the supply and demand for labour in an organization. Discuss

two such factors, and indicate their impact on either the supply of, or demand for, labour in an organization.

3. Differentiate between the internal labour supply techniques known as replacement charts and succession plans. Explain why the employer may prefer either strategy.

4. To attain a "balanced" labour demand–supply state, the HR planning team may offer advice on particular techniques to increase or lower the current supply of the labour force in an organization. Suggest two possible strategies when:

   a. there is a short-term (2–5 days) shortage of staff for scheduled afternoon shifts in a production department.

   b. there is a need to increase the number of sales associates due to the forecasted long-term popularity of a new line of cosmetics.

CRITICAL THINKING QUESTIONS

1. A number of quantitative and qualitative techniques for forecasting human resources demand were discussed in this chapter. Working in groups, identify which strategies would be most appropriate for (a) small versus large companies, (b) industries undergoing rapid change, and (c) businesses/industries in which there are seasonal variations in HR (human resources) requirements.

2. Suppose that you are the HR manager at a firm where a hiring freeze has just been declared. The plan is to downsize through attrition. Define the meaning of attrition. What steps would you take to ensure that you reap the advantages of this strategy while minimizing the disadvantages?

3. Suggest a rationale to present to the senior management team that promotes an early retirement incentive plan for workers over the age of 55. What are key considerations to mention in your presentation?

EXPERIENTIAL EXERCISES

1. Individually or in groups of three or four, act as an HR (human resources) team for your local grocery store. Develop an HR plan. Specifically forecast supply for three years, including trends in demographics, turnover trends in the industry, population forecasts for the region, competition for labour, and economic trends. Forecast demand considering population growth (clients), changes to technology or automation of work, consumer preference shifts (e.g., purchasing groceries online), and competitors in the industry.

2. Consider that you are working in a company that has just announced the termination of 20 percent of the organization's workforce. You are not affected by this action, but several of your friends will lose their jobs. This past week several other employees not affected by this job loss appear to be quite stressed out by the news. You have a good relationship with the HR representative for your work team. What might you suggest she do in this situation?

TALENT ACQUISITION

LEARNING OUTCOMES

AFTER STUDYING THIS CHAPTER, YOU SHOULD BE ABLE TO:

DEFINE talent acquisition, and **DISCUSS** the relevant components of this new perspective on traditional staffing of organizations.

ANALYZE the role of various internal and external recruitment methods.

DISCUSS strategies for recruiting a more diverse workforce.

DEFINE selection, and **DISCUSS** its strategic importance.

DEFINE reliability and validity, and **EXPLAIN** their importance in selection techniques.

DESCRIBE at least four types of testing used in selection, and **ANALYZE** the conflicting legal concerns related to alcohol and drug testing.

DESCRIBE the major types of selection interviews by degree of structure, type of content, and manner of administration.

EXPLAIN the importance of reference checking, **DESCRIBE** strategies to make such checking effective, and **ANALYZE** the legal issues involved.

5.1 TALENT ACQUISITION

Globalization and advances in technology have had a direct impact on the traditional human resources management (HRM) programming areas of recruitment and selection. Competitive labour markets and demographic impacts on current and future labour supplies require contemporary HRM departments to re-think ways to provide their organization with the right number of people at the right time with the knowledge, skills, and abilities to match the corporate mission, vision, and goals. **Talent acquisition** is an emerging HRM programming concept focused on finding, acquiring, assessing, and hiring job candidates. Traditional recruiting and selection activities are now viewed as key elements of a company's talent acquisition strategy, along with linkages to corporate marketing, HR planning, employee retention, and career development programs. The example of a recruitment notice for a Talent Acquisition Specialist in **Figure 5.1** highlights the scope of this emerging HR role.

The concept of talent acquisition is reflected throughout the following discussion of traditional and new approaches in recruitment and selection activities.

talent acquisition   An emerging HRM programming concept that is focused on finding, acquiring, assessing, and hiring job candidates.

5.2 RECRUITMENT

Recruitment is the process of searching out and attracting qualified job applicants. It begins with the identification of a position that requires staffing and is completed when résumés or completed application forms are received from an adequate number of applicants. A Watson Wyatt study found that organizations with superior recruiting practices financially outperform those with less effective programs and that successful recruiting is a strong indicator of higher shareholder value.[1]

recruitment   The process of searching out and attracting qualified job applicants, which begins with the identification of a position that requires staffing and is completed when résumés or completed application forms are received from an adequate number of applicants.

FIGURE 5.1   Sample Job Summary

Willow Tech Industries is seeking a **Talent Acquisition Specialist** to develop and leverage diverse candidate channels to connect with top talent in the national and international telecommunications sectors, as well as in postsecondary educational hubs in leading-edge technology programming.

Working with the Director, the **Talent Acquisition Specialist** will develop workforce planning and sourcing strategies that reflect Willow Tech's brand, its dynamic culture, and a results-based orientation to service and design quality. This specialist role will use superior communications skills to establish external talent pipelines and a market presence in our service areas across Canada and in key international operation centres.

The **Talent Acquisition Specialist** will advise and collaborate with HR Business Partners and hiring managers on all matters related to successful recruiting and staffing strategies. This will include designing contemporary, tech-based applicant screening methods; short-listing candidates for submission to hiring managers; guiding reference and background check processes consistent with legal and human rights parameters; and lending support to HR Business Partners in coordinating the offer process.

Willow Tech seeks a strong internal and external communicator, whose professionalism and networking abilities have earned the respect of business leaders and colleagues. Postsecondary credentials in business, human resources, or marketing, and related talent acquisition experience in telecommunications are key to the desired candidate's profile. Our ideal applicant will have demonstrated the ability to *"attract candidates that stick!"*

Developed by Gary L. Gannon
August 15, 2017

Authority for recruitment is generally delegated to HR staff members or outsourced to firms that specialize in recruitment, except in small businesses where line managers usually recruit their own staff. In large organizations where recruiting is done on a continual basis, the HR team typically includes specialists, known as **recruiters**, whose job is to find and attract qualified applicants. As globalization and fluctuations in the supply of talent lead to increased competition for the employees needed to implement strategy, recruiters are becoming increasingly critical to achieving an organization's strategic objectives.

recruiter   A specialist in recruitment whose job is to find and attract capable candidates.

Organizations continue to see value in the use of "employer of choice," such as those included in lists such as Mediacorp's "Top 100 Employers," the Hewitt Associates' "50 Best Employers," and the *Financial Post*'s "Ten Best Companies to Work for." Employers such as Scotiabank, Purolator, Tim Hortons, and many others are also applying the marketing concept of branding to strengthen their recruitment activities.[2]

Great Place to Work Institute Canada
www.greatplacetowork.ca

5.2.1 Employer Branding

A key element of talent acquisition is recognizing the importance of how an employer "brands" itself. As technology has expanded its reach to passive and active job seekers through mobile devices and professional networking sites, contemporary HR professionals are realizing the importance of marketing strategies is seeking talent. Gabriel Bouchard, founder of the Monster Canada online job board, says, "In an increasingly tight job market, employers must remain permanently visible to potential employees, establishing and maintaining relationships with potential candidates before they even begin pursuing a new job. This is particularly crucial when it comes to hard-to-fill or mission-critical positions."[3] Proactive employers try to obtain a competitive advantage in recruitment by establishing themselves as employers of choice through employer branding. The purpose of an employer brand is to attract people to apply for jobs at the organization as well as to earn the loyalty of current employees.

Employer branding is the image or impression of an organization as an employer based on the perceived benefits of belonging to the organization. It is the experience of an employee when working for a company, based on feelings, emotions, senses, realities, and benefits (functional benefits such as personal development, economic benefits such as monetary rewards, and psychological benefits such as feelings of purpose, belonging, and recognition). It is essentially a promise made to employees and their perception of how well that promise is delivered.[4] Employer branding involves three steps as summarized in **Table 5.1**.

employer branding   The image or impression of an organization as an employer based on the benefits of being employed by the organization.

Employer branding is particularly important during the recruitment process, not only for applicants who are eventually hired, but also for those not hired who are out in the marketplace communicating their experience as an applicant to other job seekers.[5] Inconsiderate recruiting practices can be brand suicide for companies. Branding includes the experiences a candidate goes through while interacting with a company throughout the recruitment process, such as[6]

- what candidates experience when they go to the company's website,
- whether HR sends an acknowledgement letter or email thanking each candidate who sends in a résumé,
- how candidates are greeted by the receptionist when they make initial contact by phone or in person, and
- whether the HR person who interviews candidates is a good spokesperson who can articulate the organization's values and culture.

TABLE 5.1 Employer Branding Steps

Step	Example
1. Define the target audience	The target group may be one of the four generations in today's workforce, the underemployed, or the four employment equity groups.
2. Develop the employee value proposition	Loblaw Companies and Fairmont Hotels offer potential employees the opportunity to participate in "green" environmental initiatives. At PCL Construction of Alberta, 80 percent of employees own stock in the company.
3. Reinforce value proposition in communication	An integrated marketing approach to internal and external communication should use various channels, such as television, radio, print, websites, social media, and so on.

Sources: A. Watanabe, "From Brown to Green, What Colour Is Your Employment Brand?" *HR Professional* (February/March 2008), pp. 47–49; M. Morra, "Best in Show," *Workplace News* (September/October 2006), pp. 17–21; R. Milgram, "Getting the Most Out of Online Job Ads," *Canadian HR Reporter* (January 28, 2008).

McDonald's used focus groups to identify the interests of one of its target markets for recruitment (young people). The results of the focus groups suggest that this target market is interested in balancing its own freedom and goals with making money. As a result, McDonald's offered flexible hours, uniform choices, scholarships, and discount cards to support its value proposition slogan "We take care of our employees." This value proposition was also communicated through television ads and a recruiting website. Following the introduction of this branding initiative, McDonald's saw a surge in the number of young people who recognized McDonald's as a great place to work.[7] With the right branding strategy, job seekers line up to apply for jobs. A successful brand results in job seekers saying, "I'd like to work there."[8]

5.3 THE RECRUITMENT PROCESS

As illustrated in **Figure 5.2**, the recruitment process has a number of steps:

1. Job openings are identified through HR planning (based on the organization's strategic plan) or manager request. Openings do arise unexpectedly, though, when managers request that a new employee be hired.

2. The job requirements are determined. This step involves reviewing the job description and the job specifications and updating them, if necessary.

FIGURE 5.2 An Overview of the Recruitment Process

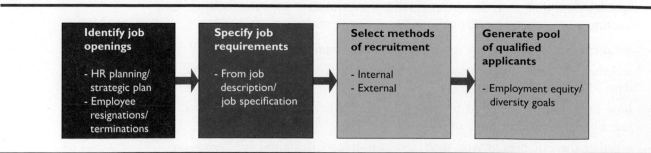

3. Appropriate recruiting source(s) and method(s) are chosen. The major decision here is whether to start with internal or external recruiting. There is no single, best recruiting technique, and the most appropriate for any given position depends on a number of factors, which will be discussed in the next section.

4. A pool of qualified recruits is generated. The requirements of employment equity legislation (if any) and the organization's diversity goals should be reflected in the applicant pool.

To be successful, a recruiter must be aware of constraints affecting the recruitment process. Constraints arise from organizational policies, such as promote-from-within policies, which mean that a recruiter cannot start recruiting externally for a specified period, even if he or she is aware that there are no suitable internal candidates. Constraints also arise from compensation policies, since they influence the attractiveness of the job to potential applicants. If there is an employment equity plan, it will specify goals for increasing recruitment from the designated groups. Monetary and non-monetary inducements offered by competitors impose a constraint, since recruiters must try to meet the prevailing standards or use alternative inducements.

The labour supply, particularly in certain sectors of the economy, serves as a constraint on recruiting activity. While Canadian government projections through the early 2020s suggest a balanced outlook for labour supply and demand in occupational categories accounting for approximately two-thirds of existing jobs, shortages of qualified workers in some occupations and regions may intensify as the labour growth rate slows post 2020.[9]

5.3.1 Recruiting from Within the Organization

Although recruiting often brings job boards and employment agencies to mind, current employees are generally the largest source of recruits. Filling open positions with inside candidates has several advantages. According to **human capital theory** (introduced in Chapter 1), the accumulation of firm-specific knowledge and experience involves a joint investment by both the employee and employer; therefore, both parties benefit from maintaining a long-term relationship. Employees see that competence is rewarded, thus enhancing their commitment, morale, and performance. Having already been with the firm for some time, insiders may be more committed to the company's goals and less likely to leave. Managers (as agents of the organization) are provided with a longer-term perspective when making business decisions. It is generally safer to promote from within, because the firm is likely to have a more accurate assessment of a person's skills and performance level than would otherwise be the case. In addition, inside candidates require less orientation than outsiders do.

Recruiting from within also has a number of drawbacks. Employees who are unsuccessful in bidding for vacant positions may become discontented. Informing unsuccessful applicants as to why they were rejected and what remedial action they might take to be more successful in the future is thus essential.[10] Managers may be required to post all job openings and interview all inside candidates, even when they already know whom they want to hire. This wastes considerable time and creates false hope for those not being generally considered. Employees may be less satisfied with and accepting of a boss appointed from within their own ranks than they would be with a newcomer; it is sometimes difficult for a

human capital theory   The accumulation of firm-specific knowledge and experience involves a joint investment by both the employee and employer; therefore, both parties benefit from maintaining a long-term relationship.

newly chosen leader to adjust to not being "one of the gang."[11] There is also a possibility of "inbreeding." When an entire management team has come up through the ranks, they may have a tendency to make decisions "by the book" and to maintain the status quo when what is needed is a new and innovative direction.

5.3.1.1 Internal Recruitment Methods

Recruiting from within can be accomplished by using job postings, human resources records, and skills inventories.

job posting   The process of notifying current employees about vacant positions.

Job Postings Job posting is a process of notifying current employees about vacant positions. Most companies now use computerized job-posting systems, where information about job vacancies can be found on the company's intranet. This involves a notice outlining the job title, duties (as listed in the job description), qualifications (taken from the job specification), hours of work, pay range, posting date, and closing date. Not all firms use intranets. Some post jobs on bulletin boards or in employee publications. As illustrated in **Figure 5.3**, there are advantages and disadvantages to using job postings to facilitate the transfer and promotion of qualified internal candidates.

Human Resources Records Human resources records are often consulted to ensure that qualified individuals are notified, individually, of vacant positions. An examination of employee files, including résumés and application forms, may uncover employees who are working in jobs below their education or skill levels, people who already have the requisite KSAs, or individuals with the potential to move into the vacant position if given some additional training.

An Ethical Dilemma

Suppose a manager has already made up his or her mind about who will be selected for an internal position. However, an internal job posting and subsequent interviews have shown another equally qualified candidate. Who should be offered the position?

Skills Inventories Skills inventories are a useful recruitment tool. Although such inventories may be used instead

FIGURE 5.3   Advantages and Disadvantages of Job Posting

Advantages

- Provides every qualified employee with a chance for a transfer or promotion.
- Reduces the likelihood of special deals and favouritism.
- Demonstrates the organization's commitment to career growth and development.
- Communicates to employees the organization's policies and guidelines regarding promotions and transfers.
- Provides equal opportunity to all qualified employees.

Disadvantages

- Unsuccessful job candidates may become demotivated, demoralized, discontented, and unhappy if feedback is not communicated in a timely and sensitive manner.
- Tensions may rise if it appears that a qualified internal candidate was passed over for an equally qualified or less qualified external candidate.
- The decision about which candidate to select may be more difficult if there are two or more equally qualified candidates.

of job postings, they are more often used as a supplement. Whether they are computerized or manual, referring to such inventories ensures that qualified internal candidates are identified and considered for transfer or promotion when opportunities arise. Such tools also serve to flag employees who may have "outgrown" their current position and are thus a turnover risk.[12]

Limitations of Recruiting from Within   It is rarely possible to fill all non-entry-level positions with current employees. Middle- and upper-level positions may be vacated unexpectedly, with no internal replacements yet qualified or ready for transfer or promotion; particularly if a replacement chart, as discussed in Chapter 4, has not been developed. Even in firms with a policy of promoting from within, potential external candidates are increasingly being considered to meet strategic objectives. Hiring someone from outside may be preferable in order to acquire the latest knowledge and expertise or to gain new ideas and revitalize the department or organization.[13]

5.3.2 Recruiting from Outside the Organization

Unless there is a workforce reduction, even in firms with a promote-from-within policy, a replacement from outside must eventually be found to fill the job left vacant once all eligible employees have been given the opportunity for transfer or promotion. In addition, most entry-level positions must be filled by external candidates (by definition, there is no one to promote up to an entry-level position). The advantages of external recruitment include the following:

- The generation of a larger pool of qualified candidates, which may have a positive impact on the quality of the selection decision

- The availability of a more diverse applicant pool, which can assist in meeting employment equity goals and timetables

- The acquisition of skills or knowledge not currently available within the organization or the introduction of new ideas and creative problem-solving techniques

- The elimination of rivalry and competition caused by employees jockeying for transfers and promotions, which can hinder interpersonal and interdepartmental cooperation

- The potential cost savings resulting from hiring individuals who already have the required skills, rather than providing extensive training

5.3.2.1 Planning External Recruitment

If external recruitment is chosen, several factors should be considered in addition to the earlier-mentioned constraints. The type of job to be filled has a major impact on the chosen recruitment method. For example, most firms normally rely on professional search firms for recruiting executive-level employees. In contrast, Internet advertising is commonly used for recruiting other salaried employees.

5.3.2.2 External Recruitment Methods

Organizations use a wide range of recruitment methods to attract interest from qualified candidates for current and future job vacancies. Such approaches range from the tradition use of job applications to contemporary, web-based sources such as job boards and social media. The following external recruitment methods illustrate the notion of "pipelines" connecting external candidate supply sources to the company's talent acquisition team.

Cold Calls: Walk-Ins and Write-Ins Individuals who go to organizations in person to apply for jobs without referral or invitation are called *walk-ins*. People who submit unsolicited résumés to organizations are known as *write-ins*. Walk-ins and write-ins are an inexpensive recruitment method. The HR department generally screens their résumés, and if an applicant is suitable, his or her résumé is retained on file for three to six months or passed on to the relevant department manager if there is an immediate or upcoming opening for which the applicant is qualified.

Job Applications and Résumés For most employers, completion of an application form or uploading a résumé into an applicant tracking system that codes and logs data is the last step in the recruitment process. These provide an efficient means of collecting verifiable historical data from each candidate in a standardized format; it usually includes information about education, prior work history, and other job-related skills. The use of online applications significantly reduces the risk of lost applications, increases the exposure level of the job ad (global reach), and minimizes the likelihood of biases associated with other forms of face-to-face recruitment. However, online application forms can also result in a large number of applications (for example, Google receives over 3 000 per day[14]); this puts pressure on staff to manage the high volume. Human Resources Information System (HRIS) software can be extremely useful here for automatically coding and storing applications.

One type of application form that can be used to predict performance is a **biographical information blank (BIB)**. Also known as a biodata form, the BIB focuses on information among a candidate's biographical data that has been found to be predictive of job success. Candidates respond to a series of questions about their background, experiences, and preferences, including willingness to travel and leisure activities. Because biographical questions rarely have right or wrong answers, BIBs are difficult to fake. Questions relating to age, gender, race, or other grounds are prohibited under human rights legislation and cannot be asked.

Many methods of recruiting from the external labour market are used. A 2010 study by Right Management of 5 858 job seekers found that the most successful way to find a job was through traditional networking, followed by online job boards. The results of the study are highlighted in **Figure 5.4**. Traditional networking includes employee referrals, former employees who have remained in contact with the organization, concentrated job fairs based on relationships formed with educational institutes, professional and trade associations, labour organizations, and military personnel. Online job boards include traditional online job boards, corporate websites, and government-initiated job boards.

Employee Referrals Some organizations encourage applications from friends and relatives of current employees by mounting an employee referral campaign. Openings are announced in the company's intranet or newsletter along with a request for referrals. Cash awards or prizes may be offered for referrals that culminate in a new hire. Because no advertising or agency fees are involved, paying referral rewards still represents a low recruiting cost.

biographical information blank (BIB)   A detailed job application form requesting biographical data pertaining to background, experiences, and preferences, and found to be predictive of success on the job. Responses are scored.

FIGURE 5.4   Most Successful Ways to Find a Job in Canada, 2012

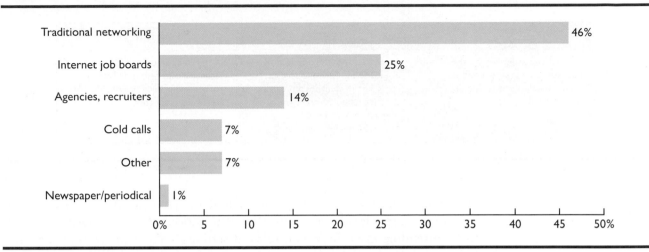

Note: Often candidates rely on more than one method (for example, networking leads to an awareness about a job posted online in a colleague's company). The above survey forced respondents to identify only one tool that they used to find their most recent job.

Source: Based on data from a survey by Right Management, published in Monika Morrow, "Networking, Not Internet Cruising, Still Lands Most Jobs for Those in Career Transition," *ThoughtWire* (May 8, 2013), www.right.com/wps/wcm/connect/right-us-en/home/thoughtwire/categories/talent-work/networking-not-internet-cruising-still-lands-most-jobs-for-those-in-career-transition (accessed July 29, 2017).

The disadvantages associated with employee referrals include the potential for inbreeding and **nepotism** to cause morale problems and dissatisfaction among employees whose referrals are not hired. Perhaps the biggest drawback, however, is that this method may result in systemic discrimination.

nepotism   A preference for hiring relatives of current employees.

Former Employees   In times of talent shortages and diminishing employee loyalty, some organizations are making efforts to keep in touch with former employees who may be interested in rejoining the organization in future. Organizations such as Microsoft, Ernst & Young, and Procter & Gamble have established alumni networks that offer benefits such as health care, job boards, and alumni parties. About 25 percent of hires at the manager level and above at Microsoft are returning employees, known as "boomerangs."[15]

Educational Institutions   Recruiting at educational institutions is extremely effective when candidates require formal training but need relatively little full-time work experience. Talent acquisition specialists see educational institutions as part of their organization's "pipeline" for sourcing candidates with the latest knowledge in their field. **Figure 5.5** lists related recruitment programming based in educational institutions.

Internship, co-op, and field placement programs can produce a win–win result. The employer has an inexpensive opportunity to assess potential employees while benefiting from the current knowledge and enthusiasm of bright, talented individuals. Because co-op students and interns have been exposed to the organization, they are less likely to leave shortly after permanent hire than recruits with no previous exposure to the firm.[16] These recognized benefits have made such programs a major recruitment method in many organizations.

Job Fairs   This recruitment strategy may be used by the organization to seek out candidates for specialized occupations or general employment openings. The

FIGURE 5.5   Examples of Talent Acquisition Pipelines from Educational Institutions

Career Fairs	Placements and Co-ops	Internships
Offered on campus where students can meet with invited employers. Fairs can be generic or specialized to specific disciplines.	Associated with the educational institution's program of studies, requiring the student to spend a specified time with an organization to gain hands-on experience in an intended career or occupation.	Offered by an organization to a student, usually in the final year of academic study or immediately following graduation.

event may be held on company premises or at a separate location. The corporate recruiters share information about the organization and job opportunities with those attending in an informal, relaxed setting. Some organizations are now holding job fairs online (known as virtual job fairs). For employers, some of the biggest payoffs of virtual career fairs are their efficiency and cost-effectiveness. Such a recruitment strategy is not limited to a single region: Job fairs can draw candidates from across the country. Moreover, employers can generate a large pool of candidates. Century 21 Real Estate, for example, received more than 230 résumés and more than 2 100 visitors during the week of a virtual job fair. Of particular interest to exhibitors is the power to promote the employer brand. Such "virtual" events offer plenty of benefits for jobseekers. No longer do candidates have to wait in line at each booth, only to find that an employer does not have any opportunities in their field. Now, by simply browsing, they can pinpoint in advance who has the right jobs matching their skills and preferences.[17]

Professional and Trade Associations   Professional and trade associations can be extremely helpful when recruiters are seeking individuals with specialized skills in such fields as IT, engineering, HR, and accounting, particularly if experience is a job requirement. Many such associations conduct ongoing placement activities on behalf of their members, and most regularly send their members newsletters or magazines in which organizations can place job advertisements. Such advertising may attract individuals who had not previously thought about changing jobs, as well as those actively seeking employment. For example, the Human Resources Professionals Association (HRPA) in Ontario has an employment service called the Hire Authority.

Hire Authority
www.hireauthority.ca

Labour Organizations   Some firms, particularly in the construction industry, obtain recruits through union hiring halls. The union maintains a roster of members (typically skilled tradespeople, such as carpenters, pipefitters, welders, plumbers, and electricians) whom it sends out on assignment as requests from employers are received. Once the union members have completed their contracted work at one firm, they notify the union of their availability for another assignment.

Canadian Union of Skilled Workers
www.cusw.ca/job-centre

Military Personnel   Military reservists are also potential recruits. The Canadian Forces Liaison Council (CFLC) is responsible for promoting the hiring of reservists by civilian employers. The CFLC's Reserve Employment Assistance Program (REAP) allows employers to place job postings for skilled personnel at more than 300 military units across the country at no charge.[18]

Canadian Forces Liaison Council
(CFLC)
www.forces.gc.ca

Print Advertising To achieve optimum results from an advertisement, the following four-point guide should be kept in mind as the ad is being constructed: attract attention; develop interest; create desire; and instigate action. There are two general types of newspaper advertisements: want ads and blind ads. **Want ads** describe the job and its specifications, the compensation package, and the hiring employer. Although the content pertaining to the job, specifications, and compensation is identical in **blind ads**, such ads omit the identity and address of the hiring employer. Although many job seekers do not like responding to blind ads because there is always the danger of unknowingly sending a résumé to the firm at which they are currently employed, such ads do result in the opening remaining confidential.

want ad A recruitment ad describing the job and its specifications, the compensation package, and the hiring employer. The address to which applications or résumés should be submitted is also provided.

blind ad A recruitment ad in which the identity and address of the employer are omitted.

5.3.2.3 Online Recruiting

The majority of companies now use *online recruitment*, and a majority of Canadian workers uses the Internet to research prospective employers, review job postings, complete online applications, and post their résumés. The Internet provides recruiters with a large audience for job postings and a vast talent pool. Online recruiting can involve accessing one or more Internet job boards, using a corporate website, or using social media sites.

Internet Job Boards Online job boards are fast, easy, and convenient, allowing recruiters to search for candidates for positions in two ways. First, companies can post a job opening online (often for a fee) and customize it by using corporate logos and adding details about the company benefits and culture. Job seekers can search through the job postings, often by job type, region, or other criteria, and apply for the position online through the job board. The popularity of Internet job boards among job seekers is high because of the number of job postings available on one site.

Second, job seekers can post their résumés on job boards, and firms can search the database. Canada has hundreds of job boards, ranging from the two largest, Workopolis and Monster, to many smaller job boards serving specific fields from tourism to medicine.[19] Job board meta-crawlers enable job seekers to search multiple job boards with one query.

The advantages of job boards include candidate assistance with self-assessment and résumé writing, and pre-screening assistance for recruiters. One problem with Internet job boards is their vulnerability to privacy breaches. Fake job postings can lead to identity theft from submitted résumés, and résumés are sometimes copied onto competing job boards or other sites.[20] As a result, job boards are now providing tips for job seekers on maintaining privacy and confidentiality.[21] In addition, the disclosure of reference persons' names and contact information on online résumés is problematic and no longer recommended.

Corporate Websites With the overabundance of applicants found on most online job boards, employers are now using their own corporate websites to recruit. Corporate "career" pages provide a single platform for recruitment that promotes the employer brand, educates the applicant about the company, captures data about the applicant, and provides an important link to job boards where a company's positions may be advertised.[22] Virtual workplace tours using video can be provided to attract top talent aligned with the employer brand.[23] Corporate websites also help the company create a pool of candidates who have already expressed interest in the organization.[24]

Active job seekers are not the only potential future employees who visit corporate websites. Customers, investors, and competitors also visit them.[25] Many of those visiting career websites are "happily employed" individuals (known as "passive" job seekers) who are likely to arrive at the career site after browsing the company's main pages for other reasons, such as research into products or services. Therefore, it is important that a firm have a prominently positioned link on the homepage leading directly to the careers section, to make it easy for passive job seekers to pursue job opportunities within the company.[26]

Social media   There is evidence that since social media first started allowing businesses to create their own accounts, organizations began to use such tools for marketing and recruitment purposes. Survey results indicate such a trend with corporate recruiters using LinkedIn, Facebook, and Twitter to a greater degree than traditional job boards. Such platforms, particularly LinkedIn, seem to be increasingly favoured by corporate recruiters as they provide more insights on a potential job candidate's interests and views based on groups they join, articles they read, or even articles they may have written.[27]

5.3.2.4 Agency Recruiters

Employment and Social Development Canada (ESDC)   Through various programs, including those for youth, Aboriginals, and persons with disabilities, ESDC helps unemployed individuals find suitable jobs and helps employers locate qualified candidates to meet their needs—at no cost to either party. The Job Bank is the largest web-based network of job postings available to Canadian employers free of charge, and it provides access to over 90 000 new jobs at any given time. Online recruitment services are offered to job seekers and employers, and labour market information and career tools are provided. ESDC also operates Job Match, a web-based recruitment tool that can match employers' skill requirements with individuals' skill sets. Job seekers receive a list of employers with a matching job vacancy, and employers receive a list of qualified candidates.[28]

Executive Search Firms   Employers use executive search firms to fill critical positions in a firm, usually middle- to senior-level professional and managerial positions. Such firms often specialize in a particular type of talent, such as executives, sales, scientific, or middle-management employees. They typically know and understand the marketplace, have many contacts, and are especially adept at contacting qualified candidates who are employed and not actively looking to change jobs (which is why they have been given the nickname "headhunters"). Generally, one-third of the fee is payable as a retainer at the outset. Compared with the value of the time savings realized by the client firm's executive team, however, such a fee often turns out to be insignificant.

Using this recruitment method has some potential pitfalls.[29] Executive search firms cannot do an effective job if they are given inaccurate or incomplete information about the job or the firm. It is therefore essential for employers to explain in detail the type of candidate required—and why.

Association of Canadian Search, Employment, and Staffing Services (ACSESS)
www.acsess.org

Private Employment Agencies   Private employment agencies are often called on to assist employers seeking clerical staff, functional specialists, and technical employees. The "staffing" business has grown into a $6 billion industry that places hundreds of thousands of job seekers each year.[30] Generally, the employer pays the agency fee. It is common for employers to pay a fee equal to 15 to 30 percent of the first year's salary of the individual hired through agency referral. This percentage may vary depending on the volume of business provided by the client and the type of employee sought.

These agencies take an employer's request for recruits and then solicit job seekers, relying primarily on Internet job boards, advertising, and walk-ins/write-ins. Employment agencies serve two basic functions: (1) expanding the applicant pool, and (2) performing preliminary interviewing and screening. It should be noted, however, that the amount of service provided varies widely, as does the level of professionalism and the calibre of staff. Although most agencies screen applicants carefully, some simply provide a stream of applicants and let the client's HR department staff do the screening.

Temporary Help Agencies   Temporary help agencies, such as Kelly Services, exist in major cities in Canada. They specialize in providing temporary workers to cover for employees who are ill, on vacation, or on leave of absence. Firms also use temporary employees to handle seasonal work, peak workloads, and special projects for which no current employees have the time or expertise. Temporary workers (temps) are agency employees and are reassigned to another employer when their services are no longer required.

Temporary employees (temps) provide employers with three major benefits: a lower cost as they generally receive less compensation and training than permanent staff; immediate replacement by the agency if performance is unsatisfactory; and a high level of motivation based on the potential opportunity for full-time employment with the agency's client

The number of temporary and freelance workers is increasing all over the world. Freelancing allows employers to match their job needs to independent workers who complete tasks on an as-needed basis.

Contract Workers   Employees who develop work relationships directly with the employer for a specific type of work or period of time are called **contract workers**.[31] For example, CAE Parc Aviation is a major supplier of contract workers to the airline industry. Airline organizations benefit from the services of contract engineers by having them cover seasonal or unplanned peaks in business, carry out special tasks or projects, and reduce the necessity for airlines to downsize permanent staff during cyclical downturns.[32]

contract workers   Employees who develop work relationships directly with the employer for a specific type of work or time period.

Many professionals with specialized skills become contract workers, including project managers, accountants, and lawyers. Some have consciously made a decision to work for themselves; others have been unable to obtain full-time employment in their field of expertise or have found themselves out of a full-time job because of cutbacks.

5.4 RECRUITING A MORE DIVERSE WORKFORCE

Recruiting a diverse workforce is not just socially responsible—it is a necessity. As noted previously, the composition of Canada's workforce is changing dramatically. Trends of particular significance include the increasing necessity of hiring older employees, a decrease in the availability of young workers, and an increase in the number of women, visible minorities, Aboriginal people, and persons with disabilities in the workforce. In addition to these four designated groups, as mentioned in Chapter 1, the integration of immigrants in the labour force is of ongoing concern. This chapter reviews the four designated groups, but the International HR chapter (Chapter 13) discusses integration of immigrants in the workforce in detail.

5.4.1 Attracting Older Workers

Hiring and retaining older employees has significant benefits. These workers typically have high job satisfaction, a strong sense of loyalty and organizational commitment, a strong work ethic, good people skills, and a willingness to work in a variety of roles, including part time.[33]

To make a company attractive to older workers, it is important to deal with stereotypical attitudes toward older workers through education, ensure that HR policies do not discourage recruitment of older workers, develop flexible work arrangements, and redesign jobs to accommodate decreased dexterity and strength. A 2008 Conference Board of Canada study found that the most common recruitment strategy for older workers was rehiring former employees and retirees. Less than 20 percent of Canadian companies use recruitment campaigns directed specifically at mature workers.[34]

5.4.2 Attracting Younger Employees

Gen Y (those born between 1982 and 2004) are influencing how employers recruit new talent. These Millennials seek employers that allow a degree of independence in decision-making and transparency in workplace policies and procedures, as well as enabling employees to achieve a desired level of work–life balance. There is also evidence that Gen Y job candidates want to work for an organization that that cares about how it impacts and contributes to society, often refusing to consider an employment offer from an irresponsible corporation.[35]

5.4.3 Recruiting Designated Group Members

Most of the recruitment methods already discussed can be used to attract members of designated groups (Aboriginal people, women, visible minorities, and persons with disabilities), provided that the employer's commitment to equality and diversity is made clear to all involved in the recruitment process—be it the employees who are asked for referrals or private employment agencies. This can also be stressed in all recruitment advertising. Alternative publications targeted at designated group members should be considered for advertising, and linkages can be formed with organizations and agencies specializing in assisting designated group members. Specific examples follow.

The Aboriginal Human Resource Council, headquartered in Saskatoon, Saskatchewan, sponsors the Aboriginal Inclusion Network, which offers a job board, résumé database, and other tools to hire, retain, and promote Aboriginal talent. The Inclusion Network is linked to 350 Aboriginal employment centres across Canada, and the number of job seekers on the network increased 70 percent from 2009 to 2011.[36]

The Society for Canadian Women in Science and Technology (SCWIST) is a not-for-profit, volunteer organization aimed at improving attitudes and stereotypes about and assisting women in scientific, technological, and engineering careers. Employers can access valuable resources such as websites, employment

Aboriginal Human Resource Council
http://aboriginalhr.ca

Canadian Council on Rehabilitation and Work
www.ccrw.org

WORKink
www.workink.com

HireImmigrants.ca
www.hireimmigrants.ca

An organization's commitment to employment equity recruiting practices is a key aspect in attracting a diverse and talented applicant pool.

agencies, and publications to attract professional women for employment opportunities in industries where they generally have a low representation.[37]

WORKink is Canada's most powerful online career development and employment portal for Canadians with disabilities. The WORKink site offers a full complement of employment and recruitment resources and services for job seekers with disabilities and for employers looking to create an inclusive workplace. WORKink is sponsored by the Canadian Council on Rehabilitation and Work. Employers can post job openings free of charge, browse résumés of people with disabilities, or access information on how to adapt the work environment to accommodate people with disabilities in their region.[38]

The Ontario Ministry of Community and Social Services sponsors a program called Paths to Equal Opportunity intended to provide links to information on removing and preventing barriers so that people with disabilities can work, learn, and play to their fullest potential. In conjunction with the Canadian Abilities Foundation, the program publishes a resource booklet called *Abilities @ Work*, which provides specific information to employers who want to find out about recruiting, interviewing, hiring, and working with people with disabilities. It also provides information to employees and job seekers with disabilities who want information on looking for work, accommodation in the workplace, and maintaining employment.

Another useful tool is the guidebook *Tapping the Talents of People with Disabilities: A Guidebook for Employers*, which is available through the Conference Board of Canada. More information on hiring people with disabilities is provided in the Workforce Diversity box.

WORKFORCE DIVERSITY

The Disconnect in Recruiting People with Disabilities

The good news is that employers want to hire people with disabilities, and qualified candidates are available. But putting employers and job seekers together needs improved coordination to create more success stories. Inclusiveness is a competitive advantage that lets an organization better connect with a diverse community and customer base. Inclusiveness provides access to a larger pool of strong job candidates in a time of skills shortages and enhances an organization's reputation as an employer of choice.

The good news is that a small number of disability organizations have made significant inroads in their regions by using employer partnerships. One example is the Dartmouth Work Activity Society in Nova Scotia, which started its new approach with just a single employer "partner" who was highly satisfied with the services provided. EmployAbilities, a full-time service agency serving Edmonton and northern Alberta for more than 35 years, has also launched a partnership-building strategy. A unique feature of the agency's approach is its partnership with the local chamber of commerce, through which it offers advice on disability issues to employers.

So why aren't more employers tapping into the wealth of human potential in people with disabilities? After all, as a group they make up roughly 13 percent of the working-age population.

Source: Based on A. Prost, "Successful Recruiting from an Untapped Source," *Canadian HR Reporter* (January 16, 2006), pp. 11–12.

5.5 RECRUITMENT METRICS

HR professionals must evaluate expenditures on the range of recruitment tools available in their talent acquisition efforts. The recognized metrics in **Figure 5.6** assist recruiters in deciding on cost-effective search tools for preferred job candidates.

FIGURE 5.6   Common Recruitment Methods

Metric	Explanation
Time lapsed per hire	Measures the number of days taken to fill a position. The length of time of particular recruitment strategies together with selection procedures contribute to this measure.
Cost per hire	The direct costs associated with different recruitment strategies together with indirect costs in the hiring process are key in determining the effectiveness of external job search methods.
Offers–applicant cost	This metric is useful when multiple job offers are extended by the organization. It reflects the quality of the applicant pool and thus shows the utility of chosen recruitment methods in assembling the candidate base.
Quality of hires and cost	The recruitment aspect of this metric focuses on the quality of résumés and applications received by the organization in response to a particular job notice.
Yield ratio	The percentage of applicants received from a particular recruitment source or the number of candidates who pass from one stage to the next screening level in the selection process.

© Andrey_Popov/Shutterstock

A panel interview is an efficient and cost-effective way of permitting a number of qualified persons to assess a candidate's KSAs.

selection   The process of choosing among individuals who have been recruited to fill existing or projected job openings.

5.6 THE STRATEGIC IMPORTANCE OF EMPLOYEE SELECTION

Selection is the process of choosing among individuals who were recruited to fill existing or projected job openings. Whether considering current employees for a transfer or promotion or outside candidates for a first-time position with the firm, information about the applicants must be collected and evaluated. Selection begins when a pool of applicants has submitted their résumés or completed application forms as a result of the recruiting process.

The selection process has important strategic significance. More and more managers have realized that the quality of the company's human resources is often the single most important factor in determining whether the firm is going to survive and be successful in reaching the objectives specified in its strategic plan. Those individuals selected will be implementing strategic decisions and, in some cases, creating strategic plans. Thus, successful candidates must fit with the strategic direction of the organization. For example, if the organization is planning to expand internationally, language skills and international experience will become important selection criteria.

When a poor selection decision is made and the individual selected for the job is not capable of acceptable performance in the job, strategic objectives will not be met. In

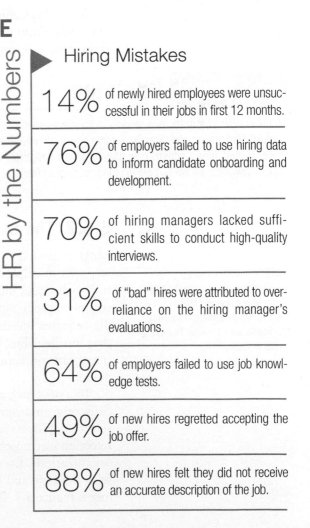

HR by the Numbers

▶ Hiring Mistakes

14% of newly hired employees were unsuccessful in their jobs in first 12 months.

76% of employers failed to use hiring data to inform candidate onboarding and development.

70% of hiring managers lacked sufficient skills to conduct high-quality interviews.

31% of "bad" hires were attributed to overreliance on the hiring manager's evaluations.

64% of employers failed to use job knowledge tests.

49% of new hires regretted accepting the job offer.

88% of new hires felt they did not receive an accurate description of the job.

addition, when an unsuccessful employee must be terminated, the recruitment and selection process must begin all over again, and the successor must be properly oriented and trained. The "hidden" costs are frequently even higher, including internal disorganization and disruption, and customer alienation. Recent research (as summarized in HR by the Numbers: Hiring Mistakes) reveals that while ideally selection should involve a clear process, in reality, the adoption and use of an appropriate selection process (as summarized in this chapter) may be problematic in many organization, often resulting in a number of hiring mistakes.

5.6.1 Supply Challenges

selection ratio   The ratio of the number of applicants hired to the total number of applicants.

Although it is desirable to have a large pool of qualified recruits from which to select applicants, this is not always possible. Certain vacant positions may be subject to a labour shortage (based on job requirements, location, work environment, and so on), while other simultaneous vacant positions may be subject to a labour surplus (due to external environment factors, training and education levels, immigration patterns, and so on). A **selection ratio** is the ratio of the number of applicants hired to the total number of applicants available, as follows:

Number of Applicants Hired : Total Number of Applicants = Selection Ratio

A small selection ratio, such as 1:2, may be indicative of a limited number of applicants from which to select, and it may also mean low-quality recruits. If this is the case, it is generally better to start the recruitment process over again, even if it means a hiring delay, rather than taking the risk of hiring an employee who will be a marginal performer at best.

A large selection ratio, such as 1:400, may indicate that the job ad is too vague, that the organization's HR team may need to automate the screening process, or that there is a need for more resources to find the right job candidate among the large number of applicants.

An Ethical Dilemma

As the company recruiter, how would you handle a request from the CEO that you hire her son for a summer job, knowing that, given current hiring constraints, the sons and daughters of other employees will not be able to obtain such positions?

5.6.2 The Selection Process

multiple-hurdle strategy   An approach to selection involving a series of successive steps or hurdles. Only candidates clearing the hurdle are permitted to move on to the next step.

Most firms use a sequential selection system involving a series of successive steps—a **multiple-hurdle strategy**. Only candidates clearing a "hurdle" (selection techniques including pre-screening, testing, interviewing, and background/reference checking) are permitted to move on to the next step. Clearing the hurdle requires meeting or exceeding the minimum requirements established for that hurdle. Thus, only candidates who have cleared all of the previous hurdles remain in contention for the position at the time that the hiring decision is being made.

To assess each applicant's potential for success in the job, organizations typically rely on a number of sources of information. The number of steps in the selection process and their sequence vary with the organization. The types of selection instruments and screening devices used are also not standardized across organizations. Even within a firm, the number and sequence of steps often vary with the type and level of the job, as well as the source and method of recruitment. **Figure 5.7** illustrates the steps commonly involved.

FIGURE 5.7   Six Typical Hurdles in the Selection Process

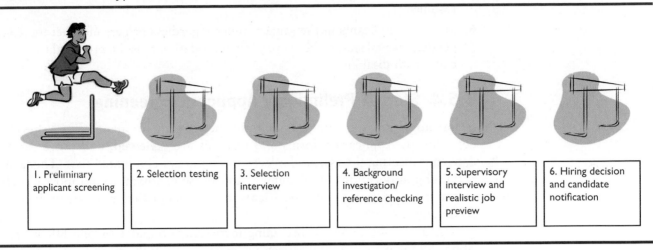

| 1. Preliminary applicant screening | 2. Selection testing | 3. Selection interview | 4. Background investigation/ reference checking | 5. Supervisory interview and realistic job preview | 6. Hiring decision and candidate notification |

At each step in the selection process, carefully chosen selection criteria must be used to determine which applicants will move on to the next step. It is through job analysis that the duties, responsibilities, and human requirements for each job are identified. By basing selection criteria on these requirements, firms can create a legally defensible hiring system.[39] Individuals hired after thorough screening against these carefully developed selection criteria (based directly on the job description and job specifications) learn their jobs readily, are productive, and generally adjust to their jobs with a minimum of difficulty.

5.6.3   Acquiring Employees and the Law

The complete recruitment and selection procedure must comply with human rights legislation. All information collected from the time an ad is posted to the time that the selection decision is made must be free of both content and questions that would, directly or indirectly, classify candidates based on any of the prohibited grounds under human rights legislation. If the selection process collects any information considered a prohibited ground for discrimination, an unsuccessful candidate may challenge the legality of the entire recruitment and selection process. In such cases, the burden of proof is on the employer. Specific guidelines regarding questions that can and cannot be asked on application forms are available through the human rights commissions in each jurisdiction.

Canadian Human Rights Commission **www.chrc-ccdp.gc.ca**

Managing the process in a legally defensible way involves keeping the following guidelines in mind:

1. Ensure that all selection criteria and strategies are based on the job description and the job specifications.

2. Do not ask questions that would violate human rights legislation, either directly or indirectly. Questions cannot be asked about candidates' marital status, child care arrangements, ethnic background, or workers' compensation history, for example.

3. Obtain written authorization for reference checking from prospective employees, and check references carefully.

4. Save all records and information obtained about the applicant during each stage of the selection process.

5. Reject applicants who make false statements on their application forms or résumés.

6. Treat all applicants in the same manner regardless of personal factors (e.g., gender, marital status). However, accommodation must be provided to applicants with disabilities.

5.6.4 Step 1: Preliminary Applicant Screening

Initial applicant screening is generally performed by members of the HR department. Application forms and résumés are reviewed, and those candidates not meeting the essential selection criteria are eliminated first. Then, the remaining applications are examined and those candidates who most closely match the remaining job specifications are identified and given further consideration.

The use of technology is becoming increasingly popular to help HR professionals improve the initial screening process, as highlighted in the Expert Opinion box. Almost all large firms or firms with high turnover use technological applications to help screen large numbers of candidates and generate short lists of individuals who will move on to the next step in the selection process.

5.6.5 Step 2: Selection Testing

Selection testing is a common screening device used by approximately two-thirds of Canadian organizations to assess specific job-related skills as well as general intelligence, personality characteristics, mental abilities, interests, and preferences.[40] Testing techniques provide efficient, standardized procedures for screening large numbers of applicants. Several thousand psychological and personality tests are on the market.[41]

5.6.5.1 The Importance of Reliability and Validity

Tests and other selection techniques are useful only if they provide reliable and valid measures.[42] All reputable tests will provide information to users about the reliability and validity of the test.

reliability   The degree to which interviews, tests, and other selection procedures yield comparable data over time; in other words, the degree of dependability, consistency, or stability of the measures used.

validity   The accuracy with which a predictor measures what it is intended to measure.

differential validity   Confirmation that the selection tool accurately predicts the performance of all possible employee subgroups, including white males, women, visible minorities, persons with disabilities, and Aboriginal people.

Reliability   The degree to which interviews, tests, and other selection procedures yield comparable data over time is known as **reliability**. Reliability is the degree of dependability, consistency, or stability of the measures used. For example, a test that results in widely variable scores when it is administered on different occasions to the same individual (for example, 60 percent, 82 percent, and 71 percent) is unreliable. Reliability also refers to the extent to which two or more methods yield the same results or are consistent. For example, applicants with high scores on personality tests for impulsivity or lack of self-control are correlated with the likelihood of failing background checks due to criminal behaviour.[43] Reliability also means the extent to which there is agreement between two or more raters (inter-rater reliability).

Validity   In the context of selection, **validity** is an indicator of the extent to which data from a selection technique, such as a test or interview, are related to or predictive of subsequent performance on the job. For example, high impulsivity is correlated with low productivity.[44] Separate validation studies of selection techniques should be conducted for different subgroups, such as visible minorities and women, to assess **differential validity**. In some cases, the technique may

Industry Viewpoint
EXPERT OPINION

1. How has HireVue used technology to change the recruitment and selection process?

HireVue pioneered digital on-demand interviewing. Most employers have been limited to traditional screening procedures, with fixed duration/schedule. Decisions were often made based on artificial thresholds (e.g., minimum education) that were not based on data, but on individual biases or competitiveness of the applicant pool. Our service allows organizations to pre-establish interview questions and access a large pool of candidates who respond to the questions via video interviews. We made it easier to view and share interviews remotely, at any pace. In addition, we allow multiple raters to score applicants and we can assess reliability of these scores. This saves money and time associated with transportation and accommodation of applicants for face-to-face screening. Similarly, applicants benefit from low barriers of entry, as they can easily access multiple jobs, upload interviews at their convenience, and keep a single profile current.

2. How does HireVue use technology to make evidence-based decisions?

We collect over 15 000 numerical features used to evaluate each

Identification:
Dr. Benjamin Taylor
Chief Data Scientist for HireVue

interview. We use this data to predict which candidate will be a top performer in the interview. Beyond that, if a company has used our service more than once, we can tailor decision criteria based on previous use of the service and largely automate the shortlisting process. The range of interview questions that companies want to use is from 5 to 30, so we assume an evidence-based approach to suggest how many questions would be ideal and how long a candidate should be given to think about or answer a question. Data collected demonstrate that minimal incremental predictive value is added when more than 15 well-crafted,

intelligent questions are used. We have also used the information to identify accuracy level of recruiters, which is a metric most organizations find useful.

3. So far, we have spoken largely about external hires. Could a system like this be used for both internal and external hires?

One of the largest airlines in the United States uses our system for internal and external screening of applicants (in addition to referrals). Although they use the same platform to test internal and external candidates, the questions asked for internal candidates have a different focus, leading to different decision models. For example, the issue of organizational or industry alignment has less variability among internal candidates. Internal candidates are more concerned with getting feedback regarding why they were not selected. Our system can use the metrics we collect to validate decisions made, increasing awareness of internal candidate selection choices (e.g., those who were offered the job scored higher on certain factors).

Source: Reprinted by permission from Benjamin Taylor.

be a valid predictor of job success for one group (such as Caucasian males) but not for other applicants, thereby leading to systemic discrimination.

Three types of validity are particularly relevant to selection: criterion-related, content, and construct validity.

Criterion-Related Validity The extent to which a selection tool predicts or significantly correlates with important elements of work behaviour is known as **criterion-related validity**. Demonstrating criterion-related validity requires proving that those who exhibit strong sales ability on a test or in an interview, for example, also have high sales on the job, and that those individuals who do poorly on the test or in the interview have poor sales results.

criterion-related validity The extent to which a selection tool predicts or significantly correlates with important elements of work behaviour.

content validity The extent to which a selection instrument, such as a test, adequately samples the knowledge and skills needed to perform the job.

construct validity The extent to which a selection tool measures a theoretical construct or trait deemed necessary to perform the job successfully.

intelligence (IQ) tests Tests that measure general intellectual abilities, such as verbal comprehension, inductive reasoning, memory, numerical ability, speed of perception, spatial visualization, and word fluency.

emotional intelligence (EI) tests Tests that measure a person's ability to monitor his or her own emotions and the emotions of others and to use that knowledge to guide thoughts and actions.

Content Validity When a selection instrument, such as a test, adequately samples the knowledge and skills needed to perform the job, **content validity** is assumed to exist. The closer the content of the selection instrument is to actual samples of work or work behaviour, the greater the content validity. For example, asking a candidate for a secretarial position to demonstrate word processing skills, as required on the job, has high content validity.

Construct Validity The extent to which a selection tool measures a theoretical construct or trait deemed necessary to perform the job successfully is known as **construct validity**. Intelligence, verbal skills, analytical ability, and leadership skills are all examples of constructs. Measuring construct validity requires demonstrating that the psychological trait or attribute is related to satisfactory job performance, as well as showing that the test or other selection tool used accurately measures the psychological trait or attribute. As an example of poor construct validity, an accounting firm was selecting applicants for auditor positions based on a test for high extroversion, when the job in fact required working alone with data. A test to select applicants with high introversion would have had higher construct validity and would have helped to avoid the high turnover rate the firm was experiencing.[45]

5.6.5.2 Tests of Cognitive Abilities

Ensuring the validity of selection tools when assessing candidates with disabilities may require accommodation of the disability. Included in the category of tests of cognitive abilities are tests of general reasoning ability (intelligence), tests of emotional intelligence, and tests of specific cognitive abilities, such as memory and inductive reasoning.

Intelligence Tests Used since the end of World War I, **intelligence (IQ) tests** are tests of general intellectual abilities (also referred to as general mental abilities).[46] They measure not a single "intelligence" trait, but rather a number of abilities, including memory, vocabulary, verbal fluency, and numerical ability. An IQ score is actually a *derived* score, reflecting the extent to which the person is above or below the "average" adult's intelligence score. Empirical research suggests that general mental ability is the strongest general predictor of job performance at one's chosen occupation.[47] Intelligence is often measured with individually administered tests, such as the Stanford-Binet test or the Wechsler test. Other IQ tests, such as the Wonderlic Personnel Test, can be administered to groups of people. These are relatively quick pen-and-paper or online tests that can be accessed for a nominal fee.

Emotional Intelligence Tests **Emotional intelligence (EI) tests** measure a person's ability to monitor his or her own emotions and the emotions of others and to use that knowledge to guide thoughts and actions. Someone with a high emotional quotient (EQ) is self-aware, can control his or her impulses, is self-motivated, and demonstrates empathy and social awareness. Many people believe that EQ, which can be modified through conscious effort and practice, is actually a more important

© Carlacastagno/Fotolia

General reasoning ability (intelligence), tests of emotional intelligence, and tests of specific cognitive abilities are all included in the category of tests of cognitive abilities.

determinant of success than a high IQ. However, there is extremely limited and somewhat highly controversial empirical evidence to support the importance of EI in the workplace.[48] Most of the research on EQ suggests that it has very limited correlations with job performance. Self-assessment tests for EQ include the Emotional Quotient Inventory (EQ-i), the EQ Map, the Mayer-Salovey-Caruso Emotional Intelligence Test (MSCEIT), and the Emotional Intelligence Questionnaire (EIQ). The Emotional Competence Inventory (ECI) is a 360-degree assessment in which several individuals evaluate one person to get a more complete picture of the individual's emotional competencies.[49]

Emotional Intelligence Consortium
www.eiconsortium.org

Specific Cognitive Abilities There are also measures of specific thinking skills, such as inductive and deductive reasoning, verbal comprehension, memory, and numerical ability. Tests in this category are often called **aptitude tests**, since they purport to measure the applicant's aptitude for the job in question, that is, the applicant's potential to perform the job, once given proper training. An example is the test of mechanical comprehension illustrated in **Figure 5.8**. It tests the applicant's understanding of basic mechanical principles. It may therefore reflect a person's aptitude for jobs—like that of machinist or engineer—that require mechanical comprehension.

aptitude tests   Tests that measure an individual's aptitude or potential to perform a job, provided he or she is given proper training.

FIGURE 5.8   Two Problems from the Test of Mechanical Comprehension

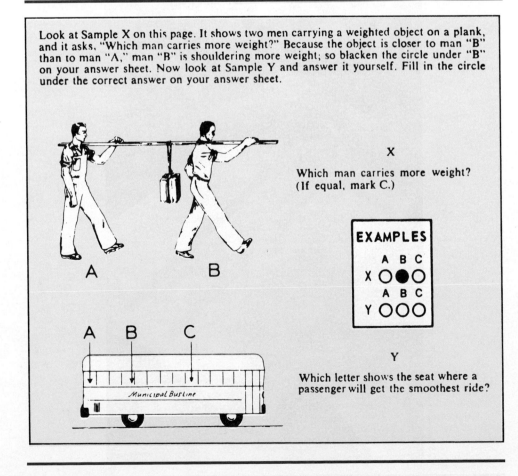

Look at Sample X on this page. It shows two men carrying a weighted object on a plank, and it asks, "Which man carries more weight?" Because the object is closer to man "B" than to man "A," man "B" is shouldering more weight; so blacken the circle under "B" on your answer sheet. Now look at Sample Y and answer it yourself. Fill in the circle under the correct answer on your answer sheet.

X

Which man carries more weight?
(If equal, mark C.)

Y

Which letter shows the seat where a passenger will get the smoothest ride?

5.6.5.3 Tests of Motor and Physical Abilities

There are many *motor abilities* that a firm might want to measure. These include finger dexterity, manual dexterity, speed of arm movement, and reaction time. The Crawford Small Parts Dexterity Test, as illustrated in **Figure 5.9**, is an example. It measures the speed and accuracy of simple judgment, as well as the speed of finger, hand, and arm movements. Other tests include the Stromberg Dexterity Test, the Minnesota Rate of Manipulation Test, and the Purdue Pegboard.

Tests of physical abilities may also be required.[50] For example, some firms are now using functional abilities evaluations (FAE) to assist with placement decisions. An FAE, which measures a whole series of physical abilities—ranging from lifting, to pulling and pushing, sitting, squatting, climbing, and carrying—is particularly useful for positions with a multitude of physical demands, such as those of firefighters or police officers.[51] Ensuring that physical abilities tests do not violate human rights legislation requires basing such tests on job duties identified through job analysis and a physical demands analysis, ensuring that the tests duplicate the actual physical requirements of the job, developing and imposing such tests honestly and in good faith, ensuring that those administering the tests

FIGURE 5.9   Crawford Small Parts Dexterity Test

© Radius Images/Alamy Stock Photo

are properly trained and administer the tests in a consistent manner, and ensuring that testing standards are objectively related to job performance.[52]

5.6.5.4 Measuring Personality and Interests

A person's mental and physical abilities are seldom sufficient to predict his or her job performance. Other factors, such as the person's motivation and interpersonal skills, are important too. Personality and interest inventories sometimes are used as predictors of such intangibles.

Personality tests measure basic aspects of an applicant's personality, such as introversion, stability, and motivation. The use of such tests for selection assumes that it is possible to find a relationship between a measurable personality trait (such as conscientiousness) and success on the job.[53] Many of these tests are *projective*. In the Thematic Apperception Test, an ambiguous stimulus (such as the one provided in **Figure 5.10**) is presented to the test taker, and he or she is asked to interpret or react to it. Because the pictures are ambiguous, the person's interpretation must come from within—the viewer supposedly *projects* into the picture his or her own emotional attitudes about life.

The Myers-Briggs Type Indicator instrument, which has been in use for more than 50 years, is believed to be the most widely used personality inventory in the world. More than 2 million assessments are administered annually in the United States alone.[54]

Research studies confirm that personality tests can help companies hire effective workers. For example, industrial psychologists often talk in terms of the "Big Five" personality dimensions as they apply to employment testing: *extroversion, emotional stability, agreeableness, conscientiousness,* and *openness to experience*.[55] These dimensions can be measured using the NEO Five-Factor Inventory (NEO-FFI) and similar tests. One study focused on the extent to which these dimensions predicted performance (in terms of job and training proficiency, for example) for professionals, police officers, managers, sales workers, and skilled/semi-skilled workers. Conscientiousness showed a consistent relationship with all performance criteria for every occupation.

personality tests   Instruments used to measure basic aspects of personality, such as introversion, stability, motivation, neurotic tendency, self-confidence, self-sufficiency, and sociability.

Psychometric Assessments
www.psychometrics.com

FIGURE 5.10   Thematic Apperception Test: How Do You Interpret It?

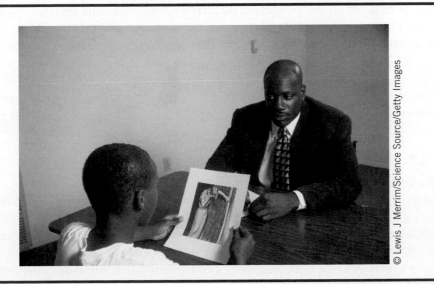

Source: Lewis J Merrim/Science Source/Getty Images

Research Psychologists Press
www.rpp.on.ca

Extroversion was a valid predictor of performance for managers and sales employees—the two occupations involving the most social interaction. Both openness to experience and extroversion predicted training proficiency for all occupations.[56]

There has been an ongoing debate in the research world on whether personality can be faked. In a test of 77 experienced assessors, over 70 percent agreed that "faking is a serious threat to the validity of personality inventory in the assessment process."[57] Evidence supports two specific trends in personality tests and faking: (1) people can fake personality inventories when they are motivated to do so, and (2) individual differences exist in the ability to fake.[58]

interest inventories   Tests that compare a candidate's interests with those of people in various occupations.

Interest inventories compare a candidate's interests with those of people in various occupations. Thus, a person taking the Strong-Campbell Interest Inventory would receive a report comparing his or her interests with those of people already in occupations, such as accountants, engineers, managers, or medical technologists. Interest inventories have many uses. One is career planning, since people generally do better in jobs involving activities in which they have an interest. Another is selection. If the firm can select people whose interests are roughly the same as those of high-performing incumbents in the jobs for which it is hiring, the new employees are more likely to be successful.[59]

5.6.5.5 Achievement Tests

achievement test   A test used to measure knowledge or proficiency acquired through education, training, or experience.

An **achievement test** is basically a measure of what a person has learned. Most of the tests taken in school are achievement tests. They measure knowledge or proficiency in such areas as economics, marketing, or HRM. Achievement tests are also widely used in selection. For example, the Purdue Test for Machinists and Machine Operators tests the job knowledge of experienced machinists with such questions as "What is meant by 'tolerance'?" Other tests are available for electricians, welders, carpenters, and so forth. In addition to job knowledge, achievement tests measure the applicant's abilities; a keyboarding test is one example.

5.6.5.6 Work Sampling

Work samples focus on measuring job performance directly and thus are among the best predictors of job performance. In developing a work-sampling test, experts first list all the possible tasks that jobholders would be required to perform. Then, by listing the frequency of performance and relative importance of each task, key tasks are identified. Each applicant then performs the key tasks, and his or her work is monitored by the test administrator, who records the approach taken. Finally, the work-sampling test is validated by determining the relationship between the applicants' scores on the work samples and their actual performance on the job. Once it is shown that the work sample is a valid predictor of job success, the employer can begin using it for selection.[60]

5.6.5.7 Management Assessment Centres

management assessment centre   A comprehensive, systematic procedure used to assess candidates' management potential that uses a combination of realistic exercises, management games, objective testing, presentations, and interviews.

At a **management assessment centre** the management potential of 10 or 12 candidates is assessed by expert appraisers who observe them performing realistic management tasks. The centre may be a plain conference room, but it is often a special room with a one-way mirror to facilitate unobtrusive observations. Examples of the types of activities and exercises include "in-basket" tests, leaderless group activities, management games, individual presentations, pen-and-pencil or computer tests, and interviews with assessors.

5.6.5.8 Situational Testing

In **situational tests**, candidates are presented with hypothetical situations representative of the job for which they are applying (often on video) and are evaluated on their responses.[61] Several of the assessment centre exercises described above are examples of situational tests. In a typical test, a number of realistic scenarios are presented and each is followed by a multiple-choice question with several possible courses of action, from which candidates are asked to select the "best" response, in their opinion.[62] The level of each candidate's skills is then evaluated, and an assessment report can be easily generated, making the simulation easier and less expensive to administer than other screening tools. Simulations also provide a realistic job preview by exposing candidates to the types of activities they will encounter on the job.

A research study of situational testing on 160 civil service employees demonstrated the validity of the situational test in predicting overall job performance as well as three performance dimensions: core technical proficiency, job dedication, and interpersonal facilitation. The situational test provided valid predictive information over and above cognitive ability tests, personality tests, and job experience.[63]

5.6.5.9 Micro-Assessments

An entirely performance-based testing strategy that focuses on individual performance is a **micro-assessment**. In a micro-assessment, each applicant completes a series of verbal, paper-based, or computer-based questions and exercises that cover the range of activities required on the job for which he or she is applying. In addition to technical exercises, participants are required to solve a set of work-related problems that demonstrate their ability to perform well within the confines of a certain department or corporate culture. Exercises are simple to develop because they are taken directly from the job.

A management game or simulation is a typical component in a management assessment centre.

situational tests   Tests in which candidates are presented with hypothetical situations representative of the job for which they are applying and are evaluated on their responses.

micro-assessment   A series of verbal, paper-based, or computer-based questions and exercises that a candidate is required to complete, covering the range of activities required on the job for which he or she is applying.

5.6.6 Physical Examination, Substance Abuse Testing, and Polygraph Tests

The use of medical examinations in selection has decreased, in part because of the loss of physically demanding manufacturing and natural resource jobs. Before 1980, 25 percent of new hires underwent a medical exam, but by 2001, only 11 percent were required to do so.[64] Three main reasons that firms may include a medical examination as a step in the selection process are as follows:

1. To determine that the applicant *qualifies for the physical requirements* of the position and, if not, to document any *accommodation requirements*;

2. To establish a *record* and *baseline* of the applicant's health for the purpose of future insurance or compensation claims; and

3. To *reduce absenteeism* and *accidents* by identifying any health issues or concerns that need to be addressed, including communicable diseases of which the applicant may have been unaware. Medical exams are permitted only after a written offer of employment has been extended (except in the case of bona fide occupational requirements, as for food handlers).

The purpose of pre-employment substance abuse testing is to avoid hiring employees who would pose unnecessary risks to themselves and others or perform below expectations. However, in Canada, employers are not permitted to screen candidates for substance abuse. Alcohol and drug addiction is considered to be a disability under human rights codes (as per Chapter 2), and an applicant cannot be discriminated against during the selection process based on a disability.[65]

A polygraph test (also referred to as a lie detector test) involves using a series of controlled questions while simultaneously assessing physiological conditions of individuals such as blood pressure, pulse, respiration, and skin conductivity, based on the assumption that deceptive responses produce different physiological responses than truthful responses. Such tests have been widely rejected by the scientific community since they have failed to produce valid or reliable results. In Ontario, the Employment Standards Act specifically prohibits use of polygraphs in pre-employment selection. Validated tests of honesty or integrity are more useful and reliable in the selection process.

5.6.7 Step 3: The Selection Interview

The interview is used by virtually all organizations for selecting job applicants. The **selection interview**, which involves a process of two-way communication between the interviewee and the interviewer, can be defined as "a procedure designed to predict future job performance on the basis of applicants' oral responses to oral inquiries."[66]

selection interview   A procedure designed to predict future job performance on the basis of applicants' oral responses to oral inquiries.

Interviews are considered to be one of the most important aspects of the selection process and generally have a major impact on both applicants and interviewers. Interviews significantly influence applicants' views about the job and organization, enable employers to fill in any gaps in the information provided on application forms and résumés, and supplement the results of any tests administered. They may also reveal entirely new types of information.

A major reason for the popularity of selection interviews is that they meet a number of the objectives of both the interviewer and interviewee. Interviewer objectives include assessing applicants' qualifications and observing relevant aspects of applicants' behaviour, such as verbal communication skills, degree of self-confidence, and interpersonal skills; providing candidates with information about the job and expected duties and responsibilities; promoting the organization and highlighting its attractiveness; and determining how well the applicants would fit into the organization. Typical objectives of job applicants include presenting a positive image of themselves, selling their skills and marketing their positive attributes to the interviewer(s), and gathering information about the job and the organization so that they can make an informed decision about the job, career opportunities in the firm, and the work environment.[67]

5.6.7.1 Types of Interviews

Selection interviews can be classified according to the degree of structure, their content, and the way in which the interview is administered.

The Structure of the Interview First, interviews can be classified according to the degree to which they are structured. In an **unstructured interview**, questions are asked as they come to mind. Thus, interviewees for the same job may or may not be asked the same or similar questions, and the interview's unstructured nature allows the interviewer to ask questions based on the candidate's last statements and to pursue points of interest as they develop. Unstructured interviews generally have low reliability and validity.[68]

The interview can also be structured. In the classical **structured interview**, the questions and acceptable responses are specified in advance and the responses are rated for appropriateness of content.[69] In practice, however, most structured interviews do not involve specifying and rating responses in advance. Instead, each candidate is asked a series of predetermined, job-related questions based on the job description and specifications. Such interviews are generally high in validity and reliability. However, a totally structured interview does not provide the flexibility to pursue points of interest as they develop, which may result in an interview that seems quite mechanical to all concerned.

Between these two extremes is the **mixed (semi-structured) interview**, which involves a combination of pre-set, structured questions based on the job description and specification, and a series of candidate-specific, job-related questions based on information provided on the application form or résumé. The questions asked of all candidates facilitate candidate comparison, while the job-related, candidate-specific questions make the interview more conversational. A realistic approach that yields comparable answers and in-depth insights, the mixed interview format is extremely popular.

5.6.7.2 The Content of the Interview

Interviews can also be classified according to the content of their questions. A **situational interview** is one in which the questions focus on the individual's ability to project what his or her *future* behaviour would be in a given situation.[70] The underlying premise is that intentions predict behaviour. For example, a candidate for a supervisory position might be asked how he or she would respond to an employee coming to work late three days in a row. The interview can be both *structured* and *situational*, with predetermined questions requiring the candidate to project what his or her behaviour would be. In a structured situational interview, the applicant could be evaluated, say, on whether he or she would try to determine if the employee was experiencing some difficulty in getting to work on time or would simply issue a verbal or written warning to the employee.

The **behavioural interview**, also known as a **behaviour description interview (BDI)**, involves describing various situations and asking interviewees how they behaved *in the past* in such situations.[71] The underlying assumption is that the best predictor of future performance is past performance in similar circumstances.

5.6.7.3 Administering the Interview

Interviews can also be classified based on how they are administered:

- Face-to-face or technology-aided (such as video conferencing or by phone)
- One-on-one or by a panel of interviewers
- Sequentially or all at once

unstructured interview An unstructured, conversational-style interview. The interviewer pursues points of interest as they come up in response to questions.

structured interview An interview following a set sequence of questions.

mixed (semi-structured) interview An interview format that combines the structured and unstructured techniques.

situational interview A series of job-related questions that focus on how the candidate would behave in a given situation.

behavioural interview or behaviour description interview (BDI) A series of job-related questions that focus on relevant past job-related behaviours.

Growing Use of Electronic

Media for Selection

76% of interviewers prefer face-to-face over video conferencing.

16.1% higher rating is secured by women compared to men in semi-structured face-to-face interviews.

68% of interviewers felt that video conferencing added no additional benefits over face-to-face interviews.

40% of interviewers felt that video conferencing made it hard to read nonverbal cues (e.g., facial expression, fidgeting).

17.4% higher rating is secured by women compared to men in semi-structured video conferences.

7.5% average higher rating is secured for interviews using video conferencing over face-to-face methods.

HR by the Numbers

panel interview An interview in which a group of interviewers questions the applicant.

Most interviews are sequential, face-to-face, and one-on-one. In recent years, the advancements of technology in recruitment have meant that candidates are rarely limited to a local region, while technological advancements allow cost-efficient access to video-conferencing technologies for interviews. Research has begun to evaluate the differences in the face-to-face versus the technology-aided interviews, as highlighted in HR by the Numbers: Growing Use of Electronic Media for Selection.

A **panel interview** involves the candidate being interviewed simultaneously by a group (or panel) of interviewers, including an HR representative, the hiring manager, and potential co-workers, superiors, or reporting employees. The key advantages associated with this technique are the increased likelihood that the information provided will be heard and recorded accurately; varied questions pertaining to each interviewer's area of expertise; minimized time and travel/accommodation expenses as each interviewee attends only one interview; reduced likelihood of human rights/employment equity violations, since an HR representative is present; and less likelihood of interviewer error, because of advanced planning and preparation.

In a *sequential* interview the applicant is interviewed by several persons in sequence before a selection decision is made. In an *unstructured sequential* interview each interviewer may look at the applicant from his or her own point of view, ask different questions, and form an independent opinion of the candidate. Conversely, in a *structured sequential* (or serialized) interview, each interviewer rates the candidate on a standard evaluation form, and the ratings are compared before the hiring decision is made.[72]

A more stressful variant of the panel interview is the *mass interview*, which involves a panel simultaneously interviewing several candidates. The panel poses a problem to be solved and then sits back and watches which candidate takes the lead in formulating an answer.

5.6.7.4 Common Interviewing Mistakes

Several common interviewing errors that can undermine the usefulness of interviews are discussed in this section. These interviewer errors can be reduced by properly planning and training interviewers on the process, as well as educating interviewers about these risks.

Poor Planning Many selection interviews are simply not carefully planned and may be conducted without having prepared written questions in advance. Lack of planning often leads to a relatively unstructured interview, in which whatever comes up is discussed. The end result may be little or no cross-candidate job-related information. The less structured the interview is, the less reliable and valid the evaluation of each candidate will be.[73]

Snap Judgments One of the most consistent literature findings is that interviewers tend to jump to conclusions—make snap judgments—during the first few minutes of the interview or even before the interview begins based on the candidates' test scores or résumé data. Thus, candidates feel pressure to start off on the right foot with the interviewer. However, snap judgments are not accurate or reliable in the selection process and should be avoided.

Negative Emphasis Many interviewers seem to have a consistent negative bias. They are generally more influenced by unfavourable than favourable information about the candidate. Also, their impressions are much more likely to change from favourable to unfavourable than vice versa. Providing information about the value or weight of criteria in the selection process can ensure that the interviewer assesses the criteria accordingly. Research also suggests that a negative emphasis exists for candidates who are unemployed at the time of recruiting.[74]

"Was the interview too early for you?"

© Cartoonresource/Fotolia

Halo Effect It is also possible for a positive initial impression to distort an interviewer's rating of a candidate, because subsequent information is judged with a positive bias. This is known as the **halo effect**. Having gained a positive impression of the candidate on one or more factors, the interviewer may not seek contradictory information when listening to the candidate's answers to the questions posed or may interpret/frame all responses positively.

halo effect   A positive initial impression that distorts an interviewer's rating of a candidate because subsequent information is judged with a positive bias.

Poor Knowledge of the Job Interviewers who do not know precisely what the job entails and what sort of candidate is best suited for it usually make their decisions based on incorrect stereotypes about what a good applicant is. Interviewers who have a clear understanding of what the job entails conduct interviews that are more effective.

Contrast (Candidate-Order) Error **Contrast or candidate-order** error means that the order in which applicants are seen can affect how they are rated. In one study, managers were asked to evaluate a candidate who was "just average" after first evaluating several "unfavourable" candidates. The average candidate was evaluated more favourably than he or she might otherwise have been because, in contrast to the unfavourable candidates, the average one looked better than he or she actually was.

contrast or candidate-order error   An error of judgment on the part of the interviewer because of his or her having interviewed one or more very good or very bad candidates just before the interview in question.

Influence of Nonverbal Behaviour Interviewers are also influenced by the applicant's nonverbal behaviour, and the more eye contact, head moving, smiling, and other similar nonverbal behaviours, the higher the ratings. These nonverbal behaviours often account for more than 80 percent of the applicant's rating. This finding is of particular concern since nonverbal behaviour is tied to ethnicity and cultural background. An applicant's attractiveness and gender also play a role. Research has shown that those rated as being more physically attractive are also rated as more suitable for employment, well ahead of those rated average-looking and those regarded as physically unattractive. Although this bias is considered to be subconscious, it may have serious implications for aging employees.[75]

Leading Some interviewers are so anxious to fill a job that they help the applicants to respond correctly to their questions by asking leading questions or guiding the candidate to the expected answer. An obvious example might be a question like "This job calls for handling a lot of stress. You can do that, right?" The leading is not always so obvious. Subtle cues regarding the preferred response, such as a smile or nod, are also forms of leading.[76]

Too Much/Too Little Talking If the applicant is permitted to dominate the interview, the interviewer may not have a chance to ask his or her prepared questions and often learns very little about the candidate's job-related skills. At the other extreme, some interviewers talk so much that the interviewee is not given enough time to answer questions. One expert suggests using the 30/70 rule: During a selection interview, encourage the candidate to speak 70 percent of the time, and restrict the interviewer speaking to just 30 percent of the time.[77]

Similar-to-Me Bias Interviewers tend to provide ratings that are more favourable to candidates who possess demographic, personality, and attitudinal characteristics similar to their own, regardless of the value of those characteristics to the job.[78] The result can be a lack of diversity in the organization and a poor fit with the job if secured.

5.6.7.5 Designing and Conducting an Effective Interview

Problems like those just described can be avoided by designing and conducting an effective interview. Combining several of the interview formats previously discussed enables interviewers to capitalize on the advantages of each.[79] To allow for probing and to prevent the interview from becoming too mechanical in nature, a semi-structured format is recommended. Given their higher validity in predicting job performance, the focus should be on situational and behavioural questions.

Although the following discussion focuses on a semi-structured panel interview, the steps described apply to all selection interviews.[80]

Planning the Interview Before the first interview, agreement should be reached on the procedure that will be followed. Sometimes all members of the team ask a question in turn; in other situations, only one member of the team asks questions and the others serve as observers. Sitting around a large table in a conference room is much more appropriate and far less stressful than having all panel members seated across from the candidate behind a table or desk, which forms both a physical and a psychological barrier. As noted earlier, special planning is required when assessing candidates with disabilities.

Establishing Rapport The main purpose of an interview is to find out as much as possible about the candidate's fit with the job specifications, something that is difficult to do if the individual is tense and nervous. The candidate should be greeted in a friendly manner and put at ease.

Asking Questions The questions written in advance should then be asked in order. Interviewers should listen carefully, encourage the candidate to express his or her thoughts and ideas fully, and record the candidate's

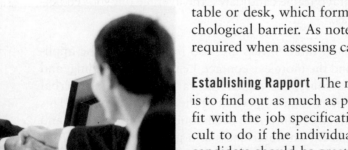

The rapport established with a job applicant not only puts the person at ease but also reflects the company's attitude toward its public.

FIGURE 5.11   Sample Structured Interview Questions

1. Describe for me one previous job responsibility that challenged you to improve your problem solving ability.
2. Tell us about a time when you contributed to a team-based activity.
3. Our company values "giving back to our community." Tell me why you think this is important.
4. In one of your previous jobs, tell us about a situation when you needed to seek advice from a colleague or supervisor in handling a difficult situation.
5. Share an example from your experience that demonstrates your leadership skills.
6. Imagine you receive a phone call late on a Friday afternoon from an angry customer who is dissatisfied with a recent encounter with your company. How would you attempt to satisfy that caller?
7. If one of your staff expressed frustration with her job, describe what steps you would take to help resolve her concerns.
8. In what way does this advertised role support your career plans?

answers briefly but thoroughly. Taking notes increases the validity of the interview process. Taking notes (1) reduces the likelihood of forgetting job-relevant information and subsequently reconstructing forgotten information in accordance with biases and stereotypes; (2) reduces the likelihood of making a snap judgment and helps to prevent the halo effect, negative emphasis, or candidate-order errors; and (3) helps to ensure that all candidates are assessed according to the same criteria.[81] Some examples of interview questions are seen in **Figure 5.11.**

Closing the Interview   Toward the end of the interview, time should be allocated to answer any questions that the candidate may have and, if appropriate, to advocate for the firm and position. It is also of use to inform the candidate about the next steps and timelines that the organization will follow at this point.

Evaluating the Candidate   Immediately following each interview, each panel member should rate the applicant's interview performance independently, based on a review of his or her notes or an observation form. Since interviews are only one-step in the process, and since a final decision cannot be reached until all assessments (including reference checking) have been completed, these evaluations should not be shared at this time.

5.6.8 Step 4: Background Investigation and Reference Checking

Background investigation and reference checking are used to verify the accuracy of the information provided by candidates on their application forms and résumés. In an ideal world, every applicant's story would be completely accurate, but in real life this is often not the case, as illustrated in **Figure 5.12.** At least one-third of applicants lie—overstating qualifications or achievements, attempting to hide negative information, or being deliberately evasive or untruthful.[82]

Unfortunately, some employers do not check references, an omission that can have grave consequences. Background checks are essential to avoid placing people in situations of unnecessary and avoidable risk, which can lead to negligent-hiring lawsuits.[83] Cases in Canada have included: a nurse who practised in a Toronto hospital for almost two years without a registered nurse qualification;

FIGURE 5.12   Top Seven Résumé Lies

1 Dates of employment

2 Job title (inflated rank)

3 Salary level

4 Criminal records

5 Education (bogus degrees, diploma mills)

6 Professional licence (MD, RN, etc.)

7 "Ghost" company (self-owned business)

Source: AccuScreen Inc., www.accuscreen.com/TOP7 (accessed May 24, 2009). Used with Permission

a manufacturing plant payroll officer who embezzled almost $2 million; and a teacher arrested for possessing child pornography.[84] Other problems can also be addressed through background checks.

Surveys indicate that at least 90 percent of Canadian organizations conduct background checks.[85] Whether employers are requesting reference information in writing or asking for such information over the telephone, questions should be written down in advance. If enough time is taken and the proper questions asked, such checking is an inexpensive and straightforward way of verifying information about the applicant. This may include current and previous job titles, salary, dates of employment, and reasons for leaving, as well as information about the applicant's fit with the prospective job and organizational culture.

5.6.8.1 Information to Be Verified

A basic background check includes a criminal record check, independent verification of educational qualifications, and verification of at least five years' employment, together with checks of three performance-related references from past supervisors. For financially sensitive positions, a credit check may also be included.

Obtaining Written Permission As a legal protection for all concerned, applicants should be asked to indicate, in writing, their willingness for the firm to check with current or former employers and other references. There is generally a section on the application form for this purpose. Many employers will not give out any reference information until they have received a copy of such written authorization. Because background checks may provide information on age or other prohibited grounds for discrimination, some employers do not conduct background checks until a conditional offer of employment has been extended.[86]

However, other employers do not hesitate to seek out information in the public domain at any time, without permission. A recent survey found that almost

© Cartoonresource/Fotolia

"Everything on your resume is true ... right?"

FIGURE 5.13   Online Postings by Job Candidates That Concern Hiring
Managers

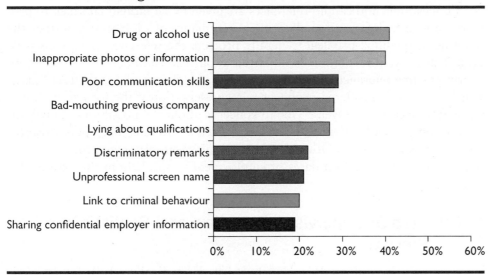

Source: R. Zupek, Is Your Future Boss Researching You Online?" CareerBuilder.ca, www.careerbuilder.ca/
blog/2008/10/09/cb-is-your-future-boss-researching-you-online (accessed May 24, 2009). Copyright Sept. 10,
2008 Career Builder, LLC. Reprinted with permission.

one-quarter of employers are using social networking sites like Facebook to
gather information on job applicants. A third of those employers find enough
negative information (such as the items listed in **Figure 5.13**) to eliminate a candidate from further consideration, and one-quarter of them find favourable content that supports the candidate's application.[87]

Privacy Considerations   Background checks should be conducted in accordance
with applicable federal or provincial statutes. Legislation related to privacy and
human rights imposes limitations on how background checks are conducted, as
well as how collected information is handled. An article in the *Canadian HR
Reporter* provides examples of these differences among Canadian provinces.[88]
For example, employers in British Columbia are not required to have the job
candidate's consent to collect personal information if such action is reasonable
for the purpose of establishing an employment relationship. However, such
employers are required to notify the candidate if they conduct such screening
procedures. BC human rights legislation also prohibits an employer from refusing to employ a candidate based on grounds of a criminal or summary conviction offense if such an occurrence is unrelated to the position and the candidate's
employment. In Quebec, an employer may only collect personal information
from a candidate directly, unless the candidate consents to collection from third
parties. Manitoba employers may not collect personal information about a candidate without the candidate's consent. In Ontario, background checks are not
limited by private sector privacy legislation, and an employer may refuse to hire
a candidate convicted of a criminal offence unless he or she received a pardon
(in which case the employer may not refuse to hire the candidate solely based on
the conviction).

5.6.8.2 Providing References

In providing reference information, the concept of *qualified privilege* is important. Generally speaking, if comments are made in confidence for a public purpose, without malice, and are honestly believed, the defense of qualified privilege exists.

If honest, fair, and candid references are given by an individual asked to provide confidential information about the performance of a job applicant, then the doctrine of qualified privilege generally protects the reference giver. This is so even if negative information is imparted about the candidate.[89] However, an overly positive reference describing an employee dismissed for theft as "trustworthy" can be considered negligent misrepresentation if the former employee steals from a new employer.[90] Due to concerns about the possibility of civil litigation, some Canadian companies have adopted a "no reference" policy regarding previous employees. Other employers limit their comments to confirming only the position held and dates of employment—especially in the case of discharged employees.[91]

5.6.9 Step 5: Supervisory Interview and Realistic Job Preview

The two or three top candidates ("short-listed") typically return for an interview with the immediate supervisor, who usually makes the final selection decision. The supervisory interview is important because the supervisor knows the technical aspects of the job, is most qualified to assess the applicants' job knowledge and skills, and is best equipped to answer any job-specific questions from the candidates. In addition, the immediate supervisor generally has to work closely with the selected individual and must feel comfortable with that person. The selected individual must fit with the current members of the department that is hiring, something that the supervisor is often best able to assess. When a supervisor makes a hiring recommendation, he or she is usually committed to the new employee's success and will try to provide assistance and guidance. If the new hire is not successful, the supervisor is more likely to accept some of the responsibility.

realistic job preview (RJP) A strategy used to provide applicants with realistic information—both positive and negative—about the job demands, the organization's expectations, and the work environment.

A **realistic job preview (RJP)** should be provided at the time of the supervisory interview. The purpose of an RJP is to create appropriate expectations about the job by presenting realistic information about the job demands, the organization's expectations, and the work environment.[92] Studies have reported that RJPs lead to improved employee job satisfaction, reduced voluntary turnover, and enhanced communication.[93] Although some candidates may choose not to accept employment with the firm after an RJP, those individuals probably would not have remained with the firm long had they accepted the job offer.[94]

5.6.10 Step 6: Hiring Decision and Candidate Notification

To make the hiring decision, HR must combine information from the multiple selection techniques used to identify the applicant who is the best fit with the selection criteria. HR staff generally play a major role in compiling all the data. It is the immediate supervisor, however, who is usually responsible for making the final hiring decision. Firms generally make a subjective evaluation of all the information gleaned about each candidate and arrive at an overall judgment. The validity and reliability of these judgments can improve by using tests that are objectively scored and by devising a candidate-rating sheet based on the weighted want criteria.

Another approach involves combining all the pieces of information according to a formula and giving the job to the candidate with the highest score. Research studies have indicated that this approach, called a **statistical strategy**, is generally more reliable and valid than a subjective evaluation.[95]

Regardless of collection methodology, all information used in making the selection decision—including interview notes, test results, reference-checking information, and so on—should be kept in a file. In the event of a human rights challenge, negligent hiring charge, or union grievance about the selection decision, such data are critical.

Following the selection decision, a job offer is extended to the successful candidate. Often, the initial offer is by telephone, but it should be followed up with a written employment offer that clearly specifies important terms and conditions of employment, such as starting date, starting salary, probation period, and so on.

Candidates should be given a reasonable length of time in which to think about the offer and not be pressured into making an immediate decision. If there are two candidates who are both excellent and the first-choice candidate declines the offer, the runner-up can then be offered the job.

> **statistical strategy**   A more objective technique used to determine which candidate the job should be offered to; involves identifying the most valid predictors and weighting them through statistical methods, such as multiple regression.

An Ethical Dilemma

As the HR manager, how much feedback should you provide to those individuals not selected for a position?

CHAPTER SUMMARY

1. Recruitment is the process of searching out and attracting qualified job applicants. It begins with the identification of a new or vacant position and is completed when résumés or completed application forms are received. In order to manage the increasing talent shortage, proactive employers are trying to obtain a competitive advantage in recruitment by establishing themselves as employers of choice through employer branding.

2. The recruitment process has four steps: First, job openings are identified through HR planning or manager request. Second, the job description and job specifications are reviewed to determine the job requirements. Third, appropriate recruiting source(s) and method(s) are chosen. Fourth, using these strategies, a pool of qualified candidates is generated.

3. Application forms have been largely replaced by online applications, on which candidates provide information on their education and experience, a brief overview of past career progress, and other information that can be used to predict whether an applicant will succeed on the job.

4. Job posting is the process of notifying existing employees about vacant positions. Human

resources records may indicate appropriate applicants for vacant positions. Skills inventories may provide even better information.

5. External recruitment methods include traditional networking, online job boards, agencies, recruiters, cold calls, social media, and print ads.

6. Selection is the process of choosing among individuals who have been recruited to fill existing or projected job openings. The purpose of selection is to find the "best" candidate. Because the quality of the company's human resources is often a competitive advantage in achieving the company's strategic objectives, selection of employees is of considerable strategic importance. Those individuals selected will be implementing strategic decisions and, in some cases, creating strategic plans. Thus, the successful candidates must fit the strategic direction of the organization.

7. Reliability (the degree to which selection techniques are dependable, consistent, and stable) and validity (which relates to accuracy) of selection tests and interviews are critically important in order to achieve effective selection

of the best candidate and to satisfy legal requirements.

8. The different types of tests used for selection include intelligence tests, emotional intelligence tests, aptitude tests, tests of motor and physical abilities, personality tests, interest inventories, achievement tests, the work-sampling technique, management assessment centres, situational testing, micro-assessments, and medical examinations. Pre-employment substance abuse testing is not permitted under human rights legislation in Canada.

9. Selection interviewing can be unstructured, structured, or semi-structured. The content varies between situational interviews (focus on future behaviour) and behavioural interviews (focus on past behaviour). Interviews can be administered on a one-on-one basis, sequentially, or by using a panel.

10. Reference checking is an important source of information about job candidates. Failure to check references can lead to negligent- or wrongful-hiring lawsuits. When providing references, the legal concept of qualified privilege means that if honest, fair, and candid references are given, the reference-giver is protected from litigation, even if negative information is imparted about the candidate. Providing falsely positive references can lead to charges of negligent misrepresentation by subsequent employers. Fear of civil litigation has led some Canadian companies to adopt a policy of "no references" or to confirm only a former employee's position and dates of employment.

MyLab Management

Visit MyLab Management to access a personalized Study Plan, Personal Inventory Assessments (PIA), and a collection of videos and assignments within MediaShare.

KEY TERMS

achievement tests *(p. 114)*
aptitude tests *(p. 111)*
behavioural interview or behaviour description interview (BDI) *(p. 117)*
biographical information blank (BIB) *(p. 96)*
blind ad *(p. 99)*
construct validity *(p. 110)*
content validity *(p. 110)*
contract workers *(p. 101)*
contrast or candidate-order error *(p. 119)*
criterion-related validity *(p. 109)*
differential validity *(p. 108)*
emotional intelligence (EI) tests *(p. 110)*
employer branding *(p. 91)*
halo effect *(p. 119)*
human capital theory *(p. 93)*
intelligence (IQ) tests *(p. 110)*
interest inventories *(p. 114)*
job posting *(p. 94)*
management assessment centre *(p. 114)*
micro-assessment *(p. 115)*

mixed (semi-structured) interview *(p. 117)*
multiple-hurdle strategy *(p. 106)*
nepotism *(p. 97)*
panel interview *(p. 118)*
personality tests *(p. 113)*
realistic job preview (RJP) *(p. 124)*
recruiter *(p. 91)*
recruitment *(p. 90)*
reliability *(p. 108)*
selection *(p. 105)*
selection interview *(p. 116)*
selection ratio *(p. 106)*
situational interview *(p. 117)*
situational tests *(p. 115)*
statistical strategy *(p. 125)*
structured interview *(p. 117)*
talent acquisition *(p. 90)*
unstructured interview *(p. 117)*
validity *(p. 108)*
want ad *(p. 99)*

REVIEW AND DISCUSSION QUESTIONS

1. Discuss the advantages and disadvantages of recruiting from within the organization. Identify and describe the three tools used in this process.

2. Brainstorm the advantages of external recruitment. Discuss the risks associated with external recruiting.

3. Name two specific situations where a private employment agency may be used for recruitment purposes.

4. Explain the differences among criterion-related validity, content validity, and construct validity.

5. Discuss an advantage for two different types of testing used in a selection process, and give an example of each.

6. Explain the difference between situational and behavioural interviews. Give examples of situational and behavioural interview questions.

CRITICAL THINKING QUESTIONS

1. What potential problems may result if the employer branding value proposition presented during the recruitment process is not reinforced once the new recruit is working for the organization? What could organizations do to avoid this situation?

2. What is a potential advantage and a possible problem in adopting a referral bonus program payable to existing employees who refer external candidates for job openings?

3. What are two advantages and two possible drawbacks of adopting an "internal applicants first" recruitment policy?

4. Assume you are the HR manager in a highly homogenous company that now seeks greater diversity in its employee demographics. What are key considerations to successfully carrying out a new recruitment strategy?

5. Suggest two appropriate forms of testing to screen candidates for a front-line supervisory role in a career path with which you have some familiarity. How are your choices relevant to assessing a candidate's "fit" for this position's job requirements?

6. What are two key considerations to build into a company policy on reference or background checks used in candidate selection?

EXPERIENTIAL EXERCISES

1. Examine three company websites associated with your career interests. Look for some specific reference on each site that matches your own set of values and beliefs. Explain why including such information on a company's website is advantageous to talent acquisition in today's job market.

2. Considering the current economic situation and using the following list of jobs, identify two sources that could be used to recruit qualified applicants:
   - Registered nurses to work in the critical-care unit of a new regional hospital
   - Carpenters to work on a new home building project
   - Chief financial officer for a Vancouver-based international engineering firm
   - Sales associate to work in an arts supply store
   - Bilingual administrative assistants for a global Canadian financial services company

3. Using the National Occupational Classification (NOC), select a job that you are familiar with and create two behavioural descriptive and two situational interview questions for short-listed candidates. For any one of these questions, identify key elements of a high quality answer you would expect from the candidate. Share this example with another member of the class.

4. Working with another student, develop a three-point argument explaining why introducing realistic job previews is beneficial to the company's talent acquisition program.

©Monkey Business Images/Shutterstock

6 ONBOARDING AND TRAINING

LEARNING OUTCOMES

AFTER STUDYING THIS CHAPTER, YOU SHOULD BE ABLE TO:

EXPLAIN how to develop an onboarding program.

DESCRIBE the five-step training process.

DISCUSS two techniques used for assessing training needs, and **DESCRIBE** how to evaluate the training effort.

EXPLAIN the strategic importance of career planning and development in the context of today's talent shortage.

EXPLAIN the evolution of career development and the impact of that on employers and employees.

The terms "orientation" and "training" are associated, but actually represent slightly different variations of employee assimilation efforts. Orientation refers to a long-term, continuous socialization process in which employee and employer expectations or obligations are considered. With a focus on organization-specific topics, orientation attempts to transfer learning into behaviour, using disciplined, consistent efforts.[1] In comparison, training refers to short-term, discrete efforts in which organizations impart information and instructions in an effort to help the recipient gain the required skills or knowledge to perform the job at an adequate level.

In addition, career planning has become a critical strategic issue for CEOs and boards of directors, as well as HR executives.[2] The aging workforce and shifts in occupations and employment patterns have created a sense of urgency regarding the development of careers for the next generation of managers and executives. Increased competition for talent is expected to create a serious challenge for retaining high-potential employees. Proactive organizations have already started to take action to manage the need for more managerial talent.

At the same time, there is an increasing need for employees who are interested in global careers, in virtual work as a key aspect of their careers, in careers that involve continuously changing technology, and in many other variations on traditional career paths. HRM activities play an important role in career planning and career development. Career-related programs help HR professionals maintain employee commitment—an employee's identification with, and agreement to pursue, the company's or the unit's strategic goals. Most employees appreciate and respond well to having their skills and potential enhanced, and to knowing that they will be more marketable. Developmental activities, such as providing the educational and training resources required to help employees identify and develop their promotion and career potential, are extremely important to younger employees today. Career-oriented firms also stress career-oriented appraisals that link the employee's past performance, career preferences, and developmental needs in a formal career plan.

6.1 BECOME A LEARNING ORGANIZATION

Learning is a survival technique for both individuals and organizations. Today, employees at all levels know that they must engage in lifelong learning to remain employable and have a satisfying career. A **learning organization** is an organization skilled at creating, acquiring, and transferring knowledge and at modifying its behaviour to reflect new knowledge and insights. The HR department is often the driving force behind ensuring that the training and development opportunities necessary to create a learning organization are in place, particularly in transferring knowledge, learning from experience, experimentation through searching for and testing new knowledge, learning from others, and systematic problem solving.

According to a Conference Board of Canada 2016 study, Canadian organizations spend, on average, $800 per employee on learning and development, accounting for approximately 1.41 percent of the organization's payroll budget. The average employee undergoes 31 hours of training and development each year.[3] Learning and development expenses in Canada are split largely between external providers, internal providers, and third-party (e.g., university) providers, as evidenced in **Figure 6.1**.

learning organization An organization skilled at creating, acquiring, and transferring knowledge and at modifying its behaviour to reflect new knowledge and insights.

FIGURE 6.1   Breakdown of Direct Learning and Development Expenditure

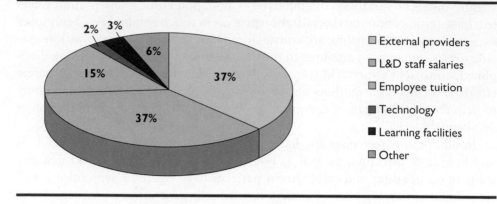

Source: Hall, Colin, and Simon Cotsman. *Learning as a Lever for Performance: Learning and Development Outlook—13th Edition.* Ottawa: The Conference Board of Canada, 2015. Used with permission

Given that training often occurs after the orientation process, this chapter first reviews the process of orienting employees, followed by a review of the training process. The last section of this chapter discusses career planning.

6.2 ONBOARDING EMPLOYEES

Once employees have been recruited and selected, the next step is onboarding (also known as orienting) them to their new company and their new job. A strategic approach to recruitment and retention of employees includes a well-integrated onboarding program, both before and after hiring.[4] New employees need a clear understanding of company policies, expectations regarding their performance, and operating procedures. In the long term, a comprehensive onboarding program can lead to reductions in turnover, increased morale, fewer instances of corrective discipline, and fewer employee grievances. It can also reduce the number of workplace injuries, particularly for young workers.[5] The bottom-line implications of successful orientation can be dramatic.

6.2.1 Purpose of Onboarding Programs

employee onboarding (orientation)   A procedure for providing new employees with basic background information about the firm and the job.

Employee onboarding (orientation) provides new employees with basic background information about the employer and specific information that they need to perform their jobs satisfactorily. At the Law Society of Upper Canada, any time a new employee walks through the door the organization acts quickly to help the person get started on the right foot. The Law Society views orientation as an investment in the retention of talent. The essence of the orientation program is to introduce people to the culture, give them a common bond, teach the importance of teamwork in the workplace, and provide the tools and information to be successful at the Law Society.[6]

socialization   The ongoing process of instilling in all employees the prevailing attitudes, standards, values, and patterns of behaviour that are expected by the organization.

Onboarding is actually one component of the employer's new-employee socialization process. **Socialization** is the ongoing process of instilling in all employees the prevailing attitudes, standards, values, and patterns of behaviour that are expected by the organization.[7] During the time required for socialization to occur, a new employee is less than fully productive. A strong onboarding program can speed up the socialization process and result in the new employee achieving full productivity as quickly as possible and reducing turnover.

Onboarding helps the employee to perform better by providing necessary information about company rules and practices. It helps to clarify the organization's expectations of an employee regarding his or her job, thus helping to reduce the new employee's first-day jitters and **reality shock** (also referred to as **cognitive dissonance**)—the discrepancy between what the new employee expected from his or her new job and its realities.

An important part of any effective onboarding program is sitting down and deciding on work-related goals with the new employee. These goals provide the basis for early feedback and establish a foundation for ongoing performance management.[8] Onboarding is the first step in helping the new employee manage the learning curve; it helps new employees become productive more quickly than they might otherwise.

Some organizations commence onboarding activity before the first day of employment. At Ernst & Young, the firm keeps in touch with people who have been hired but have not yet started work by sending them internal newsletters, inviting them to drop by for chats, and hosting dinners for them.[9] Others use onboarding as an ongoing "new-hire development process" and extend it in stages throughout the first year of employment to improve retention levels and reduce the overall costs of recruitment.[10]

Online onboarding systems that can be provided to new employees as soon as they accept the job offer are increasingly being used to engage employees more quickly and accelerate employee performance.[11] Online onboarding provides strategic benefits starting with building the brand as an employer of choice. This approach engages new hires in a personalized way and accelerates their time-to-productivity by completing benefits decisions, payroll forms, new-hire data, introduction of policies and procedures, and preliminary socialization using videos and graphics before the first day on the job, leading to a productive day one.[12]

6.2.2 Content of Onboarding Programs

Onboarding programs range from brief, informal introductions to lengthy, formal programs. In the latter, over an extended period of time. new employees are usually given the following:

- Internal publications, including employee handbooks that cover matters such as company history, current mission, activities, products, and people
- Facility tour and staff introductions
- Job-related documents, including an explanation of job procedures, duties and responsibilities, working hours, and attendance expectations; vacations and holidays; payroll, employee benefits, and pensions; and work regulations and policies such as personal use of company technology
- Expected training to be received (when and why)
- Performance appraisal criteria, including the estimated time to achieve full productivity

Note that some courts have found employee handbook contents to represent a contract with the employee. Therefore, disclaimers should be included that make it clear that statements of company policies, benefits, and regulations do not constitute the terms and conditions of an employment contract, either expressed or implied. Firms should think twice before including in the handbook such statements as "No employee will be terminated without just cause," or statements that imply or state that employees have tenure or job security based on seniority or other non-performance reasons; these could be viewed as legal and binding commitments.

6.2.3 Responsibility for Onboarding

The first day of onboarding usually involves the HR specialist, who explains such matters as working hours and vacation. The employee is also introduced to his or her new supervisor, who contributes to the orientation by explaining the exact nature of the job, introducing the person to his or her new colleagues, and familiarizing the new employee with the workplace. Sometimes, another employee at a peer level will be assigned as a "buddy" or mentor for the newly hired employee for the first few weeks or months of employment.[13] It is a good idea for the HR department to follow up with each new employee about three months after the initial orientation to address any remaining questions.

6.2.4 Special Onboarding Situations

6.2.4.1 Diverse Workforce

In an organization that has not had a diverse workforce in the past, orienting new employees from different backgrounds poses a special challenge. The values of the organization may be new to the new employees if these values were not part of their past experience. New employees should be advised to expect a variety of reactions from current employees to someone from a different background and be given some tips on how to deal with these reactions. In particular, they need to know which reactions are prohibited under human rights legislation and how to report these, should they occur. In addition, as the diversity of the internal workforce increases, existing employees can be oriented towards a broader range of employee perceptions and effective communication techniques, as highlighted in the Expert Opinion box.

6.2.4.2 Mergers and Acquisitions

Employees of a newly merged company need to receive information about the details of the merger or acquisition as part of the information on company history. They also need to be made aware of any ongoing, as-yet-unresolved difficulties regarding day-to-day operational issues related to their work. A further onboarding issue arises with respect to the existing employees at the time of the merger or acquisition: A new company culture will evolve in the merged organization, and everyone will experience a resocialization process. This presents an opportunity for the merged organization to emphasize the new organizational values and beliefs, thereby reinforcing corporate culture and furthering the new organization's business objectives.[14]

6.2.4.3 Union vs. Non-Union Employees

New employees in unionized positions need to be provided with a copy of the collective bargaining agreement and be told which information relates specifically to their particular job. They also need to be introduced to their union steward, have payroll deduction of union dues explained, and be informed of the names of union executive members. New employees, both unionized and non-unionized, need to be made aware of which jobs are unionized and which ones are not.

Academic Viewpoint
EXPERT OPINION

1. Your research focuses on social exclusion and inclusion. Can you briefly explain those concepts?

Social inclusion is a social vision. It involves the need to belong, as well as the reality of belonging. In this sense, individuals need to feel that they're contributing to society or the organization, and the organization needs to have the structures in place to promote mutual value. This includes policies, programs, and management styles that foster a sense of belonging. In order to be inclusionary, we should not view diversity management as merely a moral obligation, but rather as a core element or value of the organization.

On the other hand, social exclusion is embedded more in the social/economic/political context. When we experience exclusion we disengage, which is linked with an increase in depression symptoms and a decrease in self-esteem. In some organizations, they don't have the structures to work proactively to eliminate social exclusion. For example, there's no mechanism to stop exclusionary behaviour or support change.

2. There is a lot of discussion about the need for diversity in organizations. What are some of the major benefits

Identification:
Dr. Ann Beaton (PhD)
Canada Research Chair
in Intergroup Relations

Affiliation:
Social Sciences & Humanities,
Université de Moncton

inclusive organizations experience?

There is evidence that suggests having an inclusionary environment helps employers attract and retain employees. For example, seeing women in leadership roles promotes others to recognize the paradigm shift of the company. However, there is power in numbers, so an organization has to be careful that there is not a token female executive. An increased level of diversity in an organization reduces the sense of threat felt among the minority group.

Research also indicates a reduced incidence of mental health symptomology and increased well-being (e.g., self-esteem). Combined, these efforts can reduce turnover, thereby saving cost associated with turnover.

3. What are some of the things that an organization can do to adopt an inclusive approach to recruiting?

I. A proactive and effective recruitment strategy focused on diversity should avoid tokenism.
II. Avoid framing the increased diversity as a zero-sum game between the majority and the minority. We need to be careful that the majority group does not perceive personal or group threat. This can be done through effective communication, clear decision rules, and focus on competencies in an inclusive environment.
III. Organizations need to build a multicultural framework of values and celebrate diversity. This helps foster social cohesion, creating a sense of appreciation and knowledge regarding the differences in the workplace and in the workers. This can make contact between groups harmonious and productive, rather than self-focused.

Source: Used by permission from Dr. Ann Beaton (PhD).

6.2.4.4 Multi-Location Organizations

New employees in a multi-location company need to be made aware of where the other locations are and what business functions are performed in each location. The Ontario Ministry of Education is one such organization, and it uses a web-based, online onboarding to deliver corporate-level information.[15] All employees have equal access regardless of their location, and the same message is delivered to each one. Updates can be made instantaneously, and employees can view the information at their own pace.

IBM has been piloting two virtual onboarding programs for interns in China and India. In the Chinese pilot, US-based HR staff and Chinese interns create individual avatars to build relationships, learn about their functions, and hold meetings within Second Life (an online artificial 3-D world). In India, IBM is using another virtual tool called Plane Shift to allow virtual teams to simulate project work.[16]

6.2.4.5 Executive Integration

The onboarding process is a continuous, long-term process aimed at moulding desired behaviours and aligning the values of the employee with those of the organization. To this end, there is a formal component of onboarding that often occurs when a new employee first joins the organization. There is also an ongoing informal onboarding process, with the aim of building a strong employee bond with organizational values, history, and tradition. This can include staff involvement through mentoring or management guidance (by using high-level staff, firms communicate the importance of messages and experiences in a more meaningful way), and through employee empowerment (indoctrination of values and information to guide workplace behaviour).

Additionally, newly hired or promoted executives typically do not participate in formal onboarding activities, and there is little planning regarding how they will be integrated into their new position and company. The common assumption is that the new executive is a professional and will know what to do, but full executive integration can take up to 18 months.[17] To make things even more difficult, executives are often brought in as change agents, in which case they can expect to face considerable resistance. Thus, a lack of attention to executive integration can result in serious problems with assimilation and work effectiveness. It is common to perceive executive integration as an onboarding issue, but integration at senior levels in the organization requires an ongoing process that can continue for months as the new executive learns about the unspoken dynamics of the organization that are not covered in onboarding programs, such as how decisions are really made and who holds what type of power.[18]

An Ethical Dilemma

Is it ethical to withhold information from an incoming executive about critical problems that he or she will face?

© Maksim Pasko/Fotolia

New employees in a multi-location company need to be made aware of where the other locations are and what business functions are performed in each location.

Executive integration is of critical importance to a productive relationship between a new executive and his or her organization, and it is important to review previous successes and failures at executive integration on an ongoing basis. Key aspects of the integration process include the following:

- Identifying position specifications (particularly the ability to deal with and overcome jealousy)

- Providing realistic information to job candidates and providing support in the event of reality shock

- Assessing each candidate's previous record at making organizational transitions

- Announcing the hiring with enthusiasm
- Stressing the importance of listening as well as demonstrating competency, and promoting more time spent talking with the boss
- Assisting new executives who are balancing their work to change cultural norms while they themselves are part of the culture itself[19]

6.2.5 Problems with Onboarding Programs

A number of potential problems can arise with onboarding programs. Often, *too much information* is provided in a short time (usually one day) and the new employee is overwhelmed. New employees commonly find themselves inundated with forms to fill out for payroll, benefits, pensions, and so on. Another problem is that *little or no orientation* is provided, which means that new employees must personally seek answers to each question that arises and work without a good understanding of what is expected of them. This is a common problem for part-time and contract workers. Finally, the information provided by the HR department can be *too broad* to be meaningful to a new employee, especially on the first day, whereas the information provided by the immediate supervisor may be *too detailed* to realistically be remembered by the new employee.

6.2.6 Evaluation of Onboarding Programs

Onboarding programs should be evaluated to assess whether they are providing timely, useful information to new employees in a cost-effective manner. Three approaches to evaluating orientation programs are as follows:

1. *Employee reaction.* Interview or survey new employees for their opinion on the usefulness of the onboarding program. Also, evaluate job performance within specified time periods to assess transference of learning and behaviours where possible.

2. *Socialization effects.* Review new employees at regular intervals to assess progress towards understanding and acceptance of the beliefs, values, and norms of the organization.

3. *Cost/benefit analysis.* Compare (1) orientation costs, such as printing handbooks and time spent orienting new employees by HR staff and immediate supervisors, with (2) benefits of onboarding, including reduction in errors, rate of productivity, efficiency levels, and so on.

6.3 THE TRAINING PROCESS

Training employees involves a learning process in which workers are provided with the information and skills that they need to successfully perform their jobs. Training might mean showing a new production worker how to operate a machine, a new salesperson how to sell the firm's product, or a new supervisor how to interview and appraise employees. Whereas *training* focuses on skills and competencies needed to perform employees' current jobs, *development* is training of a long-term nature. Its aim is to prepare current employees for future jobs within the organization.

It is important to ensure that business and training goals are aligned and that training is part of an organization's strategic plan.[20] A training professional in

training   The process of teaching employees the basic skills/competencies that they need to perform their jobs.

Institute for Performance and Learning
www.performanceandlearning.ca

today's business world has to understand the organization's business, speak its language, and demonstrate the business value of training investment.[21] In today's service-based economy, highly knowledgeable workers can be the company's most important assets. Thus, it is important to treat training as a strategic investment in human capital.[22]

6.3.1 The Necessity of Training

A recent federal government report concluded that Canada's ability to remain globally competitive and manage technological change effectively is highly contingent on our ability to upgrade and renew the skills of our labour force. The assumption that youth workers alone hold the responsibility for skills development is no longer valid, and older workers must also adopt a lifelong learning approach.[23]

Already, a skills crisis has arisen in the manufacturing sector, where lack of qualified workers is a major problem. Skills in greatest need of improvement are problem solving, communications, and teamwork.[24] Training is therefore moving to centre stage as a necessity for improving employers' competitiveness. The federal government has called for businesses to increase spending on training, and business has asked the government to expand programs for professional immigrants to get Canadian qualifications in their fields. In response, the Canadian Council on Learning was created by the federal government to promote best practices in workplace learning. For example, the Quebec government has legislated that all firms with a payroll of more than $1 000 000 must spend 1 percent of payroll on employee training (or else pay a tax in the same amount).[25]

6.3.2 Training and Learning

auditory learning Learning through auditory methods such as talking and listening.

visual learning Learning through visual methods such as through pictures and print.

kinesthetic tactile learning Learning through a whole-body experience, such as learning through completing an activity.

Training is essentially a learning process. To train employees, therefore, it is useful to know something about how people learn. For example, people have three main learning styles: **Auditory learning** is learning through talking and listening; **visual learning** is learning through pictures and print; and **kinesthetic tactile learning** is learning through a whole-body experience. Training effectiveness can be enhanced by identifying learning styles and personalizing the training accordingly.[26] The following four guidelines help trainers maximize the effectiveness of the training process:

1. At the start of training, provide the trainees with an overall picture of the material to be presented. When presenting material, use as many visual aids as possible and a variety of familiar examples. Organize the material so that it is presented in a logical manner and in meaningful units. Try to use terms and concepts that are already familiar to trainees.

2. Maximize the similarity between the training situation and the work situation, and provide adequate training practice. Give trainees the chance to use their new skills immediately on their return to work. Train managers first and employees second to send a message about the importance of the training, and control contingencies by planning rewards for trainees who successfully complete and integrate the new training.[27]

3. Motivation affects training outcomes independently of any increase in cognitive ability. Training motivation is affected by individual characteristics like conscientiousness and by the training climate.[28] Therefore, it is important to

try to provide as much realistic practice as possible. Trainees learn best at their own pace and when correct responses are immediately reinforced, perhaps with a quick "Well done." For many younger employees, the use of technology can motivate learning. Simulations, games, virtual worlds, and online networking are revolutionizing how people learn and how learning experiences are designed and delivered. Learners who are immersed in deep experiential learning in highly visual and interactive environments become intellectually engaged in the experience.[29]

4. Research evidence shows that the trainee's pre-training preparation is a crucial step in the training process. It is important to create a perceived need for training in the minds of participants.[30] Also, provide preparatory information that will help to establish trainees' expectations about the events and consequences of actions that are likely to occur in the training environment (and, eventually, on the job). For example, trainees learning to become first-line supervisors may face stressful situations, high workloads, and difficult employees. Studies suggest that the negative impact of such conditions can be reduced by letting trainees know ahead of time what might occur.[31]

6.3.2.1 Legal Aspects of Training

Under human rights and employment equity legislation, several aspects of employee training programs must be assessed regarding the program's impact on designated group members.[32] For example, if relatively few women or visible minorities are selected for a training program, there may be a requirement to show that the admissions procedures are valid—that they predict performance on the job for which the person is being trained. It could turn out that the reading level of the training manuals is too advanced for many trainees for whom English is not their first language—which may result in their doing poorly in the program, regardless of their aptitude for the jobs for which they are being trained. The training program might then be found to be unfairly discriminatory. On the other hand, employees who refuse a lawful and reasonable order to attend a training program may be considered to have abandoned their position.[33]

Negligent training is another potential problem. **Negligent training** occurs when an employer fails to train adequately, and an employee subsequently harms a third party. Also, an employee who is dismissed for poor performance or disciplined for safety infractions may claim that by failing to provide adequate training, the employer was negligent.

negligent training Occurs when an employer fails to adequately train an employee who subsequently harms a third party or is disciplined for safety infractions.

6.3.3 Introduction to the Five-Step Training Process

A typical training program consists of five steps. Upon completion of the last step, there should be a feedback loop to help learning organizations engage in continuous learning.

1. Training Needs Analysis
2. Instructional and Curriculum Design
3. Validation of Training Design
4. Training Implementation
5. Evaluation of Training

International Personnel Assessment Council
www.ipacweb.org

6.3.4 Step 1: Training Needs Analysis

The first step in training is to determine what training is required, if any. The main challenge in assessing the training needs of new employees is to determine what the job entails and to break it down into subtasks, each of which is then taught to the new employee.

Task analysis and performance analysis are the two main techniques for identifying training needs.

6.3.4.1 Task Analysis: Assessing the Training Needs of New Employees

task analysis Identifying the broad competencies and specific skills required to perform job-related tasks.

Identifying the broad competencies and specific skills required to perform job-related tasks is called **task analysis**. Task analysis is used for determining the training needs of employees who are new to their jobs. Particularly with entry-level workers, it is common to hire inexperienced people and train them.[34] Thus, the aim is to develop the skills and knowledge required for effective performance—like soldering (in the case of an assembly worker) or interviewing (in the case of a supervisor).

The job description and job specifications are helpful here. These list the specific duties and skills required on the job and become the basic reference point in determining the training required to perform the job.

Some employers supplement the current job description and specification with a task analysis record form, which typically contains six types of information:

1. A list of the job's main tasks and subtasks

2. An indication of the frequency of tasks and subtasks

3. A measurable description of performance standards for each task and subtask (for instance "tolerance of 0.007 inches" or "within two days of receiving the order")

4. Conditions under which task is performed

5. The competencies and specific skills or knowledge required for each task and subtask, specifying exactly what knowledge or skills must be taught

6. The decision as to whether the task is best learned on or off the job, based on several considerations such as training objectives, methods, and resources (for example, prospective jet pilots must learn something about the plane off the job in a simulator before actually getting behind the controls)

Once the essential skills involved in doing the job are determined, new employees' proficiency in these skills can be assessed and training needs identified for each individual.

6.3.4.2 Performance Analysis: Determining the Training Needs of Current Employees

Performance analysis involves verifying whether there is a significant performance deficiency and, if so, determining whether that deficiency should be rectified through training or some other means (such as transferring the employee). The first step is to appraise the employee's performance because, to improve it, the

Profits

"It's important to note we really did try hard."

firm must first compare the person's current performance with what it should be. Examples of specific performance deficiencies follow:

"Salespeople are expected to make ten new contacts per week, but John averages only six."

"Other plants our size average no more than two serious accidents per month; we are averaging five."

Distinguishing between *can't do* and *won't do* problems is at the heart of performance analysis. First, the firm must determine whether a problem is a *can't do* problem and, if so, its specific causes. For example, the employees do not know what to do or are unaware of the standards; there are obstacles in the system (such as a lack of tools or supplies); job aids are needed; poor selection has resulted in hiring people who do not have the skills to do the job; or training is inadequate. Conversely, it might be a *won't do* problem. In this case, employees *could* do a good job if they wanted to. If so, the reward system may have to be changed, perhaps by the implementation of an incentive program.

performance analysis Verifying whether there is a significant performance deficiency and, if so, determining whether that deficiency should be rectified through training or some other means.

Establish Training Objectives   Once training needs have been identified, concrete and measurable training objectives can be established. Objectives specify what the trainee should be able to accomplish after successfully completing the training program. They thus provide a focus for the efforts of both the trainee and the trainer and provide a benchmark for evaluating the success of the training program. A training program can then be developed and implemented with the intent to achieve these objectives. These objectives must be accomplished within the organization's training budget.

6.3.5 Step 2: Instructional and Curriculum Design

After the employees' training needs have been determined and training objectives have been set, the training program can be designed. There are two major considerations in developing the instructional design: First, will learning be programmed or informal? Second, what is the medium for training? While a large portion of training occurs in the workplace (on-the-job training and apprenticeships), the option of assisted or third-party learning allows organizations to gain expertise not available in-house and may offer significant cost reductions through the benefits of economies of scale.

6.3.5.1 Programmed Learning

Whether the programmed instruction device is a textbook or a computer, **programmed learning** consists of three components:

1. Presenting questions, facts, or problems to the learner
2. Allowing the person to respond
3. Providing feedback on the accuracy of his or her answers

programmed learning   A systematic method for teaching job skills that involves presenting questions or facts, allowing the person to respond, and giving the learner immediate feedback on the accuracy of his or her answers.

The main advantage of programmed learning is that it reduces training time by about one-third.[35] Programmed instruction can also facilitate learning because it lets trainees learn at their own pace, provides immediate feedback, and (from the learner's point of view) reduces the risk of error. However, trainees do not learn much more from programmed learning than they would from a traditional textbook. Therefore, the cost of developing the manuals or software for programmed instruction has to be weighed against the accelerated but not improved learning that should occur.

6.3.5.2 Informal Learning

About two-thirds of industrial training is not formal at all but rather results from day-to-day unplanned interactions between the new worker and his or her colleagues. Informal learning may be defined as "any learning that occurs in which the learning process is not determined or designed by the organization."[36]

6.3.5.3 Workplace and Traditional Training Techniques

Traditionally, training techniques have included classroom training, on-the-job training, apprenticeship training, and job instruction training, as well as programmed learning and informal learning, discussed above, and audiovisual techniques and vestibule or simulated training, discussed below in the section on technology-enabled techniques.

Classroom Training Classroom training continues to be the primary method of providing corporate training in Canada, and lectures are a widely used method of classroom training delivery. Lecturing has several advantages. It is a quick and simple way of providing knowledge to large groups of trainees, as when the sales force must be taught the special features of a new product.

Classroom learning has evolved to maintain its relevance in the technological age. With features such as wikis, blogs, and podcasts, learning opportunities must reflect employees' new abilities and needs. Blended learning, using a combination of instructor-led training and online e-learning, has been found to provide better learning results and higher learner engagement and enthusiasm than expected. In blended learning, the in-class training becomes tightly integrated with the online experience, and the relevance to the learner is vastly improved. Thus, the classroom has evolved to include interactions with remote colleagues and instructors, e-learning in many forms, coaching, assessment, and feedback.[37]

On the Job Training On-the-job training (OJT) involves having a person learn a job by actually performing it. Virtually every employee—from mailroom clerk to company president—gets some on-the-job training when he or she joins a firm. In many companies, OJT is the only type of training available. It usually involves assigning new employees to experienced workers or supervisors who then do the actual training.[38]

OJT has several advantages: It is relatively inexpensive, trainees learn while producing, and there is no need for expensive off-job facilities like classrooms or manuals. The method also facilitates learning, since trainees learn by actually doing the job and get quick feedback about the quality of their performance.

apprenticeship   A situation in which the learner/apprentice studies under the tutelage of a master craftsperson, blending classroom instruction with on-the-job training.

Apprenticeship Training Apprenticeship basically involves having the learner/apprentice study under the tutelage of a master craftsperson. Apprenticeship training is critical today, as more than half of skilled tradespeople are expecting to retire by 2020. Federal, provincial, and territorial governments are increasing their funding of apprenticeship training programs to meet this growing need for more tradespeople.[39]

On-the-job training is structured and concrete. Here, a supervisor teaches an employee to use a drum-forming machine.

Apprentices become skilled workers through a combination of classroom instruction and on-the-job training. Apprenticeships are widely used to train individuals for many occupations, including those of electrician and plumber. In Canada, close to 170 established trades have recognized apprenticeship programs.[40]

Many jobs consist of a logical sequence of steps and are best taught step by step. This step-by-step process is called **job instruction training (JIT)**. To begin, all necessary steps in the job are listed, each in its proper sequence. Alongside each step, a corresponding "key point" (if any) should be noted. The steps show what is to be done, while the key points show how it is to be done and why. In today's service economy, job instruction training for step-by-step manual work is being superseded by behaviour modelling for service workers (see section 6.4.1.3, Focus on Life Trajectories, below).

job instruction training (JIT)   The listing of each job's basic tasks along with key points to provide step-by-step training for employees.

6.3.5.4 Technology-Enabled Training Techniques

E-Learning Electronic dependent or web-based training, called *e-learning*, is now commonly used by Canadian organizations. It is generally estimated that online training costs about 50 percent less than traditional classroom-based training. Also, online learning is ideal for adults, who learn what they want, when they want, and where they want. Online training is often the best solution for highly specialized business professionals who have little time available for ongoing education. Further, online training is ideal for global organizations that want consistent training for all employees worldwide.

However, critics point out that content management, sound educational strategy, learner support, and system administration should receive more attention, as they are often the critical determining factors in successful training outcomes. In the last few years, "learner content management systems" have been developed to deliver personalized content in small units or modules of learning. These systems complement learning management systems that are focused on the logistics of managing learning. Together, they form a powerful combination for an e-learning platform. This development is considered part of the new phase of e-learning, involving greater standardization and the emergence of norms. However, the freedom of online learning means that unless learners are highly motivated, they may not complete the training. It is estimated that learners don't complete 50 to 90 percent of online courses. In general, it is important to seek blended learning, including both personal interaction and online training tools.[41]

Audiovisual Techniques Audiovisual techniques (CDs, DVDs, computer-based techniques) can be very effective and are widely used. They can be more expensive than conventional lectures to develop, but offer some advantages. Trainers should consider using these when there is a need to illustrate how a certain sequence should be followed over time, there is a need to expose trainees to events not easily demonstrable in live lectures, or the training is going to be used organization-wide.

There are three options when it comes to audiovisual material: buying an existing product, making one, or using a production company. Businesses often have large catalogs of audiovoisual training programs on a broad range of topics from applicant interviewing to zoo management.

The advantages of audiovisual techniques include instructional consistency (unlike human trainers, computers do not have good days and bad days), mastery of learning (if the trainee does not learn it, he or she generally cannot move on to the

© NASA

Vestibule training simulates flight conditions at NASA headquarters.

video conferencing   Connecting two or more distant groups by using audiovisual equipment.

vestibule or simulated training   Training employees on special off-the-job equipment, as in airplane pilot training, whereby training costs and hazards can be reduced.

next step), flexibility for the trainee (can be scheduled when it best suits trainee) and increased trainee motivation (resulting from the responsive feedback).

Video Conferencing   Video conferencing, in which an instructor is televised live to multiple locations, is now a common method for training employees. It has been defined as "a means of joining two or more distant groups using a combination of audio and visual equipment."[42] Video conferencing allows people in one location to communicate live with people in another city or country or with groups in several places at once. It is particularly important to prepare a training guide ahead of time, as most or all of the learners will not be in the same location as the trainer. It is also important for the trainer to arrive early and test all equipment that will be used.

Vestibule or simulated training   In vestibule or simulated training is a technique by which trainees learn on the actual or simulated equipment that they will use on the job, with the training taking place off the job. Therefore, it aims to obtain the advantages of on-the-job training without actually putting the trainee on the job. Vestibule training is virtually a necessity when it is too costly or dangerous to train employees on the job. Putting new assembly-line workers right to work could slow production, for instance, and when safety is a concern—as with pilots—vestibule training may be the only practical alternative.

Vestibule training may consist of simply placing a trainee in a separate room with the equipment that he or she will actually be using on the job; however, it often involves the use of equipment simulators. In pilot training, for instance, the main advantages of flight simulators are safety, learning efficiency, and cost savings (on maintenance costs, pilot cost, fuel cost, and the cost of not having the aircraft in regular service).[43]

A new generation of simulations has been developed to simulate role-play situations designed to teach behavioural skills and emotional intelligence. Body language, facial expressions, and subtle nuances are programmed in. These new simulations offer authentic and relevant scenarios involving pressure situations that tap users' emotions and force them to act.[44]

6.3.6 Steps 3 and 4: Validation and Implementation of Training

Validation of the training program that has been designed is an often-overlooked step in the training process. In order to ensure that the program will accomplish its objectives, it is necessary to conduct a pilot study, or run-through, with a representative group of trainees. The results of the pilot study are used to assess the effectiveness of the training.

Revisions to the program can be made to address any problems encountered by the pilot group of trainees in using the training material and the experiences provided to them. Testing at the end of the pilot study can measure the extent to which the program is producing the desired improvement in skill level. If the results fall below the level of the training objectives, then more work must be undertaken to strengthen the instructional design.

Once the program has been validated, it is ready to be implemented by professional trainers. In some cases, a train-the-trainer workshop may be required to familiarize trainers with unfamiliar content or with unique and innovative new methods for presenting the training content.

6.3.7 Step 5: Training Evaluation

It is important to assess the return on investment in human capital made through training by determining whether the training has actually achieved the objectives. **Transfer of training** is the application of the skills acquired during the training program into the work environment and the maintenance of these skills over time. A number of actions can be taken before, during, and after a training program to enhance transfer of training.[45]

Before training, potential trainees can be assessed on their level of ability, aptitude, and motivation regarding the skill to be taught, and those with higher levels can be selected for the training program. Trainees can be involved in designing the training, and management should provide active support at this stage.

During the training, it is important to provide frequent feedback, opportunities for practice, and positive reinforcement. After the training program, trainees can use goal-setting and relapse-prevention techniques to increase the likelihood of applying what they have learned. Management can enhance transfer of training by providing opportunities to apply new skills and by continuing to provide positive reinforcement of the new skills while being tolerant of errors.

After trainees complete their training (or at planned intervals during the training), the program should be evaluated to see how well its objectives have been met and the extent to which transfer of training has occurred. For example, are trainees learning as *much* as they can? Are they learning as *fast* as they can? Is there a *better method* for training them? These are some of the questions that are answered by properly evaluating training efforts.

Overall, there is little doubt that training and development can be effective. Formal studies of training programs substantiate the potential positive impact of such programs. Profitable companies spend the most on training, and those rated as being among the 100 best companies to work for in Canada spend the most per employee on training.[46]

There are two basic issues to address when evaluating a training program: whether controlled experimentation will be used, and which training effect will be measured.

Controlled experimentation is the best method to use in evaluating a training program. A controlled experiment uses both a training group and a control group (that receives no training). Data (for example, on quantity of production or quality of soldered junctions) should be obtained both before and after the training effort in the training group, and before and after a corresponding work period in the control group. In this way, it is possible to determine the extent to which any change in performance in the training group resulted from the training itself, rather than from some organization-wide change like a raise in pay, which would likely have affected employees in both groups equally.

> **transfer of training**   Application of the skills acquired during the training program into the work environment and the maintenance of these skills over time.

> **controlled experimentation**   Uses both a group for which the situation is modified (e.g., the group receives training) and a group for which the situation is not modified (e.g., the group receives no training) to assess the impact of the modification.

6.3.7.1 Training Effects to Measure

Four basic categories of training outcomes can be measured:[47]

1. *Reaction.* First, evaluate trainees' reactions to the program. Did they like the program? Did they think it worthwhile?

2. *Learning.* Second, test the trainees to determine whether they learned the principles, skills, and facts that they were supposed to learn.

3. *Behaviour.* Next, ask whether the trainees' behaviour on the job has changed because of the training program. For example, are employees in the store's

complaint department more courteous towards disgruntled customers than they were previously? These measures determine the degree of transfer of training.

4. *Results.* Last, but probably most important, ask questions such as these: Did the number of customer complaints about employees drop? Did the rejection rate improve? Was turnover reduced? Are production quotas now being met? and so on. The training program may succeed in terms of the reactions from trainees, increased learning, and even changes in behaviour, but if the results are not achieved, then in the final analysis the training has not achieved its goals.

6.4 CAREER PLANNING AND DEVELOPMENT

Career Planning Exercises
www.careerstorm.com
Career Networking
www.careerkey.org

Career planning can play a significant role in retaining employees in the organization and reducing turnover of valued workers. The key factors in employee retention today are an organizational culture that values and nurtures talented employees, fair processes in "people" decisions, and managers who understand what motivates employees.[48] Employers and employees also recognize the need for lifelong learning. Retention can be strengthened by providing extensive continuing training—from basic remedial skills to advanced decision-making techniques—throughout employees' careers.

Before we proceed, it would be useful to clarify some of the terms that will be used.[49] A **career** is a series of work-related positions, paid or unpaid, that help a person to grow in job skills, success, and fulfillment. **Career development** is the lifelong series of activities (such as workshops) that contribute to a person's career exploration, establishment, success, and fulfillment. As the Workforce Diversity box illustrates, career development for older workers is just as important as it is for younger employees. **Career planning** is the deliberate process through which someone becomes aware of personal skills, interests, knowledge, motivations, and other characteristics; acquires information about opportunities and choices; identifies career-related goals; and establishes action plans to attain specific goals.

career A series of work-related positions, paid or unpaid, that help a person to grow in job skills, success, and fulfillment.

career development The lifelong series of activities (such as workshops) that contribute to a person's career exploration, establishment, success, and fulfillment.

career planning The deliberate process through which someone becomes aware of personal skills, interests, knowledge, motivations, and other characteristics; acquires information about opportunities and choices; identifies career-related goals; and establishes action plans to attain specific goals.

6.4.1 Emergent Approaches to Career Development

In the early stages of career development research, career patterns were assumed to be stable, predictable, linear, and based on hierarchies. Career stages were seen as influencing the employee's knowledge of and preference for various occupations, and were often associated with the concept that an employee's career stage could be established based on his or her age. Now, because job transitions are more frequent, occupational prospects and linear career patterns lose definability and predictability. As a result, a new concept of career development has emerged, in which the primary stakeholder of a career is the person, not the organization.[50] Therefore, a more dynamic and holistic approach to career development is emerging, with a focus on lifelong learning, flexibility, and adaptability. As a consequence, a number of individual and organizational considerations need to be taken into account.

6.4.1.1 Identify Skills and Aptitudes

Successful performance depends not only on motivation but also on ability. Whether someone has the skills to be an accountant, banker, or credit manager

WORKFORCE DIVERSITY

Career Development for Older Workers

While mandatory retirement has been largely abolished in Canada, employers often neglect career development of older workers. The "second middle age" refers to the 20-year period when an individual is between ages 60 and 80. Research has shown that they have lower rates of absenteeism, fewer accidents, higher levels of job satisfaction, and a stronger work ethic.

Here are practical career development strategies that will help keep employees fully engaged during their second middle age:

- *Adopt a new attitude:* Older workers' views are generally grounded in years of experience, but at the same time many of them reflect an open mind, a flexible and forward-thinking attitude, and a willingness to take calculated risks.

- *Provide career counselling:* People want to do work that is consistent with their values, and that taps into their interests, knowledge base, and skill set. These factors may change over the course of an individual's career, and counselling may help address this change. For example, it may help an older worker realize that returning to an earlier role could be rejuvenating, or that embarking on a completely new endeavour may be a great alternative to retirement.

- *Invest in training and development:* As long as intellectual capability is valued at the workplace, it is easy for older workers to adjust for slower mental pace and occasional memory lapse, which are typical of aging. The workplace should separate signs of aging from capacity in primary mental functions, such as language fluency, numerical ability, and spatial orientation.

© JPC-PROD/Fotolia

- *Honour the need for work–life balance:* Creative work arrangements should be considered. Things such as flexible working hours and sabbaticals enable second middle-agers to spend the necessary time with family, as well as fulfill their professional ambitions and responsibilities.

Source: Based on M. Watters of Optimum Talent/KWA Partners, "Career Development for Employees Heading into Their 'Second Middle Age,'" *Canadian HR Reporter* (February 13, 2006), p. 13.

---

will largely determine the specific occupation ultimately chosen. Therefore, the identification of each individual's skills must be based on his or her education and experience. In organizations using competency- or skill-based pay, a formal system for evaluating skills will already be in place.

For career-planning purposes, a person's aptitudes are usually measured with a test battery, such as the general aptitude test battery (GATB). This instrument measures various aptitudes, including intelligence and mathematical ability. Considerable work has been done to relate aptitudes, such as those measured by the GATB, to specific occupations.

6.4.1.2 Identify Career Anchors

Edgar Schein says that career planning is a continuing process of self-discovery.[51] As a person learns more about him- or herself, a dominant **career anchor** may become apparent. Career anchors, as their name implies, are concerns or

career anchor   A concern or value that a person will not give up if a choice has to be made.

values that a person will not give up if a choice has to be made. Schein identified eight career anchors affecting people's planning:

1. *Technical/functional:* A strong technical/functional career anchor suggests that they will make decisions enabling them to remain and grow in their chosen technical or functional fields.

2. *Managerial competence:* A strong motivation to become managers, as well as career experience, convinces them that they have the skills and values required to rise to general management positions.

3. *Creativity:* They need to build or create something that is entirely their own product—a product or process that bears their name, a company of their own, or a personal fortune that reflects their accomplishments.

4. *Autonomy and independence:* A drive to be to be on their own without being anybody's subordinate often drives them into entrepreneurial activities.

5. *Security:* A stable future with one organization that offers a good retirement program and benefits or allows them to maintain similar geographic surroundings may be important.

6. *Service/dedication:* They need to do something meaningful in a larger context.

7. *Pure challenge:* They desire to overcome impossible odds, solve unsolved problems, and beat competitors.

8. *Lifestyle:* They define their careers as a part of life and a larger lifestyle, integrating careers and personal and family concerns.

6.4.1.3 Focus on Life Trajectories

Issues of work–life balance are becoming more significant in peoples' reflections about their career aspirations. In addition, the growth in the number of people employed in the contingent workforce (temporary, part time, contractual, freelance, casual, and so on) makes managing interactions between work and life domains even more critical in career planning.

As a result, career development can be envisioned as a *life trajectory*, in which a person designs and builds his or her career and life simultaneously. This increases the importance of ensuring that employees are empowered decision makers when an organization engages in career planning. As well, the value of career development initiatives must extend beyond adding value to the employer to also include an explicit discussion of the transferability and value of the initiatives to the employee.[52]

The focus on life trajectories requires a shift in thinking about career development, as outlined below:

1. *From Traits to Context:* Research on personality traits and ability factors to guide occupation-driven careers relied on stability and predictability. In the new economy, career patterns should be viewed as professional identities that are dynamic. Understanding the range of factors that are outside of the organization's control is critical to the new approach to career development.

2. *From Prescriptive to Process:* On average, people up to the age of 36 change their jobs every two years. Traditional career paths involving a single, committed occupational choice are no longer a reality. Instead, career planners must stay informed about all of the job-specific requirements and offer a best

fit of career patterns, focusing on adding information and content to enable employees to achieve a range of career ambitions.

3. *From Linear to Non-linear:* Traditional career development was very deductive in that it assumed past employment patterns were valid predictors of future career ambitions. Thus, there is a necessary shift to a more holistic life design for career development, with an awareness of non-linear, often mutually dependant, causalities. Career plans must be frequently reevaluated and updated, involving an iterative strategy between organizational agents and employees.

4. *From Scientific to Narrative:* The old path of completing all desired education, securing a job, then establishing a family is no longer a reality for many Canadians; there is growing diversity of individual realities. Career development must empower employees to self-assess and interpret their own life experiences (often in the form of a narrative) and assist employees in making sense of their distinct perspective and implementing co-evolution.

5. *From Describing to Modelling:* Career development must adapt to individual experiences, ambitions, abilities, opportunities, and perspectives. Thus, the use of simple descriptive or scientific statistics alone undermines the complexity of career development. Career forecasting in this sense should develop a number of possible configurations and continuously monitor interacting variables to increase the success of career development.

6.4.2 Roles in Career Development

The individual, the manager, and the employer all have roles in the individual's career development. Ultimately, however, it is the *individual* who must accept responsibility for his or her own career, since workers are often seen as collaborators in the organizations that employ them.[53] This requires an entrepreneurial, goal-oriented approach that uses four key skills: self-motivation, independent learning, effective time and money management, and self-promotion.[54] Younger workers today are increasingly expecting to develop these skills by pursuing a career path that involves moving through multiple organizations.[55] **Networking** is the foundation of active career management and is essential for accessing the most valuable career resource—people. Networking is an organized process whereby the individual arranges and conducts a series of face-to-face meetings with his or her colleagues and contacts, plus individuals whom they recommend. Networking does not involve asking for a job, and it is not a one-sided encounter where only one individual benefits; rather, it is a mutual sharing process. Its objectives are to let people know about one's background and career goals, and to exchange information, advice, and referrals.[56]

networking An organized process whereby the individual arranges and conducts a series of face-to-face meetings with his or her colleagues and contacts, plus individuals whom they recommend.

Within the organization, the individual's *manager* plays a role in career development, too. The manager should provide timely and objective performance feedback, offer developmental assignments and support, and participate in career development discussions. The manager acts as a coach, an appraiser, an adviser, and a referral agent by listening to and clarifying the individual's career plans, giving feedback, generating career options, and linking the employee to organizational resources and career options.

Finally, the *employer* also plays a career development role. For example, an organization wanting to retain good employees should provide career-oriented training and development opportunities, offer career information and career programs, and give employees a variety of career options. Most employees will ultimately assess their employers on the extent to which the organization allowed them to excel and to become the people they believed they had the potential to become. How well an employer fulfills this career development role will help determine an employee's overall job satisfaction and commitment to his or her employer.[57]

6.5 MANAGING INTERNAL EMPLOYEE MOVEMENT

"They make a big deal out of promoting someone around here."

© Cartoonresource/Fotolia

Transfer and promotion decisions have important career development implications for transferred or promoted employees and substantial benefits for the organization in terms of creating a pool of potential future managers with broad experience throughout the firm. Employees may seek transfers into jobs that offer greater possibility for career advancement or opportunities for personal enrichment, or into those that are more interesting or more convenient—better hours, location of work, and so on.[58] Many organizations are recognizing that future leaders will need international experience to effectively manage their organizations in the increasingly globalized world of business, and they are providing international assignments as a career development experience. Chapter 13 includes details on how to manage international HRM.

Employers must also decide on the criteria by which to promote employees, and the way that these decisions are made will affect the employees' motivation, performance, and commitment.

6.5.1 Decision 1: Is Seniority or Competence the Rule?

From the point of view of motivation, promotion based on competence is best. However, union agreements often contain a clause that emphasizes seniority in promotions, meaning that only *substantial differences in abilities* can be taken into account in such situations.[59]

6.5.2 Decision 2: How Is Competence Measured?

If promotion is to be based on competence, how will competence be defined and measured? Defining and measuring *past* performance are relatively straightforward matters, but promotion also requires predicting the person's *potential*; thus, there must be a valid procedure for predicting a candidate's future performance. Tests and assessment centres can be used to evaluate employees and identify those with executive potential.[60]

6.5.3 Decision 3: Is the Process Formal or Informal?

Many employers still depend on an informal system whereby the availability and requirements of open positions are kept secret. Key managers make promotion decisions among employees whom they know personally and who have impressed them.[61] However, the link between performance and promotion is severed, thereby diminishing the effectiveness of promotion as a reward. Employers should establish formal, published promotion policies and procedures that describe the criteria by which promotions are awarded. Skills inventories, replacement charts, and replacement summaries (like those discussed in Chapter 4) can be used to compile detailed information about the qualifications of many employees. This ensures that (1) all qualified employees are considered for openings, and (2) promotion is more closely linked with performance in the minds of employees, which also increases the legal defensibility of the decision.

CHAPTER SUMMARY

1. A strategic approach to the recruitment and retention of employees includes a well-integrated orientation (onboarding) program both before and after hiring. New employees need a clear understanding of company policies, expectations regarding their performance, and operating procedures. Onboarding is part of the socialization process that instills in new employees the prevailing attitudes, standards, values, and patterns of behaviour that are expected by the organization. Onboarding helps to reduce reality shock—the discrepancy between what the new employee expected from his or her job and its realities.

2. The basic training process consists of five steps: needs analysis, instructional design, validation, implementation, and evaluation.

3. Two techniques for assessing training needs are (1) task analysis to determine the training needs of employees who are new to their jobs, and (2) performance analysis to appraise the performance of current employees to determine whether training could reduce performance problems.

4. Traditional training techniques include programmed learning (testing the subject on topic expertise and providing feedback on the results), informal learning (day-to-day unplanned interactions between colleagues), and workplace/traditional training techniques (formal on-the-job-training, apprenticeship training, job instruction training, and vestibule or simulated training).

5. Career planning and development is a critical strategic issue in ensuring that the supply of necessary talent is available. It involves the deliberate process through which a person becomes aware of personal career-related attributes, and the lifelong series of activities that contribute to his or her career fulfillment.

6. The evolution of career development involved identifying skills and aptitudes, and recognizing career anchors: technical/functional, managerial competence, creativity, autonomy, security, service/dedication, pure challenge, or lifestyle.

7. The focus on life trajectories involves reframing career development from traits and states to context, from prescriptive to process, from linear to non-linear, from scientific to narrative, and from descriptive to modelling. In this evolution, organizations can benefit from becoming learning organizations that use behaviour modelling, including role-playing, simulations, management games, and mentoring opportunities.

8. In evaluating the effectiveness of a training program, four categories of outcomes can be measured: reaction, learning, behaviour, and results.

9. Transfers offer an opportunity for personal and career development, but they have become more difficult to manage because of spousal and family concerns. Thus, career-transition programs for spouses are often provided. In making promotion decisions, firms have to (1) decide to promote based on seniority or competence, (2) decide how to measure competence, and (3) choose between a formal or informal promotion system.

MyLab Management

Visit MyLab Management to access a personalized Study Plan, Personal Inventory Assessments (PIA), and a collection of videos and assignments within MediaShare.

KEY TERMS

apprenticeship *(p. 140)*
auditory learning *(p. 136)*
career *(p. 144)*
career anchor *(p. 145)*
career development *(p. 144)*
career planning *(p. 144)*
controlled experimentation *(p. 143)*
employee onboarding (orientation) *(p. 130)*
job instruction training (JIT) *(p. 141)*
kinesthetic learning *(p. 136)*
learning organization *(p. 129)*
negligent training *(p. 137)*

networking *(p. 147)*
performance analysis *(p. 139)*
programmed learning *(p. 139)*
reality shock (cognitive dissonance) *(p. 131)*
socialization *(p. 130)*
task analysis *(p. 138)*
training *(p. 135)*
transfer of training *(p. 143)*
vestibule or simulated training *(p. 142)*
visual learning *(p. 136)*
video conferencing *(p. 142)*

REVIEW AND DISCUSSION QUESTIONS

1. Prepare an onboarding program checklist for your current or most recent job.

2. Choose a task you are familiar with—such as mowing the lawn or using a chat room—and develop a job instruction training sheet for it.

3. Ali Khan is an undergraduate business student majoring in accounting. He has just failed the first accounting course, Accounting 101, and is understandably upset. Explain how you would use performance analysis to identify what, if any, are Ali's training needs.

4. Think about a job you have had in the past. For this job, identify which training technique was used and reflect on reasons why you think that system was used. Next, select a different training technique from the chapter that you think would have been good to use, providing a justification as to why this would be a suitable technique.

5. Describe why career planning and development has become more strategically important. Give a brief outline of what organizations are doing to take a more strategic approach in this area.

6. What is a career anchor? Explain why you think each of the five career anchors is important today.

CRITICAL THINKING QUESTIONS

1. "A well-thought-out onboarding program is especially important for employees (like many recent graduates) who have had little or no work experience." Explain why you agree or disagree with this statement.

2. What do you think are some of the main drawbacks of relying on informal on-the-job training for teaching new employees their jobs?

3. Most training programs are not formally evaluated beyond a reaction measure. Why do you think employers do not measure the impact of training on learning, behaviour, and results more often?

4. Would you tell high-potential employees that they are on the "fast track"? How might this knowledge affect their behaviour? How might the behaviour of employees who are disappointed at not being included in management development activities be affected?

5. How do you think employees are going to respond to the new focus on career planning, given the emphasis in recent years on "being in charge of your own career"?

EXPERIENTIAL **EXERCISES**

1. Obtain a copy of an employee handbook from your employer or from some other organization. Review it, and make recommendations for improvement.

2. Working individually or in groups, follow the five-steps of the training and development process to prepare a training program for a job that one of you currently hold or have had in the past.

3. In small groups of four to six students, complete the following exercise:

   WestJet has asked you to quickly develop the outline of a training program for its new reservation clerks. Airline reservation clerks obviously need numerous skills to perform their jobs. (You may want to start by listing the job's main duties, using the information provided below.) Produce the requested training outline, making sure to be very specific about what you want to teach the new clerks and what methods and aids you suggest using to train them.

   Duties of Airline Reservation Clerks:

   Customers contact airline reservation clerks to obtain flight schedules, prices, and itineraries. The reservation clerks look up the requested information on the airline's flight schedule systems, which are updated continuously. The reservation clerk must deal courteously and expeditiously with the customer and be able to quickly find alternative flight arrangements to provide the customer with the itinerary that fits his or her needs. Alternative flights and prices must be found quickly so that the customer is not kept waiting and so that the reservation operations group maintains its efficiency standards. It is often necessary to look under various routings, since there may be a dozen or more alternative routes between the customer's starting point and destination.

4. Working in groups of four to six students, complete the following exercise:

   Determine who in your group knows how to make paper objects such as cranes, boxes, balloons, ninja darts, fortunes, boats, and so on. Select one person who is willing to be a subject matter expert (SME) to assist your group in developing an on-the-job training program to make one product.

   Using the expertise of your SME, develop, document, and validate a training plan to make the chosen product. Modify the documented plan as required after your pilot. Ensure that everyone in your group has a copy of the plan and can reliably make the product to standards. Once this is accomplished, each group member will pair up with a member of another group that made a different product. Each person in the resulting pairs will train his or her partner on how to make the products using the training plan and sample he or she created.

   Debrief the exercise as instructed.

5. Review the website of a provider of management development seminars, such as the Canadian Institute of Management. Obtain copies of recent listings of seminar offerings. At what levels of management are the seminar offerings aimed? What seem to be the most popular types of development programs? Why do you think that is the case?

6. Review all positions you have ever held. Below each position, identify core knowledge, skills, and abilities that you learned in each position. Next, identify a career you would like to be actively engaged in over the next three years. Under the future career, outline core knowledge, skills, and abilities the position would require. Now reflect on your own career trajectory to highlight your history of skill development, and identify any gaps that may exist for you to advance to your desired career in the future.

© Pressmaster/Shutterstock

7 PERFORMANCE MANAGEMENT

LEARNING OUTCOMES
AFTER STUDYING THIS CHAPTER, YOU SHOULD BE ABLE TO:

EXPLAIN the five steps in the performance management process.

DESCRIBE Seven performance appraisal methods and the pros and cons of each.

DISCUSS the major problems inhibiting effective performance appraisals.

DISCUSS 360-degree appraisal from multiple sources.

DESCRIBE the three types of appraisal interviews.

DISCUSS the future of performance management.

7.1 THE STRATEGIC IMPORTANCE OF PERFORMANCE MANAGEMENT

In any organization, achieving strategic objectives requires employee productivity above all else as organizations strive to create a high-performance culture while using a minimum number of employees. Thus, it has been suggested that better performance management represents a largely untapped opportunity to improve company profitability.[1]

Performance management is a process encompassing all activities related to improving employee performance, productivity, and effectiveness. It includes *goal setting, pay for performance, training and development, career management,* and *disciplinary action.* The performance management system must provide an integrated network of procedures across the organization that will influence all work behaviour.[2] This involves assessing employees against their individual objectives/goals, training and professional development, demonstrated competencies and behaviours, and contribution to organizational or team goals.[3] There are three major purposes of performance management: It aligns employee actions with strategic goals, it is a vehicle for culture change, and it provides input into other HR systems such as development and remuneration.[4]

In contrast, **performance appraisal** is a formal, relatively infrequent process in which an employee's performance is evaluated along a predetermined set of criteria that is quantified via a formal performance score.[5] Performance appraisals are used for a variety of decisions such as training recommendations, merit based pay increases, promotion, or termination decisions.

performance management The process encompassing all activities related to improving employee performance, productivity, and effectiveness.

performance appraisal A formal, relatively infrequent process in which an employee's performance is evaluated along a predetermined set of criteria that is quantified via a formal performance score.

7.2 THE PERFORMANCE MANAGEMENT PROCESS

Performance management is of considerable strategic importance to today's organizations because the most effective way for firms to differentiate themselves in a highly competitive, service-oriented, global marketplace is through the quality of their employees.[6] Similar to selection, the performance management process contains five steps, shown in **Figure 7.1**.[7]

FIGURE 7.1 Performance Management Process

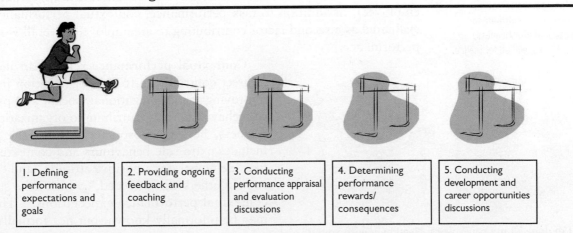

1. Defining performance expectations and goals
2. Providing ongoing feedback and coaching
3. Conducting performance appraisal and evaluation discussions
4. Determining performance rewards/consequences
5. Conducting development and career opportunities discussions

Performance appraisals in Canada are legal documents. While they should be used for planning promotions, career development, training, and performance improvement plans, they can also be required in courts when assessing wrongful termination cases. A recent survey by the Conference Board of Canada indicates that 96 percent of companies conduct performance management activities regularly, but many companies are still dealing with the reality that their performance management systems are ineffective.[8] For example, although they need to downsize poor performers, performance appraisal records indicate that all employees are performing adequately.

Robert Thorndike researched performance management processes and suggests that employment decisions (such as a performance appraisal system) must be valid, practical, reliable, and free from bias.[9] Failure to measure and use appraisal results effectively in human resource decision making and career development negates the primary purpose of performance evaluations. Effective performance management thus begins with defining the job and its performance standards, which will now be discussed.

7.2.1 Step 1: Defining Performance Expectations

Defining performance expectations and goals is a critical step in employees' understanding of how their work makes a contribution to achieving business results. Over the last 30 years, there has been more recognition that job performance is a multidimensional construct that can be split into what has become widely acknowledged as *task* versus *contextual* performance.[10]

7.2.1.1 Task Performance

task performance An individual's direct contribution to his or her job-related processes.

Task performance reflects an individual's direct contribution to his or her job-related processes. Focusing on tasks means that performance expectations are grounded in realistic job demands and align with the organization's strategic objectives and implementation plans. They may also be partially based on previous performance evaluations.

7.2.1.2 Contextual Performance

contextual performance An individual's indirect contribution to the organization in terms of improving the organizational, social, and psychological behaviours that contribute to organizational effectiveness, beyond those specified for the job.

However, as part of the movement towards more corporate social responsibility, expectations are beginning to extend beyond job skills and skills required for promotion to addressing the concept of whole person development (aligned with the direction, attitudes, motivation, and advancement opportunities of the employee). In addition to task performance, contextual performance is often evaluated as a second factor contributing to an employee's overall work-related performance.

Contextual performance reflects an individual's indirect contribution to the organization in terms of improving the organizational, social, and psychological behaviours that contribute to organizational effectiveness, beyond those specified for the job. This includes extra-role behaviours and contextual factors like "demonstrates a positive attitude" and "pitches in to help others when needed," which have surfaced as contextual performance expectations.[11] These goals may be informally known, but not formally defined, which can become problematic in performance

"I'm done all my paper work. Need help with yours?"

management. For the legitimacy of the performance management system to be maintained, employees also need to be aware of which behaviours are expected and which are discretionary.

Ultimately, the performance management process cannot be separated from performance measurement. Performance expectations need to be developed in a way that means that they are legally defensible (meaning that they are correlated with job activities), clear, and measurable. In addition, they must be communicated and supported as such by the organization. Aligned with the sales associate example, a "personal selling" activity can be measured in terms of how many dollars of sales the associate is to generate personally. "Keeping customers away from executives" can be measured with a standard of no more than 10 customer complaints per year being the sales associate's target. In general, employees should always know ahead of time how and on what basis they will be appraised. It is important to note that expectations cannot discriminate directly or indirectly against anyone on protected grounds (gender, age, disability, and so on).

In global companies, performance appraisal criteria may need to be modified to be consistent with cultural norms and values. An interesting study found that some criteria are acceptable in many cultures, as discussed in the Global HRM box.

7.2.2 Step 2: Providing Ongoing Coaching and Feedback

Traditionally, performance appraisals were conducted annually, in formalized processes, but some businesses environments are more dynamic and need to engage in more frequent or timely assessments of employee performance. There is an ongoing evolution in performance management in Canadian companies, with over 50 percent of organizations making changes to their performance management systems in the last three years.

GLOBAL HRM

Performance Appraisal Criteria in China

In the West, where individuals have an inalienable right to choose their own lifestyles and moralities, performance criteria cannot be based on personal character, but instead need to focus on more objective criteria, such as job competence, abilities, and achievements. In China, however, the attitudes and moral character of a person are regarded as highly relevant to performance. Chinese culture tends to ascribe achievement more to effort (that is, diligence, which reflects one's morality) than to ability (which, conceived as an inborn trait, requires no moral effort). These deeply rooted Confucian values in China thus lead to an emphasis on appraisals that are based upon personal attitudes and moral characteristics that appear to reflect traditional Chinese values, such as hard work, and loyalty and respect toward senior staff. Some specific examples are accepting overtime work; being punctual, careful, helpful, loyal, and respectful toward senior staff; and being persistent, adaptable, dedicated, and hard working.

Research found three performance appraisal factors that were very acceptable to Chinese employees: work dedication, work efficiency, and teamwork. Work dedication behaviours, such as punctuality, loyalty, working hard, and dedication toward one's work, exist in both Eastern and Western cultures. Employee efficiency has long been considered important to good job performance, as it is considered to be a means to achieve organizational goals. Chinese employees appear to recognize this managerial objective since they were willing to be evaluated on criteria that assess the efficiency of their work. Teamwork is a behavioural manifestation of the group orientation in Eastern cultures.

Source: R.J. Taormina and J.H. Gao, "Identifying Acceptable Performance Appraisal Criteria: An International Perspective," *Asia Pacific Journal of Human Resources*, 47, no. 1 (2009), pp. 102–125. Copyright © 2009, Australian Human Resources Institute.

The performance management changes that are taking place include an increased focus on coaching and provision of ongoing feedback, more recognition of individual development and performance while also recognizing team performance, and a decreased focus on ratings and ranking. A few of the companies surveyed indicated that updated performance management systems delinked performance from pay.[12]

In 2015, Deloitte realized that their once-a-year performance management process for the over 65 000 employees in the company was consuming over 2 million hours a year. They found that the once-a-year goals and year-end ratings were less valuable than more frequent, real-time conversations about actual performance.[13] By 2015, Accenture, PWC, and KPMG made announcements axing annual performance reviews in favour of employee development coaching strategies.[14] In this process, managers are increasingly asked to assume the role of a coach or mentor.

coaching A process for improving work performance, in a frequent-contact, hands-on process aimed at helping employees improve performance and capabilities.

Coaching is defined as a process for improving work performance, in a frequent-contact, hands-on process aimed at helping employees improve performance and capabilities.[15] It requires the manager to give guidance, encouragement, and support to an employee, and the employee to assume the role of a learner. A focus on developing people requires more frequent and informative conversations and coaching by managers, rather than annual reviews. Effective managerial coaching requires thinking, informing, empowering, assessing, advising, being professional, caring, developing others, and challenging employees for continuous improvement.[16] Some managers might not have the skills to effectively coach or struggle with the role of a manager as a coach.

Throughout the performance management process, managers and their reports should continue to address progress. It is important to have open two-way communication, and both the employee and the manager need to check in frequently throughout the performance management process to talk about progression towards goals.

It is critical to note that informal performance management, or coaching, requires a culture that supports continuous feedback in different dimensions. As organizations attempt to move away from annual performance reviews, employment law experts correctly identify the development and assessment of employees against standardized practices and objective criteria as necessary elements in the legal defence of employment-related decisions. There is also the challenge to modify goals as a project unfolds, and some employees do not value this level of ambiguity. In addition, without appraisals, managers do not have a relatively objective way to reward performance, which can lead to subjective or biased decision making. Lastly, without documentation, HR and managers have difficulty identifying and dealing with poor performers,[17] as highlighted in the Expert Opinion box.

7.2.3 Step 3: Performance Appraisal and Evaluation Discussion

The appraisal itself is generally conducted with the aid of a predetermined and formal method, like one or more of those described in this section.

7.2.3.1 Formal Appraisal Methods

graphic rating scale A scale that lists a number of traits and a range of performance for each. The employee is then rated by a score that best describes his or her level of performance for each trait.

Graphic Rating Scale The **graphic rating scale** is the simplest and most popular technique for appraising performance. It lists traits (such as reliability) and a range of performance values (from unsatisfactory to outstanding) for each one. The supervisor rates each employee by circling or checking the score that best describes his or her performance for each trait. The assigned values are then totalled.

Instead of appraising generic traits or factors, many firms specify the duties to be appraised. For a payroll coordinator, these might include being the liaison with accounting and benefits staff; continually updating knowledge regarding

Academic Viewpoint
EXPERT OPINION

1. What are some of the significant challenges when managing people globally that HR managers should be aware of?

The key challenges have changed over the years. Currently, availability of talent is critical. Companies are reporting that it is difficult to recruit people to undertake assignments. Also, the demographics of those who do go abroad are changing. We now see more women, younger people, and people without families who are more willing and interested in international mobility.

What hasn't changed is that families that accompany expatriates are still struggling to adjust to foreign locations. It becomes a catch-22 situation, given that it's hard for employees to adjust without their families (they are a great source of social support), but family adjustment can also be a source of concern or stress for the employee when family members themselves struggle to adjust. On that note, the traditional pattern of international employee mobility was focused around three-to-five-year assignments. Now, multiple alternatives such as short-term assignments or commuter assignments (Monday–Friday) are being introduced, partly with the intent of enabling employees to overcome personal or family challenges that come along with global mobility.

2. What performance management challenges are

Dr. Mila Lazarova

Identification:
Dr. Mila Lazarova (PhD)
Canada Research Chair in Global Workforce Management

Affiliation:
Beedie School of Business, Simon Fraser University

---

associated with international assignments?

This is highly dependent on the role. Higher-level employees usually report to head office, but mid-level employees might have a lack of clarity regarding what performance criteria apply to them (home or host country). In terms of higher-level expatriates evaluated by headquarters, research shows that local or context-dependent issues might not be considered fully in their performance review. For example, communication style or perceptions of leadership can all be culturally or regionally dependent, or their jobs may involve unique challenges such as delay in decision-making

due to the need to consult with local constituents such as unions that may not be well understood by their superiors. The criteria and perceptions regarding performance evaluation may vary based on who is conducting the performance evaluation.

Research identifies that in the slight majority of situations, a local or subsidiary company representative is engaged in performance evaluations of those on international assignment, and in a smaller fraction of the cases, the head office manager alone conducts the evaluation.

3. Are there options for employees who are unable to work abroad, but want global experience?

Generally, given that many of us work in a global environment, an employee would want to have some access to global experience. However, one can get such experience without changing offices. Rather than physical mobility, employees can gain some global experience through working on teams that are global or highly diverse, or through interacting with global customers or suppliers. Even if the employee cannot travel abroad, some exposure to international human resource management can be highly beneficial. This is very much the case in Canada, where we have a large immigrant population and working across cultural borders is quite common.

Source: Reprinted by permission from Dr. Mila Lazarova.

relevant legislation; maintaining payroll records, data entry, and payroll calculations; and providing ongoing responses to employee inquiries regarding payroll issues.

Alternation Ranking Method

alternation ranking method   Ranking employees from best to worst on a particular trait.

Ranking employees from best to worst on a trait or traits is another method for evaluating employees. Because it is usually easier to distinguish between the worst and best employees than to rank them, an **alternation ranking method** is popular. First, list all employees to be rated, and then cross out the names of any not known well enough to be ranked. Next, indicate the employee who is the highest on the characteristic being measured and also the one who is the lowest. Then choose the next highest and the next lowest, alternating between highest and lowest until all the employees to be rated have been ranked.

Paired Comparison Method

paired comparison method   Ranking employees by making a chart of all possible pairs of employees for each trait and indicating the better employee of the pair.

The **paired comparison method** helps to make the ranking method more precise. For every trait (quantity of work, quality of work, and so on), every employee is paired with and compared with every other employee.

Suppose that five employees are to be rated. In the paired comparison method, a chart is prepared, as in **Figure 7.2**, of all possible pairs of employees for each trait. Then, for each trait, indicate (with a + or –) who is the better employee of the pair. Next, the number of times that an employee is rated as better is added up. In **Figure 7.2**, employee Maria was ranked highest (she has the most + marks) for quality of work, while Art was ranked highest for creativity.

Forced Distribution Method

forced distribution method   Predetermined percentages of ratees are placed in various performance categories.

Jack Welch, retired chief executive officer of General Electric (GE), is most often associated with the **forced distribution method**, which places predetermined percentages of ratees in performance categories. At GE, the bell curve is used to identify the top 10 to 20 percent of the workforce

FIGURE 7.2   Ranking Employees by the Paired Comparison Method

FOR THE TRAIT "QUALITY OF WORK"

Employee Rated:

As Compared with:	A Art	B Maria	C Chuck	D Diane	E José
A Art		+	+	–	–
B Maria	–		–	–	–
C Chuck	–	+		+	–
D Diane	+	+	–		+
E José	+	+	+	–	

↑ Maria Ranks Highest Here

FOR THE TRAIT "CREATIVITY"

Employee Rated:

As Compared with:	A Art	B Maria	C Chuck	D Diane	E José
A Art		–	–	–	–
B Maria	+		–	+	+
C Chuck	+	+		–	+
D Diane	+	–	+		–
E José	+	–	–	+	

↑ Art Ranks Highest Here

Note: "+" means "better than" and "–" means "worse than." For each chart, add up the number of + signs in each column to get the highest-ranked employee.

(which are then identified as those exceeding expectations, with a focus on receiving the highest compensation increases and advancement opportunities) and the bottom 10 percent (which are identified as those not meeting expectations, with a focus on coaching for improvement or possible termination). The remaining employees, by default, are considered the backbone of the workforce and receive moderate compensation increases and development opportunities.

In 2012, 3 percent of organizations polled by the Conference Board of Canada used forced distribution, while 44 percent of organizations did not use it explicitly, but had guidelines to force a normal distribution of performance evaluations.[18] While the method allows a concentration of effort and resources on those deemed to be top performers, forced distribution has been criticized as being demotivating, since the majority of the workforce are classified as at or below average.[19] In recent years, companies like Juniper and Adobe have eliminated rating or forced ranking of employees as part of their performance appraisal system.[20]

Critical Incident Method With the **critical incident method**, the supervisor keeps a log of desirable or undesirable examples or incidents of each employee's work-related behaviour. Then, every six months or so, the supervisor and employee meet to discuss the latter's performance by using the specific incidents as examples.

This method has several advantages. It provides specific hard facts for explaining the appraisal. It also ensures that a manager thinks about the employee's appraisal throughout the year, because the incidents must be accumulated; therefore, the rating does not just reflect the employee's most recent performance. Keeping a running list of critical incidents should also provide concrete examples of what an employee can do to eliminate any performance deficiencies.

The critical incident method is often used to supplement another appraisal technique, such as a ranking system. It is useful for identifying specific examples of good and poor performance and for planning how deficiencies can be corrected. On its own, however, this method is not as useful for comparing employees, and therefore cannot contribute to decision-making regarding compensation.

Behaviourally Anchored Rating Scales A **behaviourally anchored rating scale (BARS)** combines the benefits of narratives, critical incidents, and quantified ratings by anchoring a series of quantified scales, one for each performance dimension, with specific behavioural examples of good or poor performance. The guiding principle to BARS is that by elaborating on the dimension and rating scale, it gives raters a uniform interpretation as to the types of behaviour being measured.[21] BARS usually involves a scale of nine anchors, although seven and five anchors have also been used.[22]

The midpoint scales are more difficult to develop in a standardized format than the scale extremes. Recent efforts have focused on addressing midpoint scale development to influence inter-rater reliability and inter-rater agreement.[23] The research suggests that, to increase uniform use of the scale, all levels of the scale be anchored with statements reflecting how users are to interpret them. As well, developers of the scales should be involved in the training of users to increase the consistency in how the scale is used, thus increasing the effectiveness and legal defensibility of the performance appraisal. **Figure 7.3** provides an example of a BARS for one performance dimension: "sales skills."

critical incident method   Keeping a record of uncommonly good or undesirable examples of an employee's work-related behaviour and reviewing the list with the employee at predetermined times.

behaviourally anchored rating scale (BARS)   An appraisal method that aims to combine the benefits of narratives, critical incidents, and quantified ratings by anchoring a quantified scale with specific narrative examples of good and poor performance.

FIGURE 7.3   Behaviourally Anchored Rating Scale

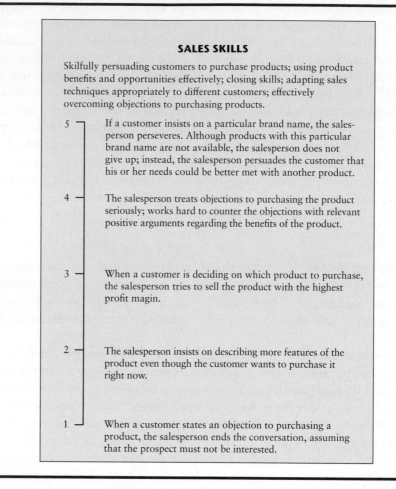

SALES SKILLS

Skilfully persuading customers to purchase products; using product benefits and opportunities effectively; closing skills; adapting sales techniques appropriately to different customers; effectively overcoming objections to purchasing products.

5 — If a customer insists on a particular brand name, the salesperson perseveres. Although products with this particular brand name are not available, the salesperson does not give up; instead, the salesperson persuades the customer that his or her needs could be better met with another product.

4 — The salesperson treats objections to purchasing the product seriously; works hard to counter the objections with relevant positive arguments regarding the benefits of the product.

3 — When a customer is deciding on which product to purchase, the salesperson tries to sell the product with the highest profit magin.

2 — The salesperson insists on describing more features of the product even though the customer wants to purchase it right now.

1 — When a customer states an objection to purchasing a product, the salesperson ends the conversation, assuming that the prospect must not be interested.

Developing a BARS can be more time-consuming than developing other appraisal tools, such as graphic rating scales. But BARS may also have important advantages:[24]

1. *A more accurate measure.* People who know the job and its requirements better than anyone else does develop BARS. The result should therefore be a good measure of performance on that job.

2. *Clearer standards.* The critical incidents along the scale help to clarify what is meant by extremely good performance, average performance, and so forth.

3. *Feedback.* The critical incidents may be more useful in providing feedback to appraisees than simply informing them of their performance rating without providing specific behavioural examples.

4. *Independent dimensions.* Systematically clustering the critical incidents into five or six performance dimensions (such as "knowledge and judgment") should help to make the dimensions more independent of one another. For example, a rater should be less likely to rate an employee high on all dimensions simply because he or she was rated high on "conscientiousness."

5. *Consistency.* BARS evaluations also seem to be relatively consistent and reliable in that different raters' appraisals of the same person tend to be similar.[25]

Management by Objectives (MBO) Stripped to its essentials, **management by objectives (MBO)** requires the manager and employee to jointly set specific measurable goals and periodically discuss progress towards these goals, aligned with a comprehensive, *organization-wide goal-setting and appraisal program*. When managers and employees set goals collaboratively, employees become more engaged and committed to the goal, leading to a higher rate of success.[26] While there is a notion that difficult goals (also referred to as "stretch goals") can increase personal growth and professional development, and improve organizational effectiveness,[27] it is important to set objectives that match the job description and the person's abilities. Goals that push an employee too far beyond his or her abilities may lead to burnout.[28] To motivate performance, the objectives must be fair and attainable.

management by objectives (MBO) Involves setting specific measurable goals with each employee and then periodically reviewing the progress made.

1. *Set the organization's goals.* Establish an organization-wide plan for the next year and set goals.
2. *Set departmental goals.* Department heads and their superiors jointly set goals for their departments.
3. *Discuss departmental goals.* Department heads discuss the department's goals with all employees in the department (often at a department-wide meeting) and ask them to develop their own individual goals; in other words, how can each employee contribute to the department's attainment of its goals?
4. *Define expected results (set individual goals).* Here, department heads and employees set short-term performance targets.
5. *Performance reviews: Measure the results.* Department heads compare the actual performance of each employee with the expected results.
6. *Provide feedback.* Department heads hold periodic performance review meetings with employees to discuss and evaluate progress in achieving expected results.

Problems to Avoid Using MBO has three potential problems. *Setting unclear, unmeasurable objectives* is the main one. Such an objective as "will do a better job of training" is useless. Conversely, "will have four employees promoted during the year" is a measurable objective. Second, MBO is *time-consuming*. Taking the time to set objectives, measure progress, and provide feedback can take several hours per employee per year, over and above the time already spent doing each person's appraisal. Third, setting objectives with an employee sometimes turns into a *tug-of-war*; managers push for higher goals and employees push for lower ones. It is thus important to know the job and the person's ability.

7.2.3.2 Mixing the Methods

Most firms combine several appraisal techniques. The quantifiable ranking method permits comparisons of employees and is therefore useful for making salary, transfer, and promotion decisions. The critical incidents provide specific examples of performance relative to expectations and can be used to develop the high and low anchors for the BARS technique.[29] Ultimately, no single solution is best for all performance management systems. Instead, resource constraints (time, money, people) and organizational factors (budget, turnover, strategy) will help determine which of the options is best for each organization.

7.2.4 Step 4: Determine Performance Rewards/ Consequences

Some time after the performance review has taken place, the manager should use the salary planning guidelines to determine the appropriate rewards or consequences, comparing actual performance against the defined levels. Performance rewards are given through merit pay or extra payment such as a cash bonus. The two most important aspects used to determine the appropriate reward/consequence are achievement of goals and how the employee meets the defined standards. Further detail on compensation and rewards is provided in Chapter 8.

7.2.5 Step 5: Career Development Discussion

Ultimately, the main objective of performance appraisals is to improve employee performance, keeping performance expectations clear and targeted on activities that build value for the organization. In dealing with employee performance issues, legal experts suggest that management follow seven steps to ensure that performance appraisals have the desired effect and are legally defensible:

1. Let the employee know that his or her performance is unacceptable, and explain your minimum expectations.
2. Ensure that your expectations are reasonable.
3. Let employees know that warnings play a significant role in the process of establishing just cause; employees must be warned and told that discharge will result if they continue to fail to meet minimum standards.
4. Ensure that you take prompt corrective measures when required; failure to do so could lead to a finding that you condoned your employee's conduct.
5. Avoid sending mixed messages, such as a warning letter together with a "satisfactory" performance review.
6. Provide the employee with a reasonable amount of time to improve performance.
7. Be prepared to provide your employees with the necessary support to facilitate improvement.[30]

formal appraisal discussion An interview in which the supervisor and employee review the appraisal and make plans to remedy deficiencies and reinforce strengths.

The essence of a performance appraisal is the feedback provided in a one-on-one conversation called the **formal appraisal discussion**. This is an interview in which the supervisor and employee review the appraisal and make plans to remedy deficiencies and reinforce strengths. Unfortunately, surveys show that fewer than half of companies describe their performance appraisal systems as effective or very effective; the reason for this is weak execution due to managers abdicating their responsibility for screening out poor performers.[31] This discussion is often avoided by supervisors and managers who have not been trained to provide constructive feedback and to deal with defensive employees. Ultimately, feedback should be ongoing, making the formal appraisal discussion one of many performance discussions.

7.2.5.1 Types of Performance Appraisal Results

There are three basic types of formal appraisal discussions, each with its own objectives:[32]

Satisfactory—Promotable Here, the person's performance is satisfactory and there is a promotion ahead. This is the easiest of the three formal appraisal discussions. The objective is to discuss the person's career plans and to develop a specific action plan for the educational and professional development that the person needs to move to the next job.

Satisfactory—Not Promotable This interview is for employees whose performance is satisfactory but for whom promotion is not possible. Perhaps there is no more room in the company; some employees are happy where they are and do not want a promotion.[33] The objective here is not to improve or develop the person but to maintain satisfactory performance.

This situation is not easy. The best option is usually to find incentives that are important to the person and are enough to maintain satisfactory performance. These might include extra time off, a small bonus, additional authority to handle a slightly enlarged job, and verbal reinforcement in the form of "Well done!"

Unsatisfactory—Correctable vs. Uncorrectable When the person's performance is unsatisfactory but correctable, the interview objective is to lay out an *action plan* (such as a performance improvement plan [PIP]) for correcting the unsatisfactory performance. A PIP highlights in writing the expectations of the employer and employee, complete with the timeline (often 30 to 90 days) required to bring performance to acceptable levels. It lists objectives, in clear and actionable terms that are considered to be reasonable, aimed at improving performance, complete with a date of follow-up and the names of parties who engaged in the conversation.

When behaviour is unsatisfactory and uncorrectable a formal written warning is required. Such written warnings serve two purposes: (1) They may serve to shake the employee out of his or her bad habits, and (2) they can help the manager defend his or her rating of the employee, both to his or her boss and (if needed) to a court or human rights commission.

7.2.5.2 Preparing for the Formal Appraisal Discussion

An important component of the performance management process is the effective use of feedback. This often happens in a formal appraisal discussion after the performance has been evaluated. There are three things to do in preparation for the interview.[34] First, assemble the data. Study the person's job description, compare the employee's performance to the standards, and review the files of the employee's previous appraisals. Next, prepare the employee. Give the employee at least a week's notice to review his or her own work, read over his or her job description, analyze problems he or she may be dealing with, and gather questions and comments for the interview. Finally, find a mutually agreeable time and place and allow plenty of time for the interview. Interviews with non-supervisory staff should take no more than an hour. Appraising management employees often takes two or three hours. Be sure that the interview is conducted in a private place where there will be no interruptions. It is important to keep in mind what is said and how it is said. The Strategic HR box provides an example of how management teams in a global company were guided on managing the formal appraisal discussion.

STRATEGIC   HR

Jaguar Land Rover Formal Appraisal Discussion Training

In 2008, an Indian conglomerate (Tata) took over the Jaguar Land Rover carmaker. This triggered a new set of management behaviours, including the redesign of the performance management process. Management was coached on techniques for managing behaviour during the formal appraisal discussion, including the following suggestions:

- Verbally acknowledge your observations—providing verbal feedback based on observations allows the individual receiving feedback to reflect on cause and effect

- Be empathetic—demonstrating sincere concern and the ability to put yourself in the other's position

- Listen actively—accurately and clearly listen to the comments being made, and reflect on the main content of the issues

- Questioning—elicit information using a variety of probing questions (open ended and closed ended)

- Communicate nonverbally—demonstrate body language that suggests and elicits open and honest information sharing

- Speak rationally, clearly, and calmly—consider the conversation a mutual exchange of information, perspectives, and challenges without being irrationally or emotionally overwhelmed or skewed

The training program is viewed as a success by management and participants alike. Jaguar Land Rover believes that managers are now equipped with the skills to implement the performance management system successfully.

Source: Based on J. Hicks, "Jaguar Land Rover Bosses Get to Grips with Performance Management: Program Teaches Practical Skills for the Workplace," *Human Resource Management International Digest* (2011), volume 19, issue 4, pp. 10–12.

7.3 PERFORMANCE APPRAISAL PROBLEMS AND SOLUTIONS

Few of the things a manager does are fraught with more peril than appraising employees' performance. Employees in general tend to be overly optimistic about what their ratings will be, and they also know that their raises, career progress, and peace of mind may well hinge on how they are rated. Thus, an honest appraisal inevitably involves an emotional component, which is particularly difficult when managers are not trained on formal appraisal discussion skills. The result is often dishonest appraisals or the avoidance of appraisals.[35]

Even more problematic, however, are the numerous structural problems that can cast serious doubt on just how fair the whole process is. Fortunately, research shows that action by management to implement a more acceptable performance appraisal system can increase employee trust in management.[36] According to several studies, the majority of organizations view their performance management systems as ineffective. What is required, instead of new techniques and methods, is more focus on the execution of performance appraisal.[37] Some of the main appraisal problems and how to solve them, as well as several other pertinent appraisal issues, will now be reviewed.

7.3.1 Validity and Reliability

Appraisal systems must be based on performance criteria that are valid for the position being rated and must be reliable, in that their application must produce consistent ratings for the same performance. Employee concerns about appraisal fairness are influenced by these characteristics of the performance appraisal system.

Criteria used in performance appraisal must be accurate, or valid, to produce useful results. Criteria must be (1) relevant to the job being appraised, (2) broad enough to cover all aspects of the job requirements, and (3) specific. For example, including a broad criterion, such as "leadership," may not be relevant to non-management jobs and may be so vague that it can be interpreted in many different ways.

Effective appraisal criteria are precise enough to result in consistent measures of performance when applied across many employees by many different raters. This is difficult to achieve without quantifiable and measurable criteria.

Day of the Zombie Performance Reviews

© Cartoonresource/Fotolia

7.3.1.1 Rating Scale Problems

Seven main problems can undermine such appraisal tools as graphic rating scales: unclear standards, the halo effect, central tendency, leniency or strictness, appraisal bias, the recency effect, and the similar-to-me bias.

Unclear Performance Standards   The problem of **unclear performance standards** is illustrated in **Table 7.1**. Although the graphic rating scale seems objective, it would probably result in unfair appraisals because the traits and degrees of merit are open to interpretation. For example, different supervisors would probably differently define "good" performance, "fair" performance, and so on. The same is true of traits, such as "quality of work" or "creativity." There are several ways in which to rectify this problem. The best way is to develop and include descriptive phrases that define each trait. For example, the form provided in **Table 7.1** fails to specify what was meant by "outstanding," "very good," and "good" quality of work. More specificity or definitions differentiating the categories will result in appraisals that are more consistent and more easily explained.

unclear performance standards   An appraisal scale that is too open to interpretation of traits and standards.

Halo Effect   The **halo effect** means that the rating of an employee on one trait (such as "gets along with others") biases the way that person is rated on other traits (such as "reliability"). This problem often occurs with employees who are especially friendly (or unfriendly) towards the supervisor. For example, an unfriendly employee will often be rated unsatisfactory for all traits rather than just for the trait "gets along well with others." Being aware of this problem is a major step towards avoiding it. Supervisory training can also alleviate the problem.[38]

halo effect   In performance appraisal, the problem that occurs when a supervisor's rating of an employee on one trait biases the rating of that person on other traits.

Central Tendency   Many supervisors have a **central tendency** when filling in rating scales. For example, if the rating scale ranges from one to seven, they tend to avoid the highs (six and seven) and lows (one and two) and rate most of their

central tendency   A tendency to rate all employees in the middle of the scale.

TABLE 7.1   A Graphic Rating Scale with Unclear Standards

	Excellent	Good	Fair	Poor
Quality of work				
Quantity of work				
Creativity				
Integrity				

Note: For example, what exactly is meant by "good," "quantity of work," and so forth?

© Bowie15/Stock Photo/123RF

With the halo effect, an employee who is friendly towards his or her supervisor may be rated more favourably on other traits.

strictness/leniency   The problem that occurs when a supervisor has a tendency to rate all employees either low or high.

appraisal bias   The tendency to allow individual differences, such as age, race, and sex, to affect the appraisal ratings that these employees receive.

Canadian Human Rights Commission
www.chrc-ccdp.ca

recency effect   The rating error that occurs when ratings are based on the employee's most recent performance rather than on performance throughout the appraisal period.

similar-to-me bias   The tendency to give higher performance ratings to employees who are perceived to be similar to the rater in some way.

employees between three and five. If a graphic rating scale is used, this central tendency could mean that all employees are simply rated "average." Such a restriction can distort the evaluations, making them less useful for promotion, salary, or counselling purposes. Ranking employees instead of using a graphic rating scale can avoid this central tendency problem, because all employees must be ranked and thus cannot all be rated average.

Strictness/Leniency   Some supervisors tend to rate all of their employees consistently high (or low), just as some instructors are notoriously high graders and others are not. Fear of interpersonal conflict is often the reason for leniency.[39] Conversely, evaluators tend to give more weight to negative attributes than to positive ones.[40] This **strictness/leniency** problem is especially serious with graphic rating scales, since supervisors are not necessarily required to avoid giving all of their employees low (or high) ratings. However, when ranking employees, a manager is forced to distinguish between high and low performers. Thus, strictness/leniency is not a problem with the ranking or forced distribution approaches.

Appraisal Bias   Individual differences among ratees in terms of a wide variety of characteristics, such as age, race, and sex, can affect their ratings, often quite apart from their actual performance.[41] In fact, research shows that less than half of performance evaluation ratings are actually related to employee performance and that most of the rating is based on idiosyncratic factors.[42] This is known as **appraisal bias**. Not only does this bias result in inaccurate feedback, but it is also illegal under human rights legislation. Although age-related bias is typically thought of as affecting older workers, one study found a negative relationship between age and performance evaluation for entry-level jobs in public accounting firms.[43] A related issue is described in the Workforce Diversity box.

Interestingly, the friendliness and likeability of an employee have been found to have little effect on that person's performance ratings.[44] However, an employee's previous performance can affect the evaluation of his or her current performance.[45] The actual error can take several forms. Sometimes the rater may systematically overestimate improvement by a poor worker or decline by a good worker, for instance. In some situations—especially when the change in behaviour is more gradual—the rater may simply be insensitive to improvement or decline. In any case, it is important to rate performance objectively. Such factors as previous performance, age, or race should not be allowed to influence results.

Recency Effect   The **recency effect** occurs when ratings are based on the employee's most recent performance, whether good or bad. To the extent that this recent performance does not exemplify the employee's average performance over the appraisal period, the appraisal is biased.

Similar-to-Me Bias   If a supervisor tends to give higher ratings to employees with whom he or she has something in common, the **similar-to-me bias** is occurring. This bias can be discriminatory if it is based on similarity in race, gender, or other prohibited grounds.

There are at least four ways in which managers can minimize the impact of appraisal problems, such as bias and central tendency. First, raters must be familiar with the problems just discussed. Understanding the problem can help to prevent it.

Second, training supervisors on how to eliminate rating errors, such as the halo effect, leniency, and central tendency, can help them avoid these problems.[46] In a typical training program, raters are shown videos of jobs being performed and are asked to rate the worker. Ratings made by each participant are then placed on a flip chart and the various errors (such as leniency and halo) are explained. For example, if a trainee rated all criteria (such as quality, quantity, and so on) about the same, the trainer might explain that a halo error had occurred. Typically, the trainer gives the correct rating and then illustrates the rating errors made by the participants.[47] According to one study, computer-assisted appraisal training improved managers' ability to conduct performance appraisal discussions with their employees.[48]

Rater training will not eliminate all rating errors or ensure absolute accuracy. In practice, several factors—including the extent to which pay is tied to performance ratings, union pressure, employee turnover, time constraints, and the need to justify ratings—may be more important than training. This means that improving appraisal accuracy calls not only for training but also for reducing outside factors, such as union pressure and time constraints.[49] It has also been found that employee reaction to current performance reviews is affected by past appraisal feedback, which is beyond the control of the current manager.[50]

Third, raters must choose the right appraisal tool. Each tool, such as the graphic rating scale or critical incident method, has its own advantages and disadvantages. For example, the ranking method avoids central tendency but can cause ill feelings when employees' performances are, in fact, all "high" (see **Table 7.2**).

TABLE 7.2   Important Advantages and Disadvantages of Appraisal Tools

	Advantages	Disadvantages
Graphic rating scale	Simple to use; provides a quantitative rating for each employee.	Standards may be unclear; halo effect, central tendency, leniency, and bias can also be problems.
Alternation ranking	Simple to use (but not as simple as graphic rating scale); avoids central tendency and other problems of rating scales.	Can cause disagreements among employees and may be unfair if all employees are, in fact, excellent.
Paired comparison method	A more precise ranking method that involves multiple traits.	Difficult to use as employee numbers increase; differences may not be noticeable enough to rank.
Forced distribution method	Ends up with a predetermined number of people in each group.	Appraisal results depend on the adequacy of the original choice of cutoff points.
Critical incident method	Helps specify what is "right" and "wrong" about the employee's performance; forces the supervisor to evaluate employees on an ongoing basis.	Difficult to rate or rank employees relative to one another; cannot be used to defend salary decisions.
Narrative form	Explicitly states improvement goals and associated outcomes or consequences.	Employees may take these too personally.
Behaviourally anchored rating scale (BARS)	Provides behavioural "anchors"; very accurate; high inter-rater reliability.	Difficult to develop.
Management by objectives	Tied to jointly agreed-upon performance objectives.	Risk of unclear performance measures, time-consuming, and inflated/deflated goals due to tug-of-war.

This food service supervisor is conducting a feedback session about an employee's performance during a major banquet to keep communications open and build employee commitment.

The fourth way to minimize the impact of errors in performance appraisals is to use multiple raters in the evaluation. Multiple raters increase the validity and accuracy of the rating by controlling for individual biases or idiosyncrasies. Also, responsibility for poor appraisals is diffused; therefore, raters are more comfortable giving a poor rating. When raters are accountable for their rating, reliability also increases.[51] As an additional benefit, multiple ratings may be more legally defensible.

7.3.1.2 The Use of Technology in Performance Appraisals

Over the past few years, web-based performance management has moved from being a leading-edge approach adopted by only large companies to a mainstream practice that is quickly becoming an industry standard among medium and small organizations.[52] It enables managers to keep computerized notes on employees, combine these with ratings on several performance traits, and then generate written text to support each part of the appraisal.

However, the true value in web-based performance management goes beyond simply automating time-consuming, tedious tasks like tracking down paper-based appraisal forms. It ultimately improves the overall performance management process, starting with higher completion rates, which can dramatically increase the value of performance management within organizations of all sizes. Performance management systems provide employees with a clear development path and a better understanding of how their goals are aligned with those of the organization, which in turn increases their support of the process. Managers have the information they need to ensure that development plans are relevant and executed. Executives have a clear picture of the organization's talent strategy and how it ties into the bottom line.

Most web-based performance management systems provide advanced reporting capabilities, which allow managers to track the status of performance management initiatives easily. Goal management functions enable organizations to link individual goals to strategic corporate goals, meaning that executives have insight into the progress being made on corporate objectives. Succession planning tools provide executives with a clear plan to build a talent pool to meet the organization's business needs and address potential attrition.

With the development of powerful, web-based tools, employee performance management has undergone a rapid evolution in a relatively short time. HR professionals are no longer mired in paperwork and other mundane administrative tasks. They have more time to focus on meeting strategic objectives, better tools to implement best practices programs, and access to critical workforce metrics they can share with their executive team.

electronic performance monitoring (EPM) Having supervisors electronically monitor the amount of computerized data an employee is processing per day and thereby his or her performance.

Electronic performance monitoring (EPM) is in some respects the ultimate in computerized appraising. Electronic performance monitoring means having supervisors electronically observe the employees' output or whereabouts. This typically involves using computer networks and wireless audio or video links to monitor and record employees' work activities. It includes, for instance, monitoring a data clerk's hourly keystrokes, tracking via GPS the whereabouts of delivery drivers, and monitoring the calls of customer service clerks.

7.4 WHO SHOULD DO THE APPRAISING?

Who should actually rate an employee's performance? Several options exist as to who can be involved in the performance management appraisal process.

7.4.1 Supervisors

Supervisors' ratings are still the heart of most appraisal systems. Getting a supervisor's appraisal is relatively easy and also makes a great deal of sense. The supervisor should be—and usually is—in the best position to observe and evaluate the performance of employees reporting to him or her and is responsible for their performance.

The best performance appraisal systems are those in which the supervisor or manager makes an ongoing effort to coach and monitor employees instead of leaving evaluation to the last minute.

7.4.2 Self

Employees' self-ratings of performance are sometimes used, generally in conjunction with supervisors' ratings. Employees value the opportunity to participate in performance appraisal, more for the opportunity to be heard than for the opportunity to influence the end result.[53] Nevertheless, the basic problem with self-ratings is that employees usually rate themselves higher than they are rated by supervisors or peers.[54] In one study, for example, it was found that when asked to rate their own job performance, 40 percent of the employees in jobs of all types placed themselves in the top 10 percent ("one of the best"), while virtually all remaining employees rated themselves either in the top 25 percent ("well above average") or at least in the top 50 percent ("above average"). Usually no more than 1 percent or 2 percent will place themselves in a below-average category, and then almost invariably in the top below-average category. However, self-ratings have been found to more accurately represent actual performance if employees know that this comparison will be made and if they are instructed to compare themselves with others.[55]

Supervisors requesting self-appraisals should know that their appraisals and their employees' self-appraisals may accentuate appraiser–appraisee differences, and rigidify positions.[56] Furthermore, even if self-appraisals are not formally requested, each employee will enter the performance review meeting with his or her own self-appraisal in mind, and this will usually be higher than the supervisor's rating.

7.4.3 Peers

The appraisal of an employee by his or her peers can be effective in predicting future management success. Peers may have more opportunity to observe ratees and to observe them at more revealing times than supervisors do. One potential problem is *logrolling*, where all the peers simply get together to rate each other highly.

Peers may have more opportunity than supervisors to observe ratees— and to observe them at more revealing times.

With more firms using self-managing teams, peer or team appraisals are becoming more popular. One study found that peer ratings had an immediate, positive impact on perceptions of open communication, motivation, group cohesion, and satisfaction, and these were not dependent on the ratio of positive to negative feedback.[57] Thus, peer appraisals would appear to have great potential for work teams.

7.4.4 Committees

Many employers use rating committees to evaluate employees. These committees usually comprise the employee's immediate supervisor and three or four other supervisors. Using multiple raters can be advantageous. Although there may be a discrepancy in the ratings made by individual supervisors, the composite ratings tend to be more reliable, fair, and valid.[58] Using several raters can help cancel out problems such as bias and the halo effect on the part of individual raters. Furthermore, when there are variations in raters' ratings, they usually stem from the fact that raters often observe different facets of an employee's performance and the appraisal ought to reflect these differences.[59] Even when a committee is not used, it is common to have the appraisal reviewed by the manager immediately above the one who makes the appraisal.

7.4.5 Subordinates

Traditionally, supervisors feared that being appraised by their employees would undermine their management authority. However, with today's flatter organizations and empowered workers, much managerial authority is a thing of the past, and employees are in a good position to observe managerial performance.[60] Thus, more firms today are letting employees anonymously evaluate their supervisors' performance, a process many call *upward feedback*.[61] When conducted throughout the firm, the process helps top managers diagnose management styles, identify potential "people" problems, and take corrective action with individual managers as required. Such employee ratings are especially valuable when used for developmental rather than evaluative purposes.[62] Managers receiving feedback from employees who identify themselves view the upward appraisal process more positively than do managers who receive anonymous feedback; however, employees (not surprisingly) are more comfortable giving anonymous responses, and those who have to identify themselves tend to provide inflated ratings.[63] Research comparing employee and peer ratings of managers found them to be comparable.[64]

Upward feedback from reporting employees is quite effective in terms of improving the supervisor's behaviour, according to the research evidence. One study examined data for 92 managers who were rated by one or more reporting employees in each of four administrations of an upward feedback survey over two and a half years. The reporting employees were asked to rate themselves and their managers in surveys that consisted of 33 behavioural statements. The feedback to the managers also contained results from previous administrations of the survey so that they could track their performance over time.

According to the researchers, managers whose initial performance level was lower than the average employee performance level improved performance by the next performance assessment and sustained this improvement two years later. Interestingly, the results also suggest that it is not necessarily the specific feedback that caused the performance improvement, because low-performing managers seemed to improve over time even if they did not receive any feedback. Instead, learning what the critical supervisory behaviours were (as a result of themselves filling out the appraisal surveys) and knowing that they might be appraised may have been enough to result in the improved supervisory behaviours. In a sense, therefore, it is the existence of the formal upward feedback program rather than the actual feedback itself that may signal and motivate supervisors to get their behaviours in line with what they should be.[65]

7.4.6 360-Degree Appraisal

Many Canadian firms are now using what is called **360-degree appraisal**, or "multisource feedback." Here, as shown in **Figure 7.4**, performance information is collected "all around" an employee—from his or her supervisors, subordinates, peers, and internal or external customers.[66] This feedback was originally used only for training and development purposes, but it has rapidly spread to the management of performance and pay.[67] The 360-degree approach supports the activities of performance feedback, coaching, leadership development, succession planning, and rewards and recognition.[68]

There are a number of reasons for the rapid growth of 360-degree appraisal, despite the significant investment of time required for it to function successfully. Today's flatter organizations employ a more open communicative climate conducive to such an approach, and 360-degree appraisal fits closely with the goals of organizations committed to continuous learning. A multiple-rater system is also more meaningful in today's reality of complex jobs, with matrix and team reporting relationships. A 360-degree appraisal can be perceived as a jury of peers, rather than the supervisor as a single judge, which enhances perceptions of fairness.[69]

Most 360-degree appraisal systems, including Internet-based 360-degree feedback systems, contain several common features. They are usually applied in a confidential and anonymous manner. Appropriate parties—peers, superiors, employees, and customers, for instance—complete survey questionnaires about

360-degree appraisal   A performance appraisal technique that uses multiple raters including peers, employees reporting to the appraisee, supervisors, and customers.

FIGURE 7.4   360-Degree Performance Appraisals

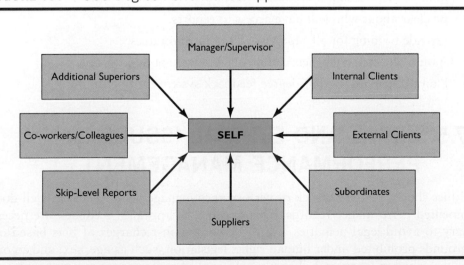

Source: Alma M. McCarthy, Thomas N. Garavan, "360° Feedback Process: Performance, Improvement and Employee Career Development," *Journal of European Industrial Training*, 25, no. 1 (2001), pp. 5–32.
© Emerald Group Publishing Limited. All rights reserved.

an individual. The questionnaires must be custom-designed and linked to the organization's strategic direction, vision, and values.[70] All this information is then compiled into individualized reports. When the information is being used for self-development purposes only, the report is presented to the person being rated, who then meets with his or her own supervisor; information pertinent for the purpose of developing a self-improvement plan is shared. When the information is being used for management of performance or pay, the information is also provided to the ratee's supervisor, and a supportive and facilitative process to follow up is required to ensure that the behavioural change required for performance improvement is made.[71]

There is a limited amount of research data on the effectiveness of 360-degree feedback. Some organizations have abandoned it for appraisal purposes because of inflated ratings and negative attitudes from employees.[72] Some studies have found that the different raters often disagree on performance ratings.[73] A recent study by researchers at Concordia University in Montreal found that 360-degree feedback is popular among Canadian employers, despite such problems as the amount of time and effort involved, lack of trust in the system by employees, and lack of fit with strategic goals and other HR practices. The results showed that organizations that successfully implemented 360-degree feedback were those that had the most clarity on what their initial objectives were. Organizations that rely exclusively on external consultants to establish 360-degree appraisal have less success than organizations that are more sensitive to contextual factors, such as the readiness of employees and the culture of the organization.[74]

An Ethical Dilemma

Is it fair to factor in employee self-ratings in 360-degree performance appraisal, when we know that these appraisals tend to be inflated?

Some experts suggest that 360-degree feedback be used for developmental purposes only.[75] In general, it is advisable to use 360-degree feedback for developmental/career-planning purposes initially, and then to determine whether the organization is ready to use it for evaluative appraisal purposes. A pilot test in one department is often recommended. Once a decision to use 360-degree appraisal has been made, organizations should consider the following advice:[76]

- Have the performance criteria developed by a representative group that is familiar with each job.
- Be clear about who will have access to reports.
- Provide training for all supervisors, raters, and ratees.
- Assure all raters that their comments will be kept anonymous.
- Plan to evaluate the 360-degree feedback system for fine-tuning.

7.5 LEGAL AND ETHICAL ISSUES IN PERFORMANCE MANAGEMENT

Ethics should be the bedrock of performance management. Accurate, well-documented performance records and performance appraisal feedback are necessary to avoid legal penalties and to defend against charges of bias based on grounds prohibited under human rights legislation, such as age, sex, and so on, as described in Chapter 2. The ultimate goal of performance management and reviews is that employees and employers alike should have a fair and similar understanding as to an employee's work effectiveness. This should be used to develop a realistic and focused plan for improvements that is honest and mutually understood.[77]

Guidelines for developing an effective appraisal process include the following:[78]

1. Conduct a job analysis to ascertain characteristics (such as "timely project completion") required for successful job performance. Use this information to create job performance standards.

2. Incorporate these characteristics into a rating instrument. (The professional literature recommends rating instruments that are tied to specific job behaviours, that is, BARS.)

3. Make sure that definitive performance standards are provided to all raters and ratees.

4. Use clearly defined individual dimensions of job performance (such as "quantity" or "quality") rather than undefined, global measures of job performance (such as "overall performance").

5. When using a graphic rating scale, avoid abstract trait names (such as "loyalty" or "honesty") unless they can be defined in terms of observable behaviours.

6. Employ subjective supervisory ratings (essays, for instance) as only one component of the overall appraisal process.

7. Train supervisors to use the rating instrument properly. Give instructions on how to apply performance appraisal standards ("outstanding," "satisfactory," and so on) when making judgments. Ensure that subjective standards are not subject to bias.

8. Allow appraisers regular contact with the employee being evaluated.

9. Whenever possible, have more than one appraiser conduct the appraisal, and conduct all such appraisals independently. This process can help to cancel out individual errors and biases.

10. Use formal appeal mechanisms and a review of ratings by upper-level managers.

11. Document evaluations and reasons for any termination decision.

12. Where appropriate, provide corrective guidance to assist poor performers in improving their performance.

Source: G. Barrett and M. Kernan. (1987). "Performance Appraisal and Terminations: A Review of Court Decisions Since Brito v. Zia with Implications for Personnel Practices," *Personnel Psychology*, 40, no. 3 (Autumn 1987), pp. 489–504. Used with permission.

7.6 THE FUTURE OF PERFORMANCE MANAGEMENT

Effective appraisals are the basis for successful performance management. Although performance appraisal is a difficult interpersonal task for managers, it cannot be eliminated.

Managers need some way to review employees' work-related behaviour, and no one has offered any concrete alternative. Despite the difficulties involved, performance management is still the basis for fostering and managing employee skills and talents, and it can be a key component of improved organizational effectiveness. Performance management techniques in high- and low-performing organizations are essentially the same, but managers in high-performing organizations tend to conduct and implement appraisals and manage performance on a daily basis more effectively.[79]

Recent research indicates that effective performance management involves

- linking individual goals and business strategy,
- showing leadership and accountability at all levels of the organization,
- ensuring close ties among appraisal results, rewards, and recognition outcomes,
- investing in employee development planning, and
- having an administratively efficient system with sufficient communication support.[80]

The key success factor for effective performance appraisal that will lead to optimum employee performance is the quality of the performance appraisal dialogue between a manager and an employee.[81] Managers need to engage in training on an ongoing basis to ensure that they are in a position to engage in high-quality formal appraisal discussions.

Overall, the solution is to create more effective appraisals, as described in this chapter. Effective appraisals are essential to managing the performance required of an organization's employees to achieve that organization's strategic objectives.

CHAPTER SUMMARY

1. The five steps in the performance management process are (1) defining performance expectations and goals, (2) providing ongoing coaching and feedback, (3) conducting performance appraisal and evaluation discussions, (4) determining performance rewards/consequences, and (5) conducting development and career opportunities discussions.

2. There are three types of formal appraisal results and associated discussions. When performance is unsatisfactory but correctable, the objective of the interview is to set out an action plan for correcting performance. For employees whose performance is satisfactory but for whom promotion is not possible, the objective of the interview is to maintain satisfactory performance. Finally, the satisfactory-and-promotable interview has the main objective of discussing the person's career plans and developing a specific action plan for the educational and professional development that the person needs to move on to the next job.

3. There are a number of performance appraisal methods. Graphic rating scales are simple to use

and facilitate comparison of employees, but the performance standards are often unclear, and bias can be a problem. Alternation ranking is a simple method that avoids central tendency, but it can be unfair if most employees are doing well. Paired comparison ensures that all employees are compared with each other, but it can also be unfair if most employees are performing similarly. Narrative forms provide concrete information to the employee but are time-consuming and can be subjective. The forced distribution method ensures differentiation of performance ratings but can be demotivating for employees classified as less than average. The critical incident method is very specific about the employee's strengths and weaknesses, and forces the supervisor to evaluate employees on an ongoing basis, but it makes it difficult to compare employees. BARS is very accurate, but is difficult and time-consuming to develop. MBO ties performance ratings to jointly agreed-upon performance objectives, but it is time-consuming to administer.

4. Appraisal problems to be aware of include unclear standards, the halo effect, central

tendency, leniency or strictness, appraisal bias, the recency effect, and the similar-to-me bias.

5. The use of 360-degree feedback has grown rapidly. Performance information is collected from the individual being appraised, his or her supervisor, other employees reporting to the person being appraised, and customers. This approach supports the activities of performance appraisal, coaching, leadership development, succession planning, and employee rewards and recognition.

6. Although appraisals can be a difficult interpersonal task for managers, they cannot be eliminated. There is no alternative method for assessing employee performance, which is essential for talent management and improved organizational effectiveness. The key success factor is the quality of the performance appraisal dialogue between managers and employees. More training on how to effectively conduct these discussions is required.

MyLab Management

Visit MyLab Management to access a personalized Study Plan, Personal Inventory Assessments (PIA), and a collection of videos and assignments within MediaShare.

KEY TERMS

360-degree appraisal *(p. 171)*
alternation ranking method *(p. 158)*
appraisal bias *(p. 166)*
behaviourally anchored rating scale (BARS) *(p. 159)*
central tendency *(p. 165)*
coaching *(p. 156)*
contextual performance *(p. 154)*
critical incident method *(p. 159)*
electronic performance monitoring (EPM) *(p. 168)*
forced distribution method *(p. 158)*
formal appraisal discussion *(p. 162)*

graphic rating scale *(p. 156)*
halo effect *(p. 165)*
management by objectives (MBO) *(p. 161)*
paired comparison method *(p. 158)*
performance appraisal *(p. 153)*
performance management *(p. 153)*
recency effect *(p. 166)*
similar-to-me bias *(p. 166)*
strictness/leniency *(p. 166)*
task performance *(p. 154)*
unclear performance standards *(p. 165)*

REVIEW AND DISCUSSION QUESTIONS

1. Describe the five steps in the performance appraisal process.

2. Explain how to ensure that the performance appraisal process is carried out ethically and without violating human rights laws.

3. Discuss the pros and cons of using different potential raters to appraise a person's performance.

4. Describe two examples of important techniques managers may use during a formal appraisal discussion.

5. Explain how to handle a defensive employee in a formal appraisal discussion.

CRITICAL THINKING QUESTIONS

1. Assume you are presenting to an upper-year group of business students and one of them asks, "Which performance appraisal system is the best?" How would you respond to that question?

2. How can the problem of inconsistency between managers who are rating workers be solved or at least diminished? Make two or more suggestions.

3. What are the challenges of the coaching method, where feedback is given more frequently and informally? Identify possible solutions to these challenges.

4. Some HR professionals avoid using BARS, given that it is so time-consuming to develop. How could the development steps be streamlined?

5. Do you agree with the use of annual performance reviews? Why or why not?

6. How might a supervisor handle a situation in which negative appraisals in the past have caused an employee to undervalue his or her performance?

7. Discuss how employees might respond to the proposed implementation of electronic performance management systems, such as call monitoring, and so on. How might an organization deal with employees' reactions?

8. How might a supervisor deal with an extremely defensive yet productive member of his or her team in the event of having to deliver the "improvement portion" of the employee's performance appraisal? What techniques would the supervisor need to use to maximize the efficacy of the appraisal and reduce the defensiveness of the employee?

EXPERIENTIAL EXERCISES

1. Working individually or in groups, develop a graphic rating scale for a retail sales associate and a fast-food restaurant manager. Reflect on the types of biases that your scale introduces inadvertently, and discuss the challenges you faced when developing the scale.

2. Working individually or in groups, develop, over a week, a set of critical incidents covering the classroom performance of one of your instructors. Categorize the critical incidents to identify themes within activities that are viewed positively and negatively. Expand on this identification by assessing how the one-week period may be affecting the results and what differences you would have expected had you selected a different week within the year to conduct the assessment.

3. Working in groups, using the National Occupational Classification (NOC) job description for cafeteria staff at a local university or college, develop a behaviourally anchored rating scale with five to eight items for the job of a chef within the cafeteria. Identify why you prioritized the items that you did.

4. Once you have drafted your form, exchange forms with another student or group. Critique and suggest possible improvements to the forms. Then with your revised form in hand, develop statements of behavioural incidents for two of your rating scale items to address the following circumstances:

- The employee has achieved outstanding results.
- The employee meets acceptable standards.
- The employee has performed very poorly in this aspect of the job.

Be prepared to share and critique statements developed by other students. Debrief the exercise as directed.

PART FOUR Total Rewards

STRATEGIC PAY PLANS

LEARNING OUTCOMES

AFTER STUDYING THIS CHAPTER, YOU SHOULD BE ABLE TO:

EXPLAIN the strategic importance of total rewards.

DEFINE pay equity, and **EXPLAIN** its importance today.

EXPLAIN in detail each of the three stages in establishing pay rates.

DISCUSS competency-based pay.

EXPLAIN under what conditions it is best to use an incentive plan.

COMPARE the three types of incentive plans.

8.1 THE STRATEGIC IMPORTANCE OF TOTAL EMPLOYMENT REWARDS

employee value proposition The total value an employee receives from the employer, including compensation, benefits, career management, workplace/lifestyle, and employee pride.

There is a new term emerging among HRM compensation professionals: **employee value proposition** (EVP). The employee value proposition may be defined as the total value an employee receives from the employer, including compensation, benefits, career management, workplace/lifestyle, and employee pride.[1] It defines the commitment the company will make to develop the employee in exchange for the effort the employee puts in to benefit the company. Borrowed from the marketing concept of customer value proposition, it has become a significant consideration as globalization and demographic changes continue to influence the attraction and retention of an organization's human talent in the second decade of the twenty-first century. Simply put, the employee value proposition asks the question, *"Why would the people our organization needs want to join, perform well and stay?"*[2]

total employment rewards An integrated package of all rewards (monetary and non-monetary, extrinsic and intrinsic) gained by employees from their employment.

Total employment rewards refers to an integrated package of all rewards gained by employees arising from their employment. These rewards encompass everything that employees value in the employment relationship. Rewards can be segmented based on the monetary (extrinsic), non-monetary (intrinsic) divide, with further differentiation between cash payments and benefits that are a cash expense for the organization but are not paid as cash to the employees, as illustrated in **Figure 8.1**.[3]

This approach considers individual reward components as part of an integrated whole to determine the best mix of rewards that are aligned with business strategy and that provide employee value, all within the cost constraints of the organization. Alignment is the extent to which rewards support outcomes that are important to achieving the organization's strategic objectives. For example, when competitive advantage requires critical attention to customer service, this behaviour should be reinforced.

FIGURE 8.1 Employment Rewards: An Integrated Package of Rewards

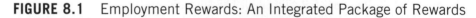

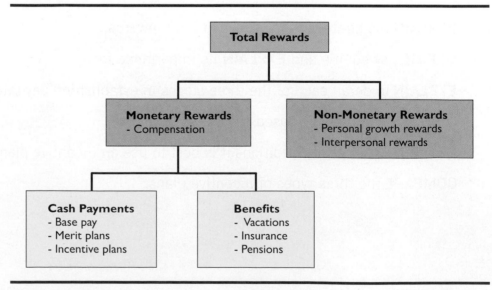

8.1.1 Components of Total Rewards

1. *Compensation.* This category includes direct financial payments in the form of wages, salaries, incentives, commissions, and bonuses. Wages, salaries, and other direct financial payments are discussed in this chapter.

2. *Benefits.* This category includes indirect payments in the form of financial benefits, such as employer-paid insurance and vacations. It also includes employee services, as discussed in the next chapter.

3. *Work–life programs.* This category of rewards relates to programs that help employees do their jobs effectively, such as flexible scheduling, telecommuting, child care, and so on.

4. *Performance and recognition.* This category includes pay-for-performance and recognition programs.

5. *Development and career opportunities.* This category of rewards focuses on planning for the advancement or change in responsibilities to best suit individual skills, talents, and desires. Tuition assistance, professional development, sabbaticals, coaching and mentoring opportunities, succession planning, and apprenticeships are all examples of career-enhancing programs.

8.2 MONEY AND MOTIVATION

Today's efforts to achieve the organization's strategy through motivated employees include fixed and variable compensation plans. **Fixed pay** represents compensation that is independent of the performance level of the individual, group, or organization. Fixed compensation includes base pay and other forms of relatively consistent compensation (for example, allowances) that satisfy the need for income stability. In contrast, **variable pay** represents any plan that links pay with productivity, profitability, or some other measure of organizational performance. Employers continue to increase their use of variable pay plans while holding salary increases or fixed compensation at modest levels. On average, organizations spend roughly 11 percent of total pay-related spending on variable pay–related expenses. More than 84 percent of Canadian employers have one or more types of variable pay plans in place.[4] As shown in **Figure 8.2**, cash bonuses or incentives are the most common form of short-term incentives, used in 87 percent of organizations that have short-term incentive plans in place.

Variable pay facilitates the management of total compensation by keeping base pay inflation controlled. The fundamental premise of variable pay plans is that top performers must get top pay to secure their commitment to the organization. Thus, accurate performance appraisal or measurable outcomes is a precondition of effective pay-for-performance plans. Employees need to understand corporate strategy and how their work as individual employees is important to the achievement of strategic objectives.[5]

Merit pay or a **merit raise** is any salary increase that is awarded to an employee based on his or her individual performance. It is different from a bonus in that it usually represents a continuing increment, whereas the bonus represents a one-time payment. Although the term "merit pay" can apply to the incentive raises given to any employees—office or factory, management or nonmanagement—the term is more often used with respect to white-collar employees, and particularly professional, office, and clerical employees.

fixed pay Compensation that is independent of the performance level of the individual, group, or organization.

variable pay Any plan that ties pay to productivity or profitability.

merit pay (merit raise) Any salary increase awarded to an employee based on his or her individual performance.

FIGURE 8.2 Variable Pay Programs, 2011

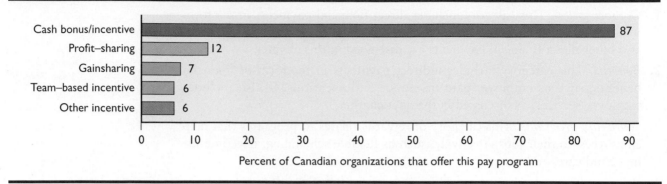

Note: n = 323; percent based on organizations with at least one annual variable pay plan in place.

Figures do not add to 100 because some respondents have more than one plan.

Source: H. McAteer, *Compensation Planning Outlook 2017* (Ottawa, ON: Conference Board of Canada, 2017); Allison Cowan and Nicole Stewart, *Compensation Planning Outlook 2011: Playing It Safe in the Face of an Unsteady Economic Recovery* (Ottawa, ON: Conference Board of Canada, 2010), p. 7, www.conferenceboard.ca/e-library/abstract.aspx?did=3797 (accessed July 31, 2017). Courtesy of Conference Board of Canada. Used with Permission.

Traditional merit pay plans have two basic characteristics: (1) Merit increases are usually granted to employees at a designated time of the year in the form of a higher base salary (or *raise*); and (2) the merit raise is usually based exclusively on individual performance, although the overall level of company profits may affect the total sum available for merit raises.[6] In some cases, merit raises are awarded in a single lump sum once a year, without changing base salary. Occasionally, awards are tied to both individual and organizational performance.

Merit pay detractors present good reasons why merit pay can backfire. If performance appraisals are viewed as unfair, so too will the merit pay that is based on them. Second, supervisors often give most employees about the same raise, either because of a reluctance to alienate some employees or a desire to give everyone a raise that will at least help them to stay even with the cost of living. Third, almost every employee thinks that he or she is an above-average performer; being paid a below-average merit increase can thus be demoralizing. Finally, some believe that merit pay pits employees against each other and harms team spirit.[7]

However, although problems like these can undermine a merit pay plan, the consensus of opinion is that merit pay can and does improve employee performance.[8] Advocates argue that only pay or other rewards tied directly to performance can motivate improved performance. They contend that the effect of awarding identical pay raises to all employees (without regard to individual performance) may actually demotivate employees, since some employees may interpret this to show that all employees are rewarded the same regardless of how they perform.

In addition, recent research reveals that base pay is regarded by employees and employers as a leading factor in attraction and retention.[9] A study of 446 organizations across Canada by Western Compensation and Benefits Consultants found that the most effective attraction strategy was offering competitive base salaries, and the top reason for turnover among employees was dissatisfaction with cash compensation. Opportunities for advancement, work–life balance programs, and competitive benefits programs are also used by over 70 percent of Canadian companies to attract talent.[10]

The Expert Opinion box Extends beyond money as a motivator to introduce the concepts of income disparity and discuss current challenges associated with the pay of young workers.

Academic Viewpoint
EXPERT OPINION

Focus: Macroeconomic effects (inflation, business cycles, financial markets, technology change, globalization), as well as determinants of aggregate employment and wages

1. Over the last two decades, how has labour income distribution changed in Canada?

There is a marked change in labour income distribution over the last two decades. Generally, skill level is rewarded with associated income levels; jobs requiring low skill levels offer low pay, while jobs requiring high skill levels offer high pay. The spread between high and low earners has increased, with a decrease in income levels of low wage earners as a major catalyst to this spread. This is a critical issue in eastern Canada. In comparison, with the recent boom in Alberta, less educated workers are still doing well, so concerns regarding income disparity and returns associated with education are less prominent in some parts of central and western Canada.

Key drivers for low income are jobs that have high repetition, routine tasks, and some level of mechanization. Due to globalization, some low-skill, low-income jobs are replaced by machines, while others are outsourced to emerging countries. Comparatively high-skilled (therefore high-earning) jobs are somewhat more protected from outsourcing and automation.

2. Your recent research finds that the wage difference between men and women shrunk in the 1980s and 1990s. What is the explanation for this?

Aligned with my response to question 1, typically jobs that were at risk

Identification:
Dr. Paul Beaudry (PhD)
Canada Research Chair in Macroeconomics, Fellow at Bank of Canada and the Royal Society of Canada, Research Associate at the National Bureau of Economics Research

Affiliation:
School of Economics, University of British Columbia

since 2000 were blue-collar, manufacturing jobs; traditionally jobs with low female representation. Technology has been an equalizing factor. With automation, cognitive abilities and technological skill levels are the primary considerations in employment, rather than physical ability. In recent years, women have been doing better than men on acquiring numeracy skills and analytical skills in postsecondary education.

3. Evidence shows that young workers often have a low level of personal savings. How can this information be used to drive management decisions about employee compensation?

The costs of education, lifestyle decisions, and income levels all play a role

in the financial pressures that young people feel. In some regions, housing affordability has reduced an employer's ability to attract and retain employees, especially young employees. The average price of a home in Canada increased 12.6 percent in the first quarter of 2017 (compared to year over year prices). In that period, Vancouver's average home (including detached, semi-detached, and condos) sold for $1.18 million, while Toronto's average home sold for $0.76 million.

This creates a situation where workers' compensation does not increase at the same rate as housing costs; as a result the cost of renting is inflated, while homeownership is increasingly expensive. To help address concerns affordability as universities recruit faculty and administration, universities are trying to build joint equity schemes to help new professors buy homes. Employers in high-cost cities might consider a similar agreement to help young workers secure homes.

Young workers need to reduce debt levels, but also want to save. An employer can share the responsibility of educated young workers on the potential associated with pension benefits and other longer term investments. These employees need information regarding investments and taxation benefits and options, in order to make an informed decision.

Source: Reprinted by permission from Dr. Paul Beaudry. Statistics on housing prices from "In Charts: Tracking House Prices in Canada's Hottest Housing Markets," *CTV News* (April 18, 2017), www.ctvnews.ca/canada/in-charts-tracking-house-prices-in-canada-s-hottest-housing-markets-1.3373632 (accessed July 18, 2017).

8.3 BASIC CONSIDERATIONS IN DETERMINING PAY RATES

Four basic considerations influence the formulation of any pay plan: union issues, compensation policy, equity, and legal requirements.

8.3.1 Union Influences on Compensation Decisions

Unions and labour relations laws also influence how pay plans are designed. Historically, wage rates have been the main issue in collective bargaining. However, other issues—including time off with pay, income security (for those in industries with periodic layoffs), cost-of-living adjustments, and pensions—are also important.[11]

The Canada Industrial Relations Board and similar bodies in each province and territory oversee employer practices and ensure that employees are treated in accordance with their legal rights. Their decisions underscore the need to involve union officials in developing the compensation package.

8.3.2 Compensation Policies

An employer's compensation policies provide important guidelines regarding the wages and benefits that it pays. A number of factors are taken into account in the development of a compensation policy, including whether the organization wants to be a leader, assume an "at market" position, or be a follower regarding pay, business strategy, and the cost of different types of compensation. Important policies include the basis for salary increases, promotion and demotion policies, overtime pay policy, and policies regarding probationary pay and leaves for military service, jury duty, and holidays. Compensation policies are usually written by the HR agent or compensation manager in conjunction with senior management contributions.[12]

8.3.3 Perceptions of Equity Internally and Externally

external equity Employees perceive their pay as fair, given the pay rates in other organizations.

internal equity Employees perceive their pay as fair, given the pay rates of others in the organization.

A crucial factor in determining pay rates is the need for equity, specifically **external equity** and **internal equity**. Research has indicated that employee perceptions of fairness are one of the two key conditions for effective reward programs.[13] Externally, pay must compare favourably with rates in other organizations or an employer will find it hard to attract and retain qualified employees. Pay rates must also be equitable internally: each employee should view his or her pay as equitable, given other pay rates in the organization.

8.3.4 Legal Considerations in Compensation

All of the 14 jurisdictions regulating employment in Canada (10 provinces, 3 territories, and the federal jurisdiction) have laws regulating compensation. Thus, HR managers must pay careful attention to which legislation affects their employees. Further, these laws are constantly changing and require continual monitoring to ensure compliance. Employment standards acts and human rights acts must also be taken into consideration, as discussed in Chapter 2. Pay equity is a major compensation issue and stems from employees' perceptions of equity. In addition, workers' compensation laws also apply.

8.4 PAY EQUITY

The purpose of **pay equity** legislation is to redress systemic gender discrimination in compensation for work performed by employees in female-dominated job classes. Pay equity requires that equal wages be paid for jobs of equal value or "worth" to the employer, as determined by gender-neutral (i.e., free of any bias based on gender) job evaluation techniques. Although such factors as differences in hours worked, experience levels, education levels, and level of unionization contribute to the wage gap, systemic discrimination is also present.[14]

Instances of pay inequity continue to occur, even in large, structured organizations. Several internal assessments of pay equity at the University of British Columbia established that on average, compensation of full-time female professors was $14 000 less than that of their male counterparts. After adjusting for confounding factors (such as specialization, tenure, etc.), a $3 000 gap in pay still existed. As a result, in 2013, the university gave all 880 tenure-tracked and tenured female faculty members a 2 percent increase in base salary in order to achieve pay equity. The increase was made retroactive to January 1, 2010, at a cost of $2 million to the university. A similar situation occurred at Western University in 2006, resulting in individual adjustments to female faculty members' salaries to compensate for the $2 200 (after adjusting for confounding factors) difference in pay between men and women. These cases highlight how the struggle for income parity between genders is far from over, and a challenge in even the most structured organizations.[15]

In addition, each jurisdiction has its own *workers' compensation laws*. The objective of these laws is to provide a prompt, sure, and reasonable income to victims of work-related accidents and illnesses. The Employment Insurance Act is aimed at protecting Canadian workers from total economic destitution in the event of employment termination that is beyond their control. Employers and employees both contribute to the benefits provided by this act. This act also provides up to 45 weeks of compensation for workers unemployed through no fault of their own (depending on the unemployment rate in the claimant's region and other factors). Maternity leave, parental leave, and compassionate care leave benefits are also provided under the Employment Insurance Act.[16]

> **pay equity**   Providing equal pay to male-dominated job classes and female-dominated job classes of equal value to the employer.

> Association of Workers' Compensation Boards of Canada
> **www.awcbc.org**

8.5 ESTABLISHING PAY RATES

In practice, the process of establishing pay rates that are both externally and internally equitable requires three stages: evaluating jobs, conducting wage/salary surveys, and combining the two pieces of information to determine pay for jobs.

8.5.1 Stage 1: Job Evaluation

Job evaluation is aimed at determining a job's relative worth. It is a formal and systematic comparison of jobs within a firm to determine the worth of one job relative to another, and it eventually results in a job hierarchy.

The basic procedure is to compare the content of jobs in relation to one another, for example, in terms of their effort, responsibility, skills, and working conditions. Job evaluation usually focuses on **benchmark jobs** that are critical to the firm's operations or that are commonly found in other organizations. Rohm and Haas, a multinational chemical company, ensures that its benchmark jobs

> **job evaluation**   A systematic comparison to determine the relative worth of jobs within a firm.

> **benchmark job**   A job that is critical to the firm's operations or that is commonly found in other organizations.

represent all the various business units and departments in the organization, are drawn from all levels of the organization, have large numbers of incumbents, are clear and well known in the industry, are stable and easily understood in terms of purpose and work content, and are visible and well understood by all employees.[17] The resulting evaluations of benchmark jobs are used as reference points around which other jobs are arranged in order of relative worth.

8.5.1.1 Compensable Factors

Jobs can be compared intuitively by deciding that one job is "more important" or "of greater value or worth" than another without digging any deeper into why in terms of specific job-related factors. This approach, called the *ranking method*, is hard to defend to employees or others who may not agree with the resulting job hierarchy. It may also be challenging when an organization has a large number of jobs. Such an approach would be relatively easy in a small business where there are only four distinct job roles. However, how could one rank 75 different jobs in a large manufacturing enterprise? As an alternative, jobs can be compared by focusing on certain basic factors that they have in common. In compensation management, these basic factors are called **compensable factors**. They are the factors that determine the definition of job content, establish how the jobs compare with one another, and set the compensation paid for each job.

Some employers develop their own compensable factors. However, most use factors that have been popularized by packaged job evaluation systems or by legislation. For example, most of the pay equity acts in Canada focus on four compensable factors: *skill*, *effort*, *responsibility*, and *working conditions*. As another example, the job evaluation method popularized by the Hay Group consulting firm focuses on four compensable factors: *know-how*, *problem solving*, *accountability*, and *working conditions*. Often, different job evaluation systems are used for different departments, employee groups, or business units. Identifying compensable factors plays a pivotal role in job evaluation. All jobs in each employee group, department, or business unit are evaluated *using the same compensable factors*. An employer thus evaluates the same elemental components for each job within the work group and is then better able to compare jobs—for example, in terms of the degree of skill, effort, responsibility, and working conditions present in each.[18]

compensable factor   A fundamental, compensable element of a job, such as skill, effort, responsibility, and working conditions.

job evaluation committee   A diverse group (including employees, HR staff, managers, and union representatives) established to ensure the fair and comprehensive representation of the nature and requirements of the jobs in question.

8.5.1.2 Job Evaluation Committee

Job evaluation is largely a judgmental process and one that demands close cooperation among supervisors, compensation specialists, and the employees and their union representatives. The main steps involved include identifying the need for the program, getting cooperation, and choosing an evaluation committee; the committee then carries out the actual job evaluation.[19]

A **job evaluation committee** is established to ensure the representation of the points of view of various organizational members who are familiar with the jobs in question, each of whom may have a different perspective regarding the nature of the jobs. The committee may include employees, HR staff, managers, and union representatives.

© Shutterstock

The job evaluation committee typically includes several employees and has the important task of evaluating the worth of each job using compensable factors.

The evaluation committee first identifies 10 or 15 key benchmark jobs. These will be the first jobs to be evaluated and will serve as the anchors or benchmarks against which the relative importance or value of all other jobs can be compared. Then the committee turns to its most important function—actually evaluating the worth of each job. For this, the committee will probably use either the job classification method or the point method.

8.5.1.3 Classification Method

The **classification/grading method** involves categorizing jobs into groups. The groups are called **classes** if they contain similar jobs or **grades** if they contain jobs that are similar in difficulty but otherwise different.

This method is widely used in the public sector. The federal government's *University Teaching* job group is an example of a job class because it contains similar jobs involving teaching, research, and consulting. Conversely, the *Audit, Commerce, and Purchasing* job group is an example of a job grade because it contains dissimilar jobs, involving auditing, economic development consulting, and purchasing.

There are several ways to categorize jobs. One is to draw up class descriptions (similar to job descriptions) and place jobs into classes based on their correspondence to these descriptions. Another is to draw up a set of classifying rules for each class (for instance, the amount of independent judgment, skill, physical effort, and so on that the class of jobs requires). Then the jobs are categorized according to these rules.

The usual procedure is to choose compensable factors and then develop class or grade descriptions that describe each class in terms of the amount or level of compensable factor(s) in jobs. The federal government's classification system, for example, employs different compensable factors for various job groups. Based on these compensable factors, a **grade/group description** is written. Then, the evaluation committee reviews all job descriptions and slots each job into its appropriate class or grade.

The job classification method has several advantages. The main one is that most employers usually end up classifying jobs anyway, regardless of the job evaluation method that they use. They do this to avoid having to work with and develop pay rates for an unmanageable number of jobs; with the job classification method, all jobs are already grouped into several classes. The disadvantages are that it is difficult to write the class or grade descriptions and considerable judgment is required in applying them. Yet many employers use this method with success.

8.5.1.4 Point Method

The **point method** is widely used in the private sector and requires identifying several compensable factors. The extent or degree to which each factor is present in the job is evaluated, a corresponding number of points is assigned for each factor, and the number of points for each factor is summed to arrive at an overall point value for the job.

1. *Preliminary steps.* To use the point method, it is necessary to have current job descriptions and job specifications based on a thorough job analysis. The foundation of the job evaluation plan is a number of compensable factors that must be agreed upon. In Canada, four compensable factors are commonly used: skill, effort, responsibility, and working conditions. These

---

classification/grading method   A method for categorizing jobs into groups.

classes   Groups of jobs based on a set of rules for each class, such as amount of independent judgment, skill, physical effort, and so forth. Classes usually contain similar jobs—all secretarial jobs, for instance.

grades   Groups of jobs based on a set of rules for each grade, whereby the jobs are similar in difficulty but otherwise different. Grades often contain dissimilar jobs, such as those of secretaries, mechanics, and firefighters.

grade/group description   A written description of the level of compensable factors required by jobs in each grade; used to combine similar jobs into grades or classes.

point method   A job evaluation method in which a number of compensable factors are identified, the degree to which each of these factors is present in the job is determined, and an overall point value is calculated.

factors are general and can mean different things in different workplaces. Therefore sub-factors of each one may also be determined to clarify the specific meaning of each factor, as shown below.

Factor	Sub-Factors
Skill	Education and Experience
	Interpersonal Skill
Effort	Physical Effort
	Mental Effort
Responsibility	Supervision of Others
	Planning
Working Conditions	Physical Environment
	Travel

Each sub-factor must be carefully defined to ensure that the evaluation committee members apply them consistently.

2. *Determine factor weights and degrees.* The next step is to decide on the maximum number of points (called "weight") to assign to each factor. Assigning factor weights is generally done by the evaluation committee. The committee members carefully study each factor and determine the relative value of the factors. For example:

Skill	30 percent
Effort	30 percent
Responsibility	30 percent
Working Conditions	10 percent
	100 percent

Then definitions of varying amounts (called "degrees" or "levels") of each sub-factor (or overall factor if no sub-factors are used) are prepared so that raters can judge the degree of a sub-factor/factor existing in a job. Thus, sub-factor "physical environment" for the factor "working conditions" might have three degrees—occasional, frequent, continuous—defined as follows:

Degree 1: Occasional—less than 30 percent of the time on an annual basis. Typically occurs once in a while, but not every day, or every day for less than 30 percent of the day.

Degree 2: Frequent—30 percent to 60 percent of the time on an annual basis. A regular feature of the job that occurs during any given day, week, or season.

Degree 3: Continuous—More than 60 percent of the time on an annual basis. Typically occurs for most of the regular work day, all year round (on average).

The number of degrees usually does not exceed five or six, and the actual number depends mostly on judgment. It is not necessary to have the same number of degrees for each factor, and degrees should be limited to the number necessary to distinguish among jobs.

TABLE 8.1   Point Method Job Evaluation Plan

Factor	Sub-Factors	Degrees 1	2	3	4		Maximum Weight Points	
Skill	Education and Experience	50	100	150	200	200		
	Interpersonal Skill	25	50	75	100	100		
							300	30%
Effort	Physical Effort	25	50	75	100	100		
	Mental Effort	50	100	150	200	200		
							300	30%
Responsibility	Supervision of Others	50	100	150		150		
	Planning	50	100	150		150		
							300	30%
Working Conditions	Physical Environment	20	40	60		60		
	Travel	10	20	30	40	40		
							100	10%
							1000	100%

3. *Assign points for each degree of each sub-factor.* Points are then assigned to each factor, as in **Table 8.1**. For example, suppose that it is decided to use a total number of 1 000 points in the point plan. Then, since the factor "skill" had a weight of 30 percent, it would be assigned a total of 30 percent of 1 000, or 300 points. This automatically means that the highest degree for each sub-factor of the skill factor would be 300 points. Points are then assigned to the other degrees for this factor, in equal amounts from the lowest to the highest degree. This step is repeated for each factor and its sub-factors, resulting in the final job evaluation plan, as shown in **Table 8.1**. All these decisions are recorded in a job evaluation manual to be used by the job evaluation committee.

4. *Evaluate the jobs.* Once the manual is complete, the actual evaluations can begin. Each job is evaluated factor by factor to determine the number of points that should be assigned to it. First, committee members determine the degree (first degree, second degree, and so on) to which each factor is present in the job. Then they note the corresponding points (see **Table 8.1**) that were assigned to each of these degrees. Finally, they add up the points for all factors, arriving at a total point value for the job. Raters generally start by rating benchmark jobs and obtaining consensus on these, and then they rate the rest of the jobs.

Point systems involve a quantitative technique that is easily explained to, and used by, employees. However, it can be difficult and time consuming to develop a point plan and to effectively train the job evaluation user group. This is one reason why many organizations adopt a point plan developed and marketed by a consulting firm. In fact, the availability of a number of ready-made plans probably accounts in part for the wide use of point plans in job evaluation.

If the committee assigned pay rates to each individual job, it would be difficult to administer, since there might be different pay rates for hundreds or even thousands of jobs. Even in smaller organizations there is a tendency to try to simplify wage and salary structures as much as possible. Therefore, the committee will probably want to group similar jobs (in terms of their number of points, for instance) into grades for pay purposes. Then, instead of having to deal with pay rates for hundreds of jobs, it might have to focus on pay rates for only 10 or 12 groupings of jobs.

A **pay grade** comprises jobs of approximately equal value or importance, as determined by job evaluation. If the point method was used, the pay grade consists of jobs falling within a range of points. If the classification system was used, then the jobs are already categorized into classes or grades. The next stage is to obtain information on market pay rates by conducting a wage/salary survey.

pay grade Comprises jobs of approximately equal value.

8.5.2 Stage 2: Conduct a Wage/Salary Survey

Compensation surveys, or **wage/salary surveys**, play a central role in determining pay rates for jobs.[20] An employer may use wage/salary surveys in three ways:

wage/salary survey A survey aimed at determining prevailing wage rates. A good salary survey provides specific wage rates for comparable jobs. Formal written questionnaire surveys are the most comprehensive.

1. Survey data are used to determine pay rates for benchmark jobs that serve as reference points or anchors for the employer's pay scale, meaning that other jobs are then paid based on their relative worth compared to the benchmark jobs.

2. Given that an increasing number of positions are paid solely based on the marketplace (rather than relative to the firm's benchmark jobs) and that there is a current shift away from long-term employment, compensation is increasingly shaped by market wages and less by how it fits into the hierarchy of jobs in one organization.[21]

3. Surveys also collect data on employee benefits, work–life programs, pay-for-performance plans, recognition plans, and so on to provide a basis on which to make decisions regarding other types of rewards.

8.5.2.1 Formal and Informal Surveys by the Employer

Most employers rely heavily on formal or informal surveys of what other employers are paying.[22] Informal telephone surveys are good for collecting data on a relatively small number of easily identified and quickly recognized jobs, such as when a bank's HR director wants to determine the salary at which a newly opened customer service representative's job should be advertised. Informal discussions among human resources specialists at regular professional association meetings are other occasions for informal salary surveys. Some employers use formal questionnaire surveys to collect compensation information from other employers, including things like number of employees, overtime policies, starting salaries, and paid vacations. Innovative compensation survey providers such as PayScale, a leader in cloud compensation and software, now allow individuals and organizations to access up-to-date salary information from a data base of 54 million individual salary profiles.[23]

PayScale, Inc.
www.payscale.com

8.5.2.2 Commercial, Professional, and Government Salary Surveys

Many employers also rely on surveys published by various commercial firms, professional associations, or government agencies. For example, Statistics Canada provides monthly data on earnings by geographic area, by industry, and by occupation. Table 8.2 provides an example of earnings data by industry and occupation, which can be used to establish pay, determine average changes, benchmark compensation, and so on. Statistics Canada also makes more detailed data regarding industry-specific benchmarks readily available.

TABLE 8.2   Average Weekly Earnings by Industry, Canada, 2016–2017 (including overtime)

	January 2016	January 2017	Jan. 2016 – Jan. 2017
Industry	$	$	% change
Industrial aggregate excluding unclassified businesses	950.42	967.15	+1.8
Goods-producing industries	1,214.68	1,242.68	+2.3
Service-producing industries	890.69	905.95	+1.7

Source: Statistics Canada, *Earnings, Average Weekly, by Industry, Monthly*, CANSIM table 281-0063, www.statcan.gc.ca/tables-tableaux/sum-som/l01/cst01/labor93a-eng.htm (accessed April 2, 2017).

The Toronto Board of Trade conducts five compensation surveys annually, covering executive; management; professional, supervisory, and sales; information technology; and administrative and support positions. The surveys include information from small, medium, and large employers in the Greater Toronto Area. A separate survey of employee benefits and employment practices is also conducted.

Private consulting or executive recruiting companies, such as Willis Towers Watson, Mercer, and Aon Hewitt, annually publish data covering the compensation of senior and middle managers and members of boards of directors. Professional organizations, such as the Chartered Professional Accountants of Canada (CPA Canada), and the Association of Professional Engineers and Geoscientists of British Columbia, survey compensation practices among members of their associations.

Salary Wizard
**http://monsterca.salary.
com/CanadaSalaryWizard/
LayoutScripts/Swzl_NewSearch.
aspx**

For some jobs, salaries are determined directly based on formal or informal salary surveys like those available from Monster.ca. In most cases, though, surveys are used to price benchmark jobs around which other jobs are then slotted based on their relative worth as determined through job evaluation.

8.5.2.3 Salary Survey Interpretation and Use

Upward bias can be a problem regardless of the type of compensation survey used. At least one compensation expert argues that the way in which most surveys are constructed, interpreted, and used leads almost invariably to a situation in which firms set higher wages than they otherwise might. For example, "companies like to compare themselves against well-regarded, high-paying, and high-performing companies," so baseline salaries tend to be biased upward. Similarly, "companies that sponsor surveys often do so with an implicit (albeit unstated) objective: to show the company [is] paying either competitively or somewhat below the market, so as to justify positive corrective action." For these and similar reasons, it is probably wise to review survey results with a skeptical eye and to acknowledge that upward bias may exist and should perhaps be considered when making decisions.[24]

Whatever the source of the survey, the data must be carefully assessed for accuracy before they are used to make compensation decisions. Problems can arise when the organization's job descriptions only partially match the descriptions contained in the survey, the survey data were collected several months before the time of use, the participants in the survey do not represent the appropriate labour market for the jobs being matched, and so on.[25]

Now all the information necessary to move to the next stage—determining pay for jobs—has been obtained.

8.5.3 Stage 3: Combine the Job Evaluation and Salary Survey Information to Determine Pay for Jobs

The final stage is to assign pay rates to each pay grade. Of course, if jobs were not grouped into pay grades, individual pay rates would have to be assigned to each job and thus make salary administration an unwieldy task. Assigning pay rates to each pay grade (or to each job) is usually accomplished with a **wage curve**, making this less complicated.

The wage curve graphically depicts the market pay rates currently being paid for jobs in each pay grade, relative to the job evaluation points for each job or grade. An example of a wage curve is presented in **Figure 8.3**. Note that pay rates are shown on the vertical axis, while the points for pay grades are shown along the horizontal axis. The purpose of the wage curve is to show the relationship between the value of the job as determined by one of the job evaluation methods and the current average pay rates for each job or grade.

There are several steps in determining pay for pay grades using a wage curve. First, find the average pay for each pay grade, since each of the pay grades consists of several jobs. Next, plot the pay rates for each pay grade, as was done in **Figure 8.2**. Then fit a line (called a "wage line") through the points just plotted. This can be done either freehand or by using a statistical method known as regression analysis. Finally, determine pay for jobs. Wages along the wage line are the target wages or salary rates for the jobs in each pay grade.

wage curve A graphic description of the relationship between the value of the job and the average wage paid for this job.

An Ethical Dilemma

What should employers do when there is a shortage of a certain type of skill and they cannot attract any workers unless they pay a market rate above the maximum of their salary range for that job? How should other jobs (without a skills shortage) in the same company in the same salary range be paid?

8.5.3.1 Developing Rate Ranges

pay ranges A series of steps or levels within a pay grade, usually based on years of service.

Most employers do not just pay one rate for all jobs in a particular pay grade. Instead, they develop **pay ranges** for each grade so that there might, for instance, be 5–7 levels or "steps" and 5–7 corresponding pay rates within each pay grade.

FIGURE 8.3   Plotting a Wage Curve

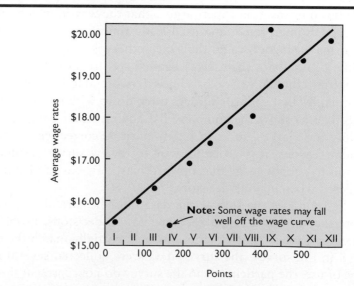

Note: The average market pay rate for jobs in each grade (Grade I, Grade II, Grade III, etc.) is plotted, and the wage curve is fitted to the resulting points.

This approach is illustrated in **Table 8.3**, which shows the hourly pay rates for any jobs located in the two initial pay grades. Employees in positions that were classified in pay grade 1 would be paid an hourly wage rate between $15.50 and $16.50 depending on the level at which they were hired into the grade, the amount of time they had been in the grade, and their merit increases (if any). Another way to depict the rate ranges for each grade is with a wage structure, as in **Figure 8.4**. The wage structure graphically depicts the range of pay rates (in this case, per hour) to be paid for each grade.

The use of pay ranges for each pay grade has several benefits. First, the employer can take a more flexible stance with respect to the labour market; for example, some flexibility makes it easier to attract experienced, higher-paid employees into a pay grade where the starting salary for the lowest step may be too low to attract such experienced people. Pay ranges also allow employers to provide for performance differences between employees within the same grade

TABLE 8.3   Sample Pay Schedule (hypothetical)

| Grade | Steps within the Pay Grade | | | | |
	1	2	3	4	5
Grade 1	$15.50	$15.75	$16.00	$16.25	$16.50
Grade 2	$16.25	$16.50	$16.75	$17.00	$17.25

FIGURE 8.4   Wage Structure

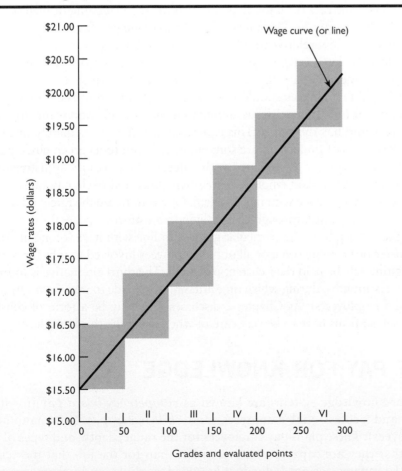

or between those with differing seniority. As in **Figure 8.4**, most employers structure their pay ranges to overlap a bit so that an employee with greater experience or seniority may earn more than an entry-level person in the next higher pay grade.

8.5.3.2 Broadbanding

broadbanding Reducing the number of salary grades and ranges into just a few wide levels or "bands," each of which then contains a relatively wide range of jobs and salary levels.

The trend today is for employers to reduce their salary grades and ranges from 10 or more down to 3–5, a process that is called **broadbanding**. Broadbanding means combining salary grades and ranges into just a few wide levels or "bands," each of which then contains a relatively wide range of jobs and salary levels.

Broadbanding a pay system involves several steps. First, the number of bands is decided on and each is assigned a salary range. The bands usually have wide salary ranges and also overlap substantially. As a result, there is much more flexibility to move employees from job to job within bands and less need to "promote" them to new grades just to give them higher salaries.

The basic advantage of broadbanding is that it injects greater flexibility into employee compensation.[26] The new, broad salary bands can include both supervisors and those reporting to them. Broadbanding also facilitates less specialized, boundaryless jobs and organizations. Less specialization and more participation in cross-departmental processes generally mean enlarged duties or capabilities and more possibilities for alternative career tracks.

8.5.4 Stage 4: Correcting Out-of-Line Rates

The actual wage rate for a job may fall well off the wage line or well outside the rate range for its grade. This means that the average pay for that job is currently too high or too low relative to other jobs in the relative pay grade. If a point falls well below the line, a pay raise for the job may be required. If the plot falls well above the wage line, pay cuts or a pay freeze may be required.

green circle pay rate A rate of pay that is below the pay range minimum.

Underpaid employees should have their wages raised to the minimum of the rate range for their pay grade, assuming that the organization wants to retain the employees and has the funds. This can be done either immediately or in several steps. Pay rates of underpaid are sometimes referred to as **green circle pay rates**. Such rates are typically associated with a need for pay equity adjustments.

red circle pay rate A rate of pay that is above the pay range maximum.

Pay rates of overpaid employees are often called **red circle pay rates,** and there are several ways to cope with this problem. One is to freeze the rate paid to employees in this grade until, through cost-of-living adjustments, general salary increases bring the other jobs in the particular grade into line with it. A second alternative is to transfer or promote some or all of the employees involved to jobs for which they can legitimately be paid their current pay rates. The third alternative is to freeze the rate for six months, during which time attempts are made to transfer or promote the overpaid employee(s). As Chapter 2 discusses, this may be a form of constructive dismissal, so firms have to be very careful when using the third option.

8.6 PAY FOR KNOWLEDGE

Pay-for-knowledge systems are known as *competency-based pay* (for management and professional employees) and *skill-based pay* (for manufacturing employees). These plans pay employees for the range, depth, and types of knowledge that they are capable of using, rather than for the job that they currently hold. Competencies are individual knowledge, skills, and behaviours that are critical to successful individual or corporate performance based on their relation to the organization's visions, values, and business strategy.[27]

Core competencies describe knowledge and behaviours that employees throughout the organization must exhibit for the organization to succeed, such as "customer service orientation" for all hotel employees. *Functional competencies* are associated with a particular organizational function, such as "negotiation skills" for salespeople, or "safety orientation" for pilots. *Behavioural competencies* are expected behaviours, such as "always walking a customer to the product they are looking for rather than pointing."[28] A pay-for-knowledge program should include the following:

- Competencies and skills—directly important to job performance—that can be defined in measurable and objective terms. Skills tend to be easier to define and measure than competencies.

- New and different competencies that replace obsolete competencies or competencies that are no longer important to job performance. If additional competencies are needed, the obsolete competency should be removed from the program.

- On-the-job training, not "in-the-classroom" training. Those who possess the competencies or skills should teach them. Also include on-the-job assessment, which can be supplemented by paper-and-pencil exams administered on the job.[29]

Construction workers today are often compensated for their work through the method of skill-based pay.

As an example, in a manufacturing plant setting, workers would be paid based on their attained skill levels. In a three-level plan,

1. Level 1 would indicate limited ability, such as knowledge of basic facts and ability to perform simple tasks without direction;

2. Level 2 would mean that the employee has attained partial proficiency and could, for instance, apply technical principles on the job; and

3. Level 3 would mean that the employee is fully competent in the area and could, for example, analyze and solve production problems.

Although only about 15 to 20 percent of workplaces use pay for knowledge at present, experts predict that the viewpoint that people, rather than jobs, provide advantages to organizations will continue to grow in popularity. They foresee the emergence of new pay systems combining competencies and market values.[30]

The greatest challenge is the measurement of competencies. As time goes on, employees often become dissatisfied if these measurements are not valid or if the people responsible for assessing competencies are considered incompetent or biased.[31] Another major employee concern is that pay be linked sufficiently to performance as well as competencies. Some compensation consultants suggest that firms should not pay for competencies at the exclusion of rewards for high performance results. For example, competencies could be linked to the determination of base salary combined with bonuses that are based on performance.[32] One final issue for many Canadian companies is that pay-for-knowledge systems do not meet pay equity requirements.[33]

8.7 DEVELOPING EFFECTIVE INCENTIVE PLANS

There are two major practical considerations in developing an effective incentive plan: when to use it and how to implement it.

8.7.1 When to Use Incentives

Before deciding to implement an incentive plan, it is important to remember several points:

1. *Performance pay cannot replace good management.* Performance pay is supposed to motivate workers, but lack of motivation is not always the culprit. Ambiguous instructions, lack of clear goals, inadequate employee selection and training, unavailability of tools, and a hostile workforce (or management) are just a few of the factors that impede performance.

2. *Firms get what they pay for.* Psychologists know that people often put their effort where they know they will be rewarded. However, this can backfire. An incentive plan that rewards a group based on how many pieces are produced could lead to rushed production and lower quality. Awarding a plant-wide incentive for reducing accidents may simply reduce the number of reported accidents.

3. *"Pay is not a motivator."*[34] Psychologist Frederick Herzberg makes the point that money only buys temporary compliance; as soon as the incentive is removed, the "motivation" disappears too. Instead, Herzberg says, employers should provide adequate financial rewards and then build other motivators, like opportunities for achievement and psychological success, into their jobs.

4. *Rewards rupture relationships.* Incentive plans have the potential for reducing teamwork by encouraging individuals (or individual groups) to blindly pursue financial rewards for themselves.

5. *Rewards may undermine responsiveness.* Since the employees' primary focus is on achieving some specific goal, like cutting costs, any changes or extraneous distractions mean that achieving that goal will be harder. Incentive plans can, therefore, mediate against change and responsiveness.

Research by two professors at the University of Alberta focused on resolving a longstanding debate about whether extrinsic rewards can backfire by reducing intrinsic motivation, or whether extrinsic rewards boost performance and enhance intrinsic motivation. The authors concluded that *careful* management of rewards does enhance performance. Common problem areas to be avoided include not tying rewards to performance, not delivering on all rewards initially promised, and delivering rewards in an authoritarian style or manner.[35]

Potential pitfalls like these do not mean that financial incentive plans cannot be useful or should not be used. Such problems do suggest, however, that goals need to be reasonable and achievable, but not so easily attained that employees view incentives as entitlements.[36] In general, any incentive plan is more apt to succeed if implemented with management support, employee acceptance, and a supportive culture characterized by teamwork, trust, and involvement at all levels.[37] This probably helps to explain why some of the longest-lasting incentive plans, like the improshare and Rucker plans, depend heavily on two-way communication and employee involvement in addition to incentive pay.

Therefore, in general, it makes more sense to use an incentive plan when units of output can be measured, the job is standardized, the workflow is regular, and delays are few or consistent. It is also important that there be a clear relationship between employee effort and quantity of output and that quality is less important than quantity, or, if quality is important, that it is easily measured and controlled.

8.7.2 How to Implement Incentive Plans

There are several specific, common-sense considerations in establishing any incentive plan. Of primary importance is "line of sight." The employee or group must be able to see their own impact on the goals or objectives for which incentives are being provided.[38]

Research indicates that seven principles support effective implementation of incentive plans that lead to superior business results:

1. Pay for performance—and make sure that performance is tied to the successful achievement of critical business goals.

2. Link incentives to other activities that engage employees in the business, such as career development and challenging opportunities.

3. Link incentives to measurable competencies that are valued by the organization.

4. Match incentives to the culture of the organization—its vision, mission, and operation principles.

5. Keep group incentives clear and simple—employee understanding is the most important factor differentiating effective from ineffective group incentive plans.

6. Over-communicate—employees become engaged when they hear the message that they are neither faceless nor expendable.

7. Remember that the greatest incentive is the work itself.

8.8 TYPES OF INCENTIVE PLANS

There are several types of incentive plans. There are organization-wide incentive plans as well as individual incentive programs providing additional compensation to employees. Organization-wide incentive plans provide monetary incentives to all employees of the organization. Examples are profit-sharing plans that provide employees with a share of the organization's profits in a specified period, and gainsharing programs designed to reward employees for improvements in organizational productivity. Non-monetary recognition programs motivate employees through praise and expressions of appreciation for their work. Informal incentives may be awarded, generally to individual employees (rather than organization-wide), for accomplishments that are not readily measured by a standard, such as "to recognize the long hours that this employee put in last month," or "to recognize exemplary customer service this week." Group incentive programs are like individual incentive plans, but they provide payments over and above base salary to all team members when the group or team collectively meets a specified standard for performance, productivity, or other work-related behaviour.

It is important to ensure that whatever incentive is being provided is appealing to the individual receiving it. Demographic factors can have an impact on what is appealing, as discussed in the Strategic HR box. Research indicates a current challenge to total employment rewards specialists is that cash is no longer the main instrument to motivate today's workforce.[39]

HRM and compensation professionals can create and implement strategic pay plans by paying attention to the following advice.

1. Identify key employee groups and their reward preferences.

2. Align compensation programs to support organizational culture and strategy.

3. Prioritize both internal and external pay equity tracking.

4. Adopt a more holistic view of performance and incentives.

5. Train managers and provide them with the right tools to aid in decision making re: compensation discussions and decisions.

6. Communicate the organization's compensation program, using marketing tactics and digital analytics, in an engaging and tailored manner to employees.

7. Use compensation software to create and improve streamlined and transparent compensation management processes.[40]

8.8.1 Organization-Wide Incentive Plans

Many employers have incentive plans in which virtually all employees can participate. These include profit-sharing, employee stock ownership, and gainsharing plans.

8.8.1.1 Profit-Sharing Plans

profit-sharing plan A plan whereby most or all employees share in the company's profits.

In a **profit-sharing plan**, most or all employees receive a share of the company's profits. A recent survey of Canadian organizations revealed 14 percent offered

---

STRATEGIC   HR

Generational Preferences in Rewards, Recognition, and Incentives

Boomers (born 1946–1964)

- Peer recognition, acknowledgement, and formal rewards from superiors

- Incentives that showcase experience and excellence

- Base and incentive pay

- Opportunities for healthy competition resulting in prizes, awards, and recognition

- Retirement and estate planning counselling

Gen X-ers (born 1965–1980)

- Personal development and skill-building experiences

- Good benefits and competitive pay

- Time off work rather than cash (e.g., paid sabbaticals)

- Flexible work schedules

- Private recognition for accomplishments

Millennials—Gen Y (born 1981–2000)

- Regular, detailed feedback on work performance

- Competitive pay

- Sabbatical leaves to work in the community

- Flexible work schedules

- Travel rewards related to business or personal choice

- Seminars and tools related to retirement planning

Source: Adapted from Allan Schweyer, "Generations in the Workforce and Marketplace: Preferences in Rewards, Recognition and Incentives," *Incentive Research Foundation* (July 2015), http://theirf.org/research/generations-in-the-workforce-marketplacepreferences-in-rewards-recognition-incentives/1427 (accessed April 5, 2017).

profit-sharing plans.[41] These plans are easy to administer and have a broad appeal to employees and other company stakeholders. In addition to helping attract, retain, and motivate workers, profit-sharing plans have tax advantages for employees, including tax deferrals and income splitting. The main weakness of profit-sharing plans is "line of sight." It is unlikely that most employees perceive that they personally have the ability to influence overall company profit. It has been found that these plans produce a one-time productivity improvement but no change thereafter. Another weakness of these plans is that they typically provide an annual payout, which is not as effective as more frequent payouts.[42]

© Pei Ling Hoo / fotolia

8.8.1.2 Employee Share Purchase/Stock Ownership Plan

Employee share purchase/stock ownership plans (ESOPs) are in place at approximately 60 percent of Canadian organizations with publicly traded stock.[43]

Profit-sharing plans are easy to administer and help to attract and motivate employees.

A trust is established to purchase shares of the firm's stock for employees by using cash from employee (and sometimes employer) contributions. Employers may also issue treasury shares to the trust instead of paying cash for a purchase on the open market. The trust holds the stock in individual employee accounts and distributes it to employees, often on retirement or other separation from service. Some plans distribute the stock to employees once a year.

employee share purchase/stock ownership plan (ESOP) A plan whereby a trust is established to hold shares of company stock purchased for or issued to employees. The trust distributes the stock to employees on retirement, separation from service, or as otherwise prescribed by the plan.

The corporation receives a tax deduction equal to the fair market value of the shares that are purchased by the trustee by using employer contributions, but not for any treasury shares issued. The value of the shares purchased with employer contributions, and of any treasury shares issued, is a taxable benefit to the employees in the year of purchase of the shares. This tax treatment can create two problems. First, if the plan requires employees to complete a certain period of service before taking ownership of the shares and the employee leaves before being eligible for ownership, the employee has paid tax on the value of shares that he or she never owns. Therefore, most plans have immediate vesting.[44] Second, if the value of the shares drops, employees may have paid tax on a greater amount than they will receive when they eventually sell the shares.

ESOPs can encourage employees to develop a sense of ownership in and commitment to the firm, particularly when combined with good communication, employee involvement in decision making, and employee understanding of the business and the economic environment.[45] For example, one employee at Creo, a digital products company in Burnaby, BC, that offers an ESOP said, "It's not just the shares. It's the way of thinking. I'm extremely happy here."[46]

National Center for Employee Ownership
www.nceo.org

8.8.1.3 Gainsharing Plans

A **gainsharing plan** is an incentive plan that engages many or all employees in a common effort to achieve a company's productivity objectives; any resulting incremental cost-saving gains are shared among employees and the company.[47] Popular types of gainsharing plans include the Rucker and improshare plans.

The basic difference between these plans is in the formula used to determine employee bonuses.[48] The Rucker formula uses sales value minus materials and

gainsharing plan An incentive plan that engages employees in a common effort to achieve productivity objectives and share the gains.

supplies, all divided into payroll expenses. It includes participative management systems that use committees. The improshare plan creates production standards for each department. It does not include a participative management component but instead considers participation an outcome of the bonus plan.

Gainsharing works well in stable organizations with predictable goals and measures of performance, but is less flexible and useful in dynamic industries that require rapid business adjustment. In general, most of their cost savings are generated in the early years.[49] For example, in 2011, US Airways announced that its employees would receive profit-sharing payouts totalling more than $47 million associated with the previous year's financial performance success. US Airways' Chair and Chief Executive Officer, Doug Parker, said, "Thank you and congratulations to our professional team members on an outstanding 2010. Our team ran a safe, reliable airline in 2010, completing more scheduled flights and delivering baggage more reliably than our network peers. Our customers have noticed the turnaround and our financial results reflect these positive results." Individual employee payouts vary by the employee's base salary and collective bargaining agreement. In addition, US Airways employees also received more than $25 million in operational incentive bonuses and individual employee recognition rewards in 2010.[50]

8.8.2 Incentives for Individuals

Many employers also have plans to motivate individuals, and these are offered based on factors that only relate to individual employees, such as their performance or length of employment.

8.8.2.1 The Annual Bonus

More than 90 percent of firms in Canada with variable pay plans provide an *annual bonus*.[51] Unlike salaries, which rarely decline with reduced performance, short-term incentive bonuses can easily result in an increase or decrease of up to 70 percent or more in total pay relative to the previous year. Three basic issues should be considered when awarding short-term incentives: eligibility, fund-size determination, and individual awards.

Eligibility Eligibility is usually decided in one of three ways. The first criterion is *key position*. Here, a job-by-job review is conducted to identify the key jobs (typically only line jobs) that have a measurable impact on profitability. The second approach to determining eligibility is to set a *salary-level* cut-off point; all employees earning over that threshold amount are automatically eligible for consideration for short-term incentives. Finally, eligibility can be determined by *salary grade*. This is a refinement of the salary cut-off approach and assumes that all employees at a certain grade or above should be eligible for the short-term incentive program. The simplest approach is just to use salary level as a cut-off.[52] The size of the bonus is usually greater for top-level executives.

How Much to Pay Out (Fund Size) Next, a decision must be made regarding the fund size—the total amount of bonus

"Due to corporate cutbacks, we're all going to have to sacrifice. Which is why I'm only playing nine holes today, instead of my customary 18."

money that will be available—and there are several formulas to do this. Some companies use a *non-deductible formula*, where a straight percentage (usually of the company's net income) is used to create the short-term incentive fund. Others use a *deductible formula* on the assumption that the short-term incentive fund should begin to accumulate only after the firm has met a specified level of earnings.

In practice, what proportion of profits is usually paid out as bonuses? In fact, there are no hard-and-fast rules about what an ideal payout size would be, and some firms do not even have a formula for developing the bonus fund. One alternative is to reserve a minimum amount of the profits, say 10 percent, for safeguarding shareholders' investments, and then to establish a fund for bonuses equal to 20 percent of the corporate operating profit before taxes in excess of this base amount. Thus, if the operating profits were $100 000, then the management bonus fund might be 20 percent of $90 000, or $18 000.

Determining Individual Awards The third issue is determining the *individual awards* to be paid. In some cases, the amount is determined on a discretionary basis, but typically a target bonus is set for each eligible position and adjustments are then made for greater or less than targeted performance. A maximum amount, perhaps double the target bonus, may be set. Performance ratings are obtained for each manager, and preliminary bonus estimates are computed. Estimates for the total amount of money to be spent on short-term incentives are thereby made and compared with the bonus fund available. If necessary, the individual estimates are then adjusted.

Many experts argue that, in most organizations, managerial and executive-level bonuses should be tied to both organizational and individual performance, and there are several ways to do this.[53] Perhaps the simplest is the *split-award method*, which breaks the bonus into two parts. Here, the manager actually gets two separate bonuses, one based on his or her individual effort and one based on the organization's overall performance. Thus, a manager might be eligible for an individual performance bonus of up to $10 000 but receive an individual performance bonus of only $8 000 at the end of the year, based on his or her individual performance evaluation. In addition, though, the person might also receive a second bonus of $8 000 based on the company's profits for the year. Thus, even if there were no company profits, the high-performing manager would still get an individual performance bonus.

One drawback to this approach is that it pays too much to the marginal performer, who, even if his or her own performance is mediocre, at least gets that second, company-based bonus. One way to get around this problem is to use the *multiplier method*. For example, a manager whose individual performance was "poor" might not even receive a company-performance-based bonus, on the assumption that the bonus should be a product of individual *and* corporate performance. When either is very poor, the product is zero.

Whichever approach is used, outstanding performers should get substantially larger awards than do other managers. They are people whom the company cannot afford to lose, and their performance should always be adequately rewarded by the organization's incentive system. Conversely, marginal or below-average performers should never receive awards that are normal or average, and poor performers should be awarded nothing. The money saved on those people should be given to above-average performers.[54]

An Ethical Dilemma

Is it ethical to provide potentially large bonuses to managers and executives on a purely discretionary basis, not necessarily related to performance?

The Conference Board of Canada
www.conferenceboard.ca

8.8.2.2 Retention Incentives

Long-term incentives are intended to motivate and reward top management for their contribution to firm's long-term growth and prosperity. As a retention effort, long-term incentives aim to create and support a long-term perspective into executive decisions. For instance, if only short-term criteria are used, a manager could increase profitability in one year by reducing plant maintenance; this tactic might, however, reduce profits over the next two or three years. This issue of long- versus short-term perspective has received considerable attention in the past several years as shareholders have become increasingly critical of management's focus on short-term returns at the expense of a long-term increase in share price.

capital accumulation programs Long-term incentives most often reserved for senior executives.

Long-term incentives are also intended to encourage executives to stay with the company by giving them the opportunity to accumulate capital (in the form of company shares) based on the firm's long-term success. Long-term incentives, or **capital accumulation programs**, are most often reserved for senior executives but have begun to be extended to employees at lower organizational levels.[55] Approximately 60 percent of Canadian private sector organizations provide long-term incentives. They are rarely provided to public sector employees.[56]

Some of the most common long-term incentive plans (for capital accumulation) in Canada are stock options, performance share unit plans, restricted share unit plans, and deferred share unit plans.[57] The popularity of these plans changes over time because of economic conditions and trends, internal company financial pressures, changing attitudes towards long-term incentives, and changes in tax law, as well as other factors. **Figure 8.5** illustrates the popularity of various long-term incentive plans.

stock option The right to purchase a stated number of shares of a company stock at today's price at some time in the future.

Stock Options The **stock option** is the most popular long-term incentive in Canada, but its use is decreasing. Forty-six percent of organizations using long-term incentives provided stock options in 2011, compared with 57 percent in 2005

FIGURE 8.5   Long-Term Incentive Plans (LTIP), by Plan Type, 2017

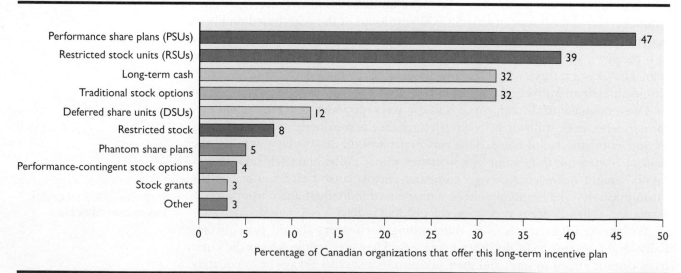

Notes: n=158; percentage based on organizations that reported having at least one LTIP in place.

Figures do not add to 100 because some respondents have more than one plan.

Source: H. McAteer, *Compensation Planning Outlook, 2017* (Ottawa: Conference Board of Canada, 2016). Reprinted with permission of Conference Board of Canada.

and 72 percent in 2002.[58] A stock option is the right to purchase a specific number of shares of company stock at a specific price at some point in the future.

Often a vesting (waiting) period is required to ensure that the employee has contributed to any increase in stock price, which also aligns the stock option with the goal of long-term retention of talent. The executive thus hopes to profit by exercising his or her option to buy the shares in the future but at today's price. The assumption is that the price of the stock will go up rather than going down or staying the same. For example, if shares provided at an option price of $20 per share are exercised (bought) later for $20 when the market price is $60 per share and sold on the stock market when the market price is $80 per share, a cash gain of $60 per share results. The difference between fair market value of the stock at the time the option is sold and the amount paid by the employee to acquire it is treated as a taxable benefit. Often, the employee benefits, since he or she is required to pay capital gains tax on only 50 percent of the gain. In comparison, from the employer's perspective, capital gains from cash incentive plans and stock purchase plans are taxed at full income inclusion levels. Thus, stock option plans are often seen as a cash windfall with no downside risk but unlimited upside potential.[59]

Proposals have been made to require that stock options be shown as an expense on company financial statements because the excessive issuing of options dilutes share values for shareholders and creates a distorted impression of the true value of a company.

Stock options are a less effective and less efficient form of compensation than direct share ownership in aligning the interests of directors with those of shareholders. Stock options do not motivate the executive to enhance long-term corporate performance. Stock-based compensation is superior to option-based compensation plans for three broad reasons:

- Stock-based compensation provides better alignment of interest of employees with shareholders (across a wide range of future share prices).

- It is a more efficient form of compensation (in terms of the perceived value received by the executive).

- It alters the capital structure in a more predictable way (with less potential dilution and more straightforward accounting treatment).[60]

Source: CPP Investment Board Proxy Voting Principles and Guidelines (February 7, 2006). Reprinted with permission.

Plans Providing Performance Share "Units"   Although the use of stock options persists, a new approach based on providing "units," tied to performance, instead of stock has become increasingly common.[61] Executives are granted a specified number of units whose value is equal to (and fluctuates with) a company's share price, subject to the organization's achievement of performance targets. A *performance share unit plan* provides units subject to the achievement of predetermined financial targets, such as profit or growth in earnings per share (often over a multiyear period). If the performance goals are met, then the value of the units is paid to the executive in cash or stock. The units have no value if the pre-established performance criteria are not met. In a *restricted share unit plan*, units are promised to the executive but will be forfeited if an executive leaves the company before a vesting period (typically three years). If the executive is still employed at the company after the vesting period, the full value of the units based on the current stock price is payable in cash or stock. In a *deferred share unit plan*, units are promised to the executive but are only payable when the executive leaves the company.

8.8.3 Incentives for Groups or Teams

Organizations require and promote teamwork and groups to help achieve their organizational goals. Therefore, there are special rewards and incentives for groups or teams.

8.8.3.1 Incentives for Salespeople (salary and/or commission)

Sales compensation plans have typically relied heavily on incentives (sales commissions), although this varies by industry. In the real estate industry, for instance, salespeople are paid entirely via commissions, while in the pharmaceutical industry, salespeople tend to be paid a salary. However, the most prevalent approach is to use a combination of salary and commissions to compensate salespeople.[62]

Realtors rely on sales commissions as their source of income.

© Kurhan / fotolia

The widespread use of incentives for salespeople is due to three factors: tradition, the unsupervised nature of most sales work, and the assumption that incentives are needed to motivate salespeople. The pros and cons of salary, commission, and combination plans follow.

Salary Plan In a salary plan, salespeople are paid a fixed salary, although there may be occasional incentives in the form of bonuses, sales contest prizes, and the like. There are several reasons to use straight salary. It works well when the main sales objective is prospecting (finding new clients) or when the salesperson is mostly involved in account servicing, such as developing and executing product training programs for a distributor's sales force or participating in national and local trade shows.[63] Jobs like these are often found in industries that sell technical products. This is one reason why the aerospace and transportation equipment industries have a relatively heavy emphasis on salary plans for their salespeople.

There are advantages to paying salespeople on a straight salary basis. Salespeople know in advance what their income will be, and the employer also has fixed, predictable sales force expenses. Straight salary makes it simple to switch territories or quotas or to reassign salespeople, and it can develop a high degree of loyalty among the sales staff. Commissions tend to shift the salesperson's emphasis to making the sale rather than to prospecting and cultivating long-term customers. A long-term perspective is encouraged by straight salary compensation.

The main disadvantage is that salary plans do not depend on results.[64] In fact, salaries are often tied to seniority rather than to performance, which can be demotivating to potentially high-performing salespeople who see seniority—not performance—being rewarded.

Commission Plan Commission plans pay salespeople in direct proportion to their sales—they pay for results and only for results. The commission plan has several advantages. Salespeople have the greatest possible incentive, and there is a tendency to attract high-performing salespeople who see that effort will clearly lead to rewards. Sales costs are proportional to sales rather than fixed, and the company's selling investment is reduced. The commission basis is also easy to understand and compute.

The commission plan also has drawbacks, however. Salespeople focus on making a sale and on high-volume items; cultivating dedicated customers and working to push hard-to-sell items may be neglected. Wide variances in income between salespeople may occur and this can lead to a feeling that the plan is inequitable. More serious is the fact that salespeople are encouraged to neglect other duties, like servicing small accounts. In addition, pay is often excessive in boom times and very low in recessions.

An Ethical Dilemma

Is it fair to compensate sales employees on a 100 percent commission basis with no financial security?

Recent research evidence presents further insights into the impact of sales commissions. One study addressed whether paying salespeople on commission "without a financial net" might induce more salespeople to leave. The participants in this study were 225 field sales representatives from a telecommunications company. Results showed that paying salespeople a commission accounting for 100 percent of pay was the situation that resulted in the highest turnover of salespersons by far. Turnover was much lower in the situation in which salespeople are paid a combination of a base salary plus commissions.[65] These findings suggest that although 100 percent commissions can drive higher sales by focusing the attention of strong-willed salespeople on maximizing sales, without a financial safety net it can also undermine the desire of salespeople to stay.

8.8.3.2 Incentives for Operations Employees

Several incentive plans are particularly well suited for use with operations employees, such as those doing production work.[66] **Piecework** is the oldest incentive plan and still the most commonly used. Earnings are tied directly to what the worker produces—the person is paid a piece rate for each unit that he or she produces. Thus, if Tom Smith gets $0.50 per piece for stamping out door jambs, then he would make $100 for stamping out 200 a day and $200 for stamping out 400.

piecework   A system of pay based on the number of items processed by each individual worker in a unit of time, such as items per hour or items per day.

Developing a workable piece-rate plan requires both job evaluation and (usually) industrial engineering. The crucial issue in piece-rate planning is the production standard, however, and this standard is usually developed by industrial engineers. With a **straight piecework plan**, Tom Smith would be paid on the basis of the number of door jambs that he produced; there would be no guaranteed minimum wage. However, after passage of employment/labour standards legislation, it became necessary for most employers to guarantee their workers a minimum wage. With a **guaranteed piecework plan**, Tom Smith would be paid the minimum wage whether or not he stamped out the number of door jambs required to make minimum wage—for example, 30 pieces if minimum wage is $15.00 per hour. As an incentive he would, however, also be paid at the piece rate of $0.50 for each unit that he produced over the number required to make minimum wage.

straight piecework plan   A set payment for each piece produced or processed in a factory or shop.

guaranteed piecework plan   The minimum hourly wage plus an incentive for each piece produced above a set number of pieces per hour.

"Piecework" generally implies straight piecework, a strict proportionality between results and rewards regardless of the level of output. Thus, in Smith's case, he continues to get $0.50 apiece for stamping out door jambs, even if he stamps out many more than planned (say, 600 per day). Other types of piecework incentive plans call for a sharing of productivity gains between worker and employer such that the worker does not receive full credit for all production above normal.[67]

The **differential piece-rate plan** is like the standard piece-rate plan with one major difference: With a piece-rate plan, the worker is paid a particular rate for each piece that he or she produces; with the differential piece-rate plan, the worker is rewarded by a *premium that equals the percentage by which his or her*

differential piece-rate plan   A plan by which a worker is paid a basic hourly rate plus an extra percentage of his or her base rate for production exceeding the standard per hour or per day. It is similar to piecework payment but is based on a percentage premium.

performance exceeds the standard. The plan assumes the worker has a guaranteed base rate. (The base rate may, but need not, equal the hourly rate determined by the job evaluation; however, it must meet or exceed the minimums established in the applicable Labour/Employment Standards Act.)

Advantages and Disadvantages   Piecework incentive plans have several advantages. They are simple to calculate and easily understood by employees. Piecerate plans appear equitable in principle, and their incentive value can be powerful since rewards are directly tied to performance.

Piecework also has some disadvantages. A main one is its somewhat unsavoury reputation among many employees, based on some employers' habits of arbitrarily raising production standards whenever they find their workers earning "excessive" wages. Since the piece rate is quoted on a per-piece basis, in workers' minds production standards become tied inseparably to the amount of money earned. When an attempt is made to revise production standards, it is met with considerable worker resistance, even if the revision is fully justified.[68]

The differential piece-rate plan has most of the advantages of the piecework plan and is fairly simple to compute and easy to understand. The incentive is expressed in units of time instead of in monetary terms (as it is with the standard piece-rate system). Therefore, there is less of a tendency on the part of workers to link their production standard with their pay. Furthermore, the clerical job of re-computing piece rates whenever hourly wage rates are re-evaluated is avoided.

Such problems as these have led some firms to drop their piecework plans and to substitute team-based incentive plans or programs, such as gainsharing (discussed above). An interesting example of how piecework and other forms of incentive pay can lead to corporate success is seen in the Lincoln Electric company.[69]

8.8.3.3 Incentives for Teams or Groups

team or group incentive plan   A plan in which a production standard is set for a specific work group and its members are paid incentives if the group exceeds the production standard.

There are several ways in which to implement **team or group incentive plans**.[70] One is to set work standards for each member of the group and maintain a count of the output of each member. Members are then paid based on one of three formulas: (1) All members receive the pay earned by the highest producer; (2) all members receive the pay earned by the lowest producer; or (3) all members receive payment equal to the average pay earned by the group. Group incentive plans have been found to be more effective when there are high levels of communication with employees about the specifics of the plan, when there is strong worker involvement in the plan's design and implementation, and when group members perceive the plan as fair.[71]

The second approach is to set a production standard based on the final output of the group as a whole; all members then receive the same pay, based on the piece rate that exists for the group's job. The group incentive can be based on either the piece rate or standard hour plan, but the latter is somewhat more prevalent.

A third option is to choose a measurable definition of group performance or productivity that the group can control. For instance, broad criteria, such as total labour hours per final product, could be used; piecework's engineered standards are thus not necessarily required here.[72]

There are several reasons to use team incentive plans. Sometimes, several jobs are interrelated, as they are on project teams. Here, one worker's performance reflects not only his or her own effort but that of co-workers as well; thus, team incentives make sense. Team plans also reinforce group planning and problem solving, and help to ensure that collaboration takes place. Group incentive plans also facilitate on-the-job training, since each member of the group has an interest in getting new members trained as quickly as possible.[73]

A group incentive plan's chief disadvantage is that each worker's rewards are no longer based solely on his or her own effort. To the extent that the person does not see his or her effort leading to the desired reward, a group plan may be less effective at motivating employees than an individual plan is.

8.8.3.4 Incentives for Senior Managers and Executives

There has been much discussion regarding executive compensation levels particularly when placed against such concomitant factors as corporate performance, restructuring, employee downsizing and shareholder dissatisfaction.[74] There are five elements in an executive/managerial compensation package: salary, benefits, short-term incentives, long-term incentives, and perquisites.[75] Salary is the cornerstone of executive compensation because it is the element on which the others are layered, with benefits, incentives, and perquisites often awarded in some proportion to base pay. There has been considerable debate regarding whether top executives are worth what they are paid. Some argue that the job of an executive is increasingly difficult. The stakes are high, and job tenure is often short. Expectations are getting higher, the questions from shareholders are more direct, and the challenge of navigating an organization through difficult economic times has never been so great.[76]

An Ethical Dilemma

Is it right that CEOs earn enormous amounts of money when most employees are getting small increases each year (sometimes even less than inflation)?

8.8.3.5 Combination Plan

There has been a definite movement away from the extremes of straight commission or fixed salary to combination plans for salespeople. Combination plans provide some of the advantages of both straight salary and straight commission plans and also some of their disadvantages. Salespeople have a floor to their earnings. Furthermore, the company can direct its salespeople's activities by detailing what services the salary component is being paid for, while the commission component provides a built-in incentive for superior performance.

However, the salary component is not tied to performance, and the employer is therefore trading away some incentive value. Combination plans also tend to become complicated, and misunderstandings can result. This might not be a problem with a simple "salary plus commission" plan, but most plans are not so simple. For example, there is a "commission plus drawing account" plan, whereby a salesperson is paid basically on commissions but can draw on future earnings to get through low sales periods. Similarly, in the "commission plus bonus" plan, salespeople are again paid primarily on the basis of commissions, but they are also given a small bonus for directed activities, like selling slow-moving items.

While concern related to turnover among sales staff due to the use of commission plans is legitimate, some level of turnover is not only predictable but actually a healthy by-product of a well-designed pay-for-performance plan. However, when does turnover among sales staff become a concern? Human resources managers should track turnover rates for those on a commission-based plan and, through exit interviews, determine the reason(s) for employees leaving the organization. These reasons for leaving, when matched against the sales staff performance levels, may cause HR compensation specialists to reconsider their incentive-base pay plan design options to assure motivational levels and retention of high-performers in their business.[77]

CHAPTER SUMMARY

1. A total rewards approach considers individual reward components as part of an integrated whole to determine the best mix of rewards that are aligned with business strategy and provide employee value, all within the cost constraints of the organization. Alignment is the extent to which rewards support outcomes that are important to achieving the organization's strategic objectives.

2. Establishing pay rates involves three stages: job evaluation (to ensure internal equity), conducting wage/salary surveys (to ensure external equity), and combining job evaluation and salary survey results to determine pay rates. Job evaluation is aimed at determining the relative worth of jobs within a firm. It compares jobs with one another based on their content, which is usually defined in terms of compensable factors, such as skill, effort, responsibility, and working conditions. Jobs of approximately equal value are combined into pay grades for pay purposes. Salary surveys collect data from other employers in the marketplace who are competing for employees in similar kinds of positions. The wage curve shows the average market wage for each pay grade (or job). It illustrates what the average wage for each grade should be and whether any present wages or salaries are out of line.

3. Competency-based pay plans provide employee compensation based on the skills and knowledge that they are capable of using, rather than the job that they currently hold.

4. The five basic elements of compensation for managers are salary, benefits, short-term incentives, long-term incentives, and perquisites.

5. Pay equity is intended to redress systemic gender discrimination as measured by the wage gap, and requires equal pay for female-dominated jobs and male-dominated jobs of equal value

(where value is determined through job evaluation).

6. Piecework is the oldest type of incentive plan. Here, a worker is paid a piece rate for each unit that he or she produces. The differential piece-rate plan rewards workers by a premium that equals the percentage by which their performance is above standard.

7. Most management employees receive a short-term incentive, usually in the form of an annual bonus linked to company or divisional profits. Long-term incentives are intended to motivate and reward top management for the firm's long-term growth and prosperity and to inject a long-term perspective into executive decisions.

8. Salary plans for salespeople are effective when the main sales objective is finding new clients or servicing accounts. Commission plans attract high-performing salespeople who see that performance will clearly lead to rewards.

9. Profit-sharing plans, employee share purchase/stock ownership plans, and gainsharing plans are examples of organization-wide incentive plans. Profit-sharing plans provide a share of company profits to all employees in the organization. The problem with such plans is that sometimes the link between a person's efforts and rewards is unclear. Stock purchase plans provide a vehicle for employees to purchase company stock with their own and sometimes employer contributions. Gainsharing plans engage employees in a common effort to achieve a company's productivity objectives in which incremental cost savings are shared among employees and the company.

MyLab Management

Visit MyLab Management to access a personalized Study Plan, Personal Inventory Assessments (PIA), and a collection of videos and assignments within MediaShare.

KEY TERMS

benchmark job *(p. 183)*
broadbanding *(p. 192)*
capital accumulation programs *(p. 200)*

classes *(p. 185)*
classification/grading method *(p. 185)*
compensable factor *(p. 184)*

differential piece-rate plan *(p. 203)*
employee share purchase/stock ownership plan
    (ESOP) *(p. 197)*
employee value proposition *(p. 178)*
external equity *(p. 182)*
fixed pay *(p. 179)*
gainsharing plan *(p. 197)*
green circle pay rate *(p. 192)*
guaranteed piecework plan *(p. 203)*
grade/group description *(p. 185)*
grades *(p. 185)*
internal equity *(p. 182)*
job evaluation *(p. 183)*
job evaluation committee *(p. 184)*
merit pay (merit raise) *(p. 179)*

pay equity *(p. 183)*
pay grade *(p. 188)*
pay ranges *(p. 190)*
piecework *(p. 203)*
point method *(p. 185)*
profit-sharing plan *(p. 196)*
red circle pay rate *(p. 192)*
stock option *(p. 200)*
straight piecework plan *(p. 203)*
team or group incentive plan *(p. 204)*
total employment rewards *(p. 178)*
variable pay *(p. 179)*
wage curve *(p. 190)*
wage/salary survey *(p. 188)*

REVIEW AND DISCUSSION QUESTIONS

1. What are the five components of total rewards?
2. Describe what is meant by the term "benchmark job."
3. Identify and briefly describe one of the basic considerations in determining pay rates in an organization.
4. Discuss one advantage and one disadvantage of each of the following job evaluation methods: ranking, classification, factor comparison, point method.
5. Explain the term "competencies," and explain the differences among core, functional, and behavioural competencies.
6. Explain what is meant by the market-pricing approach in evaluating professional jobs.
7. Explain the intention of pay equity legislation.
8. Describe the three basic issues to be considered when awarding short-term management bonuses.
9. Identify two supporting reasons for offering long-term incentives to an organization's executive staff.
10. Discuss the relative merits of compensating sales staff through a (i) salary only, (ii) commission only, and (iii) combined salary and commission plans.
11. In your view, what is a key reason employee incentive plans do not succeed?

CRITICAL THINKING QUESTIONS

1. Media reports identify significant compensation levels for Canadian corporate CEOs, at the same time as low corporate performance ratings or employee layoffs. Should anything be done about this? If "yes," what are your suggestions?
2. What are some of the potential reasons that gender-based pay discrimination is so hard to eradicate?
3. A major consulting firm recently launched a new "project managers' incentive" plan. Basically,

senior managers in the company were told to award $5 000 raises (not bonuses) to about 40 percent of the project managers in their team, based on how well they managed people on their projects and met deadlines, and the number of projects each project manager was responsible for that year. No additional criteria were provided, given the wide variance in projects and teams that the consulting firm secures in a given year. What are the potential advantages and pitfalls of such an incentive program? What areas of support or concern do you think project managers might have with the incentives? What areas of support or concern do you think senior managers might have with the incentives?

4. In making strategic pay policy decisions in a company, should the HR compensation specialist favour internal or external equity in wage and salary rates among employees?

5. Do you think that it is a good idea to reward employees with merit raises? Why or why not? If not, what approach would you take to incentive compensation?

6. Recognition can take many forms. Prepare a list of some forms of recognition that would be particularly motivational for Millennial (Gen Y) employees, and explain why you have chosen them.

EXPERIENTIAL EXERCISES

1. Visit the Starbucks Canada website, and find examples of compensation incentives offered to its employees. Using information in this chapter, prepare a rationale to support any of these incentive plans. What would you add as an additional pay incentive option for the company? Why?

2. You have been asked by the owner of your medium-size import and export company (200+ people) to develop a way to standardize pay ranges for various jobs in the company. He says he is tired of employees complaining about their pay as compared to that of others and is concerned that if he does nothing someone will complain about inequitable pay practices. Outline the steps you will follow to do this. Make sure to give a rationale for the type of job evaluation system you propose, as well as for the method you suggest to obtain comparable salary data. The jobs he is most concerned about are

   • Sales representative

   • Shipping and receiving manager

   • Multilingual sales contract negotiator

   • Accounts receivable clerk

   • Shipping clerk

3. You are the HR manager at a large construction firm headquartered in Edmonton. Most of the company's administrative staff are also in Edmonton. You have regional and local site offices across the country. Draft a memo to employees about your company's new pay-for-knowledge-and-skills policy. Make sure to document at least one fully complete section on how this policy will be administered. Your

professor may give you some ideas on what might be considered or you may create your own circumstances under which pay for knowledge and skills will be applied.

4. Working individually or in groups, develop an incentive plan for each of the following positions: web designer, hotel manager, and used-car salesperson. What factors should be taken into consideration for each job?

5. Using the Internet, locate a news media article on a national or provincial pay equity issue in Canada. Based on the situation described in the article, explain how a "green circle pay rate" solution would help to resolve the pay equity issue seen in the media account.

6. Express Automotive, an automobile mega-dealership with more than 600 employees that represents 22 brands, has just received a very discouraging set of survey results. It seems its customer satisfaction scores have fallen for the ninth straight quarter. Customer complaints included the following:

   • It was hard to get prompt feedback from mechanics by phone.

   • Salespeople often did not return phone calls.

   • The loan financing people seemed "pushy."

   • New cars were often not properly cleaned or had minor items that needed immediate repair or adjustment.

   • Cars often had to be returned to have repair work redone.

The following table describes Express Automotive's current compensation system.

Team	Responsibility	Current Compensation Method
Sales force	Persuade buyers to purchase a car.	Very small salary (minimum wage) with commissions; commission rate increases with every 20 cars sold per month.
Loan financing office	Help close the sale; persuade customer to use company finance plan.	Salary, plus bonus for each $10 000 financed with the company.
Detailing	Inspect cars delivered from factory, clean them, and make minor adjustments.	Piecework paid on the number of cars detailed per day.
Mechanics	Provide factory warranty service, maintenance, and repair.	Small hourly wage, plus bonus based on (1) number of cars completed per day and (2) finishing each car faster than the standard estimated time to repair.
Receptionists/phone service personnel	Act as primary liaison between customer and sales force, finance, and mechanics.	Minimum wage.

7. The class is to be divided into five groups. Each group is assigned to one of the five teams in column one. Each group should analyze the compensation package for its team. Each group should be able to identify the ways in which the current compensation plan (1) helps company performance or (2) impedes company performance. Once the groups have completed their analyses, the following questions are to be discussed as a class:

1. In what ways might your group's compensation plan contribute to the customer service problems?

2. Do the rewards provided by your department impede the work of other departments?

3. What recommendations would you make to improve the compensation system in a way that would likely improve customer satisfaction?

© Dmitry Kalinovsky / Shutterstock

9 EMPLOYEE BENEFITS AND SERVICES

LEARNING OUTCOMES

AFTER STUDYING THIS CHAPTER, YOU SHOULD BE ABLE TO:

EXPLAIN the strategic role of employee benefits.

DESCRIBE seven government-mandated benefits.

EXPLAIN why the cost of health insurance benefits is increasing and how employers can reduce these costs.

DESCRIBE the two categories of pension plans and the shift that is occurring in their relative popularity.

DISCUSS three types of personal employee services and six types of job-related services offered to employees.

EXPLAIN how to set up a flexible benefits program.

9.1 THE STRATEGIC ROLE OF EMPLOYEE BENEFITS

Employee benefits and services can be defined as all the indirect financial payments that an employee receives during his or her employment with an employer.[1] Benefits generally provided to all of a firm's employees include such things as time off with pay, supplementary health and life insurance, and retirement savings plans. Employee services, traditionally a minor aspect of compensation, are becoming more sought after by today's employees in the post–job security era. Research indicates that benefits do matter to employees and that, if they are aligned with business strategy, such programs can help attract and retain the right people to achieve business objectives, as highlighted in **Table 9.1**.[2]

Employee benefits are an important part of most employees' compensation, particularly given today's reality of modest salary increases.[3] Three mandatory benefits (CPP/QPP [Canada/Quebec Pension Plan]), EI premiums, and workers' compensation) account for over 50 percent of the employer portion of benefits.[4] Over half of employers indicate that from 2010 to 2011, cost of benefits in their organization rose at a rate twice the general rate of inflation.[5]

Administering benefits today represents an increasingly specialized task because workers are more financially sophisticated and demanding, and because benefit plans must comply with a wide variety of laws. Providing and administering benefits is also an increasingly expensive task. Benefits as a percentage of payroll (for public and private sectors combined) are approximately 37 percent today (compared with about 15 percent in 1953). Most employees do not realize the market value and high cost to the employer of their benefits.

As a result, cost containment of benefits is a current challenge to many organizations.

Certain benefits are mandated by law, and most Canadian companies voluntarily provide additional employee benefits such as group life insurance, health and dental care insurance, and retirement benefits. In the remainder of this chapter, government-sponsored benefits, voluntary employer-sponsored benefits, employee services, flexible benefits, and benefits administration will be discussed. **Table 9.2** provides a summary of mandated and voluntary benefits.

employee benefits   Indirect financial payments given to employees. They may include supplementary health and life insurance, vacation, pension plans, education plans, and discounts on company products.

Benefits Interface
www.benefits.org

Employee Benefit Research Institute
www.ebri.org

BenefitsLink.com
www.benefitslink.com

Benefits Canada
www.benefitscanada.ca

TABLE 9.1   Objectives of a Benefits Strategy, 2015

Objectives of Benefits Strategy	Percentage of Organizations that Rated the Objective as "Very Important"
Complying with accounting, regulatory, and company standards	53%
Containing benefits costs	45%
Attracting talent/maintaining competitive position	39%
Retaining talent/reducing turnover	37%
Increasing job satisfaction/employee engagement	33%
Enhancing employee health	30%

Source: The Conference Board of Canada. "*Benefits Benchmarking 2015*," October, 2015, p. 6. Reprinted by permission.

TABLE 9.2   Employee Benefits: Government-mandated vs. Voluntary

Government-Mandated Benefits	Voluntary Employer-Sponsored Benefits
• Employment Insurance (EI) • Pay on termination of employment • Leaves of absence • Canada/Quebec Pension Plan (CPP/QPP) • Workers' compensation • Vacations and statutory holidays • Paid breaks	• Life insurance • Supplementary health care/medical insurance • Short-term disability plans and sick leave plans • Long-term disability • Sabbaticals • Retirement benefits

9.2 GOVERNMENT-MANDATED BENEFITS

Canada has one of the world's finest collections of social programs to protect its citizens when they cannot earn income. Employers and employees, as well as general tax revenues, provide funding for these plans.

9.2.1 Employment Insurance (EI)

employment insurance (EI)   A federal program intended to provide temporary financial assistance to eligible persons who experience interruption to their work through no fault of their own.

Employment insurance (EI) is a federal program intended to provide temporary financial assistance to eligible persons who experience interruption to their work through no fault of their own. EI benefits are not payable when an employee is terminated for just cause (for example, for theft of company property); quits for no good reason; participates in a legal union strike; or is incarcerated in a jail, prison, or other institution. EI is seen as a benefit, since it provides employees who are laid off, who are terminated without just cause, or who quit their job for a justifiable reason (such as harassment) with an alternative form of government income until they secure employment.

In addition to loss of employment through no fault of the employee, eligibility is also restricted to persons who have paid into the account (for example, a contractor who does not contribute to the EI account is ineligible for the benefit), have worked a minimum number of hours in a specified time, and are willing and able to work.

The EI benefit is generally 55 percent of average earnings during the last 14 to 45 weeks of the qualifying period or a maximum weekly rate (for example, as of January 1, 2017, in the maximum weekly rate was $543),[6] whichever is lower of the two. The benefit is payable for a maximum number of weeks, depending on factors such as the regional unemployment rate. To continue receiving EI benefits, individuals must demonstrate that they are actively seeking work. Claimants are encouraged to work part time, as they can earn a portion of their EI benefit amount (e.g., 25 percent) before these earnings will be deducted from the benefit.

To receive benefits, an employee must first have worked a minimum number of hours during a minimum number of weeks called a *qualifying period* (the number of hours and weeks varies among regions of the country). Then there is a waiting period from the last day of work until benefits begin. The waiting period varies by jurisdiction but is often two weeks. If the employee received severance pay or holiday pay from the employer at the time of losing the job, these payments must run out before the waiting period begins.

The EI program is funded by contributions from eligible employees and their employers. Employee contributions are collected by payroll deduction, and employers pay 1.4 times the employee contribution. Employer contributions can be reduced if the employer provides a wage loss replacement plan for employee sick leave.

A supplemental unemployment benefit (SUB) plan is an agreement between an employer and the employees (often the result of collective bargaining) for a plan that enables employees who are eligible for EI benefits to receive additional benefits from a SUB fund created by the employer. SUB plans help employees maintain their standard of living during periods of unemployment (most often maternity leave) by receiving a combined benefit closer to their actual working wage. Most SUBs provide benefits of 90 percent of the working wage or greater.[7] Work-sharing programs are a related arrangement in which employees work a reduced workweek and receive EI benefits for the remainder of the week. The Canada Employment Insurance Commission must approve SUB plans and work-sharing programs.

9.2.2 Pay on Termination of Employment

Employment/labour standards legislation requires that employees whose employment is being terminated by the employer be provided with termination pay when they leave. The amount to be paid varies among jurisdictions and with the circumstances, as follows. Specifically, it should be noted that employees often confuse severance pay with termination pay.

9.2.2.1 Reasonable Notice Periods

An employer may provide an employee with reasonable notice of termination from their job. The length of the notice period is defined in the applicable employment standards legislation and in some cases with the common law. Such notice is not required in situations where the employer alleges just cause against the employee. The employer may elect to provide the terminated employee with **pay in lieu of reasonable notice**, offering a lump sum or wage continuance payment rather than have the individual work out the term of the notice period.

pay in lieu of reasonable notice A lump sum or wage continuance payment equal to an employee's pay for the notice period provided to employees who cease working immediately.

9.2.2.2 Severance Pay

While it is common in everyday conversation to hear the terms "termination pay" and "severance pay" used interchangeably, the latter term has specific application under law. **Severance pay** is a one-time, lump sum statutory payment at time of termination, based on the employee's length of service with the employer; it is paid *in addition* to pay in lieu of reasonable notice. Only employees in Ontario and the federal jurisdiction may be eligible for severance pay, and only in certain termination situations (no other jurisdictions mandate severance pay). For example, in Ontario, employees with five or more years of service may be eligible for severance pay if (1) the employer's annual Ontario payroll is $2.5 million or more, or (2) the employer is closing down the business and 50 or more employees will be losing their jobs within a six-month period. The amount of the severance pay is one week's pay for each year of employment (maximum 26 weeks). In the federal jurisdiction system, employees who have been employed for 12 months or more receive the greater of either two days' worth of wages for every year employed with the company or a total of five days' wages. For example, an employee who has been with the company for one year would be entitled

severance pay Payable by employers under Ontario and/or federal jurisdiction to employees terminated for reasons other than cause, in addition to the reasonable notice payment or period. Severance pay is often based on the employee's length of service and other factors (such as the total size of the annual company payroll).

to five days' worth of severance, whichever is the greater of the two above options. Severance pay is an additional payout on top of the minimum notice period requirements and applies only if the specific conditions in the applicable jurisdiction are met.

9.2.2.3 Pay for Mass Layoffs

In situations where a number of employees are terminated by the employer at one time, legislation in the federal or provincial jurisdictions will set out termination notice or pay-in-lieu-of-notice requirements for affected individuals. Severance payments for these affected employees, in addition to these termination pay requirements, may also be required under the law. The rationale behind this regulation is that larger layoffs result in longer time for re-employment, so in cases of larger layoffs the employees are given longer reasonable notice periods.

9.2.3 Leaves of Absence

All provinces and territories and the federal jurisdiction require unpaid leaves of absence to be provided to employees in certain circumstances. Maternity (pregnancy) or parental leave is provided in every jurisdiction (usually after one year of service). The amount of maternity leave is 17 or 18 weeks in each jurisdiction (15 weeks in Alberta),[8] but parental and adoption leaves range from 34 to 52 weeks. Employees who take these leaves of absence are guaranteed their old job or a similar job when they return to work. Parental leave benefits can be taken by one parent or split between both parents.

Bereavement leave on the death of a family member is provided for employees in some but not all jurisdictions. The amount of time off varies by jurisdiction and depends on the closeness of the relationship between the employee and the deceased. Bereavement leave is usually unpaid, but in some cases it can be partially or fully paid. For example, in organizations employing more than 50 persons, Ontario provides up to 10 unpaid "personal emergency leave" days per year to employees, which may be used for this purpose. The federal government and several provinces also provide family medical/compassionate care leave of absence to care and support family members who are critically ill. The length of leave and qualifying conditions vary by jurisdiction. For example, British Columbia and Ontario provide up to 8 weeks within a 26-week period. There are also new forms of leave of absence in some provinces. In 2014, Ontario created Family Caregiver Leave, Critically Ill Child Care Leave, and Crime-Related Child Death/Disappearance Leave under its Employment Standards Act. The length of these new leaves of absences and eligibility requirements is determined in each instance under legislative provisions.[9]

Some employers provide full or partial pay for all or part of legally required unpaid leaves by "topping up" what employees receive from EI, such that the total amount they receive more closely matches their regular salary. For example, in some cases of bereavement, leave may be partially or fully paid by the employer.

Having a clear procedure for any leave of absence is essential. An application form should be a key component of any such procedure. In general, no employee should be given a leave until the reason for such an absence is clearly known. If the leave is for medical or family reasons, medical certification should be obtained from the attending physician or medical practitioner. A form like this creates a record of the employee's expected return date and the fact that, without an authorized extension, his or her employment may be terminated.

Although these leaves are unpaid, it is incorrect to assume that the leave is costless to the employer. For example, one study concluded that the costs associated with recruiting new temporary workers, training replacement workers, and compensating for the lower level of productivity of these workers could represent a substantial expense over and above what employers would normally pay their full-time employees.[10]

9.2.4 Canada/Quebec Pension Plan (CPP/QPP)

The **Canada/Quebec Pension Plans (CPP/QPP)** were introduced in 1966 to provide working Canadians with a basic level of financial security on retirement or disability. Four decades later, these benefits do indeed provide a significant part of most Canadians' retirement income. Almost all employed Canadians between the ages of 18 and 65 are covered, including self-employed individuals. Casual and migrant workers are excluded, as are people who are not earning any employment income, such as homemakers or volunteers. The benefits are portable, meaning that pension rights are not affected by changes in job or residence within Canada. Both contributions and benefits are based only on earnings up to the "year's maximum pensionable earnings" (intended to approximate the average industrial wage), as defined in the legislation. Benefits are adjusted based on inflation each year in line with the consumer price index. Contributions made by employees (4.95 percent of pensionable earnings as of January 2017) are matched by employers.

Three types of benefits are provided: retirement pensions, disability pensions, and survivor benefits. The *retirement pension* is calculated as 25 percent of the average earnings (adjusted for inflation up to the average inflation level during the last five years before retirement) over the years during which contributions were made. Plan members can choose to begin receiving benefits at any time between the ages of 60 and 70. Benefits are reduced on early retirement before age 65 and are increased in the case of late retirement after age 65. A number of significant changes were initiated in 2012 that will affect CPP payouts and associated employee decisions on when to retire that HR (human resources) managers must consider. For example, there has been a move to increase the reduction level for individuals who access CPP early. In 2016, the deduction for each month that an individual collected CPP before the age of 65 was 0.6 percent. There is also an increase in the value of the payment premium for those who delay retirement to consider.

Disability benefits are paid only for severe disabilities that are expected to be permanent or to last for an extended period. The disability benefit is 75 percent of the pension benefit earned at the date of disability, plus a flat-rate amount per child. *Survivor benefits* are paid on the death of a plan member. A lump-sum payment is made to the plan member's estate, and a monthly pension is also payable to the surviving spouse and each dependent child.

9.2.5 Workers' Compensation

Workers' compensation laws provide sure, prompt income and medical benefits to victims of work-related accidents or illnesses, or to their dependants, regardless of fault. Every province and territory and the federal jurisdiction has its own

Canada/Quebec Pension Plans (CPP/QPP) Programs that provide three types of benefits: retirement income, survivor or death benefits payable to the employee's dependents regardless of age at time of death, and disability benefits payable to employees with disabilities and their dependants. Benefits are payable only to those individuals who make contributions to the plans, or to their family members.

Canada Pension Plan **www.servicecanada.gc.ca/eng/services/pensions/cpp/retirement/index.shtml**

workers' compensation Provides income and medical benefits to victims of work-related accidents or illnesses, or to their dependants, regardless of fault.

workers' compensation law. These laws impose compulsory collective liability for workplace accidents and work-related illnesses. This means that employees and employers cannot sue each other regarding the costs of workplace accidents or illnesses. Workers' compensation is, in effect, a "no-fault" insurance plan designed to help injured or ill workers get well and return to work. For an injury or illness to be covered by workers' compensation, one must only prove that it arose while the employee was on the job. It does not matter that the employee may have been at fault; if he or she was on the job when the injury or illness occurred, he or she is entitled to workers' compensation. For example, suppose all employees are instructed to wear safety goggles when working at their machines, and one does not and is injured. Workers' compensation benefits will still be provided. The fact that the worker was at fault in no way waives his or her claim to benefits.

Employers collectively pay the full cost of the workers' compensation system, which can be an onerous financial burden for small businesses. The cost varies by industry and with actual employer costs; employer premiums are tax deductible. Workers' compensation boards (or equivalent bodies) exist in each jurisdiction to determine and collect payments from employers, determine rights to compensation, and pay workers the amount of benefit to which they are entitled under the legislation in their jurisdiction. Employers and employees have some representation on these boards, but usually both parties believe they should have more control.

Association of Workers'
Compensation Boards of Canada
www.awcbc.org

Workers' compensation benefits include payment of expenses for medical treatment and rehabilitation, and income benefits during the time in which the worker is unable to work (temporarily or permanently) because of his or her disability (partial or total). Survivor benefits are payable if a work-related death occurs. All benefits are non-taxable. Although workers' compensation boards pay the claims, the premiums for most employers depend on the number of claims and on the amounts of money that are paid. Minimizing such claims is thus important. The Expert Opinion box highlights how proactive management of musculoskeletal pain can help control costs associated with disabilities. Providing awareness of accident prevention methods can also effectively help manage workers' compensation costs. These ideas are integrated with occupational health and safety (to be reviewed in Chapter 10).

9.2.6 Vacations and Holidays

Labour/employment standards legislation sets out a minimum amount of paid vacation that must be provided to employees, usually two weeks per year, but the requirements vary by jurisdiction. The actual number of paid employee vacation days also varies considerably from employer to employer. Many employers provide additional paid holidays and paid vacation over and above the amount required by law. Thus, a typical annual vacation determination policy might be as follows:

- Two weeks for the first 5 years of service
- Three weeks for 6 to 10 years of service
- Four weeks for 11 to 15 years of service
- Five weeks for 16 to 25 years of service
- Six weeks after 25 years of service

Academic Viewpoint
EXPERT OPINION

1. What causes musculoskeletal pain?

A musculoskeletal condition, such as back, neck, or knee pain at work, is actually multi-causal in nature. This is often precipitated by injury (acute trauma, i.e., falling or sprain, or non-traumatic, i.e., repetitive strain). The broader psychosocial environment in the workplace is critical for triggering and resolving musculoskeletal pain. Research demonstrates that people who are dissatisfied with work report high stress levels, and those who indicate low decision-making autonomy of the workforce are generally higher at risk for musculoskeletal pain. There are personal factors, such as general health or individual psychological characteristics (e.g., depression), that increase risk. In addition, the health-care system is another point of influence.

The timeliness and nature of the feedback or treatment is critical to ensure successful return to work. For example, if treatment is only clinical in nature, rather than integrative, that individual may be more likely to experience a longer disability or time to recovery.

2. How can musculoskeletal pain that leads to disabilities impact the workplace?

The job design should consider the physical and psychosocial aspects that trigger musculoskeletal pain. In addition, using evidence-based

Identification:
Dr. Pierre Côté (PhD)
Associate Professor and Canada Research Chair in Disability Prevention and Rehabilitation

Affiliation:
Faculty of Health Sciences, University of Ontario Institute of Technology (UOIT) and Director, UOIT–CMCC Centre for the Study of Disability Prevention and Rehabilitation

approaches to pain management can help reduce the likelihood that musculoskeletal pain will result in a disability. Most workers with musculoskeletal pain get better in a few weeks. Others require an integrated solution involving the union, the worker, and clinical stakeholders in the mix to find a solution. Research shows that when individuals return to work with multi-stakeholder intervention, they can succeed. Critical to this multi-stakeholder intervention is a negotiated stakeholder decision, rather than

a unilateral decision in which the employee and other stakeholders do not have an opportunity to express their voice or help find a middle ground.

3. What can organizations do to ensure musculoskeletal pain is proactively managed?

In the health sciences, we use the concept of primary prevention. The list is not exhaustive, but highlights some of the key points to consider. First, the psychosocial environment should be healthy, including good working relationships with managers and co-workers. Second, the organization should ensure that a culture of health and well-being is prioritized. This includes legitimizing injury. For example, if a worker is hurt they don't get labelled as a whiner. This also includes fully addressing a culture of presenteeism, which can have long-term detrimental effects on the individual and the organization.

In addition, organizational leadership is required to champion initiatives associated with management of health risks. The physical makeup of work is critical as well. Poorly configured work sections are associated with neck and upper extremity injuries. The influence of stress, demands, and work conditions needs to be managed for both onsite and remote workers.

Source: Reprinted by permission from Pierre Côté.

The number of paid statutory holidays similarly varies considerably from one jurisdiction to another, from five to nine. The most common paid holidays include New Year's Day, Good Friday, Canada Day, Labour Day, and Christmas and Boxing Day. Other common holidays include Victoria Day, Thanksgiving Day, and Remembrance Day. Additional holidays may be observed in each province, such as Family Day in Ontario, Alberta, Saskatchewan, and British Columbia, and Saint-Jean-Baptiste Day in Quebec.

There are a number of commonly paid holidays in Canada, including Thanksgiving Day.

9.2.7 Paid Breaks

While vacation requirements mandate paid time off, in terms of full days of work off, there are also mandated paid and unpaid requirements for time off within a workday at the provincial, territorial, and federal levels. For example, in Nova Scotia, an employee shift of over five hours requires a minimum 30-minute uninterrupted break. If the employee is under direct control of the employer and expected to be available for work during this time, then the break must be paid. If not, then it can be unpaid. Similar conditions apply in each jurisdiction. Contrary to popular belief, coffee or other rest breaks in addition to the eating period are often not government mandated. If the employee is free to leave the workplace, then the employer does not have to pay for the time.

9.3 VOLUNTARY EMPLOYER-SPONSORED BENEFITS

Although they are not required to do so, employers often provide many other employee benefits. There are some benefits that appear to be more valued by Canadian employees than others, based on a 2012 Mercer survey (as highlighted in **Figure 9.1**); however, offering a mix of benefits appears to be the norm in most organizations. Several of the most common types of employee benefits will now be described.

9.3.1 Life Insurance

group life insurance Life insurance provided at lower rates for all employees, including new employees, regardless of health or physical condition.

Virtually all employers provide **group life insurance** plans for their employees. As a group, employees can obtain lower rates than if they bought such insurance as individuals. In addition, group plans usually contain a provision for coverage of all employees—including new ones—regardless of health or physical condition.

In most cases, the employer pays 100 percent of the base premium, which usually provides life insurance equal to about two years' salary. Additional life insurance coverage is sometimes made available to employees on an optional, employee-paid basis. *Accidental death and dismemberment* coverage provides a fixed lump-sum benefit in addition to life insurance benefits when death is accidental. It also provides a range of benefits in case of accidental loss of limbs or sight and is often paid for by the employer.

Critical illness insurance provides a lump-sum benefit to an employee who is diagnosed with and survives a life-threatening illness. This benefit bridges the gap between life insurance and disability insurance by providing immediate funds to relieve some the financial burden associated with the illness (such as paying for out-of-country treatment or experimental treatment) or enabling employees to enjoy their remaining time by pursuing activities that would normally be beyond their financial means.[11]

FIGURE 9.1   Top Benefits Choices among Canadians

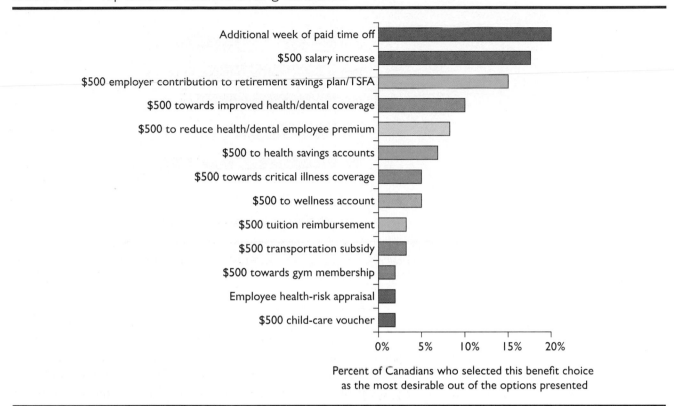

Percent of Canadians who selected this benefit choice
as the most desirable out of the options presented

9.3.2 Supplementary Health-care/Medical Insurance

Most employers provide their employees with supplementary health-care/medical insurance (over and above that provided by provincial health-care plans). Along with life insurance and long-term disability, these benefits form the cornerstone of almost all benefits programs.[12] Supplementary health-care insurance is aimed at providing protection against medical costs arising from off-the-job accidents or illness.

Most supplementary health insurance plans provide insurance at group rates, which are usually lower than individual rates and are generally available to all employees—including new ones—regardless of health or physical condition. Supplementary health-care plans provide major medical coverage to meet medical expenses not covered by government health-care plans, including prescription drugs, private or semi-private hospital rooms, private duty nursing, physiotherapy, medical supplies, ambulance services, and so on. In most employer-sponsored drug plans, employees must pay a specified amount of **deductible** expense (typically $25 or $50) per year before plan benefits begin. Many employers also sponsor health-related insurance plans that cover expenses like vision care, hearing aids, and dental services, often with deductibles. In a majority of cases, the participants in such plans have their premiums paid for entirely by their employers.[13]

deductible   The annual amount of health/dental expenses that an employee must pay before insurance benefits will be paid.

9.3.2.1 Reducing Health-Benefit Costs

Dramatic increases in health-care costs are the biggest issue facing benefits managers in Canada today. **Figure 9.2** shows how increases in medical and dental

FIGURE 9.2 Increases in Health Plan Costs, 2006–2010

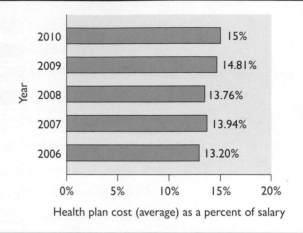

Year

2010	15%
2009	14.81%
2008	13.76%
2007	13.94%
2006	13.20%

0%   5%   10%   15%   20%

Health plan cost (average) as a percent of salary

Source: Canadian Health Care Trend Survey Results 2010 (Toronto, ON: Buck Consultants, 2010), p. 2. Courtesy of Buck Consultants Limited.

plan costs have continued to escalate since 2006. The main reasons for these increases are increased use of expensive new drugs and rising drug use by an aging population.[14] Despite government health-care plans, Canadian employers pay about 30 percent of all health-care expenses in Canada, most of this for prescription drugs.[15]

Many Canadian managers now find controlling and reducing health-care costs topping their to-do lists. The simplest approach to reducing health-benefit costs is to *increase the amount of health-care costs paid by employees*. This can be accomplished by increasing employee premiums, increasing deductibles, reducing company **co-insurance** levels (the percentage of expenses paid for by the insurance plan), instituting or lowering annual maximums on some services, or even eliminating coverage for spouses, private hospital rooms, and other benefits. An Angus Reid poll of 1 500 Canadians found that three-quarters of the respondents were willing to pay higher premiums to cover the high cost of prescription drugs.[16]

co-insurance The percentage of expenses (in excess of the deductible) that are paid for by the insurance plan.

© Pavel Losevsky/Fotolia

An onsite employee fitness centre.

Another cost-reduction strategy is to publish a *restricted list of drugs* that will be paid for under the plan to encourage the use of generic rather than more expensive brand-name drugs. New drugs may not be covered if equally effective, cheaper alternatives are available. This approach should be combined with employee education to effectively manage the demand for drugs.[17]

A third approach is *health promotion*. In-house newsletters can caution workers to take medication properly and advertise programs on weight management, smoking cessation, exercise classes, onsite massage therapy, nutrition counselling, and other wellness programs. After 10 years of providing an onsite exercise program for employees, Canada Life Assurance Company found that absenteeism dropped 24 percent for employees who exercised two to three times per week.[18] Employee assistance programs can help to combat alcohol and drug addiction and provide stress-management counselling. HR by the Numbers: Smoking and the Workplace provides a quick snapshot of the effect of smoking and the impact of smoking cessation programs in the workplace.

A fourth approach is to implement *risk-assessment* programs. CIBC and other companies are using such programs. A third party conducts a confidential survey of the health history and lifestyle choices of employees to identify common health risk factors, such as those associated with heart disease or mental health, so that problem-specific programs can be implemented.[19]

Finally, *health-care spending accounts* (HCSA) are offered by more than 90 percent of Canadian employers, either alone or in combination with a standard health care plan.[20] The employer establishes an annual account for each employee containing a certain amount of money (determined by the employer to control costs). The employee can spend the money on health-care costs as he or she wants. This provides flexibility for the employee. These accounts are governed by the Income Tax Act, which allows expenses not normally covered under employer-sponsored health-care plans (such as laser eye surgery) and defines dependants more broadly than most employer plans.[21] HCSAs are very popular with employees.

9.3.2.2 Retiree Health Benefits

Another concern is the cost of health benefits provided to retirees. These benefits typically include life insurance, drugs, and private/semi-private hospital coverage. Some continue coverage to a surviving spouse. Retiree benefit costs are already exceeding the costs for active employees in some organizations, in part because many early retirees between the ages of 50 and 65 are not yet eligible for government health benefits that start at age 65. Employers are required to disclose liabilities for retiree benefits in their financial statements. These liabilities are not required to be pre-funded and thus are at risk in the case of business failure.[22]

Employers can cut costs by increasing retiree contributions, increasing deductibles, tightening eligibility requirements, and reducing maximum payouts.[23] The last few years have seen a trend away from employer-provided retiree health benefits. This trend is expected to continue as a result of rising health-care costs, growing retiree populations, uncertain business profitability, and federal regulations that provide only limited opportunities for funding retiree medical benefits.[24]

HR by the Numbers

▶ Smoking and the Workplace

$3 396 estimated annual per-employee cost to organization associated with smoking

73% of employer health/benefit plans cover prescription smoking cessation medicines.

27% the number of additional days per year that employees who smoke are absent from work, when compared to non-smokers

40% of employer health/benefits plans cover nicotine replacement therapies like gums, lozenges, and patches

12% the average percentage of smokers employed in an organization

19% of Canadian organizations completely ban smoking on their property

Success with Workplace Smoking Cessation Programs

4–7% typical smoking quit rate without medication or counselling

27% of participants in the Alberta and Northwest Territories Lung Association workplace smoking cessation program were smoke-free one year after the end of the program.

40% of participants in the Windsor–Essex County Health Units pharmacist-led smoking cessation program were smoke-free six months after the program ended.

An Ethical Dilemma

Should it be the employer's responsibility to cover health-care costs for early retirees until they become eligible for government health-care benefits at age 65?

9.3.3 Short-Term Disability Plans and Sick Leave Plans

short-term disability and sick leave plans   Plans that provide pay to an employee when he or she is unable to work because of a non-work-related illness or injury.

Short-term disability plans (also known as salary continuation plans) provide a continuation of all or part of an employee's earnings when the employee is absent from work because of non-work-related illness or injury. Usually a medical certificate is required if the absence extends beyond two or three days. These plans typically provide full pay for some period (often two or three weeks) and then gradually reduce the percentage of earnings paid as the period of absence lengthens. The benefits cease when the employee returns to work or when the employee qualifies for long-term disability. These plans are sometimes provided through an insurance company.

Sick leave plans operate quite differently from short-term disability plans. Most sick leave policies grant full pay for a specified number of permissible sick days—usually up to about 12 per year (often accumulated at the rate of one day per month of service). Most jurisdictions require a few days of sick leave (unpaid) as a minimum standard. Sick leave pay creates difficulty for many employers. The problem is that, although many employees use their sick days only when they are legitimately sick, others simply use their sick leave as extensions to their vacations, whether they are sick or not. A 2013 study of 1 513 Canadians provides evidence as to the abuse of sick time, revealing that 54 percent of Canadians admit to calling in sick when they were not sick.[25] The reasons include feeling stressed or burned out (65 percent), needing to care for a sick child (35 percent), having too heavy a workload (13 percent), and having insufficient paid vacation days (12 percent). Limiting sick days is equally problematic in that seriously ill or injured employees get no pay once their sick days are used up; thus, the policy can encourage legitimately sick employees to come to work despite their illness.

"I'm a struggling actor hired by your insurance company. Your policy doesn't cover a real doctor."

© Andrew Genn/Fotolia

9.3.4 Long-Term Disability

Long-term disability insurance is aimed at providing income protection or compensation for loss of income because of long-term illness or injury that is not work related. The disability payments usually begin when normal short-term disability or sick leave is used up and may continue to provide income to age 65 or beyond. The disability benefits usually range from 50 to 75 percent of the employee's base pay.

The number of long-term disability claims in Canada is rising sharply. This trend is expected to accelerate as the average age of the workforce continues to rise, because the likelihood of chronic illnesses, such as arthritis, heart disease, and diabetes, increases with age. Therefore, disability management programs with a goal of returning workers safely back to work are becoming a priority in many organizations.[26] For example, employers are beginning to put more effort into managing employees with episodic disabilities, which are chronic illnesses such as HIV, lupus, multiple sclerosis, arthritis, and some cancers and mental illnesses that are unpredictable. These employees may have long periods of good health followed by unpredicted episodes of poor health.[27]

National Institute of Disability Management and Research
www.nidmar.ca

Canadian Council on Rehabilitation and Work
www.ccrw.org

Disability management is a proactive, employer-centred process that coordinates the activities of the employer, the insurance company, and health-care providers in an effort to minimize the impact of injury, disability, or disease on a worker's capacity to successfully perform the job. Maintaining contact with a worker who is ill or injured is imperative in disability management so that the worker can be involved in the return-to-work process from the beginning. Ongoing contact also allows the employer to monitor the employee's emotional well-being, which is always affected by illness or injury.[28]

Effective disability management programs include prevention, early assessment and intervention regarding employee health problems, monitoring and management of employee absences, and early and safe return-to-work policies.[29] The three most common approaches to returning a worker with a disability to work are reduced work hours, reduced work duties, and workstation modification.[30] Evaluating the physical capabilities of the worker is an important step in designing work modifications to safely reintegrate injured workers. In many cases, the cost of accommodating an employee's disability can be quite modest.

disability management A proactive, employer-centred process that coordinates the activities of the employer, the insurance company, and health-care providers in an effort to minimize the impact of injury, disability, or disease on a worker's capacity to successfully perform the job.

9.3.4.1 Mental Health Benefits

Mental health issues continue to be the leading cause of short- and long-term disability claims in Canada. Psychiatric disabilities are the fastest growing of all occupational disabilities, with depression being the most common (even though only 32 percent of those afflicted seek treatment, as they do not want to admit it to their employer).[31]

If all employees living with depression/anxiety had access to better treatments and supports, then workplace functioning would improve significantly. Mental illness can also prevent some people from entering the workforce. If all these Canadians had access to better treatments and supports, the economy could see up to 352 000 Canadians with depression/anxiety enter the workforce as fully functional employees each year until 2035. Taken together, this could potentially boost Canada's economy by up to $32.3 billion a year from improved treatment of depression and $17.3 billion a year from anxiety treatment.[32] Some of the challenges involved in improving this situation are shown in **Figure 9.3**. Only one-third of employers have implemented return-to-work programs specific to mental health. Companies such as Bell Canada, Alcan, and Superior Propane are trying to help reduce costs with prevention and early intervention programs, including psychiatric counselling and peer-support groups.[33]

Mental Health Works
Canadian Mental Health Association
www.mentalhealthworks.ca

9.3.5 Sabbaticals

A few employers provide sabbatical leaves for employees who want time off to rejuvenate or to pursue a personal goal. Sabbatical leaves are usually unpaid, but some employers provide partial or full pay. Sabbaticals can help to retain employees and to avoid employee burnout, without the employee losing job security or seniority.

9.3.6 Retirement Benefits

Employer-sponsored **pension plans** are intended to supplement an employee's government-sponsored retirement benefits, which, on average, make up 50 percent of the average Canadian's retirement income.[34] Unlike government-provided retirement benefits, employer-sponsored pension plans are pre-funded.

pension plans Plans that provide income when employees reach a pre-determined retirement age.

FIGURE 9.3 The Top Challenges in Improving How Mental Health Issues Are Addressed in the Workplace

1. Employee perceptions and stigma related to mental health issues	60%
2. Lack of front-line manager awareness	54%
3. Inability to identify suitable modified work	40%
4. Inability to introduce significant flexibility options	39%
5. Lack of tools and supports	29%
6. Lack of funds/budget for program enhancements	23%
7. Lack of senior management buy-in	20%
8. Don't know where to start	14%
9. Other	8%

Source: "What Are the Top Challenges You Face in Improving How Mental Health Issues Are Addressed in Your Workplace?" 2008 *Mental Health in the Workplace National Survey* (Toronto, ON: Mercer and Canadian Alliance on Mental Illness and Mental Health, 2008), p. 22. Reprinted with permission.

Money is set aside in a pension fund to accumulate with investment income until it is needed to pay benefits at retirement. Pension fund assets have grown rapidly over the past 40 years. Much of this money is invested in Canadian stocks and bonds because of laws restricting the investment of these assets in foreign securities.

9.3.6.1 Two Categories of Pension Plans

Pension plans fall into two categories—defined benefit pension plans and defined contribution pension plans. A **defined benefit pension plan** contains a formula for determining retirement benefits so that the actual benefits to be received are defined ahead of time. For example, the plan might include a formula, such as 2 percent of final year's earnings for each year of service, which would provide a pension of 70 percent of final year's earnings to an employee with 35 years of service.

A **defined contribution pension plan** specifies what contribution the employer will make to a retirement fund set up for the employee. The defined contribution plan does not define the eventual benefit amount, only the periodic contribution to the plan. In a defined benefit plan, the employee knows ahead of time what his or her retirement benefits will be on retirement. With a defined contribution plan, the employee cannot be sure of his or her retirement benefits until retirement, when his or her share of the money in the pension fund is used to buy an annuity. Thus, benefits depend on both the amounts contributed to the fund and the retirement fund's investment earnings.

There are two other types of defined contribution arrangements. Under a *group registered retirement savings plan* (*group RRSP*), employees can have a portion of their compensation (which would otherwise be paid in cash) put into an RRSP by the employer. The employee is not taxed on those set-aside dollars until after he or she retires (or removes the money from the plan). Most employers do not match all or a portion of what the employee contributes to the group RRSP because employer contributions are considered taxable income to

defined benefit pension plan A plan that contains a formula for determining retirement benefits.

defined contribution pension plan A plan in which the employer's contribution to the employees' retirement fund is specified.

Canadian Association for Retired Persons
www.carp.ca

Benefits and Pensions Monitor
www.bpmmagazine.com

Association of Canadian Pension Management
www.acpm.com

employees. Instead, the employer often establishes a **deferred profit-sharing plan (DPSP)** and contributes a portion of company profits into the DPSP fund, where an account is set up for each employee. No employee contributions to a DPSP are allowed under Canadian tax law. Group RRSP/DPSP combinations are popular in Canada because no tax is paid until money is received from the plans at the time of the employee's death or termination of employment (at retirement or otherwise).

As shown in **Table 9.3**, both plans are quite popular, and a few companies use combination or other forms of pension plans.

The entire area of pension planning is complicated, a result of the laws governing pensions. For example, companies want to ensure that their pension contributions are tax deductible and must therefore adhere to the Income Tax Act. The provincial and federal jurisdictions also have laws governing employer-sponsored pension plans. In some cases, the complicated and overlapping nature of federal and provincial legislation can make employers unsure whether or not to sponsor a pension plan.[35] Legislation regarding pension plans varies around the world, and Canada's regulators can learn important lessons from other countries' successes and failures, as described in the Global HRM box.

Employers must pay careful attention to their obligation to educate and inform (but not advise) plan members about pension investments. There have been cases in which plan members who were unhappy with the information provided by the employer and surprised by small benefits have sued their employers and won.

The severe economic recession that began in late 2008 resulted in major shrinkage in the value of pension funds and highlighted issues with both types of plans. For defined benefit plans, the recession necessitated major increases in contributions to pension funds in order to maintain their required funding levels.[36] Although some jurisdictions eased the funding rules temporarily to allow more time to repay funding shortfalls, defined benefit plans began to be called an "endangered species."[37] Among those who had defined contribution plans,

deferred profit-sharing plan (DPSP)   A plan in which a certain amount of company profits is credited to each employee's account, payable at retirement, termination, or death.

TABLE 9.3   Registered Pension Plans by Type, 2016

Plan type	
Defined benefit plans	57.4%
Defined contribution plans	37.5%
Composite or combination plans[1]	0.7%
Defined benefit and contribution plans[2]	4.1%
Other types of plans	0.2%
Gender	
Male	50.3%
Female	49.7%

[1] In composite or combination plans, the pension has both defined benefit and defined contribution characteristics.

[2] These plans may be for different classes of employees, or one benefit type may be for current employees and the other for new employees.

Source: Statistics Canada. Registered pension plans (RPPs) and members, by type of plan and sector (Total public and private sectors). Reproduced and distributed on an "as is" basis with the permission of Statistics Canada.

This does not constitute an endorsement by Statistics Canada of this product.

many plan members nearing retirement saw no other option but to defer retirement and continue working until the markets recovered and their pension fund account balance recovered to an amount that would provide them with the retirement income they needed. These issues created considerable debate about the adequacy of retirement savings for future generations.

When designing a pension plan, there are several legal and policy issues to consider.[38]

- *Membership requirements.* For example, at what minimum number of years of service do employees become eligible to join the plan?

- *Benefit formula* (defined benefit plans only). This usually ties the pension to the employee's final earnings, or an average of his or her last three to five years' earnings.

- *Retirement age.* Traditionally, the normal retirement age in Canada has been 65. However, since mandatory retirement is now prohibited by human rights laws across the country, employees cannot be required to retire at age 65. Some plans call for "30 and out." This permits an employee to retire after 30 years of continuous service, regardless of the person's age.

- *Funding.* The question of how the plan is to be funded is another key issue. One aspect is whether the plan will be contributory or non-contributory. In the former, contributions to the pension fund are made by both employees and the employer. In a non-contributory fund, only the employer contributes.

GLOBAL HRM

Defined Benefit Pension Problems and Solutions around the World

Many countries designed generous defined benefit social security programs between 1950 and 1970 based on fertility rates that created a stable population. The actual experience of declining populations in many countries, particularly Japan, created serious intergenerational inequity as younger employees were subsidizing older ones. Solutions included increasing contribution rates (Belgium, Canada), raising the normal retirement age to 67 (European Union), both of these (Germany), moving to defined contribution plans (Australia, France, Switzerland, United Kingdom), and even more complex protective legislation (Netherlands).

Unfortunately, none of these national actions seems to be the optimal solution to the global defined benefits plan issue. The European Union encourages the creation of pan-European pension plans whereby an employer can create a plan in one location and cover all European employees under that single plan. This encourages employee mobility and reduces administrative costs. The plans must comply with the rules from the plan's home country while still respecting some of the pension laws of other countries where employees reside or have retired. Countries such as Luxembourg, Ireland, and Belgium have tried to create the best tax and legal environment to attract these plans, but it is too early to tell if a leader will emerge.

The European Union situation is very similar to our Canadian system with its patchwork of legislation. Given Canada's population of 33 million, versus 700 million in Europe, it is clear that our pension landscape should have been more straightforward from the outset and desperately needs to be simplified. There is some hope for the future as three expert commissions in Ontario, Nova Scotia, and jointly in Alberta and British Columbia are undertaking reviews of the pension legislation in those provinces.

However, until we find better ways to enhance and preserve defined benefit plans, employers will have to make some difficult decisions. Country by country, they must choose between assuming the risks and higher administrative costs of sponsoring defined benefit plans or moving to defined contribution plans, which typically do not produce the same retirement value to each dollar spent and are less flexible as an HR tool.

Source: Adapted with permission from F. Letourneau, "Around the World in Six Pages," *Benefits Canada* (August 2008), pp. 14–19.

- *Vesting*. Employee **vesting** rights are another critical issue in pension planning. Vesting refers to the money that the employer has placed in the pension fund that cannot be forfeited for any reason; the employees' contributions can never be forfeited. An employee is vested when he or she has met the requirements set out in the plan, whereby, on termination of employment, he or she will receive future benefits based on the contributions made to the plan by the *employer* on behalf of the employee. In recent years, new rules for full and immediate vesting as well as locking-in provisions for all accrued benefits changes have been enacted at the federal level as well as by the majority of provincial pension regulations.

  vesting   A provision that employer money placed in a pension fund cannot be forfeited for any reason.

- *Portability*. Canadian employers today are required by pension legislation to make their pensions more "portable" for employees on termination of employment. **Portability** means that employees in defined contribution plans can take the money in their company pension account to a new employer's plan or roll it over into a locked-in RRSP. For defined benefit plans, the lump-sum value of the benefit earned can be transferred.

  portability   A provision that employees who change jobs can transfer the lump-sum value of the pension they have earned to a locked-in RRSP or their new employer's pension plan.

9.3.6.2 Phased Retirement

The labour shortage is resulting in employers seeking to retain older employees. At the same time, many Canadians wishing to retire early are finding that they are not in a financial position to do so and that they need to continue working to age 60, 65, or even later.[39] The idea of **phased retirement**, whereby employees gradually ease into retirement using reduced workdays or shortened workweeks, has been increasing in Canada, as shown in **Figure 9.4**. Constraints under the Income Tax Act and pension legislation in some jurisdictions are slowly being loosened, and it is now possible for older workers to receive some benefits from their pension plan while they are being paid to continue to work.[40]

phased retirement   An arrangement whereby employees gradually ease into retirement by using reduced workdays or shortened workweeks.

FIGURE 9.4   Prevalence of Phased Retirement Programs

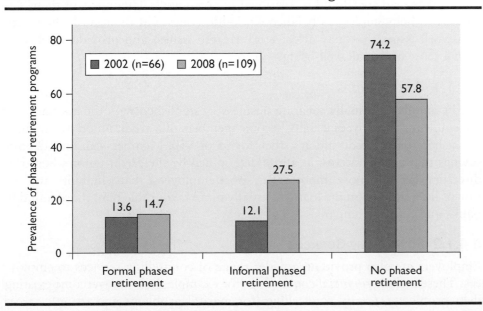

Source: K. Thorpe, *Harnessing the Power: Recruiting, Engaging, and Retaining Mature Workers* (Ottawa, ON: The Conference Board of Canada, October 2008), p. 23. Reprinted with permission

9.3.6.3 Supplemental Employee Retirement Plans (SERPs)

The Income Tax Act has not changed the maximum pension benefit permissible under the act (for tax deductibility of plan contributions) since 1976. Thus, many Canadians have their pension benefits capped at less than what their defined benefit plan formula would otherwise provide. Originally, this situation created problems only for highly paid executives, but in recent years more and more employees have been affected. **Supplemental employee retirement plans (SERPs)** are intended to provide the difference in pension benefit and thus restore pension adequacy for high earners.

An industry focused survey found that nearly three-quarters of employers provide SERPs (including about two-thirds of small employers with fewer than 500 employees). The survey also found that 53 percent of SERP sponsors cover employees below the executive level in "broad-based" plans. Most SERPs are "pay-as-you-go" plans; that is, they do not have a fund established to accumulate money to pay the benefits (because contributions are not tax deductible). However, the security of SERP benefits has been improving, as 41 percent of plans are now secured in some manner.[41]

supplemental employee retirement plans (SERPs) Plans that provide the additional pension benefit required for employees to receive their full pension benefit in cases when their full pension benefit exceeds the maximum allowable benefit under the Income Tax Act.

9.4 EMPLOYEE SERVICES

Although an employee's time off and insurance and retirement benefits account for the largest portion of an organization's benefits costs, many employers also provide a range of services, including personal services (such as counselling), job-related services (such as child-care facilities), and executive perquisites (such as company cars and planes for executives).

9.4.1 Personal Services

First, many companies provide personal services that most employees need at one time or another. These include credit unions, counselling, employee assistance plans, and social and recreational opportunities. The intent of these services is to help employees balance work–life issues, aid them in dealing with non-work issues that may affect work-related issues, and provide employees with a sense of overall well-being.

9.4.1.1 Credit Unions

Credit unions are usually separate businesses established with the assistance of the employer. Employees usually become members of a credit union by purchasing a share of the credit union's stock for $5 or $10. Members can then deposit savings that accrue interest at a rate determined by the credit union's board of directors. Perhaps more important to most employees, loan eligibility and the rate of interest paid on the loan are usually more favourable than those found in banks and finance companies.

9.4.1.2 Counselling Services

Employers are also providing a wider range of counselling services to employees. These include *financial counselling* (for example, how to overcome existing debt problems), *family counselling* (for marital problems and so on), *career counselling* (for example, analyzing one's aptitudes and deciding on a career), *job placement counselling* (for helping terminated or disenchanted employees find new jobs), and *pre-retirement counselling* (aimed at preparing retiring employees for what many find is the trauma of retiring). Many employers also make available to employees a full range of *legal counselling* services through legal insurance plans.[42]

9.4.1.3 Employee Assistance Plans (EAPs)

An **employee assistance plan (EAP)** is a formal employer program that provides employees (and often their family members) with confidential counselling or treatment programs for problems such as mental health issues, marital/family problems, work–life balance issues, stress, legal problems, substance abuse, and other addictions such as gambling. They are particularly important for helping employees who suffer

Some companies offer counselling services such as financial counselling to their employees.

workplace trauma—ranging from harassment to physical assault. There was a significant increase in EAP usage during the economic recession that began in late 2008, particularly in the areas of financial problems and stress.[43]

The number of EAPs in Canada is growing because they are a proactive way for organizations to reduce absenteeism and disability costs. A general estimate is that 10 percent of employees use EAP services. With supervisory training in how to identify employees who may need an EAP referral, usage can be expanded to more employees who need help.[44]

EAP counsellors can be employed in-house, or the company can contract with an external EAP firm.[45] It is important to assess the services provided by external EAP providers before using them, as quality levels vary. Whatever the model, an EAP provider should be confidential, accessible to employees in all company locations, and timely in providing service, and should offer highly educated counsellors and provide communication material to publicize the plan to employees. They should also provide utilization reports on the number of employees using the service and the types of services being provided, without compromising confidentiality.[46]

9.4.1.4 Other Personal Services

Finally, some employers also provide various social and recreational opportunities for their employees, including company-sponsored athletic events, dances, annual summer picnics, craft activities, and parties. In practice, the benefits offered are limited only by creativity in thinking up new benefits. For example, pharmaceutical giant Pfizer Inc. provides employees with free drugs made by the company, including Viagra.[47]

9.4.2 Job-Related Services

Job-related services aimed directly at helping employees perform their jobs, such as educational subsidies and child-care centres, constitute a second group of services.

9.4.2.1 Subsidized Child Care

The number of Canadian families with two employed parents has almost doubled in the last 40 years—from 1.0 million to 1.9 million families, from 1976 to 2015. Over that period, the proportion of families where just one parent earned

employee assistance plan (EAP) A company-sponsored program to help employees cope with personal problems that are interfering with or have the potential to interfere with their job performance, as well as issues affecting their well-being or the well-being of their families.

Canadian Centre for Occupational Health and Safety
www.ccohs.ca/oshanswers/ hsprograms/eap.html

Morneau Shepell
www.morneaushepell.com/ca

Subsidizing child-care facilities for children of employees has many benefits for the employer, including lower employee absenteeism.

a pay cheque fell by more than half, dropping from 59 percent to 27 percent. In turn, the proportion of dual-income families has nearly doubled, from 36 percent to 69 percent.[48] Subsidized child care is offered to assist in balancing these work and life responsibilities. Many employers simply investigate the child-care facilities in their communities and recommend certain ones to interested employees, but more employers are setting up company-sponsored child-care facilities themselves, both to attract young parents to the payroll and to reduce absenteeism. In this case, the centre is a separate, privately run venture, paid for by the firm. IKEA, Husky Injection Molding Systems, IBM, and the Kanata Research Park have all chosen this option. Where successful, the hours of operation are structured around parents' schedules, the child-care facility is close to the workplace (often in the same building), and the employer provides 50 to 75 percent of the operating costs. Two additional benefits are child care for mildly ill children and emergency backup child care.[49] The evidence regarding the actual effects of employer-sponsored child care on employee absenteeism, turnover, productivity, recruitment, and job satisfaction is positive, particularly with respect to reducing obstacles to coming to work and improving workers' attitudes.[50]

9.4.2.2 Elder Care

The number of seniors in Canada requiring care is expected to double between 2012 and 2031. More than one-third of the Canadian workforce is already providing informal care to a family member or friend. Many caregivers do not self-identify in such support roles so it is likely that the total reported number providing such informal support to another person is much higher. Employees fulfilling such caregiver roles experience more interruptions at work and lower productivity, and are frequently late for, or absent from, work. In 2007, the Conference Board of Canada estimated the annual cost to Canadian employers due to the resulting lost productivity was more than $1.28 billion.[51] Employees also may be less able to work overtime, travel for work, or take advantage of career-advancing opportunities such as professional development. Costs to the caregivers in terms of stress and career advancement can be significant, particularly for women at critical points in their careers. With Canada's population continuing to age, these pressures and related consequences will increase, as will the magnitude of impact on Canadian employers.

As employers become more vulnerable to elder-care issues as Canada's population ages, there are a number of supports that companies can provide to employees caring for elderly family and friends, including

- *Education*: Provide education to managers and employees about stress management and conditions afflicting the elderly, such as dementia and Parkinson's disease.
- *Flex Time*: Allow compressed workweeks, earlier or later start times, and weekend work. The notion that a nine-to-five schedule is necessary for high productivity is increasingly considered outdated, with more firms focusing on results rather than on physical presence.

- *Compassionate Care Leave*: This kind of leave (particularly paid leave) is rarely promoted in the workplace; and unpaid leave options are under used by employees, compared with child-care benefits. As a result, employees often use vacation days to take care of family members once they are out of sick leave time.

- *Programs*: Provide access to social recreation day programs for seniors. These programs usually operate during work hours, allowing seniors to socialize, exercise, challenge their minds, and enjoy planned outings. Employees who use these programs get peace of mind knowing that their loved one is cared for while they are at work and therefore are less likely to take time off to manage emergent issues.

Boomers are the "Sandwich Generation," caring for both children and elderly parents.

Depending on the type of contract that the employer negotiates, employees can pay a nominal fee for using these programs, or the employer can cover the fee directly.[52]

9.4.2.3 Subsidized Employee Transportation

Some employers also provide subsidized employee transportation. An employer can negotiate with a transit system to provide free year-round transportation to its employees. Other employers facilitate employee carpooling, perhaps by acting as the central clearinghouse to identify employees from the same geographic areas who work the same hours.

9.4.2.4 Food Services

Food services are provided in some form by many employers; they allow employees to purchase meals, snacks, or coffee onsite, usually at relatively low or subsidized prices. Even employers who do not provide full dining facilities generally make available food services, such as coffee wagons or vending machines, for the convenience of employees.

9.4.2.5 Educational Subsidies

Educational subsidies, such as tuition refunds, have long been a popular benefit for employees seeking to continue or complete their education. Payments range from all tuition and expenses to some percentage of expenses to a flat fee per year of, say, $500 to $600. Most companies pay for courses directly related to an employee's present job. Many also reimburse tuition for courses that are not job related (such as an administrative assistant taking an accounting class) that pertain to the company business, and those that are part of a degree or diploma program. In-house educational programs include remedial work in basic literacy and training for improved supervisory skills.

9.4.3 Executive Perquisites

Perquisites (perks, for short) are usually given to only a few top executives. Perks can range from the substantial to the almost insignificant. A multitude of popular perks fall between these extremes. These include management loans (which typically enable senior officers to use their stock options); salary guarantees (also known as *golden parachutes*) to protect executives if their firms are the targets of acquisitions or mergers; financial counselling (to handle top executives' investment programs); and relocation benefits, often including subsidized mortgages, purchase of the executive's current house, and payment for the actual move. A potpourri of other executive perks include outplacement assistance, company cars, chauffeured limousines, security systems, company planes and yachts, executive dining rooms, legal services, tax assistance, liberal expense accounts, club memberships, season tickets, credit cards, and subsidized education for their children. Perks related to wellness and quality of life (such as physical fitness programs) are highly valued in today's stressful environment. An increasingly popular perk offered at KPMG, TELUS, and Ernst & Young is concierge service, intended to carry out errands, such as grocery shopping or organizing a vacation, for busy executives.[53]

An Ethical Dilemma

Should the use and applicability of executive perks be made available to employees who do not qualify for these benefits?

9.5 FLEXIBLE BENEFITS PROGRAMS

Research conducted more than 30 years ago found that an employee's age, marital status, and sex influenced his or her choice of benefits.[54] For example, preference for pensions increased significantly with employee age, and preference for the family dental plan increased sharply as the number of dependants increased. Thus, benefits that one worker finds attractive may be unattractive to another. In the last 25 years in Canada, there has been a significant increase in **flexible benefits programs** that permit employees to develop individualized benefits packages by choosing their preferred benefits options. In 1980, there were no flex plans in Canada, but by 2005, 41 percent of employers offered flex benefits plans. Benefit consultants Aon Hewitt Associates report that 85 percent of Canadian employers either have a flex plan in place or expect to implement one at some point. Fifty-three percent either have a full flex plan now or are in the process of creating one.[55]

flexible benefits programs Individualized benefit plans to accommodate employee needs and preferences.

Employers derive several advantages from offering flexible benefit plans: The two most important are cost containment and the ability to meet the needs of an increasingly diverse workforce. Aon Hewitt Associates' surveys have found that over the years the most important advantage of implementing flexible benefits has been meeting diverse employee needs. However, in 2005, for the first time in survey history, the concerns about containing benefit costs increases surpassed meeting diverse employee needs as the most significant reason to implement flexible plans. In more recent surveys, 100 percent of respondents reported that their flex plans were meeting or exceeding their expectations regarding meeting employee needs, and the level of satisfaction with flex plans as a cost containment measure was 78 percent.[56]

Benefits Canada
www.benefitscanada.com

Flexible benefits plans empower the employee to put together his or her own benefit package, subject to two constraints. First, the employer must carefully limit the total cost for each total benefits package. Second, each benefit plan must include certain items that are not optional. These include, for example, Canada/Quebec Pension Plan, workers' compensation, and employment insurance. Subject to these two constraints, employees can select from the available options. Thus, a young parent might opt for the company's life and dental insurance plans, while an older employee might opt for an improved pension plan. The list of possible options that the employer might offer can include many of the benefits discussed in this chapter—vacations, insurance benefits, pension plans, educational services, and so on.

There are advantages and disadvantages to flexible benefit programs. The flexibility is, of course, the main advantage. Although most employees favour flexible benefits, some do not like to spend time choosing among available options, and some choose inappropriate benefits. Communication regarding the choices available in a flexible plan is considered the biggest challenge for employers. A majority of flex plan sponsors provide a plan website. However, even with new technology, employers still find face-to-face communication is the preferred method for providing initial information about a new flex plan.[57] The recent, rapid increase in the number of flexible plans in Canada indicates that the pros outweigh the cons.

9.6 BENEFITS ADMINISTRATION

Whether it be a flexible benefits plan or a more traditional one, benefits administration is a challenge. Even in a relatively small company with 40 to 50 employees, the administrative problems of keeping track of the benefits status of each employee can be a time-consuming task as employees are hired and separated and as they use or want to change their benefits. However, software is available to assist with this challenge. Many companies make use of some sort of benefits spreadsheet software to facilitate tracking benefits and updating information. Another approach is outsourcing benefits administration to a third-party expert. Reasons for a shift from the traditional transactional work carried out by HR staff in benefits administration include a desire to avoid substantial technology upgrading costs and re-aligning HR staff away from administrative support tasks to the core business of talent management. The major advantages are cost stabilization, lowering risk, and increased employee productivity.[58]

Canadian Pension and Benefits Institute
www.cpbi-icra.ca

9.6.1 Keeping Employees Informed

Benefits communication, particularly regarding pension plans and flexible benefits, is increasingly important as a large number of people are approaching retirement. Correct information must be provided in a timely, clear manner. Pension legislation across Canada specifies what information must be disclosed to plan members and their spouses. Court challenges concerning information on benefits plans are on the rise as people's awareness of their right to information grows.[59]

Employers select a variety of visual, oral, and written formats to effectively communicate employee benefits information. Increasingly, organizations are using intranets to ensure that up-to-date information is provided in a consistent manner to staff. Presenting a clear and concise summary of benefits can serve as an effective tool for attracting new hires and reinforcing a company's value proposition relative to other opportunities in the job market. Such communications strategies show employees how much their organization values them, helping to retain valued talent.[60]

CHAPTER SUMMARY

1. The strategic importance of employee benefits is increasing in the post-job-security era. When benefits are aligned with business strategy, they can help to attract and retain the right people to achieve business objectives.

2. Six major government-mandated benefits are employment insurance, Canada/Quebec Pension Plan, workers' compensation, vacations and holidays, leaves of absence, and pay on termination of employment.

3. Health insurance costs are rising because of expensive new drugs, rising drug use by an aging population, and reductions in coverage under provincial health-care plans. These costs can be reduced by increasing the amount of health-care costs paid by employees, establishing a restricted list of the drugs that will be paid for under the plan, implementing health and wellness promotion plans, using risk assessment programs, and offering health services spending accounts.

4. The two categories of pension plans are defined benefit plans and defined contribution plans. Defined benefit plans provide a benefit based on a formula related to years of service, and the employer assumes the investment risk associated with the pension fund assets. Defined contribution plans provide for specified contributions to a pension fund by the employer, and the benefit will vary depending on the rate of return on the pension fund assets (employees assume the investment risk).

5. Three types of personal employee services offered by many organizations include credit unions, counselling services, and employee assistance plans. Six types of job-related services offered by many employers include subsidized child care, elder care, subsidized employee transportation, food services, educational subsidies, and family-friendly benefits.

6. The flexible benefits approach allows the employee to put together his or her own benefit plan, subject to total cost limits and the inclusion of certain compulsory items. The employer first determines the total cost for the benefits package. Then a decision is made as to which benefits will be compulsory (such as Canada/Quebec Pension Plan, workers' compensation, and employment insurance). Then other benefits are selected for inclusion in the plan, such as life insurance, health and dental coverage, short- and long-term disability insurance, and retirement plans. Sometimes vacations and employee services are included as well. Then employees select the optional benefits they prefer with the money they have available to them under the total plan.

MyLab Management

Visit MyLab Management to access a personalized Study Plan, Personal Inventory Assessments (PIA), and a collection of videos and assignments within MediaShare.

KEY TERMS

Canada/Quebec Pension Plans (C/QPP) *(p. 215)*
co-insurance *(p. 220)*
deductible *(p. 219)*
deferred profit-sharing plan (DPSP) *(p. 225)*
defined benefit pension plan *(p. 224)*
defined contribution pension plan *(p. 229)*
disability management *(p. 211)*
employee assistance plan (EAP) *(p. 229)*
employee benefits *(p. 211)*
employment insurance (EI) *(p. 212)*
flexible benefits programs *(p. 232)*

group life insurance *(p. 218)*
pay in lieu of reasonable notice *(p. 213)*
pension plans *(p. 223)*
phased retirement *(p. 227)*
portability *(p. 227)*
severance pay *(p. 213)*
short-term disability and sick leave *(p. 222)*
supplemental employee retirement plans (SERPs) *(p. 228)*
vesting *(p. 227)*
workers' compensation *(p. 215)*

REVIEW AND DISCUSSION QUESTIONS

1. Name and describe the benefit(s) offered by two government-mandated employee benefit programs.

2. Explain the difference between sick leave plans and short-term disability plans.

3. Why are long-term disability claims increasing so rapidly in Canada?

4. Explain the difference between a defined benefit pension plan and a defined contribution pension plan.

5. Discuss the pros and cons of flexible benefits from both the employer and employee perspectives.

6. What are two reasons that support the delivery of online communication of employee information to Millennials?

CRITICAL THINKING QUESTIONS

1. You are applying for a job as a manager and are at the point of negotiating salary and benefits. What questions would you ask your prospective employer concerning benefits? Describe the benefits package that you would try to negotiate for yourself.

2. What is the key difference to the employer *and* the employee between a defined benefit and defined contribution pension plan sponsored by the employer?

3. You are the HR consultant to a small business with about 40 employees. Currently, the business offers only the legal minimum number of days for vacation and paid holidays and the legally mandated benefits. Using information from the Voluntary Employer-Sponsored Benefits section in the chapter, what are three benefit choices you would offer to employees? Why?

4. Name and explain two specific steps an employer may use to control health benefit costs in their company.

5. Based on details seen in the Employee Services section of the chapter, what are three personal or job-related services that would appeal to you as an employee? Why?

EXPERIENTIAL EXERCISES

1. Using your favourite search engine, locate the federal or a provincial government website dealing with maternity and parental leave benefits. Identify three important facts about such leaves of absence that an HR staff member should know when consulting with employees in their company.

2. Locate a "benefits calculator" website on the Internet, and explore the employer and employee premium costs for mandatory government benefits and voluntary employer-sponsored plans.

3. In a small group, locate several websites that outline the advantages and disadvantages of a flexible benefit plan for employees. Then collaborate with group members to build a strong case for adopting such an employee benefits approach, while at the same time raising important factors that may concern company leaders regarding this benefits strategy.

©Zulufoto/Shutterstock

10 OCCUPATIONAL HEALTH AND SAFETY

LEARNING OUTCOMES

AFTER STUDYING THIS CHAPTER, YOU SHOULD BE ABLE TO:

ANALYZE the responsibilities and rights of employees and employers under occupational health and safety legislation.

EXPLAIN WHMIS legislation.

ANALYZE in detail three basic causes of accidents.

DESCRIBE how accidents at work can be prevented.

DISCUSS five major employee health issues at work, and **RECOMMEND** how they should be handled.

EXPLAIN why employee wellness programs are becoming increasingly popular.

10.1 STRATEGIC IMPORTANCE OF OCCUPATIONAL HEALTH AND SAFETY

Health and safety initiatives are part of a strategic approach to human resources management. Service provided to clients and customers is a function of how employees are treated, and employee health, safety, and wellness management are important determinants of employee perceptions regarding fair treatment by the organization. Further, investment in disability management and proactive wellness programs create measurable bottom-line returns.[1]

Another reason that safety and accident prevention concerns managers is that the work-related accident figures are staggering. **Lost-time injury rate** measures any occupational injury or illness resulting in an employee being unable to fulfill the job's full work assignments; it does not include fatalities. According to the Association of Workers' Compensation Boards of Canada, in 2011 there were 919 deaths and 249 511 injuries resulting from accidents at work.[2] Thus, on average, more than three Canadian workers died at work each calendar day.[3] These figures do not include minor injuries that do not involve time lost from work beyond the day of the accident. Moreover, these figures do not tell the full story. They do not reflect the human suffering incurred by injured or ill workers and their families.

Ceremonies are held across Canada every April 28 to mark the National Day of Mourning for workers killed or injured on the job. In Moncton, New Brunswick, Pauline Farrell lays roses in memory of her late husband, Bill Kelly, who was killed more than 30 years ago.

Workplace health concerns are also widespread. Surveys have shown that 61 percent of Canadians believe that workplace accidents are inevitable.[4] According to the Canadian Centre for Justice Statistics, 17 percent of all self-reported incidents of violent victimization, including sexual assault, robbery, and physical assault, occur at the respondents' place of work, representing over 356 000 violent workplace incidents in Canada in one year alone or roughly 1 000 per day.[5] This statistic is particularly disturbing because workplace accidents are largely preventable.

lost-time injury rate Measures any occupational injury or illness resulting in an employee being unable to fulfill the job's full work assignments, not including any fatalities.

10.1.1 Safety Climate and Culture

Recent research suggests that organizational climate creates a social-cognitive expectation around how complex issues are resolved.[6] The large range of possible workplace injuries creates a situation in which a company cannot predict and develop a plan for every possible occupational health and safety issue. Instead, workplace policies, procedures, and practices should establish social and financial rewards to promote safe behaviour. If the company consistently prioritizes cost, speed, and production over safety, then it is difficult to develop a deep-level commitment to safety among workers. Organizational cultures that promote collaboration, open communication, and trust increase the safety climate and safety performance in the workplace, more than do organizational cultures that promote competition and meritocracy.[7]

ENTREPRENEURS and HR

Small Business Safety Calculator

On-the-job injuries cost small businesses in many other areas not covered by workers' safety boards or insurance. The Industrial Accident Prevention Association (IAPA)'s free Small Business Safety Calculator helps businesses identify and quantify these costs, including the following:

- **Incident Costs**—time to provide first aid; time for transportation to hospital/clinic/home; lost productivity of all affected workers and equipment used; cost of ambulance or taxi

- **Investigation Costs**—time to investigate the accident; time spent to complete an accident investigation report; time taken to report the incident to the WSIB and meet with WSIB officers; follow-up meetings to discuss the accident

- **Damage Costs**—time to assess the damage; time to repair or replace equipment; time to coordinate repair work; cost to dispose of damaged equipment; cost of replacement parts, equipment, or lost product

- **Replacement Costs**—time to hire or relocate replacement worker; relocation or rescheduling of another worker; trainer time for new or relocated worker; trainee time for new or relocated worker

- **Productivity Costs**—lost productivity due to disruption; time spent managing the injury claim; reduced productivity of injured worker after he or she returns to work

The IAPA Small Business Safety Calculator is modelled after one created by WorkSafeBC. It was re-engineered for use in Ontario and specifically for those companies that fall within one of IAPA's 12 industry groups: glass, stone, and ceramics; chemical and plastics; food and beverage; agri-business; high-tech; industrial auto sales; leather, rubber, and tanners; metal trades; office and related services; printing trades; textile and allied trades; and woodworking. The calculator is available online at www.iapa.ca/sbc.

Source: Adapted with permission from "Calculating the Costs of Workplace Injuries," *Canadian HR Reporter* (April 9, 2007).

10.1.2 Controlling Workers' Compensation Costs

Workers' compensation costs are often the most expensive benefit provided by an employer. For example, the average workplace injury in Ontario costs more than $59 000 in workers' compensation benefits. Indirect costs are estimated to be about four times the direct costs.[8] Each firm's workers' compensation premiums are proportional to its workers' compensation experience rate. Thus, the more claims a firm has, the more the firm will pay in premiums. A new online tool is available for small businesses in Ontario to calculate the true costs of a workplace injury, as explained in the Entrepreneurs and HR box.

10.2 BASIC FACTS ABOUT OCCUPATIONAL HEALTH AND SAFETY LEGISLATION

occupational health and safety legislation Laws intended to protect the health and safety of workers by minimizing work-related accidents and illnesses.

Occupational health and safety legislation is jurisdiction specific (provinces, territories, and the federal level), but the principle of joint responsibility is common to all jurisdictions. There is an implicit and explicit expectation that both workers and employers must maintain a hazard-free work environment and enhance the health and safety of workers.[9]

10.2.1 Purpose

These laws fall into three categories: general health and safety rules, rules for specific industries (for example, mining), and rules related to specific hazards (for example, asbestos). In some jurisdictions, these are combined into one overall law with regulations for specific industries and hazards, while in others they remain separate. The regulations are very complex and cover almost every conceivable hazard in great detail. Provisions of occupational health and safety legislation differ significantly across Canada, but most have certain basic features in common.

10.2.2 Responsibilities and Rights of Employers and Employees

In all jurisdictions, employers are responsible for taking every reasonable precaution to ensure the health and safety of their workers. This is called the **due diligence** requirement. Specific duties of the employer include filing government accident reports, maintaining records, ensuring that safety rules are enforced, and posting safety notices and legislative information.[10] In addition, if an occupational health and safety violation is reported, the employer is presumed guilty unless proven innocent (the burden of proof is reversed). A recent provincial court decision suggests that employers must enforce safe work procedures through a progressive discipline process to establish a defense of due diligence when workers do not follow safety rules and are injured on the job.[11]

Employees are responsible for taking reasonable care to protect their own health and safety and, in most cases, that of their co-workers. Specific requirements include wearing protective clothing and equipment, and reporting any contravention of the law or regulations.

Employees have three basic rights under the joint responsibility model:

- The right to know about workplace safety hazards
- The right to participate in the occupational health and safety process
- The right to refuse unsafe work if they have "reasonable cause" to believe that the work is dangerous

Reasonable cause usually means that a complaint about a workplace hazard has not been satisfactorily resolved, or a safety problem places employees in immediate danger. If performance of a task would adversely affect health and safety, a worker cannot be disciplined for refusing to do the job.

due diligence   Employers' responsibility regarding taking every reasonable precaution to ensure the health and safety of their workers.

reasonable cause   A complaint about a workplace hazard has not been satisfactorily resolved, or a safety problem places employees in immediate danger.

10.2.2.1 Joint Health and Safety Committees

The function of joint health and safety committees is to provide a non-adversarial atmosphere in which management and labour can work together to ensure a safe and healthy workplace. Most jurisdictions require a joint health and safety committee to be established in each workplace with a minimum number of workers (usually 10 or 20). In other jurisdictions, the government has the power to require that a committee be formed. Committees are usually required to consist of between 2 and 12 members, at least half of whom must represent workers. In small workplaces, one health and safety representative may be considered sufficient.

The committee is generally responsible for making regular inspections of the workplace to identify potential health and safety hazards, evaluate the hazards, and implement solutions. Hazard control can be achieved by addressing safety issues before an accident or injury happens, identifying ways in which a hazardous situation can be prevented from harming workers, and establishing procedures to ensure that a potential hazard will not recur. Health and safety committees are also responsible for investigating employee complaints, accident investigation,

Supervisors have the responsibility to ensure their workers are aware of all safety precautions they must take on the job.
© Jarp/Fotolia

development and promotion of measures to protect health and safety, and dissemination of information about health and safety laws and regulations. In Ontario, at least one management and one labour representative must be certified in occupational health and safety through a provincial training program. Committees are often more effective if the company's health and safety manager acts as an independent expert rather than as a management representative.[12]

10.2.2.2 The Supervisor's Role in Safety

Most jurisdictions impose a personal duty on supervisors to ensure that workers comply with occupational health and safety regulations. They place a specific obligation on supervisors to advise and instruct workers about safety, to ensure that all reasonable precautions have been taken to provide for the safety of all employees, and to minimize risk of injuries or illness.

Safety-minded managers must aim to instill the desire to work safely in their workers. Minimizing hazards (by ensuring that spills are wiped up, machine guards are adequate, and so forth) is important, but no matter how safe the workplace is, there will be accidents unless workers want to and do act safely. Of course, supervisors try to watch each employee closely, but most managers know that this will not work. The best (and perhaps only) alternative is to get workers to want to work safely. Then, when needed, safety rules should be enforced.[13]

Without full commitment at all levels of management, any attempts to reduce the incidence of unsafe acts performed by workers will meet with little success. The first-line supervisor is a critical link in the chain of management. If the supervisor does not take safety seriously, it is likely that his or her subordinates will not either.

10.2.3 Enforcement of Occupational Health and Safety Laws

In all Canadian jurisdictions, occupational health and safety law provides for government inspectors to periodically carry out safety inspections of workplaces. Health and safety inspectors have wide powers to conduct inspections in any workplace at any time without a warrant or prior notification and may engage in any examination and inquiry that they believe necessary to ascertain whether the workplace is in compliance with the law. Safety inspectors may order a variety of actions on the part of employers and employees, including orders to stop work or stop using tools, install first aid equipment, and stop emission of contaminants. Governments have been criticized for weak enforcement of health and safety laws, however, and several provinces have recently strengthened their inspection services.[14]

Penalties consist of fines and/or jail terms. Governments across Canada are increasingly turning to prosecution as a means of enforcing health and safety standards. In 2008, Alberta imposed a record $5 million in penalties against companies for health and safety violations.[15] Other provinces are increasing the number of charges laid against both individual managers and organizations.[16]

Canadian corporate executives and directors may be held directly responsible for workplace injuries, and in some cases corporate officers have been convicted and received prison sentences for health and safety violations.[17] The Criminal Code includes a criminal offence (known as Bill C-45 amendments, and commonly referred to as "corporate killing") that imposes criminal liability on "all persons" who direct the work of other employees and fail to ensure an appropriate level of safety in the workplace. Criminal Code convictions can be penalized by incarceration up to life in prison, and financial fines can be imposed on guilty parties.

The first company to be charged with and plead guilty to criminal negligence causing the death of a worker was Transpavé, a concrete block manufacturer in Quebec. The incident involved a young employee who was crushed by heavy machinery when he tried to remove debris jamming a stacking machine. The machine did have a safety guard device, but the device had been disabled almost two years prior to the accident. In addition, the court found that the company had inadequate programs to ensure safe operation of the machine, and there was a lack of training regarding safety and hazards in the workplace. As a result, the company was found to be negligent in its responsibility of safety in the workplace, and the company was fined $110 000.[18]

10.2.4 Occupational Health and Safety and Other Legislation

Health and safety, human rights, labour relations, and employment standards laws are in force in every jurisdiction in Canada in an interlaced web of legislation. For example, Bill 168 came into effect in 2010 as an amendment to the Ontario Occupational Health and Safety Act. The amendment has specific legislation requiring the employer to develop violence and harassment policies/programs, report and investigate violence and harassment situations, develop violence-related emergency response procedures, and deal with complaints, incidents, and threats of violence through a formalized process. Such changes to legislation may be specific or vague, local or national, and short or long term, but the role of HR in addressing and responding to changing occupational health and safety legislation will remain critical.

In addition, situations arise in which it is difficult to know which law is applicable, or which one takes precedence over another. For example, are the human rights of one employee to wear a ceremonial knife related to his or her religion more important than the safety of other employees? How much discipline is acceptable to labour arbitrators for health and safety violations? Should fights in the workplace be considered a safety hazard? Is sexual harassment a safety hazard? And how long does an employer have to tolerate poor performance from an alcoholic employee whose attempts at treatment fail? In Saskatchewan, human rights and occupational health and safety legislation overlap because sexual harassment is considered to be a workplace hazard.[19]

10.3 WHAT CAUSES ACCIDENTS?

Workplace accidents have three basic causes: (1) chance occurrences, (2) unsafe conditions, and (3) unsafe acts on the part of employees.

10.3.1 Chance Occurrences

Chance occurrences (such as walking past a plate-glass window just as someone hits a ball through it) contribute to accidents but are more or less beyond management's control. Therefore, we will focus on *unsafe conditions* and *unsafe acts*.

10.3.2 Unsafe Conditions

Unsafe conditions are a main cause of accidents. They include such factors as improperly guarded equipment; defective equipment; hazardous procedures in, on, or around machines or equipment; unsafe storage (congestion, overloading); improper illumination (glare, insufficient light); and improper ventilation (insufficient air change, impure air source).[20] These conditions are often under direct or indirect control of employers, who can take appropriate actions to minimize employee risk levels.

The basic remedy here is to eliminate or minimize the unsafe conditions. Government standards address the mechanical and physical conditions that cause accidents. Furthermore, a checklist of unsafe conditions can be used to conduct a job hazard analysis. Common indicators of job hazards include increased numbers of accidents, employee complaints, poor product quality, employee modifications to workstations, and higher levels of absenteeism and turnover.[21]

10.3.2.1 Control of Toxic Substances

Most occupational health and safety laws require basic precautions with respect to toxic substances, including chemicals, biohazards (such as HIV/AIDS and SARS), and physical agents (such as radiation, heat, and noise). An accurate inventory of these substances must be maintained, maximum exposure limits for airborne concentrations of these agents adhered to, the substances tested, and their use carefully controlled.

The **Workplace Hazardous Materials Information System (WHMIS)** is a Canada-wide, legally mandated system designed to protect workers by providing crucial information about hazardous materials or substances in the workplace. WHMIS was the outcome of a cooperative effort among the federal, provincial, and territorial governments together with industry and organized labour. The WHMIS legislation has three components:[22]

1. Labelling of hazardous material containers to alert workers that there is a potentially hazardous product inside (see **Figure 10.1** for examples of hazard symbols).

2. Material safety data sheets (MSDS) to outline a product's potentially hazardous ingredients and the procedures for safe handling of the product.

3. Employee training to ensure that employees can identify WHMIS hazard symbols, read WHMIS supplier and workplace labels, and read and apply the information on an MSDS.

In addition to unsafe conditions, three other work-related factors contribute to accidents: the *job itself,* the *work schedule,* and the *psychological climate* of the workplace. Certain jobs are inherently more dangerous than others. According to one study, for example, the job of crane operator results in about three times more accident-related hospital visits than does the job of supervisor. Similarly, the work of some departments is inherently safer than that of others. For example, an accounting department usually has fewer accidents than a shipping department.

Work schedules and fatigue also affect accident rates. Accident rates usually do not increase too noticeably during the first five or six hours of the workday. Beyond that, however, the accident rate increases quickly as the number of hours worked increases. This is due partly to fatigue. It has also been found that

Canada Safety Council
https://canadasafetycouncil.org

Workplace Hazardous Materials Information System (WHMIS) A Canada-wide, legally mandated system designed to protect workers by providing information about hazardous materials in the workplace.

WHMIS Training
www.whmis.net

FIGURE 10.1   WHMIS Class and Hazard Symbols

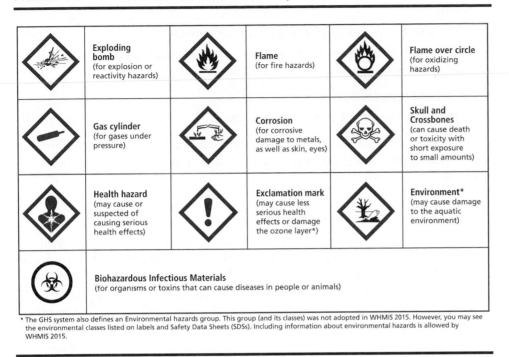

⬙	**Exploding bomb** (for explosion or reactivity hazards)	⬙	**Flame** (for fire hazards)	⬙	**Flame over circle** (for oxidizing hazards)
⬙	**Gas cylinder** (for gases under pressure)	⬙	**Corrosion** (for corrosive damage to metals, as well as skin, eyes)	⬙	**Skull and Crossbones** (can cause death or toxicity with short exposure to small amounts)
⬙	**Health hazard** (may cause or suspected of causing serious health effects)	⬙	**Exclamation mark** (may cause less serious health effects or damage the ozone layer*)	⬙	**Environment*** (may cause damage to the aquatic environment)
⊛	**Biohazardous Infectious Materials** (for organisms or toxins that can cause diseases in people or animals)				

* The GHS system also defines an Environmental hazards group. This group (and its classes) was not adopted in WHMIS 2015. However, you may see the environmental classes listed on labels and Safety Data Sheets (SDSs). Including information about environmental hazards is allowed by WHMIS 2015.

Source: Workplace Hazardous Materials Information System (WHMIS): *A Guide to the Legislation-* Appendix 11.1. Reprinted with permission.

accidents occur more often during night shifts. In addition, recent research in Canada identifies how shift work impacts employee health and safety, as summarized in HR by the Numbers: Balancing Scheduling of Employees and Health Concerns.

Finally, many experts believe that the psychological climate of the workplace affects the accident rate. For example, accidents occur more frequently in plants with a high seasonal layoff rate and those where there is hostility among employees, many garnished wages, and blighted living conditions. Temporary stress factors, such as high workplace temperature, poor illumination, and a congested workplace, are also related to accident rates. It appears that workers who work under stress or who consider their jobs to be threatened or insecure have more accidents than those who do not work under these conditions.[23]

10.3.4   Unsafe Acts

Most safety experts and managers know that it is impossible to eliminate accidents just by improving unsafe conditions. People cause accidents, and no one has found a surefire way to eliminate *unsafe acts* by employees, such as

- throwing materials;
- operating or working at unsafe speeds (either too fast or too slow);

HR by the Numbers

▶ Balancing Scheduling of Employees and Health Concerns

33% of Canadian employees work some form of shift work (e.g., rotating shifts, evenings or weekend shifts, on-call shifts, 24-hour shifts)

23% increased risk of heart attack for shift workers over non-shift workers

17.4% increased risk of coronary events for shift workers over non-shift workers

5% increased risk of stroke for shift workers over non-shift workers

20–30 average additional weight gain (in lbs.) of shift workers after 10–15 years of working shifts when compared to non-shift workers

- making safety devices inoperative by removing, adjusting, or disconnecting them;
- using unsafe equipment or using equipment unsafely;
- using unsafe procedures in loading, placing, mixing, and combining;
- taking unsafe positions under suspended loads;
- lifting improperly; and
- distracting, teasing, abusing, startling, quarrelling, and instigating horseplay.

Such unsafe acts as these can undermine even the best attempts to minimize unsafe conditions, and the progressive discipline system should be used in such situations.

10.3.5 Personal Characteristics

A model summarizing how personal characteristics are linked to accidents is presented in **Figure 10.2**. Personal characteristics (personality, motivation, and so on) can serve as the basis for certain undesirable attitudes and behaviour tendencies, such as the tendency to take risks. These behaviour tendencies can, in turn, result in unsafe acts, such as inattention and failure to follow procedures. It follows that such unsafe acts increase the probability of someone having an accident.[24] Research indicates that agreeableness and conscientiousness are positively associated with safe behaviour.[25] Research also indicates that safety climate has more of an impact on promoting safety than personal characteristics.[26]

Years of research have failed to unearth any set of traits that accident repeaters seem to have in common. Instead, the consensus is that the person who is

FIGURE 10.2 How Personal Factors May Influence Employee Accident Behaviour

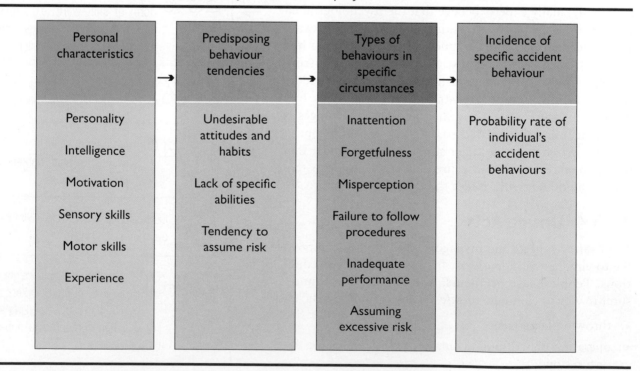

accident prone on one job may not be that way on a different job—that accident proneness is *situational*. For example, *personality traits* (such as emotional stability) may distinguish accident-prone workers on jobs involving risk; and *lack of motor skills* may distinguish accident-prone workers on jobs involving coordination. In fact, many human traits have been found to be related to accident repetition in specific situations, as the following discussion illustrates.[27]

10.3.5.1 Vision

Vision is related to accident frequency for many jobs. For example, passenger car drivers, intercity bus drivers, and machine operators who have high visual skills have fewer injuries than those who do not.[28]

10.3.5.2 Literacy

The risk of accidents is higher for employees who cannot read and understand machinery operating instructions, safety precautions, equipment and repair manuals, first aid instructions, or organizational policies on workplace health and safety. Low literacy skills potentially put workers and their co-workers in harm's way and increase the likelihood of work stoppages due to accidents or errors.[29] This situation is complicated by the fact that most workers with low literacy skills believe that their skills are good or excellent.[30]

A report by the Conference Board of Canada concluded that employers can reduce accidents by improving employees' literacy skills. They found an inverse relationship between industries requiring a high level of health and safety and investment in literacy skills.[31] This finding, together with the reality that people with lower levels of literacy often end up in more dangerous occupations like trucking, manufacturing, or construction, where literacy requirements are low compared to more intellectual jobs, clearly indicates the need for action to heighten literacy skills of workers.

10.3.5.3 Age

Accidents are generally most frequent among people between the ages of 17 and 28, declining thereafter to reach a low in the late fifties and sixties. Although different patterns might be found with different jobs, this age factor repeats year after year. Across Canada, young workers between the ages of 15 and 24 (often students in low-paying summer jobs) are over five times more likely to be injured during their first four weeks on the job than others, which raises questions about the supervision and training of young workers.[32] Suggestions regarding safety of young workers are provided in the Workforce Diversity box.

10.3.5.4 Perceptual versus Motor Skills

If a worker's perceptual skill is greater than or equal to his or her motor skill, the employee is more likely to be a safe worker than another worker whose perceptual skill is lower than his or her motor skill.[33] In other words, a worker who reacts more quickly than he or she can perceive is more likely to have accidents.

In summary, these findings provide a partial list of the human traits that have been found to be related to higher accident rates, and suggest that it seems to be possible to identify accident-prone individuals and to screen them out for specific jobs. Overall, it seems that accidents can have multiple causes. With that in mind, accident prevention will be discussed.

WORKFORCE DIVERSITY

Guiding Young Workers in Health and Safety

The Canadian Centre for Occupational Health and Safety suggests that to reduce the likelihood of accidents and injuries to young workers, the following basic steps should be observed:

1. *Assign suitable work.* Avoid assigning jobs that require long training times, a high degree of skill, a lot of responsibility, critical or risky tasks, or working alone.
2. *Understand young workers.* Young workers think differently than older and more experienced employees do. Young workers tend to take risks and are unrealistic about their own mortality; they may be reluctant to ask questions for fear of appearing unknowledgeable; and because of a lack of understanding, they may decide to make changes to the job in unexpected and possibly risky ways.
3. *Provide training.* Tell young workers not to perform any task until they have been properly trained; not to leave their work area unless they are told to do so, as other worksites may have special hazards; and to ask someone if they are unsure of anything. Make sure that any young worker who must use hazardous equipment is given detailed training on safety features. If young workers must wear protective equipment, make sure they know when they need to wear it, where to find it, how to use it, and how to care for it. Finally, provide training on what to do in case of emergency.
4. *Supervise.* Effective supervision of young workers requires that supervisors be qualified to organize and direct work; that they know the laws and regulations that apply to the job; and that they know the actual and potential hazards in the workplace.

Source: Based on "Young Workers", Canadian Centre for Occupational Health and Safety. www.ccohs.ca/products/pdf/youngWorkers.pdf.

10.4 HOW TO PREVENT ACCIDENTS

In practice, accident prevention involves minimizing unsafe conditions and reducing the incidence of unsafe acts.

10.4.1 Minimizing Unsafe Conditions

The appropriate time to begin "controlling" workplace accidents is before the accident happens, not after. This involves taking all the steps previously summarized. For example, firms should remove unsafe conditions, screen out employees who might be accident-prone for the job in question (without violating human rights legislation), and establish a safety policy and loss control goals.

Minimizing unsafe conditions is an employer's first line of defense. Safety engineers can design jobs so that physical hazards are removed or reduced. In addition, supervisors and managers play a role in reducing unsafe conditions by ensuring that employees wear personal protective equipment, an often difficult chore. However, only 4 percent of accidents stem from unsafe working conditions, and therefore more attention will be paid to accident prevention methods that focus on changing employee behaviour.

10.4.2 Reducing Incidence of Unsafe Acts

Reducing the incidence of unsafe acts is the second basic approach to accident prevention, and there are four specific actions that can help to achieve this: selection testing, top management support, training and education, and positive reinforcement.

10.4.2.1 Selection Testing

Certain selection tests can help screen out accident-prone individuals before they are hired. For example, measures of muscular coordination can be useful because coordination is a predictor of safety for certain jobs. Tests of visual skills can be important because good vision plays a part in preventing accidents in many occupations, including operating machines and driving. A test called the Employee Reliability Inventory (ERI), which measures reliability dimensions such as emotional maturity, conscientiousness, safe job performance, and courteous job performance, can also be helpful in selecting employees who are less likely to have accidents.

Employee Reliability Inventory
www.eri.com

A Canadian study conducted in a major industrial plant compared injury costs for two groups: one group of employees who were subjected to screening to assess their physical capability to perform job duties before the job offer was secured, and another group that did not require screening before the offer was made. For the screened group, injury costs over five years were $6 500, whereas for the non-screened group they were $2 073 000—a highly significant difference.[34]

Many employers would like to inquire about applicants' workers' compensation history before hiring, in part to avoid habitual workers' compensation claimants and accident-prone individuals. However, inquiring about an applicant's workers' compensation injuries and claims can lead to allegations of discrimination based on disability. Similarly, applicants cannot be asked whether they have a disability, nor can they be asked to take tests that tend to screen out those with disabilities.

Employers can ask each applicant whether he or she has the ability to perform the essential duties of the job and ask, "Do you know of any reason why you would not be able to perform the various functions of the job in question?" Candidates can also be asked to demonstrate job-related skills, provided that every applicant is required to do so. Any selection test that duplicates the physical requirements of the job at realistic levels and the type of work expected does not violate human rights law, as long as it is developed and imposed honestly and in good faith to test whether or not the applicant can meet production requirements.[35]

10.4.2.2 Top-Management Commitment

Studies consistently find that successful health and safety programs require a strong management commitment. An example of the importance of top-management commitment is provided in the Strategic HR box. This commitment manifests in senior managers being personally involved in safety activities on a routine basis, giving safety matters high priority in company meetings and production scheduling, giving the company safety officer high rank and status, and including safety training in new workers' training. For example, linking managers' bonuses to safety improvements can reinforce a firm's commitment to safety and encourage managers to emphasize safety. HR managers have an important role to play in communicating the importance of health and safety to senior management by demonstrating how it affects the bottom line.

10.4.2.3 Training and Education

Safety training is another technique for reducing the number of accidents. Reviews on workplace safety report that safety training for workers or their supervisors increases safety-conscious behaviour and reduces accidents.[36] In more complex jobs or jobs with more hazard exposure, workers should receive highly engaging training.[37] The Canadian Centre for Occupational Health and Safety and several safety associations, such as the Industrial Accident Prevention Association (IAPA), are available to partner in training efforts. The Canadian Federation of Independent Business offers online training leading to a Small Business Health and Safety (SBHS) certificate.

All employees should be required to participate in occupational health and safety training programs, and providing opportunities for employee input into the content and design of such programs is advisable. The training should include a practical evaluation process to ensure that workers are applying the acquired knowledge and following recommended safety procedures. Such training is especially appropriate for new employees.

Safety posters can also help reduce unsafe acts. However, posters are no substitute for a comprehensive safety program; instead, they should be combined with other techniques, like screening and training, to improve unsafe conditions and reduce the incidence of unsafe acts. Posters with pictures may be particularly valuable for immigrant workers if their first language is not the language of the workplace.

An Ethical Dilemma

Is it ethical to reduce costs by providing only English-language safety training to immigrant workers who speak little English?

10.4.2.4 Positive Reinforcement

Safety programs based on positive reinforcement can improve safety behaviour at work. Employees often receive little or no positive reinforcement for performing safely. One approach is to establish and communicate a reasonable goal (in terms of observed incidents performed safely) so that workers know what is expected of them in terms of good performance. Employees are encouraged to increase their performance to the new safety goal for their own protection and to decrease costs for the company. Various observers (such as safety coordinators and senior managers) walk through the plant regularly, collecting safety data. The results are then posted on a graph charting the percentage of incidents performed safely by the group as a whole, thus providing workers with feedback on their safety performance. Workers can compare their current safety performance with their assigned goal. In addition, supervisors should praise workers when they perform selected activities safely.[38]

10.4.2.5 Facilitating an Employee's Return to Work

Minimizing unsafe conditions and the incidence of unsafe acts may not completely eliminate workplace accidents. If an accident happens, employers should provide first aid, make sure that the worker gets quick medical attention, make it clear that they are interested in the injured worker and his or her fears and questions, document the accident, file any required accident reports, and encourage a speedy return to work. Perhaps the most important and effective thing an employer can do to reduce costs is to develop an aggressive return-to-work program.

The National Institute of Disability Management and Research (NIDMAR) in Victoria, British Columbia, recommends following the three Cs:

1. *Commitment* to keeping in touch with the worker and ensuring his or her return to work

2. *Collaboration* among the parties involved, including medical, family, and workers' compensation

3. *Creativity* in focusing on how to use the worker's remaining abilities on the job[39]

Specific actions to encourage early return to work can be internal or external to the organization. Internally, an employer can set up rehabilitation committees to identify modified work, including relevant stakeholders, such as the employee and his or her colleagues, HR professionals, union representatives, and managers.

Canadian Injured Workers Alliance
www.ciwa.ca

Functional abilities evaluations (FAEs) are an important step in facilitating the return to work. The FAE is conducted by a health-care professional with an aim to

- improve the chances that the injured worker will be safe on the job.

- help the worker's performance by identifying problem areas of work that can be addressed by physical therapy or accommodated through job modification.

- determine the level of disability so that the worker can either go back to his or her original job or be accommodated.[40]

Externally, the employer can work with the employee's family to ensure that they are supportive, mobilize the resources of the EAP to help the employee, ensure that physical and occupational therapists are available, and make the family physician aware of workplace accommodation possibilities.

Accident prevention continues even after an accident. Post-incident investigation and evaluation should focus not only on identifying the cause of the accident, but also on producing lessons learned that will contribute to the employer's effort to minimize unsafe conditions and reduce the incidence of unsafe acts.

The average workplace injury in Ontario costs more than $59 000 in workers' compensation benefits.

10.5 OCCUPATIONAL HEALTH AND SAFETY CHALLENGES IN CANADA

A number of health-related issues and challenges can undermine employee performance at work. These include alcoholism and substance abuse, stress and burnout, repetitive strain injuries, workplace toxins, workplace smoking, influenza pandemics, and workplace violence. Some companies take a proactive approach to managing the impact of health-related issues in the workplace, as identified in the Strategic HR box. The Expert Opinion box that follows summarizes the role of leaders in safety management.

10.5.1 Substance Abuse

The effects of substance abuse on the employee and his or her work are severe. Both the quality and quantity of work decline sharply, and safety may be compromised. When dealing with alcohol and substance abuse on

STRATEGIC HR

Fidelity Investments Canada Focuses on Employee Health

As a recent recipient of the Venngo Healthy Workplaces award, Fidelity provides a model environment of how employers can proactively promote safe workplaces through focuses on employee health and wellness. Recognizing that healthy workplaces increase employee productivity and engagement levels, while decreasing turnover and absenteeism, senior leaders champion and participate in wellness initiatives.

Internally, the company focuses on employee fitness. They have two workstations that are walking stations for employees to keep active while on conference calls; 85 percent of employees participated in an internal challenge established to get employees moving 10 000 steps per day. A monthly newsletter promotes healthy eating for working professionals. Employee gym memberships are largely reimbursed by the employer.

To balance role conflict, the company's employee assistance program (EAP) provides support for family issues (e.g., help with finding daycare centres, parenting classes, adoptive parents, etc.) and personal problems (e.g., relationship issues, stress or financial management, grief counselling, etc.).

Source: Melissa Campeau, "Venngo Healthy Workplaces Award," *HR Reporter* (September 19, 2016).

© Stokkete/Sutterstock

Alcohol and substance abuse can affect an employee's quality and quantity of work and could pose unsafe working conditions for other employees.

the job, employers must balance conflicting legal obligations. On the one hand, under human rights laws, alcoholism and drug addiction are considered to be disabilities. On the other hand, under occupational health and safety legislation, employers are responsible for maintaining due diligence. As a result, employers worry that when they accommodate an employee with an addiction, they may not be ensuring a safe work environment for other employees.[41]

In a 2016 study, almost three in four Canadian employers surveyed had a formal drug and alcohol policy, largely through urinalysis or breathalyzers.[42] Employees are often tested after an accident involving injury, a near-miss accident, as part of a monitoring program, as part of a post-treatment or post-violation condition, or based on the supervisor's referral. Drug and alcohol testing in Canada is legal only in situations where three conditions determined by the Supreme Court are met:

1. The test is rationally connected to the performance of the job.

2. The test is adopted in an honest and good-faith belief that it is necessary for the fulfillment of a legitimate work-related purpose.

3. The test is reasonably necessary to the accomplishment of the work-related purpose.[43]

Random drug tests do not measure actual impairment and are therefore unjustifiable. Arbitrary alcohol testing of one or more employees but not others is not usually justifiable, but for employees in safety-sensitive positions, such as airline pilots, it may be justifiable. "For cause" and "post-incident" testing for either alcohol or drugs may be acceptable in specific circumstances. Positive test results should generally result in accommodation of the employee. Immediate dismissal is not generally justifiable.[44]

Academic Viewpoint
EXPERT OPINION

Focus: Linking health and productivity for the workforce of the future, specifically focused on management responsibility and perspective on decision making in the workplace.

I.   Your research is really focused on putting occupational health from the leadership perspective. Why did you assume this focus?

Some people discriminate between leadership and management. Management is a formal role assigned by the organization. Managers may be leaders or may not. My research is focused on leadership. Leaders have accountability, responsibility, and influence. They need to actively construct systems to help the organization maximize its outputs.

Coming from an industrial/organizational psychology background, I realized early in my career that the conversation of employee well-being wasn't as prevalent in the business realm or in business schools. The issue of employee well-being and structures to support this are critical to organizational success and longevity. Additionally, there is a real interest in the topic from both students and leaders.

2.   What is the relationship between employees' perceptions of their managers' leadership styles and the employees' psychological well-being?

Leaders control the allocation of resources, the systems and policies that shape the organization's culture. Thus, leaders create an environment

Dr. Catherine Loughlin

Identification:
Dr. Catherine Loughlin (PhD)
Canada Research Chair in Management and on the Board of Directors at the CN Centre for Occupational Health and Safety

Affiliation:
Social Sciences and Humanities, Saint Mary's University

for employees that affects both their productivity and well-being. Research shows that employees who trust that their leaders will act in their best interest experience lower perceptions of workplace-related risks and lower resource depletion, which ultimately reduces their stress levels while increasing productivity. These workers don't consume cognitive and emotional energy trying to protect themselves.

We typically look at intrinsic and extrinsic rewards or conditions as starting points of predicting employee outcomes, but the system is constructed by leaders.

3.   What are the implications of your work in regard to provision of leadership

training as a means of minimizing workplace risks for employees?

Training of leaders is very customized, but there are a few common experiences.

I.   First, generally, leaders lack feedback. The leaders' perception of what the situation is (perceptions of priorities, culture, system, employee well-being, etc.) can be very different than what the employees perceive. While some organizations use employee surveys to collect feedback, the survey rarely provides a mechanism for individualized leader feedback. The gap analysis is required to determine required training and development initiatives for leaders.

II.   Leaders need to model behaviour through the choices that they make about resource allocation, as well as what they do (which at times can be more important than what they say). Leaders can reflect on the impact of the actions and choices they make, and how these impact employees.

III.   Leaders need to recognize that policies on paper cannot be translated into practice unless the culture is aware/aligned. For example, individual behaviour as well as group level behaviour (e.g., counterproductive behaviour, helping others) should be evaluated in performance appraisals to align with a focus on employee well-being.

Source: Reprinted by permission from Catherine Loughlin.

Recognizing the substance abuser on the job can be a challenge. The early symptoms can be similar to those of other problems and thus hard to classify; indicators range from tardiness to prolonged, unpredictable absences in later stages of addiction. Supervisors should be the company's first line of defense in combating substance abuse in the workplace, but they should not try to be company detectives or medical diagnosticians. Guidelines for supervisors should include the following:[45]

- If an employee appears to be under the influence of drugs or alcohol, ask how the employee feels and look for signs of impairment, such as slurred speech. An employee judged to be unfit for duty may be sent home but not fired on the spot.

- Make a written record of observed behaviour and follow up each incident. In addition to issuing a written reprimand, managers should inform workers of the number of warnings that the company will tolerate before requiring termination. Regardless of any suspicion of substance abuse, concerns should be focused on work performance, expected changes, and available options for help.

- Troubled employees should be referred to the company's employee assistance program.

Bellwood Health Services Inc.
www.bellwood.ca

The four traditional techniques for dealing with substance abuse are discipline, discharge/termination of employment, in-house counselling, and referral to an outside agency. Discharge or termination of employment is used to deal with alcoholism and drug problems only after repeated attempts at rehabilitation have failed. In-house counselling can be offered by the employer's medical staff or the employee assistance plan. External agencies such as Alcoholics Anonymous can also be used. In Grande Prairie, Alberta, a clinic was established by the Alberta Alcohol and Drug Abuse Commission as a result of requests from the business community for a treatment centre that could deal with workplace-specific issues. It offers quick enrollment in its 30-day alcohol treatment program or the 50-day cocaine treatment program for $175 per day, plus months of follow-up, helping 180 clients a year return to work as soon as possible.[46]

Shepell.fgi
www.shepellfgi.com

10.5.2 Mental Health in the Workplace

In Canada, the total cost of mental health problems approximates 17 percent of payroll, and the overall economic impact of work-related mental health problems is estimated to be $51 billion annually.[47] Many organizations make physical safety a priority, but too often work environments that clearly have the potential for serious consequences from stress are simply tolerated.[48] Perhaps this accounts for the fact that two-thirds of companies underestimate the prevalence of mental illness in the workplace, and only 13 percent of senior executives feel that they have a strong awareness of the impact of mental health on their workplaces.[49] However, mental health issues are the leading cause of both short- and long-term disability claims.[50] It has been estimated that if we improve treatment of employees with depression and/or anxiety resulting in these workers being fully functional at work, the Canadian economy could gain between 228 000 to 352 000 jobs annually until 2035.[51]

Workplace stress is a pervasive problem that is getting worse. Job stress has serious consequences for both the employee and the organization. The human consequences of job stress include anxiety, depression, anger, and various physical consequences, such as cardiovascular disease, headaches, and accidents. A 2016 study by the Conference Board of Canada indicates that work stress and job demands are the single largest factors contributing to sleep deprivation among Canadians.[52] Stress also has serious consequences for the organization, including reductions in productivity and increased absenteeism and turnover.[53]

Organizations begin to suffer when too many employees feel that the relentless pace of work life is neither sustainable nor healthy. Why is this happening? Employees are being asked to do more with less, creating work overload, increased time pressures, and tighter deadlines (almost one-third of Canadian workers consider themselves workaholics).[54] More people are working in "precarious" employment, such as temporary or part-time work with no benefits.[55] The sheer volume of email imposes terrific amounts of pressure and distraction on employees, taking a toll on their emotional equilibrium. The result is a corporate climate characterized by fatigue, depression, and anxiety.[56]

Job stress has two main sources: environmental factors and personal factors. First, a variety of external, *environmental factors* can lead to job stress. Two factors are particularly stress-inducing. The first is a high-demand job, such as one with constant deadlines coupled with low employee control. The second is high levels of mental and physical effort combined with low rewards in terms of compensation or acknowledgement.[57] Health-care workers, whose jobs typically include these factors, are more stressed than any other group.[58]

However, no two people react to the same job in an identical way, since *personal factors* also influence stress. For example, Type A personalities—people who are workaholics and who feel driven to always be on time and meet deadlines—normally place themselves under greater stress than do others. Similarly, one's patience, tolerance for ambiguity, self-esteem, health and exercise, and work and sleep patterns can also affect how one reacts to stress. Add to job stress the stress caused by non-job-related issues like divorce, postpartum depression, seasonal affective disorder, and work–family conflict, and many workers are problems waiting to happen.

Yet stress is not necessarily dysfunctional. Too little stress creates boredom and apathy. Performance is optimal at a level of stress that energizes but does not wear someone out.[59] Others find that stress may result in a search that leads to a better job or to a career that makes more sense given the person's aptitudes. A modest level of stress may even lead to more creativity if a competitive situation results in new ideas being generated.

"I've been feeling a lot of work related stress."

© Cartoonresource/Fotolia

10.5.2.1 Reducing Job Stress

There are things that a person can do to alleviate stress, ranging from commonsense remedies, such as getting more sleep, eating better, and taking vacation time, to more exotic remedies, such as biofeedback and meditation. Finding a more suitable job, getting counselling through an EAP or elsewhere, and planning and organizing each day's activities are other sensible responses.[60]

The organization and its HR specialists and supervisors can also play a role in identifying and reducing job stress. Offering an EAP is a major step towards alleviating the pressure on managers to try to help employees cope with stress. About 40 percent of EAP usage is related to stress at work. For the supervisor, important activities include monitoring each employee's performance to identify

An Ethical **Dilemma**

Is it ethical for an organization to create high work volume and uncertain job demands of employees during economically volatile times, if they plan to eventually lay off the employees?

symptoms of stress and then informing the person of the organizational remedies that may be available, such as EAPs, job transfers, or other counselling. Also important are fair treatment and permitting the employee to have more control over his or her job.[61]

The importance of control over a job was illustrated by the results of a study in which the psychological strain caused by job stress was reduced by the amount of control that employees had over their job. The less stressful jobs did have high demands in terms of quantitative workload, the amount of attention that the employees had to pay to their work, and work pressure; however, they also ranked high in task clarity, job control, supervisory support, and employee skill utilization. The researchers conclude that "to achieve a balanced system, that is, to reduce psychological strain, [job] demands and [ambiguity regarding the future of the job] need to be lowered, while skill utilization, task clarity, job control, and supervisor support need to be increased."[62]

HR executives need to become advocates for employee mental health within the senior management team. Today's highly valued employees who are driving corporate productivity, innovation, and performance tend to be young knowledge workers, precisely the type of worker most prone to depression and stress.[63]

burnout The total depletion of physical and mental resources caused by excessive striving to reach an unrealistic work-related goal.

Burnout Many people fall victim to **burnout**—the total depletion of physical and mental resources—because of excessive striving to reach an unrealistic work-related goal. Burnout begins with cynical and pessimistic thoughts and leads to apathy, exhaustion, withdrawal into isolation, and eventually depression.[64] Burnout is often the result of too much job stress, especially when that stress is combined with a preoccupation with attaining unattainable work-related goals. Burnout victims often do not lead well-balanced lives; virtually all of their energies are focused on achieving their work-related goals to the exclusion of other activities, leading to physical and sometimes mental collapse. This need not be limited to upwardly mobile executives; for instance, social workers caught up in their clients' problems are often burnout victims.

What can a candidate for burnout do? Here are some suggestions:

- *Break patterns.* First, survey how you spend your time. Are you doing a variety of things, or the same thing over and over? The more well-rounded your life is, the better protected you are against burnout. If you have stopped trying new activities, start them again—for instance, travel or new hobbies.

- *Get away from it all periodically.* Schedule occasional periods of introspection during which you can get away from your usual routine, perhaps alone, to seek a perspective on where you are and where you are going.

- *Reassess goals in terms of their intrinsic worth.* Are the goals that you have set for yourself attainable? Are they really worth the sacrifices that you will have to make?

- *Think about work.* Could you do as good a job without being so intense or while also pursuing outside interests?

- *Reduce stress.* Organize your time more effectively, build a better relationship with your boss, negotiate realistic deadlines, find time during the day for detachment and relaxation, reduce unnecessary noise around your office, and limit interruptions.

Workers' Compensation and Stress-Related Disability Claims All Canadian jurisdictions provide benefits for post-traumatic stress caused by a specific and sudden workplace incident. However, when it comes to chronic stress, there is very limited or no coverage, depending on the jurisdiction.[65] The rationale is that stress has multiple causes, including family situations and personal disposition. Research suggests that a significant portion of chronic stress is often work related. In particular, high-demand/low-control jobs (such as an administrative assistant with several demanding bosses) are known to be "psychotoxic." Consequently, employees who are denied workers' compensation benefits for chronic stress that they believe to be work related are suing their employers. The courts are recognizing these claims and holding employers responsible for actions of supervisors who create "poisoned work environments" through harassment and psychological abuse. Courts are finding that a fundamental implied term of any employment relationship is that the employer will treat the employee fairly and with respect and dignity and that the due diligence requirement includes protection of employees from psychological damage as well as physical harm.[66]

"Alright, I'll okay a personal day."

© Cartoonresource/Fotolia

10.5.3 Repetitive Strain Injuries

Repetitive strain injuries (RSIs) are rapidly becoming the most prevalent work-related injury because of the increasing number of "knowledge" workers who use computers. RSI is an umbrella term for a number of "overuse" injuries affecting muscles, tendons, and nerves of the neck, back, chest, shoulders, arms, and hands. Typically arising as aches and pains, these injuries can progress to become crippling disorders that prevent sufferers from working and from leading normal lives. Warning signs of RSI include tightness or stiffness in the hands, elbow, wrists, shoulders, and neck; numbness and tingling in the fingertips; hands falling asleep; and frequent dropping of tools.[67]

A variety of workplace factors can play a role in the development of RSIs, including repetition, work pace, awkward or fixed positions, forceful movements, vibration, cold temperatures, and insufficient recovery time. RSIs are costly for employers in terms of compensation claims, overtime, equipment modification, retraining, and lost productivity. As with any other workplace safety issue, employers are required under occupational health and safety law to put controls in place to prevent RSIs. British Columbia has the most rigorous requirements regarding protection of workers against RSIs, and unions are calling for other provinces to follow suit. Employers must advise and train workers about the risk of RSIs from workplace activity, identify and assess job-related RSI risk factors, encourage workers to report RSI symptoms early, and use ergonomic interventions.[68]

10.5.3.1 Ergonomics

Poorly designed workstations, bad posture, and long periods of time working on computers are common conditions leading to RSIs, and these are easily preventable. **Ergonomics** is the art of fitting the workstation and work tools to the

repetitive strain injuries (RSIs) Activity-related soft-tissue injuries of the neck, shoulders, arms, wrists, hands, back, and legs.

Human Factors and Ergonomics Society
www.hfes.org

Human Systems Inc.
www.humansys.com

ergonomics An interdisciplinary approach that seeks to integrate and accommodate the physical needs of workers into the design of jobs. It aims to adapt the entire job system—the work, environment, machines, equipment, and processes—to match human characteristics.

individual, which is necessary because there is no such thing as an average body The most important preventive measure is to have employees take short breaks every half-hour or hour to do simple stretches at their workstations.[69]

Ergonomically designed workstations have been found to increase productivity and efficiency, as well as reduce injuries. The Institute for Work and Health studied 200 tax collectors who were in sedentary, computer-intensive jobs. Workers who were given a highly adjustable chair combined with a 90-minute ergonomics training session reported less musculoskeletal pain over their workday, compared with workers who received just the training or nothing at all. Productivity increased nearly 18 percent because of the reduction in pain and more effective use of workspaces.[70]

Ergonomics will become more and more important as the workforce ages, and the physical demands of work will need to be adapted to accommodate some of the many physical changes typically associated with aging, including changes in muscular strength, hand function, cardiovascular capacity, vision, and hearing.

10.5.3.2 Video Display Terminals

The physical demands of new technologies have brought a new set of RSIs. The fact that many workers today must spend hours each day working with video display terminals (VDTs) is creating new health problems at work. Short-term eye problems, like burning, itching, and tearing, as well as eyestrain and eye soreness are common complaints among video display operators. Backaches and neck aches are also widespread among display users. These often occur because employees try to compensate for display problems like glare and immovable keyboards by manoeuvring into awkward body positions.

Researchers also found that employees who used VDTs and had heavy workloads were prone to psychological distress, such as anxiety, irritability, and fatigue. There is also a tendency for computer users to suffer from RSIs, such as *carpal tunnel syndrome* (a tingling or numbness in the fingers caused by the narrowing of a tunnel of bones and ligaments in the wrist) caused by repetitive use of the hands and arms at uncomfortable angles.[71]

General recommendations regarding the use of VDTs include giving employees rest breaks every hour, designing maximum flexibility into the workstation so that it can be adapted to the individual operator, reducing glare with devices, such as shades over windows and terminal screens, and giving VDT workers a complete pre-placement vision exam to ensure that vision is properly corrected to reduce visual strain.[72]

10.5.4   Workplace Toxins

The leading cause of work-related deaths around the world is cancer. Hundreds of Canadian workers die from occupational cancer each year.[73] There is an erroneous perception that cancer-causing agents in the workplace are disappearing. Employers often face significant costs to eliminate carcinogens in the workplace, and unions are often so preoccupied with wage and benefit increases that they don't bring the issue to the bargaining table (although the

VDTs are increasingly causing health problems such as short-term vision problems.

© Martinan/Fotolia

Canadian Labour Congress has launched an initiative to reduce work-related cancers by releasing an information kit for workers on cancer-causing materials on the job).[74] In addition to known carcinogens, such as asbestos and benzene, new chemicals and substances are constantly being introduced into the workplace without adequate testing.[75] As a response, workers' compensation laws in several provinces have been amended to provide benefits to firefighters who develop specific job-related cancers.[76]

10.5.4.1 Workplace Smoking

Smoking is a serious problem for employees and employers, as discussed in Chapter 9. Employers face higher costs for health-care and disability insurance, as smoking is associated with numerous health problems. Employees who smoke have reduced productivity and a significantly greater risk of occupational accidents than do non-smokers. Employees who smoke also expose non-smoking co-workers to toxic second-hand smoke.

Smokers who are also exposed to other carcinogens in the workplace, such as asbestos, have dramatically higher rates of lung cancer. The effects of on the job exposure to radon on lung cancer rates were found to last up to 14 years, and the cancer rates were greatly increased for smokers.[77]

Most Canadian jurisdictions have banned smoking in workplaces. Health Canada is urging employers to implement smoking cessation programs for employees to achieve better health for employees, better business results, legislative compliance, increased employee satisfaction (especially for those who do not smoke), and avoidance of litigation.[78]

10.5.4.2 Viral Pandemic

Recent major outbreaks of viral diseases like influenza have alarmed people around the world and reminded everyone that a major viral pandemic is inevitable at some time in the future. A 2006 study by the Conference Board of Canada found that although almost 80 percent of executives are concerned about the impact of a pandemic on their organization, only 4 percent of their organizations had developed a pandemic preparedness plan.[79]

HR will be a key player in responding to a pandemic as most employers are planning to continue their business operations using the existing workforce—in other words, with substantially fewer employees. Immediate decisions will be required regarding telecommuting and working at remote worksites, compensation for absent employees, and maintenance of occupational health for employees who are working on company premises.[80] Even in the plans that do exist, there is little detail on the status of quarantined employees, compensating employees who cover for absent co-workers, responding to employee refusals to work in an unsafe environment, and managing business shutdowns if health and safety officers declare the entire workplace to be unsafe.[81]

A pandemic preparedness plan should address prevention, containment, response to employee work refusals, creation of a pandemic preparation and response team, viability of continuing company operations, security of company premises, sickness/disability coverage, leaves to care for sick family members or children at home if schools are closed, and visitors to company premises.[82] Communication will be a critical component of pandemic management (likely using email, intranet, and hotlines), particularly if travel bans are imposed.[83] Unionized organizations will also need to consult their collective agreements

The Canadian Pandemic Influenza Plan

www.phac-aspc.gc.ca/cpip-pclcpi

and may wish to consult with the union when making pandemic preparedness plans.[84] Although the risk of a pandemic occurring in any one year may be small, the potential consequences are so serious that business leaders are well advised to prepare their organizations.[85]

10.5.5 Violence at Work

Workplace violence is defined by the International Labour Organization (ILO) as incidents in which an employee is abused, threatened, or assaulted in circumstances relating to work, and it includes harassment, bullying, intimidation, physical threats, assaults, and robberies. Most workplace violence arises from members of the public—customers or strangers—rather than co-workers. Canada is the fourth-worst country in the world for workplace violence (the United States is seventh) according to ILO data.[86]

The first-ever Statistics Canada report on criminal victimization in the workplace, released in 2007, indicated that one in every five violent incidents in Canada (such as physical and sexual assault, or armed robbery) occurred in the workplace. Physical assault was the most common violent incident, representing 71 percent of all incidents of workplace violence.[87] Violence against employees at work is particularly prevalent for women in health-care professions. More than one-third of nurses are physically assaulted and almost half suffer emotional abuse.[88] Reports of abuse of nurses by clinical area of practice are shown in **Figure 10.3**.

10.5.5.1 Workplace Violence and the Law

Most Canadian jurisdictions now have workplace violence legislation in place covering physical violence, and some include psychological/emotional violence as well. Human rights laws across the country prohibit various forms of harassment and bullying. Employers may be found vicariously liable for the violent acts of their employees on the basis that the employer negligently hired or negligently retained someone whom they should reasonably have known could cause the violent act; employers may also be found liable when they are aware of violent incidents and fail to respond.[89]

FIGURE 10.3   Reports of Abuse by Clinical Area of Practice

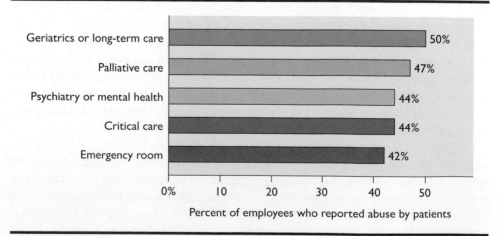

Percent of employees who reported abuse by patients

Source: Statistics Canada, Factors Related to On-the-Job Abuse of Nurses by Patients, *Health Reports,* 20, no. 2 (2009), pp. 7–19. This does not constitute an endorsement by Statistics Canada of this product.

10.5.5.2 Prevention and Control of Workplace Violence

There are several concrete steps that employers can take to reduce the incidence of workplace violence. These include identifying jobs with a high risk of violence, instituting a workplace violence policy, creating a healthy work environment, heightening security measures, training for violence reduction, and improving employee screening.

Canadian Initiative on Workplace Violence
www.workplaceviolence.ca

Identify Jobs with High Risk of Violence   Reliable predictors of workplace violence fall into three basic categories.

1. The instigator of the violence specifically enters the work environment with the intent to engage in criminal behaviour (theft, for instance) and generally has no other legitimate reason to be in the workplace. Jobs such as those of taxi drivers or gas station attendants have the highest risk for this type of violence.

2. The instigator is the recipient of a service or object offered at the targeted workplace. Jobs such as those of nurses or social workers are at risk for this type of violence.

3. The instigator is a potential or former employee (or, for example, a disgruntled employee).

Identifying and redressing these hazards and risk factors, such as installing safety shields for taxi drivers and bus drivers, can help to reduce victimization.[90]

Institute a Workplace Violence Policy   Firms should develop, support, and communicate a workplace violence policy that clearly communicates management's commitment to preventing violent incidents. The policy should state that no degree or type of violence is acceptable in the workplace; provide definitions of prohibited conduct; specify consequences of violating the policy; encourage reporting of violent incidents; include prohibitions and sanctions for retaliation or reprisal; and specify that all physical assaults will be reported to police.[91]

Create a Healthy Work Environment   A healthy work environment with professional supervision is the best way to reduce violence on the part of employees. Leaders, managers, and supervisors should express real concern for employees and treat people fairly, as acts of revenge typically occur in response to perceived injustice.[92]

Heighten Security Measures   Security precautions to reduce the risk of workplace violence include improving external lighting, using drop safes to minimize cash on hand and posting signs noting that only a limited amount of cash is on hand, installing silent alarms and surveillance cameras, increasing the number of staff members on duty, and closing establishments during high-risk hours late at night and early in the morning. In workplaces serving members of the public, some important precautions for employee safety include providing staff training in conflict resolution and defusing anger; having security staff refuse admittance to anyone who appears intoxicated, visibly angry, or threatening; and instituting a recognizable "help" signal to alert other staff members that assistance is required.[93]

Provide Workplace Violence Training   Workplace violence training explains what workplace violence is, identifies its causes and signs, and offers tips on how to prevent it and what to do when it occurs. Supervisors can also be trained to identify the typical perpetrator, who statistically speaking is most likely to be male, aged 25 to 40, bad at handling stress and a constant complainer, who tends to make verbal threats and physical or verbal outbursts, and who harbours grudges and brandishes weapons to gain attention.[94]

Improve Employee Screening Screening out potentially violent applicants means instituting a sound pre-employment investigation of all information provided. Sample interview questions to ask might include "What frustrates you?" and "Who was your worst supervisor and why?"[95] As sensible as it is to try to screen out potentially violent employees, employers who do so incur the risk of liability and lawsuits. However, human rights legislation limits the use of criminal records in hiring decisions in most jurisdictions (as outlined in Chapter 2), unless it is a bona fide occupational requirement (e.g., for a police officer's job).

10.6 EMPLOYEE WELLNESS PROGRAMS

employee wellness program A program that takes a proactive approach to employee health and well-being.

Healthy Workplace Month
www.healthyworkplacemonth.ca

There are three elements in a healthy workplace: the physical environment, the social environment, and health practices. **Employee wellness programs** take a proactive approach to all these areas of employee well-being (as opposed to EAPs, which provide reactive management of employee health problems). Wellness should be viewed as a management strategy to achieve measurable outcomes related to productivity, cost reduction, recruitment/retention, and profit. TELUS has a 50-year-old wellness program in which managers are held accountable—if absenteeism increases in their departments, their bonuses decrease![96] The company believes that a focus on wellness and enhancing corporate competitiveness are one and the same. Its long-term experience has netted a savings of three dollars for every dollar spent on wellness.

Experience has shown that wellness programs are very effective; there is overwhelming evidence that money invested in a wellness program is returned many times over.[97] For example, Seven Oaks General Hospital in Winnipeg, which has a 10-year-old Wellness Institute, reports a turnover rate of 4.5 percent, well under half of the industry average in Winnipeg of 11.9 percent.[98] A study of heart health wellness initiatives reported a return on investment of 415 percent.[99] NCR Canada saved $600 000 in direct and indirect costs during the first year of its wellness program; absenteeism was cut by more than half after 12 months and was still one-third lower after 36 months.[100]

It is predicted that over the next 25 years, prevention and wellness will be the next great leap forward in health care, as employees become more broadly recognized as the most important assets of organizations. A focus on wellness will also be driven by the shrinking workforce, an increase in postponed retirement, increased awareness of mental health, and medical and technological advances.[101]

Wellness initiatives often include stress management, nutrition and weight management, smoking

Companies are introducing employee wellness programs to promote a healthy workplace.

© Robert Kneschke/Fotolia

cessation programs, tai chi, heart health (such as screening cholesterol and blood pressure levels), physical fitness programs, and workstation wellness through ergonomics. Even simple things like providing safe bicycle lockup and change rooms or making fresh fruit and water available can make a difference.[102] Wellness and prevention efforts need to be understood and undertaken as a process—a long-term commitment to a holistic focus on the total person.

CHAPTER SUMMARY

1. Employers and employees are held jointly responsible for maintaining the health and safety of workers, including participation on joint health and safety committees. Employers are responsible for "due diligence"—taking every reasonable precaution to ensure the health and safety of their workers. Supervisors are responsible for ensuring that workplace policies are well communicated and adhered to by employees, and that employees concerns are dealt with in a safe and systematic manner. Employees are responsible for protecting their own health and safety and that of their co-workers. Employees have the right to know about workplace safety hazards, the right to participate in the occupational health and safety process, and the right to refuse unsafe work.

2. The Workplace Hazardous Materials Information System (WHMIS) is a Canada-wide, legally mandated system designed to protect workers by providing crucial information about hazardous materials and substances in the workplace. WHMIS requires labelling of hazardous material containers, material safety data sheets, and employee training.

3. There are three basic causes of accidents—chance occurrences, unsafe conditions, and unsafe acts on the part of employees. In addition, three other work-related factors—the job itself, the work schedule, and the psychological climate—also contribute to accidents.

4. One approach to preventing accidents is to improve unsafe conditions by identifying and removing potential hazards. Another approach to improving safety is to reduce the incidence of unsafe acts—for example, through selection and placement, education and training, positive reinforcement, top-management commitment, and monitoring work overload and stress.

5. Employee wellness programs aim to improve employees' health and reduce costs for sickness and disability claims, workers' compensation, and absenteeism. Wellness initiatives include physical fitness programs, smoking cessation programs, relaxation classes, and heart health monitoring.

6. Substance abuse is an important and growing health problem among employees. Techniques to deal with this challenge include disciplining, discharge, in-house counselling, and referrals to an outside agency. Stress, depression, and burnout are other potential health problems at work. Job stress can be reduced by ensuring that employees take breaks each day, providing access to counselling, and giving employees more control over their jobs. Repetitive strain injuries occur as a result of repetitive movements, awkward postures, and forceful exertion. Ergonomics is very effective at reducing RSIs.

7. Workplace toxins can be carcinogenic, and some governments are providing workers' compensation benefits to workers with job-related cancer. Employees who smoke have reduced productivity and greater health costs. Governments across Canada have increasingly banned workplace smoking. Violence against employees is a serious problem at work. Steps that can reduce workplace violence include improved security arrangements, better employee screening, and workplace violence training.

MyLab Management

Visit MyLab Management to access a personalized Study Plan, Personal Inventory Assessments (PIA), and a collection of videos and assignments within MediaShare.

KEY TERMS

burnout *(p. 254)*
due diligence *(p. 239)*
employee wellness program *(p. 260)*
ergonomics *(p. 255)*
lost-time injury rate *(p. 237)*

occupational health and safety legislation *(p. 238)*
reasonable cause *(p. 239)*
repetitive strain injuries (RSIs) *(p. 255)*
Workplace Hazardous Materials Information
    System (WHMIS) *(p. 242)*

REVIEW AND DISCUSSION QUESTIONS

1. Discuss the purpose of occupational health and safety legislation and who the agents responsible for enforcing it are.

2. Explain the differences and similarities in the roles and responsibilities of employers, supervisors, and employees in maintaining safe workplace conditions.

3. Explain factors that contribute to unsafe acts, and identify how these factors can be controlled to reduce unsafe working conditions.

4. Describe how to reduce workers' compensation costs, both before and after an accident.

5. Explain the techniques for dealing with substance abuse.

6. Analyze the legal and safety issues concerning workplace toxins.

7. Identify factors contributing to violence at work, and explain how to reduce these factors.

CRITICAL THINKING QUESTIONS

1. What is your opinion on the following question: "Is there such a thing as an accident-prone person?" How can organizations manage occupational health and safety in an organization if the answer is yes? If it is no?

2. Young people have a disproportionately high number of workplace accidents. In your opinion, what factors have contributed to this statistic? Why do you think that is? What role does the organization play in reducing workplace accidents among younger employees? What role do younger employees play in reducing workplace accidents?

3. Develop guidelines for determining the point at which to terminate an employee who shows tendencies of violence in the workplace. Assess a situation from the position of kitchen staff at a large restaurant. Reminder: Your guidelines must stay within legal limits and should also be realistic.

4. You notice that one of your employees consistently comes into work on Monday morning nursing a hangover. For most of the morning, she appears distant and reclusive. Do you approach her to discuss the situation, or do you feel that is an invasion of her privacy?

5. Given the disappointing progress in reducing workplace injuries and deaths, do you think that the "corporate killing" law should be used more aggressively?

6. Assume that you have an employee working in your company who has been treated several times already for substance abuse through the company counselling program. Today, the manager found him "stoned" again, trying to operate a piece of equipment in an unsafe manner. The manager just came to you and said, "Fire him! I've had enough! He's not only endangering himself, but other workers." The company has a policy of no substance use while at work and zero tolerance for arriving at work in an impaired state; all employees are aware of this policy and have signed off on it as part of the code of conduct. What steps can/should your company take in this circumstance?

EXPERIENTIAL EXERCISES

1. In a group of four to six students, spend about 30 to 45 minutes in and around one of the buildings on your campus identifying health and safety hazards. Research whether or not these unsafe conditions violate the applicable health and safety legislation. Develop recommendations to enhance building safety for each location, and debrief your colleagues on these recommendations.

2. Review a workplace-violence consulting website, and contact a workplace-violence consultant. Gather information on what advice is provided to clients on preventing workplace violence, and ask for a sample workplace-violence policy. Prepare a brief presentation to the class on your findings.

3. On your own, identify the workplace hazards that might be present in the following workplaces:
   - car repair and auto body shop
   - home renovations supplies and equipment storage area
   - live concert venue
   - health clinic dealing with homeless people
   - office with many employees working on computers and paper files
   - chemical plant finished-product storage area

4. Think about what these companies can and should do to ensure that their employees are safe at work. Once you have completed your own list of answers, work with a group of four or five other students to compare your lists. Brainstorm other hazards and solutions.

5. Conduct an internet search on Canadian websites to find a material safety data sheet (MSDS) for chlorine laundry bleach for home use. What have you learned that you did not know?

6. Depression has been described as a "clear and present danger" to business, as it manifests in alcoholism, absenteeism, injury, physical illness, and lost productivity. Estimates suggest that an employee with depression who goes untreated costs the company twice what treatment costs per year. A Harvard University study projects that, by 2020, depression will become the biggest source of lost workdays in developed countries; the World Health Organization predicts that depression will rank second as a cause of disability on a global basis by the same year. Young workers (aged 15 to 24) are most at risk.

7. Assuming the role of a career counsellor to newly hired graduates in a large retail company (Costco, Walmart, and so on), explain the employee and employer outcomes of stress and depression in an informed and actionable way.

CHAPTER

11

MANAGING EMPLOYEE SEPARATIONS:
Foundations of Employee Engagement, Communication, and Turnover Management

LEARNING OUTCOMES

AFTER STUDYING THIS CHAPTER, YOU SHOULD BE ABLE TO:

DEFINE voluntary and involuntary turnover, and **EXPLAIN** the impact of each turnover method.

ANALYZE important HR considerations in ensuring fairness in dismissals, layoffs, and terminations.

DEFINE wrongful dismissal, and **DISCUSS** the requirements for termination pay, including reasonable notice and severance pay where applicable.

DISCUSS the three foundations of a fair and just disciplinary process.

EXPLAIN various techniques for ensuring effective employee communication in organizations to help manage turnover.

EXPLAIN the six steps in the termination interview.

11.1 THE IMPORTANCE OF MANAGING EMPLOYEE SEPARATIONS

Issues of recruitment and selection focus on growing the human resource talent within an organization. The role of HRM is often overlooked in managing employee engagement and communication during a time of employee separations. Who leaves, how they are treated during the exit, what the cause or nature of the exit is, and how remaining employees perceive this all impacts the long-term sustainability of the organization.

This chapter first reviews employee separations by categorizing the possible causes and consequences of employee separations. Methods of reducing turnover and the negative implications of turnover on remaining employees (including legal compliance, two-way communication, and fair treatment programs) are explored later in the chapter.

11.2 MANAGING TURNOVER

An organization's labour force is in constant fluctuation as employees continuously enter and exit the workforce. Employee exits can become a huge challenge for organizations. Fifty percent of Canadian organizations admit that they experience difficulties recruiting and retaining talent.[1] Exits disrupt the organization's ability to produce and maintain the right quantity and quality of talent and derail the organization's focus on larger strategic issues. The investments in training and developing employees are lost, clients need to be reassigned, and the organization is often left with a vacancy where there is demand for work. In Canada, turnover rates vary by industry (for example, the construction industry and consumer services industries typically have the highest turnover levels, while public service has the lowest turnover levels), by the size of the company (smaller organizations typically have higher turnover rates), and by age (older workers are less likely to experience turnover than younger workers).[2]

Turnover refers to the termination of an individual's employment with an organization. Turnover can be either permanent or temporary and can be a result of action taken by either the employee or employer. There are many possible reasons for an employee to separate from a firm, including being laid off, the employee's desire to find new challenges, ineffective leadership, offers from other employers, or personal reasons.

turnover   The termination of an individual's employment with an organization.

Ultimately, the combination of having a company incur the cost of turnover as well as the cost of day-to-day operations can be economically damaging. High turnover is problematic for organizations, given that the cost of turnover ranges from 150 percent of salary to 250 percent of salary.[3] Direct costs associated with turnover are often easier to estimate given that they are more visible (for example, cost of advertising and interviewing, cost of moving expenses offered to the new candidate), while indirect costs associated with turnover are often overlooked, but are still considerable (for example, lost productivity during the employment gap, training curve productivity losses). There are four main components associated with the cost of the turnover: separation costs, vacancy costs, replacement costs, and training costs.

- Separation costs—the cost of exit interviews, administrative functions associated with the turnover, and separation or severance pay

- Vacancy costs—the net savings or cost incurred of increased overtime, the use of temporary workers, and the loss of sales associated with the vacancy
- Replacement costs—the cost of recruiting and hiring a replacement to fill the vacant position (including the cost of interviews, testing, administrative expenses, travel/moving expenses, and so on)
- Training costs—formal and informal training (including the performance differential between employees exiting the organization and their replacements)[4]

Overall, the reasons for turnover can be classified into two subgroups: voluntary and involuntary. **Voluntary turnover** is employee initiated, usually when an employee quits or retires. The decision to discontinue employment with the firm is made by the employee, without management enticement. **Involuntary turnover** is employer initiated and is usually in the form of dismissals or layoffs. Regardless, the employee has little or no personal say in this turnover decision. Employee exits from a firm are usually a mix of voluntary and involuntary turnover.

voluntary turnover Employee-initiated termination of employment, by quitting, retiring, or resigning.

involuntary turnover Employer-initiated termination of employment, such as dismissals or layoffs.

11.2.1 Voluntary Turnover

The biggest challenge of voluntary turnover is the lack of managerial control. Voluntary turnover can be functional (where bad performers leave and good performers stay), which can help reduce suboptimal organizational performance, or dysfunctional (where good performers leave and bad performers stay), which can be detrimental to a firm's success.[5]

A review of turnover research identifies predictors of voluntary turnover. Individual-level variables found to have a statistically significant relationship with voluntary job loss are (1) low organizational commitment, (2) low role clarity, (3) low tenure, (4) high role conflict, and (5) low overall job satisfaction. Additionally, as an employee ages, probability of voluntary turnover decreases, while as educational attainment of employees increases, probability of voluntary turnover also increases.[6]

A recent study of 1 400 employees and 400 managers asked each group to identify why they think employees engage in voluntary turnover; their answers are provided in **Table 11.1**. The findings indicate that insufficient pay or unfair pay practices are significant triggers for voluntary turnover. In addition, management is not completely aware of the reasons why employees leave, and thus may not be able to manage voluntary turnover effectively.

While an employer cannot always predict the reasoning behind voluntary turnover, it is important to try to understand which types of employees are likely

TABLE 11.1 Why Do Employees Engage in Voluntary Turnover? (in priority order)

According to Managers	According to Employees
Insufficient pay or unfair pay practices	Insufficient pay or unfair pay practices
A desire to pursue personal goals	A lack of honesty, integrity, ethics
An excessive workload	A lack of trust in senior leaders
A job opportunity	A lack of work–life balance
A lack of feedback or recognition	An unhealthy or undesirable culture

Source: Reprinted by permission of *Canadian HR Reporter.* © Copyright Thomson Reuters Canada Ltd., 2013, Toronto, Ontario.

to leave and why. This helps manage and prevent dysfunctional or excessive turnover. This information can be collected in exit interviews, staff surveys, and annual HR reviews.[7] Collecting this type of information can lead to trends that companies can use to screen certain types of individuals in the selection process. Additionally, these trends may lead organizations to develop methods of reducing turnover among current employees. In doing so, organizations obtain the information required to reduce turnover, retain effective employees, and decrease direct costs associated with turnover.

11.2.1.1 Quits

Quitting is legally recognized as a voluntary resignation in which the employee terminates the employment relationship, often in the form of a resignation letter. Employees often elect to leave a company based on work-related factors (for example, the employee dislikes the boss or feels that there is too much pressure or stress), or non-work-related factors (return to school, moving).[8] Either way, employee quits are most often caused by low job satisfaction.[9]

quitting Voluntary, employee-initiated resignation.

Competitive factors often play a significant role in a person's desire to resign from a company, including opportunities for employment in other organizations. Perceived job alternatives and high labour demands influence an employee's perception of ease of employment in other organizations, and are often carefully considered by the employee prior to resignation. Globalization, technological advancements, and market pressures have created an increasingly turbulent economy, and over the last few decades large-scale labour mobility has become the norm. The result has been a decline in employee job tenure and job stability.

In Canada, employment-related legislation clearly identifies employer responsibilities at the time of involuntary turnover (such as minimum notice periods and severance pay), but there also exists an equivalent employer-oriented protection in the case of employee-initiated turnover. The Employment or Labour Standards Act (ESA/LSA) may provide information regarding notice of voluntary turnover. For example, in 2017, the Ontario ESA required employees with less than two years of employment with employer to provide at least one week of notice when quitting, while those with more than two years of employment with the employer were required to provide at least two weeks' notice when quitting.

Lawsuits are rare and often limited to fiduciary employees (those employed in positions of implicit trust), as highlighted in the Strategic HR box. Of the recent cases in which the employer was awarded damages from an employee who failed to provide adequate notice, the courts suggest that termination of employment is a decision that carries a mutual obligation, and that employees should give a reasonable amount of notice to allow the employer to find a suitable replacement.[10]

11.2.1.2 Retirement

In the early 1900s, average male life expectancy was 47 years, and female life expectancy was 50 years.[11] As a result, mandatory retirement at the age of 65 was not a reality for a significant portion of the workforce. Medical discoveries, eradication of infectious diseases, and implementation of public health measures (such as water chlorination) have resulted in a significant increase in average lifespan on an international scale. According to Statistics Canada, average life expectancy for men in 2017 was 79 years, while average life expectancy for women was almost 83 years.[12]

STRATEGIC HR

Employers Owed Reasonable Notice for Voluntary Turnover

In 2008, the Supreme Court of Canada found Don Delamont, a former branch manager at RBC Dominion Securities, personally liable for almost $1.5 million in lost profit. In 2000, he had organized a mass exodus of employees from RBC to Merrill Lynch. None of the exiting employees gave reasonable notice. The Supreme Court also found that all of the employees were liable for failure to give reasonable notice of termination, resulting in an additional $40 000 in damages.

More recently, the Ontario Court of Appeal upheld an award for $20 million in damages against four key employees of GapTOPS Ltd, who quit their jobs with only two weeks of notice, immediately began working for a competitor (Forsyth), and quickly solicited clients from the previous employer. While the use of litigation against employees who fail to give reasonable notice of quitting is rare, the judicial system appears to be uphold the existing legislation protecting employers from questionable practices during employee-initiated turnover.

Sources: *Mass Exodus of Employees, Implied Duties Owed to Employers and the Supreme Court of Canada*, Norton Rose Fulbright (November 10, 2008), www.nortonrosefulbright.com/knowledge/publications/49742/mass-exodus-of-employees-implied-duties-owed-to-employers-and-the-supreme-court-of-canada; C. Chan, "Notice Is a Two-Way Street: OCA Upholds $20 Million Award against Departing Employees," *Canadian Lawyer Magazine*, April 16, 2012.

However, a combination of legal advancements on anti-discriminatory employment policies (such as age-based discrimination), labour scarcity, and peoples' desires to choose their own lifestyle, circumstances, and priorities has resulted in the abolishment of mandatory retirement in Canada. Thus, retirement is viewed as voluntary turnover rather than involuntary turnover. In 2016, the average age of retirement for public sector employees was 61.6 years, and private sector employees it was 63.8.[13] However, there is a large range of possible retirement ages, with some 40-year-olds eligible to retire from their organizations while 87-year-olds continue to be employed.

From an organizational standpoint, one of the challenges associated with the retirement of employees, is the difficulty in predicting when employees will retire. Developing succession or replacement plans around potential retirees and finding ways to transfer retiring employees' tacit and social knowledge becomes paramount to how an organization deals with retirement. Some companies are managing the labour shortage created by retiring employees by offering **retirees on call** programs, whereby retirees can come back on a part-time or as-needed basis, or by offering **phased retirement**, whereby employees gradually reduce the number of hours that they work.[14]

Court decisions have confirmed that employers do have some legal responsibility to help employees prepare for retirement.[15] Most employers provide some type of formal **pre-retirement counselling** aimed at easing the passage of their employees into retirement.[16] Retirement education and planning firms provide services to assist upcoming retirees with such issues as lifestyle goals (including part-time or volunteer work, or moving to another country), financial planning, relationship issues, and health issues. Both individual and group transition counselling are offered in seminars and workshops featuring workbooks, questionnaires, discussions, group exercises, and software products.[17]

retirees on call A program whereby retirees can continue to work on a part-time or as-needed basis.

phased retirement A program whereby potential retirees gradually reduce the number of hours worked per week over time.

pre-retirement counselling Counselling provided to employees some months (or even years) before retirement, which covers such matters as benefits advice, second careers, and so on.

The Retirement Education Centre
www.iretire.org

11.2.2 Involuntary Turnover

There are many reasons why an organization might engage in involuntary turnover. Job performance may be below acceptable standards and the organization decides to dismiss an employee. Economic or financial pressures may result in a decision to downsize through mass layoffs. The organization may be engaging in a new strategic direction and has chosen to close down or outsource one or more business units. In any of these cases, the decision to terminate employment is made by the organization and its agents, not by the individual employee.

Employee dismissal and downsizing are two of the most common situations in which employees perceive that they are treated unfairly. This reaction is not surprising given the negative ramifications to the employee in each case (job loss). The burden of proof rests with the employer in cases of dismissal or layoff. Thus, it is important for all managers and HR professionals to be aware of how to conduct involuntary turnover fairly and legally.

"There isn't enough blame to go around, there's only enough for you."

© Cartoonresource/Fotolia

Specifically, employer-initiated termination should be fair and occur after all reasonable steps to rehabilitate or salvage the employment relationship through employee discipline have failed. The legal system in Canada has repeatedly articulated the rights of employees to fair treatment, not only during the term of employment but also during the discipline and dismissal process.

A fair and just disciplinary process is based on three foundations: rules and regulations, progressive discipline, and an appeals process.

11.2.2.1 Dismissal for Just Cause

Dismissal is the most drastic disciplinary step that can be taken towards an employee and one that must be handled with deliberate care. While dismissals damage the goodwill of a company and sever the employment relationship, there are undoubtedly times when dismissal is required, and in these instances it should be carried out forthrightly.[18]

dismissal   Involuntary termination of an employee's employment.

Dismissal for just cause is considered an employer-initiated termination based on an employee's poor behaviour or performance. Therefore employers are not obligated to provide severance pay, reasonable notice of termination, or additional payments beyond what the employee has already earned (for example, earned salary and vacation time that is outstanding must be paid). In cases of dismissal for just cause, the onus of proof lies on management to prove that performance in the past was below acceptable levels and that the organization provided feedback and allowed opportunities to correct behaviours that led to poor performance (performance management was highlighted in Chapter 7).

dismissal for just cause   An employer-initiated termination based on an employee's poor behaviour; in these situations, no severance, reasonable notice periods, or additional payments beyond what the employee has already earned are owed.

There is no clear definition of what behaviour constitutes "just cause" for dismissal.[19] Any allegation of just cause must be considered using a contextual approach, looking at not only the alleged behaviour, but the entirety of the employment relationship.[20] If an employer is considering making an allegation of just cause, it is crucial to investigate fully and fairly before any decision is made. The fundamental question is whether or not the employee has irreparably harmed the relationship to the point that it would be unreasonable to expect the employer to continue the employment relationship.[21]

A set of clear expectations informs employees ahead of time as to what is and is not considered acceptable behaviour in the workplace. Employees must be informed, preferably in writing, of what behaviours or actions are not

Verbal and written warnings are examples of penalties used throughout a progress discipline process.

An Ethical Dilemma

Is it ethical to apply disciplinary action in cases of ongoing absenteeism and tardiness because of family responsibilities? What other approach could be used?

progressive discipline   A formal system to correct employee performance where penalties increase as the severity and frequency of undesirable behaviours or performance increases.

permitted. This is usually done during the employee's orientation (and included in the employee orientation handbook), or when rules or regulations in the workplace change. Examples of such rules include the following:

- Poor work performance is not acceptable. Each employee is expected to perform his or her work properly and efficiently, and to meet established standards of quality.

- Liquor and drug use is not permitted on work premises. The use of either during working hours or working under the influence of drugs or alcohol is strictly prohibited.

- Safety rules must be followed at all times.

A system of progressive penalties is the second foundation of effective discipline. **Progressive discipline** is a formal system to correct employee performance where penalties increase as the severity and frequency of undesirable behaviours or performance increases. Penalties may range from verbal warnings, to written warnings, to suspension (paid or unpaid) from the job, and finally to dismissal. The severity of the penalty is usually a function of the type of offence and the number of times the offence has occurred. For example, most companies issue warnings for the first instance of unexcused lateness. However, for chronic lateness, dismissal is the more usual disciplinary action. A sample of progressive discipline guidelines is provided in **Figure 11.1**.

Finally, there should be an appeals process as part of the disciplinary process; this helps to ensure procedural fairness. Employees should have a known set of actions and support roles to turn to if they disagree with workplace assessments; if they feel that behaviour could be excused, justified, or otherwise reconsidered; and if they feel that the penalty was inappropriate.

Employee misconduct (including theft, expense account fraud, abuse of sick leave, and so on) is a fundamental violation of the employment relationship and can constitute just cause.[22] Just cause can often be demonstrated in cases of disobedience, incompetence, dishonesty, insubordination, fighting, and

FIGURE 11.1   Progressive Discipline

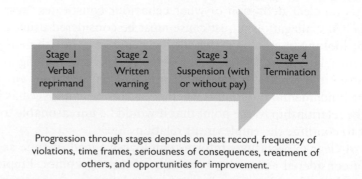

| Stage 1 | Stage 2 | Stage 3 | Stage 4 |
| Verbal reprimand | Written warning | Suspension (with or without pay) | Termination |

Progression through stages depends on past record, frequency of violations, time frames, seriousness of consequences, treatment of others, and opportunities for improvement.

persistent absence or lateness.[23] However, just cause cannot be assessed in isolation and may vary depending on the possible consequences of the misconduct, the status of the employee, and the circumstances of the case. Unfortunately, the prevalence of theft behaviour among employees is alarming, as highlighted by the HR by the Numbers feature.

Insubordination involves the wilful disregard for the boss's authority or legitimate orders, disobedience, or criticizing the boss in public. It is a form of misconduct that often provides grounds for just cause dismissal, although it may be relatively difficult to describe and to prove. To that end, it is important to communicate to employees that some acts are considered insubordination whenever and wherever they occur. These generally include the following:[24]

1. Direct disregard of the boss' authority; refusal to obey the boss's reasonable instructions—particularly in front of others

2. Deliberate defiance of clearly stated company policies, rules, regulations, and procedures

3. Public criticism of the boss; contradicting or arguing with him or her

4. Contemptuous display of disrespect—making insolent comments and portraying these feelings in terms of the employee's attitude on the job

5. Disregard for the chain of command, shown by going around the immediate supervisor or manager with a complaint, suggestion, or political maneuver

6. Participation in (or leadership of) an effort to undermine and remove the boss from power

A recent example of dismissal for just cause based on insubordination involved a Calgary stockbroker who was fired after he brought a prostitute to his office after hours and left her there alone following a dispute about payment. The woman was left alone in the reception area where she could have accessed confidential client and company data after he left. She showed up at the office the next day demanding payment, which ultimately lead in the dismissal of the stockbroker. The court said the stockbroker's conduct exhibited contempt for his employer, his co-workers, and their reputation in the business community.[25]

HR by the Numbers

▶ Prevalence of Theft Behaviour

47% of retail "inventory shrinkage" is attributable to employees[1]

$4 billion estimated annual costs of employee theft to Canadian retailers[2]

9% the amount of cabin stock Air Canada estimates it loses per year to employee theft[3]

$60K the amount one employee confessed to stealing over two years from a small retailer after a month of video monitoring by a private investigation firm[4]

10% of small and medium businesses claim that employee theft played a critical role in the eventual bankruptcy of their organizations[5]

26% of Canadian small and medium businesses report experiencing at least one workplace fraud incident in 2010, including misappropriation of inventory, assets, and cash[6]

334 the section in the Criminal Code in Canada that outlines punishment for theft

insubordination Wilful disregard or disobedience of the boss' authority or legitimate orders; criticizing the boss in public.

11.2.2.2 Layoffs

As organizations adapt to ever-changing demands, markets, technologies, and competitors, layoffs have become an accepted and familiar organizational activity. Alternative names for layoffs include "downsizing," "rightsizing," "reduction in workforce," and "mass terminations," to list just a few. A **layoff** occurs when workers are sent home for a period of time (often undefined), due to a situation in which three conditions are present: (1) There is no work available

layoff The temporary withdrawal of employment to workers for economic or business reasons.

for the employees; (2) management expects the no-work situation to be temporary and probably short term; and (3) management intends to recall the employees when work is again available.[26] Layoffs that involve unionized employees are almost always based on seniority or conditions outlined in the collective bargaining agreement. However, layoffs that occur in non-unionized environments or affect non-unionized employees occur regularly and the decision making around who gets laid off is often unclear or inconsistent.

Providing Reasonable Notice   Full-time permanent employees are hired under an implied contract, with the understanding that employment is for an indefinite period of time and may be terminated by either party only when reasonable notice is given.[27] Employers cannot fire employees at will. Canadian employers can terminate an employee's employment without reasonable notice only when just cause exists.

If an employer decides to terminate employment of an employee through a layoff or without just cause, the employer has to at least meet the minimum terms in the provincial or territorial employment or labour standards legislation (as outlined in Chapter 2). **Reasonable notice legislation** requires employers to notify employees in the event that they decide to terminate them through layoffs (i.e., without just cause). Minimum notice varies according to the size of the layoffs, with smaller layoffs requiring minimum notice based on employee tenure and mass layoffs requiring minimum notice based on total layoff size. For example, an employee in British Columbia who has worked for an employer for three consecutive years is owed at least three weeks' notice for an impending layoff or can be paid the equivalent of three weeks' worth of salary, benefits, and vacation pay if he or she is laid off. This legislation provides a minimum notice period, but employers can and often do provide more than the legislated minimum notice or pay when they lay off employees. Temporary workers, contract workers whose contracts have not been renewed, casual workers, and workers who have not completed a minimum probation period would not qualify for reasonable notice.

If there is no employment contract and just cause is not present, then a termination without reasonable notice is considered unfair and is known as **wrongful dismissal**.

Group termination laws require employers who are terminating a large group of employees to give employees more notice than that required on termination of an individual employee. The laws are intended to assist employees in situations of plant closings and large downsizings. Most jurisdictions in Canada require employers who are terminating a group of employees (some specify 10 or more, others 25 or more) within a short time to give advance notice to employees and sometimes to their union. The amount of notice varies by jurisdiction and with the number of employees being terminated, but it generally ranges from 6 to 18 weeks. The laws do not prevent the employer from closing down, nor do they require the employer to save jobs; the laws simply give employees time to seek other work or retraining by giving them advance notice of their termination.

Many employers today recognize the enormous investments that organizations make in recruiting, screening, and training their employees. As a result, they are more hesitant to lay off employees at the first signs of business decline. Instead, they are using new approaches to either limit the effects of a layoff or eliminate the layoffs entirely.

reasonable notice legislation   Laws that require employers to notify employees in the event that they decide to terminate employees through layoffs (i.e., without just cause). Minimum notice varies according to the size of the layoffs, with smaller layoffs requiring minimum notice based on employee tenure and mass layoffs requiring minimum notice based on total layoff size.

wrongful dismissal   An employee dismissal that does not comply with the law or does not comply with a written or implied contractual arrangement.

group termination laws   Laws that require an employer to notify employees in the event that they decide to terminate a group of employees.

There are several alternatives to layoffs. One such alternative is a voluntary reduction in pay, whereby all employees agree to reductions in their pay to keep everyone working. Other employers arrange to have all or most of their employees accumulate their vacation time and to concentrate their vacations during slow periods. Other employees agree to take voluntary time off, which again has the effect of reducing the employer's payroll and avoiding the need for a layoff. Another way to avoid layoffs is the use of contingent employees hired with the understanding that their work is temporary and they may be laid off at any time.[28] Finally, the work-sharing program, available through Service Canada, allows employers to reduce the workweek by one to three days, and employees can claim employment insurance for the time not worked.

11.2.2.3 Avoiding Wrongful Dismissal Accusations

A study of 996 recently fired or laid-off workers found that wrongful dismissal claims were strongly correlated with the way workers felt they had been treated at the time of termination. They also found a "vendetta effect," where the instances of wrongful dismissal claims became stronger as negative treatment became more extreme. The researchers concluded that many wrongful dismissal lawsuits could be avoided if effective human resource practices, specifically treating employees fairly, were used. Providing clear, honest explanations of termination decisions, and handling the termination in a way that treats people with dignity and respect, can be especially favourable to the company's reputation, as well as reduce the employee's negative feelings towards themselves and the company.[29]

For example, HMV in the United Kingdom gathered employees together for a mass layoff, including the employee responsible for the company's Twitter account. During the layoff announcement tweets sent out included, "We're live tweeting from the HR firing session, this is so exciting!" and "We've all been fired, in a group, of 50+ people! And those who ruined the business are safe . . . hooray!"[30]

Similarly, Burnaby, BC–based Best Buy and Future Shop shuttered up 15 locations across Canada, without giving workers any notice or warning. Employees showed up for work to find doors locked and signs on the doors saying that the location was closed effective immediately. These closures affected around 900 employees, representing 5 percent of the organization's workforce.[31]

There are several steps that can be taken to avoid wrongful dismissal suits:[32]

1. Use employment contracts with a termination clause and with wording clearly permitting the company to dismiss without cause during the probationary period.

2. Document all disciplinary action.

3. Do not allege just cause for dismissal unless it can be proven.

4. Time the termination so that it does not conflict with special occasions, such as birthdays or holidays.

5. Use termination letters in all cases, clearly stating the settlement offer.

6. Schedule the termination interview in a private location at a time of day that will allow the employee to clear out belongings with a minimal amount of contact with other employees.

7. Include two members of management in the termination meeting.

If a wrongful dismissal suit is made against the company, the firm should do the following:[33]

- Review the claim carefully before retaining an employment lawyer, and investigate for other improper conduct; ask for a legal opinion on the merits of the case; work with the lawyer and provide all relevant facts and documentation; and discuss any possible letter of reference with the lawyer.

- Never allege cause if none exists, and avoid defamatory statements.

- Consider mediation as an option, or offer to settle to save time and money.

Source: Reprinted by permission of *Canadian HR Reporter.* © Copyright Thomson Reuters Canada Ltd., 2013, Toronto, Ontario.

11.3 EMPLOYEE ENGAGEMENT AND FAIRNESS IN EMPLOYEE SEPARATIONS

Effectively managing employee separations in Canada includes a focus on both exiting employees (including legal compliance with reasonable notice periods) and remaining employees (employee engagement), as well as effective communication to all employees. On the opposite end of managing exits is an active effort to manage those who remain through active retention efforts, as highlighted in the Expert Opinion box.

employee engagement The emotional and intellectual involvement of employees in their work, such as intensity, focus, and involvement in their job and organization.

Employee engagement is a positive, fulfilling, work-related state of mind characterized by vigour, dedication, and absorption.[34] It is a heightened emotional and intellectual connection that an employee has with his or her job, organization, manager, or co-workers, that in turn influences the employee to apply additional discretionary effort.[35] Engaged employees feel a vested interest in the company's success and are both willing and motivated to perform to levels that exceed the stated job requirements.[36] To increase employee engagement, many firms give employees extensive data on the performance of and prospects for their operations.[37]

Over 30 years of organizational research clearly indicates that employees are sensitive to the treatment they receive, and that they have strong perceptions regarding the fairness of their experiences at work.[38] In respect to employee relations, experts generally define organizational justice in terms of three components: distributive justice, procedural justice, and interactional justice. **Distributive justice** refers to the fairness and justice of the outcome of a decision (Would a comparable employee have the same outcome related to the employee separation?). **Procedural justice** refers to the fairness of the process (Is the process my company uses to make decisions about terminations or employee separations fair?). **Interactional justice** refers to the manner in which managers conduct their interpersonal dealings with employees and, in particular, the degree to which they treat employees with dignity and respect as opposed to abuse or disrespect (Does my supervisor treat me with respect when assessing factors related to the separation?).

distributive justice Fairness of a decision outcome.

procedural justice Fairness of the process used to make a decision.

interactional justice Fairness in interpersonal interactions, treating others with dignity and respect.

While a focus on fairness perceptions of employees who exit an organization through employee separations is important from a legal and ethical perspective, perceptions of whether exiting employees were treated fairly and justly also affect employees who remain with the organization. For example, fair treatment of employees whose jobs are lost in layoffs is important for maintaining employee engagement on the part of the "survivors" who continue to come to

Academic Viewpoint
EXPERT OPINION

Focus: Expertise in industrial and organizational psychology, organizational commitment, performance management, employee retention, and change management

1. Some of your past research has focused on the causes of turnover. Based on this research, what can managers do to improve employee retention?

Job characteristics are important drivers of retention, and often reflected in the job scope (diversity of skills and tasks, autonomy, feedback, significance of job, etc.). These characteristics improve or enhance commitments to the organization, increasing employee retention. Managers have power and control over these characteristics. Transformational leadership has been found to improve employees' perspectives towards work, and both leaders and managers have a role in stimulating the employee. Accordingly, they can strengthen the relationship with supportive behaviour to help employees face job demands. This increases retention.

Management also act as a link to the global organization or team members. They transmit support and justice practices to their teams, which can emphasize and strengthen retention. Research has found that managers who have more networks, are more central in the organization, have values that match the organization, and are more politically astute are perceived to legitimately represent the organization. These types of managers transmit a sense of the organization to the employee, thereby strengthening the employee-to-organization relationship.

Dr. Christian Vandenberghe

Expert:
Dr. Christian Vandenberghe (PhD)
Canada Research Chair in Management of Employee Engagement and Performance

Affiliation:
Department of Management, HEC Montreal

2. What is the profile of employee engagement that is the most beneficial to employee health?

Research profiling employees' commitment on different dimensions includes affective commitment, normative commitment, and continuous commitment. We know that these types of commitment have an impact on employee health, especially affective commitment. Once employees develop an emotional/affective link to the organization, the values of the organization become part of their identity. This congruence makes work more meaningful and ensures psychologically healthy employees. There is a negative aspect to continuance commitment. When an employee stays with the organization because of limited external employment opportunities, the result is employee perceptions of alienation, frustration, anxiety, etc. The best profile is one with high levels of affective and normative commitment and a low level of continuance commitment.

3. Your research considers the emotional, moral, and instrumental nature of employee engagement. Are these equally important to employee performance?

Job performance (in-role aspects or more discretionary aspects) is influenced by organizational commitment. Research has shown that affective commitment is a strong predictor of performance. Research also consistently demonstrates that continuous commitment has very little correlation to job performance. This is partially attributable to the fact that once employees have an instrumental link to the organization, they will meet minimal requirements of doing the job, and don't invest more in doing the job better.

My research identifies that high levels of normative commitment, combined with high levels of continuous commitment, impede job performance. The negative influence may stem from a forced obligation to the company. The commitment in these situations is externally driven, and the employee experience is based on limited choices or alternative options. This is not a good motivator for driving strong performance.

Source: Reprinted by permission from Dr. Christian Vandenberghe.

work in these difficult circumstances. Communicating the news of impending layoffs is a difficult task, but ensuring interactional justice when doing so is critical to maintaining engagement on the part of the employees who will continue working for the organization.

11.3.1 Suggestion Programs

Employees can often offer well-informed, thoughtful, and creative suggestions regarding issues ranging from malfunctioning vending machines to unlit parking lots to a manager spending too much of the department's money on travel. ArcelorMittal Dofasco Inc.'s suggestion program has been a success story for decades. Employees can receive cash awards of up to $50 000, depending on the savings realized by implementing the suggestion. Suggestion programs like these have several benefits. They let management continually monitor employees' feelings and concerns while making it clear that employees have several channels through which to communicate concerns and get responses. The impact of these programs is the ability to deal with minor employee issues before they become more extreme and eventually manifest into major organizational concerns.

11.3.2 Employee Opinion Surveys

employee opinion surveys Communication devices that use questionnaires to ask for employees' opinions about the company, management, and work life.

Many firms also administer periodic anonymous **employee opinion surveys**, which ask for opinions about the company, management, and work life. For maximum benefit, surveys should be conducted regularly and the results must be provided to participants.[39] An employee satisfaction survey, called the Employee Feedback System (EFS), has been developed by the National Quality Institute and the Workplace Health Research Unit at Brock University.[40] The EFS examines 16 areas ranging from job satisfaction and co-worker cohesion to quality focus and employee commitment.

Recently, employees have begun to use blogs to express opinions about their employers, and employer concerns have arisen about damage to their reputation and possible disclosure of confidential company information. Some corporations, such as IBM, Cisco, and Sun Microsystems, have chosen to trust their employees and have suggested guidelines and specific tactics so that employees can blog without causing themselves or their employers any grief.[41] However, there are also cases in which employees have been terminated for posting negative opinions about their employer, and arbitration boards have upheld the terminations, finding that postings about managers, co-workers, and the work environment are sufficient grounds for discharge.[42] A blogging policy is recommended by legal experts and should include directions to refrain from disclosing any confidential company information or posting any embarrassing or demeaning information about the company and its employees.[43]

11.3.3 Communication from Management

Traditionally, newsletters and verbal presentations were the most effective methods used to disseminate information from the company to employees. More recently, organizations have used videos, email, and intranets.[44] Blogs can also be used by senior managers to connect with employees. When Jim Estill sold his company and became CEO of the larger combined operation, he found employees of the acquiring company "treated me like I was some sort of Martian." He started a blog (80 percent company-related content and 20 percent personal) and soon overcame the problem—staff even sent him pictures from their kids' birthday parties! In addition, staff sent the blog to vendors and customers, which elevated him in their eyes as well.[45]

11.3.4 The Termination Interview

Dismissing an employee is one of the most difficult tasks that a manager will face at work.[46] The dismissed employee, even if warned many times in the past, will often still react with total disbelief or even violence. Guidelines for the **termination interview** itself follow, based on the fairness and employee engagement research:

termination interview   The interview in which an employee is informed of the fact that he or she has been dismissed.

1. *Plan the interview.* Carefully schedule the meeting on a day early in the week, and try to avoid Fridays, pre-holidays, and vacation times. Have the employee agreement, human resources file, and release announcement (internal and external) prepared in advance. Be available at a time after the interview in case questions or problems arise, and have phone numbers ready for medical or security emergencies.

2. *Get to the point.* As soon as the employee arrives, give the person a moment to get comfortable and then inform him or her of the decision.

3. *Describe the situation briefly.* In three or four sentences, explain why the person is being let go. For instance, "Production in your area is down 4 per-cent, and we are continuing to have quality prob-lems. We have talked about these problems several times in the past three months, and the solutions are not being followed through. We have to make a change."[47] Remember to describe the situation rather than attacking the employee personally.

4. *Listen.* It is important to continue the interview until the person appears to be talking freely and seems reasonably calm about the reasons for his or her termination and the severance package that he or she is to receive. Behavioural indications can be used to help gauge the person's reaction and to decide how best to proceed. Five major reactions often occur:

An Ethical Dilemma

Is it ethical to "buy out" an undesirable employee with severance pay and a good letter of reference in order to avoid prolonged wrongful dismissal litigation, even if you know the letter is misleading to potential future employers?

- First, some employees will be *hostile and angry,* expressing hurt and disappointment. In such cases, remain objective while providing informa-tion on any outplacement or career counselling to be provided, being careful to avoid being defensive or confronting the person's anger.

- Second, some employees may react in a *defen-sive, bargaining* manner, based on their feelings of fear and disbelief. In this case, it is important to acknowledge that this is a difficult time for the employee and then provide information regarding outplacement counselling without get-ting involved in any bargaining discussions.

- Third, the employee may proceed in a *formal, controlled* manner, indicative of a suppressed, vengeful reaction and the potential for legal

Termination interviews are among the most difficult tasks that managers face, but there are guidelines for making them less painful for both parties.

© Alex Raths/istock/Thinkstock/Getty Images

action. In this case, allow the employee to ask any questions pertaining to his or her case (avoiding side issues) in a formal tone while leading into information about the outplacement counselling to be provided.

- Fourth, some employees will maintain a *stoic* façade, masking their shock, disbelief, and numbness. In this case, communicate to the employee that his or her shock is recognized and that the details can be handled later if the employee prefers. Answer any questions arising at that point and provide information on outplacement counselling.

- A fifth reaction is an *emotional* one involving tears and sadness, indicating grief and worry on the part of the employee. Allow the person to cry and provide tissues. When the person regains his or her composure, explain the outplacement counselling process.

5. *Review all elements of the severance package.* Describe severance payments, benefits, and the way in which references will be handled. However, under no conditions should any promises or benefits beyond those already in the severance package be implied. The termination should be complete when the person leaves.

6. *Identify the next step.* The terminated employee may be disoriented, so explain where he or she should go on leaving the interview. Remind the person whom to contact at the company regarding questions about the severance package or references.

11.3.5 Easing the Pain of Labour Surplus Management

Although restructuring initiatives, ranging from layoffs to mergers and acquisitions, were prevalent in the last two decades, organizations that engaged in layoffs were not consistently achieving the desired goals or financial benefits of their decisions. In a study of 6 418 workforce reductions in Fortune 500 firms over 18 years, researchers found no consistent evidence that downsizing led to improved financial performance.[48] A primary reason for this is the high cost associated with **survivor syndrome**, a range of emotions that can include feelings of betrayal or violation, guilt, or detachment. The remaining employees, anxious about the next round of terminations, often suffer stress symptoms, including depression, increased errors, and reduced performance.

To ease the financial burden of layoffs, some organizations offer **supplemental unemployment benefits (SUBs)**, which are a top-up of EI benefits to bring income levels of temporarily laid-off workers closer to their regular, on-the-job pay. SUB programs are generally negotiated through collective bargaining between the employee and employer. Benefits are payable until the pool of funds set aside has been exhausted.

Termination pay refers to a payment owed to employees by the employer when an employee is involuntarily terminated for reasons other than cause. The amount paid must meet the the minimum-notice-period payments established by labour legislation (if payment is given in lieu of reasonable notice) or follow guidelines established in common law precedent. Employees affected by termination of their employment for reasons other than cause must be given either reasonable notice or pay in lieu of reasonable notice as stipulated under applicable employment standards legislation. The specific length of employment and the resulting period of required notice are stated in federal and provincial statutes. For long-service employees, the amount of termination pay may also be affected by common law.

survivor syndrome   A range of negative emotions experienced by employees remaining after a major restructuring initiative, which can include feelings of betrayal or violation, guilt, or detachment, and can result in stress symptoms, including depression, increased errors, and reduced performance.

supplemental unemployment benefits (SUBs)   A top-up of EI benefits to bring income levels closer to what an employee would receive if on the job.

termination pay   Payment of wages from the employer to the employee at the time of involuntary termination for reasons other than cause. The amount paid must meet the minimum-notice-period payments established by labour legislation (if payment is given in lieu of reasonable notice) or follow guidelines established in common law precedent.

Legislation may also provide **severance pay** to these individuals. Specifically, employees who fall under the Ontario and/or federal jurisdiction and meet the requirements in the legislation receive severance pay in addition to reasonable notice when they are involuntarily terminated without cause. This is calculated based on the employee's length of service and other factors (such as the total size of the annual company payroll).

Executives may be protected by a *golden parachute clause* in their contract of employment; this is a guarantee by the employer to pay specified compensation and benefits in the case of termination due to downsizing or restructuring. To soften the blow of termination, *outplacement assistance*, generally offered by an outside agency, can assist affected employees in finding employment elsewhere. The issues and processes related to managing a labour surplus legally were initially discussed in Chapter 4.

severance pay   Payable by employers under Ontario and/or federal jurisdiction to employees terminated for reasons other than cause, in addition to the reasonable notice payment or period. Severance pay is often based on the employee's length of service and other factors (such as the total size of the annual company payroll).

An Ethical Dilemma

How much time, effort, and money should firms devote to helping "surviving" employees deal with downsizing? With mergers and acquisitions?

CHAPTER SUMMARY

1. Employee exits can be a huge challenge for organizations and need to be managed in way that minimizes disruption to the organization, given the high cost of turnover. Turnover can generally be organized as voluntary turnover (employee initiated, often quits/resignations or retirement) or involuntary turnover (employer initiated, often dismissal for just cause or layoffs).

2. A fair and just disciplinary process is based on three prerequisites: rules and regulations, a system of progressive penalties, and an appeals process. While insubordination and theft continue to be problematic for Canadian employers, an employer's ability to terminate an employee must abide by a fair and just discipline process.

3. Employees who are dismissed without just cause must be provided with reasonable notice. If the employee does not believe that the period of notice is reasonable, he or she may file a wrongful dismissal lawsuit.

4. Employee engagement is a positive, fulfilling, work-related state of mind characterized by vigour, dedication, and absorption.

Organizational factors such as senior leadership, opportunities for learning and development, and company image and reputation are the primary influencers of engagement. Outcomes of employee engagement include improvements in recruiting, retention, turnover, individual productivity, customer service, and customer loyalty, as well as growth in operating margins and increased profit margins and revenue growth rates.

5. Techniques for ensuring effective employee communication include suggestion programs, employee opinion surveys, and communication from management.

6. The six steps in the termination interview are to plan the interview carefully, get to the point, describe the situation, listen until the person has expressed his or her feelings, discuss the severance package, and identify the next step.

MyLab Management

Visit MyLab Management to access a personalized Study Plan, Personal Inventory Assessments (PIA), and a collection of videos and assignments within MediaShare.

KEY TERMS

dismissal *(p. 269)*
dismissal for just cause *(p. 269)*
distributive justice *(p. 274)*

employee engagement *(p. 274)*
employee opinion surveys *(p. 276)*
group termination laws *(p. 272)*

insubordination *(p. 271)*
interactional justice *(p. 274)*
involuntary turnover *(p. 266)*
layoff *(p. 271)*
phased retirement *(p. 268)*
pre-retirement counselling *(p. 268)*
procedural justice *(p. 274)*
progressive discipline *(p. 270)*
quitting *(p. 267)*
reasonable notice legislation *(p. 272)*

retirees on call *(p. 268)*
severance pay *(p. 279)*
survivor syndrome *(p. 278)*
supplemental unemployment benefits
    (SUBs) *(p. 278)*
termination interview *(p. 277)*
termination pay *(p. 278)*
turnover *(p. 265)*
voluntary turnover *(p. 266)*
wrongful dismissal *(p. 272)*

REVIEW AND DISCUSSION QUESTIONS

1. Explain why organizations today are concerned with voluntary turnover.

2. Describe the issue of reasonable notice in layoffs and how it relates to employee perspectives of fairness or intent to file wrongful dismissal lawsuits.

3. Explain how fairness in employee termination can be ensured, particularly the prerequisites to progressive discipline guidelines.

4. What are the various steps in the termination interview?

5. Discuss some of the issues that should be covered when communicating effectively with employees in the organization.

CRITICAL THINKING QUESTIONS

1. Should a company consider providing termination packages to employees who have ongoing disciplinary problems rather than taking the time and effort to go through the progressive discipline process?

2. Assume that in one department of your organization the voluntary turnover rate is double the rate that other departments have. What factors might contribute to this? What issues would you investigate? Is voluntary turnover necessarily bad and in need of correction?

3. Discuss the options presented as alternatives to layoffs. Which of these would appeal to you, your family members, and friends? Why? What challenges do these alternatives pose to organizations?

EXPERIENTIAL EXERCISES

1. Working individually or in groups, obtain copies of the student handbook for your college or university, and determine to what extent there is a formal process through which students can air grievances. Would you expect the process to be effective? Why or why not? Based on contact with students who have used the grievance process, has it been effective?

2. Working individually or in groups, determine the nature of the academic discipline process in your college or university. Does it appear to be an effective one? Based on this chapter, should any modification be made to the student discipline process?

3. A computer department employee made an entry error that ruined an entire run of computer reports. Efforts to rectify the situation produced a second batch of improperly run reports. As a result of the series of errors, the employer incurred extra costs of $2 400, plus a weekend of overtime work by other computer department staffers. Management suspended the employee for three days for negligence and also revoked a promotion for which the employee had previously been approved.

   Protesting the discipline, the employee stressed that she had attempted to correct her error in the early stages of the run by notifying the manager of computer operations of her mistake. Maintaining that the resulting string of errors could have been avoided if the manager had followed up on her report and stopped the initial run, the employee argued that she had been treated unfairly; she was being severely punished but the manager had not been disciplined at all, even though he had compounded the problem. Moreover, citing her "impeccable" work record and management's acknowledgement that she had always been a "model employee," the employee insisted that the denial of her previously approved promotion was "unconscionable."

   a. In groups, determine what your decision would be if you were the arbitrator. Why? (Your instructor will inform you of the actual arbitrator's decision when you discuss this exercise in class.)

   b. Do you think that the employer handled the disciplinary situation correctly? Why? What would you have done differently?

4. You are the HR manager in a small company that has just bought another company in your field. You learned of the purchase only when you were asked to attend a meeting this morning. Somehow, between now and tomorrow at noon, you must come up with a plan to commu nicate the purchase to your and the other organization's employees. What do you think will be the main concerns of employees in each company? Describe your first steps and the plan for the transition period between now and the closing date of the purchase.

12 LABOUR RELATIONS

LEARNING OUTCOMES

AFTER STUDYING THIS CHAPTER, YOU SHOULD BE ABLE TO:

DISCUSS the key elements of Canada's labour laws.

OUTLINE the five steps in the labour relations process.

DESCRIBE the five steps in a union organizing campaign.

OUTLINE the three ways to obtain union recognition.

DESCRIBE the three steps in the collective bargaining process.

EXPLAIN the typical steps in a grievance procedure.

DESCRIBE the impact that unionization has had on human resources management.

12.1 INTRODUCTION TO LABOUR RELATIONS

The term **labour relations** (LR) refers to the ongoing interactions between labour unions and management in organizations. A **labour union** (or **union**) is an officially recognized body representing a group of employees who have joined together to present a collective voice in dealing with management. The purposes of unionization are to influence HR policies and practices that affect bargaining unit members, such as pay and benefits; to achieve greater control over the jobs being performed, greater job security, and improved working conditions; and to increase job satisfaction and meet employees' affiliation needs. Unlike informal labour associations or teams, a union is a legally recognized entity that provides a common voice for a specific set of employees. Therefore, the agreements between the union and management teams (called collective agreements) are legally binding.

The presence of a labour union alters the relationship between employees and the firm, and has implications for planning and implementing a business strategy. Managerial discretion and flexibility in dealing with employees and in implementing and administering HR policies and procedures are reduced. For example, union seniority provisions in the **collective agreement** (**union contract**), negotiated through **collective bargaining**, govern the selection of employees for transfers, promotions, and training programs and specify the order in which employees can be laid off and recalled. Many other terms and conditions of employment for **bargaining unit** members are determined and standardized through collective bargaining, rather than being left to management's discretion.

An organization's *labour relations (LR) strategy*, one component of its HR strategy, is its overall plan for dealing with unions, which sets the tone for its union–management relationship. The decision to accept or avoid unions is the basis of an organization's LR strategy.[1] Managers in firms choosing a *union acceptance strategy* view the union as the legitimate representative of the firm's employees. Such a relationship can lead to innovative initiatives and win–win outcomes. Managers select a *union avoidance strategy* when they believe that it is preferable to operate in a non-unionized environment. Walmart is well known for its preference to remain union free (and has even closed stores that have attempted to unionize).[2] To avoid unions, some companies adopt a *union substitution approach*, in which they become so responsive to employee needs that there is no incentive for them to unionize. Alternatively, a company may adopt a *union suppression approach* when there is a desire to avoid a union at all costs (Walmart challenged the constitutionality of Saskatchewan's labour laws all the way to the Supreme Court of Canada, but lost).[3]

12.1.1 Canada's Labour Laws

Canadian labour laws have two general purposes:

1. To provide a common set of rules for fair negotiations
2. To protect the public interest by preventing the impact of labour disputes from inconveniencing the public

As with other employment-related legislation, there are 13 provincial/territorial jurisdictions, as well as federal labour relations legislation for

labour relations The ongoing interactions between labour unions and management in organizations.

labour union (union) An officially recognized association of employees practising a similar trade or employed in the same company or industry who have joined together to present a united front and collective voice in dealing with management.

collective agreement (union contract) A formal agreement between an employer and the union representing a group of employees regarding terms and conditions of employment.

collective bargaining Negotiations between a union and an employer to arrive at a mutually acceptable collective agreement.

bargaining unit The group of employees in an organization, a plant, or an industry that has been certified by a labour relations board (LRB) or recognized by an employer as appropriate for collective bargaining purposes.

Ontario Ministry of Labour
www.labour.gov.on.ca

Canadian LabourWatch Association
www.labourwatch.com

Air Canada workers on strike in 2011.

unfair labour practice   A contravention of labour relations legislation by an employer, a union, or an employee.

employees subject to federal jurisdiction. There are a number of common characteristics in the LR legislation across Canada, which can be summarized as follows:

- procedures for the certification of a union
- the requirement that a collective agreement be in force for a minimum of one year
- procedures that must be followed by one or both parties before a strike or lockout is legal
- the prohibition of strikes or lockouts during the life of a collective agreement
- the requirement that disputes over matters arising from interpretation of the collective agreement be settled by final and binding arbitration
- prohibition of certain specified **"unfair labour practices"** on the part of labour and management
- establishment of a labour relations board or the equivalent; labour relations boards are tripartite—made up of representatives of union and management, as well as a neutral chair or a vice-chair, typically a government representative

Labour relations (LR) legislation attempts to balance employees' rights to engage in union activities with employers' rights to manage. For example, managers are prohibited from interfering with and discriminating against employees who are exercising their rights under the LR legislation. One restriction on unions is that they are prohibited from calling or authorizing an unlawful strike.

12.1.2 The Labour Movement in Canada Today

business unionism   The activities of labour unions focusing on economic and welfare issues of their members, including pay and benefits, job security, and working conditions.

social (reform) unionism   Activities of unions directed at furthering the interests of their members by influencing the social and economic policies of governments at all levels, such as speaking out on proposed legislative reforms.

Two distinct philosophies have been seen throughout the history of the union movement. **Business unionism** emphasizes economic and welfare goals for members. Unions strive to ensure *job security* and to attain *improved economic conditions* and *better working conditions* for their members. However, many unions have also become involved in broader political and social issues affecting union members. Activities aimed at influencing government economic and social policies are known as **social (reform) unionism**. For example, unions have recognized the special circumstances of Aboriginal workers, as outlined in the Workforce Diversity box.

12.1.3 Types of Unions

craft union   Traditionally, a labour organization representing workers practising the same craft or trade, such as carpentry or plumbing.

industrial union   A labour organization representing all workers eligible for union membership in a particular company or industry, including skilled tradespeople.

The labour unions in Canada can be classified according to the following characteristics:

1. *Type of worker eligible for membership.* All the early trade unions in Canada were **craft unions**—associations of persons practising the same craft or trade (for example, carpenters or bricklayers). Examples in today's workforce include the United Association of Plumbers and Pipefitters or the Ontario Nurses' Association. An **industrial union** is a labour organization comprising all the workers eligible for union membership in a particular company or

WORKFORCE DIVERSITY

Collective Agreement Puts Aboriginals First

The collective bargaining agreement (CBA) at Voisey's Bay Nickel Company in Labrador includes a clause outlining order of preference for vacant positions, training opportunities, or promotions. Innu and Inuit people are on top of this order of preference, starting with those in the bargaining unit, followed by those already employed by Voisey's Bay and then by Innu and Inuit outside candidates. Among non-Aboriginals,

priority goes to Labrador residents. Those with union membership rank first, followed by Voisey's Bay employees, and then those in the community. Aboriginals make up more than half of the bargaining unit. To reflect the employee population, the CBA includes a clause categorizing National Aboriginal Day on June 21 as a paid holiday.

Source: Based on "Collective Agreement Puts Aboriginals First," *Canadian HR Reporter* (November 6, 2006).

---

industry, irrespective of the type of work performed. A contemporary example of an industrial union is Unifor.

2. *Geographical scope.* Labour unions with head offices in other countries (most often the United States) that charter branches in both Canada and one or more countries are known as *international unions*. An example of such a union is the International Brotherhood of Teamsters, which has 125 000 Canadian members. Labour unions that charter branches in Canada only and have their head office in this country are known as *national unions*. An example of such a national union is the Canadian Union of Public Employees (CUPE). There are 639 000 members across Canada. A small number of employees belong to labour unions that are purely *local* in geographical scope.

3. *Labour congress affiliation.* A third way of distinguishing among labour unions is according to affiliation with one or another central labour organization. These central organizations include the following:

   - *Canadian Labour Congress (CLC).* The CLC is the major central labour organization in Canada and has over 3.3 million affiliated union members. Most international and national unions belong to the CLC, as do all directly chartered local unions, local/district labour councils, and provincial/territorial federations of labour.

   - *Confédération des syndicats nationaux (CSN)*—in English, Confederation of National Trade Unions (CNTU). This organization is the Quebec counterpart of the CLC and has more than 300 000 members.

   - *American Federation of Labor and Congress of Industrial Organizations (AFL–CIO).* The American counterpart of the CLC is the AFL–CIO. The two organizations operate independently, but since most international unions in the CLC are also members of the AFL–CIO, a certain degree of common interest exists.

The basic unit of the labour movement in Canada is the union **local,** formed in a particular location. A union local serves as an administrative unit of a provincial, national, or international union. For HR managers and front-line supervisors, the union locals are generally the most important part of the union structure. Key players within the local are the elected officials known as **union stewards,** who are responsible for representing the interests and protecting the rights of bargaining unit employees in their department or area. The Strategic HR box discusses a recent trend of expanded memberships at the local union level in Canada.

American Federation of Labor and Congress of Industrial Organizations (AFL–CIO)
www.aflcio.org

International Labour News
www.labourstart.org

Construction Labour Relations
www.clra.org

union local   A group of unionized employees in a particular location.

union steward   A union member elected by workers in a particular department or area of a firm to act as their union representative.

STRATEGIC HR

UFCW's Social Media Campaign to Engage and Educate Young Canadian Workers

UFCW Canada stands for the United Food and Commercial Workers Canada, representing more than a quarter of a million Canadians working in every sector of the food industry as well as workers in retail, health care, hospitality, security, financial service, and related manufacturing sectors of the economy. More than 40 percent of UFCW Canada members are under the age of 30.

In March 2017, UFCW Canada launched Incite—a new initiative aimed at engaging and educating young workers across the country on their rights at work. The goal of Incite is to equip young workers with the tools and knowledge to effectively address workplace issues and common realities that young workers are facing, such as the rise of precarious work and unpredictable scheduling. Incite was unveiled at the George Brown College Labour Fair. The Incite activists conducted a number of in-class presentations to get the word out and inspire young workers to take action in their

workplace. Between presentations, the activists also engaged with students at a display area at the Labour Fair. The week-long event at the downtown Toronto college is the biggest annual labour fair at any college or university in Canada.

Incite builds on other UFCW Canada-backed young worker initiatives, including Students Against Migrant Exploitation (SAME, at www.facebook.com/samegroup) and the UFCW Canada Young Workers Internship Program (www.facebook.com/UFCWYIP). The Incite group also launched a weekly podcast discussion of topics related to young people and the world of work.

A dedicated website for Incite (www.incitemore.ca) and the use of Twitter, Facebook, and Instagram reflect UFCW's desire to serve its young membership base while also providing a savvy recruitment strategy to support union growth in Canada's service sector.

Source: Adapted from "UFCW Canada Launches Incite Initiative." UFCW Canada website. Media and News. (March 17, 2017). www.ufcw.ca/index.php?option=com_content&view=article&id=31412:ufcw-canada-launches-incite-initiative&catid=9828&Itemid=6&lang=en7, UFCW Canada.

12.1.4 Membership Trends

As of 2014, 28.8 percent of Canadian employees were unionized. While these rates have remained relatively constant at 30 percent in Canada since 1999, union density rates have varied by industry, as highlighted in **Table 12.1**. Various factors were responsible for membership decline, including a dramatic increase in service sector and white-collar jobs, combined with a decrease in employment opportunities in industries that had traditionally been highly unionized. More effective HR practices in non-unionized firms are another contributing factor.[4]

TABLE 12.1   Union Density by Industry, 2005 vs. 2015

Industry	Union Density in 2005 (percentage)	Union Density in 2015 (percentage)
Educational services	67.6	68.8
Utilities	66.7	63.0
Health care and social assistance	53.6	53.2
Transportation and warehousing	41.0	36.7
Construction	30.3	29.7
Manufacturing	29.5	23.5
Accommodation and food services	7.7	5.9

Source: The Conference Board of Canada, "*Industrial Relations Outlook 2017: Striking,*" December 2016, p. 9. Reprinted with permission.

Traditionally, unions have targeted full-time manufacturing workers (who used to be almost exclusively older males) for membership. Canadian unions are unique in that they have managed to refocus their target on membership to better align with workforce realities, as highlighted in the Expert Opinion box. As a result, the rate of decline in union membership is not nearly as significant in Canada as it is elsewhere (for example, the United States). This can be attributed to three significant issues: global competition, demographics, and the unionization of white-collar workers in Canada.

Industry Viewpoint
EXPERT OPINION

1. Given the volume and forecast for contingent workers in Canada, how can these groups be organized and gain a collective voice?

Statistically, more than half of the jobs created in the last five years in Canada have been contingent work oriented. We've had success in organizing these contingent workers because we are focused on helping find real opportunities and solutions that are specific to the type of work. For example, we recently unionized at Casino Rama in Orillia, Ontario, where a significant portion of the 1 800 jobs unionized were part time in nature.

We find that a union is instrumental in securing decent pay and benefits for people who are in non-traditional jobs, but these employees also want and need protection from unfair labour practices (such as changing scheduled work hours with minimal notice, unfair terminations, etc.), as well as assistance increasing the number of hours employees work. Through this, we can prevent situations in which an individual is required to work two to three part-time jobs with low pay and minimal benefit, in order to work the number of hours required to earn a basic level of income.

2. The new generation of workers (Gen-Y) has unique needs and perspectives

**Identification:
Mr. Jerry Dias**
President, Unifor

when compared to previous generations. How can unions address these differences?

Young people are looking at jobs differently than what may be portrayed in the media. They graduate from school and try transitioning into their careers, but often cannot find well-paying, meaningful, progressive jobs in their field. The concept of this generation being loyal to themselves over their employer might be more indicative of the employment opportunities that are presented, rather than their true desire for a career and job stability. Organized labour helps to address these concerns.

Young people today are also the first generation to have less opportunity than their parents. They are very technically savvy, so any forms of organized labour, such as ours, need to communicate using a multimedia approach (Twitter, social media, LinkedIn, websites, blogs, etc.). This generation generally values information, and appreciates both timely and accurate information.

3. What are the challenges that Unifor faces today and in the near future?

We were established in August 2013, and the recognition of the Unifor brand has been great. A big focus of the organization is to not only serve our members' needs well, but also spend time on issues of interest to the greater community. The labour movement cannot survive in isolation, and community and labour relations experience a reciprocal relationship. For example, in a recent settlement we were able to get the organization to commit funds for women's issues regarding employment in the local and regional communities, with a special focus on Aboriginal women. It is critical that we continue to gain broad-based support for the changing perception of the labour movement, and stay linked and connected with the communities we serve (members and beyond).

Source: Reprinted by permission from Mr. Jerry Dias, President, Unifo.

12.1.4.1 Global Competition

Globalization is transforming the dynamics of labour relations in Canada such that employers are being forced to become more militant, and unions are struggling to maintain their influence at the bargaining table.[5] Some unions face the difficult choice of negotiating concessions or watching jobs go to lower-cost countries.

12.1.4.2 Demographics

The focus of union collective bargaining efforts must align with the workplace demographics. The aging of the workforce and pending labour shortage affect unions as well as HR managers.[6] It has been suggested that unions and management may need to work together to attract and retain workers. Unions have also been criticized as a "movement of the old" that focuses on past glories as opposed to the challenges faced in the second decade of the twenty-first century.[7] However, unions are taking aim at Canadian youth and visible minorities to show the relevancy of the labour movement in today's economically fragile world. Initiatives such as the Ontario Federation of Labour's Workers under 30 Committee and the Canadian Union of Public Employees' research in the area of racial equality illustrate a strategic awareness of the new demographic recruitment and service planning efforts required by contemporary labour organizations in this country.[8]

12.1.4.3 Unionization of White-Collar Employees

A lack of job security and difficulties in attempting to resolve grievances have led to increased interest in unionization among white-collar workers. Service sector workers, such as those in retail stores, fast-food chains, and government agencies, as well as managers and professionals (including university/college faculty), have been targeted for organizing campaigns.[9] Since more women and young people hold such jobs, rather than manufacturing jobs, unions are now focusing more on work–family issues as well as the health and safety risks associated with white-collar jobs, such as the potential for repetitive strain injuries from working at video display terminals (computers or laptops).[10]

12.2 THE LABOUR RELATIONS PROCESS

As illustrated in **Figure 12.1**, the labour relations process consists of five steps. Each of these five steps is detailed below.

12.2.1 Step 1: Desire for Collective Representation

Based on a review of 36 research studies internationally, three classifications of reasons were developed to explain why individuals join unions:[11]

- *Dissonance-based reasons.* When expectations of work (work should be enjoyable and rewarding, for example) and the experience of work (the work environment is unpleasant and pay is low) are in conflict (dissonance), the desire to join a union is triggered. However, if dissonance is the reason for employees wanting to unionize, then they will do so only if they believe the union will be effective in remedying the associated discontent or frustration with their work expectations versus their experiences. The mere belief in such success is sometimes referred to as *instrumentality*.

FIGURE 12.1   An Overview of the Labour Relations Process

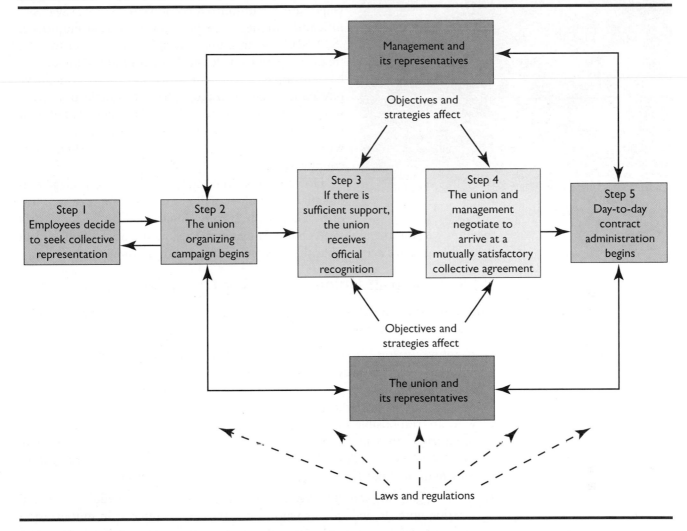

- *Utility-based reasons.* An individual's decision to join a union can also be attributed to a rational calculation of the costs and benefits of unionization, whereby individuals compare the costs and benefits of remaining non-unionized versus becoming unionized. The decision is largely based on the calculation of the cost/benefit analysis.[12]

- *Political/ideological reasons.* An individual's political or ideological beliefs may influence his or her understanding of and desire for collective versus individual negotiation of employment terms.[13]

Numerous studies suggest that age, gender, education levels, and other demographic factors are highly correlated with the desire to join a union. However, there is little consistency with the findings of the studies, except in the case of two groups: People over the age of 60 and Black workers are consistently likely to have a desire to join a union.[14] It has been theorized that this is largely due to perceptions of employment-related discrimination. Another suggestion is that each workplace is unique, so the demographic characteristics of one workforce may affect the desire to join a union in a way that is not highly generalizable or applicable to a larger population.

Promoting the benefits of unionization.

Given that, in March 2017, the average hourly wage rate for unionized employees ($29.73) was significantly higher than for non-unionized employees ($24.52),[15] being a union member does seem to offer financial benefits at least. Being a union member also has an impact on female workers' ability to achieve pay equity. On average, full-time female unionized workers earned 94 percent of the hourly wages of their male counterparts, and part-time female unionized workers earned 14 percent more than their male counterparts.[16]

However, research studies have made it clear that dissatisfaction alone will not lead to unionization. It is only when workers are dissatisfied and believe that they are without the ability to change the factors causing dissatisfaction, except through collective action, that they become interested in unionizing.[17]

12.2.2 Step 2: Union Organizing Campaign

Once interest in joining a union has been aroused, the union organizing process begins. There are five steps typically involved in this process:

1. *Employee/union contact.* A formal organizing campaign may be initiated by a union organizer or by employees acting on their own behalf. Most organizing campaigns are begun by employees who get in touch with an existing union.[18] However, large unions have a number of *union organizers* on staff who are responsible for identifying organizing opportunities and launching organizing campaigns. During these initial discussions, employees investigate the advantages of union representation, and the union officials start to gather information about the employees' sources of dissatisfaction.

2. *Initial organizational meeting.* The union organizer then schedules an initial meeting with the individuals who first expressed an interest in unionization and co-workers who subsequently express their support. Such meetings occur outside of the workplace. The aim is to identify employees who would be willing to help the organizer direct the campaign.

3. *Formation of an in-house organizing committee.* This committee comprises a group of employees who are dedicated to the goal of unionization and who are willing to assist the union organizer.

4. *The organizing campaign.* Members of the in-house committee then contact employees, present the case for unionization, and encourage as many employees as possible to sign an **authorization card**, indicating their willingness to be represented by the union in collective bargaining with the employer.

5. *The outcome.* There are a number of possible outcomes to a unionization campaign, including rejection by the majority of eligible employees. For a union to become the bargaining unit for a group of employees, it must be certified by a labour relations board (LRB) or receive official recognition from the employer.

authorization card A card signed by an employee that indicates his or her willingness to have the union act as his or her representative for purposes of collective bargaining.

12.2.2.1 Employer Response to an Organizing Campaign

There may be cases when an employer feels that the employees are considering organizing a union (some common signs of this are highlighted in **Table 12.2**). It

Labour Relations (Ontario)
www.labour.gov.on.ca/english/lr

TABLE 12.2   Signs of Organizing Activity

- The disappearance of employee lists or directories
- More inquiries than usual about benefits, wages, promotions, and other HR policies and procedures
- Questions about management's opinion of unions
- An increase in the number or nature of employee complaints or grievances
- A change in the number, composition, and size of informal groups at lunch and coffee breaks
- The sudden popularity of certain employees (especially if they are the informal leaders)
- The sudden cessation of employee conversation when a member of management approaches, or an obvious change in employees' behaviour towards members of management, expressed either formally or informally
- The appearance of strangers in the parking lot
- The distribution of cards, flyers, or pro-union buttons

Source: Based in part on "Early Signs," *Canadian HR Reporter* (November 29, 1999), p. 14.

has been suggested that the best defense against union organizing is through effective human resources management. If an organizing campaign is already underway, it may be too late to implement the HRM strategies that would have prevented a successful union drive. However, this does not mean an employer is helpless, particularly in its communications with employees.[19] If the employer prefers that the group seeking unionization retain its non-union status, a careful campaign is usually mounted to counteract the union drive. Normally, HR department staff members head up the campaign, although they may be assisted by a consultant or labour lawyer. In addition to designing a communication strategy, it is also important to provide supervisory training. Supervisors need to be informed about what they can and cannot do or say during the organizing campaign to ensure that they avoid actions that might directly or inadvertently provide fuel for the union's campaign, while at the same time refraining from violating LR legislation.

As much information about the union as possible should also be obtained pertaining to dues, strike record, salaries of officers, and any other relevant facts that might cause employees to question the benefits of unionization. Communication strategies can be planned, with the aim of reminding employees about the company's good points, pointing out disadvantages of unionization, and refuting any misleading union claims. The employer's case for remaining non-union should be presented in a factual, honest, and straightforward manner.

Under the law, employers are granted the right to do the following:

- Express their views and opinions regarding unions
- State their position regarding the desirability of remaining non-union
- Prohibit distribution of union literature on company property on company time
- Increase wages, make promotions, and take other HR actions, as long as they would do so *in the normal course of business* (in most jurisdictions, however, once an application for certification is received by the LRB, wages, benefits, and working conditions are frozen until the application is dealt with)

An Ethical Dilemma

Knowing that head office plans to close your facility if a unionization bid is successful, how should you, as a manager, respond to inquiries from employees about the impact of a union?

- Assemble employees during working hours to state the company's position, as long as employees are advised of the purpose of the meeting in advance, attendance is optional, and threats and promises are avoided (employers have no obligation to give the union the same opportunity)

12.2.3 Step 3: Union Recognition

A union can obtain recognition as a bargaining unit for a group of workers in three basic ways: (1) voluntary recognition, (2) the regular certification process, and (3) a pre-hearing vote. Bargaining rights can also be terminated in various ways.

12.2.3.1 Voluntary Recognition

Every employer in a Canadian jurisdiction, except Quebec, can voluntarily recognize a union as the bargaining agent for a group of its employees. Although fairly rare, this may occur if an employer has adopted a union acceptance strategy and believes that employees want to be represented by that union.

12.2.3.2 Regular Certification

certification The procedure whereby a labour union obtains a certificate from the relevant LRB declaring that the union is the exclusive bargaining agent for a defined group of employees in a bargaining unit that the LRB considers appropriate for collective bargaining purposes.

The normal union certification procedure is for the union to present evidence of at least a minimum level of membership support for a bargaining unit that the union has defined, in the form of signed authorization cards, to the appropriate LRB, along with an application for **certification**. The minimum level of support required to apply for certification varies by jurisdiction (e.g., Ontario and Alberta each require 40 percent of proposed bargaining unit members, while both Saskatchewan and British Columbia require 45 percent of the proposed bargaining unit members). The LRB then determines whether the bargaining unit defined by the union is appropriate for collective bargaining purposes.

representation vote A vote conducted by the LRB in which employees in the bargaining unit indicate, by secret ballot, whether or not they want to be represented, or continue to be represented, by a labour union.

In a limited number of jurisdictions, LRBs can grant *automatic certification* without a vote if the applicant union can demonstrate a high enough level of support for the proposed bargaining unit. Automatic certification may also be granted in some jurisdictions if the employer has engaged in unfair practices. If the level of support is not sufficient for automatic certification, but is above a specified minimum level (typically 40 percent, depending on jurisdiction), the LRB will order and supervise a **representation vote**.[20] Eligible employees have the opportunity to cast a secret ballot, indicating whether or not they want the union to be certified. If the union loses, another election cannot be held among the same employees for at least one year.

12.2.3.3 Pre-Hearing Votes

pre-hearing vote An alternative mechanism for certification, used in situations in which there is evidence of violations of fair labour practices early in the organizing campaign.

In most jurisdictions, a **pre-hearing vote** may be conducted if there is evidence of violations of fair labour practices early in an organizing campaign. In such a case, the LRB may order a vote before holding a hearing to determine the composition of the bargaining unit. The intent is to determine the level of support for the union as quickly as possible, before the effect of any irregularities can taint the outcome. The ballot box is then sealed until the LRB determines whether the bargaining unit is appropriate and, if so, which employees are eligible for membership. If the bargaining unit is deemed appropriate by the LRB, only the votes of potential bargaining unit members are counted, and if the majority of the ballots cast support the union, it is certified.

12.2.3.4 Termination of Bargaining Rights

All labour relations acts provide procedures for workers to apply for the **decertification** of their unions. Generally, members may apply for decertification if the union has failed to negotiate a collective agreement within one year of certification, or if they are dissatisfied with the performance of the union. The LRB holds a secret-ballot vote, and if more than 50 percent of the ballots cast (or bargaining unit members, depending on jurisdiction) are in opposition to the union, the union will be decertified. A labour union also has the right to notify the LRB that it no longer wants to continue to represent the employees in a particular bargaining unit. This is known as *termination on abandonment*. Once the LRB has declared that the union no longer represents the bargaining unit employees, any collective agreement negotiated between the parties is void.

decertification The process whereby a union is legally deprived of its official recognition as the exclusive bargaining agent for a group of employees.

12.2.4 Step 4: Collective Bargaining

Collective bargaining is the process by which a formal collective agreement is established between labour and management. The collective agreement is the cornerstone of the Canadian LR system. Both union and management representatives are required to bargain in good faith. This means that they must communicate and negotiate, that proposals must be matched with counterproposals, and that both parties must make every reasonable effort to arrive at an agreement.

Steps typically involved in the collective bargaining process include (1) preparation for bargaining, (2) face-to-face negotiations, and (3) obtaining approval for the proposed contract. There are two possible additional steps. First, when talks break down, third-party assistance is required by law. The second additional step is a strike/lockout or interest arbitration if the parties arrive at a bargaining impasse. Each of these steps will be described next.

12.2.4.1 Preparation for Negotiations

Good preparation leads to a greater likelihood that desired goals will be achieved. Preparation for negotiations involves planning the bargaining strategy and process, and assembling data to support bargaining proposals. Each party will also conduct an analysis of past grievances and review the items not achieved in the previous round of bargaining and, in the case of a first collective agreement, the union's organizing campaign promises. Data will be gathered on current wage rates and benefit plans offered by local or regional competitors, as well as from other union locals representing employees in similar industries. Cost estimates on bargaining proposals from the employer and union will be calculated and, in certain industries, contingency planning will be made related to possible strike or lock-out actions.

In addition, management negotiators will obtain input from supervisors. Union negotiators will obtain input from union stewards, obtain the company's financial information (if it is a public company), gather demographic information on their membership, and obtain input from union local members. While labour legislation sets minimum requirements for the content of a collective agreement, the list of items for negotiation between union and management representatives is typically quite lengthy. Shortlisting and prioritizing issues is critical to successful negotiations. **Figure 12.2** identifies a series of issues that are currently prioritized by management and unions.

Negotech
http://negotech.labour.gc.ca

FIGURE 12.2   Management versus Union Negotiation Issues, 2016

Management Issues	Number Identifying This among Top 3 Issues	Union Issues	Number Identifying This among Top 3 Issues
Wages	63	Wages	92
Productivity	39	Employment security	56
Organizational change	30	Health benefits	42
Health benefits	30	Outsourcing and contracting out	20
Business competitiveness	28	Employment and pay equity	19
Flexible work practices	25	Pensions	18
Pensions	24	Organizational change	15
Outsourcing and contraction out	12	Flexible work practices	12
Employment security	12	Variable pay	7
Employment and pay equity	11	Technological change	7
Technological change	10	Training and skills development	5
Variable pay	6	Productivity	4
Training and skills development	4	Business competitiveness	1
Other	13	Other	9

Note: This list of 13 potential CBA issues was given to 172 respondents or management and union representatives, who were asked to identify their top three negotiation issues. Values are the number of respondents per issue.

Source: The Conference Board of Canada, "*Industrial Relations Outlook 2017: Striking,*" December 2016, p. 9. Reprinted with permission.

© Pressmaster/Shutterstock

Negotiating a collective agreement.

Once these steps are completed, each side forms a negotiating team and an initial bargaining plan/strategy is prepared. Initial proposals are then finalized and presented for approval by either senior management or the union membership.

12.2.4.2 Face-to-Face Negotiations

Under LR legislation, representatives of either union or management are expected to provide written notice to the other party of their desire to negotiate a first collective agreement or renew an existing one. Early in the negotiating process, demands are exchanged—often before the first bargaining session. Then both negotiating teams can make a private assessment of the other team's demands. Usually, each team finds some items with which they can agree quite readily and others on which compromise seems likely. Tentative conclusions are also made regarding which items, if any, are potential strike or lockout issues.

Location, Frequency, and Duration of Meetings Negotiations are generally held at a neutral, offsite location, such as a hotel meeting room, so that there is no psychological advantage for either team and so that interruptions and work distractions can be kept to a minimum. Each side generally has another room in which intrateam meetings, known as **caucus sessions,** are held.

caucus session A session in which only the members of one's own bargaining team are present.

Generally, meetings are held as often as either or both parties consider desirable, and they last as long as progress is being made. Marathon bargaining sessions, such as those lasting all night, are not typical until conciliation has been exhausted and the clock is ticking rapidly towards the strike/lockout deadline.

Initial Bargaining Session The initial meeting of the bargaining teams is extremely important in establishing the climate that will prevail during the negotiating sessions that follow. A cordial attitude can help to relax tension and ensure that negotiations proceed smoothly. Generally, the first meeting is devoted to an exchange of demands (if this has not taken place previously) and the establishment of rules and procedures that will be used during negotiations.

Subsequent Bargaining Sessions In traditional approaches to bargaining, each party argues for its demands and resists those of the other at each negotiating session. At the same time, both are looking for compromise alternatives that will enable an agreement to be reached. Every proposal submitted must be withdrawn either temporarily or permanently, accepted by the other side in its entirety, or accepted in a modified form. Ideally, both sides should come away from negotiations feeling that they have attained many of their basic bargaining goals and confident that the tentative agreement reached will be acceptable to senior management and the members of the bargaining unit.

For each issue on the table to be resolved satisfactorily, the point at which agreement is reached must be within limits that the union and employer are willing to accept, often referred to as the **bargaining zone**. As illustrated in **Figure 12.3**, if the solution desired by one party exceeds the limits of the other party, then it is outside of the bargaining zone. Unless that party modifies its demands sufficiently to bring them within the bargaining zone, or the other party extends its limits to accommodate such demands, a bargaining deadlock is the inevitable result.

Distributive bargaining is an approach often typified as "win–lose" bargaining because the gains of one party are normally achieved at the expense of the other.[21] It is appropriately involved when the issues being discussed pertain to

bargaining zone The area defined by the bargaining limits (resistance points) of each side, in which compromise is possible, as is the attainment of a settlement satisfactory to both parties.

distributive bargaining A win–lose negotiating strategy in which one party gains at the expense of the other.

FIGURE 12.3 The Bargaining Zone and Characteristics of Distributive Bargaining

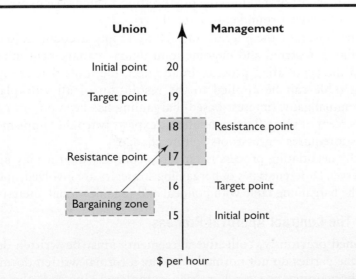

$ per hour

the distribution of things that are available in fixed amounts, such as wage increases and benefits improvements. However, it may also be used when there is a history of distrust and adversarial relations, even when dealing with issues on which a more constructive approach is possible.

As indicated in **Figure 12.3**, distributive bargaining is characterized by three distinct components: the initial point, the target point, and the resistance point. The initial point for the union is usually higher than what the union expects to receive from management. The union target point is next, and represents the negotiating team's assessment of what is realistically achievable from management. The union's bargaining zone limit is its resistance point, which represents its minimally acceptable level.

These points are essentially reversed for management. The management team's initial point is its lowest level, which is used at the beginning of negotiations. Next is its target point, the desired agreement level. Management's resistance point forms the other boundary of the bargaining zone.

integrative bargaining   A negotiating strategy in which the possibility of win–win, lose–win, win–lose, and lose–lose outcomes is recognized, and there is acknowledgement that achieving a win–win outcome will depend on mutual trust and problem solving.

Integrative bargaining is an approach that assumes that a win–win solution can be found but also acknowledges that one or both sides can be losers if the bargaining is not handled effectively.[22] Integrative bargaining strategies require that both management and union negotiators adopt a genuine interest in the joint exploration of creative solutions to common problems.

Issues pertaining to work rules, occupational health and safety concerns, and unclear contract language can often be handled effectively by using an integrative approach. These are situations in which management negotiators are not intent on retaining management rights and both sides are committed to seeking a win–win solution. Wage rates, employee benefits, and vacation entitlements are more likely to be fixed-sum issues that are handled by a distributive approach.

mutual gains (interest-based) bargaining   A win–win negotiating approach based on training in the fundamentals of effective problem solving and conflict resolution, in which the interests of all stakeholders are taken into account.

The objective of integrative bargaining is to establish a creative negotiating relationship that benefits labour and management. Becoming increasingly popular these days is a relatively new integrative approach known as **mutual gains (interest-based) bargaining**, which is another win–win approach to LR issues. All key union and management negotiators are trained in the fundamentals of effective problem solving and conflict resolution. Such training is often extended to other employees to ensure that the principles of mutual gains (interest-based) bargaining are incorporated into the organization's value system and that cooperation becomes a year-round corporate objective.[23]

Solutions must take the interests of each party into account. A joint sense of accountability is fostered and ongoing joint union–management initiatives can result from the negotiating process. In addition, the tools that are used at the bargaining table can be applied to the resolution of all workplace issues. Although mutual gains (interest-based) bargaining has been put into practice in about 40 percent of Canadian negotiations, experts warn that implementation is difficult, as it requires a grassroots culture change.[24]

Thus, the negotiating process is far more complex than it may appear to a casual observer. Different types of bargaining strategies are involved, and each side arrives at the bargaining table with political and organizational interests at stake.

12.2.4.3 The Contract Approval Process

As mentioned previously, collective agreements must be written documents. However, the parties do not normally execute a formal written document until after the bargaining process has been completed. Instead, the terms and conditions agreed to by the parties are usually reduced to a **memorandum of settlement** and submitted to the constituent groups for final approval.

Generally, final approval for the employer rests with the senior management team. In most cases, the union bargaining team submits the memorandum of settlement to the bargaining unit members for **ratification**. In some jurisdictions, ratification is required by law, and all members of the bargaining unit must be given many opportunities to cast a secret-ballot vote indicating approval or rejection of the proposed contract. If the majority of bargaining unit members vote in favour of the proposal, it goes into effect. If the proposed collective agreement is rejected, union and management negotiators must return to the bargaining table and seek a more acceptable compromise. In such instances, third-party assistance is often sought to seek agreement on key issues that were not supported in the initial ratification process.

Once approval has been received from the constituent groups, the bargaining team members sign the memorandum of settlement. Once signed, this memorandum serves as the collective agreement until the formal document has been prepared and contract administration begins. Copies of the new collective agreement are produced for union local members as well as managers in the organization.

12.2.4.4 Third-Party Assistance and Bargaining Impasses

Legislation in all Canadian jurisdictions provides for conciliation and mediation services. Although the terms *conciliation* and *mediation* are often used interchangeably, they have quite distinct and different meanings.

Conciliation is the intervention of a neutral third party whose primary purpose is to bring the parties together and keep them talking so they can reach a mutually satisfactory collective agreement. In the majority of jurisdictions, legislation provides for a conciliation process and in certain instances states that such a process is required before a legal strike or lockout. The only means available to a conciliator to bring the parties to agreement is persuasion—he or she is not permitted to have any direct input into the negotiation process or to impose a settlement. Laws also provide for the formation of a conciliation board. Conciliation is typically requested after the parties have been negotiating for some time and are starting to reach a deadlock, or after talks have broken down. The aim of conciliation is to try to help the parties avoid the hardship of a strike or lockout.[25]

Mediation is the intervention of a neutral third party whose primary purpose is to help the parties fashion a mutually satisfactory agreement. Mediation is usually a voluntary process, typically occurring during the countdown period prior to a strike or lockout, or during the strike or lockout itself. The mediator's role is an active one. It often involves meeting with each side separately and then bringing them together in an attempt to assist them in bridging the existing gaps. The mediator is allowed to have direct input into the negotiation process but cannot impose a settlement.

memorandum of settlement   A summary of the terms and conditions agreed to by the parties that is submitted to the constituent groups for final approval.

ratification   Formal approval by secret-ballot vote of the bargaining unit members of the agreement negotiated between union and management.

Ontario Ministry of Labour—Conciliation **www.labour.gov.on.ca/english/lr/faqs/lr_faq2.php**

conciliation   The often mandatory use of a neutral third party, who has no direct input in the negotiation process, to help an organization and the union representing a group of its employees communicate more effectively with the aim of coming to a mutually satisfactory collective agreement.

mediation   The often voluntary use of a neutral third party who has direct input on the negotiation process to help an organization and the union representing its employees to reach a mutually satisfactory collective agreement.

The mediator's role is an active one. It often involves meeting with each side separately and then bringing them together in an attempt to assist them in bridging the existing gaps.

When the union and management negotiating teams are unable to reach an agreement, and once the conciliation process has been undertaken (where required), the union may exercise its right to strike or request interest arbitration, and the employer may exercise its right to lock out the bargaining unit members. Alternatively, once the old collective agreement has expired, bargaining unit members may continue to work without one until talks resume and an agreement is reached.

Strikes A **strike** can be defined as a temporary refusal by bargaining unit members to continue working for the employer. When talks are reaching an impasse, unions will often hold a **strike vote**. Legally required in some jurisdictions, such a vote seeks authorization from bargaining unit members to strike if necessary. A favourable vote does not mean that a strike is inevitable. In fact, a highly favourable strike vote is often used as a bargaining ploy to gain concessions that will make a strike unnecessary. The result of a strike vote, in terms of a percentage of members who support strike action, also helps the union negotiating team members determine their relative bargaining strength. Unless strike action is supported by a substantial majority of bargaining unit members, union leaders are rarely prepared to risk a strike and must therefore be more willing to compromise, if necessary, to avoid a work stoppage.

Since a strike can have serious economic consequences for bargaining unit members, the union negotiating team must carefully analyze the prospects for its success. Striking union members receive no wages and often have no benefits coverage until they return to work, although they may draw some money from the union's strike fund. Work stoppages are also costly for employers, customers, and suppliers.

When a union goes on strike, bargaining unit members often **picket** the employer. To ensure the participation of as many picketers as possible, the union may make strike pay contingent on picket duty. Picketers stand at business entrances, carrying signs advertising the issues in dispute, and attempt to discourage people, supplies, and goods from entering or leaving the premises. The employer may seek to limit the extent of picketing by seeking a temporary court injunction.

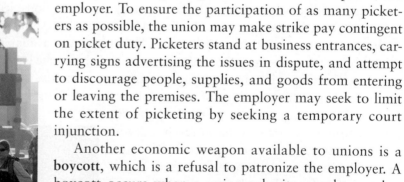

Another economic weapon available to unions is a **boycott**, which is a refusal to patronize the employer. A boycott occurs when a union asks its members, other union members, the employer's customers/clients, and supporters in the general public not to patronize the business involved in the labour dispute. Such action can harm the employer if the union is successful in gaining a large number of supporters. As with a strike, a boycott can have long-term consequences if former customers/clients develop a bias against the employer's products or services or make a change in buying habits or service provider that is not easily reversed.

The duration and ultimate success of a strike depends on the relative strength of the parties. Once a strike is settled, striking workers return to their jobs. During a labour dispute many people are put under remarkable pressure,

strike The temporary refusal by bargaining unit members to continue working for the employer.

strike vote Legally required in some jurisdictions, it is a vote seeking authorization from bargaining unit members to strike if necessary. A favourable vote does not mean that a strike is inevitable.

picket Stationing groups of striking employees, usually carrying signs, at the entrances and exits of the struck operation to publicize the issues in dispute and discourage people, supplies, and goods from entering or leaving the premises.

boycott An organized refusal of bargaining unit members and supporters to buy the products or use the services of the organization whose employees are on strike in an effort to exert economic pressure on the employer.

Striking members of the Canadian Union of Public Employees, local 3903, picket at York University in Toronto.

and relationships essential to effective post-settlement work dynamics can be tarnished—especially in firms that rely heavily on teamwork. Post-settlement work environments are often riddled with tension, derogatory remarks, and hostility.

Lockouts Although not a widely used strategy in Canada, lockouts are legally permissible. In a **lockout**, the employer temporarily prohibits the bargaining unit employees from entering the company premises, thus refusing to provide work for them, as a means of putting pressure on the union to agree to the terms and conditions being offered by management. Sometimes the employer chooses to close operations entirely, which means that non-striking employees are also affected. Most employers try to avoid this option, since doing so means that the well-being of innocent parties is threatened, and a lockout may damage the firm's public image. A brief description of the timeline and outcomes of the 2012–2013 NHL lockout are provided in the Strategic HR textbox.

> **lockout**   The temporary refusal of a company to continue providing work for bargaining unit employees involved in a labour dispute, which may result in closure of the establishment for a time.

Unlawful Strikes An unlawful strike is one that contravenes the relevant LR legislation and lays the union and its members open to charges and possible fines or periods of imprisonment if found guilty. For example, it is illegal for a union to call a strike involving employees who do not have the right to strike because of the essential nature of their services, such as nurses or police officers. In all jurisdictions, it is illegal to call a strike during the term of an existing collective agreement. A **wildcat strike** is a spontaneous walkout, not officially sanctioned by the

> **wildcat strike**   A spontaneous walkout, not officially sanctioned by the union leadership, which may or may not be legal, depending on its timing.

STRATEGIC HR

NHL Lockout Timeline (2012–2013 Season)

June 29, 2012	Initial meeting in Toronto between the NHLPA (representing NHL players for all 30 teams) and NHL management.
July 13, 2012	NHL management team puts its initial offer on the table, asking for a reduction in players' share of hockey-related revenue from 57 percent to 43 percent, and suggesting changes in contract rules.
Aug. 19, 2012	NHLPA puts its initial offer on the table: salary caps of $69 million and more revenue sharing between teams.
Sept. 13, 2012	No agreement reached. NHL Board of Governors approves potential for lockout when CBA expires.
Sept. 15, 2012	CBA expires, NHL management trigger lockouts
Jan. 6, 2013	Commissioner Gary Bettman and the NHLPA Executive Director Donald Fehr jointly announce tentative deal.
Jan. 12, 2013	NHLPA approves new CBA. Lockout officially ended.[1]

Impact of Lockout?

Of over 2 000 Canadians surveyed	41%	feel more negative about the sport after the most recent lockout
	37%	plan to spend less on merchandise
	35%	plan to watch fewer games[2]

Source: Based on CBA Talks Timeline, www.tsn.ca/nhl/feature/?id=9678, accessed June 21, 2013; & D. Friend, "NHL Brand Value Dips Thanks To 2012 Hockey Lockout, Say Study," *Huffington Press*, February 13, 2013, www.huffingtonpost.ca/2013/02/13/nhl-brand-value-drops_n_2675352.html.

An Ethical Dilemma

Is it ethical for a firm to close the establishment during a labour dispute if doing so results in non-striking employees being laid off?

Public Service Grievance
Board—Arbitration
**www.psab.gov.on.ca/english/psgb/
Arbitration.htm**

arbitration The use of an outside third party to investigate a dispute between an employer and union and impose a settlement.

interest arbitration The imposition of the final terms of a collective agreement.

interest dispute A dispute between an organization and the union representing its employees over the terms of a collective agreement.

union security clause The contract provisions protecting the interests of the labour union and dealing with the issues of membership requirements, the ability to participate in union duties at work, and, often, the payment of union dues.

union leaders, that is illegal if it occurs during the term of a collective agreement.

Interest Arbitration Arbitration involves the use of an outside third party to investigate a dispute between an employer and union and impose a settlement. A sole arbitrator or three-person arbitration board may be involved. Most arbitrators have a legal background, but there is no requirement that the arbitrator be a lawyer. An arbitration board is comprised of a representative chosen by the union and a second member selected by the employer. A third person, either agreed-to by both parties or appointed by a government authority, serves as the board chairperson. Arbitrators listen to evidence, weigh it impartially and objectively, and make a decision based on the law or the contract language.[26] Arbitration decisions are final and binding and cannot be changed or revised.

Interest arbitration may be used to settle an **interest dispute** regarding the terms of a collective agreement by imposing the terms of the collective agreement. The right to interest arbitration is legally mandated for workers who are not permitted to strike, such as hospital and nursing home employees, police officers and firefighters in most jurisdictions, and some public servants.[27] Interest arbitration is also involved when special legislation is passed ordering striking or locked-out parties back to work because of public hardship. As **Table 12.3** reveals, only about 10 percent of Canadian contracts are settled through interest arbitration.

12.2.4.5 The Collective Agreement: Typical Provisions

The eventual outcome of collective bargaining, whether negotiated by the parties or imposed by an arbitrator, is a formal, written collective agreement.

Union Recognition Clause A *union recognition clause* is required in a collective agreement. It confirms the employer's willingness to recognize a union as the sole bargaining agent for its members' terms and conditions of work and clarifies the scope of the bargaining unit by specifying the employee classifications included therein or listing those excluded.

Union Security/Checkoff Clause All Canadian jurisdictions permit the inclusion of a **union security clause** in the collective agreement to protect the interests of the labour union. This clause deals with the issue of membership requirements,

TABLE 12.3   Form of Contract Settlement Used in Collective Bargaining, 2015

Form of Contract Settlement Used	Percentage
Direct bargaining between union and employer	65.8
After conciliation	7.9
After mediation	15.8
After interest arbitration	10.4
Legislation	0.0

Source: Based on Government of Canada, Employment and Social Development in Canada. *"Overview of Collective Bargaining in Canada – 2015.* Chart 8."

the ability to participate in union duties at work, and, often, the payment of union dues. There are various forms of union security clauses:[28]

- A *closed shop* is the most restrictive form of union security. Only union members in good standing may be hired by the employer to perform bargaining unit work. This type of security clause is common in the construction industry.

- In a *union shop*, membership and dues payment are mandatory conditions of employment. Although individuals do not have to be union members at the time that they are hired, they are required to join the union on the day on which they commence work or on completion of probation.

- In a *modified union shop*, the individuals who were bargaining unit members at the time of certification or when the collective agreement was signed are not obliged to join the union, although they must pay dues, but all subsequently hired employees must do both.

- Under a *maintenance-of-membership arrangement*, individuals voluntarily joining the union must remain members during the term of the contract. Membership withdrawal is typically permitted during a designated period around the time of contract expiration. Dues payment is generally mandatory for all bargaining unit members.

- The *Rand formula* is the most popular union security arrangement. It does not require union membership, but it does require that all members of the bargaining unit pay union dues. It is a compromise arrangement that recognizes the fact that the union must represent all employees in the bargaining unit and should therefore be entitled to their financial support, but also provides the choice to join or not join the union.

- An *open shop* is a type of security arrangement whereby union membership is voluntary and non-members are not required to pay dues.

An Ethical Dilemma

Given the fact that some workers have religious or other objections to unions, is the Rand formula ethical?

No-Strike-or-Lockout Provision There must be a clause in every contract in Canada forbidding strikes or lockouts while the collective agreement is in effect. The intent is to guarantee some degree of stability in the employment relationship during the life of the collective agreement, which must be at least one year in length. In general, the duration of collective agreements in Canada is increasing. In 2015, the majority (86 percent) of collective agreements had a duration of more than three years. Over half (55.6 percent) of the settled agreements had a duration of four years or more. The proportion of those settled for two to four years fell from 46.7 percent in 2014 to 39.4 percent in 2015.[29]

Management Rights Clause The management rights clause clarifies the areas in which management may exercise its exclusive rights without agreement from the union, and the issues that are not subject to collective bargaining. It typically refers to the rights of management to operate the organization, subject to the terms of the collective agreement. Any rights not limited by the clause in the collective agreement are reserved to management.

Arbitration Clause All Canadian jurisdictions require that collective agreements contain a clause providing for the final and binding settlement, by arbitration, of all disputes arising during the term of a collective agreement. Such disputes may relate to the application, interpretation, or administration of the agreement, as well as alleged contraventions by either party.

12.2.5 Step 5: Contract Administration

After a collective agreement has been negotiated and signed, the contract administration process begins. Both union and management are required to abide by the contract provisions. It is also in day-to-day contract administration that the bulk of labour–management relations occurs. Regardless of the amount of time and effort put into the wording of the contract, it is almost inevitable that differences of opinion will arise regarding the application and interpretation of the agreement. Seniority and discipline issues tend to be the major sources of disagreement between union and management.

12.2.5.1 Seniority

seniority Length of service in the bargaining unit.

Unions typically prefer to have employee-related decisions determined by **seniority**, which refers to length of service in the bargaining unit. In many collective agreements, seniority is the governing factor in layoffs and recalls (the most senior employees are the last to be laid off and the first to be recalled) and a determining factor in transfers and promotions. In some collective agreements, seniority is also the determining factor in decisions pertaining to work assignments, shift preferences, allocation of days off, and vacation time.

Unions prefer the principle of seniority as an equitable and objective decision-making criterion, ensuring that there is no favouritism. Managers often prefer to place greater weight on ability or merit.

12.2.5.2 Discipline

Almost all collective agreements give the employer the right to make reasonable rules and regulations governing employees' behaviour and to take disciplinary action if the rules are broken. In every collective agreement, bargaining unit members are given the right to file a grievance if they feel that any disciplinary action taken was too harsh or without just cause.

By requiring proof of just cause for the disciplinary action imposed, most collective agreements restrict an employer's right to discipline employees. Since just cause is open to different interpretations, disciplinary action is a major source of grievances. Thus, disciplinary issues must be handled in accordance with the terms of the collective agreement and backed by carefully documented evidence. Even when disciplinary action is handled carefully, the union may argue that there were extenuating circumstances that should be taken into consideration. Supervisors have to strike a delicate balance between fairness and consistency.

When discipline cases end up at arbitration, two independent decisions are made. The first is whether the employee actually engaged in some form of misconduct. Then, if that question is

Grievance meetings provide an opportunity for progressively higher levels of authority in the company and union to resolve disagreements over the interpretation, application, and administration of the collective agreement.

© Pandora Studio/Shutterstock

answered in the affirmative, an assessment must be made of whether such misconduct warrants the particular discipline imposed, as well as whether such disciplinary action violated the collective agreement.

12.2.5.3 Grievance Resolution and Rights Arbitration

A **grievance** is a written allegation of a contract violation relating to a disagreement about its application or interpretation. When such alleged violations or disagreements arise, they are settled through the grievance procedure. A multistep grievance procedure, the last step of which is final and binding arbitration, is found in virtually all collective agreements. Such procedures have been very effective in resolving day-to-day problems arising during the life of the collective agreement.

The primary purpose of the grievance procedure is to ensure the application of the contract with a degree of justice for both parties. Secondary purposes include providing the opportunity for the interpretation of contract language, such as the meaning of "sufficient ability"; serving as a communications device through which managers can become aware of employee concerns and areas of dissatisfaction; and bringing to the attention of both union and management those areas of the contract requiring clarification or modification in subsequent negotiations.

Steps in the Grievance Procedure   The grievance procedure involves systematic deliberation of a complaint at progressively higher levels of authority in the company and union, and most grievance procedures provide for arbitration as a final step. Grievances are usually filed by individual bargaining unit members. If the issue under contention is one that may affect a number of union members, it may be filed as a *group grievance*. A *policy grievance* may be filed by the union when it wishes to challenge management's administration, interpretation, or application of the collective agreement. Management also has the right to use the grievance procedure to process a complaint about the union, although such use is rare. Although the number of steps and people involved at each grievance procedure vary, **Figure 12.4** illustrates a typical sequence.

As illustrated in **Figure 12.4**, the typical first step of the grievance procedure is the filing of a written complaint with the employee's immediate supervisor. If the problem is not resolved to the satisfaction of the employee at the first step, he or she may then take the problem to the next higher managerial level designated in the contract, and so on through all the steps available. Time limits are typically provided for resolution at each step. Failure to respond within the specified time limit may result in the grievance being automatically processed at the next step or being deemed to have been withdrawn or resolved. Ninety percent or more of all grievances are settled, abandoned, or withdrawn before arbitration.

Rights Arbitration   Grievances between an organization and the union that relate to the interpretation or administration of the collective agreement are known as **rights disputes**. If these cannot be resolved internally, they must be referred to arbitration for a final and binding decision. The process involved in resolving such issues is known as **rights arbitration.**

A written arbitration award is issued at the conclusion of most rights arbitration cases, indicating that the grievance has been upheld or overturned. In disciplinary cases, it is also possible for an arbitration award to substitute a penalty

grievance   A written allegation of a contract violation, filed by an individual bargaining unit member, the union, or management.

rights dispute   A disagreement between an organization and the union representing its employees regarding the interpretation or application of one or more clauses in the current collective agreement.

rights arbitration   The process involved in the settlement of a rights dispute.

FIGURE 12.4 A Typical Grievance Procedure

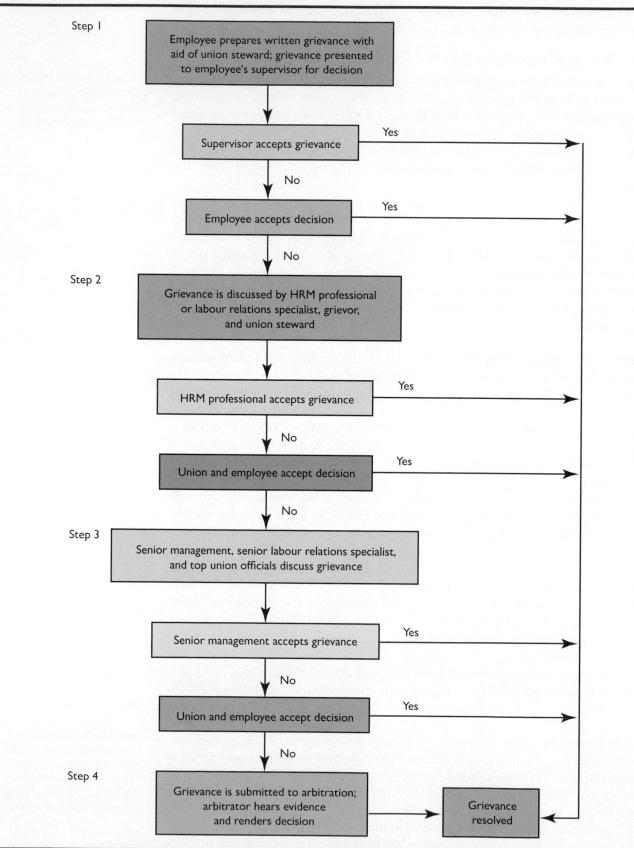

that is more or less severe than the one proposed by union or management. In cases where the disciplinary action is the termination of a unionized worker's employment, an arbitrator may order that person reinstated in his or her position and may also rule that back pay, benefits, and seniority be credited to the employee.

12.3 THE IMPACT OF UNIONIZATION ON HRM

Unionization results in a number of changes relating to HRM, all relating back to the requirements of the collective agreement. A union does have an impact on the way in which managers perform their HR responsibilities; when union leaders are treated as partners, they can provide a great deal of assistance with HR functions.

Once an organization is unionized, the HR department is typically expanded by the addition of an LR specialist or section. In a large firm with a number of bargaining units, human resources and labour relations may form two divisions within a broader department, often called "industrial relations" or "labour relations."

In a unionized setting, management has less freedom to make unilateral decisions. This change may lead managers and supervisors to feel that they have lost some of their authority, which can cause resentment, especially since they inevitably find that unionization results in an increase in their responsibilities. Supervisors are often required to produce more written records than ever before, since documentation is critical at grievance and arbitration hearings. They also benefit from training and development activities to improve their communication and conflict resolution skills.

All HR policies must be consistent with the terms of the collective agreement. Union representatives are often involved in the formulation of any policies that affect bargaining unit members—such as those pertaining to disciplinary rules and regulations—or are at least consulted as such policies are being drafted. Unionization also generally results in greater centralization of employee record keeping, which helps to ensure consistency and uniformity.

CHAPTER SUMMARY

1. Canada's labour laws provide a common set of rules for fair negotiations and ensure the protection of public interest by preventing the impact of labour disputes from inconveniencing the public. Labour relations boards across the country administer labour relations laws. These laws try to balance employees' rights to engage in union activity with employers' management rights.

2. There are five steps in the LR process: (1) employees' decision to seek collective representation, (2) the union organizing campaign, (3) official recognition of the union, (4) negotiation of a collective agreement, and (5) day-to-day contract administration.

3. The union organizing process involves five steps, which typically include (1) the employee/union contact, (2) an initial organizational meeting, (3) the formation of an in-house organizing committee, (4) an organizing campaign, and (5) the outcome—certification, recognition, or rejection.

4. There are three basic ways in which a union can obtain recognition as a bargaining unit for a group

of workers: voluntary recognition, the regular certification process, and a pre-hearing vote.

5. The three steps in the collective bargaining process are preparation for negotiations, face-to-face negotiations, and obtaining approval of union members and senior management for the proposed contract. Two possible additional steps are third-party assistance if talks break down, and a strike/lockout or interest arbitration if the parties arrive at a bargaining impasse.

6. Typical steps in a grievance procedure involve presenting a complaint or a written grievance to the worker's immediate supervisor, then to an HR/LR specialist, then to senior management, and finally to an arbitrator for final and binding rights arbitration.

MyLab Management

Visit MyLab Management to access a personalized Study Plan, Personal Inventory Assessments (PIA), and a collection of videos and assignments within MediaShare.

KEY TERMS

arbitration *(p. 300)*
authorization card *(p. 290)*
bargaining unit *(p. 283)*
bargaining zone *(p. 295)*
boycott *(p. 298)*
business unionism *(p. 284)*
caucus session *(p. 294)*
certification *(p. 292)*
collective bargaining *(p. 283)*
collective bargaining agreement (union contract or CBA) *(p. 283)*
conciliation *(p. 297)*
craft union *(p. 284)*
decertification *(p. 293)*
distributive bargaining *(p. 295)*
grievance *(p. 303)*
industrial union *(p. 284)*
integrative bargaining *(p. 296)*
interest arbitration *(p. 300)*
interest dispute *(p. 300)*
labour–management relations *(p. 283)*

labour union (union) *(p. 283)*
local *(p. 285)*
lockout *(p. 299)*
mediation *(p. 297)*
memorandum of settlement *(p. 297)*
mutual gains (interest-based) bargaining *(p. 296)*
picket *(p. 298)*
pre-hearing vote *(p. 292)*
ratification *(p. 297)*
representation vote *(p. 292)*
rights arbitration *(p. 303)*
rights dispute *(p. 303)*
seniority *(p. 302)*
social (reform) unionism *(p. 284)*
strike *(p. 298)*
strike vote *(p. 298)*
unfair labour practice *(p. 284)*
union local *(p. 285)*
union security clause *(p. 300)*
union steward *(p. 285)*
wildcat strike *(p. 299)*

REVIEW AND DISCUSSION QUESTIONS

1. Explain the difference between a craft union and industrial union.

2. Explain how either globalization or demographic challenges are influencing today's union movement in Canada.

3. Describe two key signs that managers should watch for as indications of a possible union organizing campaign.

4. Using **Figure 12.2** in the text, explain why three management or three union issues seen in this diagram may be important negotiating points in an upcoming round of collective bargaining.

5. Explain how two union security clauses help to "secure" the ongoing presence of a union in a company.

6. Explain two forms of third-party intervention known as conciliation and mediation. Then, differentiate when interest arbitration and rights arbitration procedures are used in the labour management process as seen in **Figure 12.1** in the text.

CRITICAL THINKING QUESTIONS

1. Are unions relevant in today's world? Suggest two reasons in favour or two reasons against their role in contemporary workplaces.

2. "If supervisors communicate effectively with employees, deal with their concerns, and treat them fairly, employees are far less likely to be interested in forming or joining a union." Do you agree or disagree with this statement? Why?

3. Two possible approaches to labour relations are union acceptance and union avoidance. Determine which of these strategies seems to have been adopted in a firm in which you have been employed or with which you are familiar. Provide evidence to back up your answer.

4. As the labour relations specialist, what steps would you take to prepare the firm and management team if you believed that a strike was a possible outcome of the upcoming negotiations?

5. As the human resources manager, how would you handle a situation in which a supervisor has knowingly violated the collective agreement when scheduling overtime?

EXPERIENTIAL EXERCISES

1. Assume that you are the vice-president of HR (human resources) at a relatively new non-union firm that has been experiencing rapid growth. In view of the management team's desire to remain non-union, you are asked to prepare a report to the other senior management team members making specific recommendations regarding human resources management strategies that the firm should adopt to help ensure that the employees will have no desire to unionize. Identify two key recommendations in your plan.

2. Look at two union websites, and locate information on union organizing campaigns. Which union does a better job in clearly explaining this important process to workers who may be worried about risks associated with unionizing their company?

3. Select a provincial government website dealing with labour relations. Locate an FAQ page on this site, and identify three things you learn to increase your knowledge of labour relations. Share your findings with another student or in a class presentation.

4. Using the Negotech search tool on the Government of Canada website (http://negotech.labour.gc.ca/cgi-bin/recherche-search/nego/index.aspx?GoCTemplateCulture=en-CA), compare and contrast the following provisions of two collective agreements: union recognition, management rights, union security, grievance procedures, and arbitration clauses. What do you think led to the differences? Which contract do you think in its entirety is better for employees? Why?

5. Read the following scenario and then, based on the role your team has been assigned by your instructor and the preparation time allowed, develop a negotiating strategy, including your bargaining zone, that you think will enable you to reach a fair and reasonable outcome for all parties. Before coming to the bargaining table, pick a chief negotiator for your team. Negotiate a settlement.

Scenario

ABC manufacturing is a large multinational machinery and heavy equipment manufacturer. The last two years have been very difficult, with more competition coming from offshore companies whose labour costs are much lower than those in Canada. The company is losing money and is considering whether to lay off workers in one or more of its Canadian plants, perhaps opening a new plant in Mexico or somewhere else in Central America. The union contract is up, and negotiations will begin soon.

London   Tokyo   New Delhi   New York   Berlin

CHAPTER

13

MANAGING HUMAN RESOURCES IN A GLOBAL BUSINESS

LEARNING OUTCOMES

AFTER STUDYING THIS CHAPTER, YOU SHOULD BE ABLE TO:

EXPLAIN how global movement of labour has an impact on HRM in Canada.

DESCRIBE the influence of intercountry differences on the workplace.

EXPLAIN how to improve global assignments through employee selection.

DISCUSS the major considerations in formulating a compensation plan for international employees.

DESCRIBE the main considerations in repatriating employees from abroad.

DISCUSS challenges immigrants to Canada face, and **IDENTIFY** the role of multiple stakeholders in ensuring successful integration of talent in Canada.

13.1 THE GLOBALIZATION OF BUSINESS AND STRATEGIC HR

The globalization of business is now the norm. European market unification is ongoing, and the economies of Brazil, Russia, India, and China are burgeoning (known as BRIC). Huge Canadian companies like Alcan and Molson have long had extensive overseas operations, but today the vast majority of companies are finding that their success depends on their ability to market and manage overseas operations. Thousands of Canadian corporations with international operations are now relocating employees overseas on a regular basis. These employees, called **expatriates**, are citizens of the country where the parent company is based who are sent to work in another country.

Workforce mobility programs focus on managing the recruitment, relocation, and retention of employees who complete work-related tasks and activities outside of the core or primary head office or region of the company. These programs are enabled by technological advancements, globalization, tight labour markets, and customer demands, and have a direct impact on company profits. Research by Runzheimer International shows that organizations can improve profitability by 1 to 4 percent simply by making workforce mobility management a strategic priority and by managing mobility programs in a more integrated way. This is because disjointed management of mobility programs often results in employee confusion, aggravation, frustration, and disengagement.[1]

Canada is also increasingly influenced by globalization within our borders. Roughly one in every five persons residing in Canada is foreign born. In addition, most of the labour force growth over the last decade has been attributable to immigration, and immigrants continue to be a critical component of Canada's workforce. According to Statistics Canada, an **immigrant** is a person residing in Canada who was born outside of Canada (excluding temporary foreign workers, Canadian citizens born outside of Canada, and those with student or working visas).[2]

Thus, the impact of globalization on the human resource management landscape of Canada includes both Canadians working internationally and international members (mainly immigrants) working in Canada. This chapter reviews both elements of global HRM.

expatriate   Employees who are citizens of the country where the parent company is based and are sent to work in another country.

workforce mobility   The focus on managing the recruitment, relocation, and retention of employees who complete work-related tasks and activities outside of the core or primary head office or region of the company.

immigrant   A person residing in Canada who was born outside of Canada (excluding temporary foreign workers, Canadian citizens born outside of Canada, and those with student or work visas).

13.2 HOW INTERCOUNTRY DIFFERENCES AFFECT HRM

A company that is operating units abroad requires a diverse and informed approach to HRM. Managing the HR functions in multinational companies is complicated enormously by the need to adapt HR policies and procedures to the differences among countries in which each subsidiary is based. The following are some intercountry differences that demand such adaptation: cultural, economic, legal and labour costs, and labour relations. However, this list is by no means exhaustive.[3] Political, physical, demographic, technological, and other significant factors also impact the success of labour force management globally.

13.2.1 Cultural Factors

Major studies have clarified some basic dimensions of international cultural differences. For example, societies differ in power distance—the extent to which the less powerful members of institutions accept and expect that power will be distributed unequally.[4] The institutionalization of such an inequality is higher in some countries (such as Mexico and Japan) than in others (such as Sweden and the Netherlands).

Societies also differ when it comes to individualism versus collectivism—the degree to which ties between individuals are normally distant rather than close. In more individualistic countries, such as Canada and the United States, individuals look out for themselves and their immediate families. However, in more collectivist countries, such as China and Pakistan, people's identity is strongly linked to their extended family group, and sometimes even to their work group. Interestingly, the one-child policy in China has resulted in a younger generation that is much more individualistic, known for job-hopping and lack of company loyalty.[5]

Such intercountry cultural differences have several HR implications. First, they suggest the need for adapting HR practices, such as training and pay plans, to local cultural norms. They also suggest that HR staff members in a foreign subsidiary should include host-country citizens. A high degree of sensitivity and empathy for the cultural and attitudinal demands of co-workers is always important in the selection of expatriate employees to staff overseas operations.

13.2.2 Economic Systems

In free enterprise systems, the need for efficiency tends to favour HR policies that value productivity, efficient workers, and staff cutting where market forces dictate. Moving along the scale towards more socialist systems, HR practices tend to shift towards preventing unemployment, even at the expense of sacrificing efficiency. For example, in communist Vietnam, workplace culture involves a post-lunch siesta for workers, and managers spend a lot time out of the office enhancing personal and social relationships.[6]

13.2.3 Legal Systems

Labour laws vary considerably around the world, on a variety of topics from discrimination to occupational health and safety. China continues to update its labour laws, which now include many similarities to those in the West. Discrimination is prohibited on most of the grounds commonly found in Western countries, with the exception of age. However, enforcement of labour laws is haphazard.[7]

When it comes to employee termination, the amount of notice with pay to be provided, continuation of benefits, notification of unions, and minimum length of service to qualify for severance payments vary significantly and in some cases can have a major impact on labour costs.[8]

Health and safety laws vary from non-existent in many African states to Britain's new Corporate

© Alabama Sunday/The Canadian Press

A worker walks past a broken electricity transformer in Lagos, Nigeria. Although the country has one of the world's great energy reserves, corruption and mismanagement have left Africa's oil giant chronically short of electricity.

TABLE 13.1   Unit Labour Cost (in $US) in the Manufacturing Industry by Country: Comparison with Canada, 2015

Country	Canada	United States	Japan	Taiwan	United Kingdom	Italy
Hourly compensation costs in manufacturing	30.94	37.71	23.60	9.51	31.44	31.48
Hourly direct pay costs	24.64	28.77	19.33	8.07	26.87	22.61
Hourly social insurance expenditures and labour cost	6.30	8.95	4.27	1.44	4.57	8.87
Hourly direct paid benefits cost	3.05	3.52	6.09	0	4.27	5.87
Output/Productivity (indexed)						
Output per hour	117.3	148.2	141.0	206.2	129.8	119.9
Output per employed person	115.1	138.7	141.3	199.9	133.6	112.0

Source: Based on International Comparisons of Manufacturing Productivity and Unit Labor Cost Trends, *U.S. Department of Labor, Bureau of Labor Statistics*, December 2012, www.bls.gov/ilc.

Manslaughter and Corporate Homicide Act, which tightens the rules around the liability of senior management in cases of health and safety offences.[9] On the other hand, since 2008, a number of cases of women sexually assaulted while on work trips to Dubai, UAE, have resulted in the victims being charged and fined for public intoxication and having sex outside of marriage, in some cases serving jail time for the "crime."[10] In other countries like China, worker health and safety laws exist but are largely unenforced.[11]

13.2.4   Labour Cost Factors

Differences in labour costs require clear HR interpretation and associated practices. As highlighted in **Table 13.1** below, wages are only part of the equation when considering international labour costs. A more informed review of labour productivity indicates that the cost of doing business abroad should not be viewed as a wage issue alone. In some countries, despite significantly lower wages, there may be higher unit labour costs. HR considerations such as benefits, training expenses, and turnover must be considered when evaluating labour costs.

This may also produce differences in HR practices. To maintain the competitive advantage of lower labour costs in China, the concept of investing in employees through training and development is seen as an unnecessary cost.[12] High labour costs can require a focus on efficiency and on HR practices (like pay for performance) aimed at improving employee performance.

13.2.5   Industrial Relations Factors

Industrial relations, and specifically the relationship among the workers, the union, and the employer, vary dramatically from country to country and have an enormous impact on HRM practices. In Germany, for instance, co-determination is the rule: that is, employees have the legal right to a voice in setting company policies. In this and several other countries, workers elect their own representatives to the supervisory board of the employer, and there is also a vice-president for labour at the top management level.[13] Conversely, in many other countries, the state interferes little in the relations between employers and unions. In China, for instance, company unions fall under the administration of the local Communist Party committee, which often shares long-term goals with the company; unions seldom play an effective role in labour disputes.[14]

International Labour Organization
www.ilo.org

13.2.6 Summary

These variations result in corresponding differences that make the job of managers much more complex and difficult than they are at home. International assignments thus run a relatively high risk of failing unless these differences are taken into account when selecting, training, and compensating international assignees.

13.3 GLOBAL RELOCATION

The number of expatriates working abroad is continuing to increase. One survey showed that the number of expatriates doubled between 2005 and 2008. The number of "global nomads" (employees who continuously move from country to country on multiple assignments) has also increased.[15] In addition, there has been a gradual increase in the number of female expatriates, who have long been underrepresented in the expatriate ranks.[16]

Family issues rank as the number one concern when it comes to employee relocations, and many employees are reluctant to accept expatriate assignments for this reason.[17] Employees who are considering an international assignment will also want to know how working and living in another country will affect their compensation, benefits, and taxes, and what kind of relocation assistance they will receive. From a practical perspective, some of the most pressing challenges are techniques used to recruit, select, train, compensate, and provide family support for employees who are based abroad, such as the following:

1. *Candidate identification, assessment, and selection.* In addition to the required technical and business skills, key traits to consider for global assignments include cultural sensitivity, interpersonal skills, and flexibility.

2. *Cost projections.* The average cost of sending an employee and his or her family on an overseas assignment is reportedly between three and five times the employee's pre-departure salary; as a result, quantifying total costs for a global assignment and deciding whether to use an expatriate or a local employee are essential in the budgeting process.

3. *Assignment letters.* The assignee's specific job requirements and remuneration, vacation, home leave, and repatriation arrangements will have to be documented and formally communicated in an assignment letter.[18]

4. *Compensation, benefits, and tax programs.* There are many ways in which to compensate employees who are transferred abroad, given the vast differences in living expenses around the world. Some common approaches to international pay include home-based pay plus a supplement and destination-based pay.

5. *Relocation assistance.* The assignee will probably have to be assisted with such matters as maintenance of a home and automobiles, shipment and storage of household goods, and so forth. The average cost of a permanent international relocation for a Canadian employee is between $50 000 and $100 000.[19]

6. *Family support.* Cultural orientation, educational assistance, and emergency provisions are just some of the matters to be addressed before the family is moved abroad.

The last two issues relate to the heightened focus on the spouse and family, who are vitally important in today's climate of relocation refusals. There may be concerns about, for instance, a mother-in-law's home care, the children's education, a spouse's career, and the difficulty of adjusting to new surroundings while juggling family responsibilities at the same time as focusing on the new job. Although the typical expatriate has traditionally been a male with a non-working spouse, dual-career families are now the norm. Major work–life balance relocation challenges thus include career assistance for the spouse and education and school selection assistance for the children.[20] Cross-cultural and language training programs will also probably be required. Policies for repatriating the expatriate when he or she returns home are another matter that must be addressed.

Sending employees abroad and managing HR globally are complicated by the nature of the countries into which many firms are expanding. Today's expatriates are heading to emerging economies like China and India.[21] Strategic HR involvement in the design and implementation of a global expansion strategy is required right from the start. Extensive research may be required with regard to local hiring practices, the availability of skilled labour, and employment regulations. Drivers of employee engagement vary across countries, but communication is the key to employee engagement.

DHL's Emerging Markets division was one of the first to realize this. The division serves 93 countries across 14 time zones. The countries are grouped by area to address similar needs, issues and expectations in a manageable way: Russia and the Commonwealth of Independent States; southeast Europe and North Africa; the Middle East, sub-Saharan Africa, and Turkey.

13.3.1 Why Expatriate Assignments Fail

Global mobility management is important because the cost of **expatriate assignment failure**—early return from an expatriate assignment—can reach $1 million.[22] There is some evidence that the rate of early departures, at least, is declining. This appears to be because more employers are taking steps to reduce expatriates' problems abroad. For example, they are selecting expatriates more carefully, helping spouses to get jobs abroad, and providing more ongoing support to the expatriate and his or her family.[23] As another example, some companies have formal "global buddy" programs. Here, local managers assist new expatriates with advice on things such as office politics, norms of behaviour, and where to receive emergency medical assistance.[24] Research in Canada identifies hassle factors associated with expat assignments by country, as highlighted in the Expert Opinion box.

Discovering why expatriate assignments fail is an important research task, and experts have made considerable progress. Personality is one factor. For example, in a study of 143 expatriate employees, extroverted, agreeable, and emotionally stable individuals were less likely to want to leave early.[25] Furthermore, the person's intentions are important. For example, people who want expatriate careers try harder to adjust to such a life.[26]

Non-work factors such as family pressures usually loom large in expatriate failures. In one study, managers identified the reasons for expats leaving assignments before expected (from highest to lowest impact): inability of spouse to adjust, manager's inability to adjust, other family problems, manager's personal or emotional immaturity, and inability to cope with larger overseas

expatriate assignment failure   Early return of an expatriate from a global assignment.

Academic Viewpoint
EXPERT OPINION

Focus: International strategic management, specifically joint ventures and alliances

I. Success or failure of managers in foreign investment locations is critical to success or failure of the project. Based on your research, what influences a manager's willingness to work in foreign locations?

A lot of analysis in business schools tends to take a rational, analytical perspective based on sound economic logic. Yet some of it forgets the role of the manager. The manager responsible for a foreign location needs to feel safe (personal safety, quality of water/food, transportation, etc.). This experience will be beneficial to his or her career in the organization.

One of our studies found that the longer it takes to travel between the head office and the subsidiary, the less likely it is that the subsidiary will be profitable. Executives found that the time added in transit resulted in fatigue, which led to poorer oversight of people, and reduced opportunities to develop relationships. Subsidiaries that were more than 16 hours in travel time from headquarters experienced 23 percent higher turnover than others.

Dr. Paul Beamish

Identification:
Dr. Paul Beamish (PhD)
Canada Research Chair in International Management, Executive Director of Ivey Publishing

Affiliation:
Ivey Business School, Western University

2. What is the "hassle" factor, and how can it be used by organizations?

The hassle factor is an 11-factor composite measure of travel inconveniences by country. Travel inconveniences have a negative effect on the relationship between foreign investment potential of the company and realized investment.

The hassle factor brings the manager back into the equation when organizing international expansion. Research found that difficulty travelling to and residing in certain places impacts

managerial preferences of and willingness to partake in expatriate assignments. We have currently released the hassle factor online as an interactive world map (www.hasslefactor.org), enabling organizations and individuals to explore countries of interest. This information will be updated annually.

3. As the economy continues to globalize, do you predict convergence or divergence of hassle factor scores over time?

As long as there are huge disparities in economic development, the hassle factors will persist, so I don't imagine that they will converge anytime soon. In part, this is a story of economic development; things are improving around the world, however, the change is slow and sporadic.

As a complement of this project, I established the "39 Country Initiative," in which universities in the world's 39 poorest countries are able to use Ivey's case collection at no cost. In addition, we collect and ship container loads of teaching material (mostly textbooks) to these locales. This is an example of how we can give back and help equalize access to education, which is a critical component of global progress. It helps business students in the poorest countries deal with one of the ultimate hassles: poverty.

Source: Reprinted by permission from Dr. Paul Beamish.

responsibility.[27] Managers of European firms emphasized only the inability of the manager's spouse to adjust as an explanation for the expatriate's failed assignment. Other studies similarly emphasize the effects of a dissatisfied spouse on the international assignment.[28]

Canadian companies have reported low failure rates for expatriates relative to other countries, particularly the United States, which has a failure rate of 40 to 50 percent.[29] Canadians may be more culturally adaptable than their American counterparts because they are already familiar with bilingualism and multiculturalism. In fact, Canadian executives are in demand across the globe. The country's diverse ethnic makeup has produced a generation of business leaders who mix easily with different cultures.[30]

Many employers have tried to eliminate issues that lead to expatriate assignment failures by shortening the assignment length and having the family remain at home. Expatriate assignments have traditionally been for terms of three to five years, but recently there has been a trend towards short-term global assignments instead of permanent relocations.[31] A survey by KPMG (a global consulting firm) found that short-term assignments of less than 12 months are almost as prevalent as long-term assignments (more than five years).[32]

Short-term assignment alternatives include frequent extended business trips with corresponding time spent back at home, short-term assignments of between three months and a year with frequent home leave (once every 12 weeks on average), and the dual household arrangement, where the employee's family remains at home and the employee sets up a small household for himself or herself in the foreign country. Often, firms neglect to prepare employees for short-term assignments in the same way they do for the long-term variety, which leads to problems such as lack of cross-cultural awareness, extreme loneliness, and feeling undervalued on returning to the home office.[33] Companies that provide strong support to expatriate employees stand a higher chance of success.[34]

13.4 CONSIDERATIONS IN GLOBAL HRM

Careful screening is just the first step in ensuring that a foreign assignee is successful. The employee may then require special training and, additionally, international HR policies must be formulated for compensating the firm's overseas managers and maintaining healthy labour relations.

13.4.1 Global Staffing Policy

There are three international staffing policies. An **ethnocentric staffing policy** is based on the attitude that home-country managers are superior to those in the host country, and all key management positions are filled by parent-country nationals. At Royal Dutch Shell, for instance, virtually all financial controllers around the world are Dutch nationals. Reasons given for ethnocentric staffing policies include lack of qualified host-country senior management talent, a desire to maintain a unified corporate culture and tighter control, and the desire to transfer the parent firm's core competencies (for example, a specialized manufacturing skill) to a foreign subsidiary more expeditiously.

A **polycentric staffing policy** is based on the belief that only host-country managers can understand the culture and behaviour of the host-country market, and therefore foreign subsidiaries should be staffed with host-country nationals and the home office headquarters with parent-country nationals. This may reduce the lack of local cultural understanding that expatriate managers may exhibit. It will also almost undoubtedly be less expensive. One expert estimates that an expatriate executive can cost a firm up to three times as much as a domestic executive because of transfer expenses and other expenses such as schooling for children, annual home leave, and the need to pay income taxes in two countries.

Canadian Employee Relocation Council
www.cerc.ca

The Expatriate Group
www.expat.ca

ethnocentric staffing policy
Policies that align with the attitude that home-country managers are superior to those in the host country.

polycentric staffing policy
Policies that align with the belief that only host-country managers can understand the culture and behaviour of the host-country market.

geocentric staffing policy   Policies that align with the belief that the best manager for any specific position anywhere on the globe may be found in any of the countries in which the firm operates.

A **geocentric staffing policy** assumes that management candidates must be searched for globally, on the assumption that the best manager for any specific position anywhere on the globe may be found in any of the countries in which the firm operates. This allows the global firm to use its human resources more efficiently by transferring the best person to the open job, wherever he or she may be. It can also help to build a stronger and more consistent culture and set of values among the entire global management team. Team members here are continually interacting and networking with one another as they move from assignment to assignment around the globe and participate in global development activities.

13.4.2 Selection for Global Assignments

International managers can be expatriates, locals (citizens of the countries where they are working), or third-country nationals (citizens of a country other than the parent or the host country), such as a British executive working in a Tokyo subsidiary of a Canadian multinational bank.[35] Expatriates represent a minority of managers; most managerial positions are filled by locals rather than expatriates in both headquarters and foreign subsidiary operations.

An Ethical Dilemma

How ethical is it for a multinational organization to recruit expatriate staff for managerial positions when similarly qualified staff can be identified in the host country?

There are several reasons to rely on local, host-country management talent for filling the foreign subsidiary's management ranks. Many people simply prefer not to work in a foreign country, and in general the cost of using expatriates is far greater than the cost of using local management talent. The multinational corporation may be viewed locally as a "better citizen" if it uses local management talent, and indeed some governments actually press for the localization of management. There may also be a fear that expatriates, knowing that they are posted to the foreign subsidiary for only a few years, may overemphasize short-term projects rather than focus on perhaps more necessary long-term tasks.

There are also several reasons for using expatriates—either parent-country or third-country nationals—for staffing subsidiaries. The major reason is technical competence. In other words, employers may be unable to find local candidates with the required technical qualifications. Multinationals also increasingly view a successful stint abroad as a required step in leadership development. Control is another important reason. Multinationals sometimes assign expatriates from their headquarters staff abroad on the assumption that these managers are more steeped in the firm's policies and culture and more likely to unquestioningly implement headquarters' instructions.

13.4.3 Orienting and Training Employees for Global Assignments

Cross-cultural training is very important for creating realistic expectations, which in turn are strongly related to cross-cultural adjustment.[36] A four-step approach to cross-cultural training is often used, as discussed in **Figure 13.1**.

© Jupiterimages/Stockbyte/Getty Images

Orientation and training for international assignments can help employees (and their families) to avoid "culture shock" and better adjust to their new surroundings.

FIGURE 13.1   Levels of Cross-Cultural Training

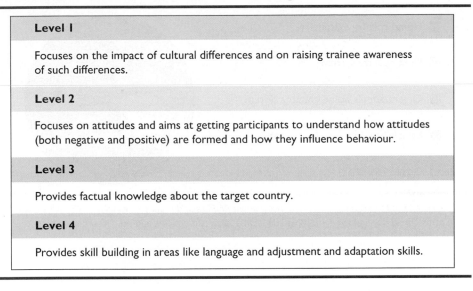

Level I
Focuses on the impact of cultural differences and on raising trainee awareness of such differences.
Level 2
Focuses on attitudes and aims at getting participants to understand how attitudes (both negative and positive) are formed and how they influence behaviour.
Level 3
Provides factual knowledge about the target country.
Level 4
Provides skill building in areas like language and adjustment and adaptation skills.

In addition to cross-cultural training, leadership development opportunities are often an important learning component of expatriate assignment.[37] At IBM, for instance, such development includes the use of a series of rotating assignments that permits overseas managers to grow professionally. At the same time, IBM and other major firms have established management development centres around the world where executives can go to hone their skills. Beyond that, classroom programs (such as those at the London Business School, or at INSEAD in France) provide overseas executives with the opportunities that they need to hone their functional and leadership skills.

13.4.4 International Compensation

International compensation management can present some unexpected and complicated problems. Compensation programs throughout a global firm must be both integrated (to maximize overall effectiveness) and differentiated (to effectively motivate and meet the specific needs of the various categories and locations of employees). On the one hand, there is logic in maintaining company-wide pay scales and policies so that, for instance, divisional marketing directors throughout the world are all paid within the same narrow range. This reduces the risk of perceived inequities and dramatically simplifies the job of keeping track of disparate country-by-country wage rates. However, most multinational companies have recognized the need to make executive pay decisions on a global level, and executive pay plans are gradually becoming more uniform.[38] As shown in **Figure 13.2**, most global assignment compensation (61 percent) is aligned to pay expatriates according to compensation levels in their own country.

However, the practice of not adapting pay scales to local markets can present an HR manager with more problems than it solves. The fact is that living in Tokyo is many times more expensive than living in Calgary, while the cost of living in Bangalore, India, is considerably lower than living in Toronto.[39] If these cost-of-living differences are not considered, it may be almost impossible to get managers to accept assignments in high-cost locations. One way to handle the

FIGURE 13.2   Approaches to Compensation for Global Assignments, 2016

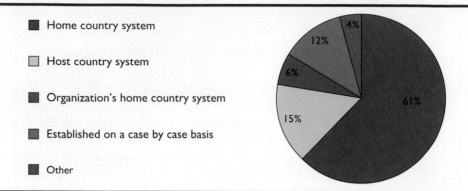

- ■ Home country system
- ☐ Host country system
- ■ Organization's home country system
- ■ Established on a case by case basis
- ■ Other

Source: Data from the *Survey 2016 Global Assignment Policies and Practices*, KPMG, p. 25, https://assets.kpmg.com/content/dam/kpmg/xx/pdf/2016/10/global-assignment-policies-and-practices-survey-2016.pdf.

problem is to pay a similar base salary companywide and then add on various allowances according to individual market conditions.[40]

Compensation professionals also face the challenge of designing programs that motivate both local employees in each country and internationally mobile employees of all nationalities. Some multinational companies deal with this problem by conducting their own annual compensation surveys. Others use a global career progression framework that includes the flexibility to accommodate local practices and still maintain organization-wide consistency.[41]

13.4.5 The Balance Sheet Approach

balance sheet approach A method of formulating expatriate pay based on equalizing purchasing power across countries.

The most common approach to formulating expatriate pay is to equalize purchasing power across countries, a technique known as the **balance sheet approach.** The basic idea is that each expatriate should enjoy the same standard of living that he or she would have had at home. The employer estimates what the cost of major expenses such as housing would be in the expatriate's home country and the equivalent cost of each in the host country. Any differences—such as higher housing expenses—are then paid by the employer.

An Ethical Dilemma

Is it ethical to pay expatriates using the balance sheet approach when local staff at the same level receive far less compensation?

In practice, this involves building the expatriate's total compensation around a limited number of considerations. For example, base salary will normally be in the same range as the manager's home-country salary. In addition, however, there might be a mobility premium. This is paid as a percentage of the executive's base salary, in part to compensate the manager for the cultural and physical adjustments that he or she will have to make.[42] There may also be several allowances, including a housing allowance and an education allowance for the expatriate's children.

13.4.6 Variable Pay

As organizations around the world have shifted their focus to individual performance differentiation, there has been a rise in the prevalence of individual performance rewards, although the widespread use of team awards remains in a few Asian countries.[43] Across the globe, over 85 percent of companies offer at least one type of broad-based variable pay program. Target bonuses for management and professional employees, as a percentage of base salary, have become quite similar globally. Although broad-based variable pay was a lot less common in the past, it has now gone global and is an integral part of the compensation landscape for management and professional employees in every region.

13.4.7 International EAPs

Employee assistance programs (EAPs) are also going global, helping expatriates take care of their mental health, which is often affected by the stressful relocation process. A worldwide survey found that more than half of expatriates are weighed down by added stress caused by longer hours, extended workdays/workweeks, and cultural differences, among other factors. Two-thirds feel the strain of managing the demands of work and the well-being of family.[44] The proactive approach is to contact employees before departure to explain the program's services; then, about three months after arrival, families are contacted again. By this time, they have usually run into some challenges from culture shock and will welcome some assistance. The expatriates and their families have then established a connection with the EAP to use for ongoing support.[45]

Problems such as homesickness, boredom, withdrawal, depression, compulsive eating and drinking, irritability, marital stress, family tension, and conflict are all common reactions to culture shock. Employees on short-term assignment without their families can experience extreme loneliness. Treatment for psychiatric illnesses varies widely around the world, as do the conditions in government-run mental health institutions, and consultation with an EAP professional who has extensive cross-cultural training may be critical in ensuring that appropriate medical treatment is obtained.[46]

13.4.8 Performance Appraisal of Global Managers

Several issues complicate the task of appraising an expatriate's performance. The question of who actually appraises the expatriate is crucial. Local management must have some input, but the appraisal may then be distorted by cultural differences. Thus, an expatriate manager in India may be evaluated somewhat negatively by his host-country bosses, who find the use of participative decision making or other behaviours to be inappropriate in their culture. However, home-office managers may be so geographically distanced from the expatriate that they cannot provide valid appraisals because they are not fully aware of the situation that the manager actually faces. Therefore, problems can arise if the expatriate is measured by objective criteria, such as profits and market share, but local events, such as political instability, undermine the manager's performance while remaining "invisible" to home-office staff.

13.4.9 Repatriation

Repatriation is the process of moving the expatriate and his or her family back home from the foreign assignment. Sometimes, repatriation can be more difficult than going abroad.[47] Up to half of expatriates leave their organization following a repatriation, usually because they are not able to use their newly developed skills and capabilities in their roles on their return.[48] Their expert knowledge and international expertise often ends up with the competition.

repatriation   The process of moving the expatriate and his or her family back home from the foreign assignment.

Several repatriation problems are very common. One is the expatriate's fear that he or she has been "out of sight, out of mind" during an extended foreign stay and has thus lost touch with the parent firm's culture, top executives, and those responsible for the firm's management selection processes. Indeed, such fears may be well founded: Many repatriates are temporarily placed in mediocre or makeshift jobs. Ironically, the company often undervalues the cross-cultural skills acquired abroad, and the international posting becomes a career-limiting, rather than career-enhancing, move. Many are shocked to find that the executive trappings of the overseas job (private schools for the children and a company car and driver, for instance) are lost on return, and that the executive is again just a small fish in a big pond. Perhaps more exasperating is the discovery that some of the expatriate's former colleagues have been more rapidly promoted while he or she was overseas. Even the expatriate's family may undergo a sort of reverse culture shock, as the spouse and children face the often daunting task of picking up old friendships and habits or starting schools anew on their return.[49]

Progressive multinationals anticipate and avoid these problems by taking a number of sensible steps:[50]

1. *Writing repatriation agreements.* Many firms use repatriation agreements, which guarantee in writing that the international assignee will not be kept abroad longer than some period (such as five years) and that on return he or she will be given a mutually acceptable job.

2. *Assigning a sponsor.* The employee should be assigned a sponsor/mentor (such as a senior manager at the parent firm's home office). This person's role is to look after the expatriate while he or she is away. This includes keeping the person apprised of significant company events and changes back home, monitoring his or her career interests, and nominating the person to be considered for key openings when the expatriate is ready to come home.

3. *Providing career counselling.* Provide formal career counselling sessions to ensure that the repatriate's job assignments on return will meet his or her needs.

4. *Keeping communication open.* Keep the expatriate "plugged in" to home-office business affairs through management meetings around the world and frequent home leave combined with meetings at headquarters. Only 18 percent of companies in a 2006 Watson Wyatt global survey had a global communication plan in place to keep employees around the world informed about what the company was doing.

5. *Offering financial support.* Many firms pay real estate and legal fees and help the expatriate to rent or in some other way to maintain his or her residence so that the repatriate and his or her family can actually return "home."

6. *Developing reorientation programs.* Provide the repatriate and his or her family with a reorientation program to facilitate the adjustment back into the home culture.

7. *Building in return trips.* Expatriates can benefit from more frequent trips to the home country to ensure that they keep in touch with home-country norms and changes during their international assignment.

13.5 MANAGING GLOBAL WORKERS WITHIN CANADA

The successful integration of immigrants and foreign workers into the Canadian labour market is increasingly becoming of interest to organizations, Canadian public policy makers, and HR professionals alike. Underemployment of immigrants and foreign workers is especially critical today, given the aging workforce, the rate of immigration to Canada (almost one in every five persons residing in Canada is foreign born), and our dependence on immigrants to maintain our labour force size. Additionally, the labour and talent scarcity further fuels the need for successful integration and utilization of immigrants in the Canadian labour force.

Canadian employers note that hiring immigrants increases the employer's language skills and innovation, and enhances the company's reputation.[51] Research has found that diverse groups make higher-quality decisions, generate more creative ideas, use more creative problem-solving techniques, and have the potential for higher rates of productivity.[52] A survey of human resources professionals found that 91 percent of respondents felt that diversity initiatives help the organization maintain a competitive advantage, largely through enhanced corporate culture, employee morale, retention, and recruitment.[53] The Conference Board of Canada suggests that the effective integration and utilization of immigrants in the workforce requires a commitment to recruiting and attracting talent, development and retention, and identifying that efforts to create an inclusive organization require multiple HR and management interventions. The summary below in **Figure 13.3** suggests that the approach to managing immigrants in the Canadian workforce should be strategic, proactive, and planned.

Immigrant workers in Canada can face unique challenges that hinder full employment or integration into the workforce. In 1980, recent male immigrants to Canada who were employed earned, on average, 85 cents for every dollar that Canadian-born males earned; by 2005, the ratio had dropped to 63 cents for every dollar.[54] In 2016, unemployment rates among new immigrants (those who have been in Canada for less than five years) were 10.2 percent for those aged 25 to 54, while the unemployment rate among those born in Canada was 5.5 percent.[55]

The unemployment level and challenges of employment represent only part of the obstacles of immigrant and foreign workforce integration in Canada. Another significant challenge is the underutilization of immigrants' skills because they are being hired for positions that they are overqualified to perform. Statistics Canada has reported that the percentage of long-term immigrants who had successfully completed a university degree and who found jobs with only low educational requirements (such as clerks, truck drivers, salespeople, cashiers, and taxi drivers) has risen steadily over the last two decades. The resulting skills mismatch puts pressure on HR departments to find the right talent needed for a position on the organization to provide more extensive training and development programs, and on society as a whole because of the lost value of experience and knowledge acquired by its members.[56]

There have been some changes to the temporary foreign workers program aimed at balancing demands for international workers with recruitment and

FIGURE 13.3   Immigrant Engagement and Employment Continuum

Stage 1 Immigrant-Friendly Attraction and Recruitment Practices	Stage 2 Immigrant-Friendly Integration and Development Practices	Stage 3 Immigrant-Friendly Retention Practices
• Expand recruitment methods beyond standard practices • Implement culturally sensitive screening practices • Provide information and pre-employment training to immigrant/international job seekers through community organizations • Offer bridging and mentoring programs to immigrant/international job seekers • Help obtain recognition of foreign qualifications through credential service agencies or in-house competency tests • Provide assistance for immigrants/international job seekers to acquire credential papers/documents	• Offer workplace mentoring programs • Provide professional language and communication skills training programs • Support and encourage the achievement of their professional goals and objectives	• Promote cultural awareness • Support affinity groups • Provide cultural diversity training • Engage executive support for diversity

Source: The Conference Board of Canada, "*Immigrant-Friendly Businesses: Effective Practices for Attracting, Integrating, and Retaining Immigrants in Canadian Workplaces,*" November 2009, p. 15. Reprinted with permission

training efforts focusing on Canadian workers. In June 2014, the Minister of Employment and Social Development and the Minister of Citizenship and Immigration announced a comprehensive overhaul of the Temporary Foreign Worker Program (TFWP) and the creation of an International Mobility Program (IMP). Employers who want to bring in workers under the TFWP will need to request employees through an approval process, using a new Labour Market Impact Assessment (LMIA). The LMIA fee also increased from $275 for every foreign worker to $1 000.

The main catalyst for the reforms was to ensure Canadians are given priority for available jobs. The reforms will limit access to the TFWP, tighten the labour market assessment needed for the program (LMA), and enforce stronger penalties for employers who violate the rules. In addition, Canadian businesses will have to make more effort to recruit and train Canadians for vacancies.[57]

A survey by Statistics Canada found that 70 percent of newcomers said they had encountered problems or barriers in the job-finding process. The results can be broadly categorized into a lack of Canadian work experience, poor transferability of foreign credentials, and a lack of literacy skills in either of the official languages (English or French).

13.5.1 Barrier 1: Lack of Canadian Experience

Work experience helps individuals develop skills in communication, work patterns, and teamwork that are recognized and valued by organizations. It can help people identify career paths and the requirements of desired positions. It can shape perceptions of the world of work and set expectations of the employer. It can also provide an opportunity for individuals to network with others, which can assist with future job search efforts.

Understandably, most employers look for familiar references when assessing candidates, such as experiences and companies that they recognize on résumés or during interviews. Often immigrants feel like they are in a Catch-22 situation; they cannot secure a job without the proven Canadian experience, and they cannot acquire the Canadian experience without securing a job.

This situation is deepened because of a lack of recognition for foreign work, which is consistently discounted in the Canadian labour market.[58] As immigrants enter the Canadian workforce, research on earnings shows low, or even zero, returns (monetary recognition) for their foreign work experience.[59] When only their Canadian work experience is taken into account, immigrants' earnings are similar to those of the Canadian-born with the same years of Canadian experience, regardless of how many years of international experience the immigrant had prior to joining the Canadian workforce. These results suggest a significant inability to transfer and recognize skills and experiences immigrants acquired in their country of origin to the Canadian labour market, representing lost value to the immigrant.

Almost two in every three new immigrants fail to find employment in the same field in which they were employed in their native country. For example, before arriving in Canada, only 10.2 percent of men and 12.1 percent of women were employed in sales and service-related occupations. Six months after arrival in Canada, 24.9 percent of men and 37.3 percent of women were employed in these occupations.[60]

Options to help overcome challenges associated with lack of Canadian experience and devaluation of foreign experience include the following:[61]

1. Educate employers, recruiters, and hiring managers to develop the necessary ability to recognize and effectively interpret skills from different countries.

2. Provide clear statements in job descriptions as to the extent and nature of work experience required to complete job requirements. Offer candidates an opportunity to demonstrate the skills in a simulated or field setting.

3. Use apprenticeships effectively. Some trades mandate apprenticeships (for example, in Ontario, there are 20 trades with a mandatory apprenticeship component), whereas others are voluntary. This creates an option whereby apprenticeships can be used to develop and evaluate the skills of foreign-trained workers. Alternatively, some provinces (like Alberta) allow immigrants with significant foreign experience in a trade the opportunity to write an exam to receive certification.

4. Partner with industry-based assessment centres (for example, Workplace Integration of Skilled Newcomers in the Trades, Internationally Educated Engineer Qualification Bridging Program) to develop bridging programs to integrate foreign experience of immigrants.

© kaloul1927/fotolia

Apprenticeships can be used to develop and evaluate the skills of foreign-trained workers.

At the same time, immigrants to Canada have a responsibility to learn about Canadian workplace norms and customs, and to present their experiences or qualifications to Canadian recruiters in a clear and effective way. There must also be an awareness of Canadian laws and regulations.

13.5.2 Barrier 2: Poor Transferability of Foreign Education or Training

While finding a job can be difficult for many, employment prospects for new immigrants are often diminished due to poor recognition of foreign qualifications. Licensing bodies of certain trades and professions may not accept foreign-obtained certification, and employers have difficulty assessing foreign education in a meaningful way.[62] In 2008, over 42 percent of new immigrants were working in occupations that required lower levels of education than those they had attained. Of Canadian-born workers, the corresponding rate was 28 percent.[63]

The result is the underutilization of foreign workers in Canada. A study of over 7 700 new immigrants found that within four years after landing in Canada, only 28 percent with foreign credentials had received recognition for these credentials (meaning that the employer/institution recognizes the credential as being legitimate within determined standards).[64] Women and older immigrants are less likely to have foreign education recognized in Canada. Also, immigrants from South Korea, the Philippines, and France have the lowest rates of full foreign credentials recognition, while immigrants from the United States and United Kingdom have the highest rates.[65]

Canadian literature on the assessment of foreign training, using prior learning assessment and recognition (PLAR) methods, is extensive. PLAR is a system meant to aide in the recognition of the learning adults acquire outside of formal Canadian education; it attempts to standardize recognition of skills and abilities in a meaningful way. Many colleges and universities in Canada rely on PLAR to evaluate foreign credentials.

13.5.3 Barrier 3: Lack of Literacy Skills

Literacy is the ability to identify, understand, interpret, create, communicate, compute, and use printed and written materials associated with varying contexts. In a global economy, it is critical that employees have the ability to express themselves in the official language(s) of the country in which they are employed. The education levels of new immigrants have been steadily rising over recent years due to changes in immigration criteria.

Literacy and adult education falls mainly under the jurisdiction of provincial and territorial governments. The federal government plays a role in developing policy and delivering some funding for literacy initiatives. In May 2007, Citizenship and Immigration Canada established the Foreign Credential Referral Office (FCRO) to guide, monitor, and facilitate the assessment of foreign credentials. In October 2010, the FCRO took over responsibility from Department of Human Resources and Skill Development Canada (HRSDC, now known as Employment and Social Development Canada [ESDC]) for the Canadian Immigrant Integration Program. That year, the FCRO aided in answering online and over-the-phone inquiries from over 25 000 immigrants.[66]

Six months after arrival in Canada, only three in every five immigrants report that they are able to speak English well or very well, and only one in every ten immigrants report the same about French.[67] Language training increases an immigrant's likelihood of gaining employment or advancing within an organization. Roughly 45 percent of new immigrants partake in language training in English once employed in Canada, and 10 percent are trained in French.[68]

Language ability has also been shown to improve labour-market outcomes among educated immigrants.[69] The earnings differential between immigrants and Canadian-born individuals would narrow by about 20 percent if immigrants had the same average literacy scores as the native born. Consequently, this would eliminate more than half of the immigrant earnings disadvantage among university educated workers alone. The variance and, in some cases, lack of literacy skills in Canada's official languages is viewed as a significant barrier to the successful integration of immigrants in the labour market.

Thus, while literacy deficiencies among immigrants have an important impact on earnings differentials, the impact is decidedly smaller than the effect of low returns associated with foreign experience among the highly educated. Controlling for literacy does not affect the relative patterns of returns to foreign- and Canadian-acquired experience. Immigration is vital to Canada's population growth and economic prosperity. Yet, while demand for their skills grows, many highly competent newcomers to Canada remain underemployed.

CHAPTER SUMMARY

1. Globalization affects human resources management in two significant ways. First, workforce mobility forces companies to focus on international recruitment, retention, and relations strategies to take advantage of the skills that workers who are not born in Canada can offer. Second, immigrants into Canada present a significant source of labour force growth, and successful integration of these immigrants can yield significant benefits for the organization.

2. Intercountry differences include cultural factors (such as power distance, individualism versus collectivism, and gender egalitarianism), economic systems, labour cost factors, and industrial relations factors. These affect HRM in a variety of ways.

3. Global relocation strategies must consider effective selection, training, compensation, labour relations, and performance appraisals for expatriates and global managers. For example, in reference to compensation, the balance sheet approach allows the employer to estimate expenses for income taxes, housing, and goods and services, and to pay supplements to the expatriate in such a way as to maintain the same standard of living that he or she would have had at home.

4. Repatriation problems are common but can be minimized. They include the often well-founded fear that the expatriate is "out of sight, out of mind" and difficulties in re-assimilating the expatriate's family back into home-country culture. Suggestions for avoiding these problems include using repatriation agreements, assigning a home-country sponsor/mentor, offering career counselling, keeping the expatriate plugged in to home-office business, building in return trips, providing financial support to maintain the expatriate's home-country residence, and offering reorientation programs to the expatriate and his or her family.

5. Newcomers to Canada face a variety of challenges associated with securing full employment. Specifically, a lack of Canadian work experience, poor transferability of foreign credentials, and a lack of language skills in English or French are seen as the greatest barriers to employment for newcomers, according to both immigrants and employers.

6. These barriers result in significant underemployment of immigrants, or a skills mismatch, which further exasperates the skills shortage that employers experience.

7. Newcomers to Canada and employers can benefit from modifying recruitment and selection procedures to offer opportunities to assess the skills of immigrants as part of the selection process, using apprenticeships effectively, partnering with assessment centres to recognize skills, and educating employers, recruiters, and managers about how to recognize and interpret skills from another country.

MyLab Management

Visit MyLab Management to access a personalized Study Plan, Personal Inventory Assessments (PIA), and a collection of videos and assignments within MediaShare.

KEY TERMS

balance sheet approach *(p. 318)*
ethnocentric staffing policy *(p. 315)*
expatriate *(p. 309)*
expatriate assignment failure *(p. 313)*
geocentric staffing policy *(p. 316)*

immigrant *(p. 309)*
polycentric staffing policy *(p. 315)*
repatriation *(p. 319)*
workforce mobility *(p. 309)*

REVIEW AND DISCUSSION QUESTIONS

1. Specifically, what are some of the uniquely international activities that an international HR manager typically engages in?

2. Explain three broad global HR challenges.

3. Discuss the reasons why expatriate assignments fail and what is being done to reduce the failure rate.

4. How does compensation of an expatriate differ from that of a home-office manager? How can some of the unique problems of compensating the expatriate be avoided?

5. Describe five actions that can be taken by expatriate managers in other countries to increase their personal safety.

6. What are the three biggest obstacles to securing full employment of immigrants and foreign workers in Canada? How can these be managed?

7. Why is the issue of underemployment of foreign-trained persons important to Canadian employers?

CRITICAL THINKING QUESTIONS

1. You are president of a small business. In what ways do you expect that being involved in international business activity will affect human resources management (HRM) in your business?

2. A firm is about to send its first employees overseas to staff a new subsidiary. The president asks why such assignments fail and what can be done to avoid such failures. Write a memo in response to these questions.

3. What can an organization do to ensure that the skills acquired on an international assignment are used when the employee returns to his or her home country?

4. How would you assess the credentials of foreign-trained persons? What agencies are available for you to contact?

5. What obstacles to successful integration of global talent do you think exist in your company? What solutions can you recommend to overcome these obstacles?

EXPERIENTIAL EXERCISES

1. Choose three traits that are useful for selecting international assignees, and create a straightforward test (not one that uses pencil and paper) to screen candidates for these traits.

2. Describe the most common approach to formulating expatriate pay. Use a library source to determine the relative cost of living in five countries this year, and explain the implications of such differences for drafting a pay plan for managers being sent to each country.

3. Either in pairs or groups of four or five, develop an outline for an initial four-hour cross-cultural training program. What training resources, tools, and processes might you use? Be prepared to give a rationale for your program.

4. Review some of the employers in your local area. What programs or approaches do they have to help recruit and evaluate international talent? If required, contact the company representatives to develop a stronger understanding of the company practices towards ensuring that immigrants are given equal opportunities for employment.

Notes

Chapter 1

1. O. Parker, *The Strategic Value of People: Human Resource Trends and Metrics* (Ottawa, ON: The Conference Board of Canada, 2006); E. Andrew, "Most Canadian Companies Are Still Not Treating Human Resources as a Serious Strategic Issue," *Workspan Focus Canada* (February 2006), pp. 14–16; S. Prashad, "All Aligned: How to Get HR on Board with Business," *HR Professional* (February/March 2005), pp. 19–29.

2. HR-related questions that line managers have to address include the following: What are our talent needs? How should we meet our talent needs? How can we do a better job of hiring? How can we develop internal talent? And finally, how can we manage our employees' career paths? (These come from Peter Cappelli, "HR for Neophytes," *Harvard Business Review* [October 2013], pp. 25–27.)

3. O. Parker, *It's the Journey That Matters: 2005 Strategic HR Transformation Study Tour.* (Ottawa, ON: The Conference Board of Canada, March 2006).

4. N. Bontis, "Made to Measure: Linking Human Capital Metrics with Organizational Performance," *HR Professional* (August/September 2007), pp. 16–20; B. Becker, M. Huselid, P.S. Pickus, and M.F. Spratt, "HR as a Source of Shareholder Value: Research and Recommendations," *Human Resource Management,* 36, no. 1 (Spring 1997), pp. 39–47; B. Becker and B. Gerhart, "The Impact of Human Resource Management on Organizational Performance: Progress and Prospects," *Academy of Management Journal,* 39, no. 4 (August 1996), pp. 779–801; M. Huselid, "The Impact of Human Resources Management Practices on Turnover, Productivity, and Corporate Performance," *Academy of Management Journal,* 38 (1995), pp. 635–672; P. Wright, G. McMahan, B. McCormick, and S. Sherman, "Strategy, Core Competence, and HR Involvement as Determinants of HR Effectiveness and Refinery," *Human Resource Management,* 37, no. 37 (1998), pp. 17–31.

5. C. Clegg, M. Patterson, A. Robinson, C. Stride, T.D. Wall, and S.J. Wood, "The Impact of Human Resource and Operational Management Practices on Company Productivity: A Longitudinal Study," *Personnel Psychology*, 61 (Autumn 2008), pp. 467–501.

6. A. Lado and M.C. Wilson, "Human Resource Systems and Sustained Competitive Advantage: A Competency-Based Perspective," *Academy of Management Review*, 19 (1994), pp. 699–727.

7. J.E. Delery and D.H. Doty, "Modes of Theorizing in Strategic Human Resource Management: Tests of Universalistic, Contingency, and Configurational Performance Predictions," *Academy of Management Journal*, 39, no. 4 (1996), pp. 802–835.

8. M. Huselid, "The Impact of Human Resources Management Practices on Turnover, Productivity, and Corporate Performance," *Academy of Management Journal*, 38 (1995), pp. 635–672.

9. This is based on Bruce Kaufman, "The Historical Development of American HRM Broadly Viewed," *Human Resource Management Review* 24, no. 3 (2014), pp. 196–218. See also D. Ulrich and J. H. Dulebohn, "Are We There Yet? What's Next for HR?" *Human Resource Management Review* 25, no. 2 (June 2015), pp. 188–204; and D.J. Cohen, "HR Past, Present and Future: A Call for Consistent Practices and a Focus on Competencies," *Human Resource Management Review* 25, no. 2 (June 2015), pp. 205–215.

10. For a book describing the history of human resource management, see, for example, Society for Human Resource Management, *A History of Human Resources: SHRM's 60-Year Journey* (Alexandra, VA: SHRM, 2008).

11. "Human Capital Critical to Success," *Management Review*, November 1998, p. 9. See also "HR 2018: Top Predictions," *Workforce Management* 87, no. 20 (December 15, 2008), pp. 20–21; and E. Lawler III, "Celebrating 50 Years: HR: Time for a Reset?" *Human Resource Management* 50, no. 2 (March–April 2011), pp. 171–173, http://dx.doi.org/10.1002/hrm.20420.

12. *Canada's Demographic Revolution: Adjusting to an Aging Population* (Ottawa, ON: The Conference Board of Canada, March 2006).

13. S. Dobson, "Business Acumen Critical for HR: Survey," *Canadian HR Reporter* (May 9, 2011).

14. S. Modi, "Is the CEO the New Chief Talent Officer in Global Recruitment and HR?" Monster Thinking (July 6, 2011), www.monsterthinking.com/2011/07/06/is-the-ceo-the-new-chief-talent-officer-in-global-recruitment-and-hr (accessed September 26, 2011).

15. R. Wright, *Measuring Human Resources Effectiveness Toolkit* (Ottawa, ON: The Conference Board of Canada, 2004); U. Vu, "The HR Leader's Contribution in an Engaged Organization," *Canadian HR Reporter* (May 22, 2006); D. Brown, "Measuring Human Capital Crucial, ROI Isn't, Says New Think-Tank Paper," *Canadian HR Reporter* (October 25, 2004), pp. 1, 4; J. Douglas and T. Emond, "Time to Pop the Question: Are Your Employees Engaged?" *WorldatWork Canadian News* (Third Quarter, 2003), pp. 12–14.

16. R. Baumruk, "The Missing Link: The Role of Employee Engagement in Business Success," *Workspan* (November 2004), pp. 48–52; N. Winter, "Tuned In and Turned On," *Workspan* (April 2003), pp. 48–52.

17. Global Workforce Study, July 2012, www.towerswatson.com/en/Insights/IC-Types/Survey-Research-Results/2012/07/2012-Towers-Watson-Global-Workforce-Study (accessed June 21, 2013).

18. D.S. Cohen, "Behaviour-Based Interviewing," *Human Resources Professional* (April/May 1997), p. 29.

19. *CCHRA Awareness Study* (Toronto, ON: CCHRA and Ekos Research Associates, 2008).

20. B.E. Becker, M.A. Huselid, and D. Ulrich, *The HR Scorecard: Linking People, Strategy and Performance* (Boston, MA: Harvard Business School Press, 2001); D. Brown, "Measuring the Value of HR," *Canadian HR Reporter* (September 24, 2001), pp. 1, 5. See also E. Beaudan, "The Failure of Strategy: It's All in the Execution," *Ivey Business Journal* 65, no. 3 (January/February 2001), pp. 64–68.

21. A. Aijala, B. Walsh, and J. Schwartz, *Aligned at the Top: How Business and HR Executives View Today's Most Significant People Challenges—And What They're Doing About It* (Deloitte Development LLC, 2007).

22. *Canada's Demographic Revolution: Adjusting to an Aging Population* (Ottawa, ON: The Conference Board of Canada, March 2006).

23. O. Parker, *The Strategic Value of People: Human Resource Trends and Metrics* (Ottawa, ON: The Conference Board of Canada, July 2006).

24. R. Kaplan and D. Norton, *The Strategy-Focused Organization: How Balanced Scorecard Companies Thrive in the New Business Environment* (Boston, MA: Harvard Business School Press, 1996); S. Mooraj, D. Oyon, and D. Hostettler, "The Balanced Scorecard: A Necessary Good or an Unnecessary Evil?" *European Management Journal* 17, no. 5 (October 1999), pp. 481–491; B. Becker, M. Huselid, and D. Ulrich, *The HR Scorecard: Linking People, Strategy and Performance* (Boston, MA: Harvard Business School Press, 2001); M. Huselid, B. Becker, and R. Beatty, *The Workforce Scorecard: Managing Human Capital to Execute Strategy* (Boston, MA: Harvard Business School Press, 2006).

25. This section on HR professional designations in Canada is based on material from the CPHR/CRHA website at www.cphr.ca. See also "An Open Invitation to HRPA," *CPHR News* (January 31, 2017), https://cphr.ca/blog/2017/01/31/an-open-invitation-to-hrpa (accessed July 7, 2017).

26. D. McDougall, "Employees Want an Ethical Work Environment," *Canadian HR Reporter* (April 10, 2000), p. 4.

27. S. Klie, "Most HR Professionals Have Been Coerced," *Canadian HR Reporter* (June 16, 2008).

28. "KPMG's Ethics Survey 2000—Managing for Ethical Practice," cited in L. Young, "Companies Not Doing Right," *Canadian HR Reporter* (April 10, 2000), p. 17.

29. Based on Walker Information Canada Inc. study, cited in J. Martin, "Studies Suggest a Link between Employees' Perception of a Firm's Ethics—and Loyalty," *Recruitment & Staffing*, Supplement to *Canadian HR Reporter* (September 20, 1999), p. G7; D. McDougall, "Employees Want an Ethical Work Environment," *Canadian HR Reporter* (April 10, 2000), p. 4.

30. Mountain Equipment Coop, July 29, 2009, www.mec.ca.

31. G. Ferris, D. Frink, and M.C. Galang, "Diversity in the Workplace: The Human Resources Management Challenge," *Human Resource Planning* 16, no. 1 (1993), p. 42.

32. Human Resources and Skills Development Canada, "Indicators of Well-being in Canada: Learning—Educational Attainment," www4.hrsdc.gc.ca/.3ndic.1t.4r@eng.jsp?iid=29.

33. A. Campbell and N. Gagnon, *Literacy, Life and Employment: An Analysis of Canadian International Adult Literacy Survey (IALS) Microdata* (Ottawa, ON: Conference Board of Canada, January 2006).

34. J. Bernier, *The Scope of Federal Labour Standards and Nontraditional Work Situations* (Submission to the Federal Labour Standards Review, October 2005), pp. 5–13.

35. M. Vartiainen, M. Hakonen, S. Koivisto, P. Mannonen, M. P. Nieminen, V. Ruohomaki, and A. Vartola, *Distributed and Mobile: Places, People and Technology* (Helsinki, Finland: Oy Yliopistokustannus University Press, 2007), p. 75.

36. C. Clark, "The World Is Flat: Work–Life Trends to Watch," *Workspan* (January 2009), pp. 17–19.

37. K. Williams, "Privacy in a Climate of Electronic Surveillance," *Workplace News* (April 2005), p. 10.

38. "Multinational Corporation," http://en.wikipedia.org/wiki/Multinational_corporation (accessed August 17, 2006).

39. S. Nolen, "Step 1: Keep Workers Alive," *Globe and Mail* (August 5, 2006), pp. B4–B5.

40. U. Vu, "Climate Change Sparks Attitude Shift," *Canadian HR Reporter* (March 26, 2007), p. 11.

41. S. Dobson, "Fairmont Finds It's Easy Being Green," *Canadian HR Reporter* (March 26, 2007).

42. R. Stringer, *Leadership and Organizational Climate* (Upper Saddle River, NJ: Prentice-Hall, 2002).

HR by the Numbers: Increased Use of Contract Workers

A. Silliker, "More Firms Hiring Contract Workers," *Canadian HR Reporter* 25, no. 9 (May 7, 2011), p. 1.

Chapter 2

1. S. Dobson, "Business Acumen Critical for HR: Survey," *Canadian HR Reporter* (May 9, 2011).

2. P. Verge and G. Vallee, "Un droit du travail? Essai sur la spécificité du droit du travail," Editions Yvon Blais, Cowansville (1997).

3. Canadian Charter of Rights and Freedoms, as part of the Constitution Act of 1982.

4. Canadian Charter of Rights and Freedoms, Section 15(1).

5. *Annual Report of the Canadian Human Rights Commission* (Ottawa, ON: Government of Canada, 1991), p. 65.

6. A. Colella, M. Hebl, and E. King, "One Hundred Years of Discrimination Research in *Journal of Applied Psychology*: A Sobering Synopsis," *Journal of Applied Psychology*, 102, no. 3 (2017), pp. 500–513, http://dx.doi.org/10.1037/apl0000084.

7. A. Colella, M. Hebl, and E. King, "One Hundred Years of Discrimination Research in *Journal of Applied Psychology*: A Sobering Synopsis," *Journal of Applied Psychology*, 102, no. 3 (2017), pp. 500–513, http://dx.doi.org/10.1037/apl0000084.

8. R.D. Arvey, T.E. Landon, S.M. Nutting, and S.E. Maxwell, "Development of Physical Ability Tests for Police Officers: A Construct Validation Approach," *Journal of Applied Psychology*, 77 (1992), pp. 996–1009, http://dx.doi.org/10.1037/0021-9010.77.6.996.

9. D. Chan and N. Schmitt, "Video-based versus Paper-and-Pencil Method of Assessment in Situational Judgment Tests: Subgroup Differences in Test Performance and Face Validity Perceptions," *Journal of Applied Psychology*, 82 (1997), pp. 143–159, http://dx.doi.org/10.1037/0021-9010.82.1.143.

10. A.P. Aggarwal, *Sex Discrimination: Employment Law and Practices* (Toronto, ON: Butterworths Canada, 1994).

11. Ontario Human Rights Commission, *Human Rights at Work* (Toronto, ON: Government of Ontario, 1999), pp. 63–64.

12. S. Rudner, "Just Cause—Back from the Dead?" *Canadian HR Reporter* (September 22, 2008); M. Bélanger and R. Ravary, "Supreme Court of Canada Sets Limits on Employer's Duty to Accommodate," *McCarthy Tétrault e-Alert* (July 24, 2008); D. Elenbaas, "Undue Hardship: Supreme Court of Canada Clarifies the Standard—or Does it?" *Ultimate HR Manual*, 39 (August 2008), pp. 1–3.

13. "Policy and Guidelines on Disability and the Duty to Accommodate," Ontario Human Rights Commission (December 2009), www.ohrc.on.ca/en/resources/Policies/PolicyDisAccom2/pdf (accessed September 26, 2011).

14. *British Columbia (Public Service Employee Relations Commission) v. BCGSEU*, [1999] 3 S.C.R. 3 at para. 68.

15. According to the US National Library of Medicine, www.ncbi.nlm.nih.gov/pubmedhealth/PMH0001295.

16. "Disability and the Duty to Accommodate: Your Rights and Responsibilities," Ontario Human Rights Commission, www.ohrc.on.ca/en/issues/disability (accessed November 23, 2011).

17. According to the Supreme Court Ruling by Brian Dickson, Chief Justice of Canada, *Janzen v. Platy Enterprises Ltd.*, 1989.

18. Based on Stephen Hammond of Harassment Solutions Inc., "The Historic Fight Against Sexual Harassment," *Canadian HR Reporter* (August 15, 2011), p. 33.

19. S. Dobson, "Tackling the Bullies," *Canadian HR Reporter* (March 9, 2009).

20. J.R. Smith, "Employers: Don't Let Workplace Harassment Catch You Off Guard," *Canadian HR Reporter* (October 22, 2007); Canadian Human Rights Commission, *Anti-Harassment Policies for the Workplace: An Employer's Guide* (Ottawa, ON: Minister of Public Works and Government Services, March 2006), p. 3.

21. J.R. Smith, "Employer's Damage Control Leads to Big-Time Damages," *Canadian HR Reporter* (June 1, 2009); "Employer Vicariously Liable for Supervisor's Abusive Conduct," *Ultimate HR Manual*, 49 (June 2009), p. 7.

22. A.P. Aggarwal, *Sexual Harassment in the Workplace*, 2nd ed. (Toronto, ON: Butterworths Canada, 1992), pp. 10–11.

23. Data from Canadian Human Rights Commission, *Anti-Harassment Policies for the Workplace: An Employer's Guide* (Ottawa, ON: Minister of Public Works and Government Services, March 2006), pp. 16–25.

24. "Construction Firms Fight B.C. Human Rights Ruling," *HR Professional* (April/May 2009), p. 13.

25. "Key Provisions of Ottawa's Same-Sex Legislation," *Canadian HR Reporter* (March 27, 2000), p. 11.

26. Canadian Human Rights Commission, www.chrc-ccdp.ca/adr/settlements/archives2/page5-en.asp (accessed August 13, 2006).

27. Canadian Human Rights Commission, www.chrc-ccdp.ca/discrimination/age-en.asp (accessed August 13, 2006).

28. Ontario Human Rights Commission, www.ohrc.on.ca/english/publicatoins/age-policy_5.shtml (accessed June 2, 2006).

29. Statistics Canada, *Table 282-0002—Labour Force Survey Estimates (LFS), by Sex and Detailed Age Group, Annual (Persons unless Otherwise Noted)*, CANSIM (January 6, 2017), www5.statcan.gc.ca/cansim/a47 (accessed July 20, 2017).

30. *Women in Canada: Work Chapter Updates*, Statistics Canada, Catalogue No. 89F0133XIE, 2006.

31. S. Klie, "Feds Discriminated Against Nurses," *Canadian HR Reporter* (February 25, 2008).

32. Statistics Canada, *Aboriginal Peoples in Canada: First Nations People, Métis, and Inuit, National Household Survey, 2011* (Ottawa, ON: Minister of Industry, 2013), www12.statcan.gc.ca/nhs-enm/2011/as-sa/99-011-x/99-011-x2011001-eng.cfm (accessed July 7, 2017).

33. Statistics Canada, *Aboriginal Peoples Technical Report, 2011 National Household Survey (NHS)*, rev. June 19, 2014 (Ottawa, ON: Minister of Industry, 2014), sec. 6.1.2, www12.statcan.gc.ca/nhs-enm/2011/ref/reports-rapports/ap-pa/ch6-eng.cfm#A_1_2 (accessed July 7, 2017).

34. Statistics Canada, "Employment," in *Aboriginal Statistics at a Glance*, 2nd ed. (Ottawa, ON: Minister of Industry, 2015), www.statcan.gc.ca/pub/89-645-x/2015001/employment-emploi-eng.htm (accessed July 7, 2017).

35. Statistics Canada, "Study: Persons with Disabilities and Employment," *The Daily* (December 3, 2014), www.statcan.gc.ca/daily-quotidien/141203/dq141203a-eng.htm (accessed July 14, 2017).

36. Statistics Canada, *Immigration and Ethnocultural Diversity in Canada*, Catalogue no. 99-010-X2011001, p. 4.

37. Statistics Canada, *Immigration and Ethnocultural Diversity in Canada*, Catalogue no. 99-010-X2011001, p. 4.

38. W. Cukier and M. Yap, *DiverseCity Counts: A Snapshot of Diversity in the Greater Toronto Area* (Toronto, ON: The Diversity Institute, Ryerson University, May 2009).

39. P. Israel, "Employee Misconduct…Employer Responsibility?" *Canadian HR Reporter* (May 20, 2002), p. 5.

40. P. Israel, "Spying on Employees…and It's Perfectly Legal," *Canadian HR Reporter* (April 21, 2003), p. 5.

41. A.P. Cleek, "Six Steps to an Effective Workplace Blogging Policy," *Ultimate HR Manual* (August 2007), pp. 6–7.

42. E. Kuzz, "More Rules for Employee Information Protection," *Canadian HR Reporter* (September 9, 2002), p. 16; D. Brown, "10 Months to Get Ready," *Canadian HR Reporter* (February 24, 2003), pp. 1, 11.

43. D. Fallows, "Technology Paves the Way for Big Brother," *Canadian HR Reporter* (April 9, 2007).

44. M. Draaisma, "Computer Use Policy in Workplace Is a Must, Says Toronto Lawyer," *Ultimate HR Manual* (May 2009), pp. 1–4; S. Rudner, "The High Cost of Internet, E-mail Abuse," *Canadian HR Reporter* (January 31, 2005),

pp. R5–R6; N. MacDonald, "You've Got E-mail Problems," *Canadian HR Reporter* (March 10, 2003), pp. G5, G10.

45. S. Dobson, "Hamilton Workers Caught in the Act," *Canadian HR Reporter* (February 25, 2013), p. 1.

46. K. Williams, "Privacy in a Climate of Electronic Surveillance," *Workplace News* (April 2005), p. 10; S. Hood, "What's Private, What's Not?" *HR Professional* (February/March 2006), pp. 20–28; P. Strazynski, "Falsely Accused Employee Gets $2.1 Million," *Canadian HR Reporter* (July 14, 2008).

Chapter 3

1. R. I. Henderson (ed.), *Compensation Management in a Knowledge-Based World* (Upper Saddle River, NJ: Prentice-Hall, 2003), pp. 135–138. See also P.W. Wright and K. Wesley, "How to Choose the Kind of Job Analysis You Really Need," *Personnel*, 62 (May 1985), pp. 51–55; C.J. Cranny and M.E. Doherty, "Importance Ratings in Job Analysis: Note on the Misinterpretation of Factor Analyses," *Journal of Applied Psychology*, 73 (May 1988), pp. 320–322.

2. C. Babbage, *On the Economy of Machinery and Manufacturers* (London: Charles Knight, 1832), pp. 169–176; reprinted in Joseph Litterer, *Organizations* (New York, NY: John Wiley and Sons, 1969), pp. 73–75.

3. J. Heerwagen, K. Kelly, and K. Kampschroer, "The Changing Nature of Organizations, Work, and Workplace," *Whole Building Design Group (WBDG), National Institute of Building Sciences* (February 2006).

4. F. Herzberg, "One More Time, How Do You Motivate Employees?" *Harvard Business Review*, 46 (January–February 1968), pp. 53–62.

5. The next two sections are based on J. Schippmann et al., "The Practice of Competency Modeling," *Personnel Psychology*, 53, no. 3 (2000), pp. 703–740; P. Singh, "Job Analysis for a Changing Workplace," *Human Resource Management Review*, 18 (2008), pp. 87–99.

6. Adapted from Richard Mirabile, "Everything You Wanted to Know About Competency Modeling," *Training and Development*, 51, no. 8 (August 1997), pp. 73–78.

7. D. Kravetz, "Building a Job Competency Database: What the Leaders Do" (Bartlett, IL: Kravetz Associates, 1997).

8. G.M. Parker, *Cross-Functional Teams: Working with Allies, Enemies and Other Strangers* (San Francisco, CA: Jossey-Bass, 2003), p. 68.

9. "Collaboration for Virtual Teams," *HR Professional* (December 2002/January 2003), p. 44.

10. Note that the PAQ (and other quantitative techniques) can also be used for job evaluation.

11. E. Cornelius III, F. Schmidt, and T. Carron, "Job Classification Approaches and the Implementation of Validity Generalization Results," *Personnel Psychology*, 37 (Summer 1984), pp. 247–260; E. Cornelius III, A. DeNisi, and A. Blencoe, "Expert and Naïve Raters Using the PAQ: Does It Matter?" *Personnel Psychology*, 37 (Autumn 1984), pp. 453–464; L. Friedman and R. Harvey, "Can Raters with Reduced Job Description Information Provide Accurate Position Analysis Questionnaire (PAQ) Ratings?" *Personnel Psychology*, 34 (Winter 1986), pp. 779–789; R.J. Harvey et al., "Dimensionality of the Job Element Inventory: A Simplified Worker-Oriented Job Analysis Questionnaire," *Journal of Applied Psychology* (November 1988), pp. 639–646; S. Butler and R. Harvey, "A Comparison of Holistic versus Decomposed Rating of Position Analysis Questionnaire Work Dimensions," *Personnel Psychology* (Winter 1988), pp. 761–772.

12. This discussion is based on H. Olson et al., "The Use of Functional Job Analysis in Establishing Performance Standards for Heavy Equipment Operators," *Personnel Psychology*, 34 (Summer 1981), pp. 351–364.

13. Human Resources Development Canada, *National Occupation Classification Career Handbook* (2003), http://noc.esdc.gc.ca/English/CH/Welcome.

aspx?ver=06&ch=03&_ga=2.150633974.1995106938.1503114446-735205063.1503114446.

14. J. Evered, "How to Write a Good Job Description," *Supervisory Management* (April 1981), p. 16.

15. *Human Rights at Work 2008*, 3rd ed. ([Toronto]: Ontario Human Rights Commission, 2008), www.ohrc.on.ca/en/book/export/html/4260.

16. P.H. Raymark, M.J. Schmidt, and R.M. Guion, "Identifying Potentially Useful Personality Constructs for Employee Selection," *Personnel Psychology* 50 (1997), pp. 723–726.

Chapter 4

1. *Imbalances between Labour Demand and Supply, 2013–2022*, Canadian Occupational Projection System, Employment and Social Development Canada, February 24, 2016, http://occupations.esdc.gc.ca/sppc-cops/c.4nt.2nt@-eng.jsp?cid=52&_ga=1.83300758.1032398791.1484510823 (accessed July 12, 2017).

2. Manitoba, *Economic Analysis and Research: Manitoba Occupational Forecasts*, Ministry of Growth, Enterprise, and Trade, www.gov.mb.ca/jec/lmi/forecasts.html (accessed July 12, 2017).

3. S. Klie, "Guesses Just Don't Cut It Anymore," *Canadian HR Reporter* (March 24, 2008).

4. B. Kreissl, "The Toughest Challenges Facing HR Departments," *Canadian HR Reporter* (December 15, 2014).

5. "10 Surprising Stats about Small Business in Canada," CBC News, October 17, 2011, www.cbc.ca/news/business/10-surprising-stats-about-small-business-in-canada-1.1083238 (accessed August 9, 2017).

6. B. Tal. "Inadequate Business Succession Planning —A Growing Macroeconomic Risk," *In Focus* (November 13, 2012), http://research.cibcwm.com/economic_public/download/if-20121113.pdf (accessed August 9, 2017).

7. M. Evans, "5 Steps to Create a Viable Succession Plan for Your Family Business," *Forbes* (August 28, 2013), www.forbes.com/sites/allbusiness/2013/08/28/5-steps-to-create-a-viable-succession-plan-for-your-family-business/#fbda1476f224 (accessed August 7, 2017).

8. HRSDC, *Looking Ahead: A 10-Year Outlook for the Canadian Labour Market (2008–2017)* (Gatineau, QC: Policy Research Directorate, 2008), http://occupations.esdc.gc.ca/sppc-cops/servlet/copspub?lang=en&curjsp=l.3bd.2t.1.3ls@-eng.jsp&curactn=dwnld&lid=1&fid=1 (accessed July 12, 2017).

9. HRSDC, *Looking Ahead: A 10-Year Outlook for the Canadian Labour Market (2008–2017)* (Gatineau, QC: Policy Research Directorate, 2008), http://occupations.esdc.gc.ca/sppc-cops/servlet/copspub?lang=en&curjsp=l.3bd.2t.1.3ls@-eng.jsp&curactn=dwnld&lid=1&fid=1 (accessed July 12, 2017).

10. A.L. Delbecq, A.H. Van DelVen, and D.H. Gustafson, *Group Techniques for Program Planning: A Guide to Nominal and Delphi Processes* (Glenview, IL: Scott Foresman, 1975).

11. G. Milkovich, A.J. Annoni, and T.A. Mahoney, "The Use of Delphi Procedures in Manpower Forecasting," *Management Science* (1972), pp. 381–388.

Chapter 5

1. "Effective Recruiting Tied to Stronger Financial Performance," *WorldatWork Canadian News* (Fourth Quarter, 2005), pp. 18–19.

2. K. Peters, "Public Image Ltd.," *HR Professional* (December 2007/January 2008), pp. 24–30; S. Klie, "Getting Employees to Come to You," *Canadian HR Reporter* (November 19, 2007), pp. 9–10; S. Klie, "Tuning into TV's Recruitment Reach," *Canadian HR Reporter* (September 25, 2006).

3. G. Bouchard, "Strong Employer Brand Can Tap Scarce Resource: Talent," *Canadian HR Reporter* (November 19, 2007), p. 10.

4. K. Peters, "Public Image Ltd.," *HR Professional* (December 2007/January 2008), pp. 24–30; G. Bouchard, "Strong Employer Brand Can Tap Scarce Resource: Talent," *Canadian HR Reporter* (November 19, 2007), p. 10; M. Morra, "Best in Show," *Workplace News* (September/October 2006), pp. 17–21; M. Shuster, "Employment Branding: The Law of Attraction!" *Workplace* (January/February 2008), pp. 14–15.

5. M. Morra, "Best in Show," *Workplace News* (September/October 2006), pp. 17–21.

6. G. Bouchard, "Strong Employer Brand Can Tap Scarce Resource: Talent," *Canadian HR Reporter* (November 19, 2007), p. 10.

7. K. Peters, "Public Image Ltd.," *HR Professional* (December 2007/January 2008), pp. 24–30; S. Klie, "Getting Employees to Come to You," *Canadian HR Reporter* (November 19, 2007), pp. 9–10.

8. S. Klie, "Getting Employees to Come to You," *Canadian HR Reporter* (November 19, 2007), pp. 9–10; M. Shuster, "Employment Branding: The Law of Attraction!" *Workplace* (January/February 2008), pp. 14–15.

9. "Labour Demand and Supply in Canada: The Big Picture," Business Council of British Columbia (August 25, 2015), www.bcbc.com/publications/2015/labour-demand-and-supply-in-canada-the-big-picture (accessed July 13, 2017).

10. D. Dahl and P. Pinto, "Job Posting, an Industry Survey," *Personnel Journal* (January 1977), pp. 40–41.

11. J. Daum, "Internal Promotion—Psychological Asset or Debit? A Study of the Effects of Leader Origin," *Organizational Behavior and Human Performance,* 13 (1975), pp. 404–413.

12. B. Kreissl, "Retaining Workers Who Have Outgrown Their Jobs," *Canadian HR Reporter* (September 5, 2016), p. 19.

13. See, for example, A. Harris, "Hiring Middle Management: External Recruitment or Internal Promotion?" *Canadian HR Reporter* (April 10, 2000), pp. 8–10.

14. L. Petrecca, "With 3000 Job Applications a Day, Google Can Be Picky," *USA Today* (May 18, 2010), www.usatoday.com/money/workplace/2010-05-19-jobs19_VA_N.htm (accessed September 9, 2012).

15. M. Sharma, "Welcome Back!" *HR Professional* (February/March 2006), pp. 38–40; E. Simon, "You're Leaving the Company? Well, Don't Be a Stranger," *Globe and Mail* (December 22, 2006), p. B16.

16. N. Laurie and M. Laurie, "No Holds Barred in Fight for Students to Fill Internship Programs," *Canadian HR Reporter* (January 17, 2000), pp. 15–16.

17. R. Waghorn, "Internet Puts New Spin on Traditional Career Fair," *Canadian HR Reporter* (November 21, 2011), p. 17.

18. L. Blake, "Ready-Trained, Untapped Source of Skilled Talent—Courtesy Canadian Forces," *Workplace*, www.workplace-mag.com (accessed December 2, 2008).

19. U. Vu, "Security Failures Expose Résumés," *Canadian HR Reporter* (May 24, 2003); P. Lima, "Talent Shortage? That Was Yesterday. Online Recruiters Can Deliver More Candidates for Your Job Openings and Help You Find Keepers," *Profit: The Magazine for Canadian Entrepreneurs* (February/March 2002), pp. 65–66; "Online Job Boards," *Canadian HR Reporter* (February 11, 2002), pp. G11–G15.

20. U. Vu, "Security Failures Expose Résumés," *Canadian HR Reporter* (May 24, 2003).

21. S. Bury, "Face-Based Recruiting," *Workplace* (September/October 2008), pp. 19–21.

22. G. Stanton, "Recruiting Portals Take Centre Stage in Play for Talent," *Canadian HR Reporter* (September 25, 2000), pp. G1–G2.

23. A. da Luz, "Video Enhances Online Job Ads," *Canadian HR Reporter* (February 11, 2008).

24. D. Brown, "Canadian Government Job Boards Lag on Best Practices," *Canadian HR Reporter* (January 13, 2003), p. 2.

25. "Corporate Spending Millions on Ineffective Web Recruiting Strategies," *Canadian HR Reporter* (September 25, 2000), p. G5.

26. A. Snell, "Best Practices for Web Site Recruiting," *Canadian HR Reporter* (February 26, 2001), pp. G7, G10.

27. Social Media vs. Job Boards—The Future of Recruiting," Onrec: The Online Recruitment Resource (March 11, 2015), www.onrec.com/news/statistics-and-trends/social-media-vs-job-boards-the-future-of-recruiting (accessed July 13, 2017).

28. Job Bank, Government of Canada, www.jobbank.gc.ca (accessed July 13, 2017).

29. J.A. Parr, "7 Reasons Why Executive Searches Fail," *Canadian HR Reporter* (March 12, 2001), pp. 20, 23.

30. Statistics Canada, *The Daily* (April 8, 2005); Association of Canadian Search, Employment and Staffing Services (ACSESS), "Media Kit: Media Fact Sheet," www.acsess.org/NEWS/factsheet.asp (accessed May 31, 2009).

31. A. Ryckman, "The 5 Keys to Getting Top Value from Contractors," *Canadian HR Reporter* (December 2, 2002), p. 25; S. Purba, "Contracting Works for Job Hunters," *Globe and Mail* (April 24, 2002).

32. "Flexible Staffing in the Aerospace Industry," *Airfinance Journal I Aircraft Economic Yearbook* (2001), pp. 14–17.

33. L. Cassiani, "Looming Retirement Surge Takes on New Urgency," *Canadian HR Reporter* (May 21, 2001), pp. 1, 10.

34. K. Thorpe, *Harnessing the Power: Recruiting, Engaging, and Retaining Mature Workers* (Ottawa, ON: Conference Board of Canada, 2008).

35. J. Meister, "The Future of Work: Corporate Social Responsibility Attracts Top Talent," *Forbes* (June 2, 2012), www.forbes.com/sites/jeannemeister/2012/06/07/the-future-of-work-corporate-social-responsiblity-attracts-top-talent/#ed9c5783f954 (accessed July 13, 2017).

36. Inclusion Network, www.inclusionnetwork.ca (accessed May 31, 2009); Aboriginal Human Resource Council, http://aboriginalhr.ca (accessed May 31, 2009).

37. Society for Canadian Women in Science and Technology, www.harbour.sfu.ca/scwist/index_files/Page1897.htm (accessed May 31, 2009); C. Emerson, H. Matsui, and L. Michael, "Progress Slow for Women in Trades, Tech, Science," *Canadian HR Reporter* (February 14, 2005), p. 11.

38. WORKInk, www.workink.com (accessed May 31, 2009).

39. C. Kapel, "Giant Steps," *Human Resources Professional* (April 1993), pp. 13–16.

40. S.A. Way and J.W. Thacker, "Selection Practices: Where Are Canadian Organizations?" *HR Professional* (October/November 1999), p. 34.

41. L.J. Katunich, "How to Avoid the Pitfalls of Psych Tests," *Workplace News Online* (July 2005), p. 5; *Testing and Assessment—FAQ/Finding Information About Psychological Tests*, APA Online, www.apa.org/science/faq-findtests.html (accessed August 1, 2006).

42. M. McDaniel et al., "The Validity of Employment Interviews: A Comprehensive Review and Meta-analysis," *Journal of Applied Psychology*, 79, no. 4 (1994).

43. "Hiring: Psychology and Employee Potential," *HR Professional* (August/September 2008), p. 16.

44. "Hiring: Psychology and Employee Potential," *HR Professional* (August/September 2008), p. 16.

45. S. Bakker, "Psychometric Selection Assessments," *HR Professional* (April/May 2009), p. 21.

46. R.M. Yerkes, *Psychological Examining in the U.S. Army*, vol. 15, *Memoirs of the National Academy of Sciences* (Washington DC: U.S. Government Printing Office, 1921).

47. F.L. Schmidt and J. Hunter, "General Mental Ability in the World of Work: Occupational Attainment and Job Performance," *Journal of Personality and Social Psychology*, 86, no. 1 (2004), 162–173.

48. M. Zeidner, I. G. Matthews, and R.D. Roberts, "Emotional Intelligence in the Workplace: A Critical Review," *Applied Psychology: An International Review*, 53, no.3 (2004), pp. 371–399.

49. "Emotional Intelligence Testing," *HR Focus* (October 2001), pp. 8–9.

50. Results of meta-analyses in one recent study indicated that isometric strength tests were valid predictors of both supervisory ratings of physical performance and performance on work simulations. See B.R. Blakley, M. Quinones, M.S. Crawford, and I.A. Jago, "The Validity of Isometric Strength Tests," *Personnel Psychology*, 47 (1994), pp. 247–274.

51. C. Colacci, "Testing Helps You Decrease Disability Costs," *Canadian HR Reporter* (June 14, 1999), p. G4.

52. K. Gillin, "Reduce Employee Exposure to Injury with Pre-Employment Screening Tests," *Canadian HR Reporter* (February 28, 2000), p. 10.

53. This approach calls for construct validation, which, as was pointed out, is extremely difficult to demonstrate.

54. Myers-Briggs Type Indicator (MBTI) Assessment, www.cpp.com/products/mbti/index.asp (accessed May 31, 2009).

55. See, for example, D. Cellar et al., "Comparison of Factor Structures and Criterion Related Validity Coefficients for Two Measures of Personality Based on the Five-Factor Model," *Journal of Applied Psychology*, 81, no. 6 (1996), pp. 694–704; J. Salgado, "The Five Factor Model of Personality and Job Performance in the European Community," *Journal of Applied Psychology*, 82, no. 1 (1997), pp. 30–43.

56. M.R. Barrick and M.K. Mount, "The Big Five Personality Dimensions and Job Performance: A Meta-Analysis," *Personnel Psychology*, 44 (Spring 1991), pp. 1–26.

57. C. Robie, K. Tuzinski, and P. Bly, "A Survey of Assessor Beliefs and Practices Related to Faking," *Journal of Managerial Psychology* (October 2006), pp. 669–681.

58. C. Robie, "Effects of Perceived Selection Ratio on Personality Test Faking," *Social Behavior and Personality*, 34, no. 10 (2006), 1233–1244.

59. E. Silver and C. Bennett, "Modification of the Minnesota Clerical Test to Predict Performance on Video Display Terminals," *Journal of Applied Psychology*, 72, no. 1 (February 1987), pp. 153–155.

60. L. Siegel and I. Lane, *Personnel and Organizational Psychology* (Homewood, IL: Irwin, 1982), pp. 182–183.

61. J. Weekley and C. Jones, "Video-Based Situational Testing," *Personnel Psychology*, 50 (1997), p. 25.

62. J. Weekley and C. Jones, "Video-Based Situational Testing," *Personnel Psychology*, 50 (1997), pp. 26–30.

63. D. Chan and N. Schmitt, "Situational Judgment and Job Performance," *Human Performance*, 15, no. 3 (2002), pp. 233–254.

64. S. Klie, "Screening Gets More Secure," *Canadian HR Reporter* (June 19, 2006).

65. Canadian Human Rights Commission, *Canadian Human Rights Commission Policy on Alcohol and Drug Testing* (June 2002).

66. M. McDaniel et al., "The Validity of Employment Interviews: A Comprehensive Review and Meta-Analysis," *Journal of Applied Psychology*, 79, no. 4 (1994), p. 599.

67. J.G. Goodale, *The Fine Art of Interviewing* (Englewood Cliffs, NJ: Prentice Hall Inc., 1982), p. 22; see also R.L. Decker, "The Employment Interview," *Personnel Administrator,* 26 (November 1981), pp. 71–73.

68. M. Campion, E. Pursell, and B. Brown, "Structured Interviewing: Raising the Psychometric Properties of the Employment Interview," *Personnel Psychology,* 41 (1988), pp. 25–42.

69. M. McDaniel et al., "The Validity of Employment Interviews: A Comprehensive Review and Meta-Analysis," *Journal of Applied Psychology,* 79, no. 4 (1994), pp. 599–616.

70. M. McDaniel et al., "The Validity of Employment Interviews: A Comprehensive Review and Meta-Analysis," *Journal of Applied Psychology,* 79, no. 4 (1994), p. 601.

71. M. McDaniel et al., "The Validity of Employment Interviews: A Comprehensive Review and Meta-Analysis," *Journal of Applied Psychology,* 79, no. 4 (1994), p. 601.

72. "Lights, Camera…Can I Have a Job?" *Globe and Mail* (March 2, 2007), p. C1; A. Pell, *Recruiting and Selecting Personnel* (New York, NY: Regents, 1969), p. 119.

73. J.G. Goodale, *The Fine Art of Interviewing* (Englewood Cliffs, NJ: Prentice Hall, 1982), p. 26.

74. G.C. Ho, M. Shih, D.J. Walters and T.L. Pittinsky, "The Stigma of Unemployment: When Joblessness Leads to Being Jobless," UC Los Angeles: The Institute for Research on Labor and Employment (2011), www.escholarship.org/uc/item/7nh039h1; K. Kroft, F. Lange and M.J. Notowidigdo, "Duration Dependence and Labor Market Conditions: Theory and Evidence from a Field Experiment," NBER Working Paper No. 18387 (September 2012).

75. See R.D. Arvey and J.E. Campion, "The Employment Interview: A Summary and Review of Recent Research," *Personnel Psychology,* 35 (1982), pp. 281–322; M. Heilmann and L. Saruwatari, "When Beauty Is Beastly: The Effects of Appearance and Sex on Evaluation of Job Applicants for Managerial and Nonmanagerial Jobs," *Organizational Behavior and Human Performance,* 23 (June 1979), pp. 360–722; C. Marlowe, S. Schneider, and C. Nelson, "Gender and Attractiveness Biases in Hiring Decisions: Are More Experienced Managers Less Biased?" *Journal of Applied Psychology,* 81, no. 1 (1996), pp. 11–21; V. Galt, "Beauty Found Not Beastly in the Job Interview," *Globe and Mail* (April 15, 2002).

76. A. Pell, "Nine Interviewing Pitfalls," *Managers* (January 1994), p. 29; T. Dougherty, D. Turban, and J. Callender, "Confirming First Impressions in the Employment Interview: A Field Study of Interviewer Behavior," *Journal of Applied Psychology,* 79, no. 5 (1994), p. 663.

77. See A. Pell, "Nine Interviewing Pitfalls," *Managers* (January 1994), p. 29; P. Sarathi, "Making Selection Interviews Effective," *Management and Labor Studies,* 18, no. 1 (1993), pp. 5–7; J. Shetcliffe, "Who, and How, to Employ," *Insurance Brokers' Monthly* (December 2002), pp. 14–16.

78. G.J. Sears and P.M. Rowe, "A Personality-Based Similar-to-Me Effect in the Employment Interview: Conscientious, Affect-versus-Competence Mediated Interpretations, and the Role of Job Relevance," *Canadian Journal of Behavioural Sciences,* 35 (January 2003), p. 13.

79. This section is based on E.D. Pursell, M.A. Campion, and S.R. Gaylord, "Structured Interviewing: Avoiding Selection Problems," *Personnel Journal,* 59 (1980), pp. 907–912; G.P. Latham, L.M. Saari, E.D. Pursell, and M.A. Campion, "The Situational Interview," *Journal of Applied Psychology,* 65 (1980), pp. 422–427; see also M. Campion, E. Pursell, and B. Brown, "Structured Interviewing: Raising the Psychometric Properties of the Employment Interview," *Personnel Psychology,* 41 (1988), pp. 25–42; J.A.

Weekley and J.A. Gier, "Reliability and Validity of the Situational Interview for a Sales Position," *Journal of Applied Psychology,* 72 (1987), pp. 484–487.

80. A. Pell, *Recruiting and Selecting Personnel* (New York, NY: Regents, 1969), pp. 103–115.

81. W.H. Wiesner and R.J. Oppenheimer, "Note-Taking in the Selection Interview: Its Effect upon Predictive Validity and Information Recall," *Proceedings of the Annual Conference Meeting. Administrative Sciences Association of Canada* (Personnel and Human Resources Division, 1991), pp. 97–106.

82. V. Tsang, "No More Excuses," *Canadian HR Reporter* (May 23, 2005); L.T. Cullen, "Getting Wise to Lies," *Time* (May 1, 2006), p. 27.

83. V. Tsang, "No More Excuses," *Canadian HR Reporter* (May 23, 2005); L.T. Cullen, "Getting Wise to Lies," *Time* (May 1, 2006), p. 27.

84. L. Fischer, "Gatekeeper," *Workplace News* (August 2005), pp. 10–11.

85. T. Humber, "Recruitment Isn't Getting Any Easier," *Canadian HR Reporter* (May 23, 2005).

86. C. Hall and A. Miedema, "But I Thought You Checked?" *Canadian HR Reporter* (May 21, 2007).

87. R. Zupek, "Is Your Future Boss Researching You Online?" CareerBuilder.ca, www.careerbuilder.ca/blog/2008/10/09/cb-is-your-future-boss-researching-you-online (accessed May 24, 2009).

88. A. Silliker, "1 in 8 New Hires Unsuccessful," *Canadian HR Reporter* (February 25, 2013), pp. 3, 10.

89. J.R. Smith, "Damaging Reference Survives Alberta Privacy Challenge," *Canadian HR Reporter* (January 28, 2008).

90. A.C. Elmslie, "Writing a Reference Letter—Right or Wrong?" *Ultimate HR Manual,* 44 (January 2009), pp. 1–3.

91. A. Moffat, "The Danger of Digging Too Deep," *Canadian HR Reporter* (August 11, 2008); see also P. Israel, "Providing References to Employees: Should You or Shouldn't You?" *Canadian HR Reporter* (March 24, 2003), pp. 5–6; T. Humber, "Name, Rank and Serial Number," *Canadian HR Reporter* (May 19, 2003), pp. G1, G7.

92. J.A. Breaugh, "Realistic Job Previews: A Critical Appraisal and Future Research Directions," *Academy of Management Review,* 8, no. 4 (1983), pp. 612–619.

93. P. Buhler, "Managing in the '90s: Hiring the Right Person for the Job," *Supervision* (July 1992), pp. 21–23; S. Jackson, "Realistic Job Previews Help Screen Applicants and Reduce Turnover," *Canadian HR Reporter* (August 9, 1999), p. 10.

94. S. Jackson, "Realistic Job Previews Help Screen Applicants and Reduce Turnover," *Canadian HR Reporter* (August 9, 1999), p. 10.

95. B. Kleinmutz, "Why We Still Use Our Heads Instead of Formulas: Toward an Integrative Approach," *Psychological Bulletin,* 107 (1990), pp. 296–310.

HR by the Numbers: Hiring Mistakes

A. Silliker, "1 in 8 New Hires Unsuccessful: Survey," *Canadian HR Reporter* (February 25, 2013), pp. 3, 10.

HR by the Numbers: Growing Use of Electronic Media for Selection

D.S. Chapman and P.M. Rowe, "The Impact of Videoconference Technology, Interview Structure, and Interviewer Gender on Interviewer Evaluations in the Employment Interview: A Field Experiment," *Journal of Occupational and Organizational Psychology,* 74 (2001), pp. 279–298.

Chapter 6

1. M. Akdere and S. Schmidt, "Measuring the Effects of Employee Orientation Training on Employee Perception," *The Business Review* (Summer 2007), pp. 322–327.

2. Towers Perrin, *Talent Management: The State of the Art* (Toronto, ON: Towers Perrin, 2005); E. Chadnick, "Is HR Prepared to Keep the Keepers?" *Canadian HR Reporter* (January 29, 2007).

3. C. Hall and S. Cotsman, *Learning as a Lever for Performance: Learning and Development Outlook*, 13th ed. (Ottawa, ON: The Conference Board of Canada, 2015).

4. B.W. Pascal, "The Orientation Wars," *Workplace Today* (October 2001), p. 4.

5. B. Pomfret, "Sound Employee Orientation Program Boosts Productivity and Safety," *Canadian HR Reporter* (January 25, 1999), pp. 17–19.

6. L. Shelat, "First Impressions Matter—A Lot," *Canadian HR Reporter* (May 3, 2004), pp. 11, 13.

7. G. Chao et al., "Organizational Socialization: Its Content and Consequences," *Journal of Applied Psychology*, 79, no. 5 (1994), pp. 730–743.

8. S. Jackson, "After All That Work in Hiring, Don't Let New Employees Dangle," *Canadian HR Reporter* (May 19, 1997), p. 13.

9. A. Macaulay, "The Long and Winding Road," *Canadian HR Reporter* (November 16, 1998), pp. G1–G10.

10. "Employee Onboarding Guides New Hires," *Workspan* (January 2009), p. 119.

11. D. Chhabra, "What Web-Based Onboarding Can Do for Your Company," *Workspan* (May 2008), pp. 111–114.

12. D. Chhabra, "What Web-Based Onboarding Can Do for Your Company," *Workspan* (May 2008), pp. 111–114.

13. R. Harrison, "Onboarding: The First Step in Motivation and Retention," *Workspan* (September 2007), pp. 43–45.

14. D. Barnes, "Learning Is Key to Post-Merger Success," *Canadian HR Reporter* (July 12, 1999), pp. 16–17.

15. C. Gibson, "Online Orientation: Extending a Welcoming Hand to New Employees," *Canadian HR Reporter* (November 30, 1998), pp. 22–23.

16. "Onboarding: Virtual Orientation at IBM," *HR Professional* (August/ September 2008), p. 12.

17. D. Brown, "Execs Need Help Learning the Ropes Too," *Canadian HR Reporter* (April 22, 2002), p. 2.

18. D. Brown, "Execs Need Help Learning the Ropes Too," *Canadian HR Reporter* (April 22, 2002), p. 2.

19. "The Critical Importance of Executive Integration," *Drake Business Review* (December 2002), pp. 6–8.

20. S. Mingail, "Employers Need a Lesson in Training," *Canadian HR Reporter* (February 11, 2002), pp. 22–23.

21. U. Vu, "Trainers Mature into Business Partners," *Canadian HR Reporter* (July 12, 2004), pp. 1–2.

22. V. Galt, "Training Falls Short: Study," *Globe and Mail* (July 9, 2001), p. M1.

23. *Knowledge Matters: Skills and Learning for Canadians* (Government of Canada, 2002), p. 3, www11.sdc.gc.ca/sl-ca/doc/summary.shtml (accessed June 7, 2006).

24. A. Tomlinson, "More Training Critical in Manufacturing," *Canadian HR Reporter* (November 4, 2002), p. 2.

25. D. Brown, "PM Calls for Business to Spend More on Training," *Canadian HR Reporter* (December 16, 2002), pp. 1, 11; D. Brown, "Budget Should Include More for Training: Critics," *Canadian HR Reporter* (March 10, 2003), pp. 1–2; D. Brown, "Legislated Training, Questionable Results," *Canadian HR Reporter* (May 6, 2002), pp. 1, 12.

26. N.L. Trainor, "Employee Development the Key to Talent Attraction and Retention," *Canadian HR Reporter* (November 1, 1999), p. 8.

27. M. Belcourt, P.C. Wright, and A.M. Saks, *Managing Performance through Training and Development*, 2nd ed. (Toronto, ON: Nelson Thomson Learning, 2000); see also A.M. Saks and R.R. Haccoun, "Easing the Transfer of Training," *Human Resources Professional* (July–August 1996), pp. 8–11.

28. J.A. Colquitt, J.A. LePine, and R.A. Noe, "Toward an Integrative Theory of Training Motivation: A Meta-Analytic Path Analysis of 20 Years of Research," *Journal of Applied Psychology*, 85 (2000), pp. 678–707.

29. M. Georghiou, "Games, Simulations Open World of Learning," *Canadian HR Reporter* (May 5, 2008).

30. K.A. Smith-Jentsch et al., "Can Pre-Training Experiences Explain Individual Differences in Learning?" *Journal of Applied Psychology*, 81, no. 1 (1986), pp. 100–116.

31. J.A. Cannon-Bowers et al., "A Framework for Understanding Pre-Practice Conditions and Their Impact on Learning," *Personnel Psychology*, 51 (1988), pp. 291–320.

32. Based on K. Wexley and G. Latham, *Developing and Training Human Resources in Organizations* (Glenview, IL: Scott, Foresman, 1981), pp. 22–27.

33. G. Na, "An Employer's Right to Train," *Canadian HR Reporter* (October 6, 2008).

34. J.C. Georges, "The Hard Realities of Soft Skills Training," *Personnel Journal*, 68, no. 4 (April 1989), pp. 40–45; R.H. Buckham, "Applying Role Analysis in the Workplace," *Personnel*, 64, no. 2 (February 1987), pp. 63–65; J.K. Ford and R. Noe, "Self-Assessed Training Needs: The Effects of Attitudes towards Training, Management Level, and Function," *Personnel Psychology*, 40, no. 1 (Spring 1987), pp. 39–54.

35. G.N. Nash, J.P. Muczyk, and F.L. Vettori, "The Role and Practical Effectiveness of Programmed Instruction," *Personnel Psychology*, 24 (1971), pp. 397–418.

36. N. Day, "Informal Learning Gets Results," *Workforce* (June 1998), p. 31.

37. S. Williams, "'Classroom' Training Alive and Changing," *Canadian HR Reporter* (October 6, 2008).

38. K. Wexley and G. Latham, *Developing and Training Human Resources in Organizations* (Glenview, IL: Scott, Foresman, 1981), p. 107.

39. "Apprenticeship Grant Gets Going," *Canadian HR Reporter* (January 25, 2007); "New Funding for Apprenticeships," *Canadian HR Reporter* (May 3, 2004), p. 2; "Ontario Boosts Apprenticeship Program with $37 Million Investment," *Canadian HR Reporter* (April 7, 2000); ThinkTrades (Alberta Aboriginal Apprenticeship Project), www.thinktrades.com/candidates.htm (accessed June 13, 2006).

40. "German Training Model Imported," *BNA Bulletin to Management* (December 19, 1996), p. 408; L. Burton, "Apprenticeship: The Learn While You Earn Option," *Human Resources Professional* (February/March 1998), p. 25; H. Frazis, D.E. Herz, and M.W. Harrigan, "Employer-Provided Training: Results from a New Survey," *Monthly Labor Review*, 118 (1995), pp. 3–17.

41. O. Diss, "Deploying a New E-Learning Program?" *HR Professional* (October–November 2005), p. 16.

42. M. Emery and M. Schubert, "A Trainer's Guide to Videoconferencing," *Training* (June 1993), p. 60.

43. K. Wexley and G. Latham, *Developing and Training Human Resources in Organizations* (Glenview, IL: Scott, Foresman, 1981), p. 141; see also R. Wlozkowski, "Simulation," *Training and Development Journal*, 39, no. 6 (June 1985), pp. 38–43.

44. W. Powell, "Like Life?" *Training & Development* (February 2002), pp. 32–38; see also A. Macaulay, "Reality-Based Computer Simulations Allow Staff to Grow through Failure," *Canadian HR Reporter* (October 23, 2000), pp. 11–12.

45. M. Belcourt, P.C. Wright, and A.M. Saks, *Managing Performance through Training and Development*, 2nd ed. (Toronto, ON: Nelson Thomson Learning, 2002), pp. 188–202.

46. M. Belcourt, P.C. Wright, and A.M. Saks, *Managing Performance through Training and Development*, 2nd ed. (Toronto, ON: Nelson Thomson Learning, 2002), p. 9.

47. D. Kirkpatrick, "Effective Supervisory Training and Development," Part 3, "Outside Programs," *Personnel*, 62, no. 2 (February 1985), pp. 39–42. Among the reasons training might not pay off on the job are a mismatching of courses and trainees' needs, supervisory slip-ups (with supervisors signing up trainees and then forgetting to have them attend the sessions when the training session is actually given), and lack of help in applying skills on the job.

48. S. O'Neal and J. Gebauer, "Talent Management in the 21st Century: Attracting, Retaining and Engaging Employees of Choice," *WorldatWork Journal* (First Quarter, 2006), pp. 6–17.

49. F. Otte and P. Hutcheson, *Helping Employees Manage Careers* (Englewood Cliffs, NJ: Prentice Hall, 1992), pp. 5–6.

50. M. Duarte, "O indivíduo e a organização: Perspectivas de desenvolvimento" (The Individual and the Organization: Perspectives of Development)," *Psychologica (Extra-Série)* (2004), pp. 549–557.

51. E.H. Schein, "Organizational Psychology Then and Now: Some Observations," *Annual Review of Organizational Psychology and Organizational Behavior*, 2, no. 1 (2015), 1–19.

52. M. Savickas, L. Nota, J. Rossier, J. Dauwalder, M. Duarte, J. Guichard, S. Soresi, R. Van Esbroeck, and A. Van Vianen, "Life Designing: A Paradigm for Career Construction in the 21st Century," *Journal of Vocational Behavior* (May 2009), pp. 239–250.

53. M. Duarte, "O indivíduo e a organização: Perspectivas de desenvolvimento" (The Individual and the Organization: Perspectives of Development)," *Psychologica (Extra-Série)* (2004), pp. 549–557.

54. W. Enelow, *100 Ways to Recession-Proof Your Career* (Toronto, ON: McGraw-Hill, 2002), p. 1.

55. P. Linkow, "Winning the Competition for Talent: The Role of the New Career Paradigm in Total Rewards," *Workspan* (October 2006), pp. 28–32.

56. M. Watters and L. O'Connor, *It's Your Move: A Personal and Practical Guide to Career Transition and Job Search for Canadian Managers, Professionals and Executives* (Toronto, ON: HarperCollins, 2001).

57. J. Rogers, "Baby Boomers and Their Career Expectations," *Canadian Business Review* (Spring 1993), pp. 13–18.

58. R. Chanick, "Career Growth for Baby Boomers," *Personnel Journal*, 71, no. 1 (January 1992), pp. 40–46.

59. D. Quinn Mills, *Labor–Management Relations* (New York, NY: McGraw-Hill, 1986), pp. 387–396.

60. G. Dessler, *Winning Commitment* (New York, NY: McGraw-Hill, 1993), pp. 144–149.

61. J. Famularo, *Handbook of Modern Personnel Administration* (New York, NY: McGraw-Hill, 1972), p. 17.

Chapter 7

1. J.T. Rich, "The Solutions for Employee Performance Management," *Workspan* (February 2002), pp. 32–37.

2. J.A. Rubino, "Aligning Performance Management and Compensation Rewards Successfully," *WorldatWork Canadian News* (Fourth Quarter, 2004), pp. 12–16.

3. Conference Board of Canada, *Performance Management: Turning Individual Stress to Organizational Strategy* (Ottawa, ON: Conference Board of Canada, 2012), p. 2.

4. P. Nel, O. Van Dyk, G. Haasbroek, H. Schultz, T. Sono, and A. Werner, *Human Resource Management* (Cape Town, South Africa: Oxford University Press, 2004).

5. A.S. DeNisi and K.R. Murphy, (2017). "Performance Appraisal and Performance Management: 100 Years of Progress?" *Journal of Applied Psychology*, 102, no. 3 (2017), pp. 421–433,http://dx.doi.org/10.1037/apl0000085.

6. D. Brown, "HR Improving at Performance Management," *Canadian HR Reporter* (December 2, 2002), pp. 1, 14.

7. "The Performance-Management Process," *Workspan* (October 2006), p. 96.

8. J. Cooper and S. Jackson, *Human Resources Trends and Metrics: Talent Management Benchmarking*, 4th ed. (Ottawa, ON: The Conference Board of Canada, 2017).

9. R. Thorndike, "Concepts of Culture-Fairness," *Journal of Educational Measurement* (Summer, 1971), pp. 63–70.

10. S. Motowidlo and J. Van Scotter, "Evidence That Task Performance Should Be Distinguished from Contextual Performance," *Journal of Applied Psychology* (November 1993), pp. 475–480.

11. R. Tett, K. Fox, and P. Palmer, "Task and Contextual Performance as Formal and Expected Work Behaviors," Paper presented at the 18th annual Society of Industrial Organizational Psychologists Conference (Orlando, FL, April 2002).

12. J. Cooper and S. Jackson, *Human Resources Trends and Metrics: Talent Management Benchmarking*, 4th ed. (Ottawa, ON: The Conference Board of Canada, 2017).

13. M. Buckingham and A. Goodall, "Reinventing Performance Management," *Harvard Business Review* (April 2015), https://hbr.org/2015/04/reinventing-performance-management.

14. P. Cappelli and A. Tavis, "The Performance Management Revolution," *Harvard Business Review* (October 2016), https://hbr.org/2016/10/the-performance-management-revolution.

15. A.D. Ellinger, R.G. Hamlin, and R.S. Beattie, "Behavioural Indicators of Ineffective Managerial Coaching: A Cross-National Study," *Journal of European Industrial Training*, 32, no. 4 (2008), pp. 240–257; B. Redshaw, "Do We Really Understand Coaching? How Can We Make It Work Better?" *Industrial and Commercial Training*, 32, no. 3 (2000), pp. 106–108.

16. R.S. Beattie, "Line Managers and Workplace Learning: Learning from the Voluntary Sector," *Human Resource Development International*, 9, no. 1 (2006), pp. 99–119.

17. P. Cappelli and A. Tavis, "The Performance Management Revolution," *Harvard Business Review* (October 2016), https://hbr.org/2016/10/the-performance-management-revolution.

18. Conference Board of Canada, *Performance Management: Turning Individual Stress to Organizational Strategy* (Ottawa, ON: Conference Board of Canada, 2012).

19. C.L. Hughes, "The Bell-Shaped Curve That Inspires Guerrilla Warfare," *Personnel Administrator* (May 1987), pp. 40–41.

20. D. Rock and B. Jones, "Why More and More Companies Are Ditching Performance Ratings," *Harvard Business Review* (September 8, 2015), https://hbr.org/2015/09/why-more-and-more-companies-are-ditching-performance-ratings.

21. D. Bernardin and P. Smith, "A Clarification of Some Issues Regarding the Development and Use of Behaviorally Anchored Ratings Scales (BARS)," *Journal of Applied Psychology,* 66 (August 1981), pp. 458–463.

22. D. Bownas and H. Bernardin, "Critical Incident Technique," in S. Gael (ed.), *The Job Analysis Handbook for Business, Industry, and Government* (New York, NY: Wiley, 1988), pp. 1120–1137.

23. N. Hauenstein, R. Brown, and A. Sinclair, "BARS and Those Mysterious, Missing Middle Anchors," *Journal of Business and Psychology,* 25, no. 4 (May 2010), pp. 663–672.

24. J. Goodale and R. Burke, "Behaviorally Based Rating Scales Need Not Be Job Specific," *Journal of Applied Psychology,* 60, no. 3 (June 1975), 389–391.

25. K.R. Murphy and J. Constans, "Behavioral Anchors as a Source of Bias in Rating," *Journal of Applied Psychology,* 72, no. 4 (November 1987), pp. 573–577.

26. E. Mone and M. London, *Employee Engagement through Effective Performance Management: A Manager's Guide* (New York, NY: Routledge, 2009).

27. S. Kerr and S. Landouer, "Using Stretch Goals to Promote Organizational Effectiveness and Personal Growth: General Electric and Goldman Sachs," *Academy of Management Executive* (November 2004), pp. 134–138.

28. C. Maslach and M. Leiter, "Early Predictors of Job Burnout and Engagement," *Journal of Applied Psychology,* 93, no. 3 (May 2008), pp. 498–512, http://dx.doi.org/10.1037/0021-9010.93.3.498.

29. M. Levy, "Almost-Perfect Performance Appraisals," *Personnel Journal,* 68, no. 4 (April 1989), pp. 76–83.

30. D.B. Jarvis and R.E. McGilvery, "Poor Performers," *HR Professional* (June/July 2005), p. 32.

31. D. Brown, "Performance Management Systems Need Fixing: Survey," *Canadian HR Reporter* (April 1, 2005), pp. 1, 10.

32. See also J. Greenberg, "Using Explanations to Manage Impressions of Performance Appraisal Fairness," *Employee Responsibilities and Rights Journal,* 4, no. 1 (March 1991), pp. 51–60.

33. R.G. Johnson, *The Appraisal Interview Guide* (New York, NY: AMACOM, 1979), ch. 9.

34. J. Block, *Performance Appraisal on the Job: Making It Work* (New York, NY: Executive Enterprises Publications, 1981), pp. 58–62; see also T. Lowe, "Eight Ways to Ruin a Performance Review," *Personnel Journal,* 65, no. 1 (January 1986).

35. C. Howard, "Appraise This!" *Canadian Business* (May 23, 1998), p. 96.

36. E. Farndale, V. Hope-Hailey, and C. Kelliher, "High Commitment Performance Management: The Roles of Justice and Trust," *Personnel Review,* 40, no. 1 (2011), pp. 5–23.

37. E. Mone, C. Eisinger, K. Guggenheim, B. Price, and C. Stine, "Performance Management at the Wheel: Driving Employee Engagement in Organizations," *Journal of Business and Psychology,* 26, no. 2 (May 2011), pp. 205–212.

38. K.S. Teel, "Performance Appraisal: Current Trends, Persistent Progress," *Personnel Journal,* 59, no. 4 (April 1980), pp. 296–316.

39. D. Brown, "Performance Management Systems Need Fixing: Survey," *Canadian HR Reporter* (April 11, 2005), pp. 1, 10; M. Waung and S. Highhouse, "Fear of Conflict and Empathic Buffering: Two Explanations for the Inflation of Performance Feedback," *Organizational Behavior and Human Decision Processes,* 71 (1997), pp. 37–54.

40. Y. Ganzach, "Negativity (and Positivity) in Performance Evaluation: Three Field Studies," *Journal of Applied Psychology,* 80 (1995), pp. 491–499.

41. T.J. Maurer and M.A. Taylor, "Is Sex by Itself Enough? An Exploration of Gender Bias Issues in Performance Appraisal," *Organizational Behavior and Human Decision Processes,* 60 (1994), pp. 231–251; see also C.E. Lance, "Test for Latent Structure of Performance Ratings Derived from Wherry's (1952) *Theory of Ratings,*" *Journal of Management,* 20 (1994), pp. 757–771.

42. S.E. Scullen, M.K. Mount, and M. Goff, "Understanding the Latent Structure of Job Performance Ratings," *Journal of Applied Psychology,* 85 (2001), pp. 956–970.

43. A.M. Saks and D.A. Waldman, "The Relationship between Age and Job Performance Evaluations for Entry-Level Professionals," *Journal of Organizational Behavior,* 19 (1998), pp. 409–419.

44. W.C. Borman, L.A. White, and D.W. Dorsey, "Effects of Ratee Task Performance and Interpersonal Factors in Supervisor and Peer Performance Ratings," *Journal of Applied Psychology,* 80 (1995), pp. 168–177.

45. K. Murphy, W. Balzer, M. Lockhart, and E. Eisenman, "Effects of Previous Performance on Evaluations of Present Performance," *Journal of Applied Psychology,* 70, no. 1 (1985), pp. 72–84; see also K. Williams, A. DeNisi, B. Meglino, and T. Cafferty, "Initial Decisions and Subsequent Performance Ratings," *Journal of Applied Psychology,* 71, no. 2 (May 1986), pp. 189–195.

46. S. Appelbaum, M. Roy, and T. Gillilan, "Globalization of Performance Appraisals: Theory and Applications," *Management Decision,* 49, no. 4 (2011), pp. 570–585.

47. J. Hedge and M. Cavanagh, "Improving the Accuracy of Performance Evaluations: Comparison of Three Methods of Performance Appraiser Training," *Journal of Applied Psychology,* 73, no. 1 (February 1988), pp. 68–73.

48. B. Davis and M. Mount, "Effectiveness of Performance Appraisal Training Using Computer Assistance Instruction and Behavior Modeling," *Personnel Psychology,* 37 (Fall 1984), pp. 439–452.

49. T. Athey and R. McIntyre, "Effect of Rater Training on Rater Accuracy: Levels of Processing Theory and Social Facilitation Theory Perspectives," *Journal of Applied Psychology,* 72, no. 4 (November 1987), pp. 567–572.

50. M.M. Greller, "Participation in the Performance Appraisal Review: Inflexible Manager Behavior and Variable Worker Needs," *Human Relations,* 51 (1998), pp. 1061–1083.

51. R. Arvey, and J. Campion, "The Employment Interview: A Summary and Review of Recent Research," *Personnel Psychology,* 35 (June 1982), pp. 281–322; W. Wiesner and S. Cronshaw, "A Meta-Analytic Investigation of the Impact of Interview Format and Degree of Structure on the Validity of the Employment Interview," *Journal of Occupational Psychology,* 61, no. 4 (1988), pp. 275–290; K. Murphy, and J. Cleveland, *Understanding Performance Appraisal: Social, Organizational, and Goal-Based Perspectives* (Thousand Oaks, CA: Sage, 1995).

52. P. Loucks, "Plugging into Performance Management," *Canadian HR Reporter* (February 26, 2007).

53. B.D. Cawley, L.M. Keeping, and P.E Levy, "Participation in the Performance Appraisal Process and Employee Reactions: A Meta-Analytic Review of Field Investigations," *Journal of Applied Psychology,* 83 (1998), pp. 615–633.

54. J.W. Lawrie, "Your Performance: Appraise It Yourself!" *Personnel,* 66, no. 1 (January 1989), pp. 21–33; includes a good explanation of how self-appraisals can be used at work. See also A. Furnham and P. Stringfield, "Congruence in Job-Performance Ratings: A Study of 360° Feedback Examining Self, Manager, Peers, and Consultant Ratings," *Human Relations,* 51 (1998), pp. 517–530.

55. P.A. Mabe III and S.G. West, "Validity of Self-Evaluation of Ability: A Review and Meta-Analysis," *Journal of Applied Psychology,* 67, no. 3 (1982), pp. 280–296.

56. J. Russell and D. Goode, "An Analysis of Managers' Reactions to Their Own Performance Appraisal Feedback," *Journal of Applied Psychology,* 73, no. 1 (February 1988), pp. 63–67; M.M. Harris and J. Schaubroeck, "A Meta-Analysis of Self–Supervisor, Self–Peer, and Peer–Supervisor Ratings," *Personnel Psychology,* 41 (1988), pp. 43–62.

57. V.V. Druskat and S.B. Wolff, "Effects and Timing of Developmental Peer Appraisals in Self-Managing Work Groups," *Journal of Applied Psychology,* 84 (1999), pp. 58–74.

58. M.M. Harris and J. Schaubroeck, "A Meta-Analysis of Self–Supervisor, Self–Peer, and Peer–Supervisor Ratings," *Personnel Psychology,* 41 (1988), pp. 43–62.

59. W.C. Borman, "The Rating of Individuals in Organizations: An Alternate Approach," *Organizational Behavior and Human Performance,* 12 (1974), pp. 105–124.

60. H.J. Bernardin and R.W. Beatty, "Can Subordinate Appraisals Enhance Managerial Productivity?" *Sloan Management Review* (Summer 1987), pp. 63–73.

61. M. London and A. Wohlers, "Agreement between Subordinate and Self-Ratings in Upward Feedback," *Personnel Psychology,* 44 (1991), pp. 375–390.

62. M. London and A. Wohlers, "Agreement between Subordinate and Self-Ratings in Upward Feedback," *Personnel Psychology,* 44 (1991), p. 376.

63. D. Antonioni, "The Effects of Feedback Accountability on Upward Appraisal Ratings," *Personnel Psychology,* 47 (1994), pp. 349–355.

64. T.J. Maurer, N.S. Raju, and W.C. Collins, "Peer and Subordinate Performance Appraisal Measurement Equivalence," *Journal of Applied Psychology,* 83 (1998), pp. 693–702.

65. R. Reilly, J. Smither, and N. Vasilopoulos, "A Longitudinal Study of Upward Feedback," *Personnel Psychology,* 49 (1996), pp. 599–612.

66. K. Nowack, "360-Degree Feedback: The Whole Story," *Training and Development* (January 1993), p. 69; for a description of some of the problems involved in implementing 360-degree feedback, see M. Budman, "The Rating Game," *Across the Board,* 31, no. 2 (February 1994), pp. 35–38.

67. C. Romano, "Fear of Feedback," *Management Review* (December 1993), p. 39; see also M.R. Edwards and A.J. Ewen, "How to Manage Performance and Pay with 360-Degree Feedback," *Compensation and Benefits Review,* 28, no. 3 (May/June 1996), pp. 41–46.

68. G.P. Latham, J. Almost, S. Mann, and C. Moore, "New Developments in Performance Management," *Organizational Dynamics,* 34, no. 1 (2005), pp. 77–87; R. Brillinger, "The Many Faces of 360-Degree Feedback," *Canadian HR Reporter* (December 16, 1996), p. 21.

69. J.F. Milliman, R.A. Zawacki, C. Norman, L. Powell, and J. Kirksey, "Companies Evaluate Employees from All Perspectives," *Personnel Journal,* 73, no. 11 (November 1994), pp. 99–103.

70. R. Brillinger, "The Many Faces of 360-Degree Feedback," *Canadian HR Reporter* (December 16, 1996), p. 20.

71. R. Brillinger, "The Many Faces of 360-Degree Feedback," *Canadian HR Reporter* (December 16, 1996), p. 20.

72. D.A. Waldman, L.A. Atwater, and D. Antonioni, "Has 360-Degree Feedback Gone Amok?" *Academy of Management Executive,* 12 (1998), pp. 86–94.

73. P.E. Levy, B.D. Cawley, and R.J. Foti, "Reactions to Appraisal Discrepancies: Performance Ratings and Attributions," *Journal of Business and Psychology,* 12 (1998), pp. 437–455.

74. M. Derayeh and S. Brutus, "Learning from Others' 360-Degree Experiences," *Canadian HR Reporter* (February 10, 2003), pp. 18, 23.

75. A.S. DeNisi and A.N. Kluger, "Feedback Effectiveness: Can 360-Degree Appraisal Be Improved?" *Academy of Management Executive,* 14 (2000), pp. 129–139.

76. T. Bentley, "Internet Addresses 360-Degree Feedback Concerns," *Canadian HR Reporter* (May 8, 2000), pp. G3, G15.

77. L. Axline, "Ethical Considerations of Performance Appraisals," *Management Review* (March 1994), p. 62.

78. G. Barrett and M. Kernan, "Performance Appraisal and Terminations: A Review of Court Decisions Since Brito v. Zia with Implications for Personnel Practices," *Personnel Psychology,* 40, no. 3 (Autumn 1987), pp. 489–504.

79. J. Kochnarski and A. Sorenson, "Managing Performance Management," *Workspan* (September 2005), pp. 20–37.

80. E.E. Lawler and M. McDermott, "Current Performance Management Practices," *WorldatWork Journal,* 12, no. 2 (2003), pp. 49–60.

81. D. Bell, J. Blanchet, and N. Gore, "Performance Management: Making It Work Is Worth the Effort," *WorldatWork Canadian News,* 12, no. 11 (Fourth Quarter, 2004), pp. 1, 27–28.

Chapter 8

1. "Enhancing Your Employee Value Proposition," Mercer website, www.mercer.com/about-mercer/lines-of-business/talent/employee-value-proposition.html (accessed March 31, 2017).

2. R. Wagner, "An 'Employee Value Proposition' Mindset Just Might Fix Employee Engagement," *Forbes* (January 23, 2017), www.forbes.com/sites/roddwagner/2017/01/23/an-employee-value-proposition-mindset-just-might-fix-employee-engagement/#2bcf2efc4c3d (accessed July 18, 2017).

3. S. O'Neal, "Total Rewards and the Future of Work," *Workspan* (January 2005), pp. 18–26; S. Watson, "Total Rewards: Building a Better Employment Deal," *Workspan* (December 2003), pp. 48–51.

4. A. Cowan, *Compensation Planning Outlook 2011* (Ottawa, ON: Conference Board of Canada, 2011).

5. P.K. Zingheim and J.R. Schuster, *Pay People Right! Breakthrough Reward Strategies to Create Great Companies* (San Francisco, CA: Jossey-Bass, 2000); D. Brown, "Top Performers Must Get Top Pay," *Canadian HR Reporter* (May 8, 2000), pp. 7, 10; V. Dell'Agnese, "Performance-Based Rewards, Line-of-Sight Foster Ownership Behaviour in Staff," *Canadian HR Reporter* (October 8, 2001), p. 10.

6. S. Minken, "Does Lump Sum Pay Merit Attention?" *Personnel Journal* (June 1988), pp. 77–83; J. Newman and D. Fisher, "Strategic Impact Merit Pay," *Compensation and Benefits Review* (July–August 1992), pp. 38–45.

7. J. Pfeffer and R.I. Sutton, *Hard Facts, Dangerous Half-Truths, and Total Nonsense* (Boston MA: Harvard Business School Press, 2006).

8. W. Seithel and J. Emans, "Calculating Merit Increases: A Structured Approach," *Personnel,* 60, no. 5 (June 1985), pp. 56–68; D. Gilbert and G. Bassett, "Merit Pay Increases Are a Mistake," *Compensation and Benefits Review,* 26, no. 2 (March–April 1994), pp. 20–25.

9. C. Hathaway, S. Varney, and T. Smith, "Unlocking Value from Effective Compensation Management," Willis Towers Watson (January 27, 2017), www.willistowerswatson.com/en/insights/2017/01/unlocking-value-from-effective-compensation-management (accessed July 18, 2017).

10. "Employee Attraction and Retention," Western Compensation and Benefits Consultants, www.wcbc.ca/news/attractionretention (accessed September 26, 2011).

11. "GM, Daimler-Chrysler Workers Ratify Agreements," *Workplace Today* (December 1999), p. 11.

12. R. Sahl, "Job Content Salary Surveys: Survey Design and Selection Features," *Compensation and Benefits Review* (May–June 1991), pp. 14–21.

13. M.A. Thompson, "Rewards, Performance Two Biggest Words in HR Future," *WorldatWork Canadian News,* 10 (2002), pp. 1, 2, 11; A.Tekleab, K. Bartol, and W. Liu, "Is It Pay Levels or Pay Raises that Matter to Fairness and Turnover?" *Journal of Organizational Behaviour,* 26 (December 2005), pp. 899–921.

14. D. Brown, "StatsCan Unable to Explain Gender Wage Gap," *Canadian HR Reporter* (January 31, 2000), p. 3.

15. A. Silliker, "UBC Giving 2 Percent Raise to All Tenure-Stream Female Faculty," *Canadian HR Reporter* (March 11, 2013), Vol. 26(5), p. 3.

16. J. Dawe, "Compassionate Care Benefit: A New Alternative for Family Caregivers," *Workplace Gazette* (Summer 2004); S. Klie, "Feds Expand Eligibility for Compassionate Care," *Canadian HR Reporter* (July 17, 2006).

17. E. Sibray and J.B. Cavallaro, "Case Study: Market Data and Job Evaluation Equals the Best of Both Worlds," *Workspan* (July 2007), pp. 27–30.

18. For example, a quantitative job analysis technique like the position analysis questionnaire generates quantitative information on the degree to which the following five basic factors are present in each job: having decision making/communication/social responsibilities, performing skilled activities, being physically active, operating vehicles or equipment, and processing information.

19. H. Risher, "Job Evaluation: Validity and Reliability," *Compensation and Benefits Review,* 21 (January–February 1989), pp. 22–36.

20. S. Werner, R. Konopaske, and C. Touhey, "Ten Questions to Ask Yourself about Compensation Surveys," *Compensation and Benefits Review,* 31 (May/June 1999), pp. 54–59.

21. P. Cappelli, *The New Deal at Work: Managing the Market-Driven Workforce* (Boston, MA: Harvard Business School Press, 1999).

22. S. Werner, R. Konopaske, and C. Touhey, "Ten Questions to Ask Yourself about Compensation Surveys," *Compensation and Benefits Review,* 31 (May/June 1999), pp. 54–59.

23. Canada NewsWire, "New Report Shows Certified Human Resources Professional (CHRP) Designation Translates to Higher Earnings and More Promotions," (September 12, 2013).

24. F.W. Cook, "Compensation Surveys Are Biased," *Compensation and Benefits Review* (September–October 1994), pp. 19–22.

25. K.R. Cardinal, "The Art and Science of the Match, or Why Job Matching Keeps Me Up at Night," *Workspan* (February 2004), pp. 53–56; S. Werner, R. Konopaske, and C. Touhey, "Ten Questions to Ask Yourself about Compensation Surveys," *Compensation and Benefits Review,* 31 (May/June 1999), pp. 1–6; see also U. Vu, "Know-How Pays in Comp Surveys," *Canadian HR Reporter* (April 7, 2003), p. 13.

26. D. Hofrichter, "Broadbanding: A 'Second Generation' Approach," *Compensation and Benefits Review* (September–October 1993), pp. 53–58; see also G. Bergel, "Choosing the Right Pay Delivery System to Fit Banding," *Compensation and Benefits Review,* 26 (July–August 1994), pp. 34–38.

27. C. Bacca and G. Starzmann, "Clarifying Competencies: Powerful Tools for Driving Business Success," *Workspan* (March 2006), pp. 44–46.

28. C. Bacca and G. Starzmann, "Clarifying Competencies: Powerful Tools for Driving Business Success," *Workspan* (March 2006), pp. 44–46.

29. P.K. Zingheim and J.R. Schuster, "Reassessing the Value of Skill-Based Pay," *WorldatWork Journal* (Third Quarter, 2002), pp. 42–49.

30. P.K. Zingheim, J.R. Schuster, and M.G. Dertien, "Measuring the Value of Work: The 'People-Based' Pay Solution," *WorldatWork Journal* (Third Quarter, 2005), pp. 42–49.

31. S. St.-Onge, "Competency-Based Pay Plans Revisited," *Human Resources Professional* (August/September 1998), pp. 29–34; J. Kochanski and P. Leblanc, "Should Firms Pay for Competencies: Competencies Have to Help the Bottom Line," *Canadian HR Reporter* (February 22, 1999), p. 10.

32. F. Giancola, "Skill-Based Pay—Issues for Consideration," *Benefits & Compensation Digest,* 44, no. 5 (May 2007), pp. 10–15.

33. D. Tyson, *Canadian Compensation Handbook* (Toronto, ON: Aurora Professional Press, 2002).

34. R.J. Long, "Ensuring Your Executive Compensation Plan Is an Asset Rather Than a Liability," *Canadian HR Reporter* (October 19, 1998), pp. 15–16; see also D. Brown, "Bringing Stock Options Back to the Surface," *Canadian HR Reporter* (May 7, 2001), p. 2.

35. J. Cameron and W.D. Pierce, *Rewards and Intrinsic Motivation: Resolving the Controversy* (Westport, CT: Bergin & Garvey, 2002); see also G. Bouchard, "When Rewards Don't Work," *Globe and Mail* (September 25, 2002), p. C3.

36. P.K. Zingheim and J.R. Schuster, *Pay People Right! Breakthrough Reward Strategies to Create Great Companies* (San Francisco, CA: Jossey-Bass, 2000).

37. S. Gross and J. Bacher, "The New Variable Pay Programs: How Some Succeed, Why Some Don't," *Compensation and Benefits Review* (January–February 1993), pp. 55–56; see also G. Milkovich and C. Milkovich, "Strengthening the Pay–Performance Relationship: The Research," *Compensation and Benefits Review* (November–December 1992), pp. 53–62; J. Schuster and P. Zingheim, "The New Variable Pay: Key Design Issues," *Compensation and Benefits Review* (March–April 1993), pp. 27–34.

38. D. Belcher, *Compensation Administration* (Englewood Cliffs, NJ: Prentice Hall, 1973), pp. 309–310.

39. S. A. Hewlett, L. Sherbin, and K. Sumberg, "How Gen Y and Boomers Will Re-shape Your Agenda," *Harvard Business Review* (July–August, 2009), pp. 71–76.

40. C. Hathaway, S. Varney, and T. Smith, "Unlocking Value from Effective Compensation Management," Willis Towers Watson (January 27, 2017), www.willistowerswatson.com/en/insights/2017/01/unlocking-value-from-effective-compensation-management (accessed July 18, 2017)

41. H. McAteer, *Compensation Planning Outlook* 2017 (Ottawa, ON: The Conference Board of Canada, 2016).

42. B. Duke, "Are Profit-Sharing Plans Making the Grade?" *Canadian HR Reporter* (January 11, 1999), pp. 8–9.

43. C. Baarda, *Compensation Planning Outlook 2006* (Ottawa, ON: Conference Board of Canada, 2006).

44. R. Murrill, "Executive Share Ownership," *Watson Wyatt Memorandum,* 11, no. 1 (March 1997), p. 11.

45. P. Robertson, "Increasing Productivity through an Employee Share Purchase Plan," *Canadian HR Reporter* (September 20, 1999), pp. 7, 9.

46. C. Beatty, "Our Company: Employee Ownership May Sound Drastic, But It Can Work," *HR Professional* (June/July 2004), p. 20.

47. B.W. Thomas and M.H. Olson, "Gainsharing: The Design Guarantees Success," *Personnel Journal* (May 1988), pp. 73–79; see also "Aligning Compensation with Quality," *Bulletin to Management, BNA Policy and Practice Series* (April 1, 1993), p. 97.

48. T.A. Welbourne and L. Gomez Mejia, "Gainsharing Revisited," *Compensation and Benefits Review* (July–August 1988), pp. 19–28.

49. P.K. Zingheim and J.R. Schuster, "Value Is the Goal," *Workforce* (February 2000), pp. 56–61.

50. "US Airways Employees to Get Profit Sharing Checks," *Entertainment Close-Up* (March 19, 2011).

51. A. Cowan, *Compensation Planning Outlook 2009* (Ottawa, ON: Conference Board of Canada, 2009).

52. B.R. Ellig, "Incentive Plans: Short-Term Design Issues," *Compensation Review*, 16, no. 3 (Third Quarter, 1984), pp. 26–36; B. Ellig, *Executive Compensation—A Total Pay Perspective* (New York, NY: McGraw-Hill, 1982), p. 187.

53. F.D. Hildebrand Jr., "Individual Performance Incentives," *Compensation Review*, 10 (Third Quarter, 1978), p. 32.

54. F.D. Hildebrand Jr., "Individual Performance Incentives," *Compensation Review*, 10 (Third Quarter, 1978), pp. 28–33.

55. P. Brieger, "Shareholders Target CEO Compensation," *Financial Post* (April 7, 2003), p. FP5; see also S.M. Van Putten and E.D. Graskamp, "End of an Era? The Future of Stock Options," *Compensation and Benefits Review* (September–October 2002), pp. 29–35; N. Winter, "The Current Crisis in Executive Compensation," *WorldatWork Canadian News* (Fourth Quarter, 2002), pp. 1–3; R.M. Kanungo and M. Mendonca, *Compensation: Effective Reward Management* (1997), p. 237.

56. A. Cowan, *Compensation Planning Outlook 2011* (Ottawa, ON: Conference Board of Canada, 2011).

57. R. Levasseur and D. D'Alessandro, "Preparing for Changes in Executive Compensation," *Workspan Canada: Workspan Focus* (January 2009), pp. 101–104.

58. A. Cowan, *Compensation Planning Outlook 2011* (Ottawa, ON: Conference Board of Canada, 2011).

59. R. Murrill, "Executive Share Ownership," *Watson Wyatt Memorandum*, 11, no. 1 (March 1997), p. 11.

60. *CPP Investment Board Proxy Voting Principles and Guidelines* (February 7, 2006).

61. R. Levasseur and D. D'Alessandro, "Preparing for Changes in Executive Compensation," *Workspan Canada: Workspan Focus* (January 2009), pp. 101–104.

62. J. Tallitsch and J. Moynahan, "Fine-Tuning Sales Compensation Programs," *Compensation and Benefits Review*, 26, no. 2 (March–April 1994), pp. 34–37.

63. J. Steinbrink, "How to Pay Your Sales Force," *Harvard Business Review*, 57 (July–August 1978), pp. 111–122.

64. T.H. Patten, "Trends in Pay Practices for Salesmen," *Personnel*, 43 (January–February 1968), pp. 54–63; see also C. Romano, "Death of a Salesman," *Management Review*, 83, no. 9 (September 1994), pp. 10–16.

65. D. Harrison, M. Virick, and S. William, "Working without a Net: Time, Performance, and Turnover under Maximally Contingent Rewards," *Journal of Applied Psychology*, 81 (1996), pp. 331–345.

66. R. Henderson, *Compensation Management* (Reston, VA: Reston, 1979), p. 363. For a discussion of the increasing use of incentives for blue-collar employees, see, for example, R. Henderson, "Contract Concessions: Is the Past Prologue?" *Compensation and Benefits Review*, 18, no. 5 (September–October 1986), pp. 17–30; see also A.J. Vogl, "Carrots, Sticks and Self-Deception," *Across-the-Board*, 3, no. 1 (January 1994), pp. 39–44.

67. D. Belcher, *Compensation Administration* (Englewood Cliffs, NJ: Prentice Hall, 1973), p. 314.

68. T. Wilson, "Is It Time to Eliminate the Piece Rate Incentive System?" *Compensation and Benefits Review* (March–April 1992), pp. 43–49.

69. D. Cable, "Strange Success," *Business Strategy Review* (March 1, 2008), pp. 45–47, http://dx.doi.org/_10.1111/j.1467-8616.2008.00517.x.

70. A. Saunier and E. Hawk, "Realizing the Potential of Teams through Team-Based Rewards," *Compensation and Benefits Review* (July–August 1994), pp. 24–33; S. Caudron, "Tie Individual Pay to Team Success," *Personnel Journal*, 73, no. 10 (October 1994), pp. 40–46.

71. L.N. McClurg, "Team Rewards: How Far Have We Come?" *Human Resource Management*, 40 (Spring 2001), pp. 73–86; see also A. Gostick, "Team Recognition," *Canadian HR Reporter* (May 21, 2001), p. 15.

72. K. Bartol and L. Hagmann, "Team-Based Pay Plans: A Key to Effective Teamwork," *Compensation and Benefits Review* (November–December 1992), pp. 24–29.

73. J. Nickel and S. O'Neal, "Small Group Incentives: Gainsharing in the Microcosm," *Compensation and Benefits Review* (March–April 1990), p. 24; see also J. Pickard, "How Incentives Can Drive Teamworking," *Personnel Management* (September 1993), pp. 26–32; S. Caudron, "Tie Individual Pay to Team Success," *Personnel Journal* 73, no. 10 (October 1994), pp. 40–46. For an explanation of how to develop a successful group incentive program, see K.D. Scott and T. Cotter, "The Team That Works Together Earns Together," *Personnel Journal*, 63 (March 1984), pp. 59–67.

74. "Bombardier Defers Executive Compensation Plan after Backlash," *CBC News* (April 3, 2017), www.cbc.ca/news/business/bombardier-executive-compensation-1.4052533 (accessed April 5, 2017); S. Deveau, "Air Canada CEO Took Home More than $9.5-million in 2012," *Financial Post* (May 31, 2013), http://business.financialpost.com/news/transportation/air-canada-ceo-took-home-more-than-9-5-million-in-2012 (accessed April 5, 2017).

75. Canadian Press, "CP Rail Cuts Executive Perks, Revises Compensation after Shareholder Criticism," *Toronto Star* (March 16, 2017), www.thestar.com/business/2017/03/16/cp-rail-cuts-executive-perks-revises-compensation-after-shareholder-criticism.html (accessed April 5, 2017).

76. S. Barton and K. Gribben, *When Is It Time to Get Worried about High Sales Force Turnover?* (Compensation Consulting, Aon Consultants, 2015) https://radford.aon.com/aon.radford/media/files/articles/2015/high_sales_force_turnover.pdf?ext=.pdf (accessed April 6, 2017).

Chapter 9

1. F. Hills, T. Bergmann, and V. Scarpello, *Compensation Decision Making* (Fort Worth, TX: The Dryden Press, 1994), p. 424; see also L.K. Beatty, "Pay and Benefits Break Away from Tradition," *HR Magazine*, 39 (November 1994), pp. 63–68.

2. R.K. Platt, "A Strategic Approach to Benefits," *Workspan* (July 2002), pp. 23–24.

3. S. Beech and J. Tompkins, "Do Benefits Plans Attract and Retain Talent?" *Benefits Canada* (October 2002), pp. 49–53.

4. The Conference Board of Canada, "Benefits Benchmarking 2012" (October 2012).

5. The Conference Board of Canada, "Benefits Benchmarking 2012" (October 2012).

6. Employment and Social Development Canada, "EI Regular Benefits—How Much You Could Receive," Government of Canada website (accessed July 19, 2017).

7. "EI Top-Ups Common—Survey," Canadian HR Reporter (February 23, 1998), p. 15.

8. Alberta, "Maternity Leave and Parental Leave," Employment Standards: Rights and Responsibilities at Work series (July 2014), http://work.alberta.ca/documents/Maternity-Leave-and-Parental-Leave.pdf (accessed April 20, 2018).

9. S. Rudner, "New Statutory Leave in Ontario: Additional Rights Provided in Specific Circumstances," *Canadian HR Reporter* (October 14, 2014), www.hrreporter.com/columnist/canadian-hr-law/archive/2014/10/14/new-statutory-leaves-in-ontario (accessed April 20, 2017).

10. D. Gunch, "The Family Leave Act: A Financial Burden?" *Personnel Journal* (September 1993), p. 49.

11. S. Pellegrini, "Considering Critical," *Benefits Canada* (April 2002), pp. 71–73.

12. "Employee Benefits in Small Firms," *BNA Bulletin to Management* (June 27, 1991), pp. 196–197.

13. "Employee Benefits," *Commerce Clearing House Ideas and Trends in Personnel* (January 23, 1991), pp. 9–11.

14. S. Dobson, "Health-Care Costs Maintain Dramatic Rise," *Canadian HR Reporter* (July 13, 2009).

15. *Canadian Health Care Trend Survey Results 2009* (Toronto, ON: Buck Consultants).

16. C. Kapel, "Unitel Asks Employees to Share Costs," *Canadian HR Reporter* (June 17, 1996), p. 17; see also J. Sloane and J. Taggart, "Runaway Drug Costs," *Canadian HR Reporter* (September 10, 2001), pp. 17–18; "Deductibles Could Be Making a Comeback," *Canadian HR Reporter* (February 26, 2001), pp. 2, 16.

17. J. Norton, "The New Drug Invasion," *Benefits Canada* (June 1999), pp. 29–32.

18. S. Felix, "Healthy Alternative," *Benefits Canada* (February 1997), p. 47; A. Dimon, "Money Well Spent," *Benefits Canada* (April 1997), p. 15.

19. A. Dimon, "Money Well Spent," *Benefits Canada* (April 1997), p. 15.

20. D. Jones, "Accounting for Health: The Present and Future of HCSAs and Other Consumer-Driven Health Care Products in Canada," *Benefits Canada* (January 2009), pp. 21–23.

21. J. Taggart, "Health Spending Accounts: A Prescription for Cost Control," *Canadian HR Reporter* (October 22, 2001), pp. 16, 18; see also "How Spending Accounts Work," *Canadian HR Reporter* (February 24, 2003), p. 16.

22. K. Gay, "Post-Retirement Benefits Costing Firms a Fortune," *Financial Post* (June 2, 1995), p. 18; S. Lebrun, "Turning a Blind Eye to Benefits," *Canadian HR Reporter* (February 24, 1997), p. 2; S. Pellegrini, "Keep Benefits Costs Low by Assessing Retiree Health," *Canadian HR Reporter* (June 14, 1999), pp. 9–10; M. Warren, "Uncovering the Costs," *Benefits Canada* (November 1996), p. 41; G. Dufresne, "Financing Benefits for Tomorrow's Retirees," *Canadian HR Reporter* (April 6, 1998), p. 11.

23. A. Khemani, "Post-Retirement Benefits Liability Grows," *Canadian HR Reporter* (November 4, 1996), p. 17; see also M. Warren, "Retiree Benefits Come of Age," *Benefits Canada* (May 2000), pp. 73–77.

24. *2008 Post-Retirement Trends* (Toronto, ON: Mercer Human Resources Consulting).

25. I. Ray-Ghosal & L. Shafee, "New Survey Finds 54 Percent of Canadians Admitting to Playing Hookey from Work: Feeling Burned or Stressed Out Cited as Key Reason," Kronos Press Release, May 15, 2013.

26. W. Pyper, "Aging, Health and Work," *Perspectives on Labour and Income* (Spring 2006), p. 48; S. Klie, "Private Health Coverage Enters Benefits Realm," *Canadian HR Reporter* (September 12, 2005), pp. 1, 22.

27. "Managing Episodic Disabilities Course," *HR Professional* (February–March 2009), p. 18.

28. A. Blake, "A New Approach to Disability Management," *Benefits Canada* (March 2000), pp. 58–64; P. Kulig, "Returning the Whole Employee to Work," *Canadian HR Reporter* (March 9, 1998), p. 20; see also A. Gibbs, "Gearing Disability Management to the Realities of Working Life," *Canadian HR Reporter* (December 2, 2002), p. G7.

29. J. Curtis and L. Scott, "Making the Connection," *Benefits Canada* (April 2003), pp. 75–79.

30. N. Rankin, "A Guide to Disability Management," *Canadian HR Reporter* (March 22, 1999), pp. 14–15.

31. *Staying@Work: Effective Presence at Work,* 2007 Survey Report–Canada (Toronto, ON: Watson Wyatt); "Mental Health Claims on the Rise in Canada," *WorldatWork Canadian News* (Third Quarter, 2005), pp. 15–16; D. Brown, "Mental Illness a Top Concern but Only Gets Band-Aid Treatment," *Canadian HR Reporter* (May 9, 2005), pp. 1, 3; "Mental Health Biggest Workplace Barrier, Women Say," *Canadian HR Reporter* (January 17, 2005), p. 2.

32. The Conference Board of Canada, "Unmet Mental Health Care Needs Costing Canadian Economy Billions," news release 17-20 (September 1, 2016), www.conferenceboard.ca/press/newsrelease/16-09-01/unmet_mental_health_care_needs_costing_canadian_economy_billions.aspx (accessed April 24, 2017).

33. J. Melnitzer, "Down and Out," *Workplace News* (September/October 2005), pp. 20–23; M. Burych, "Baby Blues," *Benefits Canada* (October 2000), pp 33–35.

34. B. Hayhoe, "The Case for Employee Retirement Planning," *Canadian HR Reporter* (May 20, 2002), p. 18.

35. J. Nunes, "Defined Benefit or Defined Contribution, It's Always Costly," *Canadian HR Reporter* (November 5, 2001), pp. 7, 9.

36. S. Klie, "Little Guarantee for Ontario Pensions," *Canadian HR Reporter* (May 4, 2009); S. Dobson, "Costs Top List of Concerns for DB Plan Sponsors: Survey," *Canadian HR Reporter* (March 24, 2008).

37. A. Scappatura, "DB Plans Endangered," *Canadian HR Reporter* (June 15, 2009); T. Humber, "The Death of the DB Pension," *Canadian HR Reporter* (March 23, 2009); S. Dobson, "Ottawa Provides Pension Relief," *Canadian HR Reporter* (December 15, 2008); D. Birschel, "Alberta and British Columbia Provide Pension Solvency Relief," *Benefits Quarterly*, 25, no. 2 (2009), p. 66.

38. T. Piskorski, "Minimizing Employee Benefits Litigation through Effective Claims Administration Procedures," *Employee Relations Law Journal*, 20, no. 3 (Winter 1994–95), pp. 421–431.

39. A. Rappaport, "Phased Retirement: An Important Part of the Evolving Retirement Scene," *Benefits Quarterly*, 25, no. 2 (2009), pp. 38–50; R. Castelli, "Phased Retirement Plans, *HR Professional* (December 2008/ January 2009), p. 23.

40. D. Brown, "New Brunswick Nurses Find Phased Retirement Solution," *Canadian HR Reporter* (September 22, 2003), pp. 1, 12; Y. Saint-Cyr, "Phased Retirement Agreements," *Canadian Payroll and Employment Law News*, www.hrpao.org/HRPAO/HRResourceCentre/LegalCentre/ (accessed July 11, 2005).

41. *Towers Perrin 2004 SERP Report: Supplementary Pensions Under Pressure* (Toronto, ON: Towers Perrin).

42. L. Burger, "Group Legal Service Plans: A Benefit Whose Time Has Come," *Compensation and Benefits Review,* 18 (July–August 1986), pp. 28–34.

43. "Financial Distress Impacts Health and Productivity: Employees Turning to EAP for Help," Shepell-fgi Research Group, 2009 Series, 5, no. 1; A. Scappatura, "EAP Use Soars as Economy Tanks: Study," *Canadian HR Reporter* (March 23, 2009); "Requests for Help through EAP Up Significantly," *Workspan* (February 2009), p. 13.

44. J. Hobel, "EAPs Flounder without Manager Support," *Canadian HR Reporter* (June 2, 2003), p. 7; P. Davies, "Problem Gamblers in the Workplace," *Canadian HR Reporter* (November 4, 2002), p. 17; A. Sharratt, "When a Tragedy Strikes," *Benefits Canada* (November 2002), pp. 101–105.

45. R. Csiernik, "The Great EAP Question: Internal or External?" *Canadian HR Reporter* (August 20, 2007).

46. R. Csiernik, "What to Look for in an External EAP Service," *Canadian HR Reporter* (May 31, 2004), p. 7; D. Sharar, "With HR Chasing Lowest Price, EAPs Can't Improve Quality," *Canadian HR Reporter* (May 31, 2004), pp. 6, 8; A. Davis, "Helping Hands," *Benefits Canada* (November 2000), pp. 117–121.

47. "100 Best Companies to Work For," *Fortune* (January 2000), http://money.cnn.com/magazines/fortune/fortune_archive/2000/01/10/271718/index.htm (accessed September 4, 2012).

48. Statistics Canada, "The Rise of the Dual-earner Family with Children: Canadian Megatrends," *The Daily* (May 30, 2016), www.statcan.gc.ca/pub/11-630-x/11-630-x2016005-eng.htm (accessed April 24, 2017).

49. S. Dobson, "Is Backup Care Worth the Investment?" *Canadian HR Reporter* (November 3, 2008); D. Brown, "Bringing the Family to Work," *Canadian HR Reporter* (November 6, 2000), pp. 19–20.

50. "Employer-Sponsored Child Care Can Be Instrumental in Attraction and Retention," *Workspan* (January 2009), p. 10.

51. G. Hermus, C. Stonebridge, L. Thériault, and F.Bounajm, *Home and Community Care in Canada: An Economic Footprint* (Ottawa, ON: Conference Board of Canada, 2012), p. iii, www.conferenceboard.ca/cashc/research/2012/homecommunitycare.aspx (accessed July 21, 2017).

52. C. Tinglin, "How to Help Employers with Eldercare Responsibilities," *Benefits Canada* (April 3, 2014), www.benefitscanada.com/benefits/health-benefits/benefits-column-care-package-50185 (accessed April 24, 2017).

53. B. Jaworski, "'I'll Have My People Call Your People,'" *Canadian HR Reporter* (March 27, 2006).

54. W. White and J. Becker, "Increasing the Motivational Impact of Employee Benefits," *Personnel* (January–February 1980), pp. 32–37; B. Olmsted and S. Smith, "Flex for Success!" *Personnel*, 66, no. 6 (June 1989), pp. 50–55.

55. B. McKay, "The Flexible Evolution," *Workplace News* (January/February 2006), pp. 14–15.

56. B. McKay, "The Flexible Evolution," *Workplace News* (January/February 2006), pp. 14–15.

57. D. Brown, "Everybody Loves Flex," *Canadian HR Reporter* (November 18, 2002), pp. 1, 11; R. Dawson and B. McKay, "The Flexibility of Flex," *WorldatWork Canadian News* (Fourth Quarter, 2005), pp. 1, 6–13.

58. B. Smith. "HR Is Going from In-House to Out-of-House," *Benefits Canada* (November 17, 2015), www.benefitscanada.com/benefits/health-wellness/hr-is-going-from-in-house-to-out-of-house-73246 (accessed April 25, 2017).

59. N. Chaplick, "Enter at Your Own Risk," *Benefits Canada* (May 2000), pp. 37–39; see also M. Reid, "Legal Aid," *Benefits Canada* (June 2000), pp. 46–48; S. Deller, "Five Hot Survival Tips for Communicating Benefits," *Canadian HR Reporter* (July 13, 1998), pp. 9, 19.

60. R. Taylor, "The Benefits Are the Message," *Canadian HR Reporter* (January 12, 2009).

HR by the Numbers: Smoking and the Workplace

The Conference Board of Canada, "Smoking Cessation and the Workplace: Briefing 2—Smoking Cessation Programs in Canadian Workplaces" (June 2013); American Cancer Society, "A Word About Quitting Success Rates" (January 17, 2013), www.cancer.org/healthy/stayawayfromtobacco/guidetoquittingsmoking/guide-to-quitting-smoking-success-rates (accessed June 21, 2013).

Chapter 10

1. D. Brown, "Wellness Programs Bring Healthy Bottom Line," *Canadian HR Reporter* (December 17, 2001), pp. 1, 14.

2. Association of Workers' Compensation Boards of Canada, *Tables of Accepted Time-Loss Injuries/Diseases and Fatalities—Age, Industry, Jurisdiction*, www.awcbc.org/common/assets/nwisptables/all_tables.pdf.

3. Association of Workers' Compensation Boards of Canada, www.awcbc.ca (accessed July 15, 2009); "Working to Death—Millions Die Each Year Due to Work-Related Accidents and Diseases," *IAPA Press Release* (April 19, 2006), www.iapa.ca/about_iapa/2006_apr19_press.asp (accessed June 20, 2006).

4. H. Bryan, "Attitude Is Everything," *WorkSafe Magazine* (October 2005), p. 18.

5. S. De Léséleuc, "Criminal Victimization in the Workplace," Canadian Centre for Justice Statistics Profile Series (2004), http://downloads.workplaceviolencenews.com/criminal_victimization_in_the_workplace.pdf (accessed September 26, 2011).

6. D.A. Hofmann, M.J. Burke, and D. Zohar, "100 Years of Occupational Safety Research: From Basic Protections and Work Analysis to a Multilevel View of Workplace Safety and Risk," *Journal of Applied Psychology*, 102, no. 3 (2017), pp. 375–388, http://dx.doi.org/10.1037/apl0000114.

7. D.A. Hofmann and A. Stetzer, "The Role of Safety Climate and Communication in Accident Interpretation: Implications for Learning from Negative Events," *Academy of Management Journal*, 41, no. 6 (1988), pp. 644–657; D. Zohar, "A Group-level Model of Safety Climate: Testing the Effect of Group Climate on Microaccidents in Manufacturing Jobs," *Journal of Applied Psychology*, 85, no. 4 (2000), pp. 587–596.

8. M. Morra, "Fun, with Caution," *Workplace* (March/April 2008), p. 1; L. Scott, "Measuring Employee Abilities," *Benefits Canada* (September 2002), pp. 41–49.

9. T.A. Opie and L. Bates, *1997 Canadian Master Labour Guide* (Toronto: CCH Canada, 1997), pp. 1015–1034.

10. C.A. Edwards and C.E. Humphrey, *Due Diligence under the Occupational Health and Safety Act: A Practical Guide* (Toronto, ON: Carswell/Thomson Canada, 2000).

11. N. Keith, "The Omniscient Employer: The Need to See the Unforeseeable," *Workplace* (March/April 2008), pp. 16–19.

12. M. Pilger, "Conducting a Hygiene Assessment," *Canadian HR Reporter* (April 10, 2000), pp. G3, G4; J. Montgomery, *Occupational Health and Safety* (Toronto, ON: Nelson Canada, 1996), p. 97; D. Brown, "Joint H&S Committees: An Opportunity, Not a Nuisance," *Canadian HR Reporter* (October 20, 2002), pp. 7, 10.

13. P. Strahlendorf, "What Supervisors Need to Know," *OH&S Canada* (January/February 1996), pp. 38–40; N. Tompkins, "Getting the Best Help from Your Safety Committee," *HR Magazine,* 40, no. 4 (April 1995), p. 76.

14. J. Grant and D. Brown, "The Inspector Cometh," *Canadian HR Reporter* (January 31, 2005), pp. 13, 17; "It's Time to Wake Up to Health and Safety: Ministry of Labour Increases Number of Inspectors," *Safety Mosaic,* 8 (Spring 2005), pp. 5–6.

15. "Alberta Imposes Record Penalties for OH&S Violations," *Workplace*, www.workplace-mag.com/Alberta-imposes-record-penalties-for-ohs-violations.html (accessed July 16, 2009).

16. S. Klie, "Individuals Targeted under OHS," *Canadian HR Reporter* (March 12, 2007); R. Stewart, "Legal Duties of the Front Line," *Canadian HR Reporter* (March 12, 2007).

17. "Employer Jailed for H&S Violation," *Canadian HR Reporter* (April 8, 2002), p. 2; see also T. Humber, "Putting the Boss Behind Bars?" *Canadian HR Reporter* (April 7, 2003).

18. "Quebec Employer First to Be Criminally Convicted in Death of Worker," *Canadian HR Reporter* (February 7, 2008); "C-45 Conviction Nets $110K Fine," *Canadian HR Reporter* (April 7, 2008).

19. K. Prisciak, "Health, Safety & Harassment?" *OH&S Canada* (April/May 1997), pp. 20–21.

20. *A Safety Committee Man's Guide*, Catalog no. 872684, Aetna Life and Casualty Insurance Company.

21. J. Roughton, "Job Hazard Analysis," *OH&S Canada* (January/February 1996), pp. 41–44.

22. J. Montgomery, *Occupational Health and Safety* (Toronto, ON: Nelson Canada, 1996), p. 34.

23. A. Fowler, "How to Make the Workplace Safer," *People Management*, 1, no. 2 (January 1995), pp. 38–39.

24. *A Safety Committee Man's Guide*, Catalog no. 872684, Aetna Life and Casualty Insurance Company; E. McCormick and J. Tiffin, *Industrial Psychology* (Englewood Cliffs, NJ: Prentice Hall, 1974).

25. J.M. Beus, L.Y. Dhanani, and M.A. McCord, "A Meta-Analysis of Personality and Workplace Safety: Addressing Unanswered Questions," *Journal of Applied Psychology*, 100 (2015), pp. 481–498, http://dx.doi.org/10.1037/a0037916; S. Clarke and I.T. Robertson, "A Meta-Analytic Review of the Big Five Personality Factors and Accident Involvement in Occupational and Non-occupational Settings, *Journal of Occupational and Organizational Psychology*, 78 (2005), pp. 355–376.

26. D.A. Hofmann, M.J. Burke, and D. Zohar, "100 Years of Occupational Safety Research: From Basic Protections and Work Analysis to a Multilevel View of Workplace Safety and Risk," *Journal of Applied Psychology* (2017, January 26), advance online publication, http://dx.doi.org/10.1037/apl0000114.

27. E. McCormick and J. Tiffin, *Industrial Psychology* (Englewood Cliffs, NJ: Prentice Hall, 1974), pp. 522–523; David DeJoy, "Attributional Processes and Hazard Control Management in Industry," *Journal of Safety Research*, 16 (Summer 1985), pp. 61–71.

28. E. McCormick and J. Tiffin, *Industrial Psychology* (Englewood Cliffs, NJ: Prentice Hall, 1974), p. 523.

29. A. Campbell, *All Signs Point to Yes: Literacy's Impact on Workplace Health and Safety* (Ottawa, ON: The Conference Board of Canada, 2008).

30. S. Dobson, "Evidence of Link between Literacy, Safety," *Canadian HR Reporter* (December 1, 2008).

31. A. Campbell, *All Signs Point to Yes: Literacy's Impact on Workplace Health and Safety* (Ottawa, ON: The Conference Board of Canada, 2008).

32. "IAPA Wins First Place at International Film and Multimedia Festival," *Workplace* (July 18, 2008).

33. M. Blum and J. Nayler, *Industrial Psychology* (New York, NY: Harper & Row, 1968), p. 522.

34. L. Scott, "Measuring Employee Abilities," *Benefits Canada* (September 2002), pp. 41–49.

35. K. Gillin, "Reduce Employee Exposure to Injury with Pre-Employment Screening Tests," *Canadian HR Reporter* (February 28, 2000), p. 10.

36. M.J. Burke, S.A. Sarpy, K. Smith-Crowe, S. Chan-Serafin, R.O. Salvador, and G. Islam, "Relative Effectiveness of Worker Safety and Health Training Methods," *American Journal of Public Health*, 96 (2006), pp. 315–324, http://dx.doi.org/10.2105/AJPH.2004.059840; D. Zohar, "The Effects of Leadership Dimensions, Safety Climate, and Assigned Priorities on Minor Injuries in Work Groups," *Journal of Organizational Behavior*, 23 (2002), pp. 75–92.

37. D. Zohar, "The Effects of Leadership Dimensions, Safety Climate, and Assigned Priorities on Minor Injuries in Work Groups," *Journal of Organizational Behavior*, 23 (2002), pp. 75–92.

38. M. Shaw, "Rewarding Health and Safety," *Canadian HR Reporter* (December 2, 2002), pp. 19–20.

39. A. Dunn, "Back in Business," *Workplace News* (April 2005), pp. 16–17.

40. Ergomed Solutions and C. Colacci, "Meet Your Return to Work Obligations with a Functional Abilities Evaluation," *Canadian HR Reporter* (April 10, 2000), p. G5.

41. C. Hall, "Sobering Advice," *Workplace News*, 11, no. 10 (November/December 2005), pp. 11–12.

42. Conference Board of Canada, *Problematic Substance Use and the Canadian Workplace* (Ottawa, ON: The Conference Board of Canada, 2016).

43. *British Columbia (Public Service Employee Relations Commission) v. B.C.G.S.E.U.*, (1999) 176 D.L.R. (4th) 1 (S.C.C.) [*Meiorin*].

44. Policy on Drug and Alcohol Testing, Ontario Human Rights Commission, www.ohrc.on.ca/en/resources/Policies/PolicyDrugAlch (accessed July 16, 2009).

45. D. McCutcheon, "Confronting Addiction," *HR Professional* (June/July 2009), p. 39.

46. D. O'Meara, "Sober Second Chance," *Alberta Venture*, 9, no. 2 (March 2005), http://albertaventure.com/2005/03/sober-second-chance/?year=2005 (accessed September 4, 2012).

47. A. Nicoll, *Time for Action: Managing Mental Health in the Workplace* (Toronto, ON: Mercer Human Resources Consulting, 2008); L. Duxbury and C. Higgins, *Exploring the Link between Work–Life Conflict and Demands on Canada's Health Care System: Report Three* (Ottawa, ON: Public Health Agency of Canada, March 2004).

48. D. Crisp, "Leaders Make the Difference," in A. Shaw, "Toxic Workplaces as Bad as Unsafe Ones," *Canadian HR Reporter* (April 21, 2008).

49. A. Nicoll, *Time for Action: Managing Mental Health in the Workplace* (Toronto, ON: Mercer Human Resources Consulting, 2008).

50. *Staying@Work: Effective Presence at Work: 2007 Survey Report: Canada* (Toronto, ON: Watson Wyatt).

51. C. Stonebridge and G. Sutherland, *Healthy Brains at Work: Estimating the Impact of Workplace Mental Health Benefits and Programs* (Ottawa, ON: Conference Board of Canada, 2016).

52. G. Hepburn, C. Boyer, and L. Chenier, *Running on Empty: Understanding Fatigue in the Workplace* (Ottawa, ON: Conference Board of Canada, 2016).

53. *Mental Health at Work: Booklet 1* (IRSST, Laval University, 2005).

54. Statistics Canada, "Study: Workaholics and Time Perception," *The Daily* (May 15, 2007).

55. "Is Your Job Making You Sick?" *Canadian HR Reporter* (September 17, 2008).

56. J.W. Simpson, "Psychopaths Wear Suits, Too," *National Post* (May 10, 2006), p. WK6; A. Gill, "The Psychopath in the Corner Office," *Globe and Mail* (May 27, 2006), p. F1; "Push for Productivity Taking Its Toll," *Canadian HR Reporter* (November 6, 2001), p. 15; D. Brown, "Doing More with Less Hurts Employees and Productivity," *Canadian HR Reporter* (October 7, 2002), pp. 3, 13; A. Sharratt, "Silver Linings," *Benefits Canada* (March 2003), pp. 51–53.

57. J. Santa-Barbara, "Preventing the Stress Epidemic," *Canadian HR Reporter* (March 8, 1999), p. 19; see also A. Chiu, "Beyond Physical Wellness: Mental Health Issues in the Workplace," *Canadian HR Reporter* (February 26, 2001), p. 4; L. Hyatt, "Job Stress: Have We Reached the Breaking Point?" *Workplace Today* (January 2002), pp. 14, 15, 37.

58. "Health Care Workers Most Stressed," *Canadian HR Reporter* (November 15, 2007).

59. P. Crawford-Smith, "Stressed Out," *Benefits Canada* (November 1999), pp. 115–117.

60. *Stress at Work: Taking Control* (Industrial Accident Prevention Association, 2002); J. Newman and T. Beehr, "Personal and Organizational Strategies for Handling Job Stress: A Review of Research and Opinion," *Personnel Psychology* (Spring 1979), pp. 1–43; see also Bureau of National Affairs, "Work Place Stress: How to Curb Claims," *Bulletin to Management* (April 14, 1988), p. 120.

61. T. Humber, "Stress Attack," *Canadian HR Reporter* (February 10, 2002), pp. G1, G10; M. Shain, "Stress and Satisfaction," *OH&S Canada* (April/May 1999), pp. 38–47.

62. P. Carayon, "Stressful Jobs and Non-Stressful Jobs: A Cluster Analysis of Office Jobs," *Ergonomics*, 37, no. 2 (1994), pp. 311–323.

63. *Workplace Mental Health Indicators: An EAP's Perspective*, series 1, vol. 1, no. 1 (Shepell-fgi Research Group, 2005).

64. A. Pihulyk, "When the Job Overwhelms," *Canadian HR Reporter* (January 14, 2002), p. 11.

65. P. Kishchuk, *Yukon Workers' Compensation Act Subsection 105.1 Research Series: Expansion of the Meaning of Disability* (March 2003).

66. M. Gibb-Clark, "The Case for Compensating Stress Claims," *Globe and Mail* (June 14, 1999), p. M1; L. Young, "Stressed Workers Are Suing Employers," *Canadian HR Reporter* (May 3, 1999), pp. 1, 6; D. Brown, "Liability Could Extend to Mental Damage," *Canadian HR Reporter* (October 9, 2000), pp. 1, 8.

67. J. Hampton, "RSIs: The Biggest Strain Is on the Bottom Line," *Canadian HR Reporter* (February 10, 1997), pp. 15.

68. "Prevent Workplace Pains and Strains! It's Time to Take Action!" Ontario Ministry of Labour, www.labour.gov.on.ca/english/hs/ergonomics/is_ergonomics.html (accessed May 25, 2006).

69. S.B. Hood, "Repetitive Strain Injury," *Human Resources Professional* (June/July 1997), pp. 29–34.

70. "Ergonomic Intervention Improves Worker Health and Productivity," *Institute for Work and Health* (December 15, 2003), www.iwh.on.ca/media/ergonomic.php (accessed July 8, 2006); "Ergonomic Intervention Improves Worker Health and Productivity," *Workplace News* (February 2004), p. 16.

71. J.A. Savage, "Are Computer Terminals Zapping Workers' Health?" *Business and Society Review*, 84 (Winter 1994), pp. 41–43.

72. S. Tenby, "Introduction to Ergonomics: How to Avoid RSI—Repetitive Strain Injury," Disabled Women's Network Ontario, http://dawn.thot.net/cd/20.html (accessed May 25, 2006).

73. U. Vu, "Steel Union Gathers Workplace Cancer Data," *Canadian HR Reporter* (June 2, 2008).

74. "Unions Stress Cancer Prevention," *Canadian HR Reporter* (February 28, 2005), p. 2.

75. D. Brown, "Killer Toxins in the Workplace," *Canadian HR Reporter* (April 23, 2001), pp. 1, 12.

76. A. Scappatura, "Enhanced Coverage for Firefighters," *Canadian HR Reporter* (May 18, 2009).

77. "EI Granted in Second-Hand Smoke Case," *Canadian HR Reporter* (May 19, 2003), p. 3; see also M.M. Finklestein, "Risky Business," *OH&S Canada* (September/October 1996), pp. 32–34.

78. T. Humber, "Snuffing Out Smoking," *Canadian HR Reporter* (April 11, 2005), p. 19, 23; *Towards Healthier Workplaces and Public Places* (Health Canada, 2004).

79. C. Hallamore, *A State of Unpreparedness: Canadian Organizations' Readiness for a Pandemic* (Ottawa, ON: The Conference Board of Canada, June 2006).

80. C.C. Cavicchio, "Action Plan for Dealing with a Global Pandemic," *The Conference Board Executive Action Series* (May 2009).

81. C. Hallamore, *A State of Unpreparedness: Canadian Organizations' Readiness for a Pandemic* (Ottawa, ON: The Conference Board of Canada, June 2006).

82. R.A. Macpherson, E. Ringsels, and H. Singh, "Swine Influenza: Advice for Employers Preparing for a Pandemic," *McCarthy Tetrault e-Alert* (April 29, 2009), http://news.mccarthy.ca/en/news_template_full.asp?pub_code=4502&news_code=1066 (accessed April 29, 2009).

83. C.C. Cavicchio, "Action Plan for Dealing with a Global Pandemic," *The Conference Board Executive Action Series* (May 2009).

84. D.J. McKeown and K. Ford, "The Importance of People-Focused Pandemic Planning," *Workplace News* (September/October 2006).

85. C. Harden, "Preparing for a Pandemic: The Total Rewards Angle," *Workspan* (July 2006).

86. W.H. Glenn, "Workplace Violence: An Employees' Survival Guide," *OH&S Canada* (April/May 2002), pp. 26–31.

87. S. De Leseleuc, *Criminal Victimization in the Workplace*, Catalogue no. 85F0033MIE, no. 013 (Canadian Centre for Justice Statistics, 2004).

88. "Male Nurses More Likely to Be Assaulted by Patients: StatsCan," *Canadian HR Reporter* (April 16, 2009).

89. S. Dobson, "Sexual Assault Prompts OHS Charge," *Canadian HR Reporter* (December 15, 2008); L. De Piante, "Watch Out for Dangerous Employees," *Canadian HR Reporter* (October 22, 2007); A. Feliu, "Workplace Violence and the Duty of Care: The Scope of an Employer's Obligation to Protect against the Violent Employee," *Employee Relations Law Journal*, 20, no. 3 (Winter 1994/95), pp. 381–406; G. French and P. Morgan, "The Risks of Workplace Violence," *Canadian HR Reporter* (December 18, 2000), pp. 27–28.

90. M.M. LeBlanc and E.K. Kelloway, "Predictors and Outcomes of Workplace Violence and Aggression, *Journal of Applied Psychology*, 87, no. 3 (June 2002), 444–453.

91. L. De Piante, "Watch Out for Dangerous Employees," *Canadian HR Reporter* (October 22, 2007).

92. S. Klie, "Screening New Hires Won't End Workplace Violence, Study Says," *Canadian HR Reporter* (November 21, 2005), pp. 1, 3; K. Acquino et al., "How Employees Respond to Personal Offense: The Effect of the Blame Attribution, Victim Status, and Offender Status on Revenge and Reconciliation in the Workplace," *Journal of Applied Psychology*, 86, no. 1 (2001), pp. 52–59.

93. A. Tomlinson, "Re-evaluating Your Workplace: Is It Safe and Secure?" *Canadian HR Reporter* (February 25, 2002), pp. 3, 12; L. Martin and D. Tona, "Before It's Too Late," *OH&S Canada* (April/May 2000), pp. 52–53.

94. P. Viollis and C. Mathers, "Companies Need to Re-engineer Their Cultural Thinking about Workplace Violence," *Canadian HR Reporter* (March 14, 2005), p. 19; D. Anfuso, "Workplace Violence," *Personnel Journal* (October 1994), p. 71; see also L. Martin and D. Tona, "Before It's Too Late," *OH&S Canada* (April/May 2000), pp. 52–53; H. Bloom, "Workplace Violence: The Myth That We're Helpless," *Workplace Today* (January 2002), pp. 36–37; W.H. Glenn, "Workplace Violence: An Employees' Survival Guide," *OH&S Canada* (April/May 2002), pp. 26–31.

95. D. Anfuso, "Workplace Violence," *Personnel Journal* (October 1994), pp. 66–77.

96. L. Young, "Managers at B.C. Telus Held Accountable for Wellness," *Canadian HR Reporter* (February 28, 2000), p. 9.

97. J. Taggart and J. Farrell, "Where Wellness Shows Up on the Bottom Line," *Canadian HR Reporter* (October 20, 2003), pp. 12, 15.

98. S. Klie, "Seven Oaks Hospital Relies on Healthy Staff," *Canadian HR Reporter* (October 23, 2006).

99. E. Buffett, "Healthy Employees Translate into Profits," *Canadian HR Reporter* (April 9, 2007).

100. A. Tomlinson, "Healthy Living a Remedy for Burgeoning Employee Absentee Rates," *Canadian HR Reporter* (March 25, 2002), pp. 3, 12.

101. S. Pellegrini, "The Next 25 Years: Wellness," *Benefits Canada* (June 2002), pp. 83–85.

102. C. Warren, "Healthy Competition Boosts Workplace Wellness," *Workplace News* (November/December 2007).

HR by the Numbers: Balancing Scheduling of Employees and Health Concerns

M.V. Vyas, A.X. Garg, A.V. Iansavichus, J. Costella, A. Donner, L.E. Laugsand, I. Janszky, M. Mrkobrada, G. Parraga, and D.G. Hackam,. 2012. "Shift work and vascular events: systematic review and meta-analysis", *British Medical* Journal, 345, 2012, pp 1–11, doi: https://doi.org/10.1136/bmj.e4800.

Chapter 11

1. A. Cowan and N. Stewart, *Compensation Planning Outlook 2011: Playing It Safe in the Face of an Unsteady Economic Recovery*, (Ottawa, ON: The Conference Board of Canada, October 2010).

2. Statistics Canada, "Permanent Layoffs, Quits and Hirings in the Canadian Economy 1978 to 1995," Business and Labour Market Analysis Division, www.statcan.gc.ca/pub/71-539-x/71-539-x1995001-eng.pdf (accessed September 26, 2011).

3. W.F. Cascio, *Responsible Restructuring: Creative and Profitable Alternatives to Layoffs* (San Fransico, CA: Barrett-Koehler, 2002).

4. W.F. Cascio, *Costing Human Resources: The Financial Impact of Behavior in Organizations* (Boston, MA: PWS-Kent, 1991).

5. J. Johnson, R.W. Griffeth, and M. Griffin, "Factors Discrimination Functional and Dysfunctional Sales Force Turnover," *Journal of Business & Industrial Marketing*, 15, no. 6 (January 2000), pp. 399–415.

6. R.W. Griffeth, P.W. Hom, and S. Gaertner, "A Meta-Analysis of Antecedents and Correlates of Employee Turnover: Update, Moderator Tests, and Research Implications for the Next Millennium," *Journal of Management*, 26, no. 3 (June 2006), pp. 463–488.

7. M. Stovel and N. Bontis, "Voluntary Turnover: Knowledge Management Friend or Foe?" *Journal of Intellectual Capital*, 3, no. 3 (2002), pp. 303–322.

8. W.H. Mobley, R.W. Griffeth, H.H. Hand, and B.M. Meglino, "Review and Conceptual Analysis of the Employee Turnover Process," *Psychological Bulletin*, 86, no. 3 (May 1979), pp. 493–522.

9. P.W. Hom and A.J. Kinicki, "Toward a Greater Understanding of How Dissatisfaction Drives Employee Turnover," *Academy of Management Journal*, 44, no. 5 (October, 2001), pp. 975–987.

10. B. Prentice, "When Can an Employer Sue an Employee for Damages?" *Employment Update January 2013* (January 16, 2013), p. 1.

11. S. Norris and T. Williams, "Healthy Aging: Adding Years to Life and Life to Years," Government of Canada (October 27, 2000), http://dsp-psd.pwgsc.gc.ca/Collection-R/LoPBdP/BP/prb0023-e.htm (accessed September 26, 2011).

12. Statistics Canada, "Life Expectancy," *Aboriginal Statistics at a Glance* (November 30, 2015), www.statcan.gc.ca/pub/89-645-x/2010001/life-expectancy-esperance-vie-eng.htm (accessed May 12, 2017).

13. Statistics Canada, "Labour Force Survey Estimates (LFS), Retirement Age by Class of Worker and Sex," CANSIM 282-0051 (January 6, 2017), www5.statcan.gc.ca/cansim/a26?lang=eng&id=2820051 (accessed August 8, 2017).

14. "Mandatory Retirement Fades in Canada," CBC News (October 18, 2010), www.cbc.ca/news/canada/story/2009/08/20/mandatory-retirement-explainer523.html (accessed September 26, 2011).

15. G. Golightly, "Preparing Employees for Retirement Transitions," *HR Professional* (December 1999/January 2000), pp. 27–33.

16. *1995 Canadian Dismissal Practices Survey* (Toronto, ON: Murray Axmith & Associates).

17. G. Golightly, "Preparing Employees for Retirement Transitions," *HR Professional* (December 1999/January 2000), pp. 27–33.

18. J. Famularo, *Handbook of Modern Personnel Administration* (New York, NY: McGraw-Hill, 1972), pp. 65.3–65.5.

19. N.C. MacDonald, "Progressing towards Just Cause," *Canadian HR Reporter* (September 22, 2008).

20. S. Rudner, "Just Cause Termination Still Not Clearcut," *Canadian HR Reporter* (March 23, 2009).

21. D. Bambrough and M. Certosimo, "Worker Fraud Usually Justifies Dismissal," *Canadian HR Reporter* (October 23, 2006).

22. D. Bambrough and M. Certosimo, "Worker Fraud Usually Justifies Dismissal," *Canadian HR Reporter* (October 23, 2006).

23. L. Cassiani, "Dishonesty Not Always Enough to Terminate," *Canadian HR Reporter* (August 13, 2001), pp. 3, 6; P. Israel, "Firing an Employee for Dishonesty? Put Things in Context First," *Canadian HR Reporter* (August 12, 2002), p. 5.

24. J. Famularo, *Handbook of Modern Personnel Administration* (New York, NY: McGraw-Hill, 1972), pp. 65.4–65.5.

25. "Good Broker, Bad Decision," *Canadian HR Reporter* (July 17, 2006).

26. K.S. Cameron. "Investigating Organizational Downsizing: Fundamental Issues," *Human Resource Management*, 33 (1994), pp. 183–188.

27. E.E. Mole, *Wrongful Dismissal Practice Manual* (Toronto, ON: Butterworths Canada, 1993), ch. 7.

28. Commerce Clearing House, *Personnel Practices/Communications* (Chicago, IL: CCH, 1992), p. 1410.

29. E.A. Lind, J. Greenberg, K.S. Scott, and T.D. Welchans, "The Winding Road from Employee to Complainant: Situational and Psychological Determinants of Wrongful Dismissal Claims," *Administrative Science Quarterly*, 45 (2000), pp. 557–590.

30. S. Dobson, "'We're Live from the HR Firing Session!'" *Canadian HR Reporter*, 26, no. 4 (February 25, 2013), p. 1.

31. A. Silliker, "Is There a Better Way to Close a Store?" *Canadian HR Reporter*, 26, no. 5 (March 11, 2013), p. 1.

32. J. McAlpine, "10 Steps for Reducing Exposure to Wrongful Dismissal," *Canadian HR Reporter* (May 6, 2002), p. 8.

33. E. Caruk, "What to Do If a Wrongful Dismissal Action Hits," *Canadian HR Reporter* (May 6, 2002), p. 10.

34. A. Saks, "Engagement: The Academic Perspective," *Canadian HR Reporter* (January 26, 2009).

35. J. Gibbons, *Employee Engagement: A Review of Current Research and Its Implications* (New York, NY: The Conference Board, 2006).

36. *Engaging Employees to Drive Global Business Success: Insights from Mercer's What's Working™ Research* (New York, NY: Mercer, 2007).

37. Based on D. McElroy, "High Tech with High Touch: A New Communication Contract," *Canadian HR Reporter* (April 7, 1997), p. G6.

38. Y. Cohen-Charash and P.E. Spector, "The Role of Justice in Organizations: A Meta-Analysis," *Organizational Behavior and Human Decision Processes*, 86 (November 2001), pp. 278–321.

39. D. Jones, "What If You Held a Survey and No-One Came?" *Canadian HR Reporter* (July 16, 2001), pp. 19, 22.

40. D. Brown, "Getting the Hard Facts in Employee Attitude and Satisfaction," *Canadian HR Reporter* (November 1, 1999), p. 2.

41. A. Massey, "Blogging Phobia Hits Employers," *Canadian HR Reporter* (September 26, 2005), pp. 15, 17.

42. L. Harris, "Staffer Fired after Bad-Mouthing Colleagues, Management in Blog," *Canadian HR Reporter* (September 8, 2008); S.E. Sorenson, "Employee Blogging," *HR Professional* (April/May 2008), p. 16.

43. L. De Piante, "Blogging Guidelines for Employees: A Necessity in the Workplace," *Canadian HR Reporter* (April 23, 2007); S. Crossley and M. Torrance, "Indiscriminate Blogging and the Workplace," *Workplace News* (November/December 2007), pp. 12–13.

44. D. McElroy, "High Tech with High Touch: A New Communication Contract," *Canadian HR Reporter* (April 7, 1997), p. G6.

45. S. Klie, "Blogs Connect CEOs with Employees, Clients," *Canadian HR Reporter* (November 17, 2008).

46. D. Bell, "No Easy Way to Say 'You're Fired,'" *Canadian HR Reporter* (June 15, 2009); J. Coil III and C. Rice, "Three Steps to Creating Effective Employee Releases," *Employment Relations Today* (Spring 1994), p. 92.

47. S. Milne, "The Termination Interview," *Canadian Manager* (Spring 1994), pp. 15–16.

48. W.F. Cascio and C.E. Young, "Financial Consequences of Employment Change Decisions in Major U.S. Corporations: 1982–2000," in K.P. DeMeuse and M.L. Marks (eds.), *Resizing the Organization* (San Francisco, CA: Jossey-Bass, 2003), pp. 131–156.

HR by the Numbers: Prevalence of Theft Behaviour

1. A. Britnell, "Stop Employee Theft," *Canadian Business Online* (July 16, 2003), www.canadianbusiness.com (accessed May 29, 2006); J. Towler, "Dealing with Employees Who Steal," *Canadian HR Reporter* (September 23, 2002), p. 4.

2. "Employee Theft on the Rise: A Thorn in the Side for Retailers Says Survey," *The Huffington Post Canada*, October 31, 2012.

3. "Air Canada Searches Employee Rooms," *Canadian HR Reporter* (February 10, 2003), p. 2.

4. J. Divon, "Why More Employees Are Stealing from You," *The Globe and Mail*, November 26, 2012.

5. J. Divon, "Why More Employees Are Stealing from You," *The Globe and Mail*, November 26, 2012.

6. J. Divon, "Why More Employees Are Stealing from You," *The Globe and Mail*, November 26, 2012.

Chapter 12

1. L. Suffield and G.L. Gannon, *Labour Relations*, 4th ed. (Toronto, ON: Pearson, 2016).

2. S. Klie, "Wal-Mart Closes Union Shop in Quebec," *Canadian HR Reporter* (November 3, 2008).

3. L. Harris, "Union-Proof: How Some Employers Avoid Organized Labour," *Canadian HR Reporter* (October 22, 2007).

4. R. Morissette, G. Shellenberg, and A. Johnson, "Diverging Trends in Unionization," *Perspectives on Labour and Income,* 17, no. 2 (Summer 2005); U. Vu, "Low Membership Keeps Unions on the Defensive," *Canadian HR Reporter* (February 13, 2006), pp. 4, 9.

5. C. Hallamore, "Globalization Shifts the Ground in Labour Relations," *Inside Edge* (Spring 2006), p. 14; see also C. Hallamore, *Industrial Relations Outlook 2006: Shifting Ground, Shifting Attitudes* (Ottawa, ON: Conference Board of Canada, 2006).

6. C. Hallamore, *Industrial Relations Outlook 2007: Finding Common Ground through the War for Workers* (Ottawa, ON: The Conference Board of Canada, 2007); S. Klie, "Labour Market Should Unite Business, Unions," *Canadian HR Reporter* (February 27, 2007).

7. J. Allemang, "The Sorry State of Our Unions," *The Globe and Mail* (March 24, 2012), www.theglobeandmail.com/news/national/the-sorry-state-of-our-unions/article535618/?page=all (accessed April 28, 2017).

8. Ontario Federation of Labour, *Issues: Young Workers* (March 20, 2017), http://ofl.ca/index.php/category/issues/young-workers/ (accessed April 28, 2017); Canadian Union of Public Employees, *Racial Equality and Research*, https://cupe.ca/issues-research (accessed April 28, 2017).

9. S. Greenhouse, "How to Get Low Wage Workers into the Middle Class," *The Atlantic* (August 2015), www.theatlantic.com/business/archive/2015/08/fifteen-dollars-minimum-wage/401540/ (accessed April 29, 2017).

10. L. Harris, "Unions Taking Up the Mantle of Women's Issues," *Canadian HR Reporter* (August 11, 2008); L. Harris, "Youthful Proposition from Unions," *Canadian HR Reporter* (October 20, 2008).

11. H.N. Wheeler and J.A. McClendon, "The Individual Decision to Unionise," in G. Strauss et al. (eds.), *The State of the Unions* (Madison, WI: Industrial Relations Research Association, 1991).

12. H.S. Farber and D.H. Saks, "Why Workers Want Unions: The Role of Relative Wages and Job Characteristics," *Journal of Political Economy*, 88, no. 21 (April 1980), pp. 349–369.

13. J. Kelly, *Rethinking Industrial Relations: Mobilization, Collectivism, and Long Waves* (London, UK: Routledge, 1998).

14. H.N. Wheeler and J.A. McClendon, "The Individual Decision to Unionise," in G. Strauss et. al. (eds.), *The State of the Unions* (Madison, WI: Industrial Relations Research Association, 1991).

15. Statistics Canada, Average Hourly Wages of Employees by Selected Characteristics and Occupation, Unadjusted Data, by Province (monthly) (April 4, 2017), www.statcan.gc.ca/tables-tableaux/sum-som/l01/cst01/labr69a-eng.htm (accessed April 29, 2017).

16. Statistics Canada, "Unionization Rates in First Half of 2007 and 2008" (March, 3, 2010), www.statcan.gc.ca/pub/75-001-x/topics-sujets/unionization-syndicalisation/unionization-syndicalisation-2008-eng.htm (accessed September 26, 2011).

17. C. Fullager and J. Barling, "A Longitudinal Test of a Model of the Antecedents and Consequences of Union Loyalty," *Journal of Applied Psychology,* 74, no. 2 (April 1989), pp. 213–227; A. Eaton, M. Gordon, and J. Keefe, "The Impact of Quality of Work-Life Programs and Grievance Systems Effectiveness on Union Commitment," *Industrial and Labor Relations Review,* 45, no. 3 (April 1992), pp. 592–604.

18. L. Young, "Union Drives: Initiated Within, Prevented Within," *Canadian HR Reporter* (November 29, 1999), pp. 2, 14.

19. J. Knight, "What You Can Do If a Union Comes Knocking," *Canadian HR Reporter* (October 2013), p. 5.

20. A.W.J. Craig and N.A. Solomon, *The System of Industrial Relations in Canada*, 5th ed. (Toronto, ON: Prentice Hall Canada, 1996), p. 217; L. Suffield and G.L. Gannon, *Labour Relations*, 4th ed. (Toronto, ON: Pearson, 2016).

21. L. Suffield and G.L. Gannon, *Labour Relations*, 4th ed. (Toronto, ON: Pearson, 2016).

22. L. Suffield and G.L. Gannon, *Labour Relations*, 4th ed. (Toronto, ON: Pearson, 2016).

23. L. Suffield and G.L. Gannon, *Labour Relations*, 4th ed. (Toronto, ON: Pearson, 2016).

24. U. Vu, "Interest Wanes on Interest-Based?" *Canadian HR Reporter* (February 28, 2006), pp. 6, 9.

25. L. Suffield and G.L. Gannon, *Labour Relations*, 4th ed. (Toronto, ON: Pearson, 2016).

26. L. Suffield and G.L. Gannon, *Labour Relations*, 4th ed. (Toronto, ON: Pearson, 2016).

27. M. Gunderson and D.G. Taras, *Union–Management Relations in Canada* (Toronto, ON: Pearson Education Canada, 2009), p. 351; L. Suffield and G.L. Gannon, *Labour Relations*, 4th ed. (Toronto, ON: Pearson, 2016).

28. L. Suffield and G.L. Gannon, *Labour Relations*, 4th ed. (Toronto, ON: Pearson, 2016).

29. Government of Canada, Employment and Social Development Canada, *Overview of Collective Bargaining in Canada—2015* (Ottawa, ON: Statistics Canada, July 2016).

Chapter 13

1. R. Runzheimer and G. Harper, "Workforce Mobility Management Saves Money and Increases Efficiency," *Workspan* (December 2007), pp. 76–81.

2. "Definition of 'Immigrant,'" Statistics Canada (November 2010), www.statcan.gc.ca/pub/81-004-x/2010004/def/immigrant-eng.htm (accessed September 26, 2011).

3. "Oil and Water," *Canadian Business* (November 8–21, 2004), pp. 14, 16; "Expect Corruption Overseas," *Canadian HR Reporter* (September 23, 2002), p. 9.

4. R.J. House, P.J. Hanges, M. Javidan, P.W. Dorfman, and V. Gupta, *Culture, Leadership, and Organizations: The GLOBE Study of 62 Societies* (Thousand Oaks, CA: Sage, 2004); G. Hofstede, "Cultural Dimensions in People Management," in V. Pucik, N. Tichy and C. Barnett (eds.), *Globalizing Management* (New York, NY: John Wiley & Sons, 1992), p. 143.

5. S. Klie, "HR around the World," *Canadian HR Reporter* (November 6, 2006); K. King-Metters and R. Metters, "Misunderstanding the Chinese Worker," *The Wall Street Journal* (July 7, 2008), p. R11.

6. R. Little, "Foreigners Explore Pros and Cons behind Vietnamese Work Ethic," *Vietnam News* (August 7, 2008), http://vietnamnews.vnagency.com.vn/showarticle.php?num=)!SAY080808 (accessed September 4, 2008).

7. A. Yeo, "A Brief Look at the PRC Employment Promotion Law," *Human Resources* (December 2007), pp. 29–31; J. Yan, "A Snapshot of Chinese Employment Law," *Canadian HR Reporter* (November 6, 2006); "China's New Labor Contract Law," *Workspan* (March 2008), p. 12.

8. D. Matthews, *Severance Practices around the World.* (Philadelphia, PA: Right Management, 2008); G. Avraam, A. Ishak, and T. Appleyard, "Terminating Employees around the World," *Canadian HR Reporter* (April 6, 2009).

9. "Britain Introduces Corporate Manslaughter Act," *Canadian HR Reporter* (April 16, 2008).

10. N. Goulding, J.Z. Deaton and L. Smith-Park, "Dubai Ruler Pardons Norwegian Woman Convicted after She Reported Rape," *CNN* (July 22, 2013), www.cnn.com/2013/07/22/world/meast/uae-norway-rape-controversy/index.html?hpt=hp_t1 (accessed July 22, 2013).

11. A. Macaulay, "Culture, Safety and Privacy Norms abroad Present Challenges for HR," *Canadian HR Reporter* (November 6, 2006).

12. E. Kelly, "The New Frontier," *HR Professional* (August/September 2008), pp. 24–28.

13. E. Gaugler, "HR Management: An International Comparison," *Personnel* (August 1988), p. 28.

14. Wharton School, "Made in China," *Human Resource Executive Online* (February 26, 2008).

15. *2008/2009 Benefits Survey for Expatriates and Globally Mobile Employees* (New York, NY: Mercer, 2009).

16. M. Sim and L. Dixon, "Number of Women Expats Increasing," *Canadian HR Reporter* (May 21, 2007).

17. T. Shelton, "A Best-of-Breed Approach: Addressing the ROI and Retention Challenges of Global Workforce Management," *Workspan* (April 2009), pp. 50–54.

18. J. Head, "How Paper Can Protect International Relocations," *Canadian HR Reporter* (March 13, 2006).

19. *2005 Employee Relocation Survey: Domestic, Cross-Border & International Relocations* (Toronto, ON: Canadian Employee Relocation Council, 2005).

20. *2005 Employee Relocation Survey: Domestic, Cross-Border & International Relocations* (Toronto, ON: Canadian Employee Relocation Council, 2005).

21. *Global Relocation Trends: Survey Report 2008.* GMAC Global Relocation Services.

22. G.N. Abbott, B.W. Stening, P.W.B. Atkins, and A.M. Grant, "Coaching Expatriate Managers for Success: Adding Value beyond Training and Mentoring," *Asia-Pacific Journal of Human Resources,* 44, no. 3 (2006), pp. 295–317.

23. G. Insch and J. Daniels, "Causes and Consequences of Declining Early Departures from Foreign Assignments," *Business Horizons,* 46, no. 6 (November–December 2002), pp. 39–48.

24. E. Krell, "Budding Relationships," *HR Magazine,* 50, no. 6 (June 2005), pp. 114–118.

25. P. Caliguri, "The Big Five Personality Characteristics as Predictors of Expatriates' Desire to Terminate the Assignment and Supervisor-Rated Performance," *Personnel Psychology,* 53, no. 1 (Spring 2000), pp. 67–88.

26. J. Selmer, "Expatriation: Corporate Policy, Personal Intentions and International Adjustment," *International Journal of Human Resource Management,* 9, no. 6 (December 1998), pp. 997–1007.

27. C. Hill, *International Business: Competing in the Global Marketplace* (Burr Ridge, IL: Irwin, 1994), pp. 511–515.

28. C. Solomon, "One Assignment, Two Lives," *Personnel Journal* (May 1996), pp. 36–47; M. Harvey, "Dual-Career Couples during International Relocation: The Trailing Spouse," *International Journal of Human Resource Management,* 9, no. 2 (April 1998), pp. 309–330.

29. B.J. Punnett, "International Human Resources Management," in A.M. Rugman (ed.), *International Business in Canada: Strategies for Management* (Toronto, ON: Prentice Hall Canada, 1989) , pp. 330–346; L.G. Klaff, "Thinning the Ranks of the 'Career Expats,'" *Workforce Management* (October 2004), pp. 84–87.

30. V. Galt, "World Loves to Milk Canada's Executive Pool," *Globe and Mail* (September 5, 2005), p. B10.

31. S. Cryne, "The Changing World of the Relocation Specialist," *Canadian HR Reporter* (March 8, 2004), pp. 13, 15; G. Reinhart, "Preparing for Global Expansion: A Primer," *Canadian HR Reporter* (March 14, 2005), pp. 14, 17.

32. *Survey 2011 Global Assignment Policies and Practices* (KPMG, 2011), p. 9, www.kpmginstitutes.com/taxwatch/insights/2011/pdf/gapp-survey-2011.pdf.

33. Z. Fedder, "Short-Sighted Thinking Shortchanges Short-Term International Assignments," *Canadian HR Reporter* (September 25, 2000), p. 20.

34. S. Cryne, "The Changing World of the Relocation Specialist," *Canadian HR Reporter* (March 8, 2004), pp. 13, 15.

35. J.D. Daniels and L.H. Radebaugh, *International Business* (Reading, MA: Addison-Wesley, 1994), p. 767; A. Phatak, *International Dimensions of Management* (Boston, MA: PWS-Kent, 1989), pp. 106–107.

36. A. Bross, A. Churchill, and J. Zifkin, "Cross-Cultural Training: Issues to Consider During Implementation," *Canadian HR Reporter* (June 5, 2000), pp. 10, 12.

37. E.M. Norman, "How Multinationals Doing Business in Asia Can Develop Leadership Talent during a Recession," *Workspan* (May 2009), pp. 35–43.

38. "More Multinationals Embracing Centralized Compensation Structures," *Workspan* (November 2006), p. 10; C. Reynolds, "Global Compensation and Benefits in Transition," *Compensation and Benefits Review* (January/February 2000), pp. 28–28; J.E. Richard, "Global Executive Compensation: A Look at the Future," *Compensation and Benefits Review* (May/June 2000), pp. 35–38.

39. L. Laroche, "Negotiating Expatriate Packages," *Canadian HR Reporter* (November 20, 2000), pp. 15, 19.

40. J. Cartland, "Reward Policies in a Global Corporation," *Business Quarterly* (Autumn 1993), pp. 93–96; L. Mazur, "Europay," *Across-the-Board* (January 1995), pp. 40–43.

41. K. Bensky, "Developing a Workable Global Rewards System," *Workspan* (October 2002), pp. 44–48.

42. A. Phatak, *International Dimensions of Management* (Boston, MA: PWS-Kent, 1989), p. 134; see also L. Laroche, "Negotiating Expatriate Packages," *Canadian HR Reporter* (November 20, 2000), pp. 15, 19.

43. K. Abosch, J. Schermerhorn, and L. Wisper, "Broad-Based Variable Pay Goes Global," *Workspan* (May 2008), pp. 56–62.

44. "Expatriates, Families Face Different Stressors Than Stateside Counterparts," *Workspan* (October 2008), p. 18.

45. V. Frazee, "Keeping Your Expats Healthy," *Global Workforce* (November 1998), pp. 18–23; see also B. Barker and D. Schulde, "Special EAP Helps Expatriates Face International 'Culture Shock,'" *Canadian HR Reporter* (November 29, 1999), p. 20; L. O'Grady, "Using Technology to De-stress on International Assignment," *Canadian HR Reporter* (September 24, 2001), pp. 8, 12; R. Melles, "Lost in Translation," *Canadian HR Reporter* (March 8, 2004), p. 14; E.C. Heher, "Anticipating the Psychological Effects of Expatriate Life," *Workspan* (May 2006), pp. 54–56.

46. A. Bross and G. Wise, "Sustaining the Relocated Employee with an International EAP," *Canadian HR Reporter* (November 29, 1999), pp. 18, 19, 21.

47. C. Storti, *The Art of Coming Home* (Boston, MA: Nicholas Brealey Publishing, 2001); S. Cryne, "Homeward Bound," *Canadian HR Reporter* (March 9, 2009).

48. "Views of Employees and Companies Differ on International Assignments," *Workspan Focus Canada 2006*, pp. 22–24; L. Stroh, "Predicting Turnover among Repatriates: Can Organizations Affect Retention Rates?" *International Journal of Human Resource Management*, 6, no. 2 (May 1995), pp. 443–456.

49. J. Keogh, "A Win–Win, from Start to Finish," *Workspan* (February 2003), pp. 36–39; D. Brown, "Companies Undervaluing Skills Learned during Relocation," *Canadian HR Reporter* (February 28, 2000), pp. 15, 21; J. Hobel, "The Expatriate Employee Homecoming," *Canadian HR Reporter* (June 1, 1998), pp. G5, G11.

50. D. McCutcheon, "Repatriation: Bringing Home the Troops," *HR Professional* (April/May 2009), pp. 33–34; P. Stanoch and G. Reynolds, "Relocating Career Development," *Canadian HR Reporter* (May 5, 2003), pp. 13, 15; L.M, "Global Talk," *HR Professional* (June/July 2006), p. 12.

51. S. Lopes and Y. Poisson, "Bringing Employers into the Immigration Debate: Survey and Roundtable," *Public Policy Forum* (2004), www.toronto.ca/metropolis/metropolistoronto2005/pdf/lopesetal_audc.pdf (accessed September 26, 2011).

52. C.C. Miller, L.M. Burke, and W.H. Glick, "Cognitive Diversity among Upper Echelon Executives: Implications for Strategic Decision Processes," *Strategic Management Journal*, 19, no.1 (January 1998), pp. 39–58; S.K. Horwitz and I.B. Horwitz, "The Effects of Team Diversity on Team Outcomes: A Meta-Analytic Review of Team Demography," *Journal of Management*, 33, no. 6 (December 2007), pp. 987–1015.

53. Society for Human Resources Management Survey Programme, 2001, p. 16.

54. Statistics Canada, "Earnings Differences between Immigrants and the Canadian-Born—The Role of Literacy Skills," (May 1, 2009), www.statcan.gc.ca/pub/81-004-x/2008005/article/10798-eng.htm (accessed September 26, 2011).

55. Statistics Canada, "Labour Force Characteristics by Immigrant Status of Population aged 25 to 54, and by Educational Attainment" (January 6, 2017), www.statcan.gc.ca/tables-tableaux/sum-som/l01/cst01/labor90a-eng.htm.

56. CanadaImmigrants.com, "Canada Immigrants' Earning Statistics," www.canadaimmigrants.com/immigrants_earnings.asp.

57. Immigration and Citizenship Canada, "Hire a Temporary Worker" (June 12, 2017), www.cic.gc.ca/english/hire/worker.asp (accessed August 8, 2017).

58. G. Picot and A. Sweetman, "The Deteriorating Economic Welfare of Immigrants and Possible Causes: Update 2005," Statistics Canada, Catalogue No. 11F0019MIE, No. 262.

59. Statistics Canada, "Earnings Differences between Immigrants and the Canadian-Born—The Role of Literacy Skills" (May 1, 2009), www.statcan.gc.ca/pub/81-004-x/2008005/article/10798-eng.htm (accessed September 26, 2011).

60. Statistics Canada, "Longitudinal Survey of Immigrants to Canada: Process, Progress and Prospects," Housing, Family and Social Statistics Division (October 2003), http://dsp-psd.pwgsc.gc.ca/Collection/Statcan/89-611-X/89-611-XIE2003001.pdf (accessed September 26, 2001).

61. G. Larose and G. Tillman, "Valorizing Immigrants' Non-Canadian Work Experience," (Ottawa, ON: Work and Learning Knowledge Centre, 2009).

62. M. Fernando, "The Non-Accreditation of Immigrant Professionals in Canada: Societal Dimensions of the Problem," *Metropolis* (September 15, 1999), http://canada.metropolis.net/research-policy/conversation/MATAPAPER.html (accessed September 26, 2011).

63. J. Gilmour, "The 2008 Canadian Immigrant Labour Market: Analysis of Quality of Employment," Statistics Canada, Labour Statistics Division (November 23, 2009), www.statcan.gc.ca/pub/71-606-x/71-606-x2009001-eng.pdf (accessed August 11, 2010).

64. J. Gilmour, "The 2008 Canadian Immigrant Labour Market: Analysis of Quality of Employment," Statistics Canada, Labour Statistics Division (November 23, 2009), www.statcan.gc.ca/pub/71-606-x/71-606-x2009001-eng.pdf (accessed August 11, 2010).

65. J. Gilmour, "The 2008 Canadian Immigrant Labour Market: Analysis of Quality of Employment," Statistics Canada, Labour Statistics Division (November 23, 2009), www.statcan.gc.ca/pub/71-606-x/71-606-x2009001-eng.pdf (accessed August 11, 2010).

66. "Progress Report 2010," Foreign Credentials Referral Office, Government of Canada (August 5, 2011), www.credentials.gc.ca/fcro/progress-report2010.asp#bfn07.

67. C. Grondin, "Knowledge of Official Languages among New Immigrants: How Important Is It in the Labour Market?" Statistics Canada (April 2007), www.statcan.gc.ca/pub/89-624-x/89-624-x2007000-eng.pdf (accessed September 26, 2011).

68. C. Grondin, "Knowledge of Official Languages among New Immigrants: How Important Is It in the Labour Market?" Statistics Canada (April 2007), www.statcan.gc.ca/pub/89-624-x/89-624-x2007000-eng.pdf (accessed September 26, 2011).

69. M. Adamuti-Trache and R. Sweet, "Exploring the Relationship between Educational Credentials and the Earnings of Immigrants," *Canadian Studies in Population*, 32, no. 2 (2005), pp. 177–201.

Glossary

360-degree appraisal A performance appraisal technique that uses multiple raters including peers, employees reporting to the appraisee, supervisors, and customers.

A

achievement test A test used to measure knowledge or proficiency acquired through education, training, or experience.

alternation ranking method Ranking employees from best to worst on a particular trait.

appraisal bias The tendency to allow individual differences, such as age, race, and sex, to affect the appraisal ratings that these employees receive.

apprenticeship A situation in which the learner/apprentice studies under the tutelage of a master craftsperson, blending classroom instruction with on-the-job training.

aptitude tests Tests that measure an individual's aptitude or potential to perform a job, provided he or she is given proper training.

arbitration The use of an outside third party to investigate a dispute between an employer and union and impose a settlement.

attrition The normal separation of employees from an organization because of resignation, retirement, or death.

auditory learning Learning through auditory methods such as talking and listening.

authorization card A card signed by an employee that indicates his or her willingness to have the union act as his or her representative for purposes of collective bargaining.

B

balance sheet approach A method of formulating expatriate pay based on equalizing purchasing power across countries.

balanced scorecard A measurement system that translates an organization's strategy into a comprehensive set of performance measures.

bargaining unit The group of employees in an organization, a plant, or an industry that has been certified by a labour relations board (LRB) or recognized by an employer as appropriate for collective bargaining purposes.

bargaining zone The area defined by the bargaining limits (resistance points) of each side, in which compromise is possible, as is the attainment of a settlement satisfactory to both parties.

behavioural interview or behaviour description interview (BDI) A series of job-related questions that focus on relevant past job-related behaviours.

behaviourally anchored rating scale (BARS) An appraisal method that aims to combine the benefits of narratives, critical incidents, and quantified ratings by anchoring a quantified scale with specific narrative examples of good and poor performance.

benchmark job A job that is critical to the firm's operations or that is commonly found in other organizations.

biographical information blank (BIB) A detailed job application form requesting biographical data pertaining to background, experiences, and preferences, and found to be predictive of success on the job. Responses are scored.

blind ad A recruitment ad in which the identity and address of the employer are omitted.

bona fide occupational requirement (BFOR) A justifiable reason for discrimination based on business necessity (that is, the discrimination is required for the safe and efficient operation of the organization) or a requirement that can be clearly defended as intrinsically required by the tasks an employee is expected to perform.

boycott An organized refusal of bargaining unit members and supporters to buy the products or use the services of the organization whose employees are on strike in an effort to exert economic pressure on the employer.

broadbanding Reducing the number of salary grades and ranges into just a few wide levels or "bands," each of which then contains a relatively wide range of jobs and salary levels.

burnout The total depletion of physical and mental resources caused by excessive striving to reach an unrealistic work-related goal.

business unionism The activities of a labour union focusing on economic and welfare issues of its members, including pay and benefits, job security, and working conditions.

C

Canada/Quebec Pension Plans (C/QPP) Programs that provide three types of benefits: retirement income, survivor or death benefits payable to the employee's dependants regardless of age at time of death, and disability benefits payable to employees with disabilities and their dependants. Benefits are payable only to those individuals who make contributions to the plans, or to their family members.

capital accumulation programs Long-term incentives most often reserved for senior executives.

career A series of work-related positions, paid or unpaid, that help a person to grow in job skills, success, and fulfillment.

career anchor A concern or value that a person will not give up if a choice has to be made.

career development The lifelong series of activities (such as workshops) that contribute to a person's career exploration, establishment, success, and fulfillment.

career planning The deliberate process through which someone becomes aware of personal skills, interests, knowledge, motivations, and other characteristics; acquires information about opportunities and choices; identifies career-related goals; and establishes action plans to attain specific goals.

caucus session A session in which only the members of one's own bargaining team are present.

central tendency A tendency to rate all employees in the middle of the scale.

certification Recognition for having met certain professional standards. For unions, certification is the procedure whereby a labour union obtains a certificate from the relevant LRB declaring that the union is the exclusive bargaining agent for a defined group of employees in a bargaining unit that the LRB considers appropriate for collective bargaining purposes.

change agents Specialists who lead the organization and its employees through organizational change.

Charter of Rights and Freedoms Federal law enacted in 1982 that guarantees fundamental freedoms to all Canadians.

classes Groups of jobs based on a set of rules for each class, such as amount of independent judgment, skill, physical effort, and so forth. Classes usually contain similar jobs—all secretarial jobs, for instance.

classification/grading method A method for categorizing jobs into groups.

coaching A process for improving work performance, in a frequent contact, hand on process aimed at helping employees improve performance and capabilities.

co-insurance The percentage of expenses (in excess of the deductible) that are paid for by the insurance plan.

collective bargaining Negotiations between a union and an employer to arrive at a mutually acceptable collective agreement.

collective agreement (union contract) A formal agreement between an employer and the union representing a group of employees regarding terms and conditions of employment.

compensable factor A fundamental, compensable element of a job, such as skill, effort, responsibility, and working conditions.

competencies Demonstrable characteristics of a person that enable performance of a job.

competency-based job analysis Describing a job in terms of the measurable, observable behavioural competencies an employee must exhibit to do a job well.

conciliation The often mandatory use of a neutral third party who has no direct input on the negotiation process to help an organization and the union representing a group of its employees communicate more effectively with the aim of coming to a mutually satisfactory collective agreement.

construct validity The extent to which a selection tool measures a theoretical construct or trait deemed necessary to perform the job successfully.

content validity The extent to which a selection instrument, such as a test, adequately samples the knowledge and skills needed to perform the job.

contextual performance An individual's indirect contribution to the organization in terms of improving the organizational, social, and psychological behaviours that contribute to organizational effectiveness, beyond those specified for the job.

contingent/non-standard workers Workers who do not have regular full-time employment status.

contract workers Employees who develop work relationships directly with the employer for a specific type of work or period of time.

contrast or candidate-order error An error of judgment on the part of the interviewer because of his or her having interviewed one or more very good or very bad candidates just before the interview in question.

controlled experimentation Uses both a group for which the situation is modified (e.g., the group receives training) and a group for which the situation is not modified (e.g., the group receives no training) to assess the impact of the modification.

craft union Traditionally, a labour organization representing workers practising the same craft or trade, such as carpentry or plumbing.

criterion-related validity The extent to which a selection tool predicts or significantly correlates with important elements of work behaviour.

critical incident method Keeping a record of uncommonly good or undesirable examples of an employee's work-related behaviour and reviewing the list with the employee at predetermined times.

D

decertification The process whereby a union is legally deprived of its official recognition as the exclusive bargaining agent for a group of employees.

deductible The annual amount of health/dental expenses that an employee must pay before insurance benefits will be paid.

deferred profit-sharing plan (DPSP) A plan in which a certain amount of company profits is credited to each employee's account, payable at retirement, termination, or death.

defined benefit pension plan A plan that contains a formula for determining retirement benefits.

defined contribution pension plan A plan in which the employer's contribution to the employees' retirement fund is specified.

Delphi technique A judgmental forecasting method used to arrive at a group decision, typically involving outside experts as well as organizational employees. Ideas are exchanged without face-to-face interaction, and feedback is provided and used to fine-tune independent judgments until a consensus is reached.

diary/log Daily listings made by employees of every activity in which they engage, along with the time each activity takes.

differential or unequal treatment Treating an individual or group differently in any aspect of terms and conditions of employment based on any of the prohibited grounds.

differential piece-rate plan A plan by which a worker is paid a basic hourly rate plus an extra percentage of his or her base rate for production exceeding the standard per hour or per day. It is similar to piecework payment but is based on a percentage premium.

differential validity Confirmation that the selection tool accurately predicts the performance of all possible employee subgroups, including white males, women, visible minorities, persons with disabilities, and Aboriginal people.

disability A protected ground in human rights legislation, including a wide range of conditions, some which are visible and some which are not. A disability may be present from birth, caused by an accident, or develop over time.

disability management A proactive, employer-centred process that coordinates the activities of the employer, the insurance company, and healthcare providers in an effort to minimize the impact of injury, disability, or disease on a worker's capacity to successfully perform his or her job.

discrimination As used in the context of human rights in employment, a distinction, exclusion, or preference based on one of the prohibited grounds that has the effect of nullifying or impairing the right of a person to full and equal recognition and exercise of his or her human rights and freedoms.

discrimination because of association Denial of rights because of friendship or other relationship with a protected group member.

dismissal Involuntary termination of an employee's employment.

dismissal for just cause An employer-initiated termination based on an employee's poor behaviour; in these situations, no severance, reasonable notice periods, or additional payments beyond what the employee has already earned are owed.

distributive bargaining A win–lose negotiating strategy in which one party gains at the expense of the other.

distributive justice Fairness of a decision outcome.

due diligence Employers' responsibility regarding taking every reasonable precaution to ensure the health and safety of their workers.

E

early retirement or buyout programs Strategies used to accelerate attrition that involve offering attractive buyout packages or the opportunity to retire on full pension with an attractive benefits package.

electronic performance monitoring (EPM) Having supervisors electronically monitor the amount of computerized data an employee is processing per day and thereby his or her performance.

emotional intelligence (EI) tests Tests that measure a person's ability to monitor his or her own emotions and the emotions of others and to use that knowledge to guide thoughts and actions.

employee assistance plan (EAP) A company-sponsored program to help employees cope with personal problems that are interfering with or have the potential to interfere with their job performance, as well as issues affecting their well-being or the well-being of their families.

employee benefits Indirect financial payments given to employees. They may include supplementary health and life insurance, vacation, pension plans, education plans, and discounts on company products.

employee engagement The emotional and intellectual involvement of employees in their work, and the intensity, focus, and involvement they bring to their jobs and organizations.

employee opinion surveys Communication devices that use questionnaires to ask for employees' opinions about the company, management, and work life.

employee onboarding (orientation) A procedure for providing new employees with basic background information about the firm and the job.

employee share purchase/stock ownership plan (ESOP) A plan whereby a trust is established to hold shares of company stock purchased for or issued to employees. The trust distributes the stock to employees on retirement, separation from service, or as otherwise prescribed by the plan.

employee value proposition The total value an employee receives from the employer, including compensation, benefits, career management, workplace/lifestyle, and employee pride.

employee wellness program A program that takes a proactive approach to employee health and well-being.

employer branding The image or impression of an organization as an employer based on the benefits of being employed by the organization.

employment equity program A detailed plan designed to identify and correct existing discrimination, redress past discrimination, and achieve a balanced representation of designated group members in the organization.

employment insurance (EI) A federal program intended to provide temporary financial assistance to eligible persons who experience interruption to their work through no fault of their own.

employment (labour) standards legislation Laws present in every Canadian jurisdiction that establish minimum employee entitlements and set a limit on the maximum number of hours of work permitted per day or week.

empowerment Providing workers with the skills and authority to make decisions that would traditionally be made by managers.

environmental scanning Identifying and analyzing external opportunities and threats that may be crucial to the organization's success. In the context of human resources management, environmental scanning is an assessment of external factors influencing the organization's ability to find and secure talent from the external labour market, including economic, competitive, legislative, social, technological, and demographic trends.

equal pay for equal work Specifies that an employer cannot pay male and female employees differently if they are performing the same or substantially similar work.

equality rights Section 15 of the Charter of Rights and Freedoms, which guarantees the right to equal protection and benefit of the law without discrimination.

ergonomics An interdisciplinary approach that seeks to integrate and accommodate the physical needs of workers into the design of jobs. It aims to adapt the entire job system—the work, environment, machines, equipment, and processes—to match human characteristics.

ethics The principles of conduct governing an individual or a group; specifically, the standards you use to decide what your conduct should be.

ethnocentric staffing policy Policies that align with the attitude that home-country managers are superior to those in the host country.

expatriate Employees who are citizens of the country where the parent company is based and are sent to work in another country.

expatriate assignment failure Early return of an expatriate from a global assignment.

external equity Employees perceive their pay as fair, given the pay rates in other organizations.

F

fixed pay Compensation that is independent of the performance level of the individual, group, or organization.

flexible benefits programs Individualized benefit plans to accommodate employee needs and preferences.

forced distribution method Predetermined percentages of ratees are placed in various performance categories.

formal appraisal discussion An interview in which the supervisor and employee review the appraisal and make plans to remedy deficiencies and reinforce strengths.

Functional Job Analysis (FJA) A quantitative method for classifying jobs based on types and amounts of responsibility for data, people, and things. Performance standards and training requirements are also identified.

G

gainsharing plan An incentive plan that engages employees in a common effort to achieve productivity objectives and share the gains.

geocentric staffing policy Policies that align with the belief that the best manager for any specific position anywhere on the globe may be found in any of the countries in which the firm operates.

glass ceiling An invisible barrier, caused by attitudinal or organizational bias, that limits the advancement opportunities of qualified designated group members.

grade/group description A written description of the level of compensable factors required by jobs in each grade; used to combine similar jobs into grades or classes.

grades Groups of jobs based on a set of rules for each grade, whereby the jobs are similar in difficulty but otherwise different. Grades often contain dissimilar jobs, such as those of secretaries, mechanics, and firefighters.

graphic rating scale A scale that lists a number of traits and a range of performance for each. The employee is then rated by a score that best describes his or her level of performance for each trait.

green circle pay rate A rate of pay that is below the pay range minimum.

grievance A written allegation of a contract violation, filed by an individual bargaining unit member, the union, or management.

group life insurance Life insurance provided at lower rates for all employees, including new employees, regardless of health or physical condition.

group termination laws Laws that require an employer to notify employees in the event that they decide to terminate a group of employees.

guaranteed piecework plan The minimum hourly wage plus an incentive for each piece produced above a set number of pieces per hour.

H

halo effect A positive initial impression that distorts an interviewer's rating of a candidate because subsequent information is judged with a positive bias. In performance appraisal, the problem that occurs when a supervisor's rating of an employee on one trait biases the rating of that person on other traits.

harassment Unwelcome behaviour that demeans, humiliates, or embarrasses a person and that a reasonable person should have known would be unwelcome.

hiring freeze A common initial response to an employee surplus; openings are filled by reassigning current employees, and no outsiders are hired.

human capital The knowledge, education, training, skills, and expertise of an organization's workforce.

human capital theory The accumulation of firm-specific knowledge and experience involves a joint investment by both the employee and employer; therefore, both parties benefit from maintaining a long-term relationship.

human resources management (HRM) The management of people in organizations to drive successful organizational performance and achievement of the organization's strategic goals.

human resources planning (HRP) The process of forecasting future human resources requirements to ensure that the organization will have the required number of employees, at the right time, with the necessary skills, knowledge, and abilities to meet its strategic objectives.

human rights legislation Jurisdiction-specific legislation that prohibits intentional and unintentional discrimination in employment situations and in the delivery of goods and services.

I

immigrant A person residing in Canada who was born outside of Canada (excluding temporary foreign workers, Canadian citizens born outside of Canada, and those with student or work visas).

incumbent Individual currently holding the position.

industrial engineering A field of study concerned with analyzing work methods; making work cycles more efficient by modifying, combining, rearranging, or eliminating tasks; and establishing time standards.

industrial union A labour organization representing all workers eligible for union membership in a particular company or industry, including skilled tradespeople.

insubordination Wilful disregard for the boss's authority or legitimate orders, disobedience, or criticizing the boss in public.

integrative bargaining A negotiating strategy in which the possibility of win–win, lose–win, win–lose, and lose–lose outcomes is recognized, and there is acknowledgement that achieving a win–win outcome will depend on mutual trust and problem solving.

intelligence (IQ) tests Tests that measure general intellectual abilities, such as verbal comprehension, inductive reasoning, memory, numerical ability, speed of perception, spatial visualization, and word fluency.

interactional justice Fairness in interpersonal interactions, treating others with dignity and respect.

interest arbitration The imposition of the final terms of a collective agreement.

interest dispute A dispute between an organization and the union representing its employees over the terms of a collective agreement.

interest inventories Tests that compare a candidate's interests with those of people in various occupations.

internal equity Employees perceive their pay as fair, given the pay rates of others in the organization.

involuntary turnover Employer-initiated termination of employment, such as dismissals or layoffs.

J

job A group of related activities and duties, held by a single employee or a number of incumbents.

job analysis The procedure for determining the tasks, duties, and responsibilities of each job, and the human attributes (in terms of knowledge, skills, and abilities) required to perform it.

job description A list of the duties, responsibilities, reporting relationships, and working conditions of a job—one product of a job analysis.

job design The process of improving organizational efficiency and employee satisfaction through technological and human considerations.

job enlargement (horizontal loading) A technique to relieve monotony and boredom that involves assigning workers additional tasks at the same level of responsibility to increase the number of tasks they have to perform.

job enrichment (vertical loading) Any effort that makes an employee's job more rewarding or satisfying by adding more meaningful tasks and duties.

job evaluation A systematic comparison to determine the relative worth of jobs within a firm.

job evaluation committee A diverse group (including employees, HR staff, managers, and union representatives) established to ensure the fair and comprehensive representation of the nature and requirements of the jobs in question.

job instruction training (JIT) The listing of each job's basic tasks along with key points to provide step-by-step training for employees.

job posting The process of notifying current employees about vacant positions.

job rotation A technique to relieve monotony and employee boredom that involves systematically moving employees from one job to another.

job sharing A strategy that involves dividing the duties of a single position between two or more employees.

job specification A list of the "human capital requirements," that is, the requisite knowledge, skills, and abilities needed to perform the job—another product of a job analysis.

K

kinesthetic tactile learning Learning through a whole-body experience, such as learning through completing an activity.

KSAs Knowledge, skills, and abilities.

L

labour relations The ongoing interactions between labour unions and management in organizations.

labour union (union) An officially recognized association of employees practising a similar trade or employed in the same company or industry who have joined together to present a united front and collective voice in dealing with management.

layoff The temporary or permanent withdrawal of employment to workers for economic or business reasons.

learning organization An organization skilled at creating, acquiring, and transferring knowledge and at modifying its behaviour to reflect new knowledge and insights.

leave of absence Allows an employee who may be interested in taking time away from work for a variety of reasons (e.g., personal, educational, etc.) to have a set period of time away from his or her position without pay, but with a guarantee that their job will be available upon return.

lockout The temporary refusal of a company to continue providing work for bargaining unit employees involved in a labour dispute, which may result in closure of the establishment for a time.

lost-time injury rate Measures any occupational injury or illness resulting in an employee being unable to fulfill the job's full work assignments, not including any fatalities.

M

management assessment centre A comprehensive, systematic procedure used to assess candidates' management potential that uses a combination of realistic exercises, management games, objective testing, presentations, and interviews.

management by objectives (MBO) Involves setting specific measurable goals with each employee and then periodically reviewing the progress made.

management inventories Records summarizing the qualifications, interests, and skills of management employees, along with the number and types of employees supervised, duties of such employees, total budget managed, previous managerial duties and responsibilities, and managerial training received.

Markov analysis A method of forecasting internal labour supply that involves tracking the pattern of employee movements through various jobs and developing a transitional probability matrix.

mediation The often voluntary use of a neutral third party who has direct input on the negotiation process to help an organization and the union representing its employees to reach a mutually satisfactory collective agreement.

memorandum of settlement A summary of the terms and conditions agreed to by the parties that is submitted to the constituent groups for final approval.

merit pay (merit raise) Any salary increase awarded to an employee based on his or her individual performance.

metrics Statistics used to measure activities and results.

micro-assessment A series of verbal, paper-based, or computer-based questions and exercises that a candidate is required to complete, covering the range of activities required on the job for which he or she is applying.

mixed (semi-structured) interview An interview format that combines the structured and unstructured techniques.

multiple-hurdle strategy An approach to selection involving a series of successive steps or hurdles. Only candidates clearing the hurdle are permitted to move on to the next step.

mutual gains (interest-based) bargaining A win–win negotiating approach based on training in the fundamentals of effective problem solving and conflict resolution, in which the interests of all stakeholders are taken into account.

N

National Occupational Classification (NOC) A reference tool for writing job descriptions and job specifications. Compiled by the federal government, it contains comprehensive, standardized descriptions of about 30 000 occupations organized into 500 Unit Groups according to four skill levels and ten skill types.

negligent training Occurs when an employer fails to adequately train an employee who subsequently harms a third party or is disciplined for safetl infractions.

nepotism A preference for hiring relatives of current employees.

networking An organized process whereby the individual arranges and conducts a series of face-to-face meetings with his or her colleagues and contacts, plus individuals whom they recommend.

nominal group technique A decision-making technique that involves a group of experts meeting face to face. Steps include independent idea generation, clarification and open discussion, and private assessment.

O

occupation A collection of jobs that share some or all of a set of main duties.

occupational health and safety legislation Laws intended to protect the health and safety of workers by minimizing work-related accidents and illnesses.

occupational segregation The existence of certain occupations that have traditionally been male dominated and others that have been female dominated.

organization chart A "snapshot" of the firm, depicting the organization's structure in chart form at a particular point in time.

organizational climate The prevailing atmosphere that exists in an organization and its impact on employees.

organizational culture The core values, beliefs, and assumptions that are widely shared by members of an organization.

organizational structure The formal relationships among jobs in an organization.

P

paired comparison method Ranking employees by making a chart of all possible pairs of employees for each trait and indicating the better employee of the pair.

panel interview An interview in which a group of interviewers questions the applicant.

pay equity Providing equal pay to male-dominated job classes and female-dominated job classes of equal value to the employer.

pay grade Comprises jobs of approximately equal value.

pay in lieu of reasonable notice A lump sum or wage continuance payment equal to an employee's pay for the notice period provided to employees who cease working immediately.

pay ranges A series of steps or levels within a pay grade, usually based on years of service.

pension plans Plans that provide income when employees reach a pre-determined retirement age.

performance analysis Verifying whether there is a significant performance deficiency and, if so, determining whether that deficiency should be rectified through training or some other means.

performance appraisal A formal, relatively infrequent process in which an employee's performance is evaluated along a predetermined set of criteria that is quantified via a formal performance score.

performance management The process encompassing all activities related to improving employee performance, productivity, and effectiveness.

personality tests Instruments used to measure basic aspects of personality, such as introversion, stability, motivation, neurotic tendency, self-confidence, self-sufficiency, and sociability.

phased retirement A program whereby potential retirees gradually reduce the number of hours worked per week over time.

physical demands analysis Identification of the senses used and the type, frequency, and amount of physical effort involved in a job.

picket Stationing groups of striking employees, usually carrying signs, at the entrances and exits of the struck operation to publicize the issues in dispute and discourage people, supplies, and goods from entering or leaving the premises.

piecework A system of pay based on the number of items processed by each individual worker in a unit of time, such as items per hour or items per day.

point method A job evaluation method in which a number of compensable factors are identified, the degree to which each of these factors is present in the job is determined, and an overall point value is calculated.

polycentric staffing policy Policies that align with the belief that only host-country managers can understand the culture and behaviour of the host-country market.

portability A provision that employees who change jobs can transfer the lump-sum value of the pension they have earned to a locked-in RRSP or their new employer's pension plan.

position The collection of tasks and responsibilities performed by one person.

Position Analysis Questionnaire (PAQ) A questionnaire used to collect quantifiable data concerning the duties and responsibilities of various jobs.

precedent The decision or interpretation of a court of another jurisdiction can act as a persuasive authority regarding how legislation is to be interpreted and applied in other jurisdictions.

pre-hearing vote An alternative mechanism for certification, used in situations in which there is evidence of violations of fair labour practices early in the organizing campaign.

pre-retirement counselling Counselling provided to employees some months (or even years) before retirement, which covers such matters as benefits advice, second careers, and so on.

primary sector Jobs in agriculture, fishing and trapping, forestry, and mining.

procedural justice Fairness of the process used to make a decision.

process chart A diagram showing the flow of inputs to and outputs from the job under study.

productivity The ratio of an organization's outputs (goods and services) to its inputs (people, capital, energy, and materials).

profit-sharing plan A plan whereby most or all employees share in the company's profits.

programmed learning A systematic method for teaching job skills that involves presenting questions or facts, allowing the person to respond, and giving the learner immediate feedback on the accuracy of his or her answers.

progressive discipline A formal system to correct employee performance where penalties increase as the severity and frequency of undesirable behaviours or performance increases.

promotion Movement of an employee from one job to another that is higher in pay, responsibility, or organizational level, usually based on merit, seniority, or a combination of both.

Q

quitting Voluntary, employee-initiated resignation.

R

ratification Formal approval by secret-ballot vote of the bargaining unit members of the agreement negotiated between union and management.

ratio analysis A forecasting technique for determining future staff needs by using ratios between some causal factor (such as sales volume) and the number of employees needed.

realistic job preview (RJP) A strategy used to provide applicants with realistic information—both positive and negative—about the job demands, the organization's expectations, and the work environment.

reality shock (cognitive dissonance) The state that results from the discrepancy between what the new employee expected from his or her new job and its realities.

reasonable accommodation The adjustment of employment policies and practices that an employer may be expected to make so that no individual is denied benefits, disadvantaged in employment, or prevented from carrying out the essential components of a job because of grounds prohibited in human rights legislation.

reasonable cause A complaint about a workplace hazard has not been satisfactorily resolved, or a safety problem places employees in immediate danger.

reasonable notice legislation Laws that require employers to notify employees in the event that they decide to terminate employees through layoffs (i.e., without just cause). Minimum notice varies according to the size of the layoffs, with smaller layoffs requiring minimum notice based on employee tenure and mass layoffs requiring minimum notice based on total layoff size.

recency effect The rating error that occurs when ratings are based on the employee's most recent performance rather than on performance throughout the appraisal period.

recruiter A specialist in recruitment whose job is to find and attract capable candidates.

recruitment The process of searching out and attracting qualified job applicants, which begins with the identification of a position that requires staffing and is completed when résumés or completed application forms are received from an adequate number of applicants.

red circle pay rate A rate of pay that is above the pay range maximum.

reduced workweek Employees work fewer hours and receive less pay.

regression analysis A statistical technique involving the use of a mathematical formula to project future demands based on an established relationship between an organization's employment level (dependent variable) and some measurable factor of output (independent variable).

regulations Legally binding rules established by special regulatory bodies created to enforce compliance with the law and aid in its interpretation.

reliability The degree to which interviews, tests, and other selection procedures yield comparable data over time; in other words, the degree of dependability, consistency, or stability of the measures used.

repatriation The process of moving the expatriate and his or her family back home from the foreign assignment.

repetitive strain injuries (RSIs) Activity-related soft-tissue injuries of the neck, shoulders, arms, wrists, hands, back, and legs.

replacement charts Visual representations of who will replace whom in the event of a job opening. An organizational chart format is typically used to depict reporting relationships, relevant jobs, and job incumbents. Such charts indicate the current performance level of the employee and his or her promotion potential.

replacement summaries Lists of likely replacements for each position and their relative strengths and weaknesses, as well as information about current position, performance, promotability, age, and experience.

representation vote A vote conducted by the LRB in which employees in the bargaining unit indicate, by secret ballot, whether or not they want to be represented, or continue to be represented, by a labour union.

restitutional remedies Monetary compensation for the complainant to put him or her back to the position he or she would be in if the discrimination had not occurred (this includes compensation for injury to dignity and self-respect); a written letter of apology may be required.

retirees on call A program whereby retirees can continue to work on a part-time or as-needed basis.

rights arbitration The process involved in the settlement of a rights dispute.

rights dispute A disagreement between an organization and the union representing its employees regarding the interpretation or application of one or more clauses in the current collective agreement.

S

scatter plot A graphical method used to help identify the relationship between two variables.

secondary sector Jobs in manufacturing and construction.

selection The process of choosing among individuals who have been recruited to fill existing or projected job openings.

selection interview A procedure designed to predict future job performance on the basis of applicants' oral responses to oral inquiries.

selection ratio The ratio of the number of applicants hired to the total number of applicants.

seniority Length of service in the bargaining unit.

severance pay Payable by employers under Ontario and/or federal jurisdiction to employees terminated for reasons other than cause, in addition to the reasonable notice payment or period. Severance pay is often based on the employee's length of service and other factors (such as the total size of the annual company payroll).

sexual annoyance Sexually related conduct that is hostile, intimidating, or offensive to the employee but has no direct link to tangible job benefits or loss thereof.

sexual coercion Harassment of a sexual nature that results in some direct consequence to the worker's employment status or some gain in or loss of tangible job benefits.

sexual harassment Offensive or humiliating behaviour that is related to a person's sex, as well as behaviour of a sexual nature that creates an intimidating, unwelcome, hostile, or offensive work environment or that could

reasonably be thought to put sexual conditions on a person's job or employment opportunities.

short-term disability and sick leave Plans that provide pay to an employee when he or she is unable to work because of a non-work-related illness or injury.

similar-to-me bias The tendency to give higher performance ratings to employees who are perceived to be similar to the rater in some way.

situational interview A series of job-related questions that focus on how the candidate would behave in a given situation.

situational tests Tests in which candidates are presented with hypothetical situations representative of the job for which they are applying and are evaluated on their responses.

skills inventories Manual or computerized records summarizing employees' education, experience, interests, skills, and so on, which are used to identify internal candidates eligible for transfer or promotion.

social (reform) unionism Activities of unions directed at furthering the interests of their members by influencing the social and economic policies of governments at all levels, such as speaking out on proposed legislative reforms.

social responsibility The implied, enforced, or felt obligation of managers, acting in their official capacities, to serve or protect the interests of groups other than themselves.

socialization The ongoing process of instilling in all employees the prevailing attitudes, standards, values, and patterns of behaviour that are expected by the organization.

staffing table A pictorial representation of all jobs within the organization, along with the number of current incumbents and future employment requirements (monthly or yearly) for each.

stare decisis Decisions of a higher court can act as the binding authority on a lower court decisions within that same jurisdiction.

statistical strategy A more objective technique used to determine whom the job should be offered to; involves identifying the most valid predictors and weighting them through statistical methods, such as multiple regression.

stock option The right to purchase a stated number of shares of a company stock at today's price at some time in the future.

straight piecework plan A set payment for each piece produced or processed in a factory or shop.

strategy The company's plan for how it will balance its internal strengths and weaknesses with external opportunities and threats to maintain a competitive advantage.

strictness/leniency The problem that occurs when a supervisor has a tendency to rate all employees either low or high.

strike The temporary refusal by bargaining unit members to continue working for the employer.

strike vote Legally required in some jurisdictions, it is a vote seeking authorization from bargaining unit members to strike if necessary. A favourable vote does not mean that a strike is inevitable.

structured interview An interview following a set sequence of questions.

succession planning The process of ensuring a suitable supply of successors for current and future senior or key jobs so that the careers of individuals can be effectively planned and managed.

supplemental employee retirement plans (SERPs) Plans that provide the additional pension benefit required for employees to receive their full pension benefit in cases when their full pension benefit exceeds the maximum allowable benefit under the Income Tax Act.

supplemental unemployment benefits (SUBs) A top-up of EI benefits to bring income levels closer to what an employee would receive if on the job.

survivor syndrome A range of negative emotions experienced by employees remaining after a major restructuring initiative, which can include feelings of betrayal or violation, guilt, or detachment, and can result in stress symptoms, including depression, increased errors, and reduced performance.

systemic remedies Forward-looking solutions to discrimination that require respondents to take positive steps to ensure compliance with legislation, with respect to both the current complaint and any future practices.

T

talent acquisition An emerging HRM programming concept that is focused on finding, acquiring, assessing, and hiring job candidates.

task analysis Identifying the broad competencies and specific skills required to perform job-related tasks.

task performance An individual's direct contribution to his or her job-related processes.

team A small group of people with complementary skills who work toward common goals for which they hold joint responsibility and accountability.

team or group incentive plan A plan in which a production standard is set for a specific work group and its members are paid incentives if the group exceeds the production standard.

team-based job designs Job designs that focus on giving a team, rather than an individual, a whole and meaningful piece of work to do and empowering team members to decide among themselves how to accomplish the work.

termination Permanent separation from the organization for any reason.

termination interview The interview in which an employee is informed of the fact that he or she has been dismissed.

termination pay Payment of wages from the employer to the employee at the time of involuntary termination for reasons other than cause. The amount paid must meet the minimum-notice-period payments established by labour legislation (if payment is given in lieu of reasonable notice) or follow guidelines established in common law precedent.

tertiary or service sector Jobs in public administration, personal and business services, finance, trade, public utilities, and transportation/communications.

tort law Primarily judge-based law, whereby the precedent and jurisprudences set by one judge through his or her assessment of a case establishes how similar cases will be interpreted, as either intentional torts or unintentional torts.

total employment rewards An integrated package of all rewards (monetary and non-monetary, extrinsic and intrinsic) gained by employees arising from their employment.

training The process of teaching employees the basic skills/competencies that they need to perform their jobs.

transfer Movement of an employee from one job to another that is relatively equal in pay, responsibility, or organizational level.

transfer of training Application of the skills acquired during the training program into the work environment and the maintenance of these skills over time.

trend analysis The study of a firm's past employment levels over a period of years to predict future needs.

turnover The termination of an individual's employment with an organization.

U

unclear performance standards An appraisal scale that is too open to interpretation of traits and standards.

underemployment Employment in a job that does not fully utilize one's knowledge, skills, and abilities (KSAs).

undue hardship The point to which employers are expected to accommodate employees under human rights legislative requirements.

unfair labour practice A contravention of labour relations legislation by an employer, a union, or an employee.

unintentional/constructive/systemic discrimination Discrimination that is embedded in policies and practices that appear neutral on the surface and are implemented impartially, but have an adverse impact on specific groups of people for reasons that are not job related or required for the safe and efficient operation of the business.

union local A group of unionized employees in a particular location.

union security clause The contract provisions protecting the interests of the labour union and dealing with the issues of membership requirements, the ability to participate in union duties at work, and, often, the payment of union dues.

union steward A union member elected by workers in a particular department or area of a firm to act as their union representative.

unstructured interview An unstructured, conversational-style interview. The interviewer pursues points of interest as they come up in response to questions.

V

validity The accuracy with which a predictor measures what it is intended to measure.

variable pay Any plan that ties pay to productivity or profitability.

vestibule or simulated training Training employees on special off-the-job equipment, as in airplane pilot training, whereby training costs and hazards can be reduced.

vesting A provision that employer money placed in a pension fund cannot be forfeited for any reason.

video conferencing Connecting two or more distant groups by using audiovisual equipment.

visual learning Learning through visual methods such as through pictures and print.

voluntary turnover Employee-initiated termination of employment, by quitting, retiring, or resigning.

W

wage curve A graphic description of the relationship between the value of the job and the average wage paid for this job.

wage/salary survey A survey aimed at determining prevailing wage rates. A good salary survey provides specific wage rates for comparable jobs. Formal written questionnaire surveys are the most comprehensive.

want ad A recruitment ad describing the job and its specifications, the compensation package, and the hiring employer. The address to which applications or résumés should be submitted is also provided.

wildcat strike A spontaneous walkout, not officially sanctioned by the union leadership, which may or may not be legal, depending on its timing.

work sharing Employees work three or four days a week and receive EI benefits on their non-workday(s).

work simplification An approach to job design that involves assigning most of the administrative aspects of work (such as planning and organizing) to supervisors and managers, while giving lower-level employees narrowly defined tasks to perform according to methods established and specified by management.

workers' compensation Provides income and medical benefits to victims of work-related accidents or illnesses, or to their dependants, regardless of fault.

workforce mobility The focus on managing the recruitment, relocation, and retention of employees who complete work-related tasks and activities outside of the core or primary head office or region of the company.

Workplace Hazardous Materials Information System (WHMIS) A Canada-wide, legally mandated system designed to protect workers by providing information about hazardous materials in the workplace.

wrongful dismissal An employee dismissal that does not comply with the law or does not comply with a written or implied contractual arrangement.

Name and Organization Index

A

Aboriginal Inclusion Network, 102
Accenture, 156
Alberta Alcohol and Drug Abuse Commission, 252
Alcan, Inc., 223, 309
American Federation of Labor and Congress of Industrial Organizations (AFL–CIO), 285
Aon Hewitt, 189
ArcelorMittal Dofasco Inc., 276
Association of Canadian Search, Employment, and Staffing Services (ACSESS), 100

B

Barrett, G., 173
Beamish, Paul, Dr., 314
Beaton, Ann, Dr., 133
Beaudry, Paul, Dr., 181
Bell Canada, 223
Bell Mobility, 33
Bernardi, Lauren, 22
Best Buy, 273
Bhinder, case of, 34–35
Bouchard, Gabriel, 91
British Columbia Human Rights Tribunal, 34
Burnaby, 197, 273
Byres, N., 27

C

Canada Life Assurance Company, 220
Canadian Border Services Agency, 41
Canadian Centre for Justice Statistics, 237
Canadian Council of Human Resources Associations (CCHRA), 9
Canadian Council on Learning, 136
Canadian Council on Rehabilitation and Work, 102, 222
Canadian Forces Liaison Council (CFLC), 98
Canadian Human Rights Commission, 30, 35, 107
Canadian Industrial Relations Association, 9
Canadian Labour Congress (CLC), 257, 285
Canadian National Railway (CN), 34

Canadian Union of Public Employees (CUPE), 285
Chan, C., 268
Chhinzer, Nita, 21, 36
Cisco, 276
City of Boisbriand, 31
Communauté urbaine de Montréal, 31
Concordia University, 172
Confédération des syndicats nationaux (CSN), 285
Conference Board of Canada, 102, 103, 129, 130, 154, 159, 230, 245, 252, 257, 294, 321
Construction Safety Association, 9
Côté, Pierre, Dr., 217
Cowan, Allison, 180
Cox, C.H., 8
Cox, D.M., 8

D

Deloitte, 156
Dessler, Gary, 21
Dias, Jerry, 287
Dolson, Scott, Dr., 55, 77

E

Ernst & Young, 97, 131, 232
Estill, Jim, 276

F

Facebook, 14, 100, 286
Foreign Credential Referral Office (FCRO), 324
Future Shop, 273

G

Gannon, Gary L., 90
Gao, J. H., 155
GapTOPS Ltd., 268
Garavan, Thomas N., 171
Greater Toronto Area, 39
Group Benefits Associate (GBA), 10

H

Hackett, Rick, Dr., 3–4
Heisz, A., 14
Henderson, Richard I., 52
Hewitt Associates, 232
Hicks, J., 164
HMV, 273
Human Resources Professionals Association (HRPA), 13, 98
Husky Injection Molding Systems, 230

I

IBM Canada, 134, 230, 276
IKEA, 230
Industrial Accident Prevention Association (IAPA), 9, 238
INSEAD, 317
Instagram, 286
Institute for Performance and Learning, 9
Institute for Work and Health, 256
International Brotherhood of Teamsters, 285

J

Jaguar Land Rover, 164

K

Kanata Research Park, 230
Kernan, M., 173
KPMG, 156, 232, 318

L

Law Society of Upper Canada, 130
Lazarova, Mila, Dr., 157
Letourneau, F., 226
Lincoln Electric, 204
LinkedIn, 100, 287
London Business School, 317
Loughlin, Catherine, Dr., 251

M

McAteer, H., 180, 200
McCarthy, Alma M., 171
McDonald's, 92
Mercer, 189
Merrill Lynch, 268
Merrim, Lewis J., 113
Microsoft, 97
Milgram, R., 92
Molson, 309
Monster, 99
Monster.com (Monster Canada), 91, 189
Morra, M., 92
Mountain Equipment Co-op (MEC), 11

N

Notten, G., 14

O

Office of the Privacy Commissioner of Canada, 42
Ontario-based Human Resources Professionals Association (HRPA), 9
Ontario Human Rights Tribunal, 35

Ontario Ministry of Community and Social Services, 103
Ontario Ministry of Education, 133

P

Paquin, Renee, 85
Parker, Doug, 198
Pharos Restaurant, 32
Procter & Gamble, 97
Prost, A., 104
PWC, 156

R

Registered Professional Recruiter (RPR), 10
Reserve Employment Assistance Program (REAP), 98
Roman Catholic Church, 29
Royal Canadian Mounted Police, 29
Royal Dutch Shell, 315
Runzheimer International, 309

S

Seven Oaks General Hospital (Winnipeg), 260
Silliker, A., 42
Situ, J., 14
Smith, Tom, 203
Society for Canadian Women in Science and Technology (SCWIST), 102
Stewart, Nicole, 180
Sun Microsystems, 276
Superior Propane, 223
Supreme Court of Canada, 25, 29, 31, 32, 33

T

Taormina, R. J., 155
Tata, 164
Taylor, Benjamin, Dr., 109
TELUS, 232
Thorndike, Robert, 154
Thorpe, K., 227
Toronto Board of Trade, 189
Towers Watson, 189
Toyota, 15
Troilo, Palmerino, 31
Twitter, 14, 100, 286, 287

U

United Food and Commercial Workers (UFCW), 286
University of Alberta, 194

V
Vandenberghe, Christian, Dr., 275
Voisey's Bay Nickel Company, 285

W
Watanabe, A., 92
Watson Wyatt, 90, 320
Watters, M., 145
Welch, Jack, 158

Western Compensation and Benefits Consultants, 180
WORKink, 103
Workopolis, 99

Workplace Health Research Unit (Brock University), 276
Workplace Safety and Insurance Board (WSIB) (Ontario), 238

Subject Index

boldface = key term
f = figure
t = table

A

Abilities @ Work, 103
Aboriginal people
  differential treatment of, 37
  First Nations' rights, 25
  recruiting, 101–102
  in the workforce, 12, 39,
    100
absenteeism, 5, 116
accidental death and
    dismemberment
    coverage, 218
accident prevention
  employee's return to work,
    248–249
  incidence of unsafe acts,
    reducing, 246
  positive reinforcement, 248
  selection testing, 247
  top-management
    commitment, 247
  training and education,
    247–248
  unsafe conditions,
    minimizing, 246
accidents in workplace
  chance occurrences, 241
  personal characteristics,
    244–245, 244*f*
  reducing, 116
  unsafe acts, 243–244
  unsafe conditions, 242–243,
    243*f*
accommodations, 108, 110,
    115
accounting scandals, 7
achievement tests, 114
acquisitions and mergers, 132
action plans, 163
addiction, 116. *See also*
    substance abuse
adult education, 324
advertising, 48, 95, 96, 99,
    101, 102
age
  sexual orientation, 35
  and career development, 144
  discrimination, 27, 35
  employee accident
    behaviour, 245
  and workplace diversity, 12
agency recruiters, 100–101
agreeableness, 66, 113
alcohol addiction, 116
alternation ranking method,
    158, 167*t*
alumni networks, 97
American Federation of Labor
    and Congress of
    Industrial Organizations
    (AFL–CIO), 285

annual bonus. *See also*
    incentive plans
  eligibility, 198
  fund size, 198–199
  individual awards,
    determining, 199
applicants. *See* candidates
applications, job, 96
  online, 96
appraisal. *See* appraisal bias;
    appraisal methods;
    appraisal problems;
    appraisal tools
appraisal bias, 166
appraisal methods. *See also*
    appraisal problems;
    formal appraisal
    discussion
  alternation ranking method,
    158
  behaviourally anchored
    rating scale (BARS),
    159–160, 160*f*
  critical incident model, 159
  forced distribution model,
    158–159
  graphic rating scale,
    156–158
  management by objectives
    (MBO), 161
  midpoint scales, 159
  mixing, 161
  paired comparison method,
    158, 158*f*
  use of technology, 168, 171
  web-based, 168
  work sampling, 114
appraisal problems. *See also*
    appraisal methods
  appraisal bias, 166
  avoiding, 161, 167–168
  central tendency, 165–166
  rating scale problems,
    165–168
  recency effect, 166
  similar-to-me bias, 166–168
  strictness/leniency, 166
  unclear performance
    standards, 165, 165*t*
  validity and reliability,
    164–168
appraisal tools, advantages and
    disadvantages of, 167*t*
apprenticeship training,
    140–141
aptitude tests, 111
arbitration, 300
arbitration clause, 301
assembly lines, 53
association
  discrimination because
    of, 28
  freedom of, 25
associations by province and
    designation, HR, 10*t*

attitude, positive, 154
attrition, 83
audiovisual techniques,
    141–142
auditory learning, 136
authority, 49, 54, 91, 170
authorization card, 290
automatic certification, 292
autonomy, 31, 54, 57, 146

B

baby boomers, 13*t*
background checks,
    121–124, 125
balanced scorecard, 8
balance sheet approach, 318
bargaining. *See* collective
    bargaining; distributive
    bargaining
bargaining unit, 283
bargaining zone, 295
behavioural competencies, 193
behavioural interview, 117
**behaviourally anchored rating
    scale (BARS)**, 159–160,
    160*f*, 167*t*
**behaviour description
    interview (BDI)**, 117
bell curve, 158–159
benchmark job, 183
benefits. *See* employee benefits
bereavement leave, 214
Big Five personality
    dimension, 113–114
Bill C-45 amendments, 241
**biographical information
    blank (BIB)**, 96
blended learning, 140, 141
blind ad, 100
blogging, by employees, 41
**bona fide occupational
    requirement (BFOR)**,
    28–29
boycott, 298
branding, 91–92
broadbanding, 192
bullying, 32–33
bureaucratic structure, 49–50,
    51*f*
burnout, 254
business ally, 6–7
business unionism, 284
buyout programs, 83–84

C

Canada
  complaints received by
    Canadian Human Rights
    Commission in 2016, 26*f*
  direct learning expenditure
    in, 129, 130*f*
  economy in, 12
  employment legislation in,
    21–24, 21*f*, 23*f*

employment trends in, 12
  government jurisdictions,
    15, 23–24
  job openings in, 70
  most successful ways to find
    a job in, 97*f*
  multiculturalism in, 34
  privacy in, 41–42
  women in business in, 38*f*
  workforce diversity in, 12
**Canada/Quebec pension plans
    (CPP/QPP)**, 215
Canadian labour laws,
    283–284
candidate-order error, 119
candidates
  availability of, 72–73
  external, 73
  internal, 73–75, 94–95
  notification of, 124–125
**capital accumulation
    programs**, 200
carbon footprints, 16
career, 144
career anchor, 145–146
career counselling, 228
career development, 144–148.
    See also career planning
    and development
**career planning and
    development**
  appraisal problems and
    solutions, 164–168
  career counselling, 145
  career development
    discussion, 162–163
  career management, 48,
    153
  for CEOs and executives,
    129
  evolution of, 144–147
  new approaches to, 146
  for older workers, 145
  and performance
    management, 162–163
  roles in, 147–148
  use of interest inventories
    in, 114
  value of, 144
carpal tunnel syndrome, 256
caucus session, 294
CDs, used for training, 141
central tendency, 165–166
certification, 9, 292
chance occurrences, in
    accidents, 241
change
  administrative, 78
  product, 52
  technological, 52, 72, 78,
    129
change agents, 6
**Charter of Rights and
    Freedoms**, 23–25, 37
Chief HR Officer (CHRO), 7

Chief Talent Officer, 7
child care facilities, 72
China, performance appraisal criteria in, 155
classification/grading method, 185
climate change, 16
closed shop, 301
coaching, 155–156, 171
cognitive abilities, testing of, 110–111
cognitive dissonance, 131, 132
co-insurance, 220
cold calls, 96
collaboration, 249
collective agreement, 283
    contract settlement used in, 300t
    union recognition clause, 300
    union security/checkoff clause, 300
collective bargaining, 283
    collective bargaining agreement, 300–302
    contract approval process, 296–297
    face-to-face negotiations, 294–296, 295f
    preparation for negotiations, 293–294, 294f
    third-party assistance and bargaining impasses, 297–300
collective representation, desire for, 288–290
    dissonance-based reasons, 288
    political/ideological reasons, 289
    utility-based reasons, 289
colour discrimination, 34
combination plans, 205
commission plans, 202–203
commitment, 248
committees, appraisal by, 170
communication
    benefits, 233
    from management, 276–277
compassionate care leave, 231
compensable factor, 184
compensation, 2, 24, 48. *See also* pay rates
    costs, workers', 238
    incentive, 2
    laws, workers', 183
    legal considerations in, 182
    policies, 182
    specialists, 66
    union influences on decisions, 182
compensation professionals, 318
competence, 148
competencies
    analysis of, 54–56
    general, 56

for HR professionals, 4–7
    task functional, 56
    technical, 56
competency-based job analysis, 54–57
competency-based pay, 192
complaints, 26f
conciliation, 297
Confédération des syndicats nationaux (CSN), 285
conflicts of interest, 10
conscience, freedom of, 25
conscientiousness, 113
construct validity, 110
content validity, 110
contextual performance, 154–155
contingent/non-standard workers, 13–14
contingent workforce, 4
contract administration
    discipline, 302–303
    grievance resolution and rights arbitration, 303–305, 304f
    seniority, 302
contract law, 24
contract workers, 101
contrast or candidate-order error, 119
controlled experimentation, 143
core competencies, 56, 193
corporate social responsibility, 10–11
corporations, multinational, 15
cost/benefit analysis, 135
cost per hire, 104f
counselling, career, 145
counselling services, 228–229
craft union, 284
Crawford Small Parts Dexterity Test, 112, 112f
creativity, 146, 165, 249
credible activist, 5
credit checks, 122
credit unions, 228
crime, 10
criterion-related validity, 109
critical illness insurance, 218
critical incident model, 159, 167t
cross-cultural training, 316, 317f
culture, of organization, 2
culture and change steward, 5
culture and globalization, 310
curriculum design, 139–142
customer service, 168

D

damage, to equipment, 54
data analytics, 4
data control, 15
decertification, 293
dedication, 115, 146, 155
deductible, 219

deferred profit-sharing plan (DPSP), 225
deferred share unit plan, 201
defined benefit pension plan, 224
defined contribution pension plan, 224
Delphi technique, 78, 81–82
demographics, 3, 72, 288
deregulation, 52
designations, 9–10
development, 48. *See also* career planning and development
development expenditures, 130f
diary/log, 60
differential or unequal treatment, 28
differential piece-rate plan, 203
differential validity, 108–109
direct learning expenditure, 130f
disability. *See also* persons with disabilities
    defined, 30
    discrimination because of, 30–31, 37
disability management, 223
disability pensions, 215
discipline, 302–303
    disciplinary action, 153
discrimination
    against Aboriginal people, 37
    because of age, 35
    because of association, 28
    because of race and colour, 34
    because of religion, 34–35
    defined, 27
    freedom from, 25, 27
    indirect, 27
    intentional, 27–28
    laws against, 25
    against persons with disabilities, 30–31, 37
    systemic remedies for, 36
    unintentional, 28
    against visible minorities, 12, 37, 102
    against women, 37
dismissal, 269. *See also* termination
dismissal for just cause, 269–271
distributive bargaining, 295
distributive justice, 274
diversity. *See* workforce diversity
drug addiction, 116
drug and alcohol testing, 116
due diligence, 239
due process, right to, 25
duties and responsibilities, 63–64
duty to accommodate, 31–32
DVDs, used for training, 141

E

early retirement, 83–84
    forced, 84
eastern cultures, values in, 155
economic conditions, 12, 71, 76–77
economic systems, 310
economic trends, 3
ecosystem fragility, 16
education
    cooperative, 97
    educational priorities, 72
    e-learning, 140
    of the workforce, 13
educational institutions, recruitment at, 97
educational subsidies, 231
efficiency, 53, 155
elder care, 230–231
e-learning, 140, 141
electronic monitoring, 41–42
electronic performance monitoring (EPM), 168
Emotional Competence Inventory (ECI), 111
Emotional Intelligence Questionnaire (EIQ), 111
emotional intelligence (EI) tests, 110–111
Emotional Quotient Inventory (EQ-i), 111
emotional stability, 66, 113
employee assistance plan (EAP), 229
    international, 319
employee benefits
    administration, 233
    to alumni networks, 97
    Canada/Quebec pension plans (CPP/QPP), 215
    choices among Canadians, 219f
    defined, 211
    employment insurance (EI), 212–213
    executive perquisites, 231–232
    flexible, 232–233
    government-mandated, 212–218
    government-mandated *vs.* voluntary, 212t
    job-related services, 229–231
    leaves of absence, 214–215
    life insurance, 218
    long-term disability insurance, 222–223
    mental health benefits, 223, 224f
    objectives of, 211t
    paid breaks, 218
    pay for mass layoffs, 214
    pay on termination of employment, 213–214
    personal services, 228–229
    phased retirement, 227
    reasonable advance notice periods, 213
    reduction in, 12

employee benefits (*continued*)
retirement benefits, 223–227
sabbatical leaves, 223
severance pay, 24, 213–214
short-term disability plans, 222
sick leave plans, 222
supplemental employee retirement plans (SERPs), 228
supplementary health-care/medical insurance, 219–222
vacations and holidays, 216–217
voluntary employer-sponsored, 218–228
workers' compensation, 215–216
employee engagement, 5
communication from management, 276–277
distributive justice, 274
employee opinion surveys, 276
interactional justice, 274
labour surplus management, pain of, 278–279
procedural justice, 274
suggestion programs, 276
termination interview, 277–278
employee feedback system (EFS), 276
employee opinion surveys, 276
employee reliability inventory (ERI), 247
employees. *See also* employee benefits; employee engagement; employee selection; recruitment; retention
accident behaviour, 244–245, 244*f*
discontented, 93
employer expectations of, 21
empowerment of, 2, 6, 17
former, 97
internal movement of, 148–149
involvement of, 2
misconduct, 270
onboarding, 130–135
performance assessment of, 48
productivity of, 2
quality and nature of, 78
relieving monotony and boredom for, 54
responsibilities and rights of, 239
return to work, 248–249
screening, 260
selection, 3
self-appraisal by, 169
surveillance of, 15, 41–42
training of, 5–6
union *vs.* non-union, 132

employee selection. *See also* selection interview; selection testing
background investigation/reference checking, 121–124
candidate notification, 124–125
criteria development for, 107
evaluation form for, 118
hiring decision, 124–125
legal considerations, 107–108
multiple-hurdle strategy, 106–107, 107*f*
preliminary applicant screening, 108
reaction to, 135
realistic job preview, 124
selection ratio, 106
supervisory interview, 124
supply challenges, 106
employee separations
dismissal for just cause, 269–271
employee engagement and fairness in, 274–279
golden parachute clause, 232, 279
importance of, 265
involuntary turnover, 268–274, 270*f*
layoff, 271–273
quitting, 267
retirement, 267–268
turnover management, 265–274
voluntary turnover, 266–268, 266*t*
wrongful dismissal accusations, avoiding, 273–274
employee services. *See also* employee benefits; occupational health and safety
executive perquisites, 231–232
job-related services, 229–231
personal services, 228–229
employee share purchase/stock ownership plan (ESOP), 197. *See also* incentive plans
employee value proposition (EVP), 178
employee wellness programs, 260–261
employer branding, 91–92
employer branding steps, 92*t*
employers
employee expectations of, 21
health and safety responsibilities of, 33
role in career development, 147–148
employment, 84
employment agencies, private, 100–101
Employment Equity Act, 39

employment equity legislation, 15, 37, 93
employment equity program, 37
employment insurance (EI), 84, 212
Employment Insurance Act, 183
Employment or Labour Standards Act (ESA/LSA), 267
employment rewards. *See* incentive plans; rewards programs
Employment Standards Act (ESA), 23, 24, 39–40, 48, 116
employment (labour) standards legislation, 39–41
empowerment, 17
engagement. *See* employee engagement
entrepreneurs and HR job analysis and job descriptions, 64
environmental issues, 11, 16
environmental scanning, 6, 71–72
EQ Map, 111
equality rights, 25
equal pay for equal work, 38
ergonomics, 54, 255
ethics
and human resource management, 10–11, 13
and performance management, 172–173
ethnocentric staffing policy, 315
executive perquisites, 231–232
executives, integration of, 134–135
executive search firms, 100
expatriate, 309
expatriate assignment failure, 313
external candidates, forecasting supplies of, 76–78
external equity, 182
extroversion, 113, 114

F
face-to-face negotiations, 294–296, 295*f*
initial bargaining session, 295
location, frequency, and duration of meetings, 294–295
subsequent bargaining sessions, 295–296
family businesses, and succession planning, 75
family counselling, 228
feedback, 155–156, 160, 166, 167, 171
360-degree, 172
upward, 170
field placement programs, 97
financial counselling, 228
financial resources, of departments, 78

finger dexterity, 112
First Nations' rights, 25
fixed pay, 179
flat structure, 49–50, 51*f*, 57
flexible benefits programs, 232–233
food services, 231
forced distribution model, 158–159
formal appraisal discussion, 162
preparing for, 163
types of, 162–163
freedoms, fundamental, 25
functional abilities evaluations (FAE), 112–113, 249
functional competencies, 193
Functional Job Analysis (FJA), 59
future human resources needs, 78–82

G
gainsharing plan, 197–198. *See also* incentive plans
Gap analysis, 82
gender identity, in BC Human Rights Code, 27
General Aptitude Test Battery (GATB), 145
general competencies, 56. *See also* core competencies
generational differences, 12, 13*t*. *See also* age
Generation X-ers, 13*t*
Generation Y-ers, 13*t*, 102
Gen X-ers. *See* Generation X-ers
Gen Y-ers. *See* Generation Y-ers
geocentric staffing policy, 316
glass ceiling, 37
global assignments
orientation and training for, 316–317, 317*t*
selection for, 316
global competition, 52, 288
global HRM
balance sheet approach, 318
global staffing policy, 314–315
international compensation management, 317–318, 318*f*
international employee assistance programs, 319
orientation and training for global assignments, 316–317, 317*t*
performance appraisal criteria in China, 155
performance appraisal of global managers, 319
repatriation, 319–320
selection for global assignments, 316
variable pay, 318–319
globalization, 3. *See also* expatriate
of business and human resource, 309

cultural factors, 310
economic systems, 310
impact on HRM, 15
industrial relations
factors, 311
intercountry differences
on HRM, 309–311
labour cost factors,
311, 311t
legal systems, 310–311
relocation, 312–315
global managers, performance
appraisal of, 319
global staffing policy, 314–315
global warming, 16
global workers management,
in Canada, 321–325,
322t
lack of Canadian
experience, 322–324
lack of literacy skills,
324–325
poor transferability of
foreign education or
training, 324
goals
of CEOs, 5
individual, 153
organizational, 3f, 49, 129,
161
golden parachute clause, 232,
279
government. *See also*
legislation
and the balance between
employee and employer
needs, 21f
and human resource
management, 15
government-mandated benefits
Canada/Quebec pension
plans (CPP/QPP), 215
employment insurance (EI),
212–213
leaves of absence, 214–215
paid breaks, 218
pay on termination of
employment, 213–214
vacations and holidays,
216–217
workers' compensation,
215–216
grade/group description, 185
grades, 185
graphic rating scale, 156–158,
165–166, 165t, 167t
green circle pay rate, 192
grievance, 303, 304f
gross rate of return on
capital, 2
group incentive programs, 195
group interviews, 58
group life insurance, 218
group registered retirement
savings plan (group
RRSP), 224
group termination laws, 272
guaranteed piecework plan,
203

H
halo effect, 119, 165
harassment, 32–33
bullying, 32–33
sexual, 33
health and safety laws, 310
health and safety programs.
See occupational health
and safety
health-benefit costs, 219–221
health care, 72
health-care spending accounts
(HCSA), 221
health promotion, 220
high-performance work
system, 56
hiring decisions, 124–125
hiring freeze, 83
horizontal loading, 53
human capital, 2, 136
human capital theory, 93
human resource competencies,
4–7
business ally, 6 7
credible activist, 5
culture and change
steward, 5
operational executor, 6
strategy architect, 6
talent manager and
organizational
designer, 5–6
human resource
professionals, job
description for, 61f
human resources
operational *vs.* strategic, 8t
records, 94
Human Resources
Information System
(HRIS) software, 96
**human resources management
(HRM)**
continuing evolution of, 7
defined, 2
designations, 9–10
early stages, 3
economic conditions and, 12
environmental concerns
and, 16
ethics and, 10–11, 13
evolution of, 3–8
external environmental
influences on, 11–16
globalization and, 15
and government, 15
internal and external
environmental influences
on, 11t
internal environmental
influences on, 16–17
labour market issues, 12–14
management practices and,
17
organizational culture
and, 16
professionalism in, 9–11
strategies of, 2, 3f
and technology, 14–15

**human resources planning
(HRP)**
forecasting demand, 78–82
forecasting supply of
external candidates,
76–78
forecasting supply of
internal candidates,
73–75
fundamentals of, 47–48
importance of, 70–72
model, 71f
planning and implementing
programs, 82–86
qualitative approaches,
81–82
quantitative approaches,
79–81
relationship with strategic
planning, 70–71
steps in, 72
human rights, key metrics, 30f
human rights legislation,
26–37
case examples, 30–35
compensation and, 48
differential or unequal
treatment, 28
discrimination because of
association, 27–28
enforcement of, 35–37
and the hiring process,
107–108
and job descriptions, 65
permissible discrimination,
28–29
provincial, 15, 26
reasonable accommodation,
29
unintentional
discrimination, 28

I
illiteracy, 13
immigrant, 39, 77, 309
immigrant engagement and
employment continuum,
322t
immigrant workers in Canada,
321
in-basket exercise, 114
incentive plans. *See also*
rewards programs
annual bonus, 198–199
combination plans, 205
employee share purchase/
stock ownership plans
(ESOP), 197
gainsharing plan, 197–198
implementation of, 195
for individuals, 198–205
for operations employees,
203–204
organization-wide, 196–198
performance share unit
plan, 201
profit-sharing plan, 196–197
retention incentives,
200–201

for salespeople, 202–203
for senior managers and
executives, 205
stock option, 200–201
for teams or groups,
204–205
types of, 195–205
when to use, 194–195
incident costs, 238
income levels, in Canada, 14f
Income Tax Act, 24, 228
incumbent, 58, 59
individual, responsibilities,
147
individual awards, 199
individual incentive programs
annual bonus, 198–199
retention incentives,
200–201
individual interviews, 58
Industrial Accident
Prevention Association
(IAPA), 248
industrial engineering, 53
industrial psychologists, 113
industrial relations, 311
industrial union, 284
informal incentives, 195
information
availability and accuracy of,
72
verification of, 62, 122–123
Institute for Work and Health,
256
instructional design, 139–142
insubordination, 271
integrative bargaining, 296
intelligence (IQ) tests, 110
interactional justice, 274
interest arbitration, 300
interest dispute, 300
interest inventories, 113, 114
internal equity, 182
internal theft, 10
international compensation
management, 317–318,
318f
International Labour
Organization (ILO), 258
international unions, 285
internships, 97, 98f
interviews. *See also* selection
interview
group, 58
guidelines for, 58–59
individual, 58
job analysis, 58–59, 62
management assessment,
114
mass, 118
negative emphasis in, 119
situational, 117
supervisory, 58, 124
intranet, 94, 96
intrepreneurship, 4
inventories, skills and
management, 73
involuntary turnover, 266,
268–274, 270f

J

job, 47. *See also* job analysis; job design; jobs

job analysis
collection of information for, 58–62
communication and preparations for revisions, 66
competency-based, 54–57
defined, 47
reviewing relevant organizational information, 49–50
selection of jobs to be analyzed, 50, 52–57
in small businesses, 64
steps in (summary), 49
traditional *vs.* competency-based, 57
using interviews, 58–59, 62
using multiple sources of information, 62
using observations, 60, 62
using questionnaire, 59, 62
verifying information, 62
writing job descriptions, 62–64
writing job specifications, 64

job analysis information, uses of, 47–48, 47*f*
job applications, 96
job boards, Internet, 99
job candidates. *See also* candidates
evaluation after interview, 121
objectives of, 116
passive, 100
job characteristics model, 57
job descriptions, 47, 48, 62–64, 63*f*, 107
competency-based, 66
and human rights legislation, 65
for small business, 64
writing competency-based, 64

job design, 52–53
defined, 52
team-based, 57
job enlargement, 53–54
job enrichment, 54, 57
job evaluation, 183
job evaluation committee, 184
job fairs, 97–98
job instruction training (JIT), 141
job performance. *See* appraisal methods
job placement counselling, 228
job posting, 94
advantages and disadvantages of, 94*f*
job-related services
educational subsidies, 231
elder care, 230–231
food services, 231

subsidized child care, 229–230
subsidized employee transportation, 231
job rotation, 54, 57
jobs
activities of, 155
analysis of, 50, 52–57
human requirements for, 65–66
identification of, 62–63
poor knowledge of, 119
requirements of, 93
summaries of, 63
workflow of, 52*f*
job sharing, 84
job specification form, completing, 66
job specifications, 65–66, 107
job stress, 253–255
reducing, 253–254
joint health and safety committees, 239–240

K

kinesthetic tactile learning, 136
knowledge, skills, and abilities (KSAs), 39, 48, 94
KSAOs (knowledge, skills, abilities, and other characteristics), 66

L

labour congress affiliation, 285
labour cost factors, 311, 311*t*
labour costs, lowering, 5
labour force, trends in, 73
labour laws. *See* legislation
labour market conditions, 77
Labour Market Impact Assessment (LMIA), 322
labour market issues, 12–14, 77
labour movement in Canada, 284
labour organizations, 96, 98. *See also* union
labour relations (LR), 24, 48. *See also* labour relations process
Canadian labour laws, 283–284
labour movement in Canada, 284
labour unions, types of, 284–285
membership trends, 286–288, 286*t*
labour relations process
collective bargaining, 293–302, 294*f*, 295*f*
contract administration, 302–305
desire for collective representation, 288–290
overview, 289*f*

union organizing campaign, 290–292
union recognition, 292–293
labour supply
balancing supply and demand, 82, 83*f*
challenges of, 106
external solutions, 76–78, 86
forecasting future needs, 78–82
internal solutions, 73–75, 86
labour equilibrium, 83
selection ratio, 106
shortage, 85–86, 93, 106
strategic HR, 77
surplus, 83–85, 106
labour surplus management, pain of, 278–279
labour union, 283. *See also* union
language ability, 325
layoff, 84, 271–273
leaderless group discussions, 114
leadership
competencies, 56
development, 171
and ethics, 10
learner content management systems, 141
learning
informal, 140
styles of, 136
learning organization, 129
leave of absence, 84–85
leaves of absence, 214–215
legal counselling, 229
legal issues, in performance management, 172–173
legal systems, 310–311
legislation. *See also* human rights legislation; occupational health and safety
and Aboriginals, 39
contract law, 24
employment equity, 15, 37, 93
employment-related, 15, 21
Employment Standards Act (ESA), 23, 24, 116
and environmental scanning, 71
and human resources, 15
pay equity, 15, 24, 48
and people with disabilities, 39
respecting employee privacy, 41–42
and visible minorities, 39
and women, 38
leniency/strictness, 166
lie detector tests, 116
life insurance, 218
life trajectories, 146–147
line managers, 66
literacy, 245, 324
literacy levels, in Canada, 14*f*
loans, 231

lockout, 299
log (or diary), 60
logrolling, 169
long-term disability insurance
disability management, 223
mental health benefits, 223, 224*f*
objectives, 222
long-term incentive plans (LTIP), 200, 200*f*
lost-time injury rate, 237
loyalty
client/customer, 10
employee, 10, 16, 91, 97, 101, 136, 155

M

maintenance-of-membership arrangement, 301
Major Groups (of occupations), 61, 62
management, 17. *See also* senior managers
line managers, 66
management practices, 17
role in career development, 147–148
management assessment centre, 114
management by objectives (MBO), 161, 167*t*
management games, 114
management inventories, 73
management rights clause, 301
managers. *See* management
manual dexterity, 112
market conditions
labour, 77
occupational, 78
market trends, 71
Markov analysis, 75, 76*f*
material safety data sheets (MSDS), 242
maternity leaves, 214
matrix structure, 49, 50, 51*f*, 57
maximum hours, 48
Mayer-Salovey- Caruso Emotional Intelligence Test (MSCEIT), 111
mediation, 297
medical examinations, 115–116
memorandum of settlement, 297
mental health
benefits, 223, 224*f*
in workplace, 252–255
mergers and acquisitions, 132
merit pay (merit raise), 179–180
metrics, 8, 14, 168
recruitment, 104, 104*f*
micro-assessment, 115
military service, 98
minimum wage, 15, 23, 24
Minnesota Rate of Manipulation Test, 112
Minor Groups (of occupations), 61, 62

minorities (visible and ethnic) in the workforce, 12. *See also* visible minorities
minority language education rights, 25
mixed (semi-structured) interview, 117
modified union shop, 301
money and motivation, 179–180, 180f
motivation, 136–137
motor abilities, 112
multicultural heritage, 25
multicultural heritage rights, 25
multiple-hurdle strategy, 106–107, 107f
multiplier method, 199
mutual gains (interest-based) bargaining, 296

N
narrative form, 167t
National Occupational Classification (NOC), 60–62, 64
Job Description for Specialists in Human Resources, 61f
National Occupation Classification Career Handbook, 60
national unions, 285
negligent training, 137
negotiations
face-to-face, 294–296, 295f
preparation for, 293–294, 294f
NEO Five-Factor Inventory (NEO–FFI), 113
nepotism, 97
networking, 147
traditional, 96
nominal group technique, 78, 81
non-monetary recognition programs, 195
non-standard/contingent workers, 13–14
nonverbal communication, 119, 164
no-strike-or-lockout provision, 301

O
objective tests, 114
occupation, 61
occupational health and safety
accident prevention, 246–249
accidents, causes of, 241–246
burnout, 254
challenges in Canada, 249–260
chance occurrences, 241
employee wellness program, 260–261
ergonomics, 255–256

mental health in workplace, 252–255
personal characteristics, 244–245, 244f
repetitive strain injuries (RSI), 255–256
safety climate and culture, 237
smoking in workplace, 257
stress, job-related, 253–255
substance abuse, 249–252
unsafe acts, 243–244
unsafe conditions, 242–243, 243f
video display terminals (VDT), 256
violence at work, 258–260, 258f
viral pandemic, 257–258
workers' compensation costs, 238
workplace toxins, 256–258
occupational health and safety legislation, 23, 24, 238
enforcement of, 240–241
joint health and safety committees, 239–240
occupational health and safety and other legislation, 241
purpose, 238–239
responsibilities and rights of employers/employees, 239
supervisor's role in safety, 240
occupational market conditions, 78
occupational segregation, 37
offers–applicant cost, 104f
older workers, attracting, 102
onboarding, 130–135. *See also* orientation
executive integration, 134–135
program content, 131–132
responsibility for, 132
special situations, 132–135
onboarding programs
evaluation of, 135
problems with, 135
online applications, 96
online postings, by job candidates, 123f
Ontario Occupational Health and Safety Act, 241
on-the-job training (OJT), 140
openness to experience, 113, 114
open shop, 301
operational executor, 6
operational human resources, 8t
operations employees, incentives for, 203–204
opportunities, external, 6
organizational behaviours, 154
organizational climate, 16–17
organizational culture, 16

organizational designer, 5–6
organizational information, reviewing, 49–50
organizational strategy, 66
organizational structure, 49–50, 51f
types of, 49–50, 51f
organization chart, 49–50, 50f, 64
organizations, multilocation, 133–134
organization-wide incentive plans. *See also* incentive plans
employee share purchase/ stock ownership plans (ESOP), 197
gainsharing plan, 197–198
profit-sharing plans, 196–197
orientation, 129. *See also* onboarding
outplacement assistance, 279
overtime pay, 15, 48

P
paid breaks, 218
paired comparison method, 158, 158f, 167t
panel interview, 118
parental leave benefits, 214
pay equity, 15, 24, 48, 183
pay-for-knowledge, 192–193
pay for mass layoffs, 214
pay for performance, 153
pay grade, 188, 198
pay in lieu of reasonable notice, 213
pay on termination of employment
golden parachute clause, 232, 279
pay for mass layoffs, 214
reasonable notice periods, 213
severance pay, 213–214
pay ranges, 90
pay rates
broadbanding, 192
classification/grading method, 185
compensable factors, 184
compensation, legal considerations in, 182
compensation decisions, union influences on, 182
compensation policies, 182
correcting out-of-line rates, 192
equity internally and externally, perceptions of, 182
formal and informal surveys by employer, 188
job evaluation, 183–185
job evaluation and salary survey information, combining, 190–192
job evaluation committee, 184–185

overtime, 15, 48
point method, 185–188, 187t
rate ranges, 190–192
reduction of, 12
salary survey interpretation and use, 189
salary surveys, commercial, professional, and government, 188–189
severance, 24
wage/salary survey, 188–189, 189t
peaceful assembly, freedom of, 25
peers, as appraisers, 169–170
pension plans, 24, 223. *See also* retirement benefits
perceptual *vs.* motor skills, 245
performance analysis, 138–139
performance appraisal of global managers, 319
performance appraisals, 2, 153
in China, 155
performance expectations, 154–155
performance improvement plan (PIP), 163
performance management, 153
choice of appraisers, 169–172
defining performance expectations, 154–155
determining performance rewards/consequences, 162
elements of, 153
evaluation discussion, 156–161
formal written warnings, 163
future of, 173–174
legal and ethical issues in, 172–173
performance appraisal, 156–161
process of, 56, 153–163, 153f
providing ongoing coaching and feedback, 155–156
standards for, 48
strategic importance of, 153
training, 164, 169
web-based, 168
performance measures, corporate, 8
performance share unit plan, 201
performance standards, 65
perquisites (perks), 231–232
personal characteristics. *See also* accidents in workplace
age, 245
and employee accident behaviour, 244–245, 244f
literacy, 245
perceptual *vs.* motor skills, 245
vision, 245

Personal Information
    Protection and Electronic
    Documents Act
    (PIPEDA), 41
Personality-Related Position
    Requirements Form
    (PPRF), 65
personality tests, 113–114
personality types, and the
    hiring process, 113
personal services
    counselling services,
        228–229
    credit unions, 228
    employee assistance plan
        (EAP), 229
personnel management, 3
persons with disabilities.
        See also disabilities
    discrimination against, 37
    as job applicants, 108
    in the workforce, 12, 39
phased retirement, 227, 268
physical appearance, and
    interviews, 119
physical demand analysis, 65
physical environment, 64
picket, 298
piecework, 203
point method, 185
political instability, 52
pollution, 16
polycentric staffing policy, 315
polygraph tests, 116
portability, 227
position, 47
**Position Analysis
    Questionnaire**, 59
positive reinforcement, 248
posters, safety, 248
post–industrial revolution, 3
precedent, 23
pre-hearing vote, 292
pre-retirement counselling,
    229, 268
presentations, individual, 114
press, freedom of, 25
primary sector, 12
print advertising, 99
prior learning assessment and
    recognition (PLAR)
    methods, 324
privacy rights, 10, 15, 41, 123
procedural justice, 274
process chart, 50, 52*f*
productivity
    changes in, 79
    in the corporate
        environment, 2, 8, 12
    decrease in, 70
    increase in, 79
    job specialization and, 53
    monitoring, 42
    onboarding programs and,
        131–132, 135
    pay based on, 38
    and performance
        management, 153
professional organizations, 98

profitability, improving, 153
profit-sharing plan, 196.
        See also incentive plans
programmed learning, 139
progressive discipline, 270,
    270*f*
projected turnover, 78
promotion, 86, 148–149
    guidelines for, 167, 148
    merit-based, 86
psychiatric disabilities, 223
psychological behaviours, 154
public trust, 10
punctuality, 155
Purdue Pegboard, 112
Purdue Test for Machinists
    and Machine Operators,
    114

Q
qualified privilege, 123–124
qualifying period, 212
qualitative analysis, 78, 81–82
quality of hires and cost, 104*f*
quantitative analysis, 78,
    79–81
quasi-judicial bodies, decisions
    of, 71
questionnaires, 59, 62, 65
questions
    for employee selection, 107
    in interviews, 120–121
    leading, 119–120
quitting, 267

R
race, 34
Rand formula, 301
ranking method, 184
ratification, 297
rating committees, 170
rating scales, 165, 165*t*
ratio analysis, 79
reaction time, 112
realistic job preview
    (RJP), 124
**reality shock (cognitive
    dissonance)**, 131, 132
reasonable accommodation, 29
reasonable cause, 239
reasonable notice for volun-
    tary turnover, 268
reasonable notice legislation,
    272
recency effect, 166
recognition, 171
recruiter, 66, 91, 93. *See also*
    recruitment
    agency recruiters, 100–101
recruiting. *See* recruitment
recruitment, 5. *See also*
    recruiter
    and employer branding,
        91–92
    external, 95–99
    and human resource
        management, 2, 5, 90–92
    internal methods, 94–95
    methods, 93

metrics, 104, 104*f*
    of a more diverse
        workforce, 101–104
    online, 99–100
    within the organization,
        93–95
    from outside organization,
        95–101
    from outside the system,
        95–101
    overview of process, 92*f*
    the recruitment process,
        92–93, 92*f*
    and selection, 2, 5
    sources, 93
red circle pay rates, 192
reduced workweek, 84
reduction in pay and benefits,
    12
references
    checking, 107, 121–124
    evaluating the candidate, 121
    providing, 123–124
referrals, 96–97, 102, 147
regression analysis, 80–81
    example (relationship
        between hospital size and
        number of registered
        nurses), 80*f*
regular certification, 292
regulations, 24
relationships
    of employees, 5, 40, 59, 62,
        134
    of employers, 91
    matrix and team-reporting,
        171
reliability, 108
    of appraisals, 164–168
religion
    discrimination because of,
        34–35
    freedom of, 25
repatriation, 319
repetitive strain injuries (RSI)
    ergonomics, 255–256
    video display terminals
        (VDT), 256
replacement charts, 73–74
replacement costs, 266
replacement summaries, 73–74
representation vote, 292
Reserve Employment
    Assistance Program
    (REAP), 98
responsibilities, and duties,
    63–64
restitutional remedies, 36–37
restricted share unit plan, 201
restructuring, 48
résumés, 96, 98, 99
    résumé lies, 122*f*
retention, 5, 12, 16, 86, 130,
    131, 144
retention incentives
    long-term incentive plans
        (LTIP), 200, 200*f*
    performance share unit
        plan, 201

stock option, 200–201
retiree health benefits, 221
retirees on call, 268
retirement, 77, 267–268.
        See also retirement benefits
retirement benefits. *See also*
    pension plans
    categories of, 224–227,
        225*t*
    phased retirement, 227,
        227*f*
    supplemental employee
        retirement plans (SERP),
        228
retirement pension, 215
return on assets, 2
return on equity, 2
rewards programs, 171.
        See also incentive plans
rights, fundamental, 25
rights arbitration, 383
rights dispute, 383
risk-assessment programs, 221
Rucker formula, 198

S
sabbatical leaves, 223
safety and health programs.
        See occupational health
        and safety
safety climate and culture,
    237–238
safety training, 247–248
salary continuation plans. *See*
    short-term disability
    plans
salary grade. *See* pay grade
salary guarantees, 231–232
salary plan, 202
salary survey. *See* wage/salary
    survey
salespeople, incentives for
    commission plans, 202–203
    salary plan, 202
sandwich generation. *See* baby
    boomers
scandals, 7
scatter plots, 79–80
screening process.
        See selection testing
secondary sector, 12
second middle age, 145
security, of information, 10
security precautions in
    workplace, 259
selection, 5, 6, 105. *See also*
    employee selection;
    selection interview;
    selection testing
selection interview
    administering, 117–118
    behavioural (behaviour
        description), 117
    closing, 121
    common mistakes, 118–120
    content of, 117
    contrast or candidate-order
        error, 119, 121
    designing, 120–121

face-to-face, 117, 118
halo effect, 119, 121
mixed (semi-structured) interview, 117
negative emphasis, 119, 121
nonverbal behaviour, 119
panel, 118
planning, 120
poor knowledge of job, 119
poor planning of, 118
questions, asking, 120–121, 121*f*
rapport, establishing, 120
sample structured questions for, 121*f*
sequential, 118
similar-to-me bias, 120
situational, 117
snap judgments, 118–119
structured, 117, 118
talking too much/too little, 120
technology aided, 117, 118
types of, 116–117
unstructured, 117, 118
selection ratio, 106
selection testing
 and accidents, 247
 aptitude tests, 111
 automated, 106
 cognitive abilities, 110–111
 emotional intelligence (EI) test, 110–111
 intelligence tests, 110
 interest inventories, 113, 114
 management assessment centre, 114
 micro-assessments, 115
 motor and physical abilities, 112
 objective tests, 114
 personality tests, 113–114
 physical examination, 115–116
 situational testing, 115
 work sampling, 114
self-appraisals, 169
self-management, 169
seniority, 148, 302
senior managers and executives, incentives for, 205
separation costs, 265
service economy, 52
service sector (tertiary sector), 12
severance pay, 24, 213, 279
sexual annoyance, 33
sexual coercion, 33
sexual harassment, 33
sexual orientation, discrimination because of, 35
short-term disability plans, 222
sick leave plans, 222
similar-to-me bias, 166–168
simulated training, 142
situational interview, 117
situational tests, 115
skill-based pay, 192

skills inventories, 94–95, 159
skills inventories, 73
small business, job analysis questionnaire for, 64
Small Business Health and Safety (SBHS) certificate, 248
small business safety calculator, 238
smoking in workplace, 257
snap judgments, in interviews, 118–119
social behaviours, 154
social concerns, 72
social handicapping, 31–32
socialization, 130, 135
social networking sites, 123
social responsibility, 11, 16
social (reform) unionism, 284
split-award method, 199
staffing table, 82
stakeholders, confidence among, 10
Stanford-Binet test, 110
stare decisis, 22–23
statistical strategy, 125
statutory holidays, 23
stock option, 200
straight piecework plan, 203
strategic HR, 9*t*
 evolving role of, 7
 Jaguar Land Rover formal appraisal discussion training, 164
 pumping up people supply, 77
strategic planning, 2, 3*f*
 relationship with human resources planning, 70–71
 and training, 136
strategy, 6
strategy architect, 6
stress, job-related, 253–255
 reducing, 253–254
stress-related disability claims, workers' compensation and, 254–255
strictness/leniency, 166
strike, 298
strike vote, 298
Stromberg Dexterity Test, 112
Strong-Campbell Interest Inventory, 114
structured interview, 117, 118
subordinates, appraisal by, 170–171
subsidized child care, 229–230
subsidized employee transportation, 231
substance abuse, 249–252
succession planning, 7, 74–75, 171
suggestion programs, 276
supervisors
 as appraisers, 169
 in safety issues, 240
supervisory interviews, 58, 124

supplemental employee retirement plans (SERP), 228
supplemental unemployment benefit (SUB) plan, 213, 278
supplementary health-care/ medical insurance
 health-benefit costs, reducing, 219–221
 retiree health benefits, 221
supply and demand, balancing, 82, 83*f*
supply challenges, 106
surveys. *See* wage/salary survey
survivor benefits, 215
survivor syndrome, 278
sustainability, 16
systemic remedies, 36

T
talent, identification of, 7
talent acquisition, 48, 90
talent manager, 5–6
Tapping the Talents of People with Disabilities: A Guidebook for Employers, 103
task analysis, 138
task performance, 154
tasks
 functional competencies, 56
 rotation of, 54, 57
team
 cross-functional, 17
 defined, 57
 objectives of, 153
 organizing around, 6
 self managing, 169
team-based job designs, 57
team or group incentive plan, 204
teamwork, 155
technology
 changes in, 52, 72, 78, 129
 and HR functions, 7
 and human resources management, 14–15
 in performance appraisals, 168, 171
 technical competencies, 56
technology for performance management, 4
Temporary Foreign Worker Program (TFWP), 322
temporary help agencies, 101
temporary workers (temps), 101
termination
 defined, 84
 wrongful dismissal, 154, 272
termination interview, 277–278
termination on abandonment, 293
termination pay, 278
tertiary or service sector, 12

testing
 of cognitive abilities, 110–111
 of job applicants, 108–115
 of motor and physical abilities, 112
 reliability of, 108
 validity of, 108–110
Test of Mechanical Comprehension, problems from, 111*f*
Thematic Apperceptions Test, 113, 113*f*
threats, external, 6
360-degree appraisal, 171–172, 171*f*
time constraints, 167
time lapsed per hire, 104*f*
time wasted, 41
top-management commitment, 247
tort law, 24
total employment rewards, 178, 178*f*
total rewards, components of, 179
toxic substances, control of, 242
toxins in workplace
 smoking, 257
 viral pandemic, 257–258
trade organizations, 98
traditionalists, 13*t*
training. *See also* training process
 for appraisals, 169
 audiovisual techniques, 141–142
 classroom, 140
 computer-based, 141
 costs, 266
 and development, 135, 153
 effects to measure, 143–144
 of employees, 5–6
 and ethics, 10
 evaluation of, 143–144
 implementation of, 142
 and learning, 136–137
 legal aspects of, 137
 necessity of, 136
 negligent, 137
 online, 140
 for performance management, 164, 169
 for specific jobs, 48, 129
 strategic HR, 164
 transfer of, 143
 validation of, 142
 for workplace violence, 259–260
training needs analysis, 138–139
training process
 curriculum design, 139–142
 evaluation and follow-up, 143–144
 five-step, 137
 implementation, 142

training process (*continued*)
  instructional design, 139–142
  task analysis, 138
  training needs analysis, 138–139
  validation, 142
transfer, 86, 148
transfer of training, 143
trend analysis, 79
turnover
  costs of, 265–266
  HR practices and, 2, 86
  involuntary, 268–274, 270*f*
  projected, 78
  reasons for, 167
  reducing, 5, 130
  voluntary, 266–268, 266*t*

U
unclear performance standards, 165, 165*t*
underemployment, 39
undue hardship, 29
unemployment, 12
unequal treatment, 28.
  See also discrimination
unfair labour practice, 284
unintentional/constructive/systemic discrimination, 28
union
  avoidance strategy, 283
  certification, 292
  density by industry, 2005 *vs.* 2015, 286*t*
  and employee contact, 290
  employer response to organizing campaign, 290–292
  impact on human resource management, 305
  in-house organizing committee, 290
  international, 285
  and job descriptions, 48
  membership trends in, 286–288, 286*t*
  organizers, 290
  organizing campaign, 290–292
  pressure from, 167
  recognition, 292–293
  recruiting through, 98
  relationship with management, 24

termination of bargaining rights, 293
  types of, 284–285
  of white-collar employees, 288
union local, 285
union recognition clause, 300
union security clause, 300
union shop, 301
union steward, 285
union suppression approach, 283
Unit Groups (of occupations), 61–62
unlawful strike, 299
unsafe acts, 243–244, 246
unsafe conditions. *See also* accidents in workplace
  cause of accidents, 242–243, 243*f*
  minimization of, 246
unstructured interview, 117, 118

V
vacancy costs, 266
vacations and holidays, 216–217
vacation time, 23, 24
  entitlement to, 15
  pay rate for, 40
validity
  of appraisal criteria, 164–168
  and the selection process, 108–110
values
  assessment of, 153
  Eastern *vs.* Western, 155
  traditional Chinese, 155
variable pay, 179, 180f, 318–319
vertical loading, 54
vestibule or simulated training, 142
vesting, 227
video conferencing, 14, 142
video display terminals (VDT), 256
video surveillance, 42
violence at work
  defined by International Labour Organization (ILO), 258
  and law, 258

prevention and control of, 259–260
  reports of abuse by clinical area of practice, 258, 258*f*
viral pandemic, 257–258
visible minorities, 12, 37, 102
vision, 245
visual learning, 136
voluntary employer-sponsored benefits
  life insurance, 218
  long-term disability insurance, 222–223, 224*f*
  retirement benefits, 223–228
  sabbatical leaves, 223
  short-term disability plans, 222
  sick leave plans, 222
  supplementary health-care/medical insurance, 219–221, 220*f*
voluntary recognition, 292
voluntary turnover, 266–268, 266*t*

W
wage curve, 190
  plotting, 190f
wages, unpaid, 41
wage/salary survey
  commercial, professional, and government, 188–189
  formal and informal surveys by employer, 188
  interpretation and use, 189
walk-ins, 96
want ad, 99
websites, corporate, 99–100.
  See also intranet
Wechsler test, 110
western cultures, values in, 155
wildcat strike, 299
women
  attracting, 102–103
  in business (Canadian), 38*f*
  discrimination against, 37
  in the workforce, 12, 38
Wonderlic Personnel Test, 110
workers. *See also* employees
  contingent, 13–14

as human capital, 2
  non-standard, 13–14
workers' compensation, 215–216
  costs, 238
  and stress-related disability claims, 254–255
  workforce diversity, 12
workflow, of a job, 52*f*
workforce, aging, 129
workforce diversity, 12, 37–39, 101–104, 132
  career development for older workers, 145
  gender identity in BC Human Rights Code, 27
  people with disabilities, recruiting, 104
workforce mobility, 309
working conditions, 64
workplace accidents. *See* accidents in workplace
Workplace Hazardous Materials Information System (WHMIS), 242, 243*f*
workplace investigators, 36
  selection of, 36*f*
workplace legislation.
  See legislation
workplace toxins. *See* toxins in workplace
workplace violence.
  See violence at work
work sampling, 114
work sharing, 84
work simplification, 53
work team. *See* team
write-ins, 96
writing competency-based job descriptions, 64
written permission, obtaining, 122–123
written warnings, formal, 163
wrongful dismissal, 154, 272
wrongful dismissal accusations, avoiding, 273

Y
yield ratio, 104*f*
younger employees, attracting, 102
young workers in health and safety, guiding, 246